A DESCRIPTIVE CATALOGUE OF THE ORIENTAL MSS. BELONGING TO THE LATE E. G. BROWNE

A DESCRIPTIVE CATALOGUE OF THE ORIENTAL MSS. BELONGING TO THE LATE E. G. BROWNE

BY

EDWARD G. BROWNE

M.A., M.B., F.B.A., F.R.C.P.

Sir Thomas Adams's Professor of Arabic
and Fellow of Pembroke College
in the University of
Cambridge

COMPLETED & EDITED
WITH A MEMOIR OF THE AUTHOR
AND A BIBLIOGRAPHY OF
HIS WRITINGS

BY

REYNOLD A. NICHOLSON

Fellow of Trinity College
Cambridge

CAMBRIDGE

AT THE UNIVERSITY PRESS

1932

CAMBRIDGE UNIVERSITY PRESS
Cambridge, New York, Melbourne, Madrid, Cape Town, Singapore,
São Paulo, Delhi, Dubai, Tokyo, Mexico City

Cambridge University Press
The Edinburgh Building, Cambridge CB2 8RU, UK

Published in the United States of America by Cambridge University Press, New York

www.cambridge.org
Information on this title: www.cambridge.org/9780521158466

First published 1932
First paperback edition 2010

A catalogue record for this publication is available from the British Library

ISBN 978-0-521-04343-4 Hardback
ISBN 978-0-521-15846-6 Paperback

TABLE OF CONTENTS

ERRATA AND ADDENDA

P. 3, l. 1. *After* pp. 13–16 *add* [pp. 12–15 in the original edition].

P. 14, l. 13. *For* 'Ísá *read* 'Ísà.

P. 23, foot-note. *Insert* 1 *before* Read.

P. 28. *For* 82 (page-number) *read* 28.

P. 115, note. *After* p. 184 *add* [p. 168 in the original edition].

P. 124, l. 20. For *Lala-báshí* read *Lálá-báshí.*

P. 126, l. 3 from foot. *For* al-Yázají *read* al-Yázijí.

P. 150, ll. 4–5. I have translated the passage referring to the *sufra-sabzí* or "Feast for the Daughter of the Fairy King" in an article entitled "Some Notes on Arabian and Persian Folklore" (*Folk-Lore*, vol. XLI, No. 4, pp. 355–358).

P. 164, l. 7. *For* 'Ísá *read* 'Ísà.

P. 169, l. 14 and p. 170, l. 11. For *Kámilu'ṣ-Ṣaná'at* read *Kámilu'ṣ-Ṣiná'at.*

P. 200, l. 12. *For* Jaldakí *read* Jildakí.

P. 201, l. 6. *For* Sháhmírzáda *read* Sháhmírzádí.

P. 268, l. 19. *Delete* and probably he belongs to the 19th century.
Ṭarzí was an Afshár Turk, born near Urúmiyya in Ádharbáyján, who flourished in the reigns of Sháh Ṣafí and Sháh 'Abbás II (A.D. 1629–1667). His *Díwán*, with an excellent biographical notice, in which the editor praises his originality as a poet, was published by the "Tamaddun" Press in 1309/1891.

P. 276, l. 19. The *Kamálu'l-Balágha* of al-Yazdádí was printed in Cairo in 1341/1922.

P. 278, l. 13 from foot. For *Naqli'ẓ-Ẓiráf* read *Nuqli'ẓ-Ẓiráf.*

P. 293, l. 2. *Add* The text has been edited and translated by C. D. Cobham in *J.R.A.S.*; Vol. XXIX, 1897, pp. 81–101, where further information is given concerning Umm Ḥarám, her shrine, and the MSS. of this work.

INTRODUCTION

Born on February 7, 1862, Edward Granville Browne came of good English stock, a Gloucestershire family "producing soldiers and business men, with divines and doctors of medicine in former generations," but leaving no record that might seem to anticipate their descendant's genius for Orientalism. His schooldays were less happy than those of most boys, for even then he went his own ways, which could not be fitted into any orthodox system of work and play. Browne was destined for engineering, his father's profession, and accordingly left Eton before he was sixteen. What first turned his thoughts to the East was the Russo-Turkish war of 1877–8; admiration for the bravery of the Turks and disgust with the attempts made in this country "to confound questions of abstract justice with party politics" started him upon the study of the Turkish language. From that day he never looked back. On coming up to Pembroke College, Cambridge, in 1879, though Medicine claimed most of his time, he began to read Arabic with Professor E. H. Palmer and later with Professor William Wright, while Persian (one of the subjects for the Indian Languages Tripos which he took in 1884) was rapidly mastered with the help of "a very learned but very eccentric old Persian," Mírzá Muḥammad Báqir of Bawánát, then living in Limehouse. A visit to Constantinople in 1882, after passing his second examination for the M.B., gave him a glimpse of the promised land; but now it was Persia on which his heart was set. When he went down from Cambridge to work for three years in London hospitals, he found consolation in the poetry of Persian mystics, in the society of Persian friends, and above all in the dream that some day he would make a pilgrimage to Shíráz and Iṣfahán. That dream came true sooner than he had dared to hope. In May, 1887, he was elected Fellow of his College and the way to the East lay open before him.

A Year amongst the Persians, published in 1893, reflects his experiences and impressions with extraordinary vividness. Every one knows this fascinating book, in which the inmost spirit of Persia and the Persian people is revealed by a young Englishman who, incomparably beyond any other Western traveller, had absorbed it and made it part of his own feeling and thinking. Hence the book is a revelation of Browne himself; already we see his whole-hearted sympathy with the Oriental mind and, conversely, the fixed point of view from which his judgements on the West were formed and delivered. His falling in with the Bábís, though some readers may have regretted it, was a great piece of luck; for who else could have won their confidence, learned so much about them, and penetrated into the mysteries of their faith as he did? On returning to Cambridge with many precious manuscripts, he became University Lecturer in Persian, a post which he held till 1902, when he succeeded Charles Rieu as Sir Thomas Adams's Professor of Arabic.

I first met him in 1891 and well remember how I was struck by his appearance and personality, so attractive and so unlike anything I had expected. At that time he had few pupils, mostly beginners, and some of us found his methods a little disconcerting. Impatient of grammar and syntax, he would read and translate with amazing speed, only pausing to take up a point that interested him, which he would illustrate by anecdotes and quotations and draw out into an eloquent digression lasting as often as not to the end of the hour. But he possessed in a singular degree the born teacher's gift of communicating enthusiasm to his pupils; and when he saw that they desired knowledge for its own sake, he would spare no pains to remove their difficulties and help them in every possible way. As time went on, his teaching and organizing activities encroached more and more upon his leisure for literary work. He founded and directed a school, with Oriental instructors, where probationers for the Levant Consular Service and the Egyptian and Soudan Civil Services received special training in Arabic, Persian, and Turkish. During Term, lectures would keep him busy the whole morning, and to these, in his later years, there was added the supervision of Government of India Research Students, who produced admirable work under his guidance and inspiration. In 1904 the foundation of the E. J. W. Gibb Memorial Trust set on foot a great enterprise, in which Browne naturally took the leading part, for publishing editions and translations of Oriental texts. Besides contributing several important volumes and collaborating with Mírzá Muhammad Khán of Qazwín and others in many more, he was actively and often very intimately concerned in one way or another not only with most of the forty-five volumes which appeared before 1926 but also with some of those that have been published since. Indeed the whole series is as much a memorial to Browne as to Gibb himself.

In 1906 came the most fortunate event in his life, his marriage to Alice Blackburne-Daniell, and thenceforth he was always associated in the minds of those who knew him with his home, Firwood, and the delightful library where he and his wife entertained a host of friends from far and near. The same year witnessed the publication of the second volume of his *Literary History of Persia*; but then the work was broken off by his enthusiastic championship of Persia in her struggle for independence, followed after a brief interval by the world-war. What this catastrophe meant to him may be gathered from the words he wrote on the death of Charles Rieu, his predecessor in the Chair of Arabic at Cambridge—"in the realm of science at least we see some foreshadowing of that universal brotherhood of mankind which elsewhere is but dreamed of and hoped for, wherein the limitations of nationalities and tongues vanish away, and even East and West, so widely separated by thought, custom, feeling, and belief, are reconciled in the Light of that Knowledge which is the Creator's Supreme Attribute and the student's ultimate goal." After the war, scholars of many nations joined in writing a volume of Oriental Studies, which was presented to him on February 7, 1922, his sixtieth birthday. At this time he was busy with his manuscripts, and in a paper read on November 14 in the same year, he refers to "the Catalogue, with facsimiles and photographs, which I hope to publish before long." Though he wrote as easily as he talked, it must always remain a mystery how he contrived to get through the work he did, without ever denying himself to friends, pupils, or any one who sought his help. But he had felt the strain; there was a limit even to *his* output of energy. Two years later he collapsed and slowly sank till he passed away on January 5, 1926.

Of Browne's character and achievements as a scholar I will write briefly because they speak for themselves. He was the most human of men, and if he ranks among the greatest Orientalists it is because he was also, I suppose, the greatest humanist who has ever devoted himself to studying the life, thought, and literature of the East. He was no grammarian, and philology did not interest him except incidentally. He would have admitted the value of grammar as a necessary discipline for scholars to whom exact linguistic knowledge is either an end in itself or a means of promoting philological studies; but his own mastery of three Oriental languages was not gained by those methods against which as a schoolboy he had instinctively revolted. In his view, to know a language was to possess its literature, and through the literature a key to the minds and hearts of men; hence, though he admired profound scholarship, however "pure," he himself really cared for it in proportion as it was capable of being used to throw light upon Islamic, and especially Persian, culture and civilization. During the forty years which he spent in illuminating this immense subject, he was continually drawing information from the best sources available, including, besides books and manuscripts, a large number of Oriental correspondents and personal friends; for he spoke and wrote Arabic, Persian, and Turkish with equal facility, while they were charmed to find in him one who was familiar with their thoughts and sympathized with their ideals. As may be seen from the Bibliography (pp. xii–xv), the whole of Browne's literary work, not excepting his Lectures on Arabian Medicine, is concerned with Persia and falls into three main divisions:

I. Works on Religion.
II. Works on Literature and History.
III. Works on Politics and Journalism.

The religious works are the earliest, the political the fewest, while the most numerous and extensive belong to the domain of literary history. No attempt will be made to describe them in detail; there is only room for some general remarks under each head.

I. Browne's indifference (to use no stronger word) to Sunní theology was not surprising, but it is characteristic of him that, without ignoring the orthodox Shí'a, he was far more attracted by its heretical sects: Ismá'ílís, Ḥurúfís, and Bábís. These mysterious and fantastic doctrines excited his curiosity, and their appeal to him became irresistible when he saw them inspiring a faith for which its votaries were ready to suffer torture and death. To me, at any rate, his enthusiasm for the Bábís has never seemed difficult to understand, nor its consequences to be a matter for regret. That he should eagerly grasp the opportunity given him to study on the spot, and in close touch with members of the sect, a typically Persian religion, which, though no longer in its infancy, was still young enough to feel growing pains; that he should realize its interest and historical importance to students of Comparative Religion; and that he should therefore exert himself to collect, examine, edit, and translate its earliest documents and records—all this is only what any one who knew Browne must have expected of him. His work on Bábism may be supplemented in the future; it can never be superseded. I am not sure whether, taking a long view, we ought not to regard it as the most original and valuable of all his contributions to our knowledge of Persia. The *Maqála-i-Shakhṣí Sayyáḥ* ("A Traveller's Narrative"), edited and translated in 1891, the *Ta'ríkh-i-Jadíd* ("New History"), translated in 1893, which is a later and garbled recension of the same author's *Nuqṭatu'l-Káf*, edited by Browne from the unique Paris MS. in 1910, bring out striking analogies between the history and historical records of Bábism and those of the early Christian Church. *Materials for the Study of the Bábí Religion* (1918), his last book on the subject which he had made his own, gives an account of many new and hitherto unpublished documents in his possession and includes a chapter on the Bahá'í propaganda in America. His magnificent collection of Bábí MSS. is described on pp. 53–87 of the present Catalogue.

II. About 1900 the *Literary History of Persia*, which Browne had contemplated since he was in his teens, took definite shape. The work, as he conceived it, was not to be a History of Persian Literature in the narrower sense; it should deal with "the manifestations of the national genius in the fields of Religion, Philosophy, and Science"; with ideas and movements rather than books; and, of course, not exclusively with books written in Persian. According to the arrangement made with his publisher, the complete work was to consist of a single volume of 500 pages; but few of Browne's friends, and certainly none of his pupils, can have been astonished when in 1902 a volume of the stipulated size duly appeared, comprising the Prolegomena to a History of Persian Literature and carrying the work no further than A.D. 1000. The second volume (1906) covers the period of three hundred years from Firdawsí to Sa'dí; the third and fourth, entitled respectively *Persian Literature under Tartar Dominion* and *Persian Literature in Modern Times*, were published by the Cambridge University Press in 1920 and 1924. Browne had embarked on what he afterwards called "the labour of a life-time." For the most part, he found it necessary to provide his own materials. The History is built on his multifarious researches before and during the twenty-two years which elapsed between the appearance of the first and last of its four volumes. These researches produced a great number of subsidiary publications, amounting to many thousands of pages and constituting, by themselves, a service of unparalleled importance to Persian studies. I need only mention his three catalogues of the Muḥammadan MSS. in the Cambridge University Library; his editions of the *Lubáb* of 'Awfí and the *Tadhkira* of Dawlatsháh; his translations of the *Chahár Maqála* and the *Ta'ríkh-i-Guzída*; and his numerous articles in the *Journal of the Royal Asiatic Society*. In this way he traversed a vast extent of ground; and the deficiency of printed and lithographed texts he supplied, so far as was practicable, with original matter derived from the rare manuscripts which he was continually adding to his private Collection. Since it is always interesting to see how the personality and work of a famous scholar impress those who, though not of his own race, are specialists in the same branch of learning, I will give the gist of some critical remarks on the *Literary History* by a distinguished German savant, Professor Franz Babinger, who enjoyed Browne's friendship and, on his death, contributed an appreciative notice to the Oriental journal *Der Islam* (vol. XVI, 1927, pp. 114–122). The writer regards Browne as "one of the greatest (bedeutendsten) Orientalists of all time," and declares that the verdict passed on the History by the Anglo-Saxon world is entirely justified, though elsewhere, perhaps, the work would have received more censure than praise. "How fortunate for Browne that he thought and wrote as a true Englishman!" Too much, however, is left to chance; the book is unequal; "man kann es als eine Reihe von Essays bezeichnen, die der Verfasser über ihm lieb gewordene Gestalten geschrieben hat"; moreover, a certain capriciousness, excusable in the circumstances, is shown in the author's choice of the sources which he has utilized. Without disputing the justice of these criticisms from an academic standpoint, I cannot admit that they are relevant here. Browne himself would have swept them aside. It was not his object to compile an exhaustive and systematic work either on the lines of Brockelmann's *History of Arabic Literature* or on any other plan. He ranges freely along the paths to which his tastes and predilections beckon him, but there is a method in his wanderings, and those who accompany him to the end will feel that they have surveyed the historical evolution of the Persian people and have obtained such a wide and commanding view of Persian thought and literature as they could hardly have imagined to be possible in the limits of a single book.

III. The principles which impelled Browne to follow the fortunes of the Persian national movement of 1905–1909 with intense sympathy, take an active part in organizing and influencing British opinion, and devote two considerable volumes to writing the history of the "Risorgimento" and illustrating its character, are expressed in the following sentences. "Whether it be a question of individuals or nations, the destruction of a distinctive type is a loss to the universe and therefore an evil." "There can be no doubt that politically both Greece and Italy profited much from a sympathy largely based on a recognition of what human civilization owed them for their contributions to art and literature. It is my contention that Persia stands in the same category and that her disappearance from the society of independent states would be a misfortune not only to herself but to the whole human race." The fact that his *Persian Revolution* is deeply coloured by the fervour with which he held these convictions, as well as by the origin of some of the papers and letters whence he drew the materials for his narrative, does not impair its authority as a faithful and masterly presentation of the events described. During the years 1909–1912, when the crisis was at its height, he published several pamphlets, of which the titles are given below. In his *Press and Poetry of Modern Persia* the literary side of the movement is attractively exhibited in text and translation.

BIBLIOGRAPHY

The following Bibliography is based on the list of Browne's writings at the end of his *Materials for the Study of the Bábí Religion* (1918), but differs from it in some respects. It comprises all his own books, editions, and translations; the articles which he contributed to the *J.R.A.S.* (*Journal of the Royal Asiatic Society*); his political pamphlets and his papers read to and published by the Persia Society. These, together with a few more, have been classified and arranged chronologically under three heads, *viz.*: I. **Persian Religion**; II. **Persian Literature, History, Science, and Travel**; III. **Persian Politics and Journalism.** The titles of books, of which the Introductions alone were written by Browne[1], are not included; and I have also omitted E. J. W. Gibb's *History of Ottoman Poetry*, of which Vols. II–VI were edited by Browne after the author's death. Although the present Bibliography is not complete, it contains, I hope, nearly everything of importance except reviews of books, letters published in newspapers, and a few scattered articles. Of these last, two, though not included in the Bibliography, deserve mention here. The first is a paper entitled, "On the Turkish Language and Turkish Philology" (*Transactions of the Philological Society*, 1882–1884, pp. 544–572); the second, "A Chapter from the History of Cannabis Indica," published in the *St Bartholomew's Hospital Journal* for March, 1897.

I. PERSIAN RELIGION

1. **The Bábís of Persia.** I. Sketch of their History, and Personal Experiences among them. II. Their Literature and Doctrines. *J.R.A.S.*, Vol. XXI, 1889, pp. 485–526 and 881–1009.
2. **A Traveller's Narrative written to illustrate the Episode of the Báb.** Edited in the original Persian and translated into English, with an Introduction and Explanatory Notes.

[1] The most important of these Introductions were written for the Persian texts edited by Mírzá Muḥammad of Qazwín in the E. J. W. Gibb Memorial Series: Vol. VIII, the *Marzubán-náma* (1909); Vol. X, *al-Mu'jam fí Ma'áyíri Ash'ári'l-'Ajam* (1909); Vol. XI, the *Chahár Maqála* (1910); and Vol. XVI, 1 and 2, the *Ta'ríkh-i-Jahán-gushá* (1912 and 1916). Browne also contributed Introductions to the reprint of Morier's *Hajji Baba* (1895) in the Series of English Classics edited by W. E. Henley; to *The Life and Teaching of Abbas Effendi* by Myron H. Phelps (New York, 1903); and to *Dar-ul-Islam* (1904), a record of a journey through ten of the Asiatic provinces of Turkey, by his friend Sir Mark Sykes.

Vol. I, Persian Text, pp. ٢١١ + iv. Vol. II, English Translation and Notes, pp. lv + 447. Cambridge University Press, 1891.

3. Ṣúfiism in *Religious Systems of the World* (Swan Sonnenschein, 1892), pp. 314–332.

4. **Some Remarks on the Bábí Texts edited by Baron Victor Rosen.** *J.R.A.S.*, Vol. XXIV, 1892, pp. 259–332.

5. **Catalogue and Description of 27 Bábí Manuscripts.** *J.R.A.S.*, Vol. XXIV, 1892, pp. 433–499 and 637–710.

6. **Ta'ríkh-i-Jadíd or New History of Mírzá 'Alí Muḥammad the Báb.** Translated from the Persian, with an Introduction, Illustrations and Appendices. Pp. liii + 459 + ٢٦. Cambridge University Press, 1893.

7. **Personal Reminiscences of the Bábí Insurrection at Zanján in 1850.** Translated from the Persian. *J.R.A.S.*, Vol. XXIX, 1897, pp. 761–827.

8. **Some Notes on the Literature and Doctrines of the Ḥurúfí Sect.** *J.R.A.S.*, Vol. XXX, 1898, pp. 61–89.

9. **Further Notes on the Literature of the Ḥurúfís and their connection with the Bektáshí Order of Dervishes.** *J.R.A.S.*, Vol. XXXIX, 1907, pp. 533–581.

10. **Báb, Bábís** in the *Encyclopaedia of Religion and Ethics*, edited by James Hastings, Vol. II, 1909, pp. 299–308.

11. **The Kitáb-i-Nuqṭatu'l-Káf,** being the earliest history of the Bábís, compiled by ḤÁJJÍ MÍRZÁ JÁNÍ of Káshán between the years 1850 and 1852. Edited from the unique Paris MS. (Suppl. Pers. 1071). Pp. عج + ٢٩٧ + xcv. E. J. W. Gibb Memorial Series, Vol. XV, 1910.

12. **The Religious Influence of Persia,** a paper read before the Persia Society on May 20, 1914. Pp. 57–72 of a collection of four papers published for the Society.

13. **Materials for the Study of the Bábí Religion.** Pp. xxiv + 380. Cambridge University Press, 1918.

II. PERSIAN LITERATURE, HISTORY, SCIENCE, AND TRAVEL

1. **A Year amongst the Persians:** Impressions as to the Life, Character and Thought of the People of Persia, received during twelve months' residence in that country in the years 1887–8. Pp. x + 594. London, A. and C. Black, 1893. Reprinted, with a Memoir by Sir E. Denison Ross (Cambridge University Press, 1926).

2. **Description of an Old Persian Commentary on the Qur'án.** *J.R.A.S.*, Vol. XXVI, 1894, pp. 417–524.

3. **Some Notes on the Poetry of the Persian Dialects.** *J.R.A.S.*, Vol. XXVII, 1895, pp. 773–825.

4. **A Catalogue of the Persian Manuscripts in the Library of the University of Cambridge.** Pp. xl + 472. Cambridge University Press, 1896.

5. **A Specimen of the Gabrí Dialect of Persia.** *J.R.A.S.*, Vol. XXIX, 1897, pp. 103–110.

6. **The Sources of Dawlatsháh,** with some Remarks on the Materials available for a Literary History of Persia, and an Excursus on Bárbad and Rúdagí. *J.R.A.S.*, Vol. XXXI, 1899, pp. 37–69.

7. **Yet More Light on 'Umar-i-Khayyám.** *J.R.A.S.*, Vol. XXXI, 1899, pp. 409–420.

8. **The Chahár Maqála** ("Four Discourses") of Nidhámí-i-'Arúḍí-i-Samarqandí, translated into English. *J.R.A.S.*, Vol. XXXI, 1899, pp. 613–663 and 757–845. *See* No. 28 *infra*.

9. **A Hand-list of the Muḥammadan Manuscripts in the Library of the University of Cambridge.** Pp. xviii + 440. Cambridge University Press, 1900.

10. **Some Account of the Niháyatu'l-irab fí Akhbári'l-Furs wa'l-'Arab,** particularly of that part which treats of the Persian Kings. *J.R.A.S.*, Vol. XXXII, 1900, pp. 195–259.

11. **Biographies of Persian Poets,** contained in Ch. V, § 6, of the *Ta'ríkh-i-Guzída* or "Select History" of Ḥamdu'lláh Mustawfí of Qazwín. *J.R.A.S.*, Vol. XXXII, 1900, pp. 721–762, and Vol. XXXIII, 1901, pp. 1–32.

12. **The Tadhkiratu'sh-Shu'ará** ("Memoirs of the Poets") of Dawlatsháh of Samarqand. Edited by E. G. BROWNE. Pp. يا + 621 + 16. Persian Historical Texts Series, Vol. I. Luzac & Co., 1901.

13. **Account of a rare manuscript History of Iṣfahán,** presented to the Royal Asiatic Society on May 19, 1827, by Sir John Malcolm. *J.R.A.S.*, Vol. XXXIII, 1901, pp. 411–446 and 661–704.

14. **A Literary History of Persia.**
   Vol. I, from the earliest times until Firdawsí. Pp. xiv + 521. London, T. Fisher Unwin, 1902.
   Vol. II, from Firdawsí to Sa'dí. Pp. xiv + 568. London, T. Fisher Unwin, 1906.
   Vol. III, **Persian Literature under Tartar Dominion** (A.D. 1265–1502). Pp. xi + 586. With 12 illustrations. Cambridge University Press, 1920.
   Vol. IV, **Persian Literature in Modern Times** (A.D. 1500–1924). Pp. ix + 530. With 16 illustrations. Cambridge University Press, 1924.
   The whole work is now issued by the Cambridge University Press in four volumes, uniform in style and appearance.

15. **Catalogue of Two Collections of Persian and Arabic Manuscripts,** preserved in the India Office Library. By E. D. ROSS and E. G. BROWNE. Pp. vii + 189. London, 1902.

16. **Account of a rare manuscript History of the Seljúqs** in the Schefer Collection of MSS. in the Bibliothèque Nationale at Paris. *J.R.A.S.*, Vol. XXXIV, 1902, pp. 567–610 and 849–887.

17. **The Lubábu'l-Albáb** (the oldest Biography of Persian Poets, compiled about A.D. 1221) by Muḥammad 'Awfí. Edited by E. G. BROWNE and MÍRZÁ MUḤAMMAD of Qazwín. Vol. I, pp. كه + ۴۳۳ + xi. Vol. II, pp. و + ۴۷۲ + 78. Persian Historical Texts Series, Vols. II and IV. Luzac & Co., 1903 and 1906.

18. **Note on the Contents of the Ta'ríkh-i-Jahán-gushá** of 'Aṭá Malik-i-Juwayní. *J.R.A.S.*, Vol. XXXVI, 1904, pp. 27–43.

19. **An Abridged Translation of the History of Ṭabaristán** of Muḥammad ibn Ḥasan ibn Isfandiyár. Pp. xv + 356. E. J. W. Gibb Memorial Series, Vol. II, 1905.

20. **Náṣir-i-Khusraw, Poet, Traveller, and Propagandist.** *J.R.A.S.*, Vol. XXXVII, 1905, pp. 313–352.

21. **Mas'úd-i-Sa'd-i-Salmán,** by MÍRZÁ MUḤAMMAD IBN 'ABDU'L-WAHHÁB of Qazwín. Translated by E. G. BROWNE. *J.R.A.S.*, Vol. XXXVII, 1905, pp. 693–740, and Vol. XXXVIII, 1906, pp. 11–51.

22. **A Hand-list of the Turkish and other printed and lithographed books** presented by Mrs E. J. W. Gibb to the Cambridge University Library. Pp. viii + 87. Cambridge University Press, 1906.

23. **Suggestions for a complete edition of the "Jámi'u't-Tawáríkh"** of Rashídu'd-Dín Faḍlu'lláh. *J.R.A.S.*, Vol. XL, 1908, pp. 17–37.

24. **The Ta'ríkh-i-Guzída** ("Select History") of Ḥamdu'lláh Mustawfí, reproduced in facsimile from a MS. written in A.D. 1453, with an abridged translation by E. G. BROWNE and

Indices by R. A. NICHOLSON. Vol. I (facsimile), pp. يجٓ + ۸۵۳ + xix. Vol. II, pp. xxi + 237 + ۲۸۶. E. J. W. Gibb Memorial Series, Vols. XIV, 1 and XIV, 2, 1910 and 1913.

25. **The Literature of Persia,** a Lecture delivered to the Persia Society on April 26, 1912. Pp. 43.

26. **The Persian Manuscripts of the late Sir Albert Houtum-Schindler, K.C.I.E.** *J.R.A.S.*, Vol. XLIX, 1917, pp. 657–694.

27. **Persian Literature under Tartar Dominion,** 1920. *See* No. 14 *supra.*

28. **Revised Translation of the Chahár Maqála** ("Four Discourses") **of Nizámí-i-'Arúḍí of Samarqand,** followed by an abridged translation of Mírzá Muḥammad's Notes to the Persian text. Pp. 184 + xv. E. J. W. Gibb Memorial Series, Vol. XI, 2, 1921. *See* No. 8 *supra.*

29. **Arabian Medicine,** being the FitzPatrick Lectures delivered at the College of Physicians in 1919 and 1920. Pp. viii + 138, with Frontispiece. Cambridge University Press, 1921.

30. **Note on an apparently unique Manuscript History of the Ṣafawí Dynasty of Persia.** *J.R.A.S.*, Vol. LIII, 1921, pp. 395–418.

31. **Supplementary Hand-list of the Muḥammadan Manuscripts** preserved in the Libraries of the University and Colleges of Cambridge. Pp. xi + 348. Cambridge University Press, 1922.

32. **Persian Literature in Modern Times,** 1924. *See* No. 14 *supra.*

33. **The Tajáribu's-Salaf, a Persian version of the Arabic Kitábu'l-Fakhrí,** composed by Hindú-sháh ibn Sanjar aṣ-Ṣáḥibí al-Kíráni in 723/1323. *J.R.A.S.*, *Centenary Supplement*, 1924, pp. 245–254.

34. **A Parallel to the Story, in the Mathnawí of Jalálu'd-Dín Rúmí, of the Jewish King who persecuted the Christians.** *Islamica* (April, 1926), Vol. II, fasc. 1, pp. 129–134.

III. PERSIAN POLITICS AND JOURNALISM

1. **A Brief Narrative of Recent Events in Persia,** followed by a translation of "The Four Pillars of the Persian Constitution." Pp. 101. Luzac & Co., 1909.

2. **The responsibility of the Russian Government for the "chaos" now existing in Persia.** Pp. 11. For private circulation only. Newcastle-upon-Tyne, 1909.

3. **The Persian Revolution of 1905–1909.** Pp. xxvi + 470. With 46 illustrations. Cambridge University Press, 1910.

4. **The Persian Crisis of December, 1911,** how it arose and whither it may lead us, compiled for the use of the Persia Committee, privately printed at the University Press, Cambridge, and published on New Year's Day, 1912. Pp. 18.

5. **The Reign of Terror at Tabríz:** England's Responsibility: with Photographs and a brief Narrative of the events of December, 1911, and January, 1912, compiled for the use of the Persia Committee and published in October, 1912, by Messrs Taylor, Garnett, Evans, & Co., Blackfriars Street, Manchester, and Messrs Luzac & Co., London. Pp. 15.

6. **The Persian Press and Persian Journalism,** a Lecture delivered to the Persia Society on May 23, 1913. Pp. 28.

7. **The Press and Poetry of Modern Persia,** partly based on the Manuscript Work of Mírzá Muḥammad 'Alí "Tarbiyat" of Tabríz. Pp. xl + 357 + ٥. Cambridge University Press, 1914.

8. **The Persian Constitutional Movement.** *Proceedings of the British Academy*, Vol. VIII, 1917–1918, pp. 311–330. Read on February 6, 1918.

All Orientalists will regret that Browne did not live to finish and see in type the Catalogue of his Oriental Manuscripts, upon which he had been engaged for several years before his last illness, and which is now published in accordance with injunctions given by him to his literary executors, Dr Ellis Hovell Minns of Pembroke College and myself. We have done our best to carry out his wishes, and since I am writing on behalf of us both, it is an obvious duty to say a few words here regarding my colleague's share in the work. On him fell the main burden of making the preliminary arrangements for its publication, and though he has taken no part in preparing it for the press, he has helped to settle many points of difficulty which arose in connection with it, and at every stage his collaboration has proved invaluable. Without entering into the reasons which determined our choice of the Cambridge University Press as publishers, perhaps I may say that we took into account the probability that the Browne Collection will ultimately find a permanent home in the University Library, as well as the fact that Browne's three catalogues of the Muḥammadan MSS. in the Library were published by the University Press. The Trustees of the E. J. W. Gibb Memorial Fund agreed to contribute the sum of £150 towards the cost of publication in return for an equivalent number of copies, which will be presented to Oriental scholars and institutions in different parts of the world; and a further sum of £50 was promised by the Managers of the E. G. Browne Memorial Fund. The materials handed over to us comprised (1) the entire Collection of Oriental Manuscripts; (2) a slip-catalogue, dated July, 1922, containing the titles and brief descriptions of most of these MSS.; (3) a catalogue, written on 311 pages of foolscap, containing 386 articles in their final form. It is this, supplemented by 82 articles for which I am responsible, that is published in the present volume.

Now, in the first place, something should be said concerning the formation, contents, and character of the Browne Collection. It began modestly enough with two volumes of Persian Poetry, namely, the *Laylá ú Majnún* of Maktabí (**V. 44**), which Browne acquired on his first visit to Constantinople in 1882—this, by the way, is almost the only one of his MSS. that contains miniatures—and a copy of the *Búsṭán* with Súdí's Turkish translation and commentary, purchased soon afterwards from Quaritch. The real nucleus, however, was formed in 1888, his "year amongst the Persians," and the period immediately following, when his keen interest in the Bábí movement led to the acquisition of about 30 MSS. bearing on the history and doctrines of the sect, a number which subsequently was more than doubled, as on his return from Persia he kept up an active correspondence with both Azalís and Bahá'ís; and even after this had slackened, he continued to receive copies of their latest books and tracts at frequent intervals till within a year or two of his death. From 1890 onwards the Collection expanded steadily, but although 39 MSS., of which nearly half belong to Classes **V** and **W** (Persian and Turkish Poetry), were purchased, for the most part between 1901 and 1911, from J. J. Naaman of

Baghdád, it received its most important accessions during and after the European War. In January, 1917, Browne acquired *en bloc* the small but valuable collection of Schindler MSS., 64 in all, which he has described in the *Journal of the Royal Asiatic Society* (October, 1917, p. 657 foll.). Sir Albert Houtum-Schindler possessed a singularly deep and extensive knowledge of Persia, where he spent over forty years of his life in the service of the Persian Government. His tastes were objective; hence in this group of MSS., as Browne remarks, "historical, biographical, and geographical works enormously preponderate; the remaining volumes represent lexicography, anecdotes, and various scientific subjects, *viz.*, medicine, astronomy, music, and notably mineralogy and the natural history of precious stones." As the provenance of the Schindler MSS. is not always stated in the Catalogue, I append a complete list of the class-marks under which they are described: **C 1**; **D 8**; **G 6**, **G 8**, **G 10–12**, **G 14**, **G 15**, **G 17**; **H 2–4**, **H 6**, **H 8**, **H 10–12**, **H 14–17**, **H 19**, **H 21**, **H 22**; **I 1–4**, **I 6**, **I 7**; **J 5**, **J 6**, **J 8**, **J 18**; **K 2**, **K 3**, **K 5–9**; **L 1–3**, **L 6**; **N 1**; **O 3**; **P 12**, **P 13**, **P 29–32**; **R 1**; **S 3**, **S 5**; **V 59**, **V 69**; **X 4**, **X 6**; **Y 3**; **Sup. 3**, **Sup. 4**.

A collector of very different type was Ḥájjí 'Abdu'l-Majíd Belshah (*ob.* 1923), whose name appears oftener than any other in the pages of this Catalogue. Though, like many professional dealers in Oriental manuscripts, he may sometimes have been inclined to overestimate their worth, "his *flair* for good books was only equalled by his energy in seeking them out," and the present Collection (not to speak of those in the British Museum and the India Office Library) is indebted to him for many of its choicest treasures. From Belshah, directly or indirectly, Browne obtained at least 100 MSS., the great majority of which were purchased in 1920. About half of them are works on Medicine (26), Shí'a Theology (12), and Mysticism (9), while Arabic and Persian Poetry are represented by 15 volumes and Mathematics and Astronomy by 5. Further large acquisitions, the last of their kind, were made in December, 1923, and January, 1924, when 57 MSS. were bought from the Trustees of the British Museum.

The facts which have been noticed indicate the provenance of some 330 MSS., *i.e.* over two-thirds of the whole Collection. Many others, including five acquired (May, 1901) at the sale of a Bektáshí dervish's effects, were picked up at auctions in London, Constantinople and elsewhere, or purchased from booksellers and private individuals. An extraordinarily high proportion—not less, I think, than 75 or 80—were personal gifts to Browne from his friends. Dr Riẓá Tevfíq, the well-known Turkish patriot, philosopher, and man of letters, presented him with 31 volumes; a great many gifts of this kind came from Persia; and the same generosity, which he never failed to appreciate, was shown by many of his English and European friends, such as (to mention only a few names), Mr Guy le Strange, E. J. W. Gibb, Sir Albert Houtum-Schindler, Professor A. von Le Coq of Berlin, Mr H. L. Rabino, Sir Mark Sykes, Professor E. H. Minns, C. D. Cobham, and Rev. W. St Clair Tisdall.

The motives and considerations by which Browne was guided in forming his Collection are apparent from numerous passages in his works. He points out that "those whose studies are concerned with Western literature, whether ancient or modern, often hardly realize how dependent the Orientalist is on manuscript materials. Of most important ancient and mediaeval Western writings some tolerable printed edition exists, even though it be rare and not equal to the highest standard of textual accuracy. But in the case of Oriental, especially Persian, books of reference it is far otherwise; many indispensable works exist only in manuscript and can only be consulted in large libraries like the British Museum." When he described Sir Albert Houtum-Schindler's MSS. as "a working library, containing many very rare books carefully selected during a long period of time...for a definite purpose of study, and clearly reflecting the outlook of him who formed it," he was no doubt conscious that these words might be applied with the same propriety to his own Collection. In his view a manuscript was primarily a scientific instrument, and unless it had some intrinsic value as such, its merits as an object of art would seldom kindle his enthusiasm, though he was not insensible to the charms of calligraphy when they met his eye, for example, in a fine old Persian codex of the 13th century. It was his thirst for knowledge, and the depth and breadth of his interest in Islam, that created the Collection and gave it so much of the personal character and individuality that we find everywhere in his writings, just as it was his study of the materials which he gradually accumulated in the course of his life-work that enabled him to strike off from the familiar highways of Orientalism and penetrate into regions hitherto little known or altogether unexplored.

The total number of MSS. designated by class-marks is 468. Some are in two or more volumes, and the number of separate works is, of course, very much greater, as many MSS. contain several by one or more than one author. Taking a general survey of their subject-matter, we observe that Religion, including Theology and Mysticism, claims 149; Poetry 115; History and Biography 76; Medicine and Natural Science 43; while the remnant are distributed in comparatively small numbers under such heads as Geography and Travels, Philosophy, Lexicography, and Belles-Lettres. No one need be told that the most prominent features of the Collection coincide with those aspects of Islam by which Browne was mainly attracted. The **Shaykhí and Bábí MSS.** alone would suffice to make it memorable; probably they constitute the fullest and richest assemblage of original documents relating to these sects that exists in any public or private library in the world. Among them are the *Maqála-i-Shakhṣí Sayyáḥ* (**F 56**), of which the text, accompanied by an English translation, was published by Browne in 1891; the *Ta'ríkh-i-Jadíd* (**F 55**), which he translated two years afterwards; the *Ṣaḥífa bayna'l-Ḥaramayn* (**F 7**), one of the earliest writings of the Báb, with a note by Ṣubḥ-i-Azal on the disposal of the Báb's remains; and a collection of letters written by the Báb to various persons (**F 21**). **Ḥurúfí** literature, the subject of two articles by Browne in the *Journal of the Royal Asiatic Society*, is also strongly represented. Measured in terms of MSS., his preference for Shí'a as opposed to Sunní religious literature is something like nine to one, and 22 volumes on **Ṣúfism** do not go far towards restoring the balance. These comprise a Persian translation of the *Fuṣúṣu'l-Ḥikam* (**D 1**) made in 744/1343–4; an excellent old copy (768/1367) of the *Mirṣádu'l-'Ibád* of Najmu'd-Dín Dáya (**D 3**); and two autographs, *viz.*, a polemic against the Ṣúfís, entitled *Maṭá'inu'ṣ-Ṣúfiyya* (**D** 16), which was composed in 1221/1806 by Muḥammad Rafí' of Tabriz, and a treatise (**D 17**) written in 1887 by 'Abdu'lláh Muḥammad Zamán in answer to nine questions on Ṣúfí terminology and doctrine which Browne had submitted to his eccentric friend, Mírzá Muḥammad Báqir of Bawánát. Several other religious works in the Collection are remarkable for their antiquity or rarity, and an old anonymous Persian Commentary on the *Qur'án* (**A 1**) seems to be unique.

Among the **Historical and Biographical MSS.**, attention may be drawn to the *Tajáribu's-Salaf* (**G 3**), a Persian version of the *Kitábu'l-Fakhrí*, described by Browne in the Centenary Volume of the Royal Asiatic Society (1924); a complete copy, apparently the only one extant, of an enormous general history in Persian entitled *Khuld-i-Barín* (**G 14**); a fine and ancient copy, dated 542/1148, of Shahristání's *Kitábu'l-Milal wa'n-Niḥal* (**H 1**); the very rare *Silsilatu'n-Nasab-i-Ṣafawiyya* (**H 12**) on the Ṣafawí kings and their ancestors; the original Arabic treatise, entitled *Risála fí Maḥásini Isfahán*, by al-Máfarrúkhí, together with the Persian translation of the same (**I 1** and **I 2**); and the *Qiṣaṣu'l-Anbiyá* (**J 21**), translated into Persian from the Arabic of Abu'l-Ḥasan al-Búshanjí, in which there occurs an account of St Paul that forms the subject of the last article written by Browne before his death (see *Islamica*, April, 1926, pp. 129–134). A most instructive and probably unique collection of letters by the famous statesman and historian, Rashídu'd-Dín Faḍlu'lláh, is preserved in the *Munsha'át-i-Rashídí* (**L 1**).

Next to the Bábí MSS., I think the most characteristic group is that composed of 28 works on **Medicine and Medical Science**, a domain in which Browne renewed the studies of his youth and felt himself to be inspired by the traditions of what he always regarded as "a great and noble profession." The rare books belonging to this class include the *Kitábu'l-Fákhir* of Rází (**P 2**); eleventh century copies of 'Alí ibn 'Ísá's *Tadhkiratu'l-Kaḥḥálín* (**P 3**) and the *Maqála fí Khalqi'l-Insán* (**P 4**) of Sa'íd ibn Hibati'lláh; part of Book III of the *Qánún* of Avicenna (**P 5**), transcribed by the eminent physician Hibatu'lláh ibn Ṣá'id (*ob.* 560/1164); and the encyclopaedic *Dhakhíra-i-Khwárazmsháhí* (**P 16**), complete in one volume, as well as portions of the same work dating from the thirteenth and fourteenth centuries (**P 17–19**). Among the remaining **Scientific MSS.** the *Zíju'l-Mufrad* (**O 1**), a unique work on astronomy and chronology, deserves particular notice; there are also some *tansúq-náma's* or Persian lapidaries (**P 29–33**). **Persian Poetry**, the largest single class in the Collection, though less rich in quality than many others, contains the *Gházán-námá* (**V 28**), an extremely rare account of the reign of Gházán Khán the Mongol, composed in 758/1357; the complete works of 'Aṭṭár (**V 7**) and Jamálí or Pír Jamál (**V 38**); ancient copies of the *Díwán* of Qásimu'l-Anwár (**V 35**) and the *Tuḥfatu'l-Aḥrár* of Jámí (**V 41**); some uncommon *Díwáns*, *e.g.*, those of Jahán (**V 32**), Muḥyí (**V 46**), Shaykh Ṣáfí (**V 56**), Maẓhar (**V 57**), Mír Naṣr Nawá (**V 84**), Ṭarzí (**V 86**); three valuable Anthologies (**V 65**, **V 68**, **V 88**); and a Kurdish *mathnawí* entitled Kitáb-i-Mullá Paríshán (**V 62**).

Inadequate as it is, the foregoing review will have served to show the importance of the Collection for students of Islamic literature and literary history. I can now proceed to explain the arrangement of the Catalogue, or rather let Browne himself explain it by quoting a passage in which, with his usual mastery of details, he sets forth the principles and practice that he has followed.

"Now even a few hundred manuscripts, if they are to be readily available for reference, must be catalogued, and for this purpose each one must bear a class-mark for identification and a size-mark to indicate location. It would, of course, be more convenient if the books could be arranged simply according to subject; but owing to the difference of size this would involve a great waste of space on the shelves, and those volumes must stand together which are approximately of the same height. The system which I have adopted for the size-marks... is that used in the Cambridge University Library, according to which a book is marked **8** when it is over 7 and under 8 inches in height, and so on. Since a book marked **8** should go into a shelf 8 inches in height, directly it exceeds this height, no matter by how little, it becomes **9**. Under each size the books are arranged in order of class-marks, so that the double indication of size-mark and class-mark enables a book to be located immediately. The question of class-marks is rather less simple, and the system must be adapted to the extent and character of the collection.... I therefore decided to group the subjects under the 26 letters of the Roman alphabet; in each subject to arrange the books in chronological order; and when one book was represented by more than one MS., to put the older before the later copy. In arranging the classes, I followed on the whole the order adopted in Dr Rieu's excellent Catalogues of the Persian, Arabic, and Turkish MSS. in the British Museum, except that I placed non-Muḥammadan religious books at the end, under **Z**, instead of at the beginning, under **A**....Also I made no differentiation according to language, for Muḥammadan learning and culture is so essentially one that its vehicle is, comparatively speaking, a matter of indifference[1]."

So much for the method of classification. The reader will see at once that, for instance, the MS. designated as **Q 4** (9) occupies the fourth place in Class **Q** and is over eight, but not more than nine, inches in height. As finally arranged the Classes, with the number of MSS. in each, are as follows:

[1] From an unpublished paper, entitled *A Persian Library*, which Browne read before the Royal Asiatic Society on November 14, 1922.

A. Qur'áns and Commentaries.	3 MSS.	**P.** Medicine, Natural Science, Mineralogy, etc.	35 MSS.
B. Sunní Theology, etc.	13 MSS.	**Q.** Occult Sciences.	6 MSS.
C. Shí'a Theology, etc.	23 MSS.	**R.** Art, Calligraphy, Music, etc.	5 MSS.
D. Mysticism.	22 MSS.	**S.** Dictionaries.	10 MSS.
E. The Older Heretical Sects.	21 MSS.	**T.** Acrostics, Rhyme, Rhetoric, etc.	5 MSS.
F. Shaykhí and Bábí MSS.	67 MSS.	**U.** Arabic Poetry.	11 MSS.
G. General History.	19 MSS.	**V.** Persian Poetry.	94 MSS.
H. History of Special Periods, Dynasties, etc.	23 MSS.	**W.** Turkish Poetry.	10 MSS.
I. Local Histories.	11 MSS.	**X.** Stories and Epistolary Models.	14 MSS.
J. Biographical Works.	23 MSS.	**Y.** Collectanea, Miscellanea, and Unclassified.	12 MSS.
K. Geography and Travels.	9 MSS.	**Z.** Non-Islamic Books.	1 MS.
L. Official Papers, Letters, etc.	6 MSS.	**Sup.** (Supernumerary)[1].	9 MSS.
M. Encyclopaedias.	2 MSS.		
N. Philosophy.	6 MSS.		
O. Mathematics and Astronomy.	8 MSS.		

When the written Catalogue, containing Browne's description of 386 of these 468 MSS., came into my hands, I found that it was in perfect order so far as it went, and that all I had to do was to re-write some words here and there which might have puzzled the compositors, make a few trivial corrections, insert a few foot-notes[2], and verify the references. If the claims of other work have sometimes prevented me from discharging the last-mentioned duty as thoroughly as I could have wished, it must be added that numerous tests of the author's accuracy have almost invariably confirmed my respect for it. But unfortunately the Catalogue, as he left it, was incomplete. I had to ascertain the extent of the deficiency, and in the summer of 1926, after the MSS. had been deposited in the University Library, my friend Mr Guy le Strange, who was also one of Browne's oldest and most valued friends, undertook the arduous task of arranging the volumes on the shelves. By grouping together those of the same size *seriatim* and drawing up a table to show the location of each group, he made it easy for me to find any particular MS. that might be wanted; moreover, he noted cases where the same class-mark had been assigned to two MSS. or where MSS. which had been entered in the Catalogue were no longer traceable. I am glad to have an opportunity of recording my gratitude to Mr le Strange for the time and trouble which he devoted to this labour of love in circumstances that rendered it peculiarly toilsome.

The 84 MSS.[3] of which the written Catalogue gave no account bear the following class-marks: **D 21**, **D 22**; **F 65**, **F 66**, **F 66***; **H 23**; **L 6**; **N 6**; **S 9**, **S 10**; **U 10**,

[1] See the Appendix. The nine MSS. of this Class were discovered among Browne's lithographed editions of Oriental texts by Mr Reuben Levy, University Lecturer in Persian, whilst he was engaged in preparing a Hand-list of the latter.

[2] These are enclosed in square brackets, to distinguish them from foot-notes written by the author himself.

[3] Two MSS., designated by the class-marks **V 74** and **Y 2**, are not included in the Collection.

U 11; V 69, V 69*, V 70, V 70*, V 71, V 71*, V 72–91; W 1–10; X 1–14; Y 1–12; Z 1; Sup. 1–9. Over a dozen were obtained by gift or purchase at various dates between 1898 and 1917, but most were recent acquisitions[1]. As a rule, I have described them briefly, since on the whole they are uninteresting and, though they contribute to the catholicity of the Collection, have scarcely repaid me for many tedious hours spent in their company. The two Indices will, I hope, be found useful. The first contains only the titles of MSS. described in the Catalogue; the second, the names of authors, copyists, and other persons, titles of books, and some general references. In the Catalogue the following abbreviations have occasionally been employed:

A.S.B. Persian Catalogue or A.S.B.P.C. = Concise Descriptive Catalogue of the Persian Manuscripts in the Collection of the Asiatic Society of Bengal, by W. Ivanow (Calcutta, 1924).

B.M.P.C. = Catalogue of Persian MSS. in the British Museum, by C. Rieu.

B.M.T.C. = Catalogue of Turkish MSS. in the British Museum, by C. Rieu.

I.O. Persian Catalogue or I.O.P.C. = Catalogue of Persian MSS. in the India Office Library, Vol. 1, by H. Ethé.

J.R.A.S. = *Journal of the Royal Asiatic Society.*

As has been explained above, I am particularly indebted to Professor E. H. Minns and Mr Guy le Strange for the help they have given me in the preparation of this work; but there are also other friends and colleagues to whom I wish to express my thanks—to Mr R. Levy for discovering and calling my attention to several MSS. which had been mislaid; to Mr E. Edwards of the British Museum for his notices (*Browne Presentation Volume*, pp. 137–149) of certain MSS. in the Collection; and to the University Librarian, Mr A. F. Scholfield, for facilities in making use of the Library, for his interest in the work, and for his promptness and courtesy in disposing of many questions with which I troubled him. A final word of gratitude is due to the Staff of the Cambridge University Press for the care and skill that made the correction of the proofs, if not a light task, at least an exceptionally pleasant one of its kind.

[1] A list at the end of the slip-catalogue (on which Browne's later manuscript catalogue was based) gives the titles of 23, and is preceded by a note stating that they were bought as a residue from the Trustees of the British Museum on January 17, 1924.

REYNOLD A. NICHOLSON

February 7, 1932

A. QUR'ÁNS AND COMMENTARIES.

A. 1 (9).

A *Qur'án*, imperfect at the beginning, lacking *súras* I–V and part of VI, written in a very peculiar hand, unlike any that I have seen, attributed by the vendor, the late Ḥájjí 'Abdu'l-Majíd Belshah, to the seventh (thirteenth) century, but by the experts of the British Museum to the seventeenth or eighteenth century of our era.

Ff. 275 of 21·6 × 12·8 c. and 12 ll.; n. d.

A. 2 (10).

A Persian commentary on the *Qur'án*, defective at beginning and end, of unknown authorship, but probably composed in the eleventh and transcribed in the thirteenth century of the Christian era. It begins with *súra* XXXVIII, 20, and ends with *súra* XCV. The margins of some of the pages, especially in the earlier part of the volume, are filled with Turkish verses. There is one serious dislocation, *súra* LV being omitted in its proper place and inserted after *súra* LXXXIX, where there is a considerable lacuna and further dislocations, for *súra* XCVI follows, and after that *súras* XCIV and XCV. As a specimen of the style, and for purposes of comparison, the commentary on the first ten verses of *súra* LXXX (عَبَسَ وَتَوَلَّى) is here given from ff. 233[b]–234[a]. After the continuous text of these ten verses, which it is unnecessary to reproduce here, the commentary proceeds thus:

آورده اند که روزی عبد الله بن امّ مکتوم و اورا عبد الله بن شریح گفتندی مردی بود مکفوف نابینا بنزدیك رسول خدای آمد و صنادید قریش چون عتبه بن ربیعه و ابو جهل بن هشام و عبّاس بن المطّلب و غیر ایشان حاضر بودند رسول عَم با ایشان سخن میگفت و از سرِ حرص بر ایمانِ ایشان خودرا بایشان داده بود و دعوة میکرد ابن امّ مکتوم نمیدانست که ایشان حاضر اند و رسول با ایشان سخن میگوید روی برسول آورد و گفت یا رسول الله اَقرِءنِی وعَلِّمنی ممّا عَلَّمَكَ الله از آنچ خدای بتو آموختهاست بر من خوان و مرا بیاموز و این سخن مکرّر گردانید رسول خدای روی از وی بگردانید کراهتِ آنرا که سخن قطع میبایست کردن بآخر نا رسیده و نیز از برای آن تا کافران نگویند که اتباعِ محمّد و مُجِیبان دعوتِ او نابینایان و سفله اند خدای تعالی این آیات فرستاد و گفت عَبَسَ وَتَوَلَّى پس از آن هرگاه که وی آمدی رسول خدای ویرا گرامی داشتی و گفتی مرحبًا ای آنکسی که خدای تعَ از برای وی با من عتاب کرد و دو نوبت ویرا بر مدینه خلیفه گردانید و پس از آن در روی هیچ درویشی روی ترش نگردانید و فراپیش هیچ توانگری نیامد، جمعی مفسّران چنین گفته اند که این عُبُوس از رسول خدای بود و او بود که روی ترش کرد امّا محقّقان گفته اند که رسول نبود که روی

ترش کرد بلکه مردی بود اُمَوی بنزدیك رسول حاضر بود چون این مرد نابینا آنجا آمد وی خودرا فراهم گرفت و اعراض کرد و روی ترش گردانید عبوس و اعراضی که از جملهٔ صفات مذمومه است و منفر اگر در بعضی علما و فقها گویند منفر باشد فکیف در حق رسول و خدای تعالی رسول‌را ازین جمله تنزیه کرده است و گفته وَلَوْ كُنْتَ فَظًّا غَلِيظَ ٱلْقَلْبِ لَٱنْفَضُّوا مِنْ حَوْلِكَ و بحسن خُلق و کرم و طبع وصف کرده است وَإِنَّكَ عَلَى خُلُقٍ عَظِيمٍ تا در خبر آمده است که رسول عمَ دست در دست غلام سیاه نهادی کریه الخلق و الرّایحة از کرم روا نداشتی (f. 234ᵃ) که دست خود از دست وی دور گرداند تا هم آن غلام آغاز کردی و دست از دست رسول ببردی حق سبحانه و تعالی از آن مرد اُمَوی خبر داد و گفت وی روی ترش کرد و فراهم کشید و اعراض کرد از آن سبب که نابینا یعنی ابن امّ مکتوم بوی آمد آنگه التفات کرد با رسول که روی بایشان آورده بود و با یکی ازیشان سخن میگفت از حرص آنك باشد که وی ایمان آرد تا دیگران نیز ایمان آورند گفت ای محمّد تو چه دانی و ترا چه شناسا گردانید بحال این کافر که وی ایمان خواهد آورد و باسلام پاکیزه خواهد گشت و مطموع تو حاصل خواهد آمد یا خود وی پند خواهد گرفت و موعظت و پند تو ویرا سود خواهد کرد و گفته اند معنی اینست که چه چیز ترا بحال این نابینا عالم گردایند که باشد که وی تو آنچ ویرا تلقین کنی و بیاموزی از شریعت پاکیزه شود یا خود متّعظ گردد و پند تو قبول کند پس موعظت تو و پند تو ویرا سود کند آنگه گفت أَمَّا مَنِ ٱسْتَغْنَى امّا آنکس که توانگر باشد تو فرا پیش وی روی و رُوی بوی آری چون عتبه و شیبه یا عبّاس عبد المطّلب و چه باشد بر تو اگر پاکیزه نشود و ایمان نیارد بر تو جز از رسانیدن رسالت چیزی دیگر نیست و امّا آن کس که پیش تو آید بشتاب در طلبِ خیر و تعلّم شرایع و او از خدای میترسد یا از کافران و ایذاء ایشان تو خودرا از وی مشغول سازی٬

Many of the early traditionists are cited, but few books. Amongst these few the commentary of Abú Isḥáq ibn Muḥammad ath-Tha'labí (d. 427/1036)[1] seems to be one of the latest. The authority of the *Tafsíru Ahli'l-Bayt*, or explanation of the Imáms, is also occasionally invoked[2].

Ff. 267 of 23·5 × 16·4 c. and 23 ll.; fine old *naskh*, the Arabic text in a larger hand.

A. 3 (8).

رَوْضاتِ لندنی و فَوْحاتِ انجمنی کنایت از قرآن معطّر٬

A versified Persian commentary on the twenty-six *súras* of the *Qur'án* revealed, according to the author's belief, in the first year of the Prophet's mission. This is the original, and, I believe, the only copy of this curious book, which was given to me by the author, Mírzá Muḥammad Báqir of Bawánát in Fárs, called Ibráhím Ján

---

[1] See Brockelmann, vol. I, p. 350. It is cited on f. 53ᵇ of the MS., third and fourth lines from the bottom.

[2] *E.g.* on f. 55ᵃ, third line from the bottom.

Mu'aṭṭar, concerning whom some information will be found on pp. 13–16 of my *Year amongst the Persians*. As stated in the prose preface, he began it on January 15, 1883, completed it on May 24 of the same year, and presented it to me a few days before his departure from England for Beyrout about the end of 1884.

The MS. comprises 179 ff. of 14 × 11 c. and 16 ll., and is throughout written in the author's clear *naskh* hand. The prose preface (ff. 2^b–3^a) is followed by a versified preface entitled "Breezes of the Garden" (*Nasá'im-i-Rawḍa*) consisting of thirteen "Breezes" (*Nasím*), each containing from seven to twelve verses (*Shamím*). These are entitled as follows:

(١) عرضِ حالِ معطّر، (٢) ذوقِ وصالِ معطّر، (٣) بنای رازِ معطّر، (۴) رَهِ نیازِ معطّر، (٥) پذیرشِ معطّر، (٦) پوزشِ معطّر، (٧) اختیارِ معطّر، (٨) افتخارِ معطّر، (٩) تسلّای معطّر، (١٠) تمنّای معطّر، (١١) شورِ معطّر، (١٢) فتورِ معطّر، (١٣) مکتبِ معطّر،

Next follows the "Entrance of the Garden" (*Madkhal-i-Rawḍa*), or "Mu'aṭṭar's Alphabet" (*Abjad-i-Mu'aṭṭar*), wherein each of the twenty-eight letters of the Arabic alphabet is the subject of three or four verses, the whole of this section (ff. 13^a–19^a) comprising one hundred verses, of which the following may serve as a specimen:

مدخلِ روضه،
ابجدِ معطّر،
١٠٠ شمیم
(ا = ١)

١ گویند الف اصلش، گاوِ علف‌خوار است،
باقر الف دارد، پس گاویش کار است،

٢ چون گاوِ موساوی، ذبحش شده واجب،
خاکسترِ جسمش، تقدیسِ اخیار است،

٣ یك تا شده از کُلّ، فرد آمده در قُل،
گویا چو ابراهیم، در قُلّش اکثار است،

(ب = ٢)

۴ با اصلش از بیت است، پس خانه‌اش آباد،
ابیاتِ او هر یك، بیت الله آثار است،

٥ معمورِ جاویدان، چون عُمْرِ جاویدی،
هر گوشهٔ حُسْنش، تحسینِ معمار است،

٦ دو آمده شاخش، و اعلا شده کاخش،
قرنین نفّاخش، از نفخه سرشار است،

The remainder of the book contains the commentary on the twenty-six short *súras* in verses like the above, each verse of each *súra* being explained in seven stanzas, with an additional strophe in each case for the *Bismi'lláh*, and a short prose introduction. The term "commentary" is, however, misleading, for the Persian verses are not so much an explanation of the Sacred Text as a short sermon on it, setting forth the eccentric author's theological ideas in his own fantastic style. As a specimen *Fawḥa* VI of *Dawḥa* XIX (or, in plain language, verse 4 of *súra* XC) is here given in its entirety (f. 102[a]):

فوحه ٦

(لَقَدْ خَلَقْنَا ٱلإِنْسَانَ فِي أَحْسَنِ تَقْوِيمٍ،)

٣٦ بی شبهه انسان‌را، در احسنِ تقویم،
ما آفریدستیم، وز چشمِ بد دور است،

٣٧ خیلِ ملایك‌را اعوانِ او کردیم،
مستنصرِ ما خود همواره منصور است،

٣٨ در اوّل و آخر انسانِ ما فرد است،
دیروز و فردا کو؟ آنجا که این هور است،

٣٩ در خوشهٔ انگور از دانه تعداد است،
در صورت و معنی هر دانه انگور است،

٤٠ در ذوق اگر آئی بی دانه فرمائی،
کو خوشه و کو رز کم دیده[1] مخمور است،

٤١ من تاكِ آن باغم کز من شد او پُر تاك،
این جزءِ کُل‌دان سخت در حیطه محصور است،

٤٢ در مکّه و عکّه از هر طرف مسجود،
در لندن و شیراز هر گوشه منظور است،

---

[1] *K'am dída* = *ki dída-am*, "for my eye."

B. SUNNÍ THEOLOGY, ETC.

B. 1 (9).

المقصد الأسنى فى معانى اسمآء الله الحسنى

Al-Maqṣadu'l-Asnà [not *-Aqṣà*, as written in the colophon of f. 85[b]] *fí Ma'ání Asmá'i'lláhi'l-Ḥusnà* ("the Ultimate Goal, on the Meanings of the Most Comely Names of God"), by Abú Ḥámid Muḥammad ibn Muḥammad al-Ghazálí (b. 451/1059, d. 505/1111). See Brockelmann's *Gesch. d. Arab. Litt.*, vol. I, p. 421, No. 5; and Ahlwardt's Berlin Arabic Catalogue, vol. II, pp. 500–501 (Nos. 2219–2220).

Ff. 86 of 20·8 × 15 c. and 17 ll.; clear but ungraceful *nasta'líq* with rubrications; transcription completed on Ṣafar 19, 973 (Sept. 15, 1565). This is one of the MSS. collected by the late Ḥájjí 'Abdu'l-Majíd Belshah which fell to my share in the fourth partition of the same at the British Museum on Nov. 12, 1920.

B. 2 (9).

عقائد النّسفى

The *'Aqá'id* ("Beliefs" or "Doctrines") of Abú Ḥafṣ Najmu'd-Dín 'Umar ibn Muḥammad ibn Aḥmad an-Nasafí (b. 460/1068, d. 537/1142). See Brockelmann, vol. I, p. 427, No. 1; and Ahlwardt's Berlin Arabic Catalogue, vol. II, p. 404, Nos. 1953–4. This well-known work occupies ff. 1[b]–97[a] of the MS., and is followed (on ff. 98[b]–121[a]) by a similar but anonymous work, bearing the ungrammatical title in red—هذه الكتاب عقيده. I think that this MS. was one of several brought back from Russia (Kazan) by Dr Ellis H. Minns.

Ff. 121 of 21·2 × 16·2 c. and 15 ll.; fair *nasta'líq* written within margins ruled in red, and transcribed, the first part in 1246/1830 and the second in A.D. 1827, by Khalaf ibn Sulaymán al-Marjání, evidently somewhere in Turkistán or Asiatic Russia.

B. 3 (11)

رمز الحقائق فى شرح كنز الدقائق

The *Ramzu'l-Ḥaqá'iq*, a commentary by Badru'd-Dín Maḥmúd al-'Ayní (d. 855/1451) on the *Kanzu'l-Ḥaqá'iq* of Ḥáfiẓu'd-Dín Abu'l-Barakát 'Abdu'lláh ibn Aḥmad an-Nasafí (d. 710/1310). See Brockelmann, vol. II, p. 197, l. 2.

Ff. 150 of 25·3 × 16·5 c. and 22 ll.; coarse but clear *nasta'líq* with rubrications in a kind of large Kúfic hand. There is no date or colophon, and the MS. seems to be incomplete at the end, but, like the last, it was evidently transcribed in Turkistán or Asiatic Russia, probably early in the nineteenth century. I think that it also was one of the MSS. brought back from Russia (Kazan) by Dr Ellis H. Minns.

B. 4 (10).

شواهد النبوّة لمولانا عبد الرحمن الجامی،

A very fine MS. of the *Shawáhidu'n-Nubuwwa* ("Evidences of Prophethood") composed by Mullá Núru'd-Dín 'Abdu'r-Raḥmán Jámí in 885/1480–1, a date indicated by the chronogram تَمَّمْتُهُ ("I completed it") in some verses at the end of the book, beginning:

لك الحمد والشكر يا ذا الجلال، که وصفِ تمامی گرفت این مقال،
درآن وقتم اتمامِ آن دست داد، که تَمَّمْتُهُ بود تاریخ سال،

For a brief account of the contents of this work, see my *Persian Literature under Tartar Dominion*, pp. 512–513, and Rieu's Persian Catalogue, p. 146.

Ff. 271 of 24·2 × 18·5 c. and 17 ll.; fine, large, clear *naskh* within gold and blue lines; undated, but transcribed before 970/1562–3, when, according to the following note on f. 271ᵇ, it or its owner had the honour of "kissing the hands" of Sulṭán Sulaymán "the Magnificent" at Kútáhiya in Asia Minor:

در سیزدهم ماه ذی القعده سنه ٩٧٠ در محروسهٔ کوتاهیه بشرفِ دستبوسی حضرت سلطانِ عالمیان عمدهٔ سلاطین زمان زبدهٔ خواقینِ آلِ عثمان مشرّف و مستسعد شدیم والحمد لله علی ذلك وأصلّی وأسلّم علی سیّدنا محمّد وآله وصحبه والسّلام، حرّر فی ثالث عشر شهر ذی القعدة الحرام لسنة سبعین وتسعمائة،

I bought the MS. for £3. 10*s*. 0*d*. from Naaman of Baghdád on May 7, 1903.

B. 5 (8).

رسائل السّیوطی،

The following ten tracts by Jalálu'd-Dín 'Abdu'r-Raḥmán as-Suyúṭí (b. 849/1445, d. 911/1505), concerning whose life and very numerous works see Brockelmann, vol. II, pp. 143–158:

(1) *Arba'ún^a Ḥadíth^an* ("Forty Traditions"), ff. 2^a–4^b. Dated Rajab, 967/April, 1560.

(2) *Raf'u'l-Khidr 'an qaṭ'i's-Sidr*, ff. 5^a–7^a. Brockelmann, *loc. cit.*, p. 155, No. 243. Dated the same as the last.

(3) Questions put to the Imám ash-Sháfi'í, ff. 7^b–9^a. No colophon.

(4) *Qaṣída...fi'n-Naḥw*, a poem on grammar (ff. 10^a–12^b), but there seems to be a lacuna or dislocation after f. 10, and ff. 11–12 appear to contain the conclusion of a tract entitled *Al-Musháraʻa ila'l-Muṣáraʻa.*

(5) *Buzúghu'l-hilál fi'l-khiṣáli'l-mujíbat^i li'ẓ-ẓalál*, ff. 13^a–18^b. See Brockelmann, *loc. cit.*, p. 147, No. 35. Dated 10 Shawwál, 964/8 August, 1557.

(6) *Wuṣúlu'l-amání bi-uṣúli't-tahání*, ff. 19^a–22^a. See Brockelmann, *loc. cit.*, p. 153, No. 191. Dated 19 Rajab, 967/15 April, 1560.

(7) *Kitábu'l-ináfa fí rutbati'l-Khiláfa*, ff. 22^a–23^a: n. d.

(8) *Az-Zahru'l-básim fí-má yarúḥu fíhi'l-Ḥákim*, ff. 24^a–25^b.

(9) *Sihámu'l-Iṣába fi'd-Da'awáti'l-mujába* (or Answers to Prayer), ff. 26^a–30^a. See Brockelmann, *loc. cit.*, p. 147, No. 38. Copied by Abu'l-Luṭf ibn Ibráhím, and completed on 13 Ramaḍán, 964/10 July, 1557.

(10) *Maṭla'u'l-Badrayn fí-man yu'tà Ajrayn*, ff. 31^a–35^a. See Brockelmann, *loc. cit.*, p. 147, No. 37. Dated the same as the preceding.

Ff. 35 of 18 × 13·5 c. and 17 ll.; clear *nasta'líq* with rubrications; bought with others of the Belshah MSS. on Nov. 12, 1920.

B. 6 (9).

الزهر المنثور على شرح الصّدور فى احوال الموتى والقبور

Az-Zahru'l-Manthúr, a commentary by 'Abdu's-Salám ibn Ibráhím al-Laqání on as-Suyúṭí's work on the state of the Dead in their tombs, entitled *Sharḥu'ṣ-Ṣudúr fí Aḥwáli'l-Mawtà wa'l-Qubúr*. For the text and its author (d. 911/1505) see Brockelmann, vol. II, p. 146, No. 30; and for the commentator, who died 1078/1668, *ibid.*, p. 307.

After the *Bismi'lláh* the commentary begins quite abruptly:

قوله ابو نُعيم اسمه احمد بن عبد الله' قوله مجاهد بن جبر الخ

Ff. 178 of 21·3 × 15·5 c. and 17 ll.; good, clear *naskh* within red lines and with rubrications; many marginal notes; copied in 1126/1714.

This commentary might be a help to understanding the text, but is of little value or interest without it.

B. 7 (8) and B. 8 (7).

دلائل الخيرات

Two copies of the well-known devotional work entitled *Dalá'ilu'l-Khayrát* by Abú 'Abdi'lláh Muḥammad al-Jazúlí (d. 870/1465). See Brockelmann, vol. II, pp. 252–253.

B. 7 comprises ff. 85 of 17·7 × 11 c. and 13 ll.; good *naskh* with rubrications within red and gold lines; copied at Karkúk in 1197/1783 by Muḥammad Amín al-Anasí.

B. 8, given to me in August, 1909, by Dr Riḍá Tawfíq, comprises 108 ff. of 16·6 × 11·5 c. and 11 ll., is written in a good, clear *naskh*, fully pointed, with punctuation in red, and has no date or colophon.

B. 9 (9).

(١) التنبيهات العليّة على وظائف الصّلوة القلبيّة،
(٢) مصباح الشريعة ومفتاح الحقيقة،

(1) *At-Tanbíhátu'l-'aliyya 'alá Waẓá'ifi'ṣ-Ṣaláti'l-qalbiyya*, a treatise on silent or inward Prayer, by Zaynu'd-Dín ibn 'Alí ibn Aḥmad ash-Shámí al-'Ámilí, who wrote it in 951/1544. See Brockelmann, vol. II, p. 325. This occupies ff. 1^b–24^b of the MS., and is followed by

(2) *Miṣbáḥu'sh-Sharí'at wa-Miftáḥu'l-Ḥaqíqat*, a treatise ascribed to the Imám Ja'far aṣ-Ṣádiq and comprising one hundred chapters. It begins:

الحمد لله الّذى نوّر قلوب العارفين بذكره وقدّس ارواحهم بسرّه آلخ

occupies ff. 25^b–44^a, and is dated 23 Sha'bán, 1246/Feb. 6, 1831.

Ff. 44^b–46^a are occupied by a short treatise, partly in Arabic and partly in Persian, by Mullá Muḥsin-i-Fayḍ of Káshán.

The MS. comprises 46 ff. of 21·2 × 14·8 c. and 27 ll. written in small clear *naskh* with rubrications, but the Persian on ff. 44^b–46^a in small neat *ním-shikasta*. Dated on f. 44^a 23 Sha'bán, 1246/Feb. 6, 1831. One of the Belshah MSS. obtained on Nov. 12, 1920.

B. 10 (9).

A Turkish devotional work, containing (1) some of the shorter *súras* of the *Qur'án* and sundry Arabic prayers with Turkish translation and explanation (ff. 1[b]–23[b]); (2) *Aḥwál-i-Qiyámat*, on the Resurrection, in Turkish (ff. 25[b]–63[b]), in 38 chapters incomplete at end; (3) *Maqámát-i-Awliyá*, on the Stations of the Saints (ff. 64[b]–75[a]), in 18 chapters; followed by several other similar treatises, all in Turkish.

Ff. 131 of 20·8 × 14·5 c. and 13–21 ll., written in a coarse *nasta'líq* with rubrications, undated. Given to me by Dr Riḍá Tawfíq in Constantinople in the spring of 1908.

B. 11 (8).

رسالة فى آداب البحث، وغيره،

An Arabic treatise on the Ethics of Controversy (*Ádábu'l-Baḥth*), followed by glosses on the same. The treatise (ff. 1[b]–5[a]) appears to be that of as-Samarqandí (d. 690/1291: see Brockelmann, vol. I, p. 468, and Ahlwardt's Berlin Arabic Catalogue, vol. IV, pp. 519–520, Nos. 5272–3), while the glosses seem to be those of Mas'úd ar-Rúmí (d. 840/1436: see Brockelmann, *loc. cit.*, and Ahlwardt, *loc. cit.*, Nos. 5275 *et seqq.*) or one of his commentators.

Ff. 46 of 18·6 × 12·2 c. and 15–17 ll.; poor but clear *nasta'líq* with rubrications; dated 995/1587 on ff. 5[a] and 45[b]. Given to me by Dr Riḍá Tawfíq in August, 1909.

B. 12 (9).

كتاب مجموع مناشير سيّدنا الامام محمّد المهدى،

A large collection of proclamations issued by Muḥammad ibn Sayyid 'Abdi-'lláh, the Mahdí of the Súdán, given to me by Mr Vincent R. Woodland of the Súdán Civil Service, who described it in the accompanying note as a "MS. of the Mahdí's and Khalífa's Proclamations. Typical Súdán calligraphy. Captured by me in house of Dervish suspect near Dobha in 1907."

The dates of these proclamations, all of which appear to emanate from the Mahdí, not from his Khalífa, vary between 1298/1881 and 1304/1886–7. They vary much in length, and while most are addressed to his followers generally, some are specifically addressed to such leading men as the Qáḍi'l-Islám Aḥmad 'Alí, 'Abdu'r-Raḥmán an-Nujúmí, Ḥamdán Abú 'Anja, etc. One of these is addressed to the *Wálí* or Ruler (f. 314[a]) and one to the theologians (*'ulamá*) of Egypt (f. 308[a]).

The following passage (ff. 143ᵇ–144ᵃ), in which the use of the term "Dervishes" (*Daráwísh*) to denote the Mahdí's followers is forbidden, is of some interest, and may serve as a specimen of the style:

... ولا بُدَّ من اعلام جميع الاخوان مع الأمرا والمقاديم أن يتركوا تسمية الأنصار بالدراويش لأنّ هذه التسمية لهم وَهْمٌ وخروجٌ عن الصَّواب لأنّ الّذين سمّوهم بها سمّوهم لتسميتهم(? ابناء الآخرة ونسبتهم الى عدم العقل والادراك مع انّ من لم ينْح نَحْوَهُمْ هم الّذين لا عقل لهم اذ هو التدبير فى الفانيات وذلك ذهاب عقل اذ المدبّر للباطل ليس له عقلٌ (f. 144ᵃ) ويحقّ أن يسمّوا بالدراويش ابناء الدنيا الّذين يعلمون ظاهرًا من الحيوة الدنيا وهم عن الآخرة هم غافلون[1] فمن سمّى الأنصار دراويش بعد هذا يجرى عليه حكم التعيير والقذف بل أشدّ لأنّه نسب اهل العقل و الأعمال الّتى أمر الله بها الى السّفاهة ويقرب ذلك الى النفاق والكفر والسّلام، فى جمادى الآخرة سنة ١٣٠١[2]

Ff. 376 of 21·8 × 15 c. and 15 ll.; coarse, clear *naskh* with rubrications. The date at the end (1304/1886–7) probably refers to the concluding proclamation, not to the time of transcription.

B. 13 (8).

رسائل شرعيّة

Half a dozen Arabic tracts, some imperfect, on various theological and legal topics, mostly anonymous and undated. The last (pp. 101–116) on Analogy (*Qiyás*) is by Muḥammad Báqir ibn Muḥammad Akmal, who, according to Brockelmann (vol. II, p. 411), died about 1098/1687.

The MS., one of the Belshah collection, was transcribed in 1178/1764–5 (see pp. 40, 55 and 100) and comprises 118 pp. of 19·4 × 12·2 c. and 16 ll., and is written throughout in a clear Persian *naskh*.

C. SHÍ'A THEOLOGY, ETC.

C. 1 (10).

روضة الأبرار (ترجمة نهج البلاغة)

The *Nahju'l-Balágha* ("Way of Eloquence") is believed by nearly all Muḥammadan men of letters to contain the actual homilies and sayings of 'Alí ibn Abí Ṭálib, compiled by his descendant ash-Sharífu'l-Murtaḍà (b. 355/966: d. 436/1044), to whom European scholars generally assign the authorship of the work (Brockelmann, vol. I, pp. 404–5). The book therefore enjoys a high reputation, especially

[1] [*Qur'án*, XXX, 6].   [2] April, 1884.

amongst the Shí'a, and the present is not the only Persian paraphrase and commentary on it which exists: see Rieu's Persian Catalogue, pp. 18–19.

This Persian translation was made by a certain 'Alí ibn Ḥasan az-Zuwárí apparently in the year 647/1249–50. His short Introduction runs as follows (after the doxology):

و بعد، مخفی نیست که بعد از کلام حضرت ربّ العالمین و سیّد المرسلین کلام معجز نظام امیر المؤمنین است صلوات الله علیهما وآلهما الطیّبین که بصنوف فصاحت و فنون بلاغت مشحونست سیّما کتاب نهج البلاغة که مشتمل بر معانی لطیفهٔ شریفه و نکات غریبهٔ عجیبه که مرغ فکر هیچ فصیح در فضای آن نمی تواند پرید و اندیشهٔ هیچ بلیغ بحرم سرای آن نمی تواند رسید و لیکن غوّاصان بحور معانی بقدر وسع و توانائی درری و غرری چند از آن دریای بی پایان بساحل بیان آورده‌اند که هر کس بحسب قابلیّت و استعداد ازو محظوظ گشتند و بحکم ما لا یُدْرَكُ کُلّه لا یُتْرَكُ کُلّه بندهٔ حقیر بی مقدار علی بن حسن الزّواری غفر الله تعالی ذنوبه وستر عیوبه بجهت عموم فائده مرتکب ترجمهٔ آن شد که موسوم است بروضة الابرار بر وجه اختصار که انسب است برای استحضار ومن الله التوفیق وهو خیر رفیق و جامع این کتاب شریف حضرت من خصّه الله تعالی بالمواهب العلیّة والمناقب الجلیلة ذی الحسبین ابی الحسن السیّد رضیّ الدّین محمّد بن الحسین بن موسی بن محمّد بن موسی بن ابراهیم بن موسی الکاظم است علیهم السّلام، سیّد رحمه الله میفرماید آلخ

It will be seen from the conclusion of the above extract that the compilation of the *Nahju'l-Balágha* is here ascribed not to ash-Sharífu'l-Murtaḍá but to his brother ash-Sharífu'r-Raḍí.

This fine MS. was bought by me from the heirs of the late Sir A. Houtum-Schindler at the beginning of 1917. He bought it in December, 1906. In 1270/1854 it was in the possession of Kayúmarth Mírzá; in 1787 of Charles Boddam of Calcutta; in 1198/1784 of Shamsu'd-Dawla Muníru'l-Mulk, and in 1019/1610–11 of Sulṭán Muḥammad of Kashmír. It comprises 497 ff. of 24·2 × 16·9 c. and 23 ll. The Arabic text is written in clear *naskh* and pointed; the Persian translation is good *nasta'líq*, with rubrications and some marginal notes and glosses. There is no colophon or date, but the writing appears to be of the fifteenth century of our era.

C. 2 (12).

غُرَر الحکم و دُرَر الکلم،

Ghuraru'l-Ḥikam wa-Duraru'l-Kilam, another collection of sayings ascribed to 'Alí ibn Abí Ṭálib and compiled by 'Abdu'l-Wáḥid ibn Muḥammad ibn 'Abdi'l-Wáḥid al-Ámidí at-Tamímí (f. 2^b, ll. 8 and 9 from the bottom). See Brockelmann, vol. I, p. 44, and Ahlwardt, Nos. 8661–2 (vol. VII, p. 590). Written in a large *naskh* hand in the upper margin of ff. 3ᵇ–66ᵃ is a smaller collection of ‘Alí’s sayings, entitled *Nathru’l-La’álí*, arranged alphabetically, ten sayings being assigned to each letter.

Ff. 124 of 28·8 × 18·2 c. and 20 ll. to page: excellent modern Persian *naskh*, fully pointed, with rubrications; transcribed by Ghulám-Riḍá, poetically surnamed Ḥayrán, and concluded 17 Rajab, 1254/6 October, 1838. One of the Belshah MSS. acquired in the spring of 1920.

C. 3 (11).

من خطب امير المؤمنين علىّ بن ابى طالب،

A volume, lacking 16 ff. at the beginning and an unknown number at the end, containing, apparently, extracts from the addresses and homilies of the Imám ‘Alí ibn Abí Ṭálib with running Persian translation and commentary. It begins abruptly on what is now f. 1ᵃ (= f. 17):

... سخت (?) ملاحظه مشابهت است بينهما در علوّ و كون وعلياهنّ سقفًا محفوظًا و زبرين آنرا گردانيد سقف نگاه داشته از استراق سمع شياطين از اخبار غيبرا، از ابن عبّاس منقولست كه قبل ازين شياطين محجوب نبودند از سموات بلكه متصاعد ميشدند و از ملائكه كه اخبار لوح محفوظرا درس مينمودند سخنان ميربودند و بزمين آمده با دوستان خود از كاهنان ميگفتند در زمانى كه حضرت عيسى على نبيّنا وعليه السّلام متولّد شد ممنوع شدند از جميع آسمانها و بجهت رجم ايشان شهب ثاقب مقرّر شد

This MS. was given to me at Kirmán in the summer of 1888. It comprises about 276 ff. (numbered 17–288, 290 and a final leaf of which the number is illegible except the last figure, 5) of 25·5 × 12·7 c. and 21 ll.; neat *ta‘líq*, the Arabic in a larger *naskh* hand and overlined with red. In the margins are some glosses, notes and variants.

C. 4 (6).

الصّحيفة الكاملة،

A collection of prayers and doxologies ascribed to the Fourth Imám of the Shí‘a, ‘Alí ibnu’l-Ḥusayn commonly called Zaynu’l-‘Ábidín. See Brockelmann, vol. I, p. 44; and Ahlwardt’s Berlin Arabic Catalogue, vol. III, pp. 376–377, Nos. 3769–70, where the book is fully described.

This MS. belonged to my former colleague Shaykh Ḥasan of Tabríz, who gave it to me when he left Cambridge in June, 1911. It contains 194 ff. of 13·5 × 7·5 c. and 11 ll., is written in an excellent modern Persian *naskh*, fully pointed, with rubrications, and was transcribed by Muḥammad Amín of Ná'ín, who completed it on 11 Sha'bán, 1087/20 October, 1676. In the second colophon on f. 193[b] the alternative title of *Zubúru Áli Muḥammad wa-Injílu Ahli'l-Bayt* is given. The text is divided into two parts at f. 176. The first part ends, like the Berlin MS. No. 3769, with the prayer for the dispersal of sorrows, at the end of which is written:

تمّت الصّحيفة الشريفة الكاملة بعون الله وتوفيقه،

The succeeding portion is entitled (f. 176[b]):

وممّا أُلْحِقَ ببعض نسخ الصّحيفة وكان من تسبيحه اعنى زين العابدين عليه السّلام،

Opposite this in the margin, also written in red, are the words:

نقل من خطّ الشّيخ الشّهيد رحمه الله صَحّ

C. 5 (14).

(١) نور العَيْن فى مَشْهد الحُسَين،

(٢) قرّة العين فى أخذ ثأر الحُسَين،

(1) *Núru'l-'Ayn fí Mashhadi'l-Ḥusayn* (pp. 2–83), an account of the martyrdom of the Imám Ḥusayn ibn 'Alí at Karbalá and its attendant circumstances, by Abú Isḥáq al-Isfará'iní. This is a different work from the book bearing the same title described by Ahlwardt, vol. v, p. 429, No. 6129. It begins after the title:

الحمد لله الّذى خلق محمّدًا صلّى الله عليه وسلّم قبل الخلق الأوّلين، وحمله واختاره واصطفاه من ساير العالمين الخ... امّا بعد فيقول الامام العالم العلّامة ابو اسحق الاسفراينى انّه طلب منّى (p. 3) أن أروى ما ورد فى مصرع الحسين عم فألّفْتُ هذا الكتاب وسمّيته نور العين فى مشهد الحسين،

There is no division into chapters, but each new topic is generally introduced by the words "says the narrator" (قال الرّاوى). The following are the chief topics: Death of the Prophet (p. 3); Mu'áwiya and al-Ḥusayn (p. 4); Mu'áwiya's testament to Yazíd (p. 5); Death of Mu'áwiya (p. 6); al-Ḥusayn's letter to Yazíd (p. 7); al-Ḥusayn and the people of Kúfa (p. 11); Muslim goes to Kúfa (p. 13); al-Ḥusayn goes to Kúfa (p. 19); Death of Muslim (p. 29); the Battle of Karbalá (p. 34); Death of al-Ḥusayn (p. 50); Revolt of al-Mukhtár (p. 52); al-Ḥusayn's family after his death (p. 52); the Head of al-Ḥusayn (p. 70); ends on p. 83.

(2) *Qurratu'l-'Ayn fí akhdhi tha'ri'l-Ḥusayn* (pp. 84–111), an account of how the death of al-Ḥusayn was avenged by al-Mukhtár, by Shaykh 'Abdu'lláh ibn Muḥammad, beginning:

قال الشيخ الامام العالم العلّامة عبد الله بن محمّد الحمد لله ربّ العالمين الخ ...
و بعد، فانّى لمّا اطّلعتُ على نور العين فى مشهد الحسين اعقبته بهذا الكتاب ووسمته اذا رسمته
بقرّة العين فى اخذ ثار الحسين فأقول الخ

Pp. 111 of 35 × 21·2 c. and 20 ll.; large, clear, modern *naskh* with rubrications; copied for Muḥammad Ḥasan Khán *Ṣaní'u'd-Dawla* (whose book-plate it also bears) in 1289/1872–3 by Sayyid Muḥammad 'Alí of Khwánsár, *Rúz-náma-nawís*.

C. 6 (13).

كشف الغمّة فى معرفة الأئمّة،

Kashfu'l-Ghumma fí ma'rifati'l-A'imma ("the Dispelling of Doubt, on the knowledge of the Imáms"), by 'Alí ibn 'Ísá al-Irbilí, who, according to the *Rawḍátu'l-Jannát* (p. 369 of the Ṭihrán lithograph), was one of the leading Shí'a divines of the seventh Muḥammadan (thirteenth Christian) century. Although this book is highly esteemed and much quoted by the Shí'a, copies appear to be rare in Europe, for none is mentioned by Ahlwardt, Brockelmann, or Rieu. The date of composition is given at the end (f. 439^b), but owing to the mutilation of the last six leaves (ff. 435–40) only the words "...ty and six hundred" (...ن وستّمائةٍ) are legible, with the day of the month, Ramaḍán 20.

The MS., bought in the spring of 1920 at the Belshah sale, is unfortunately defective at the beginning, but gives the title of the book on f. 3^b, l. 11. It was transcribed by Ḥasan ibn Muḥammad ibn Ḥasan as-Sinjárí, and completed in Rabí' I, 913 (July–August, 1507). It comprises 440 ff. of 30 × 22 c. and 23 ll., and is written in a large, clear *naskh*, the headings in larger and heavier characters, and there are numerous marginal notes and glosses. It is divided into two parts (*Juz'*), of which the first, ending on f. 160^b, is entirely concerned with the Prophet and 'Alí ibn Abí Ṭálib, with some subsidiary matter, such as a section on the excellence and nobility of the Banú Háshim (ff. 12^a–14^b), and another on the limitation of the Imámate to their family and of the number of the Imáms to twelve (ff. 21^b–23^b). The second part (ff. 161^b–439^b) begins with accounts of Fáṭima (ff. 166^a *et seqq.*) and Khadíja (ff. 183^a *et seqq.*), and then treats systematically of the remaining eleven Imáms as follows: Al-Ḥasan, f. 186^a; al-Ḥusayn, f. 217^a; 'Alí Zaynu'l-'Ábidín, f. 248^a; Muḥammad Báqir, f. 264^a; Ja'far aṣ-Ṣádiq, f. 279^b; Músá al-Káẓim, f. 303^b; 'Alí ar-Riḍá, f. 323^a; Muḥammad Taqí, f. 351^a; 'Alí an-Naqí, f. 363^b; Ḥasan al-'Askarí, f. 375^b; the Imám Mahdí, f. 390^a.

Amongst the numerous authorities quoted are the following: the *Kitábu'l-Firdaws* of Shírawayhi of Daylam (d. 509/1115: see Brockelmann, I, 344); *Kitábu'l-Yawáqít*; the *Manáqib* of al-Khwárizmí; the *Kifáyatu't-Ṭálib fí Manáqibi 'Alí ibn Abí Ṭálib*; the *Musnad* of Aḥmad ibn Ḥanbal (d. 241/855: see Brockelmann, I, 181–3); the *Sunan* of Abú Dáwud Sulaymán ibnu'l-Ash'ath; the *Kashsháf* of az-Zamakhsharí (d. 538/1143: Brockelmann, I, 289–90); the *Manáqib* of Shaykh Kamálu'd-Dín ibn Ṭalḥa; the *Kitábu'l-Futúḥ*; the *Ḥilyatu'l-Awliyá* of al-Ḥáfiẓ Abú Nu'aym (d. 430/1038: see Brockelmann, I, 362), and the abridgement of it by Jamálu'd-Dín Abu'l-Faraj ibnu'l-Jawzí (d. 597/1200) known as *Ṣifatu* (here *Ṣafwatu*) *'ṣ-Ṣafwa* (Brockelmann, I, 362 and 503); the *Kitábu'l-Irshád* by ash-Shaykhu'l-Mufíd (d. 413/1022; see Brockelmann, I, 188); the *Kitábu'd-Dalá'il* by al-Ḥimyarí; the *Kitábu'l-Kharáj* of Quṭbu'd-Dín ar-Ráwandí; and the *Tadhkira* of Ibn Ḥamdún (d. 562/1167: see Brockelmann, I, 280–1).

C. 7 (8).

الفصول المهمّة فى معرفة الأئمّة.

Another work on the Twelve Imáms, entitled *Al-Fuṣúlu'l-muhimma fí ma'rifati-'l-A'imma*, defective at the beginning and consequently lacking the author's name which, however, as we learn from Brockelmann (II, 176) is Núru'd-Dín 'Alí ibn Muḥammad ibnu'ṣ-Ṣabbágh (d. 855/1451). For description of contents see Ahlwardt's Berlin Arabic Catalogue, vol. IX, pp. 212–213, Nos. 9671–2.

Ff. 202 of 18·5 × 12 c. and 18 ll.; good *naskh* with rubrications, dated 9 Rabí' I, 1178/Sept. 14, 1861; scribe, 'Abdu'l-'Azíz ibn Sa'íd [ibn] al-Ḥájj Aḥmad an-Najjár. Bought on Nov. 12, 1920, from the Belshah collection.

C. 8 (9).

(١) فهرست اسماء علماء الشيعة.

(٢) معالم العلماء.

(1) *Fihristu asmá'i 'Ulamá'i'sh-Shí'a* (ff. 1^b–35^b), an Index of the names of Shí'a divines, arranged alphabetically, by Shaykh Muntajabu'd-Dín Abu'l-Ḥasan 'Alí ibn 'Ubaydi'lláh ibnu'l-Ḥasan ibnu'l-Ḥusayn ibn Bábawayhi of Qum, who wrote it as a supplement to the *Fihrist* of aṭ-Ṭúsí. See Ahlwardt's Berlin Arabic Catalogue, vol. IX, p. 454, No. 10048, and the *Kashfu'l-Ḥujub* of Sayyid I'jáz Ḥusayn (Calcutta, 1330/1912), p. 407, No. 2250.

(2) *Ma'álimu'l-'Ulamá* (ff. 37^b–83^a), another similar work by Shaykh Rashídu'd-Dín Muḥammad ibn 'Alí ibn Shahr-áshúb as-Sarawí al-Mázandarání (d. 588/1192).

See Ahlwardt, *loc. cit.*, No. 10047; Brockelmann, I, 405; *Kashfu'l-Ḥujub*, p. 532, No. 2991.

Ff. 83 of 21 × 15·5 c. and 15 ll., fair *naskh* with rubrications. The date (Rajab 613/Oct.–Nov. 1216) and scribe's name (Muḥammad ibn Muḥammad ibn 'Alí al-Ḥamdání al-Qazwíní) contained in the first colophon (on f. 35[b]) evidently refer to the original MS. from which this quite modern copy was made, and with which it was subsequently collated. A note at the end (f. 83[a]) written and sealed by one Muḥammad Ṣábiḥ ibn 'Abdi'l-Wási' al-Ḥusayní, and dated Jumádà I, 1118/Aug.–Sept., 1706, states that this MS. formerly belonged to the celebrated Shaykh Bahá'u'd-Dín al-'Ámilí, one of the most noted theologians of the reign of Sháh 'Abbás the Great, and contains notes and glosses in his handwriting. Acquired at the sale of the Belshah MSS. in the latter part of 1920.

C. 9 (10).

(١) اعتقادات الاماميّة لابن بابويه،
(٢) مكارم الاخلاق للطبرسى،

This MS. comprises two parts with separate pagination, viz.:

(1) The Beliefs of the Imámiyya (or Shí'a) by Abú Ja'far Muḥammad ibn 'Alí ibnu'l-Ḥusayn ibn Músà Bábawayhi of Qum (d. 381/991: see Brockelmann, I, 187). The contents are stated in the *Kashfu'l-Ḥujub*, p. 51, No. 239, but the initial doxology there given is different. This copy begins, after the *Bismi'lláh*:

الحمد لله ربّ العالمين وصلّى الله على محمّد وآله الطيّبين الطّاهرين، باب فى صفة اعتقاد الاماميّة، قال الشيخ ابو جعفر محمّد بن على بن الحسين بن موسى بابويه القُمى الفقيه المصنّف لهذا الكتاب اعلم انّ اعتقادنا فى التّوحيد آلخ

This Arabic treatise ends on p. 87, and is followed (pp. 88–104) by another, of which the first part (pp. 88–94), in Arabic, contains Traditions as to the merit acquired by the visitation of the tomb of the eighth Imám 'Alí ar-Riḍá at Mashhad, while the second part (pp. 94–104), in Persian, describes how that visitation should be performed.

(2) On the virtues and noble qualities of the Prophet (464 pp., defective at end) by Shaykh Abú Naṣr al-Ḥasan ibn Abí 'Alí al-Faḍl ibn al-Ḥasan aṭ-Ṭabarsí. See the *Kashfu'l-Ḥujub*, p. 548, No. 3086, where the initial words exactly correspond with this MS. The work is divided into twelve chapters, each containing several sections, and breaks off in the course of Section 5 of Chapter XII, the last two sections being completely lost.

The MS. is written throughout in the same hand, a legible *naskh* with rubrications. A note of ownership on the title-page is dated 20 Shawwál, 1243/5 May, 1828. It is from the Belshah collection.

C. 10 (8).

ثواب الاعمال لابن بابويه،

The *Thawábu'l-A'mál* (ff. 1ᵇ–117ᵇ), or "Rewards of Actions," by the same Ibn Bábawayhi who wrote the work described above, followed (ff. 121ᵇ–180) by the *'Iqábu'l-A'mál*, or "Punishments of Actions," by the same author. See the *Kashfu'l-Ḥujub*, p. 149, No. 733, and p. 382, No. 2120.

Ff. 180 of 19·5 × 12·5 c. and 17 ll.; clear ***naskh*** with rubrications. The first colophon (on f. 117ᵇ) is dated 21 Shawwál, 1034/27 July 1625, and the second (on f. 180ᵃ) 8 Dhu'l-Qa'da, 1034 (August 12, 1625). This MS. was acquired at the third partition of the Belshah MSS. in the spring of 1920.

C. 11 (11).

تلخيص المقال (الأقوال) فى تحقيق احوال الرّجال،

A Biographical Dictionary of Shí'a traditionists, entitled *Talkhíṣu'l-Maqál* (or *-Aqwál*) *fí taḥqíqi aḥwáli'r-Rijál*, by Mírzá Muḥammad ibn 'Alí ibn Ibráhím al-Astarábádí, who wrote it in 988/1580. See Rieu's British Museum Arabic Supplement, Nos. 634–635; Brockelmann, vol. II, p. 385; *Kashfu'l-Ḥujub*, p. 138, No. 689.

Ff. 250 of 25·7 × 13 c. and 25 ll.; legible ***naskh*** with rubrications and many marginal notes; transcribed in 1053/1643. This MS. also was acquired at the third partition of the Belshah MSS. in the spring of 1920.

C. 12 (9).

كتاب الرّجال،

An anonymous and untitled *Kitábu'r-Rijál*, or Dictionary of persons, both men and women, who transmitted traditions from the Prophet and the Imáms. After the very brief doxology it begins:

...امّا بعد، فانّى قد اجبْتُ الى ما تكرّر سؤال الشيخ الفاضل فيه من جمع كتاب يشتمل على اسماء الرجال الّذين رووا عن النبى صؐ وعن الأئمّة عليهم السلام من بعده الى زمن القايم عؑ ثمّ اذكر بعد ذلك من تأخّر زمانه عن الأئمّة عليهم السلام من رواة الحديث او من عاصرهم ولم يرْو عنهم وأُرتّب ذلك على حروف المعجم الّتى اوّلها الهمزة وآخرها الياء ليقرب على ملتمسه طلبه ويسهل عليه حفظه الخ

The book is divided into a number of unnumbered chapters, each dealing with the persons who transmitted traditions first from the Prophet and afterwards from each of the Imáms, and the names in each chapter are arranged alphabetically, a mere list without any particulars. A brief table of contents has been prefixed by Mírzá Bihrúz, formerly Persian Lecturer at Cambridge.

Pp. 258 of 21 × 12·6 c. and 15 ll.; small and fairly clear *nasta'líq* with rubrications; dated Rabí' I, 1283/July–Aug., 1866. One of the Belshah MSS. bought in November, 1920.

C. 13 (13).

نسمة السّحر بذكر من تشيّع وشعر، (جلد ٢)

Notices of Shí'a poets who wrote in Arabic, by Yúsuf ibn Yaḥyà al-Yamaní aṣ-Ṣan'ání, compiled in 1111/1700. See Brockelmann, vol. II, p. 403, and Ahlwardt's Berlin Arabic Catalogue, vol. VI, pp. 502–503, No. 7423. This MS. contains only the second half of the work, beginning with the letter ط.

Ff. 210 of 30·8 × 21 c. and 25 ll.; coarse but legible *naskh*; dated 6 Jumádà II, 1324/July 28, 1906. One of the Belshah MSS. bought in the spring of 1920.

C. 14 (14).

كتاب الاستبصار فيما اختلف فيه من الاخبار،

The *Istibṣár*, a well-known work on Shí'a traditions by Muḥammad ibnu'l-Ḥasan aṭ-Ṭúsí (d. 459/1067). See Brockelmann, vol. I, p. 405; Ahlwardt's Berlin Arabic Catalogue, vol. II, pp. 108–110, Nos. 1272–6. The book has been lithographed at the Ja'fariyya Press, Lucknow, without date, in two vols. of 172 pp. and 364 pp. respectively, concluding (pp. 360–363) with an account of the eminent author.

Ff. 342 of 33·7 × 19·7 c. and 28 ll.; large, clear *naskh* with rubrications, within gilt and coloured marginal lines; transcribed by Muḥammad Muḥsin ibn Niẓám ash-Sharaf, and completed in the middle of Jumádà II, 1077/December, 1666. Bought at the Belshah sale in January, 1920.

C. 15 (13).

كتاب الانوار النّعمانيّة فى بيان معرفة النشأة الانسانيّة،

The *Kitábu'l-Anwári'n-Nu'mániyya*, on the life and growth of the human soul from before birth until death, and after death, by Ni'matu'lláh al-Ḥusayní al-Jazá'irí, beginning, after the *Bismi'lláh*:

نحمده بنعمته على نعمآئه، ونصلّى على عبده المقرّب لديه محمّد وآله، وبعد، فانّ المذنب
الحقير، صاحب الخطأ والتقصير، قليل البضاعة، وكثير الاضاعة، نعمة الله الحسينى، عفى الله عن

ذنوبه، وستر منه فاضحات عيوبه، لـمّا فرغ من كتابَيْه غـايـة المرام، فى شرح تهذيب الاحكام،
و كشف الاسرار، فى شرح الاستبصار، تاقت نفسه الى تأليف كـتـاب غريب، على نمط عجيب، لـمر
يكتب فى زبر الأوّلين، ولـم تسمح به قريحة أحدٍ من المتأخّرين، يكون للأُمّى واعظًا ومؤنسًا،
وللعالم مطرحًا ومجلسًا، ينتفع منه كلّ أحد على قدر رتبته، ويستضىء به كـلّ من أراد دفع
ظلمته، يشتمل على تفصيل احوال الانسان قبل خلقته، ويبين شأنه الى يوم ولوج حفرته، ويعقبه
بذكر احو اله يوم دخوله ناره او جنّته، بـل يفصّل فيه أحوال الدنيا وأَهْلها قبل وجودها، وبعد
وجودها، وبعد مـا يكتب عليه الفنآء، مستمدّين من الله التوفيق، لرفع الاحتياج الى المخلوقين
بحصول اسباب الغنا، و سمّيته كـتـاب الانوار النعمانيّة، فى بيان معرفة النشأة الانسانيّة، راجيًا مـنـه
سبحانـه أن يُجيرنـا مـن اهوال البرزخ والحساب، وأن يجعله مقبولاً عـنـد اصفيائه اولى الألـبـاب،
وقـد التزمنا أن لا نذكر فيه الاّ مـا أخذناه عن ارباب العصمة الطـاهرين عليهم السّلام أو ما صحّ
عندنا من كتب النـاقلين فانّ كتب التواريخ اكثرها قـد نقله الجمهور من تواريخ اليهود، ولهذا
كـان أكثر مـا فيها الأكـاذيب الفاسدة والحكايات الباردة، وقـد رتّبناه على ابواب ثلثة، الباب الأوّل
فيما قبل ولادة الانسان، الـبـاب الـثـانى فى احوالـه بعد ولادته الى وقت موته، الـبـاب الـثـالث فيما
بعد الموت الى دخوله الجنّة او النار،

The three divisions of the book indicated above are not very clearly marked, but there are a great number of sections dealing with a great variety of matters, metaphysical, theological, historical, physical, ethical, eschatological, etc., each entitled *Núr* ("Light"). At the end of the book (ff. 329^a–334^a) the author gives his autobiography, headed:

خاتمة، فى مجمل احوال مؤلّف هذا الكتاب وهو نعمة الله الحسينى الجزائرى،

This autobiography is given in full in a Persian translation in the *Qiṣaṣu'l-'Ulamá* of Muḥammad ibn Sulaymán of Tanakábun (Ṭihrán lithographed edition of 1304/1886, pp. 330–341). In it the author tells us that he was born in 1050/1640–1, and composed this book in 1089/1678. He was the author of numerous other works besides this, and the two others (*Gháyatu'l-Marám* and *Kashfu'l-Asrár*) which he mentions in the preface quoted above, and a list of them is given at the end of the autobiography. He was one of the favourite pupils of the great Shí'a *mujtahid* Mullá Muḥammad Báqir-i-Majlisí, and helped him in the compilation of the great *Biḥáru'l-Anwár* ("Oceans of Light").

This MS. is written throughout in a very clear and good *naskh*, with numerous marginal notes and references and rubrications. It was transcribed by Muḥammad ibn Muḥammad Ṣádiq ash-Sharíf al-Músawí al-Khwánsárí, and completed in the middle of Jumádà II, 1265/May, 1849. Ff. 346 of 30·5 × 20·5 c. and 31 ll.

C. 16 (9).

(۱) انیس الموحّدین، (۲) حدیقة المتّقین،

Two Persian works on Shí'a doctrine, viz. (1) the *Anísu'l-Muwaḥḥidín* of Mullá Mahdí ibn Abí Dharr-i-Niráqí (ff. 3^b–60^b), and the *Ḥadíqatu'l-Muttaqín* of Mullá Muḥammad Taqí-i-Majlisí (ff. 61^b–291^a).

(1)

A biography of Mullá Muḥammad Mahdí-i-Niráqí, father of the better known Mullá Aḥmad-i-Niráqí, is given (No. 24) in the *Qiṣaṣu'l-'Ulamá*, but no date is recorded, and though a book called *Anís* (on jurisprudence) is mentioned, it can hardly be the present work, which is purely theological. It begins, after the *Bismi'lláh*:

انیسِ موحّدین و جلیس مجرّدین سپاس بیقیاس و ستایش رفیع الاساس یگانه ایست جلّ شانه که ابداعِ ممکنات و اختراعِ مکوّنات محضِ ظهور و مرحمت اوست الخ

The book is divided into five chapters, dealing with (1) the Existence of God; (2) the Divine Attributes; (3) the Prophetic Function; (4) the Imámate; (5) the Future Life, as follows:

باب اوّل در اثبات صانع تعالی شانه (f. 4^a)،

باب دویم در صفات باری و درین باب یك مقدّمه و دو فصل است (f. 12^a)،

مقدّمه در کیفیّت صفات باری (f. 12^a)،

فصل اوّل در صفات ثبوتیّه (f. 15^b)،

فصل دویم در صفات سلبیّه (f. 20^a)،

باب سیم در نبوّت و این باب مشتمل است بر چهار فصل (f. 22^a)،

فصل اوّل در وجوب بعثت انبیا (f. 22^a)،

فصل دویم در عصمت انبیا (f. 24^a)،

فصل سیم در طریق معرفت نبی (f. 25^a)،

فصل چهارم در اثبات نبوّت ختم النبیّین صلّی الله علیه وآله (f. 26^a)،

باب چهارم در امامت و این باب مشتمل است بر یك مقدّمه و هفت فصل (f. 31^a)،

مقدّمه در ذکر اختلافاتی که در امامت شده (f. 31^a)،

فصل اوّل در اثبات احتیاج بامام (f. 32^b)،

فصل دویم در اینکه امامت از اصول دین است (f. 36^b)،

فصل سیم در اینکه در امامت عصمت شرط است (f. 37^a)،

فصل چهارم در اینکه امام باید افضل از رعیّت باشد (f. 37^b)،

فصل پنجم در اثبات اینکه امام باید منصوص باشد (f. 38ª)'

فصل ششم در اثبات خلافت علی [و اولاد او] علیهم السّلام (f. 38ᵇ)'

فصل هفتم در اثبات امامتِ سایر أئمّه (f. 56ᵇ)'

باب پنجم در معاد (f. 58ª)'

The transcription was completed on 12 Rabí' I, 1216/July 23, 1801, by Muḥammad Zamán ibn Muḥammad Ṣádiq of Shíráz.

(2)

Mullá Muḥammad Taqí ibn Maqṣúd 'Alí al-Majlisí, who was born in 1003/1594–5 and died in 1070/1659–60, was one of the greatest and most famous of the later Shí'a doctors of Persia. Full accounts of him are given in the *Rawḍátu-'l-Jannát* (lith. Ṭihrán, 1306/Jan. 1889), pp. 129–131, and in the *Qiṣaṣu'l-'Ulamá*, No. 36, while the present work is mentioned in the *Kashfu'l-Ḥujub*, p. 195, No. 1008. It begins after the *Bismi'lláh* and the brief doxology:

...امّا بعد، چنین گوید اضعف عباد الله الغنی محمّد تقی مجلسی الاصفهانی که این رساله ایست در بیان عبادات بواسطهٔ التماس جمعی از برادران مؤمنین ایّدهم الله تعالی لسلوک منهاج الصالحین و نامیدم آنرا بحدیقة المتّقین فی معرفة احکام الدّین لارتفاع معارج الیقین مرتّب بر مقدّمه و پنج باب و خاتمه

The Introduction (*Muqaddama*, ff. 61ᵇ–65ª) treats of the virtues of Prayer.
Chapter I (ff. 65ª–139ª): on Purification (*Aḥkám-i-Ṭahárat*).
,, II (ff. 139ª–229ª): on the rules of Prayer (*Aḥkám-i-Namáz*).
,, III (ff. 229ª–260ª): on Alms (*Aḥkám-i-Zakát u Khums*).
,, IV (ff. 260ª–*et seqq.*): on Fasting (*Aḥkám-i-Rúza*).
,, V (apparently missing): on Pilgrimage (*Aḥkám-i-Ḥajj u Ziyárát*).
Conclusion (*Khátima*, also missing): on rules governing acts other than acts of devotion which all believers should know.

The book was perhaps never finished, but there is no defect in the MS., which ends with two short lines (without colophon) and the word تمّ ("Finis") thrice repeated.

C. 17 (7).

رسالة لمحمّد باقر بن محمّد تقی المجلسی،

An untitled Arabic tract by Mullá Muḥammad Báqir-i-Majlisí, the son of Mullá Muḥammad Taqí mentioned in the last article, than whom he was even more famous as a theologian. Begins:

الحمد لله الّذی سهّل لنا سلوك شرایع الدین وأوضح أعلامه وبیّن لنا مناهج الیقین فأكمل بذلك علینا انعامه الخ

The tract, which is divided into two chapters, opens with a general exhortation to faith and good works "in this age wherein the paths have become doubtful to men and the ways dark"

فی هذا الزّمان الّذی اشتبه علی النّاس الطرق وأظلم علیهم المسالك...

The author fiercely denounces the Philosophers, Aristotelians and Platonists alike, as followers of "an infidel Greek"; and the Ṣúfís both for their pantheistic doctrines and their monastic institutions.

Chapter I (f. 7ª) deals with matters connected with the principles of doctrine:

الباب الأوّل فیما یتعلّق باصول العقاید،

" II (f. 20ª) deals with practice:

الباب الثّانی فیما یتعلّق بکیفیّة العمل،

Ff. 35 of 16·8 × 9·4 c. and 15 ll.; excellent modern *naskh*. A note of ownership on f. 1ª is dated Shawwál, 1277/April–May, 1861. This MS. was bought at the Belshah sale on November 12, 1920.

C. 18 (9).

مفاتیح الشرایع

An Arabic treatise on Jurisprudence (*fiqh*) entitled *Mafátiḥu'sh-Sharáyi'* by Muḥammad ibn Murtaḍà, better known as Mullá Muḥsin-i-Fayḍ. This MS. would appear to be an autograph, for the colophon (f. 199ª) runs:

هذا اتمام المفاتح وهو تاریخ اتمامها (١٠٤٢) وفرغ منه مؤلّفه العبد الضعیف المسکین المستکین محمّد بن مرتضی المدعوّ بمُحْسِن احسن الله حاله وجعل الی الرفیق الاعلی مآله والحمد لله اوّلاً وآخراً،

In effect, the words *Itmámu'l-Mafátiḥ* give A.H. 1042 (A.D. 1632–3) as the date of composition, which was also the date of transcription, and it seems clear that this MS. is actually the autograph of the author, whose biography is given in the *Rawḍátu'l-Jannát*, pp. 542–549, and No. 76 in the *Qiṣaṣu'l-'Ulamá*[1]. He died in 1091/1680, aged about 84, wrote numerous works both in Arabic and Persian, and was the favourite pupil and son-in-law of the great philosopher Mullá Ṣadrá of Shíráz. The present work, which is mentioned in the *Rawḍátu'l-Jannát* (p. 545) begins:

الحمد لله الّذی هدانا لدین الاسلام وسنّ لنا الشرایع والاحکام الّخ

Ff. 199 of 20·3 × 13·8 c. and 23 ll., written in a small and ungraceful but scholarly *ta'líq* with rubrications and numerous marginal notes and glosses.

[1] Brockelmann's notice of him (II, 406) is very inadequate. It occupies only three lines and only one of his works is mentioned.

C. 19 (12).

شرح کتاب التوحید من اصول الکافی،

The Commentary of the eminent Mullá Ṣadrá of Shíráz (d. 1050/1640) on the *Kitábu't-Tawḥíd*, or Book treating of the Divine Unity, of the *Uṣúlu'l-Káfí* of al-Kulayní (d. 328/939), both in Arabic. Concerning the *Káfí* and its author, see Brockelmann, vol. I, p. 187, and Ahlwardt's Berlin Arabic Catalogue, vol. II, pp. 108–110, Nos. 1272–6. In the Lucknow lithographed edition of 1302/1884–5 the *Kitábu't-Tawḥíd* occupies pp. 40–95. For Mullá Ṣadrá see my *Persian Literature in Modern Times*, pp. 429–432, and references there given. Begins after the *Bismi'lláh*:

کتاب التوحید سبحانك اللّهمّ وبحمدك توحّدت فی ذاتك فحسر عن ادراكك انسان كلّ عارف وتفرّدت فی صفاتك فقصر عن نعتك لسان كلّ واصف الخ...... امّا بعد فلمّا كان المقصد الاوّل من بعثة الانبیاء والرسل بالكتب الالهیّة والنوامیس الشرعیّة انّما هو جذب الخلق الی الواحد الحقّ الخ

Ff. 210 of 29·2 × 17·5 c. and 30 ll.; dated in the colophon Rabí' II, 1257/May–June, 1841; good, clear, modern Persian *naskh*.

C. 20 (10).

مصابیح القلوب،

A Persian manual of Shí'a theology entitled *Maṣábíḥu'l-Qulúb* ("Lamps of the Hearts") by Mullá Ḥasan of Sabzawár. It comprises 53 sections, of which the contents are enumerated on ff. 3^b–4^b. The book is unsystematic and discursive, dealing chiefly with the virtues of the Prophet and the Imáms, the merits of various actions and qualities, the Resurrection, etc. It begins:

شکر و سپاس و ثنا و حمد بی منتها خدائی‌را سزاست که منزّهست از ادراك و افهام و اوهام و متعالی است از حوادثِ لیالی و حروفِ[1] ایّام الخ

Ff. 148 of 23 × 16 c. and 25 ll.; small, neat *naskh* with rubrications; copied by Muḥammad Báqir ibn 'Abdi'r-Riḍá ibn 'Alí 'Askar of Kázarún, who states in the colophon on f. 148ª that he began it in 1229/1814 and finished it in Rabí' II,

[1] Read صروف.

1257/June, 1841, "and this," he concludes, "is of the strangest and most wonderful things":

شروع کردن و ابتدا نمودن در استکتاب این کتاب در سنه هزار و دویست و بیست و نُه و منتها رسیدن و تمام گردیدن او در سنه هزار و دویست و پنجاه و هفت از هجرت نبوی گذشته وهذا من العجایب و الغرایب سبحان الله٬

This is one of the Belshah MSS. acquired in the third partition of the same in the spring of 1920.

C. 21 (4).

An oblong note-book of 39 ff. of 17 × 9·5 c., containing various prayers, traditions, etc. in Arabic and Persian, written in a large and clear but immature hand, without any particular system or order.

C. 22 (5).

Another oblong note-book of 189 ff. of 21·5 × 11·5 c., containing a variable number of lines, written in various indifferent though fairly legible hands, *naskh* and *ta'líq*. The contents of the book are various pieces in prose and verse intended for recitation in the month of Muḥarram. Given to me by Mr Rabino, formerly British Consul at Rasht.

C. 23 (5).

A similar oblong note-book of 34 ff. of 21·5 × 12 c., containing a variable number of lines in various hands. A short treatise on lucky and unlucky days occupies the beginning of the book (ff. 2[b]–18[a]), the remainder of which is filled with various prayers, charms, etc. The volume has been rebound in an ornamental Persian cover better than it deserves.

D. MYSTICISM.

D. 1 (11).

نصوص الخصوص فی ترجمة الفصوص

A fine old MS. containing a Persian translation of the famous *Fuṣúṣu'l-Ḥikam* of Shaykh Muḥyi'd-Dín Ibnu'l-'Arabí, with commentary, composed by Ruknu'd-Dín of Shíráz in 744/1343–4, and transcribed two years later. No other copy of this work, entitled *Nuṣúṣu'l-Khuṣuṣ fí tarjamati'l-Fuṣúṣ*, seems to be known. Begins after the *Bismi'lláh*:

حمد فزون از حدّ و شکر برون از عدّ حضرت با عظمت اللهرا که نقش عالم و آدم محض جود و کرم از مکمن غیب عدم بقلم فیض اقدم بر لوح علم قِدم رسم صورة بوذ انداخت الخ

Nineteen lines lower the author mentions his name and gives some account of himself in verses, many of which are imperfect owing to the mutilation of the lower part of this first leaf :

و امّا بعد حمد الله والصلوة على رسول الله والسلام على اولياء الله چنين گويد بيت كمترى از هركه هست اندر انام، بندهٔ حق ركن شيرازى بنام، كز اوان كوذكى تا اين زمان، بوذ و هستم عارفانرا من غلام، چون نبوذم لايق خدمت ازآن، من نهم زآن گامكى بر جاى گام، چون كه ديذم راهشان بر حالشان، معتقد گشتم بجستم بر دوام، عشقبازى با خيال رويشان، ...منتظر تا يابم از الفاظشان، درّ شهوار معانى در كلام، يافتم من عاقبت در لفظ شيخ، قطب اقطاب...اعرابيش نسبت شذ تمام، جوهرى بس بُلعجب نامش فصوص، ختم عرفان يافت ازو[1] انتظام، الخ

After a short explanation of the "Five Planes" (حضرات خمس) the text, translation and commentary begin about the middle of f. 3ª (the second written page). As a specimen I have given the passage immediately following the doxology.

امّا بعد، فانّى رأيْتُ رسول الله صَلّعم فى مبشرّة أُرِيتُهَا فى العشر الآخر من محرّم سنة سبع وعشرين وستّمائة بمحروسة دمشق وبيده كتابٌ فقال لى هذا كتاب فصوص الحكم خُذْهُ واخرج به الى الناس ينتفعون به،[2] سبب اظهار اين كتاب و معانى مكشوفه بر شيخ رضى الله عنه و كيفيّة ظهور و اطّلاع او برآن بيان ميكند كه در خواب نموده شد بوى جمال رسول صَلّعم درين تاريخ مذكور بمحروسهٔ دمشق حرسها الله عن الآفات در صورتى كه با وى كتابى بوذ و اورا گفت كه اين كتاب فصوص الحكم است اين‌را فرا گير و در ميان مردمان بيرون آور و بنماى تا بخوانند و بدانند و بآن انتفاع يابند، پس بنابر اين مقدّمه شيخ رضى الله عنه در افشآء اين اسرار و خطاب و ابراز و اظهار اين كتاب از حضرة رسالة مأمور باشذ و الّا افشآء اين اسرار نفرموذى كه اوليآء الله امنآء الله اند و بر ايشان تستّر احوال و كتمان اسرار لازم باشذ خاصّه نهان داشتن چنين معانى غريبه و اسرار عجيبه امّا چون اين واقعه از شايبهٔ ريب خالى بوذ و بزيور يقين حالى بحكم حديث من رآنى فقد رآنى فانّ الشيطان لا يتمثّل بصورتى وفى رواية لا يتمثّل بى و بيننده صاحب كشف بوذ و مميّز خواطر رحمانى از خواطر شيطانى پس اظهار آن چنانچه بوذ ضرورى شذ و المأمور معذور، و مؤيّدى ديگر بر تحقّق اين معنى و اعتماد برآن حديث اعتبار مبشّرات است در آن قصّه كه رسول صَلّعم خبر فرموذ كه بعد از من وحى از عالم منقطع گردذ الّا المبشّرات فقالوا وما المبشّرات يا رسول الله قال الرؤيا الصالحة يريها المؤمن و مارا در ايمان و كمال ايمان شيخ قدّس سرّه هيچ شبهتى نيست و نيز أُرِيتُهَا بصيغهٔ مجهول بيان كرد تا اشاره باشذ بر آنك اورا در آن غرض نفسانى نبوذه و از خيالات شيطانى مبرّا بوذه و مبشّرة صفة موصوف محذوفست يعنى رؤيا مبشّرة و اين از آن الفاظست كه آنرا با موصوف وى استعمال نكنند همچنانچه بطحا كه آنرا با موصوف وى كه ارض است استعمال نكنند و نگويند كه ارض بطحا و قوله بمحروسة متعلّق است برأيت يعنى رأيته فى محروسة دمشق

[1] [Read از وى.]

[2] Muḥarram, 627 corresponds with Nov.–Dec. 1229. The Arabic text of the *Fuṣúṣ* is throughout written in red.

The text ends (on f. 236[b]) with twelve Persian verses, followed by six more which have been struck out to be replaced by six others written in the same hand in the margin and under the colophon. The first four of these, which give the date of composition of the work (Muḥarram, 743/June–July, 1342), run thus:

...چون سخن رسید بپایان واجب شذ گزاردن شکر...ـمت آن اگرچه بصذ هزار زبان اداءٓ یکی از هزاران نتوان...امکان نظم

بحقّ حق که حمدِ حق زجان گویم نه چندانی، که حصرِ آن توان کردن بحسبة...

محرّم بُذ ز سالِ جیم و میم آنکه بذال اندر، که توفیقم رفیق آمذ رسانیذم بپایانی،

کتابی کو بظاهر بحر و باطن دُر همی مانذ، چنین جوهر نیابذ کس بعمر خود ز هر کانی،

فصوصش نام و خاتم دان چو داری بهره از عرفان، چنان دانم که این خاتم نیابذ جز سلیمانی،

The colophon gives the date of completion as Tuesday, 14 Shawwál, 746/7 Feb., 1346, and the name of the copyist as Abu'l-Ḥasan 'Alí ibn 'Alí Muḥammad ibn Muḥammad al-'Amúya ash-Shírází. The following and final leaf (f. 237) contains a dedication of the book to some eminent and learned theologian, not specifically named, who had befriended the author, and to whose library he presented this copy for the use of himself and of all deserving students:

و این کتابرا بخزانهٔ کتب وی فرستاذم تا اگر طالبی که مستحقّ و امین طالب مکنون این بوذ از مطالعه وی دریغ نفرمایذ،

Ff. 237 of 26·4 × 19·6 c. and 33 ll.; good typical *naskh* of the period, the Arabic text in red in rather larger characters. One of 47 MSS. bought of Ḥájjí 'Abdu'l-Majíd Belshah in January, 1920.

D. 2 (9).

شرح فصوص الحکم (ترکی)

A Turkish commentary on the *Fuṣúṣu'l-Ḥikam* of Shaykh Muḥyi'd-Dín Ibnu'l-'Arabí by Aḥmad Bí-ján Yázijí-Oghlu, who flourished about the middle of the ninth Muḥammadan (fifteenth Christian) century at Gallipoli. See Rieu's Turkish Catalogue, pp. 17–18 and 105–107; Gibb's *History of Ottoman Poetry*, vol. I, pp. 390 *et seqq.*, especially p. 406, where, however, the commentary on the *Fuṣúṣ* is wrongly ascribed to Aḥmad's brother *Muḥammad*. That this is an error plainly appears from the following passage immediately succeeding the doxology in our MS.:

...وبعده محبّ العلماء وخادم الفقراء یازیجی اوغلی احمد بیجان عفی الله عنهما دار الجهاد و احسن البلاد کلیبولیده اولردی حق تعالی اڭا و جمیع اهل ایمانه رحمت ایلسون آمین یا ربّ العالمین، سبب تالیف کتاب اولدر کم بنوم اولو قرنداشم یازیجی اوغلی شیخ... سلّمه الله تعالی

ایتدی بر گون گگلمر بگا ایتدی کمر (f. 2ª) اگرچه فصوص غایت یوجه مرتبه‌در عقولِ راسخینه و لکن
غایت فتنه‌در قلوبِ ناسخینه شول اعتبارجه کمر بعضی سوزلری شرعه مخالف‌در و دخی ترتیب
انبیآء ترتیب اوزرنه دگلدر آلخ

The proper title of the book seems to be *Muntahà*, for the author says a little further on (f. 2ᵇ, last line):

وَ بُو كِتَابُكْ آدِنی مُنْتَهَی دِیُو آد وِرْدُمر زیرا که فصوص‌دن (f. 3ª) و اصطلاحاتِ صُوفِیَدَن و منازل
السایرندن (*sic*) و تفسیر کبیردن... حتّی عَرَصَاتِ معاده و جنّات‌آباد وَرِنْجَه اشبو کتابده جمع
اولندی، آیْلَه اولسه جمیع خلقوك منتهاسی اولدی بفضل الله تعالی،

The MS., which is unfortunately defective at the end and consequently has no date or colophon, comprises 314 ff. of 22 × 15 c. and 15 ll., and is written throughout in a good, clear *naskh*, fully pointed, the Arabic passages in red, and the titles of sections in red and in larger characters. Given to me by Dr Riḍá Tawfíq at Constantinople in April, 1908.

D. 3 (11).

مرصاد العباد من المبدأ الی المعاد،

A fine old copy of the *Mirṣádu'l-'Ibád* of Najmu'd-Dín Dáya, who completed it at Síwás in Asia Minor in Rajab 620/1223. See Rieu's Persian Catalogue, pp. 38–39. In this MS. the author's name is given as follows (f. 231ª):

ابو بکر بن عبد الله بن محمّد بن شاهاوور الاسدی الرازی

This beautiful old MS. was transcribed in Cairo and finished on 10 Jumádà II, 768/11 Feb., 1367, by Ḥájjí Muḥammad ibn Muḥammad ibn Sa'd an-Nakhjuwání. It contains 233 ff. of 25 × 18 c. and 17 ll.; large, clear *naskh* with rubrications. This was one of 47 MSS. bought of the late Ḥájjí 'Abdu'l-Majíd Belshah in January, 1920.

D. 4 (12).

جواهر الاسرار ن شرح المثنوی،

A well-known commentary on the *Mathnawí* of Jalálu'd-Dín Rúmí entitled *Jawáhiru'l-Asrár* ("Gems of Mysteries") by Ḥusayn ibn Ḥasan of Khwárizm (d. 849/1436–7). See Rieu's Persian Catalogue, p. 588; Ethé's Bodleian Persian Catalogue, col. 519; etc. This MS., like **Add. 14,051** of the British Museum, contains the usual introductory matter and ten preliminary discourses, followed by the commentary on Book I (f. 46ᵇ), Book II (f. 132ᵇ), and Book III (f. 196ᵇ). Whether the commentary on the three remaining books was ever written I do not know.

This MS. fell to my share in the third partition of the Belshah MSS. in the spring of 1920. It comprises 306 ff. of 28·3 × 18·5 c. and 25 ll.; small, neat *ta'líq* with rubrications; transcription completed in Jumádà II, 1066/April, 1656.

D. 5 (10).

شرح دفتر سوم مثنوى

The commentary of Surúrí on Book III of the *Mathnawí*. Concerning the commentator, whose proper name was Muṣliḥu'd-Dín Muṣṭafà ibn Sha'bán, and who was tutor to Sulṭán Sulaymán's son, Prince Muṣṭafà, and died in 969/1561–2 at the age of seventy-two, see Rieu's Persian Catalogue, p. 606.

This MS., which I bought in Constantinople on April 23, 1908, comprises 244 ff. of 25·5 × 14·3 c. and 32 ll., and is written in a legible Turkish *nasta'líq* with rubrications. The transcription was completed in Rabí' I, 1089/May, 1678.

D. 6 (10).

مقدّمهٔ فهرست مثنوى در احوال مولوى معنوى،

A table of the entire contents of the *Mathnawí* (ff. 128ᵇ–170ᵇ), to which is prefixed (ff. 1ᵇ–124ᵇ) a very interesting critical examination of Ṣúfí doctrine in general and of the teachings of the *Mathnawí* in particular, with especial regard to the charges of heresy levelled against them by certain Shí'a theologians, especially Mullá Muḥammad Ṭáhir of Qum[1], composed by Muḥammad Shafí', son of the eminent Shaykh Bahá'u'd-Dín al-'Ámilí, about the year 1185/1771–2[2]. The earlier portion of these Prolegomena (to f. 82ᵇ) deals chiefly with the various reproaches (مطاعن) brought against Jalálu'd-Dín Rúmí by his detractors and the replies to them made by his defenders, both sides being stated very fairly. Thus an attempt is made in ch. I (f. 10ᵇ) to prove that he was a Shí'a; in chs. II and III (ff. 11ᵇ and 13ᵃ) to explain away his apparent apology for Ibn Muljam, the murderer of 'Alí, whom he represents as acting under the compulsion of a fate which he cannot escape, and as being comforted by his victim with a promise of intercession at the Last Day:

لیك بیغم شو شفیعِ تو منم، خواجهٔ روحم نه مملوكِ تنم، ...
هیچ بغضی نیست در جانم ز تو، ز آنكه این‌را من نمیدانم ز تو،

[1] His biography is given in the *Rawḍátu'l-Jannát* (pp. 336–337), but not the date of his death. He was very bitter against the Ṣúfís, and had many controversies with Mullá Muḥammad Taqí-i-Majlisí on the subject.

[2] This date is mentioned on f. 121ᵇ as the current date at the time of writing.

Ch. IV (f. 17^{a}), a very long one, deals with the doctrine of Pantheism (*Waḥdatu 'l-Wujúd*), and cites the opinions of a number of thinkers, such as Shaykh Shabistarí, his commentator Láhijí, Mír Dámád, Jámí, Jalálu'd-Dín Dawání, Muḥammad Báqir-i-Majlisí, etc. No further chapters seem to be indicated until we reach the conclusion (*Khátima*, f. 82^{b}), containing short notices of eminent Ṣúfís and philosophers from the earliest times (Uways al-Qaraní, Kumayl, Ḥasan of Baṣra, Málik Dínár, Dhu'n-Nún of Egypt, Báyazíd of Bisṭám, al-Ḥalláj, etc.) down to Shaykh Bahá'u'd-Dín al-'Ámilí, Mír Abu'l-Qásim-i-Findariskí, Mullá Ṣadrá, Mullá Muḥsin-i-Fayḍ, and other notable thinkers of the Ṣafawí period. This book contains a great deal of interesting material, and would well deserve fuller study. Begins after the *Bismi'lláh* (f. 1^{b}):

لولا نفحات عطر روض القدم، لولا لمعات شمس نور الكرم،
ما كان من الوجود قطعا أثر، والعالم فى جبّ ظلام العدم،[1]

عالم همه موجود ز أسماء خداست، هستی نبود آنچه درین ارض و سماست،
پیدائی ذرّات ز خورشید بود، نبود چو فروغ مهر پرتو بکجاست،

After the doxology, which fills the best part of three pages, the author mentions his name as follows (f. 2^{b}, penultimate line):

و بعد بعرض ناظران این کلام و مطالعه کنندگان این ارقام میرساند، خادم صفّه نشینان بارگاهِ اهل معنی، ابن المرحوم بهآء الدین محمّد العاملی محمّد شفیع الحسینی که صورت این خیال چنین در مرآتِ خاطر مرتسم گردید... الخ

The author then enumerates (f. 3^{a}) a number of authorities of whom he has made use, and expresses his desire to write dispassionately and without prejudice about the *Mathnawí*, of which he is neither the indiscriminate admirer nor the hostile critic:

الحاصل راقم اینحروف که نه مادح مثنوی معنوی و نه قادح مولوی رومی است خواست که کتاب مثنوی‌را بنظر انصاف بدون عصبیّت و اعتساف بیند و گلهای فوایدش‌را چیند،

In his notice of Sháh Ni'matu'lláh (ff. 96^{b}–98^{a}) the author quotes a curious poem in which that eminent gnostic is said to have foretold the names and reigns of all the Ṣafawí kings. It begins:

ای عزیزان شور و غوغا در جهان خواهد گرفت، غصّه و غم از زمین تا آسمان خواهد گرفت،
چون ز هجرت نُهصد و نه سال و کسری بگذرد، فاش در عالم همه راز نهان خواهد گرفت،
شاه اسمعیل بن حیدر[2] بوده باشد شهریار، خاك پایش در جهان کحل عیان خواهد گرفت،

and ends:

از کلامِ حق و قولِ مصطفی گویم خبر، آنچه از امروز تا آخر زمان خواهد گرفت،

---

[1] These Arabic verses are marked in red لمحرّره (by the author), and the succeeding Persian quatrain لمسوّده (by the copyist).

[2] [The metre requires اسمعیلِ حیدر.]

The author then sketches the history of the Ṣafawís down to the end of the dynasty, and alludes to the subsequent reigns of Nádir Sháh and Karím Khán-i-Zand, and to his rivals Ázád Khán the Afghán and Muḥammad Ḥasan Khán-i-Qájár.

The MS. comprises 171 ff. of 23×14·5 c. and 21 ll. The Prolegomena (ff. 1^b–124^b) are written in a neat Persian *ta'líq* with rubrications and numerous marginal indications of topics which greatly facilitate reference: the titles and numerous Arabic citations are in a larger *naskh* hand, and generally in red. This part of the book ends abruptly with the title:

عارف ربّانی آقا محمّد بیدابادی اصفهانی

followed by an erasure of the remaining half page. The Table of Contents (ff. 128^b–170^b) is written in four columns, partly in red in the *naskh*, and partly in black in the *ta'líq* hand. The date 1178/1764–5 occurring in the colophon must apparently be taken as the date when the work was begun.

D. 7 (9).

(۱) انیس المُریدین، (۲) کنز السّالکین،

Two Persian prose treatises, of religious and mystical contents, ascribed[1] to the well-known Shaykh 'Abdu'lláh Anṣárí of Herát (b. 396/1005–6; d. 481/1088–9).

(1) The first treatise (ff. 7^b–121^a) is entitled (f. 8^a, l. 1) *Anísu'l-Murídín wa-Shamsu'l-Majális*, and the author's name occurs immediately after the doxology (f. 7^b, ll. 3–4). It appears from the first page (f. 7^b), which unfortunately presents many lacunae caused by a defective original, that the author wrote this book, containing the story of Joseph, at the request of certain friends. The basis of it is supplied by the *Súratu Yúsuf* in the *Qur'án*, of which the author first speaks, describing the circumstances in which it was revealed, and the number of verses (111), words (1887), and letters (766,000) which it contains. The Arabic text and its Persian translation are interrupted by many digressions and anecdotes of Prophets, Saints, etc.

(2) The second treatise (ff. 121^b–320^b) is headed, in a different hand from the text, "*Kanzu's-Sálikín* of Khwája Anṣárí," but this title does not seem to be mentioned in the work itself, which begins:

حمد بیحدّ اللّهی‌را و درود بیعدّ پادشاهی‌را که بر داشت از دیدهٔ دلها رمد ورفع السماء بغیر عمد[2] الخ

In this seemingly unsystematic treatise there is no division into chapters; it is written in a rather ornate style with numerous pieces of verse interspersed, and in the latter part are a good many lacunae evidently arising from a defective original.

Ff. 322 of 20·5×15 c. and 17 ll.; clear, modern Persian *naskh* with rubrications; no date or scribe's name. This was one of twenty MSS. which fell to my share at the second division of the Belshah MSS. in the spring of 1920.

---

[1] [Mr R. Levy has shown (*J.R.A.S.* for January, 1929, pp. 103 *et seqq.*) that the *Anísu'l-Murídín* was written after the death of Anṣárí.]

[2] [*Qur'án*, XIII, 2.]

D. 8 (6).

مقالات شیخ رکن الدّین علآء الدّوله سمنانی،

Discourses of Shaykh Ruknu'd-Dín 'Alá'u'd-Dawla of Simnán (d. 736/1335–6), beginning abruptly after a brief doxology:

...وبعده بدانکه این فواید چندست که شیخ رکن الحقّ والدّین علاء الدّوله سمنانی قدّس الله سرّه میفرمود و امیر اقبال می‌نوشته‌اند و بعضی از آن اینست والسّلام علی من اتّبع الهدی

Each discourse is preceded by the word *Majlis*, or *Majlis-i-dígar* in red letters, and the person to whom it was addressed is usually indicated, *e.g.*:

و حضرت شیخ قدّس سرّه شیخ علی مصری‌را پیش خود نشانده بود و از هر نوع کلمات میفرمود الخ

In the second *Majlis* (ff. 2ª–3ª) mention is made of "Shaykh Ṣadru'd-Dín who is in Ardabíl"; in another (f. 34ª) of Shaykh Sa'du'd-Dín Ḥamawí; in another (f. 37ª) of Shaykh Muḥyi'd-Dín Ibnu'l-'Arabí, etc. The discourses were collected and reduced to writing by Iqbál Sháh of Sístán.

The MS., which came from the library of the late Sir A. Houtum-Schindler, formerly belonged to Prince Farhád Mírzá *Mu'tamadu'd-Dawla*, who bestowed it in Rabí' II, 1286/July–Aug., 1869, on a certain Áqá 'Abdí. It comprises 98 ff. of 14·7 × 8 c. and 14 ll., and is written throughout in a small, neat, good and clear *ta'líq* with rubrications; no date or colophon.

D. 9 (9).

كتاب الكبريت الأحمر فى بيان علوم الكشف الأكبر،

The *Kitábu'l-Kibríti'l-Aḥmar* ("Book of the 'Red Sulphur'"—*i.e.* the Philosophers' Stone)[1] by Shaykh 'Abdu'l-Wahháb ibn Aḥmad ibn 'Alí al-Anṣárí ash-Sha'rání (d. 973/1565), an abridgement of the same author's *Lawáqiḥu'l-Anwári 'l-Qudsiyya*, which in turn is an abridgement of Shaykh Muḥyi'd-Dín Ibnu'l-'Arabí's *al-Futúḥátu'l-Makkiyya*. See Brockelmann, vol. II, pp. 335–338; Ahlwardt's Berlin Arabic Catalogue, vol. III, pp. 104–105, No. 3047.

This MS. was one of those acquired in the spring of 1920 at the third division of the Belshah collection. It comprises 214 ff. of 20·6 × 14·6 c. and 21 ll.; coarse, clear *naskh* with rubrications; dated Thursday, 3rd of Rabí' II, 1019/June 25, 1610; copyist 'Umar ibn Aḥmad ibn Muḥammad... known as Ibn Jibrá'íl al-Búṣírí. The work itself, as appears from the concluding paragraph, was completed on Sunday the 21st of Ramaḍán, 942/13th of March, 1536.

[1] [The usual title is *Kitábu'l-Kibríti'l-Aḥmar fí bayáni 'Ulúmi'sh-Shaykhi'l-Akbar.*]

D. 10 (9).

لبّ الشّروح (شرح گلشن راز)

Lubbu'sh-Shurúḥ ("the Marrow of Commentaries"), a selected commentary on the *Gulshan-i-Ráz* ("Rose-garden of Mystery") of Shaykh Maḥmúd-i-Shabistarí compiled by Muḥammad ibn Muḥammad called 'Alá'í of Shíráz from the four following commentaries, each of which is denoted by an appropriate symbol:

(1) *Nasá'im-i-Gulshan* ("Breezes of the Rose-garden") by Niẓámu'd-Dín Maḥmúd of Shíráz, called *ad-Dá'í* (denoted by عی).

(2) *Mafátíḥu'l-I'jáz* of Shaykh Shamsu'd-Dín Muḥammad Núr-bakhshí of Láhiján (جی), concerning whom see Rieu's Persian Catalogue, pp. 650–651.

(3) A commentary by Ḥusámu'd-Dín Ḥasan of Bitlís (لی).

(4) A commentary by Bábá Ni'matu'lláh of Nakhjuwán (نی).

The verses of the original poem are written in red, and the explanations and elucidations of each of the four commentators immediately follow, beginning with the easiest (نی), and ending with the most difficult (عی).

The text is incomplete at the end, the last verse commentated being No. 376 (out of 1008) of Whinfield's edition. The MS., which I bought from Naaman for £3 on May 1, 1901, comprises 182 ff. of 22·5×16·5 c. and 16 ll.; large, clear *nasta'líq* with rubrications; no colophon or date. The following title and verse are inscribed in red ink on f. 1[a]:

كتاب لبُّ الشّروح تأليف علائى بن مُحبّى الشريف الشيرازى الحسينى عفى عنه'
در جمعِ شروحِ گلشنِ راز' اين لُبِّ شروحِ هست ممتاز'

D. 11 (9).

زبدة الحقايق لعين القضاة الهمدانى

The *Zubdatu'l-Ḥaqá'iq* ("Cream of Verities") of 'Aynu'l-Quḍát al-Hamadání (d. 525/1131 or 533/1138/9), concerning whom see Rieu's Persian Catalogue, pp. 411–412 and references there given[1]. This work, written in Persian with numerous Arabic citations (written in red) from the *Qur'án* and Traditions, appears to be addressed to neophytes in the Ṣúfí doctrine, and to have no division into chapters. It begins after the usual brief doxology:

...تمهيد اصل اوّل بدانكه در حقِّ صورت بينان و ظاهر جويان با مصطفى صلعم خطاب باين آمد كه وَتَرٰيهُمْ يَنْظُرُونَ إِلَيْكَ وَهُمْ لَا يُبْصِرُونَ اى عزيز ميگويم مگر اين آيت در قرآن نخواندهٔ يا نديدهٔ كه قَدْ جَاءَكُمْ مِنَ ٱللهِ نُورٌ وَكِتَابٌ مُبِينٌ محمّدرا نور ميخواند و قرآن كه كلام خداى

[1] [This is the same work as that described by Ethé, I. O. Persian Catalogue, col. 980, No. 1793, under the title *Tamhîdât-i 'Ain-alḳuḍât*; see also his Bodleian Persian Catalogue, No. 1247.]

است نور میخواند که فَاتَّبِعُوا النُّورَ الَّذِی أُنْزِلَ مَعَهُ تو از قرآن حروف سیاه بینی بر کاغذ سفید
پس کاغذ و مداد و سطرها نور نیست پس القرآن کلام الله غیر مخلوق کدامست'

Ff. 148 of 20·9 × 14·5 c. and 15 ll.; large, clear *naskh*, the Arabic sentences written in red and fully pointed, the Persian also fully pointed for the first few pages. The scribe's name is not given, but his work was finished in the middle of Rabí' II, 999/February, 1591. The MS. was bought for £3 from Naaman on May 7, 1903.

D. 12 (7).

اشعّة اللّمعات

The *Ashi''atu'l-Lama'át*, a well-known commentary composed by Jámí in 886/1481–2 on the *Lama'át* of 'Iráqí (d. 686/1287–8 or 688/1289). See Rieu's Persian Catalogue, pp. 593–594.

Ff. 88 of 17 × 11 c. and 17 ll.; clear but ungraceful *nasta'líq*, with rubrications; dated 5 Rabí' I, 983/June 14, 1575. This was one of 13 MSS. bought from J. J. Naaman in May, 1902, for £25.

D. 13 (9).

A collection of seven Ṣúfí tracts, the first six in Turkish, the last in Arabic. The MS., which was given to me by Dr Riḍá Tawfíq in August, 1909, comprises 138 ff. of 21 × 15·5 c. and 19 ll., is written throughout in a good, clear Turkish *naskh*, and is dated (f. 134[a]) 1148/1735–6. The contents are as follows:

(1) An anonymous Turkish poem of 51 verses on the personal appearance of the Prophet Muḥammad (ff. 2[b]–3[b]), followed by a Turkish prose tract (ff. 3[b]–12[b]) on the same subject.

(2) The *'Ibrat-numá*, a Turkish treatise in mixed prose and verse (ff. 13[b]–30[b]) by Lámi'í (d. 937/1530–1 or 938/1531–2), concerning whom see E. J. W. Gibb's *History of Ottoman Poetry*, vol. III, pp. 20–34.

(3) Another Turkish treatise entitled *Kanzu's-Sálikín wa-Qabála-i-Ganji'l-'Arifín* (*sic*! ff. 31[a]–42[b]) on cosmogony, etc., containing 25 verses near the beginning, but otherwise in prose.

(4) Another Turkish treatise (ff. 42[b]–63[b]) in 23 sections, the titles of which are in Persian, beginning abruptly:

سَنُرِیهِمْ آیاتنا فی الآفاق وفی انفسهم حتّی یتبیّن لهم انّه الحقّ' ای طالب بل و آگاه اول که
آفاقده نشانلر واردر سنگ نفسکده دخی واردر الخ

(5) Another Turkish treatise (ff. 64[a]–81[b]) ascribed to Ḥájjí Bektásh, beginning after the doxology:

...امّا بعد اول اسرار سوزلو و گولر يوزلو، ترتيب معرفت و گنج حقيقت، صاحب علوم اول قطب الاقطاب سلطان حاجى بكتاش ولى الخ

(6) Another Turkish treatise (ff. 82[a]–127[b]) entitled *Manáqibu'l-Jawáhir*, composed, as we learn from a verse at the end (f. 127[b], l. 3), in 932/1525–6.

(7) An Arabic tract, ascribed in the colophon at the end to Shaykh Muḥyi 'd-Dín Ibnu'l-'Arabí (ff. 127[b]–134[a]), beginning:

الحمد لله الّذى لم يكن قبل وحدانيّته قبل الّا والقبل هو ولم يكن بعد وحدانيّته بعد الّا والبعد هو الخ

D. 14 (10).

الانسان الكامل (ترجمهٔ تركيّه)،

A Turkish translation by 'Abdu'l-Báqí of the *Insánu'l-Kámil* ("Perfect Man") of 'Abdu'l-Karím ibn Ibráhím al-Jílí (b. 767/1365–6, d. circa 811/1408–9). Concerning him and his doctrine, see Shaykh Muḥammad Iqbál's *Development of Metaphysics in Persia* (London: Luzac, 1908), pp. 150–174, and Dr R. A. Nicholson's *Studies in Islamic Mysticism* (Cambridge, 1921, ch. II, pp. 77–142); also Brockelmann, vol. II, pp. 205–206. Begins:

انّ أجلى ما يتجلّى به الاعيان و احلى ما يتحلّى اليه الانسان حمد من ابدع من كنوز هويّته حقايق جواهر الهويّات آية دالّة على احديّة هويّة الذات الخ...وبعد، تاج العارفين سراج السالكين عبد الكريم الجيلى رحمة الله عليه وعلى ساير المحقّقين وجميع المؤمنين حضرتلرينك تأليفاتندن الانسان الكامل اسميله مسمّى تصنيف لطيف بى همتالرى لسان تركى ايله ادا و املا اولنه سهل الأخذ واضح المعنى بر اثر دلربا اولوردى ديو بعضى احباب رغبت‌نما اولمغين بو عبد فقير بو خصوصده همّت درونم پيدا و خواهش دل هويدا اولوب اجتلاب دعاء صوفيّه و فقرا اُمّيديله اولا خطبهٔ بى نظيرى بعينه عربى تسطير اولنوب فصل الخطابدن صكره زبان تركى اوزره تعبير و تقرير و تحريره ابتدا اولندى ومن الله الاعانة والافاضة والتوفيق والهداية الى سواء الطريق واستمدّ منه الفهم الدقيق ولسان التحقيق،

This MS., which was given to me in August, 1909, by Dr Riḍá Tawfíq, comprises 142 ff. of 23·6 × 15·4 c. and 25 ll.; is written throughout in clear, neat Turkish *naskh* with rubrications; and was copied in 1309/1891–2 from an original dated 1157.

D. 15 (7).

رسالة الحضرات الخمس

(1) A Turkish treatise on the "Five Planes" of Being (*Ḥadarát-i-Khams*) of the Ṣúfís, composed at the end of Sha'bán, 1132/6 July, 1720, by Shaykh Ismá'íl Ḥaqqí of Broussa at the request of some of his Turkish friends. It begins:

فيض ثنا گلزار تقديسى شاداب و روضهٔ رسولى سيراب قلدقدنصكره بو فقير شيخ اسمعيل حقّى البروسوى الاسكدارى لا زال زامداد من طرف حضرت البارى بو وجهله نقشبند صحيفهٔ تقرير و طرّه آويز ورقهٔ تحرير اولور كه بيڭ يوز اوتوز ايكى شعبانى سلخنده اشارت الهيّه ايله دمشق الشامدن هجرت و مدينهٔ اسكدارده طويلهزن اقامت اولديغمده جانب رومدن بعض اخوان حضرات خمسڭ لسان تركى اوزره شرحنى استدعا و حلّ مشكلاتنى رجا ايتدكلرنده من قطع رجاء من ارتجى قطع الله رجاءه مضموننددن حذرًا اسعاف مرام قلندى و بياننه تصدّى اولنوب اسمى رسالة الحضرات (f. 2ª) دنلدى، اسأل الله أن يجعلنى من اهل فيضه الخاصّ ويشرّفنى بسرّ الاخلاص،

This treatise ends on f. 48ᵇ, and is followed by three traditions of the Prophet and a verse of the *Qur'án*.

(2) A Turkish treatise on certain questions connected with the *Futúḥátu'l-Makkiyya* of Shaykh Muḥyi'd-Dín Ibnu'l-'Arabí (ff. 51ᵇ–93ᵇ), entitled *Lubbu'l-Lubb wa-sirru's-Sirr* ("the kernel of the Kernel and mystery of the Mystery"). This is followed by a short vocabulary (ff. 94ª–95ᵇ) of Ṣúfí metaphors, and several Ṣúfí poems in Turkish, mostly by Naqshí Efendi 'Ikrimání (حضرت نقشى عكرمانى), but one each by Oghlán Shaykhí Ibráhím Efendi and Ghaybí.

This MS. was given to me at Constantinople in April, 1908, by Dr Riḍá Tawfíq, and was, I suspect, copied by him. It contains in the margins some philosophical notes by him in French. Ff. 104 of 17×12 c. and 15 ll., good, clear, modern Turkish *naskh* with rubrications, no date or colophon.

D. 16 (9).

مطاعن الصوّفيّه

A violent attack on the Ṣúfís and their doctrines entitled *Maṭá'inu'ṣ-Ṣúfiyya*, composed in Ramaḍán, 1221/Nov.–Dec. 1806 (f. 27ᵇ), by Muḥammad Rafí' ibn Muḥammad Shafí' of Tabríz (f. 5ª). This MS., which appears to be an autograph, was completed on the 22nd of Jumádá II, 1222/27 August, 1807, and was one of those bought by me from the late Ḥájjí 'Abdu'l-Majíd Belshah in January, 1920.

It comprises 176 ff. of 21 × 15·5 c. and 22 ll., and is written in a small, neat *naskh* with rubrications. The actual text begins, after the Arabic doxology:

...امّا بعد به ارباب بصیرت مخفی نیست که همواره شیطان در اغوای بنی نوع انسان کمال
سعی و اهتمام و در تخریب بنیان دین و ایمان کوشش تمام دارد الخ

A full table of contents occupying four pages and a half (ff. 1ᵇ–3ᵇ) is prefixed, of which the following is a summary.

Introduction (f. 5ᵇ). The vanity and heresy of the Ṣúfí doctrine proved by traditions derived from the Imáms, the unanimous opinion of the Shí'a, and the considered judgment of the theological doctors, both Shí'a and Sunní, including amongst the former the Shaykh-i-Mufíd, al-Kulayní, Ibn Bábawayhi, at-Ṭúsí, 'Alamu'l-Hudà, Sayyid Murtaḍà ar-Rází, 'Allámа-i-Ḥillí, Ibn Ḥamza, Shaykh 'Alí 'Abdu'l-'Ál, his son Shaykh Ḥasan, etc.; of the moderns Mullá Aḥmad of Ardabíl, Mullá Muḥammad Báqir-i-Majlisí, Sayyid Ni'matu'lláh al-Jazá'irí, etc.; and of contemporaries Muḥammad Báqir of Bihbihán, Shaykh Yúsuf al-Baḥrání, and Shaykh Muḥammad Mahdí al-'Ámilí. Amongst the Sunní doctors are mentioned ad-Damírí, an-Nasafí, az-Zamakhsharí, and Ruknu'd-Dín 'Alá'u'd-Dawla-i-Simnání.

Chapter I (f. 21ᵇ). Why the Ṣúfís were so called; when they first appeared; and how their doctrines spread. Emphasis is laid on the fact that nearly all the prominent Ṣúfís were Sunnís, while they were held in detestation by the Shí'a.

Chapter II (f. 31ᵃ). Concerning the doctrines and observances of these misguided people. This chapter is chiefly taken from the *Ḥadíqa* ("Garden") of Mullá Aḥmad of Ardabíl, and, in its latter part, from the *'Aynu'l-Ḥayát* ("Fountain of Life") of Mullá Muḥammad Báqir-i-Majlisí. Twenty-one sects or schools of the Ṣúfís are specially discussed.

Chapter III (f. 47ᵃ). Account of twenty of the leading Ṣúfís, beginning with Abú Háshim and Sufyánu'th-Thawrí and ending with al-Ḥalláj, Shams-i-Tabríz, and Mullá Ṣadrá of Shíráz, with a supplementary note (*takmíl*) on "the accursed Núr 'Alí."

Chapter IV (f. 98ᵇ). Setting forth the evils of the doctrines and practices of the Ṣúfís, and their incompatibility with the Holy Law of Islám. This chapter is divided into five sections (*faṣl*) and five topics (*maṭlab*).

Chapter V (f. 154ᵃ). On the necessity of interpreting allegorically (*ta'wíl*) certain traditions and verses of the *Qur'án* which appear to favour the opinions and doctrines of the Ṣúfís. (Ten such traditions and four such verses are dealt with.)

Conclusion (f. 172ᵃ). On the necessity of religious controversy, of enjoining virtue and repressing vice, of avoiding intercourse with heretics and sinners, and of cursing and repudiating such.

This MS. was one of 47 bought of the late Ḥájjí 'Abdu'l-Majíd Belshah in January, 1920. It comprises 176 ff. of 21×15·5 c. and 22 ll., and is written in a small, neat Persian *naskh* with rubrications. The colophon, giving the dates of the composition of the work and the completion of this copy, is as follows (f. 176[a]) :

قد وقع الفراق (*read* الفراغ) من تأليف هذه الرسالة الموسومة بمطاعن الصوفيّه بيد مؤلّفها الفقير المحتاج الى رحمة الله الغفور البديع ابن محمّد شفيع محمّد رفيع التبريزى حشرهما الله مع مواليهما فى شهر الله المبارك سنة احدى وعشرين بعد المائتين والالف الهجريّة ١٢٢١

قد تمّ تسويدها فى الثانى والعشرين من شهر جمادى الثانى سنة
اثنين وعشرين و مائتين بعد الالف من هجرة
النبويّة عليه وآله آلاف الثناء والتحيّة،

D. 17 (9).

Answers to nine questions on Ṣúfí doctrine and terminology by 'Abdu'lláh Muḥammad Zamán. These questions were addressed by me to Mírzá Muḥammad Báqir of Bawánát (see pp. 2–3 *supra*) at Beyrout about 1886, and he and Ḥájjí Muḥammad Ḥusayn of Ná'in, commonly called " Ḥájjí Pír-záda, submitted them to the author, who, in response to their request, composed the treatise of which this is the original autograph. The circumstances are briefly stated as follows in the Preface (f. 5[a]) after the doxology :

امّا بعد، فلا يخفى على ضماير ارباب العرفان انّ الّذى بعثنى على تسطير آرآء اصحاب الايقان فى هذه الاوراق الّتى الّفْتُها والصحف الّتى سطرْتُها هو ورود المسائل العرفانيّة الآتية الّتى اوردها نخبة الاذكياء المستر ادورد جُرْج برونى الانكليزى الى مشرعة المعانى والأسرار سبكتها فى تسعة مبانى يد الافكار وهى هذه على الاجمال هداه الله سوآء الطريق وأذاقه حلاوة التحقيق (f. 5[b])، المسئلة الاولى الاعيان الثّابتة و الثانية التعيّن واللا تعيّن والثالثة حضرات الخمس والرابعة نفس الرّحمن [والخامسة البرزخ] والسادسة النكاح السارى فى جميع الذرارى والسابعة العمآء والثامنة صاحب الوقت والتاسعة البرزخيّة الكبرى، هذا ولمّا وردت هذه الاسئلة المذكورة فآستوردها عندنا زبدة الفضلاء الميرزا محمّد باقر المعطّر البواناتى سلّمه الله تعالى ليتمكّن من لدنّا من الأجوبة وكان يدعونى الى تحريرها ويسئلنى عن صرف الهمّة نحو اختصارها والاقتصار على بيان معانيها وكشف استارها حسب اللّغة وانّى قد كنت أضرب عن الشرح اللّغوى صفحًا وأطوى دون مرامه كشحًا علمًا منّى بأنّه تحصيل حاصل وشرح تحته بلا طائل لوجود (f. 6[a]) الكتب اللغويّة والمعانى العرفيّة عند السائل ولمّا شاهدت من انّ السائل المعزّز اليه قد تعالت همّته العالية على استطلاع طوالع الانوار وتقاومت عزائمه الجليلة باستكشاف خبيّات الأسرار ولمّا تبيّن لنا ذلك من كتابه المنيف المرقوم بخطّه الشّريف الموسوم لحضرة نتيجة الصدق والصّفاء الحاجّ محمّد حسين نائنى الملقّب به پيرزاده أيّده الله تعالى ثمّ راجعْتُ النظر اليه وطالعْتُ ما استقرّ فيه من المواهب الالهيّة ولمّا لاحظْتُ عباراته الروحانيّة الدالّة على الاشارات الربّانيّة الموصلة الى الحقيقة الحقّة والولاية المطلقة حينئذٍ شاهدْتُ مباديها ومقاصدها من فصله الخطاب الى ختمه المستطاب أنّ الحقّ سبحانه (f. 6[b]) اختار كاتبه لمعارف الوحدانيّة واصطفاه

لمواهبه اللدنيّة فأنتصبْتُ لشرح الكتاب وناديْتُ من بعيد يا اولى الالباب بقوله تعالى انّما نُطْعمكم لوجه الله لا نُريد منكم جزاءً ولا شكورا (شعر) فللارض من كأس الكرام نصيب، الخ

The MS. comprises 159 ff. of 20·8 × 13·2 c. and 13 ll., and is written in a large, coarse, legible *ta'líq*. Seven blank pages (ff. 8ª–11ª) intervene between the Preface and the body of the book. Although the text is in Arabic, numerous passages of Persian poetry are quoted. The copying of the MS. was completed on the 22nd of Sha'bán, 1304/May 16, 1887, at Beyrout.

D. 18 (9).

بيان طريقت نقشبنديّه

A brief account in Persian of the Rules of the Naqshbandí Order of Dervishes, beginning, after a short Arabic doxology:

بعد از حمد و صلوة باعث تحرير اين چند سطور آنكه چون بعضى ياران التماس كردند كه سبقهاى طريقهٔ نقشبنديّهٔ عليّهٔ مجدّديّه قدّس الله تعالى اسرارهمرا بترتيب از ابتدا با انتهى (تا انتها *read*) بايد نوشت هرچند جناب حضرت مجدّد الف ثانى و حضرت عروة الوثقى قدّس الله تعالى اسرارهما و ديگر ابنا و نباير و خلفاء ايشان اجمالًا و تفصيلًا (p. 3) مكتوبات در طريق حاجت بنوشتن ديگر نيست ليكن اجابتًا (*sic*) للملتمس چند سطور در بيان طريقهٔ مبارك نقشبنديّه نوشته ميشود الخ

Pp. 22 of 21·5 × 13·1 c. and 15 ll.; good, clear *naskh*, with overlinings in red and punctuation in gold. The following colophon occurs on pp. 19–20:

تمّت هذه الرسالة الشريفة من مجدّد الزمان قطب العالم وارث حضرت رسول الله صَلّعم حضرت شاه فضل احمد معصومى فى ليلة الاربعا من يد كمترين غلامان ارشاد نويس حضرت صوفى خواجه فاروقى بنابر توجّه خواهش خاطر خادم خاندان صادق الاعتقاد حاجى الحرمين الشريفين حاجى نعمت الله البخارى فى تأريخ شهر صفر الخير سنه ۲۲۲،

This appears to be one of the Belshah MSS., but its source is not indicated.

D. 19 (10).

من تاليف افضل الدّين الكاشانى

This MS., obtained at the fourth partition of the Belshah MSS. on Nov. 12, 1920, comprises ff. 238 of 24·2 × 14 c. and 15 ll., and is for the most part written in a large, clear *naskh* with rubrications, though some portions are written in *ta'líq*. It was transcribed in 1161–2/1748–9 by one Muḥammad ibn Muḥammad 'Álim for the Nawwáb Mírzá Ṣafawí Khán, and contains the following writings of Bábá Afḍalu'd-Dín of Káshán (d. 707/1307–8):

(1) A short account of the author in Persian, followed by a selection of his poems, especially his quatrains (ff. 1^b–12^a).

(2) The *Minháju'l-Mubín* ("Clear Way") on Logic, in Arabic (ff. 13^a–75^b).

(3) Persian translation of the above (ff. 76^a–140^b).

(4) The *Madáriju'l-Kamál* ("Grades of Perfection"), in Arabic (ff. 142^a–172^a).

(5) Persian translation of the same (ff. 176^b–216^a).

(6) *Mabádí-i-Uṣúl* in Persian (ff. 216^b–225^b).

(7) *Khujista Andarz* ("Fortunate Counsel"), in Persian (ff. 226^a–229^a).

(8) Another short tract by Bábá Afḍal in Persian (ff. 229^b–230^a).

(9) and (10). Two more short tracts in Persian (ff. 230^b and 231^a).

(11) *Daf'u Makháfati'l-Mawt* ("Repelling the Fear of Death"), in Arabic (ff. 231^b–235^a).

(12) Persian letter to a friend (ff. 236^a–237^b).

See Rieu's Persian Catalogue, pp. 829–831, and 739 for the quatrains. Of the above-mentioned works only the Persian *Madáriju'l-Kamál* is mentioned. In the brief biography now prefixed to the volume (for, as the numbering of the leaves, 236–248, shows, it originally came at the end) Bábá Afḍal is said to have died at a village near Káshán in Rajab, 666/March–April, 1268, where his tomb is still an object of veneration.

D. 20 (9).

دُرر مقالات بابا طاهر

An Arabic commentary by an anonymous author on some of the Arabic sayings of the celebrated Saint Bábá Ṭáhir, called *'Uryán* ("the Naked"), a contemporary of Ṭughril the Saljúq, and author of the popular quatrains in dialect concerning whom see vol. II of my *Literary History of Persia*, pp. 259–260. Begins:

من دُرر مقالات العالم الربّانی بابا طاهر،
بسم الله الرّحمن الرّحیم وبه نستعین،

الحمد لله الواحد الأحد الصمد الّذی لم یلد ولم یولد الّخ ... امّا بعد، فما لا ریب فیه (f. 3^a) لظهوره اصطفاء الحقّ بعض عباده علی بعضٍ باطّلاع سرائرهم علی بعض اسراره واشراق ضمایرهم بطوالع انواره فکما خصّ الانبیاءَ بالوحی خصّ الاولیاء بالالهام الفارق بین الحقّ والباطل، ففاز منهم الصوفیّة علی ما الهمهم به من المنح العرفانیّة، والعطایا الوجدانیّة، فوضعوا له اصطلاحات یشیر الیه تغادیا عن اطّلاع الاغیار علی تلك الاسرار، واکتفوا بالاشارة عن العبارة لمن بعضها من الاحرار، فان یکفیه الاشارة وقد فتح الله علیّ ببرکة محبّتی ایّاهم، وایثاری لهداهم، وطریقهم وتمسّکی بصحّة

عقيدتهم باباً من الفهم لما يشيرون اليه من معانى التوحيد ومسالك التفريد، حتّى يستنشق منّى
عرف الوجدان مشامّ (f. 3^b) اهل الارادة لهولاء السّادة ثمّ لمّا اتّفق اختيارى بمحروسة همدان حماها الله
عن الحدثان واحتظيْتُ بملاقات اهلها من الاخوان والخُلّان وظهر بتباشير تعارف الأرواح تألّف
الاشباح وجدْتُ فيهم مسكةً من الدّين وبقيّةً من طلب اليقين واستكشافًا عن آثار الطريقة وأسرار
الحقيقه الّتى ركدت فى هذا الزمان ريحها وخبت مصابيحها ودبّ فيه الاندراس واستولى عليها
الانطماس وآنسْتُ منهم شغفًا بآلبحث عن معانى الكلمات المرويّة عن الشيخ الربّانى والعارف
الحقّانى المعروف بابا طاهر رحمة الله عليه فاقترحوا علىّ أن اكشف لهم عن وجوه حقايقها وأرفع
منارًا على طرايقها وأحْجمْتُ (f. 4^a) على الاقدام على ذلك لمّا وجدْتُها بعيدة الغور غير منكشفة للنظر
على الفور وضمنْتُ لهم أن أكتب لها شرحًا اذا ابت الى منقلبى وحطّ علىّ تعبى فها أنا واف بما
وعدْتُ بتوفيق الله أكتب لها شرحًا يحلّ معاقدها ويقرّر قواعدها واضمّنه بما يسمح به الوقت
ويفتح لى معانيها بعد رتّبْتُ لها ترتيبًا يقرب به التّناول على متعاطيها منها قول الشيخ فى العلم قوله
العلم دليل المعرفة يدلّ عليها فاذا جاءت المعرفة سقطت الرؤية و بقى حركات العلم بالمعرفة أقول
بيان ذلك انّه أراد أن يفرّق بين علم المعرفة الّذى يدلّ على معرفة الصانع بمطالعة صنعه هو دليل
المعرفة لا عينها و لهذا العلم (f. 4^b) بسبب انتقاله من الأثر الى المؤثّر حركة خالية عن المعرفة قبل
حصول عينها آلخ

The remainder of the book consists entirely of quotations from the sayings of Bábá Ṭáhir followed by the commentator's explanation, the word قوله being prefixed to the former, and أقول to the latter.

Ff. 196 of 21 × 13·5 c. and 12 ll.; large, clear, good modern Persian *naskh* with rubrications; no date or colophon. This MS. was one of those bought from the late Ḥájjí 'Abdu'l-Majíd Belshah in January, 1920.

D. 21 (11).

This MS. comprises a number of Persian works on Ṣúfism, some of which are rare, together with several miscellaneous pieces chiefly mystical in character. The contents are as follows:

(1) A letter in Persian from the Ottoman Sulṭán Murád III (?) to Sháh 'Abbás the Ṣafawí (ff. 1^b–2^a).

(2) A mystical tract without title or author's name (ff. 2^b–8^b). It begins:

سبحان الله اين چه گوهر گرانمايه و اين چه اختر بلندپايه است كه آشنايان وحى و الهام اورا
بسخن موسوم گردانيده‌اند

(3) The *Majálisu'l-'Ushsháq* (ff. 10^b–62^b), biographical notices, 77 in this copy, of famous Ṣúfís by Sulṭán Ḥusayn b. Bayqará of Herát (d. 911/1505–6). See Rieu's Persian Catalogue, p. 351; Ethé, I. O. Persian Catalogue, No. 1870.

(4) *Kanzu'l-'Áshiqín* (ff. 63b–90b) by Shaykh Muḥyi'd-Dín aṭ-Ṭúsí, who died in Ḥalab in 830/1426–7 (see Rieu's Persian Catalogue, p. 1078a). The present work, of which another copy is described by Ivanow, A. S. B. Persian Catalogue, No. 1238, consists of ten *Majális*, *viz.* :

(۱) در عشق و محبّت (۲) در بکا و ریاضات (۳) در رحمت حق و شفاعت (۴) در سکرات موت و شدّت قبر (۵) در حقوق مسلمانان (٦) در حقوق همسایه (۷) در فضیلت جمعه (۸) در کسب حلال و فضیلت آن (۹) در عدل و احسان (۱۰) در سخاوت و فضل

The author states that he was a descendant of the Imám (Abú Ḥámid Muḥammad) al-Ghazálí and that he derived the materials for this treatise from the *Iḥyá*, the *Kímiyá-i Sa'ádat*, and other writings of his famous ancestor. Transcribed in 1009/1600–1 at Band Súrat by Abú Muḥammad b. Fatḥ.

(5) *Risála-i Chihil Majlis* (ff. 90b–111b), an interesting and valuable collection of forty discourses on mystical subjects by Shaykh Ruknu'd-Dín 'Alá'u'd-Dawla of Simnán (d. 736/1335–6), compiled by Iqbál b. Sábiq al-Sijistání.

(6) Exhortations and counsels addressed by the Prophet to 'Alí b. Abí Ṭálib (ff. 111b–113b).

(7) *Jawáhiru'th-Thamína* (ff. 113b–124a), a compilation of sayings and discourses on Ṣúfism by the Chishtí Shaykh 'Alí b. 'Abdi'l-Malik b. Qáḍíkhán al-Muttaqí (see Rieu, Persian Catalogue, p. 356), who died in 975/1567–8. The author says that after he had compiled a work in Arabic entitled *Jawámi'u'l-Kilam fi'l-Mawá'iẓ wa-'l-Ḥikam*, it occurred to him to write a work of the same kind in Persian for the benefit of all and sundry, comprising citations from the sayings of Shaykh 'Abdu'lláh al-Anṣárí, the *Mir'átu'l-'Árifín* of Prince Mas'úd-i Bak (see Rieu, Persian Catalogue, p. 632), the *Nuzhatu'l-Arwáḥ*, etc., and to this he gave the title of *Jawáhiru'th-Thamína* ("The Precious Jewels"). It is arranged according to the alphabetical order of the subjects of which it treats : thus the first group of sections deals with اخلاص, اتّحاد, انصاف ; the second group with برّ الوالدین, بذل الروح, and so on. The transcription of this copy was completed on Jumádà II, 1009/9 December, 1600. Another copy of the same work is described by Ivanow, A. S. B. Persian Catalogue, No. 1254, under the title of *Jawámi'u'l-Kilam*.

(8) *Silku's-Sulúk* (ff. 124b–153b), a treatise on the progress of the Ṣúfí towards union with God, by Ḍiyá (Ḍiyá'u'd-Dín) an-Nakhshabí, who died in 751/1350–1. See Rieu, Persian Catalogue, p. 41 ; Ethé, I. O. Persian Catalogue, Nos. 1838–9 ; Ivanow, A. S. B. Persian Catalogue, Nos. 1200–3. The work is divided into 151 *silk* ("bead-strings") and begins with the explanation of a number of technical terms (*iṣṭiláḥát*).

(9) *Nuzhatu'l-Arwáḥ* (ff. 154b–173b), a well-known treatise on the same subject as the preceding work, by Ḥusayn b. 'Álim b. 'Alí b. Abi'l-Ḥasan al-Ḥusayní, generally known as Fakhru's-Sádát (see Rieu, Persian Catalogue, p. 40), who died in 718/1318–9.

(10) *Fál-i manẓúm* (f. 174ᵃ), a poem of twenty-six verses in the *hazaj* metre on omens. 'Alí b. Abí Ṭálib is quoted as authority for the rules and directions which are given.

Begins :

امیر المومنین شاه ذو عالم، که باشد سوی او راه دو عالم

(11) Two Arabic invocations (f. 174ᵃ). The first, which is said to be uttered by Ilyás and Khiḍr when they take leave of each other after their meeting at 'Arafát on the day of 'Arafa, is introduced by a list of the blessings which it brings and the misfortunes which it averts.

(12) *Tafá'ul-i 'aṭsa* (f. 174ᵇ), rules for taking omens from sternutation on each day of the week according to the quarter of the horizon whence the sneeze is heard.

(13) *Lawámi'* (ff. 175ᵇ–181ᵇ), a Persian commentary by 'Abdu'r-Raḥmán Jámí on certain verses of the *Khamriyya* ("Wine Ode") of Ibnu'l-Fáriḍ. See Rieu, Persian Catalogue, p. 808.

(14) Qaṣídas and ghazals by al-Murtaḍà al-Maghfúr Amír-i Ḥájj (ff. 182ᵇ–193ᵇ). I am unable to identify the author. Many of the poems are in praise of 'Alí b. Abí Ṭálib.

Begins :

نماز شام کز آثار امر کن فیکون، هزار نقش بر آرد سپهر بو قلمون

(15) *Munsha'át* of Mírzá Muḥammad Riḍá'í (?), a collection of letters in ornate style (ff. 195ᵇ–209ᵇ).

Begins :

یا رب نفسی ده که ثنا پردازم، وین نغمه بآهنگ سزا پردازم

Ff. 210 of 26 × 15·5 c. and, for the most part, 35 ll. running obliquely across the page. The bulk of the volume is written in small *nasta'líq*. Ff. 12–153 are numbered ٧١٢-٥٦٨ and must originally have formed part of a much larger volume. The margins are damaged in places but have been carefully repaired.

D. 22 (7).

رساله فی مراتب الثلاثة من التصوّف

A Persian treatise, consisting of a *Muqaddama* and three *Uṣúl*, on the three grades of the mystical life by Khwája Ṣá'inu'd-Dín 'Alí Tarika (Turka) al-Iṣfahání, who died in 835/1431–2. The first grade, described as the Way of the *Akhyár*, is *'ibádat*, culminating in *'ilmu'l-yaqín*; the second, *viz.* the Way of the *Abrár*, is *'ubúdiyyat*, culminating in *'aynu'l-yaqín*; and the third, *viz.* the Way of the *Muḥaqqiqán* and *Sábiqán*, which is left without a name in this MS., culminates in *ḥaqqu'l-yaqín*. See Rieu, Persian Catalogue, pp. 42, 774, 833, where other works by the author are mentioned.

Ff. 15 of 17·7 × 10·2 c. and 15 ll. Small neat *naskh*. No colophon or date.

E. THE OLDER HERETICAL SECTS.

(ISMÁ'ÍLÍS, NUṢAYRÍS, DRUZES, AND ḤURÚFÍS.)

E. 1 (10).

كتاب فضايح الباطنيّة للغزالى،

A transcript of the unique British Museum Arabic MS. **OR.** 7782[1] containing al-Ghazálí's refutation of the Báṭiní or Ismá'ílí heresy, made for me by an Indian copyist named Ismá'íl 'Alí in 1913. Photographs of the original were afterwards taken at the instance of the late Mr H. F. Amedroz and sent to the late Professor Ignaz Goldziher of Budapest[2], who subsequently published an admirable account of this important and interesting work entitled *Streitschrift des Gazālī gegen die Bāṭinijja-Sekte* (No. 3 of the De Goeje-Stiftung, E. J. Brill, Leyden, 1916). The existence of this masterly monograph (which includes 80 pp. of selected passages from the Arabic text) renders any further account of the work superfluous.

My transcript is written in a large *naskh*, which, like the original, is almost entirely devoid of diacritical points, the copyist having been instructed to transcribe the original as exactly as possible, without seeking to improve it. It comprises 252 ff. of 22·5 × 17 c. and about 21 lines, and appears to have been completed in December, 1912, although not delivered until the following year.

E. 2 (8).

حقيقة حقّ اليقين فى معرفة سرّ الاسرار،

A collection of Nuṣayrí tracts and prayers, written in a large, clear, modern *naskh*, fully but often incorrectly pointed, without date or colophon, and comprising 222 ff. of 18 × 12·5 c. and 10 ll. This MS. was presented to me in July, 1895, by the late Mírzá Áqá Khán of Kirmán, then resident at Constantinople, who described it as a book of the Druzes of the Lebanon, "who," he adds, "keep their religion very secret." Having consulted M. René Dussaud's *Histoire et Religion des Noṣairis* (Paris, 1900), I am disposed to assign it to that sect rather than to the Druzes. There are numerous blank leaves throughout the MS. which do not, however, interrupt the continuity of the text, as shown by the catch-words. The only general title of the book occurs on f. 1ᵇ as follows:

كتاب مجموع حقيقة حقّ اليقين فى معرفة سرّ الأسرار مولانا على امير المؤمنين،

[1] Acquired in November, 1912. [2] In January, 1914.

Glorification of 'Alí is mingled with reprobation of the first two Caliphs: thus on f. 44^b occurs a passage entitled:

'خبر ضلال و وبال یعنی ابو بکر و عمر لعنهم الله تعالی'

A brief account of the twelve Imáms occupies ff. 199^b–203^b. The Arabic is throughout the volume very incorrect.

ḤURÚFÍ BOOKS.

[The remaining MSS. in this class represent the literature of the Ḥurúfí sect, of which a general account will be found on pp. 365–375 and 449–452 of my *Persian Literature under Tartar Dominion.* Eleven of these MSS. have been already described in a paper entitled *Further Notes on the Literature of the Ḥurúfís and their connection with the Bektáshí Order of Dervishes* which I published in the *Journal of the Royal Asiatic Society* for July, 1907 (vol. XXXIX, pp. 533–581). This paper was supplementary to an article published in the same periodical for 1898 (vol. XXX, pp. 61–94) and entitled *Some Notes on the Literature and Doctrines of the Ḥurúfí Sect.* In what follows I shall refer to the latter as *Some Notes* and to the former as *Further Notes.* Of the last-named there is a *tirage-à-part* in which the pages are numbered 1–49, instead of 533–581 as in the complete volume, and references to both systems of pagination will be given when it is cited.]

E. 3 (7).

This is the MS. "(14) **A. 41**" described on pp. 19 (551)–22 (554) of *Further Notes,* being one of five bought in Constantinople in May, 1901, at the sale of the effects of a Bektáshí dervish. It comprises 205 ff. of 15·5 × 10·5 c. and 13 ll. and is written in a neat *nasta'líq* of the sixteenth Christian century. It contains 17 tracts in verse and prose, of which the most important is the *Khuṭbatu'l-Bayán* (ff. 26^b–181^a) in Turkish, the colophon of which is dated 983/1575–6.

E. 4 (7).

This MS., bought with the last in May, 1901, is that described on pp. 22–23 (554–555) of *Further Notes* under the heading "(15) **A. 42.**" It comprises 88 ff. of 17·4 × 12·1 c. and 13 ll., and is written in a neat, modern Turkish *riq'a* (the date 15 Jumádà I, 1282/6 Oct. 1865, occurs in a colophon on f. 78^b). It contains seven tracts, of which the chief are the *Ákhirat-náma* of Firishta-záda (ff. 8^b–15^b), and the *Kitáb-i-Nuqṭati'l-Bayán* of Shaykh-záda (ff. 19^b–78^b).

E. 5 (7).

This is the MS. "(16) **A. 43**" described on pp. 23–26 (555–558) of *Further Notes.* It was one of seven (originally marked W. 113 and W. 124–129) bought of

J. J. Naaman in September, 1901, comprises 134 ff. of 17·5 × 12·2 c. and 17 ll., and is written in a small, neat Turkish *riq'a*, undated. Its chief contents are the *Bishárat-náma* of Rafí'í (ff. 11[b]–54[a]), the *Hidáyat-náma* of Firishta-záda (ff. 89[b]–112[b]), the *Ganj-náma* of Rafí'í (ff. 115[b]–120[a]), and finally the *Shahriyár-náma* of Panáhí (ff. 121[b]–131[a]), composed in 860/1456.

E. 6 (6).

This MS., originally marked W. 126, was bought with **E. 5** in September, 1901, but is omitted in *Further Notes*. It comprises 120 ff. of 14·7 × 10·4 c. and 17 ll., and is written in a small, legible *ta'líq*. It contains two treatises in Turkish, the first (ff. 1[b]–20[a]) imperfect at the end, the second (ff. 21[a]–120[a]) at the beginning, both without title or indication of authorship. The first begins:

الحمد لله الّذی فاطر السّموات والأرض جاعل الملائکة رسلًا اولی أجنحةٍ مثنی و ثلاث و رباع یزید فی الخلق ما یشاء ان الله علی کلّ شیٔ قدیر یعنی اجنحهٔ ملائکه که مثنی و ثلاث و رباع واقع اولمشدر کلمهٔ الهی‌در که مرتبهٔ کتابتده که مرتبهٔ خلقدر بقرینهٔ یزید فی الخلق ما یشاء که کتابتدر حروف منقوطه‌دن که بونلردر ب ت ث ج الی آخره ایکی ایکی اوچ اوچ و درت درت حرف نقطه‌ایله گلمشدر الخ

The occurrence of the characteristic Ḥurúfí symbols for the numbers 28 and 32, and the citations from Ḥurúfí poems like the *'Arsh-náma-i-Iláhí* prove that the second (acephalous) tract emanates from the professors of that doctrine.

E. 7 (7).

This MS., which was given to me at Constantinople by Dr Riḍá Tawfíq in April, 1908, comprises 277 pp. of 15·7 × 10·8 c. and 15 ll., is written in a very poor *ta'líq*, dated (on p. 186) the middle of Sha'bán, 1133/June, 1721, and contains two Persian Ḥurúfí poems, the *Qiyámat-náma* (pp. 1–186) and the *Tawḥíd-náma* (pp. 1–84), both by Faḍlu'lláh's Khalífa *al-'Alí al-A'lá*. The first begins:

قیامةنامهٔ علیّ اعلا

آغاز سخن ز فضل الله، کردیم که اوست هادیٔ راه،
ای طالبِ راه حق بتحقیق، از فضل خدا بجوی توفیق،

The second begins:

توحیدنامهٔ علیّ الاعلا

بود واجب در جمیع کارها، حمد و شکر کاشف اسرارها،
پادشاه صورت و معنی که بود، بر همه واجب براء او سجود،

E. 7* (8).

A copy of the above-mentioned *Qiyámat-náma* labelled with the title of the book and name of the author as above in the Arabic character, under which is written in English "adequately copied from an old Manuscript by Dr Riza." On the other cover the book is labelled in English, "Quotations (3rd Book) on Ontological Questions." The book is an ordinary note-book of 20·2×16·6 c. and 18 ll., of which 62 leaves (about half the book) are written on, but on one side only, so far as the poem is concerned, the opposite page being reserved for notes and comments, which, however, have only been supplied in a few cases (*e.g.* on p. 57[b]). Shorter notes in Turkish are placed beside and beneath the text. The book was given to me by Dr Riḍá (Riẓá) Tawfíq at the same time as **E. 7**, the original from which it was evidently copied, as shown by the following calculation of the time required for copying the poem:

قیامتنامه هر گون بش صحیفه استنساخ ایدلمك و هفتده درت گون مشغول اولمق شرطیله طقوز هفتده اتمام ایدیله بیلهجكدر،

This indicates an original of 180 pp., and this poem in **E. 7** actually fills 186 pp.

E. 8 (7).

This MS., also given to me at Constantinople in April, 1908, by Dr Riḍá Tawfíq, comprises 165 ff. of 16·4×10·5 c. and 12–16 ll., is written in different Turkish *naskh* hands, all legible, and is dated in the colophon on f. 165[a] Shawwál 29, 1193/Nov. 9, 1779. It contains the five following tracts:

(1) Questions put to Mullá Sa'íd by a dervish in 994/1586 as to the reasons for various regulations as to the performance of prayers, etc., with the answers in Turkish (ff. 4[b]–16[b]). Dated Muḥarram, 1192/Feb. 1778.

(2) The *Ákhirat-náma* of Firishta-oghlu (ff. 17[b]–72[b]), in Turkish prose, dated the beginning of Dhu'l-Qa'da, 1191/Dec. 22, 1776. I have two other MSS. of this work (**E. 4** and **E. 13**), and there is another in the British Museum (**Or. 5961**).

(3) A Turkish *mathnawí* poem by "Lá Makání" (ff. 74[b]–97[b]), beginning:

زهی صانع كه خاكی آدم ایلر، كف و دود سیاهی عَلم ایلر،

(4) Another Turkish prose treatise (ff. 98[b]–128[b]) entitled *Kitáb-i-Mawlá Iláhí*, beginning:

حمد جمیل بی حدّ و شكر جزیل بی عدّ اول خالق كونَیْن و رزّاق الثقلَیْن الخ

Copied in Jumádà I, 1182/Sept.–Oct., 1768.

(5) Another Turkish prose treatise entitled *Tuḥfatu'l-'Ushsháq* (ff. 129[b]–165[a]), beginning, after the very incorrect Arabic doxology:

امّا بعده، بلكل و آگاه اولغیل كی حقّ سبحانه و تعالی كلام قدیمنده بیورر وما خلقْتُ الجنّ و الانس الّا لیعبدون ای لیعرفون ای لیوحّدون دیرلر یعنی بیورر جنّله انسی یراتمدم الّا بڭا عبادت اتمكچون یراتدم ظاهرًا معناسی بودر كی دیدك الخ

E. 9 (9).

جاودان كبير

A good and complete MS. of the *Jáwidán-i-Kabír* of Faḍlu'lláh the Ḥurúfí, the principal book of the sect which he founded. It is fully described on pp. 69–86 of my *Catalogue of the Persian Manuscripts in the Cambridge University Library.* See also *Further Notes*, p. 11. The present MS. was bought at Constantinople for £5 in April, 1910, and contains at the end (ff. 304ª–309ª) the vocabulary of dialect words occurring in the text.

Ff. 310 of 20·5×14·7 c. and 21 ll.; neat *nasta'líq* with rubrications.

E. 10 (9).

عشق نامهٔ فرشته زاده

This MS., bought with six others from J. J. Naaman in September, 1901, is fully described under the heading "(19) B. 15 (*Turkish*)" on pp. 27–28 (559–560) of *Further Notes.* It comprises 90 ff. of 22·2×13·2 c. and 21 ll., and is written in a large, clear *naskh*, ff. 2ᵇ–3ᵇ and 81ª–85ᵇ in a more modern *ta'líq*, with rubrications, undated. It contains the *'Ishq-náma* of 'Abdu'l-Majíd ibn Firishta 'Izzu'd-Dín, commonly called "Firishta-záda" (ff. 5ᵇ–85ᵇ), preceded by the *Miftáḥ*, or Key to the contractions occurring in the Ḥurúfí writings (ff. 2ᵇ–3ᵇ), and the *Sirru'l-Mufradát* (ff. 4ª–5ᵇ).

E. 11 (9).

ديوان عرشى

The Turkish *Díwán* of the Ḥurúfí poet 'Arshí. This is one of four MSS. bought for £15 from J. J. Naaman on May 22, 1901, and is briefly described under the heading "(20) C. 6 (*Turkish*)" on p. 28 (p. 560) of *Further Notes.*

Ff. 90 of 22·8×14·7 c. and 19 ll.; good *nasta'líq* with rubrications, n. d.

E. 12 (9).

ديوان محيى الدّين ابدال

The Turkish *Díwán* of another Turkish Ḥurúfí poet Muḥyi'd-Dín Abdál, bought with **E. 11**, and described under the heading "(21) C. 7 (*Turkish*)" in *Further Notes*, p. 28 (p. 560).

Ff. 40 of 22·1×16·2 c. and 23 ll.; good, clear, Turkish *naskh* with rubrications; copied by one Luṭfí in 1270/1853–4.

E. 13 (10).

This MS. was one of six (of which I acquired five) bought at Constantinople in May, 1901, at the sale of a Bektáshí dervish's effects. It is described under the heading "(22) C. 8 (*Turkish*)" on pp. 28–30 (560–562) of *Further Notes*, and contains (1) a Turkish *mathnawí* poem by Turábí (ff. 1^{b}–30^{a}) in 32 chapters; (2) a Turkish tract on the manner of Creation (ff. 33^{b}–38^{b}); (3) the *Manáqib* of Ḥájjí Bektásh (ff. 38^{b}–71^{a}), followed by the *Wiláyat-náma* of Ḥájim Sulṭán (ff. 71^{b}–72^{a}); (4) the *Ákhirat-náma* of Firishta-záda (ff. 73^{b}–76^{b}); (5) a treatise on the Letters (ff. 76^{b}–90^{b}); (6) several other fragments in Turkish (ff. 91^{a}–104^{a}), of which the most important is an account of the spiritual affiliation of Ḥájjí Bektásh and the diffusion of his Order.

Ff. 104 of 23·7 × 14·3 c. and 19 ll.; good, clear, modern Turkish *nasta'líq* with rubrications; no colophon or date.

E. 14 (10).

(١) فقرنامه، (٢) فيض نامه، (٣) تراش نامه،

This MS. was one of the four bought of J. J. Naaman on May 22, 1901, and is described under the heading "(23) C. 9 (*Turkish*)" on pp. 30–31 (562–563) of *Further Notes*. It contains, besides an untitled tract (ff. 1^{b}–17^{a}), the *Faqr-náma* of Vírání Dedé (ff. 17^{a}–51^{b}), the *Fayḍ-náma* (ff. 51^{b}–76^{a}), and the *Tirásh-náma* (ff. 76^{a}–77^{a}).

Ff. 79 of 22·8 × 13·3 c. and 21 ll.; large, clear Turkish *naskh* with rubrications; dated 1059/1649.

E. 15 (10).

عيون الهداية

This MS. was one of the five bought at Constantinople in May, 1901, at the sale of a Bektáshí dervish's effects, and is described under the heading "(24) C. 10 (*Turkish*)" on p. 31 (563) of *Further Notes*. It begins with about four pages of Arabic (ff. 1^{b}–3^{b}) invoking blessings on the twelve Imáms, and then continues in Turkish:

راقم تسويدات المنّان صحايف عصيان كريدى رسمى بكتاشى ناتوان بو طرزيله تحقيق بيان حال و بو نهجيله شرح ما فى البال ايدر الخ

There are numerous quotations from the *Qur'án* and Traditions, and at least one from the Gospels, and the reader is continually addressed *Imdi, 'azíz-i-man* ("Now my dear Friend").

Ff. 82 of 22·8 × 15·5 c. and 15 ll.; fair Turkish *naskh* with rubrications. Author, Kirídí Rasmí-i-Bektáshí; copyist, Maḥmúd Bábá.

E. 16 (8).

فضيلت نامه

This MS. was bought from J. J. Naaman on May 7, 1903, for £4, and is described under the heading "(25) C. 11 (*Turkish*)" in *Further Notes*, pp. 31–32 (563–564). It contains a Turkish *mathnawí* poem in the hexameter *Hazaj* metre, chiefly in praise of 'Alí, by a poet who uses the pen-name of Yamíní. This poem fills ff. 1–229, and was copied in Sha'bán, 1218/end of 1803. It is followed by other poems by Shaykh-oghlu, Nasímí, etc. (ff. 230^{b}–262^{b}).

Ff. 262 of 19·8 × 14 c. and 17 ll.; bad *ta'líq* with rubrications within gold margins.

E. 17 (10).

رسالهٔ دل دانا

This MS. was one of the five bought with **E. 15** at Constantinople in May, 1901, and is described under the heading "(26) C. 12 (*Turkish*)" on p. 32 (564) of *Further Notes*. The author of the poem (or poems, for there seem to be at least two in different metres) is Shaykh Ibráhím Efendi al-Oghlání of Áq-saráy. The first begins (f. 1^{b}):

الٓها علمنه یوق حدّ و غایت، خدایا وصفنه یوق هیچ نهایت،

The second begins (f. 33^{a}):

عالم و آدمده ظاهر اولان ذات بی همتا دیر، بو ایکیسندن دخی ذاتیله هر مستثنادر،

Ff. 110 of 23·4 × 17 c. and 19 ll.; good Turkish *nasta'líq* with rubrications; transcribed in 1285/1868–9.

E. 18 (9).

A volume containing six Ḥurúfí and Ṣúfí tracts in prose and verse, some printed and some manuscript, all given to me by Dr Riḍá Tawfíq at Constantinople in April, 1908. They are as follows:

(1) Firishta-záda's *'Ishq-náma* (Turkish), copied in 1265/1849 in a small, neat Turkish *naskh* with rubrications. Ff. 79 of 20·4 × 14 c. and 23 ll. This is followed by a continuous MS. of 114 ff. of 22·3 × 14·5 c. and 21 ll. written in a very clear but rather stilted *naskh*, with rubrications, containing the four following works.

(2) The *Bishárat-náma* of Rafí'í (ff. 1^{b}–37^{a}). See *Further Notes*, p. 24 (556), but in this copy two more *bayts* follow that which concludes the other copy, the last one here being:

خیریله اِل قالدره سوی سما، فاتحه اوقویه ایلیه ثنا،

تمّت الرسالة،

اوقویانی دگلیه‌نی یازه‌نی، فضلك ایله یارلغه قیل یا غنی،

ای بو نسخهٔ اوقویان متّقی، بر دعا نطقندن اومار ناطقی،

(3) The *Fayḍ-náma* (ff. 38^b–64^b), which, as appears from the last line of the conclusion (*tatimma*, f. 63^b), is by Mitháli:

تتمّهٔ رسالهٔ مثالی فرماید

ای مثالی مختصر قیل سوزی وار، فهم ایدر هر کیمکه عقلی اولدی یار،

For another copy of this poem, see **E. 14** *supra*.

(4) Another Turkish poem by Panáhí (ff. 65^b–72^b), beginning:

ابتدا در ابتدا در ابتدا، ابتدادن حاصل اولدی انتها،
ابتدا گلدی کلام لا ینام، فی و ضاد و لام حقدن والسّلام،

This is dated 1244/1828–9.

(5) The Turkish *Díwán* of Muḥíṭí Bábá (ff. 73^b–114^b), concluding with 72 quatrains, followed by these verses:

جمله یارانه و محبّانه، جانیله دلدن ایلرم اکرام،
اومارز کیم فراموش ایتمیه‌لر، عهد کیم قیلدیلر بزمله تمام،
دیده‌دن گرچه اولمشز غائب، لیك دلده مقرّر اولدی مقام،
فضل حقدن بو در تمنّامز،
کاوله‌وز بزده وصلله دلکام،

(6) The printed text of the *Gulshan-i-Tawḥíd* ("Rose-garden of the Divine Unity"), a Persian versified commentary on the *Mathnawí*, in the metre of the original, by the Mevleví (Mawlawí) dervish Sháhidí, printed at Constantinople in Jumádà I, 1298/April, 1881, beginning:

حمد لا یحصی ثنای بی قیاس، بی نهایت منّت و بی حدّ سپاس،

Ff. 181 of 22·2×14·5 c. and 25 ll. Printed from a MS. transcribed 361 years before the current date, *i.e.* in 937/1530–1.

E. 19 (9).

A volume containing five Ḥurúfí and Ṣúfí tracts in prose and verse, some printed and some manuscript, of which Nos. 1 and 2 (ff. 1–96) were bought from a dealer in Paris in January, 1909, while the remainder (Nos. 3–5) were given to me by Dr Riḍá Tawfíq at Constantinople in April, 1908. That Nos. 1 and 2 have also passed through his hands is shown by a descriptive note in French in his hand on f. 1^b.

(1) Two or three Ṣúfí-Ḥurúfí tracts in Turkish (ff. 2^a–68^a), the first being only the concluding page (f. 2^a) of one containing replies to numerous hypothetical questions, each prefaced by the words "If they ask..." (اگر صورسه‌لر که)[1]; the second (ff. 2^b–7^a) beginning, after the doxology:

...امّا بعد، بو مختصرك تألیفنه سبب اول اولدیکه بو فقیرك والدی الّخ

[1] It seems to be a verbatim copy, omitting the last five lines, of f. 12^a *infra*.

the third (ff. 7ᵇ–68ᵃ) beginning, after the doxology:

...امّا بعد، بیلك كه بو فقیرك خیلی شوقی وار ایدی قطب الاولیا سلطان ابو سعید ابو الخیرك قدّس الله روحه رباعینك معانیسنی بلمكه و رباعی بو در كه –

حورا بنظارهٔ نگارم صف زد، رضوان ز تعجّب كفِ خود بر كف زد،

آن خال سیاه برآن رخان مطرف زد، ابدال ز بیم چنگ در مصحف زد،

(2) The *Ṭaríqat-náma* ("Book of the Path") by Sulṭán Ashraf-záda (ff. 70ᵇ–96ᵃ), beginning:

قال الله تعالى أطيعوا الله وأطيعوا الرّسول وأولى الأمر منكم يعنى الله تعالى بيوردكم مطيع اولك اللّهه

Written in a small, ugly *ta'líq*, with rubrications, and dated 1258/1842.

(3) The *Fayḍ-náma-i-Iláhí*, a Turkish Ḥurúfí poem by Mitháli Bábá (ff. 102ᵇ–130ᵃ), preceded by a prose treatise entitled *Miftáḥu'l-Ghayb* ("the Key of the Unseen"), dated Rabí' II, 1261/April, 1845. There are numerous annotations in French and Turkish in the margins by Dr Riḍá Tawfíq.

(4) A Turkish treatise (Bektáshí) in mixed prose and verse by Wahbí (Vehbí) Bábá, lithographed at Cairo in 1290/1873–4, and containing 95 pp. The title-page bears the following curious inscription:

اشبو رساله وهبى بابا اسميله تمهير اولنميانلرينه ساخته نظريله باقيلهجقدر، سنه ۱۲۹۰ بمطبعة الحجر الفاخرة بمدينة مصر القاهرة،

(5) The *'Ishq-náma* ("Book of Love"), a Persian *mathnawí* poem ascribed to Jalálu'd-Dín Rúmí, with the Turkish prose translation and explanation of 'Alí Bahjat, printed at Constantinople in 1301/1883–4, and comprising 24 pp. In the Persian prose preface the title *Rumúzu'l-'Árifín* ("Riddles of the Gnostics") is given to the work. The poem begins:

عشق پنهان دزد خانه ازوست، سوی صحرا و كنج خانه ازوست،

Every verse, except the last two of the poem, begins with the word عشق ("Love"), and is immediately followed by the Turkish prose translation and commentary.

E. 20 (9).

A collection of five Ḥurúfí and Ṣúfí tracts, manuscript, printed and lithographed, bound together in one volume. They are as follows:

(1) The Discourses (*Maqálát*) of Ḥájjí Bektásh in Turkish. A MS. of 20 ff. of 20·3×13·5 c. and 19 ll., good *naskh* with rubrications, no colophon, date or note of acquisition.

(2) The "Interpreter of the Nations" (*Tarjumánu'l-Umam*) by Ibn Ṣadri'd-Dín of Shírwán. The preface only is in Arabic, the remainder of the text in Turkish. Begins, after the doxology:

وبعد، فهذا مختصر فى بيان مقالات اهل العالم، والمذاهب المختلفة لطوايف الأمم اوردتها على سبيل الاجمال مجتنبًا عن التطويل والاملال، أمرنى به من لا يسعنى الّا موافقته لانّه أحاط بى نعمه وملاطفته اعنى الوزير الأعظم والدستور الأفخم الّذى عمّ إحسانه وفشا، حضرت محمّد پاشا، اللّهمّ اجعل شموس دولته على فلك الوزارة مضيئةً، وبدور نفوس ساير الوزراء من انوار تدبّره مستضيئةً، ورتّبتُهُ على مقدّمةٍ وعشرة أبوابٍ وخاتمةٍ،

Ch. I (f. 2[a]) deals with the Mu'tazila; ch. II (f. 4[a]) with the Khawárij; ch. III (f. 5[b]) with the Shí'a; ch. IV (f. 9[b]) with the different varieties of the *Maláḥida*, or heretics of the Ismá'ílí school; ch. V (f. 11[a]) with the Karrámiyya; ch. VI (f. 11[a]) with the *Mushabbiha* or Anthropomorphists; ch. VII (f. 11[b]) with the Murji'a; ch. VIII (f. 12[a]) with the *Najjáriyya*; ch. IX (f. 12[b]) with the Determinists or partisans of Predestination (*Jabariyya*); ch. X (f. 12[b]) with the heretical Ṣúfís (*Maláḥidatu'ṣ-Ṣúfiyya*), amongst whom, says the author, are included most of the Mevleví (Mawlawí), Gulshaní and Bektáshí dervishes. The Conclusion (*Khátima*) deals with the six *Firaq-i-Nájiya*, or groups which shall find salvation, viz. the usual four orthodox sects together with the Sufyánís and the Thawrís. Ff. 15 of 19 × 14 c. and 20 ll.; good *naskh* with rubrications; no colophon, date, or note of acquisition.

(3) A commentary on the *qaṣída* of the old Turkish mystical poet Yúnus Imré by Miṣrí Efendi, lithographed in 1268/1851–2, without indication of place, and given to me by Dr Riḍá Tawfíq in August, 1909. Pp. 17 of 20 × 12·5 c. and 22 ll.; fair *naskh*, fully pointed. Concerning Yúnus Imré see E. J. W. Gibb's *History of Ottoman Poetry*, vol. I, pp. 164–175, and a very elaborate and scholarly study in Turkish by Kyüprülü-zádé Muḥammad Fu'ád, Professor of the History of Turkish Literature in the University of Constantinople, in his work entitled *Ilk Mutaṣawwiflar* ("the First Ṣúfís"), published at Constantinople in 1918. The second part of this book (pp. 205–394) is almost wholly devoted to this old mystic.

(4) Another manuscript copy of the *'Ishq-náma* of Firishta-záda, but containing only the first seven of the thirty-two chapters into which the work is divided. Ff. 42 of 18·5 × 13 c. and 14 ll.; fair Turkish *riq'a* hand with rubrications; no colophon, date, or note of acquisition.

(5) A printed edition of the Turkish prose and verse works of Víráni (Wíráni) Bábá, without indication of date or place of production, only a final note that it was produced for the "salvation-finding group of the Bektáshí Path":

تمّت الرسالة المرغوبهٔ ويرانى بابا بندهٔ آل عبا سلاطين گروه ناجيهٔ طريق بكتاشيه قدّس الله سرّهم تمام شد،

Pp. 98 of 18· × 12·5 c. and 19 ll.

F. SHAYKHÍ AND BÁBÍ MSS.

This large class, denoted by the letter **F**, comprises some sixty-five MSS., of which **F. 1–5** represent the older Shaykhí school of Shaykh Aḥmad al-Aḥsá'í and Sayyid Káẓim of Rasht, in which both Mírzá 'Alí Muḥammad the Báb and Ḥájjí Muḥammad Karím Khán of Kirmán pursued their earliest studies. The latter, the head of the later Shaykhí school, is represented by one MS. only (**F. 6**); the former by seventeen (**F. 7–23**). One of his early disciples, Mullá Rajab 'Alí *Qahír*, is represented by **F. 24**, and another, Mullá Muḥammad 'Alí of Bárfurúsh, called *Janáb-i-Quddús*, by part of **F. 43**. The remainder include three volumes of Miscellanea (**F. 25–27**), some eighteen of the works of Mírzá Yaḥyà *Ṣubḥ-i-Azal* (**F. 35–52**), some eight or nine of the writings of Bahá'u'lláh and his son and successor 'Abbás Efendi 'Abdu'l-Bahá (**F. 29–34**, **56**, **58** and **59**), and a certain number of historical and controversial works by other Bábí writers.

In the *Journal of the Royal Asiatic Society* for 1892 (pp. 433–499 and 637–710) I published an article entitled *Catalogue and Description of* 27 *Bábí Manuscripts* containing full particulars of my acquisitions at that date, since when the number has been more than doubled. A reference to that article (indicated as *Catalogue and Description*) will suffice for the MSS. there mentioned, which were arranged in five groups, according to the place whence they were obtained, viz.

(1)	MSS. obtained in Persia in 1887–8,	marked	**BBP. 1–8.**
(2)	,, ,, Famagusta (Cyprus)	,,	**BBF. 1–11.**
(3)	,, ,, 'Akká (Syria)	,,	**BBA. 1–5.**
(4)	,, ,, Constantinople	,,	**BBC. 1–4.**
(5)	Supplementary MSS.	,,	**BBS. 1.**

The new class-marks assigned to these twenty-seven MSS. are as follows:

BBP. 1 = F. 58.	**BBP. 2.**	**BBP. 3 = F. 30.**
BBP. 4 = F. 29.	**BBP. 5 = F. 55.**	**BBP. 6 = F. 31.**
BBP. 7 = F. 22.	**BBP. 8 = F. 12.**	
BBF. 1 = F. 14.	**BBF. 2 = F. 15.**	**BBF. 3 = F. 23.**
BBF. 4 = F. 43.	**BBF. 5 = F. 39.**	**BBF. 6 = F. 8.**
BBF. 7 = F. 9.	**BBF. 8 = F. 10.**	**BBF. 9 = F. 16.**
BBF. 10 = F. 17.	**BBF. 11 = F. 45.**	
BBA. 1 = F. 56.	**BBA. 2 = F. 59.**	**BBA. 3 = F. 32.**
BBA. 4 = F. 33.	**BBA. 5 = F. 25^{8}.**	
BBC. 1 = F. 53^{1}.	**BBC. 2 = F. 53^{2}.**	**BBC. 3 = F. 13.**
BBC. 4 = F. 11.	**BBS. 1 = F. 27^{1}.**	

Here follows the description of the hitherto undescribed MSS.

F. I[1] (9).

شرح الزّيارة الجامعة (الجزؤ الأوّل)،

Part I of the Commentary on the *Ziyáratu'l-Jámi'atu'l-Kabíra*, preceded on ff. 6^a–8^b by a tract by Sayyid Káẓim of Rasht, beginning, after the brief doxology:

...امّا بعد، فيقول العبد الفقير الحقير الفانى كاظم بن قاسم الحسينى الرشتى أنّ بعض الاخوان حرسه الله عن نوايب الزمان قد أمرنى أن أملى على الحديثين الآتيين الشريفين ما يخطر بالبال وقد امتثلت أمره مع كمال اختلال الحال وتبلبل البال وتعارض الأحوال والميسور لا يسقط بالمعسور وإلى الله ترجع الأمور الخ

Ff. 195 of 20·5 × 14·7 c. and 19 ll.; small, neat *naskh*, unpointed. The topics dealt with in the text are sometimes indicated by headlines or entries in the margins. The transcription was completed in Ramaḍán, 1256/November, 1840, and the title of the book is given in the colophon as above. It is not clear whether the Commentary on the *Ziyárat* which forms the bulk of the volume (ff. 9^b–195^a) is the first part of Shaykh Aḥmad al-Aḥsá'í's work, of which the second and third parts are represented by the two succeeding MSS., or is part of another by Sayyid Káẓim, his disciple and successor. No note as to place or date of acquisition.

F. I[2] (9).

شرح الزّيارة الجامعة الكبيرة (الجزؤ الثانى)،

Part II of the Commentary on the *Ziyáratu'l-Jámi'atu'l-Kabíra* of Shaykh Aḥmad al-Aḥsá'í, beginning, after the brief doxology:

...امّا بعد، فيقول العبد المسكين احمد بن زين الدّين انّ هذه جزء الثانى من شرح الزيارة الجامعة الكبيرة

Ff. 162 of 20·3×14·2 c. and 19 ll.; uniform in style and script with the volume last described, but ending abruptly without colophon or date. No note of acquisition.

F. 2 (9).

شرح الزّيارة الجامعة (الجزؤ الثالث)

Part III of the same Commentary, beginning, after the *Bismi'lláh*:

قال العبد المسكين احمد بن زين الدّين قال عَـ بأبى انتم وأُمّى وأهلى ومالى الخ

In the colophon on f. 144^b it is stated that Shaykh Aḥmad al-Aḥsá'í composed this work in Shawwál, 1229/Sept.–Oct. 1814, and that this copy of Part III (which is to be followed by Part IV) was completed on the 6th of Rabí' II, 1233/Feb. 13, 1818.

Ff. 144 of 21×15·5 c. and 22 ll.; clear *ta'líq*, unpointed. This was one of the Belshah MSS. bought at the fourth partition on Nov. 12, 1920.

F. 3 (9).

شرح الفوائد للاحسائى وغيره

Three treatises by Shaykh Aḥmad al-Aḥsá'í and one by Mullá Ṣadrá.

(1) Shaykh Aḥmad's commentary on his own *Fawá'id* (ff. 1^b–108^a), written at the request of Mullá Mashhad ibn Ḥasan 'Alí. No colophon.

(2) Commentary by the same on the *Risálatu'l-'Ilm* (ff. 113^a–137^b), transcribed in 1238/1822–3.

(3) Answer of the same to certain questions propounded by Sayyid Ḥasan al-Khurásání (ff. 138^b–163^b).

(4) A treatise by Muḥammad ibn Ibráhím of Shíráz, commonly known as Mullá Ṣadrá (ff. 166^b–208^a), without title, date or colophon, beginning:

سبحانك اللّهم يا مبدع المبادى والعلل وغاية الثوانى والاول الخ

This MS. was also one of the Belshah MSS. bought on Nov. 12, 1920. It comprises 208 ff. of 20·7 × 15 c. and 15–23 ll. in various *ta'líq* hands.

There is a good edition of the *Sharḥu'l-Fawá'id* lithographed in Persia (probably at Tabríz) and completed on the 17th of Dhu'l-Qa'da, 1272/July 21, 1856. It is there stated that the book was composed in 1197/1783. The *Fawá'id*, thirteen in number, end on p. 323, and are followed (pp. 323–333) by the reply of Sayyid Káẓim of Rasht to a question addressed to him by a certain Mírzá Muḥammad Shafí'.

F. 4 (8).

Two Arabic tracts by the same Shaykh Aḥmad al-Aḥsá'í, both transcribed in 1264/1848, and followed on ff. 59^b and 60^a by two inscribed circles entitled respectively the "Circle of Reason" or "Scale of Virtues" (*Dá'iratu'l-'Aql* or *Kaffatu'l-Ḥasanát*) and the "Circle of Ignorance" or "Scale of Vices" (*Dá'iratu'l-Jahl* or *Kaffatu's-Sayyi'át*).

The first tract begins after the short doxology:

...امّا بعد، فيقول العبد المسكين أحمد زين الدّين إنّى لمّا رأيْتُ كثيرًا من الطلبة يتعمّقون فى المعارف الالهيّة ويتوهّمون انّهم تعمّقوا فى المعنى الخ

The second begins abruptly after the *Bismi'lláh*:

فی الاشارة الی بیان کیفیّة تکوّن الموجودات وتنزّلاتها فی مراتب ظهوراتها آلخ

Ff. 62 of 17·6 × 11·3 c. and 17 ll.; rather coarse but legible *naskh*; no note of place or date of acquisition.

F. 5 (9).

Persian translation by Muḥammad Raḍí ibn Muḥammad Riḍá of an Arabic treatise written by Sayyid Káẓim of Rasht in reply to certain questions addressed to him by an unnamed enquirer, beginning:

بعد از حمد و ستایش خداوندی که رحمت جمیلش متحیّرینرا دلیل و رأفت جزیلش طالبینرا هادیٔ سبیل است و درود نا معدود بر رسول رادش محمّد مصطفی و ائمّهٔ هدی علیهم السّلام که خلاصهٔ وجود و از آفرینش مقصود هستند بنگارش مراد میپردازد که اینرساله ایست از رشحات قلم معجز رقم جناب علّامه عالم و عماد اعظم ملاذ الاسلام والمسلمین آیة الله علی العالمین قوام الملّة والدّین قطب العلماء والعارفین حاجی سیّد کاظم دام فیضه که در جواب سؤالی بیان فرموده اند و این فقیر کثیر التقصیر متمسّکًا بذیل ارادته محمّد رضی بن محمّد رضا طاب ثراه حسب الاشارهٔ جمعی از مخادیم کرام به ترجمهٔ آن اقدام کرد بنحویکه فهم آن بر خواصّ و عوامّ آسان باشد سؤال سائل و جواب آنفخر افاضلرا بفارسی نقل نموده امّید که در حضرت طالبین موقع قبول یابد٬

Here follow eight lines of the Arabic text, written throughout in red, beginning, after the *Bismi'lláh*:

الحمد لله الّذی أرشد من استرشده الی سبیل الرّشاد وأوصل من استهداه الی أقصی الغایة وأعلی المراد آلخ

The questions chiefly concern the attitude which the simple Shí'a believer should adopt towards the rival sects or schools of the Uṣúlís, Akhbárís, and Bálásarís on the one hand, and the Shaykhís or *Kashfís* on the other (f. 4[b]). This leads to an account of the life and teachings of Shaykh Aḥmad ibn Zayni'd-Dín al-Aḥsá'í, the founder of the Shaykhí school and predecessor of the author Sayyid Káẓim of Rasht, who is eulogized in the following terms (f. 7[a]):

...لهذا میگوئیم در جواب سؤال سائل سلّمه الله تعالی که فمنهم من سمّی نفسه شیخیًّا وکشفیًّا مراد از شیخی و کشفی اصحاب شیخ اعظم و عماد اقوم و نور اتمّ و جامع أعظم عزّ الاسلام والمسلمین رکن المؤمنین الممتحنین آیة الله فی العالمین المبطل لمخترعات الصوفیّین والمزیّف لأغالیط أوهام الحکماء (f. 7[b]) الاوّلین المبیّن للطریقة الحقّة الّتی أتی بها سیّد المرسلین وخاتم النبیّین والشارح لبعض مقامات الائمّة الطاهرین مظهر الشریعة وشارح الطریقة بسرّ الحقیقة شیخنا

وأستادنا وعمادنا الشيخ احمد بن زين الدّين الاحسائى اعلى الله مقامه است و مقصود از جمعى
که ایشانرا کشفیّه نامیده‌اند منسوبان آنجنابست بجهة اینکه خداوند عالم کشف کرده‌است
پردهٔ جهل‌را از نظر و قلوب آنها و ایشانند کسانیکه کشف شده‌است از ضمایر آنها ظلمت شکوك
و شبهات الخ

Apparently the author prefers the sect or school which he represents to be called *Kashfí* rather than *Shaykhí*, for he says (f. 8[b]):

مراد از اسم شیخیّه که در اینروزها اینفرقه‌را بدان اسمی نامند چنانکه اثنا عشریّه‌را برافضیّه کسانی
هستند که منسوبند بر این شیخ جلیل و عالم نبیل فهو الشیخ احمد بن زین الدّین بن ابرهیم بن
صغر بن واغر بن راشد بن دهیم بن شمروخ الصغر المسطرفى الاحسائى وحید عصره و یگانهٔ دهره
که اخذ کرده‌است علومرا از معدنش و بر داشته‌است از منبعش که عبارت باشد از ائمّهٔ طاهرین الخ

What he means by Shaykh Aḥmad having "drawn knowledge from its source, to wit the pure Imáms" is that first the Imám Ḥasan and subsequently the Prophet himself appeared to him in dreams and imparted to him spiritual knowledge. He seems to have been driven from 'Iráq by the fanaticism of the Wahhábís, and to have gone to Persia with the intention of visiting Mashhad. He remained some time at Yazd, where his teaching attracted much attention, and drew round him the most notable of the 'Ulamá. Finally his fame reached the ears of Fatḥ-'Alí Sháh, who invited him to Ṭihrán, and, having become acquainted with him, wished him to take up his abode there, but he declined this honour, and preferred to return to Yazd, where he remained for five years. Having resolved to visit the Holy Shrines in 'Iráq, he journeyed by way of Iṣfahán, where he remained forty days and made the acquaintance of many eminent doctors, including his biographer. Then he went to Kirmánsháh, where he was so well received by the Prince Governor that he returned thither after accomplishing his visit to the Holy Shrines, and took up his residence there for some time. After quoting a number of *ijázas* and other testimonials of distinguished theologians, in which they testify to Shaykh Aḥmad's learning and piety, the author proceeds to enumerate 97 of his works (ff. 20[b]–26[a]), beginning with the *Sharḥu'l-Jámi'ati'l-Kabíra* mentioned above (**F. 1**[1], **1**[2] and **2**), commentaries on two of Mullá Ṣadrá's works (*al-Ḥikmatu'l-'Arshiyya* and the *Mashá'ir*), and his own *Fawá'id* and its commentary (**F. 3**).

Ff. 69 of 21·6×12·8 c. and 22 ll.; excellent modern *naskh*, the Arabic passages in red and fully pointed; copied by Mírzá Mahdí ibn Ibráhím of Rasht and completed at the beginning of Rajab, 1308/Feb. 10, 1901. Given to me by the Nawwáb Mírzá 'Abbás-qulí Khán.

F. 6 (5).

المنتخب للحاجّ محمّد كريم خان

A small Arabic treatise on supererogatory prayers and other religious obligations, etc., entitled *al-Muntakhab* ("the Select") by Ḥájjí Muḥammad Karím (or perhaps his son), the head of the later Shaykhí school after the breaking away of the Bábís, beginning:

بسم الله الرّحمن الرحيم و سلام على آل ابرهيم،

و بعد، يقول العبد الأثيم محمّد بن محمّد كريم عفى الله عنهما إنّى وجدْتُ الأدعية المأثورة عن اهل العصمة كثيرة وكتب الأصحاب بها مشحونة الخ

The author speaks of Sayyid Káẓim of Rasht as "our most learned Lord and Master" (f. 22^b), and quotes a prayer of his (ff. 44^b *et seqq.*). The tract comprises seven chapters.

This MS. was given to me in Kirmán in the summer of 1888, and comprises 80 ff. of 10·8 × 6·5 c. and 12 ll. It is written in a small, neat *naskh* with rubrications and numerous marginal notes and glosses in Arabic and Persian, and was copied in 1296/1879.

BÁBÍ, BAHÁ'Í AND AZALÍ MSS. (F. 7–F. 66).

F. 7 (9).

صحيفة بين الحرمين

This *Ṣaḥífat bayna'l-Ḥaramayn*, or "Tract [revealed] between the two [Holy] Shrines" is one of the earliest writings of Mírzá 'Alí Muḥammad the Báb. It is in Arabic, is addressed to Ḥájjí Sayyid 'Alí of Kirmán, and begins after the *Bismi'lláh*:

انّ هذا كتاب قد نزل على الأرض المقدّسة بين الحرمَيْن من لدن علىّ حكيم، ثمّ فصّلت على يد الذكر هذا صراط الله فى السّموات والأرض على دعآء السآئل الحاجّ سيّد علىّ الكرمانى فى سبع آيات محكمات بإذن الله على قسطاس مبين، الخ

The only other copy of this rare book which I have seen belongs to the Leyden Library, bears the class-mark **No. 2414**[10], and was copied in Jumádà II, 1263/May, 1847, while the Báb was still living. The present copy was made in Cyprus by Riḍwán 'Alí ("Constantine the Persian"), the son of Mírzá Yaḥyà *Ṣubḥ-i-Azal*, was completed on December 26, 1905, and was given to me by the late Mr Claude Delaval Cobham, formerly Commissioner of Larnaca in Cyprus. It comprises 128 pp. (5 or 6 of which are blank) of 20×12·7 c. and 11 ll., written in clear *naskh* within red rules. At the end (unfortunately bound upside down) is a note in Persian by *Ṣubḥ-i-Azal* on the disposal of the Báb's remains, and a letter dated July 10 [? 1907] from Mr Cobham to myself which accompanied the manuscript.

F. 8 (8) = **BBF. 6.**

تفسیر سورة البقرة،

The Báb's commentary on the second *Súra* of the *Qur'án* (*Súratu'l-Baqara*). See *Catalogue and Description*, pp. 493–499.

F. 9 (6) = **BBF. 7.**

تفسیر سورة العصر،

The Báb's commentary on the *Súratu'l-'Aṣr* (*Qur'án*, CIII). See *Catalogue and Description*, pp. 637–642.

F. 10 (7) = **BBF. 8.**

تفسیر سورة الکوثر،

The Báb's commentary on the *Súratu'l-Kawthar* (*Qur'án*, CVIII). See *Catalogue and Description*, pp. 643–648.

F. 11 (9) = **BBC. 4.**

تفسیر سورة یوسف (قیّوم الأسماء)،

The Báb's commentary on the *Súratu Yúsuf* (*Qur'án*, XII), also called *Qayyúmu'l-Asmá*. See *Catalogue and Description*, pp. 699–701, and also the *J.R.A.S.* for April, 1892, pp. 261–268.

F. 12 (5) = **BBP. 8.**

بیان فارسی،

A MS. of the Báb's Persian *Bayán*, given to me in Rafsinján near Kirmán on August 22, 1888. See *Catalogue and Description*, pp. 450–451.

F. 13 (6) = **BBC. 3.**

بیان فارسی،

Another MS. of the Persian *Bayán*, bought for me at Constantinople in August, 1891. See *Catalogue and Description*, pp. 698–699.

F. 14 (8) = BBF. 1.

من آثار البيان (مناجات)،

Prayer, from the Arabic *Bayán*, constituting the second of the "Five Grades." See *Catalogue and Description*, pp. 451–462.

F. 15 (9) = BBF. 2.

شؤون خمسه،

Specimen of each of the "Five Grades" of the Báb's writings. See *Catalogue and Description*, pp. 462–470.

F. 16 (9) = BBF. 9.

تفسير الاسماء (الجلد الثانى)

Vol. II of the Báb's "Commentary on the [Divine] Names." See *Catalogue and Description*, pp. 648–656.

F. 17 (9) = BBF. 10.

من كتاب أسماء كلّ شىء (الجلد الأوّل)،

Vol. I of the "Book of the Names of All Things," apparently the companion volume to that last described, in spite of the difference in title. See *Catalogue and Description*, pp. 657–659.

F. 18 (9).

كتاب الأسماء

Another voluminous "Book of Names," extending from ch. I of *Wáḥid* VIII to ch. 18 of *Wáḥid* XIX, beginning:

الباب الأوّل من الواحد الثّامن من الشهر الثّامن من السنة فى معرفة اسم المرشد وله اربع مراتب الأوّل فى الأوّل، بسم الله الأرشد الأرشد الله لا اله الّا هو الأرشد الأرشد قُلْ الله أرشد فوق كلّ ذا إرشاد لن يقدر أن يمتنع عن مليك سلطان ارشاده من أحد لا فى السموات ولا فى الأرض ولا ما بينهما آلخ

The whole book is like this, each "Name" being treated in this way and given a whole series of derived forms, theoretically possible though not actually in use, and each chapter being, apparently, set apart for a particular day of each of the nineteen months into which the Bábí year is divided. In some cases the name of the person for whose benefit a chapter was "revealed" is specified in the margin, *e.g.*:

فی أرض الصّاد یوصل الی حرف الرّاء والبآء الشهیر بالنّهری (p. 273)،

نزل فی لیلة الاستقلال للفتحعلی فی أرض الاعلی (p. 430)،

بمولانا الکریم یحفظ الأصل یرسل السّواد لمعلّم الصّبیّ وفیه اتمام للحجّة (p. 466)،

السیّد رحیم فی الصّاد (p. 510)،

للطبیب الهمدانی قد أراد السرور والغور درر الکلمات (p. 526)،

لأخ الشهیدین المهدی والباقر الکندی (p. 536)،

Pp. 584 of 21·1 × 14·6 c. and 19 ll.; legible *naskh*; dated 22nd of Jumádà II, 1330/June 9, 1912. Received from Mírzá Muṣṭafà on June 3, 1913.

F. 19 (9).

کتاب الأسماء

Another volume of the "Book of Names" uniform with the preceding, of which, apparently, it constitutes the earlier portion, since it begins with ch. 10 of *Wáḥid* II, and ends with ch. 19 of *Wáḥid* VII. The missing portion, therefore, includes the whole of *Wáḥid* I and the first nine chapters of *Wáḥid* II. These "Books of Names" are quite unreadable except to the devout believer.

Pp. 768 of 21·1 × 14·7 c. and 19 ll., written in the same hand as the preceding, collated with the "trustworthy original" (نسخة معتبرة), and completed on the 23rd of Sha'bán, 1330/August 7, 1912. Received from Mírzá Muṣṭafà with the preceding volume on June 3, 1913.

F. 20 (9).

Another Arabic Bábí book of the same type as the last, but not arranged in *Wáḥids*. The chapters vary greatly in length. Each begins with the *Bismi'lláh*, but the Divine Attributes following this formula vary in each case. The MS. has no title, note of acquisition, or colophon, and begins:

بسم الله الرّحمن المنّان السلطان المستعان،

سبحان الّذی خلق السّموات والأرض وما بینهما بأمره کن فیکون، آلخ

Ff. 111 of 20 × 12·5 c. and 19 ll., written in a neat and legible *naskh*. The MS. appears to have been acquired on April 2, 1922.

F. 21 (9).

Thirty-two letters from the Báb, all in Arabic, to the following persons:

(1) In answer to one of the believers (p. 1).
(2) Unspecified (p. 3).
(3) [In answer to] a question of Sayyid Yaḥyà [of Dáráb], the "First Wáḥid" (p. 9).
(4) Explaining a statement of Sayyid Káẓim of Rasht (p. 26).
(5) To Sayyid Yaḥyà "Wáḥid" (p. 35).
(6) Explanation of the و in the verse (*Qur'án*, XXXVII, 1) والصّافّات (p. 44).
(7) Continuation and conclusion of the above (p. 60).
(8) Explanation of the دائرة الايقع (= 1 + 10 + 100 + 1000) (p. 63).
(9) Answer to Shaykh Náṣiru'd-Dín of Karbalá, written in 1264/1848 (p. 65).
(10) On the بسيط الحقيقة (p. 77).
(11) Answer to the Mu'tamadu'd-Dawla [Minúchihr Khán] (p. 88).
(12) Answer to the Governor of Shúshtar (p. 93).
(13) Answer to a student on the queries in the *Qur'án* (p. 100).
(14) On the Ascension (*Mi'ráj*) in the Land of Ṣád (Iṣfahán) (p. 104).
(15) Explanation of a tradition of the Imám Riḍá (p. 106).
(16) Answer to Ḥájjí Muḥammad, written from Mákú (p. 108).
(17) Answer to an enquirer in Iṣfahán (p. 111).
(18) Answer to Sayyid Asadu'lláh of Qazwín (p. 115), dated Jumádà I, 1263/ April-May, 1847, from "the Prison in the Mountain" (p. 116).
(19) Answer to Mullá Rajab 'Alí [*Janáb-i-Qahír*] (p. 120).
(20) Answer to Sayyid Aḥmad Áqá-záda (p. 126).
(21) Answer to Mírzá Muḥammad 'Alí (p. 127).
(22) Answer to Mírzá 'Abdu'l-Wahháb Munshí (p. 131).
(23) Answer to the father of Sayyid Ḥusayn, written from Mákú (p. 133).
(24) To Janáb-i-Ṭáhira (Qurratu'l-'Ayn), from Mákú (p. 135).
(25) Answer to Mullá Aḥmad Abdál, from Mákú (p. 138).
(26) To Sayyid Abu'l Ḥasan, commentary on the Morning Prayer (p. 143).
(27) Commenting on the "Verse of Light" (آية النّور) (p. 155).
(28) Answer to Asad (p. 171).
(29) To Mírzá Najaf-qulí (p. 189).
(30) To two persons from "the Land of Paradise" (لاثنين من أرض الجنّة) (p. 192).
(31) To Mullá Aḥmad (p. 196).
(32) Letter to the '*Ulamá* (p. 224).

Pp. 232 of 21·4×14·4 c. and 19 ll.; clear, legible *naskh*, dated the 5th of Dhu'l-Qa'da, 1330/Oct. 16, 1912; received from Mírzá Muṣṭafà on Nov. 4, 1912.

F. 22 (5) = BBP. 7.

دلائل سبعه وغيره،

A small volume containing (1) the *Ziyárat-náma*; (2) the *Lawḥ-i-Naṣír*; (3) the *Dalá'il-i-sab'a* or "Seven Proofs"; and (4) various Bábí poems and epistles. See *Catalogue and Description*, pp. 444–449.

F. 23 (9) = BBF. 3.

من آثار البيان

A volume containing sixty-five pieces, some in Persian but mostly in Arabic, fully described in the *Catalogue and Description*, pp. 470–483.

F. 24 (9).

كتاب ملّا رجبعلى قهير،

Mullá Rajab 'Alí, called *Qahír* (the numerical equivalent of both names being 315) was a prominent follower of the Báb, and afterwards of Mírzá Yaḥyà *Ṣubḥ-i-Azal*. He is said to have been murdered by some of Bahá'u'lláh's followers at Baghdád or Karbalá. See my *Traveller's Narrative to illustrate the Episode of the Báb*, vol. II, pp. 356, 359, 363 and 371.

This book, written partly in Arabic but chiefly in Persian, comprises four chapters, beginning on ff. 7[b], 17[b], 31[b], and 66[b] respectively. It contains allusions to Mírzá Yaḥyà *Ṣubḥ-i-Azal* (*e.g.* f. 21[b]), the *Dalá'il-i-sab'a* or "Seven Proofs" (f. 22[b]: see **F. 23** *supra*), Mírzá Asadu'lláh called *Janáb-i-Dayyán* (f. 44[b]), etc. The Arabic exordium begins:

بسمه الدائم القديم الباقى الّذى كلّ له خاضعون،

تعالى من تجلّى عن افق الصفات بنور الذات على اقاليم اراضى المبدعات من الممكنات الّخ

Chapter 1 (f. 7[a]), which is in Persian, begins:

بدانيد اى سالكان سبيل هدايت و سداد و طالبان طريق درايت و رشاد سقاكم الله ربّكم الأعلى من رحيق نوره فى كأس (f. 7[b]) ظهوره كه اعتقاد به نشأة اخرى و دار جزاء اوّل مايزى است بين ملّيين و غيرهم الّخ

Ff. 82 of 20·5 × 13·2 c. and 17 ll.; clear *naskh*, unpointed; no date or colophon. Received from Mírzá Muṣṭafà, Feb. 11, 1913.

F. 25 (9).

A volume of miscellaneous Bábí documents of different dates, sizes and writings. The contents are as follows:

(1) A letter in Persian from Ṣubḥ-i-Azal's son Riḍwán 'Alí, dated May 27, 1897, accompanying sundry Bábí documents, which immediately follow, viz. three letters from Ṣubḥ-i-Azal to unnamed correspondents; a letter from the late Mr Claude Delaval Cobham, dated April 9, 1897; a small tract on the "Names of God, from *alif* to *yá*"; prayers and incantations deemed efficacious for alleviating various ailments and misfortunes (pp. 139); names of the nineteen Bábí months; other talismans and letters, including two addressed by Ṣubḥ-i-Azal to "Báqir the enemy," presumably Muḥammad Báqir of Iṣfahán, who was one of Bahá'u'lláh's followers exiled to Cyprus with Azal, and who died there in 1872; a short Arabic tract by Ṣubḥ-i-Azal; answer by the same to fourteen questions propounded by M. Nicolas. All these documents were received together from Riḍwán 'Alí on June 7, 1897.

(2) Three Bábí tracts copied and sent to me by Mírzá Muṣṭafà, and received on June 3, 1913. The first, comprising 94 pp., is described in the scribe's prefatory note as an explanation of the *Súratu'l-Ḥamd*, and a full account of its acquisition in 1303/1885–6 is given. It is written in Persian, in a style resembling the Persian Bayán, and is divided into *Wáḥids*, but irregularly. The second is a copy of a letter written by the *Mutawallí-báshí*, or Head Custodian, of Qum to Mírzá Músà, the brother of Bahá'u'lláh, on the Bahá'í-Azalí controversy. The third and fourth are copies of two letters written in 1330–1/1912–13 from Kirmán to Shaykh Muḥammad Mahdí, the elder brother of Shaykh Aḥmad Rúḥí of Kirmán, who was put to death at Tabríz on July 17, 1896. The latter contains several poems, one of which indicates as the successor of Ṣubḥ-i-Azal (who died at Famagusta in Cyprus in April, 1912) his grandson Ḥájjí Mírzá Aḥmad, entitled *Miṣbáḥu'l-Ḥukamá* and originally named Rúḥu'lláh ("the Spirit of God"), the son of Áqá-yi-Núru'lláh, commonly known as Ḥájjí Mírzá Muḥammad Ḥasan the physician of Rasht. The following verse is the most explicit:

در هزار و سیصد و سی و یکی سازد جلوس،
قائمِ صُبْح ازل آنکو ازل خواندش پسر،

The implication of these documents is that the Commentary on the *Súratu'l-Ḥamd* (or *-Fátiḥa*) was that known to have been written by the Báb and that it foretells in a very enigmatic manner the future of the church he founded. The fifth document in this group is a photograph of Ṣubḥ-i-Azal's autograph of a passage to which reference is made in the title of the poem cited above.

(3) Extracts from the Báb's *Shu'ún-i-Khamsa* ("Five Grades") transcribed by Ṣubḥ-i-Azal's son Riḍwán 'Alí and sent to me by the late Claude Delaval Cobham in February, 1904, with a letter dated February 4 of that year.

(4) A list of Ṣubḥ-i-Azal's writings, drawn up for me by his son Riḍwán 'Alí in March, 1896.

(5) An account of the death of Ṣubḥ-i-Azal in April, 1912, written by his son Riḍwán 'Alí for Mr Cobham, followed by a list of twenty of his works, translated by myself into English from the original mentioned in the last paragraph.

(6) The original autograph Persian Narrative of the Bábí Insurrection at Zanján written at my request by 'Abdu'l-Aḥad of Zanján, one of Ṣubḥ-i-Azal's followers resident in Cyprus, of which I published an English translation in the *J.R.A.S.* for 1897, vol. XXIX. The original was completed in Ramaḍán, 1309/April, 1892, and comprises 26 ff. On the blank leaves at the end are some notes by myself of information verbally imparted.

(7) A copy of the Báb's "Seven Proofs" (*Dalá'il-i-Sab'a*) made by myself and submitted to Ṣubḥ-i-Azal, who has marked some corrections on it. I submitted it to him in Cyprus in 1890. Ff. 66, written on one side only.

(8) A letter dated Jan. 29, 1891, from Ḥájjí Muḥammad; another dated Jan. 22, of the same year, from Bahá'u'lláh's son Mírzá Badí', both accompanying a very well written copy of the "Tablet of Good Tidings" (*Lawḥ-i-Bishárát*) fully described under the class-mark **BBA. 5** in my *Catalogue and Description*, pp. 676–679. Bound between this and the two letters is the copy of Bahá'u'lláh's Testament (*Kitábu 'Ahdí*) to which reference is made at p. 710 *ad calc.* of the article above mentioned.

(9) A list of the descendants of Mírzá Buzurg, the father of Bahá'u'lláh and Ṣubḥ-i-Azal, communicated to me in June, 1912, by Mírzá Muṣṭafá.

F. 26 (9).

Another composite volume containing two printed works by Hippolyte Dreyfus the *Essai sur le Béhaïsme* (Paris, 1909, pp. 138); and *l'Épître au Fils du Loup par Bahâou'llâh* (Paris, 1913, pp. xvii + 185). These are followed by a tract in Persian lithographed in April, 1902, in Egypt, and comprising 223 pp., entitled:

این رساله ایست که جناب خادم ابهی علیه منکلّ بهآء ابهآه در جواب نامهٔ جناب سمیّ جهرمی علیه بهآء الله وعنایته مرقوم داشته آلخ

The only manuscript portion of the contents is the biography of Bahá'u'lláh written in Arabic by Muḥammad Jawád of Qazwín in 1322/1904, the translation of which constitutes the first part (pp. 1–112) of my *Materials for the Study of the Bábí Religion* (Cambridge, 1918). Some account of it will be found at pp. viii–x of the same work. The original is written in a neat *ta'líq*, comprises 87 pp. of 18·2 × 11·8 c. and 17 ll., and was completed in Ṣafar, 1322/April, 1904.

F. 27 (9).

Another composite volume, containing:

(1) The *Istidláliyya*, or Evidences of the Truth of the Bábí-Bahá'í Religion, composed by Mírzá Abu'l-Faḍl of Gulpáyagán, addressed especially to the Jews, and sent to me by a Persian Jew of Bukhárá named 'Azízu'lláh in 1309/1891–2, in which year also it was transcribed. See under **BBS.** 1 (its former class-mark) on pp. 701–705 of my *Catalogue and Description*.

(2) The *Qaṣída-i-Alifiyya* of Mírzá Aslam of Núr, explaining the peculiar terminology of the Bábís in a Persian poem rhyming throughout in *alif*, whence the name. It should comprise 19 "Unities" (*Wáḥid*) of 19 verses each, but actually breaks off abruptly after verse 8 of the eleventh "Unity." For further particulars see my *Materials*, pp. 228–229.

(3) A specimen of Ṣubḥ-i-Azal's "Revelation-writing" (*Khaṭṭ-i-nuzúlí*), containing a portion of the *Akhláqu'r-Rúḥániyyín* ("Ethics of the Spiritually-minded"), with transcript of the opening passage by Shaykh Aḥmad Rúḥí of Kirmán, who presented it to me.

(4) Part (64 ff.) of an account of the Bábí Religion and Philosophy entitled *Faṣlu'l-Khiṭáb fí tarjamati Aḥwáli'l-Báb*. It should comprise four sections (*faṣl*), and a conclusion, but breaks off abruptly in the middle of the third section. See my *Materials*, p. 226. This and the two following (also incomplete) were sent to me from Constantinople by Shaykh Aḥmad Rúḥí of Kirmán.

(5) The beginning (8 ff. only) of a Persian account of the Indian saint (مقدّس هندی) Rámchand, professedly translated from the Sanskrit, but containing only part of the first of the three sections which the treatise should comprise.

(6) Part (ff. 1–40) of the *Ḥikmatu'l-Ishráq* of Shaykh Shihábu'd-Dín Suhrawardí called *al-Maqtúl* ("the murdered"), received from Shaykh Aḥmad of Kirmán in July, 1892. Concerning this remarkable mystic, see Brockelmann, vol. 1, pp. 437–438.

(7) A brief account in Persian of the wrongs suffered by Muḥammad 'Alí at the hands of his brother 'Abbás Efendi 'Abdu'l-Bahá, addressed to one Ẓahír in 1316/1898–9. It comprises only 6 written pages and is a "Jellygraph." Received from Muḥammad Jawád of Qazwín in April, 1901.

(8) The second half only of a Persian polemical tract directed against 'Abbás Efendi by a partisan of his brother Muḥammad 'Alí, very probably Mírzá Jawád himself, from whom I received it in September, 1901. This portion comprises only pp. 16–31, and concludes with the death of Janáb-i-Khádimu'lláh (who had been in constant attendance on Bahá'u'lláh since 1269 (1852–3)) on May 5, 1901. The first half of the tract was either never received or has been mislaid.

(9) A Persian letter of two pages addressed by 'Abbás Efendi 'Abdu'l-Bahá to Mírzá 'Alí Akbar-i-Mílání, dated 22 Jumádà II, 1329/May 26, 1901.

(10) Four Persian letters from ‘Abbás Efendi ‘Abdu’l-Bahá, *viz.* (1) a general Epistle on Education (pp. 1–4); (2) an Epistle to the Persian believers on the fanatical hatred of the *‘ulamá* towards the Bahá’ís (pp. 4–7); (3) an Epistle on Immortality addressed to ‘Aynu’l-Ḥukamá of Mashhad (pp. 8–10); (4) an Epistle to "*Janáb-i-Qábil*" (pp. 11–16), replying to certain objections raised by the materialists.

(11) A lithographed Persian tract of 16 pp. describing the "Dreadful Event" which befell Janáb-i-Khádimu’lláh in the garden at ‘Akká at the hands of ‘Abbás Efendi ‘Abdu’l-Bahá in May, 1897, entitled:

واقعهٔ هائلهٔ خادم ابهی در روضهٔ مبارکهٔ علیا،

See my *Materials*, pp. 197–198, and cf. pp. 88 and 230.

(12) Sundry Persian letters from ‘Abbás Efendi ‘Abdu’l-Bahá and one in French from M. Hippolyte Dreyfus acquired in the summer of 1911.

(13) A curious printed pamphlet of 35 pp. in French, printed in Cairo in June, 1902, written by Gabriel Sacy (who died very suddenly in Cairo on the night of Saturday, March 21, 1903), and entitled *Du Règne de Dieu et de l’Agneau connu sous le nom de Babysme.* See my *Materials*, pp. 185–186.

F. 28 (9).

A collection of seven Bábí manuscript documents in Persian, received from the copyist Mírzá Muṣṭafà in October, 1912. They are uniform in writing and size (21·6×14 c. and 18 ll.), but Nos. 3–7 have their own separate pagination. They are as follows:

(1) A history of the Bábí Insurrection at Shaykh Ṭabarsí in Mázandarán, entitled *Waqáyi‘-i-Mímiyya*, by Sayyid Muḥammad Ḥusayn ibn Muḥammad Hádí of Zuwára, poetically named *Mahjúr* (pp. 1–92). For description of this and the two following tracts dealing with the same topic, see my *Materials*, pp. 237–243.

(2) An account of the death or "martyrdom" of Mullá Ḥusayn of Bushrawayh, by the same writer as the last (pp. 92–110), partly in prose and partly in verse. See *Materials*, *loc. cit.* The colophon is dated Ramaḍán 21, 1330/Sept. 3, 1912.

(3) Another account of the Mázandarán Insurrection (pp. 1–128), said to be by Luṭf-‘Alí Mírzá, a Qájár prince. No colophon.

(4) The *Risála-i-Máshá’a’lláh* (pp. 1–24), described as a refutation of Mírzá Nuṣrat’s *Risála-i-Inshá’a’lláh*, and ascribed in the title to Sayyid Burhánu’d-Dín of Balkh, but in reality, according to Mírzá Muṣṭafà the scribe, written by Mírzá Áqá Khán of Kirmán in Rajab, 1310/Jan. 1893. The colophon is dated 1 Shawwál, 1330/Sept. 13, 1912.

(5) The biography of the above-mentioned Mírzá Áqá Khán (pp. 1–13), taken from the Náẓimu’l-Islám’s lithographed *Ta’ríkh-i-Bídári-yi-Írániyán* ("History of the Awakening of the Persians"). He was born in 1270/1853–4 and was put to

death at Tabríz on July 17, 1896, together with Shaykh Aḥmad "Rúḥí" of Kirmán and Khabíru'l-Mulk, on suspicion of complicity in the assassination of Náṣiru'd-Dín Sháh. See my *Persian Revolution*, pp. 93–96.

(6) The *Ṣaḥífa-i-Riḍawiyya* (pp. 1–5), in Arabic, ascribed to the Báb and beginning:

الصحيفة السادسة فى الخطب وهى مرتّبة بأربعة عشر خطبة ‘

الخطبة الأولى ‘

هذه الخطبة قد انشأت فى كلّ ما سطر فى ذلك الكتاب ليكون الكلّ بذلك

من الشاهدين ‘

بسم الله الرحمن الرّحيم ‘

الحمد لله الّذى خلق الماء بسرّ الانشاء وأقام العرش على المآء الّخ

In the latter part of this tract the author enumerates his writings (fourteen in number) produced during the two years succeeding the Manifestation (1260–2/1844–6), *viz.* (1) the *Kitábu'l-Aḥmadiyya*, explaining the first part of the *Qur'án*; (2) the *Kitábu'l-'Alawiyya*, containing 700 *súras*, each of seven verses; (3) the *Kitábu'l-Ḥasaniyya*; (4) the *Kitábu'l-Ḥusayniyya*, explaining the *Súratu Yúsuf* in 111 *súras* (one for each verse of the original), each containing 42 verses. The remaining ten bear the title of *Ṣaḥífa* instead of *Kitáb*, and are called after the remaining nine Imáms and Fáṭima; *i.e.* a book is dedicated to each of the "Fourteen Sinless ones" (*Chahárdah Ma'ṣúm*). The Báb speaks at the end of other books which "passed out of my hands and were stolen on the Pilgrimage journey," and exhorts anyone who finds them to preserve them most carefully:

و امّا ما خرج من يدى وسرق فى سبيل الحجّ قد ذكر تفصيله فى صحيفة الرضويّة فمن وجد منه شيئًا وجب عليه حفظه فيا طوبى لمن استحفظ كلّ ما نزل من لدىّ بالواح طيّبة على احسن خطّ فوالّذى أكرمنى آياته [انّ] حرفا منها أعزّ لدىّ من ملك الآخرة والاولى واستغفر الله ربّى عن التحديد بالقليل وسبحان الله ربّ العرش عمّا يصفون وسلام على المرسلين والحمد لله ربّ العالمين ‘

(7) Arabic letters (18 pp.) written by the Báb during the earlier period of his mission to (1) the Sharíf Sulaymán and the people of Mecca (pp. 1–2); (2) to Ḥájjí Sulaymán Khán; (3) from Bushire to the King of Persia (pp. 3–5); (4) in answer to Mírzá Ḥasan the historiographer (*Waqáyi'-nigár*) "in the Land of Ṣád" (Iṣfahán).

F. 29 (6) = BBP. 4.

كتاب اقدس

A copy of the *Kitáb-i-Aqdas* given to me at Shíráz on April 2, 1888. See my *Catalogue and Description*, p. 440.

F. 30 (7) = BBP. 3.

Another copy of the *Kitáb-i-Aqdas* made for me at Shíráz in April, 1888. See my *Catalogue and Description*, p. 440.

F. 31 (8) = BBP. 6.

Another copy of the *Kitáb-i-Aqdas*, together with the *Alwáḥ-i-Salátín* and other *Alwáḥ* ("Tablets") and poems, obtained at Kirmán on July 29, 1888. See my *Catalogue and Description*, p. 444, and the same volume of the *J.R.A.S.* (April, 1892), pp. 284–291.

F. 32 (7) = BBA. 3.

صحائف پارسيّه، کلمات فردوسيّه، طرازات، تجلّيات، لوح اقدس،

A collection of Bahá'í "Tablets" (*Alwáḥ*), including some in pure Persian, besides the *Kalimát-i-Firdawsiyya*, *Ṭirázát*, *Tajalliyát*, and the *Lawḥ-i-Aqdas*. See my *Catalogue and Description*, pp. 666–671.

F. 33 (7) = BBA. 4.

کلمات مکنونهٔ فاطميّه،

The "Hidden Words of Fáṭima, with three 'Tablets'" specially addressed to the Zoroastrians. See my *Catalogue and Description*, pp. 671–676.

F. 34 (11).

A scrap-book containing photographic reproductions of "Tablets" (*Alwáḥ*) emanating from Bahá'u'lláh and 'Abdu'l-Bahá, corrected, arranged and presented to me on July 28th, 1921, by Mírzá Yuḥanná Dáwud. The album comprises 18 ff. of 25·3×20·4 c. and 31 *Alwáḥ*, each furnished with a short description in Persian in the hand of Mírzá Yuḥanná, to whom many of them are addressed. Of those which are dated the dates range between 1910 and 1920.

F. 35 (9).

ديوان ازل

A copy of the *Díwánu'l-Azal*, concerning which see my *Materials*, p. 214. This MS. comprises 551 ff. of 19·6×12 c. and 19 ll.; is written in a large, clear *naskh*, unpointed, with rubrications; is dated 18 Shawwál, 1319/Jan. 28, 1902, and was transcribed by Muḥammad 'Alí ibn Muḥammad Ḥusayn. It appears to have been acquired on April 2, 1922, but I am not sure from what source.

F. 36.

Another copy of the same *Díwánu'l-Azal*, followed by another of Ṣubḥ-i-Azal's writings entitled *Ṣaḥífa-i-Wajdiyya*, both in Arabic, copied for me in instalments between August, 1896, and May, 1897, by Azal's son Riḍwán 'Alí. The *Díwán*, which fills ff. 2^b–382^b, is incomplete, and breaks off abruptly at a point corresponding to f. 297^b, l. 7 of the MS. (**F. 37**), to be next mentioned. The *Ṣaḥífa*, in the same handwriting but on different paper, white instead of blue, and of a better quality, comprises 40 ff., and ends with the following colophon, dated only according to the Bábí computation:

قد تمّت هذه الصحيفة الجليلة وهى اسمها وجديّة وكانت خطب النكاحيّة فى ليل السّابع والعشر من شهر القدرة فى سنه[٤٨] بيانيّة

٣١٢٥٣١١٣٧٦ ٥٣٣١٦٨٥

كتبه الحقير الفقير رضوانعلى

The whole MS. comprises 422 ff. of 20·6 × 12·5 c. and 14 ll., and is written throughout in a large, clear *naskh*, unpointed. At the end are bound in three Persian letters from Riḍwán 'Alí, one received on Sept. 29, 1896, another in May, 1897, and the third undated; and a letter in English from the late Mr C. D. Cobham, dated Larnaca, Nov. 18, 1896.

F. 37 (8).

A third copy of the *Díwánu'l-Azal*, which, though considerably fuller than the last, is also incomplete and ends abruptly. It comprises 380 ff. of 19·4 × 12 c. and 14 ll. and is written in the same large, clear *naskh* hand as the last, but contains no indication of the date of acquisition, though it too reached me from Cyprus. Of these three MSS. **F. 35** only is complete, for it comprises 551 ff., and the end of **F. 37** (which is less defective than **F. 36**) corresponds to f. 355^b, l. 12, so that **F. 35** contains nearly 200 ff. more than **F. 37**. Before the title **F. 35** has بسم الله الأمنع الأقدس, omitted by the other two MSS., but all three agree in what follows, *viz.*:

لا اله الّا الله

ديوان الأزل

روح الاحتجاج اهيّه

بسمه المتعالى المحبوب

سبحان من أظهر وجهه بالهدى والحقّ وآتاكم ذكرى ورحمة وبعث نفسه نقطة الاولى وأمركم أن تتّبعوا آيات البيان الخ

F. 38 (9).

صحائف الازل،

This MS. of the *Ṣaḥá'ifu'l-Azal*, if it ever existed, is not now to be found, and I suspect that it was only an alternative title of another Azalí MS.

F. 39 (8) = BBF. 5.

آثار ازليّه،

A collection of Ṣubḥ-i-Azal's Persian writings. See my *Catalogue and Description*, pp. 492–493.

F. 40 (9).

ذيل بيان فارسى،

A continuation of the Báb's Persian *Bayán* by Ṣubḥ-i-Azal, beginning with *Wáḥid* IX, chapter 11 (at the point where the original *Bayán* terminated), and extending to *Wáḥid* XI, chapter 19. This supplement was presumably undertaken by Ṣubḥ-i-Azal in conformity with a statement by the Báb that his successor and vicegerent would continue or complete the *Bayán*, of which he therefore composed only half, *viz.* nine *Wáḥids* and a half out of nineteen. Begins abruptly:

الباب الحادى والعشر من الواحد التاسع فى أن لا يبيعون عناصر الرباع ولا تشرونها، ملخّص اينباب آنكه خداوند عالم جلّ اسمه از فضل غير متناهى وجود لا يتناهى خود من اجل مخلوق خود عناصر رباع را آفريده الخ

Ff. 122 of 20 × 12·8 c. and 14 ll.; good, clear *naskh*, unpointed; received from Cyprus on December 4, 1896.

F. 41 (6).

لمعات الأزل

Another work of Ṣubḥ-i-Azal's in Arabic, entitled *Lama'át* ("Flashes"), in 28 sections (corresponding to the number of letters in the Arabic alphabet), written "in the style of *Áyát*" (verses of the *Qur'án*), and beginning:

بسم الله الأحد الفرد القديم،

تلك آيات بيّنات ورحمة من ربّك لأن يهدى النّاس بآيات الله ويكون الّذين آمنوا فى دين الله من الشاكرين،

Ff. 414 of 12·8 × 10 c. and 18 ll.; copied by Ṣubḥ-i-Azal's son Riḍwán 'Alí in his usual large, clear *naskh*, and dated only in the Bábí fashion "the night of the sixth of the month of Jamál of the Bayání months in the year 45."

و من الكور ١٣   الدور الأبد فى ليلة العشرين

I have omitted to note the date when the MS. was received.

F. 42 (8).

نغمات الرّوح (الجلد الثّانى)،

Vol. II of Ṣubḥ-i-Azal's *Naghamátu'r-Rúḥ* ("Songs of the Spirit"), also copied for me in August or September, 1896, by Riḍwán 'Alí, whose accompanying letter (undated) is bound in the volume. Begins:

بسمه الباقى الملك الديموم المستعان،

الحمد لله ممسك السمآء بقدرته ومسكن الأرض بمشيّته ومرفع الجبال بعزّته ومشهق الآكام بقوّته ومجرى البحور بحكمته وخالق النّفوس بديموميّته آلخ

Ff. 152 of 18·5 × 13·2 c. and 14 ll.; large, clear *naskh*, unpointed; dated only in the Bábí fashion "the day of *Istijlál*, the fifteenth of the month of God *an-Núr*, in the forty-fourth year of the years which God hath determined in the *Bayán*," etc.

F. 43 (9) = BBF. 4.

آثار قُدسيّه، نغمات الرّوح، لئالى و مجالى،

A full account of this MS., received from Ṣubḥ-i-Azal with a letter written on Feb. 4, 1890, is given in my *Catalogue and Description*, pp. 483–491. It contains (1) five specimens of the Arabic writings of *Janáb-i-Quddús*, *i.e.* Ḥájjí Mullá Muḥammad 'Alí of Bárfurúsh, one of the Báb's most notable early disciples, who was put to death at Bárfurúsh in the summer of 1849 after the fall of Shaykh Ṭabarsí (ff. 1ᵇ–20ᵇ); (2) the second volume of Ṣubḥ-i-Azal's *Naghamátu'r-Rúḥ* (ff. 22ᵇ–101ᵇ), agreeing, except as regards the colophon, with that described immediately above; (3) the *La'álí u Majálí* of Ṣubḥ-i-Azal (ff. 106ᵇ–203ᵇ), an imitation of the *Sententiæ* of 'Alí ibn Abí Ṭálib; (4) a short piece of Arabic without title, apparently also by Ṣubḥ-i-Azal.

F. 44 (8).

كتاب طوبى،

A Persian poem of some seven thousand verses composed in imitation of the *Mathnawí* by Ṣubḥ-i-Azal, and entitled *Kitáb-i-Ṭúbà*. A full table of contents (ff. 6[b]–13[a]) is prefixed. Begins:

نطقِ جان بشنو ز دستان‌ساز من، این نوای جان و این آواز من،

Pp. 588 of 19·2×15 c. and 13 ll.; clear, large *ta'líq* with rubrications; copied by Riḍwán 'Alí and completed on March 11, 1897, and given to me by Mr C. D. Cobham in August, 1906. See my *Materials*, pp. 215–216.

F. 45 (9) = BBF. 11.

مرآة البيان،

The *Mir'átu'l-Bayán*, another of Ṣubḥ-i-Azal's Arabic works, of which a full account will be found in my *Catalogue and Description*, pp. 660–662. It was copied for me in 1891 and received in instalments during this and the following year. It comprises 678 ff. of 20·75×13·5 c. and 14 ll.

F. 46 (9).

كتاب الهياكل،

Another of Ṣubḥ-i-Azal's Arabic works entitled *Kitábu'l-Hayákil*, containing 1001 *haykals*, grouped in hundreds, beginning:

بسم الله الأمنع الأهدى،

الحمد لله الّذى ما حمده غيره ولا يشهد على ذلك من أحد جعل النّاس فى درجات شتّى،

Ff. 514 of 20·5×12·5 c. and 14 ll.; good, clear *ta'líq*, except the final pages which are in *naskh*; copied by Riḍwán 'Alí and completed on the 24th of Jumádà I, 1310/Dec. 14, 1892.

F. 47 (9).

صحائف الازل

Ṣaḥá'ifu'l-Azal, being ejaculatory prayers and devotional exercises in Arabic by Ṣubḥ-i-Azal. The volume is divided into two parts with separate pagination, the first comprising 314 pp., the second 292 pp., of 20·7 × 13 c. and 12 ll. It was copied by Riḍwán 'Alí and sent to me by him in January, 1900. The first part begins:

صحيفة الأوسعيّة

بسم الله الأجمل الأوسع،

الهى لا واسع الّا انت ولا موسع غيرك ضاق علىّ الأمر واحاطت علىّ سوآت الدهر الخ

The second part, entitled *Ṣaḥífatu'l-Maráyá*, begins:

هو الله الملك الحقّ العدل السلطان القديم، الهى انت الّذى تبدع خلقا بدعا وتخترع ذرءًا خرعا الخ

F. 48–52.

These five Azalí MSS. were bought from Mr W. J. Ansell, formerly Collector of Customs at Larnaca, Cyprus, on February 18, 1918.

F. 48 (8).

لحظات،

Laḥaẓát, an Arabic devotional work, apparently by Ṣubḥ-i-Azal, containing 202 sections, or *súras*, each beginning with the *Bismi'lláh*, the two Attributes varying in each case. The first, dated 21 Shawwál, 1315/March 15, 1898, with the corresponding Bábí date:

يوم الاثنين الثانى من دورة الرسل...عيد العظمة والكمال عيد الخمسين من ظهورات البيانيّة

begins:

بسم الله الأرفع الاعلى الله لا اله الّا هو الأمنع الاجلى الحمد لله الّذى بيده ما فى الآخرة والاولى الخ

Ff. 230 of 19·8 × 12·7 c. and 15 ll., small, hastily written *nasta'líq*; no date or colophon.

F. 49 (8).

كلمات بيانيّه،

Kalimát-i-Bayániyya, consisting of Arabic *súras*, each bearing a special title (*Súratu'l-Bayán*, *Súratu'n-Nuqṭa*, *Súratu'l-Qisṭás*, etc.), in imitation of the *Qur'án*. Groups of letters, such as اهع, حَسَ, are prefixed to some of them. They appear to consist entirely of pious rhapsodies and to contain no material of historical or doctrinal importance.

Ff. 682 of 19 × 12 c. and 14 ll., large, clear *naskh*, unpointed; dated at end 5 Dhu'l-Qa'da, 1312/30 April, 1895, with the corresponding Bábí dates:

بيانيّة ٤٧ كلمات ١٢ كور ١٦ دورهٔ حروف ٩

One of Mr W. J. Ansell's letters is pasted in at the end of the volume.

F. 50 (8).

لوامع،

Another Arabic devotional work by Ṣubḥ-i-Azal, comprising 95 sections entitled *Lawámi'*.

Ff. 162 of 19·7 × 14 c. and 15 ll.; small *nasta'líq*; no colophon except the mysterious numerals:

٣١٢٥٣١١٣٧٦ ٥٣٣١٦٨٥

Another letter from Mr Ansell, dated 20 November, 1917, is pasted in at the end of the volume.

F. 51 (8).

سطعات،

Another similar Arabic work comprising 267 sections entitled *Saṭa'át*.

Ff. 328 of 18·5 × 13·2 c. and 14 ll.; small, hastily written *nasta'líq*; no colophon except the same series of numerals given above.

F. 52 (8).

اللواحظ والنفائح،

Another similar Arabic work entitled *al-Lawáḥiẓ wa'n-Nafá'iḥ*, comprising 506 chapters or *súras*. The last of these ends on f. 213b with the same series of numerals as the two preceding MSS., except that at the end the letters لله are substituted for ٥٣٣. This is followed by a short piece apparently commemorating the death on Muḥarram 24, 1329/Jan. 25, 1911, of a Bábí woman related to Ṣubḥ-i-Azal, and beginning:

بسم الله الأقرب الأوسع، ذكر كتاب للورقة التّى رفعت الى الله ورجعت الى ربّها فى ليلة ٢٤ محرّم ذلك اليوم سنة ١٣٢٩ وقضت أيّامها وكان الأمر فى شأنها من لدى الله مقضيًّا،

Ff. 214 of 20 × 12·7 c. and 15 ll.; large, clear *naskh*; dated in colophon 23 Ramaḍán, 1328/28 September, 1910.

F. 53 (10) (2 vols.) = BBC. 1–2.

هشت بهشت،

This important work, the *Hasht Bihisht*, or "Eight Paradises," is fully described in my *Catalogue and Description of* 27 *Bábí Manuscripts*, pp. 680–697. Vol. I deals with the philosophy and theory of the Báb's doctrines, vol. II with its practice and certain matters connected with the history of the sect, especially the quarrel between Bahá'u'lláh and Ṣubḥ-i-Azal, the author (whose identity is uncertain) being a violent partisan of the latter. This is one of the most interesting of the later Bábí books, and was probably written by Shaykh Aḥmad Rúḥí of Kirmán, or his friend and fellow-sufferer Mírzá Áqá Khán of Kirmán, or by both in conjunction. This copy was made for me by the former in 1891.

F. 54 (8) (2 vols.).

هشت بهشت،

Another copy of the preceding work, also in two volumes, received from Mírzá Muṣṭafà on August 8, 1913. Vol. I of this copy contains a preface of 24 pp. which is lacking in the preceding copy. It is ascribed to a certain Mírzá Jawád of Shíráz, and begins:

ربّ وفّقنی بالاتمام،

جنگ هفتاد و دو ملّت همه‌را عذر بنه، چون ندیدند حقیقت رهِ افسانه زدند،

حکایت

قهوه‌خانهٔ در شهر صورت بود که پس از ظهر بسیاری از غرباء آنجا جمع می شدند الخ

There follows a long discussion on religion between a Brahmin, a Zoroastrian, a Jew, a Catholic, a Protestant, a Sunní, a Shí'a, a Shaykhí, a Bahá'í, a Confucian, and other representatives of the chief creeds, the final summing up being effected by the above-mentioned Mírzá Jawád. The preface ends:

سخن میرزا جواد اینجا ختم شد،

The text, as described on p. 685 of my *Catalogue and Description*, begins on p. 25, but is preceded by the following note, which ascribes the authorship to Mírzá Jawád of Shíráz, not, as asserted by Ḥájjí Shaykh Aḥmad of Kirmán (*Catalogue and Description*, pp. 683–685), to the venerable Ḥájjí Sayyid Jawád of Karbalá:

خلاصهٔ اقوال حکمای اسلامیّه از قول میرزا جواد شیرازی که در مقابل تحقیقات مرید کانفسیوس در قهوه‌خانهٔ شهر صورت بیان نمود وهی هذه

موسوم بحکمت نظری،

The *Fihrist*, or Glossary of Bábí terminology (*Catalogue and Description*, pp. 690–692), is missing at the end, since it was, as the copyist explains in a final note, lacking in the author's autograph from which he made his transcription:

. مخفی نبوده باشد که این کتاب از روی خطّ خودِ مصنّف نوشته شد و فهرست اصطلاحات که اسم برده مرقوم نداشته بود و در جای دیگر هم بدست نیآمد و مقابله شد بدقّت،

Pp. 538 of 20·4 × 13·8 c. and 19 ll.; clear *naskh* with rubrications; dated 22 Rajab, 1331/25 June, 1913.

The second volume (**F. 54**[2]), dealing with the ordinances and practical philosophy of the *Bayán*, corresponds both as regards beginning and end with the copy previously described, and is dated 25 Jumádà I, 1331/May 3, 1913. It also professes to have been transcribed from the author's autograph, made in 1312/1894–5. It is uniform in script and style with the companion volume, and comprises 440 pp. of 21·4 × 14·8 c.

F. 55 (9) = BBP. 5.

تأریخ جدید،

This MS. is fully described on pp. 440–444 of my *Catalogue and Description*, where references are given to other places where its authorship and contents are discussed. I copied out the whole text (amounting to 283 large pages) and collated it throughout with the British Museum MS. **Or. 2942** (obtained from Mr Sidney Churchill on Oct. 10, 1885), noting all variants. This work I completed on April 11, 1891, intending to publish it, but I only published the English translation, under the title of *The Ta'ríkh-i-Jadíd or New History of Mírzá 'Alí Muḥammad the Báb...with an Introduction, Illustrations and Appendices* (Cambridge University Press, 1893). The discovery of Ḥájjí Mírzá Jání of Káshán's *Nuqṭatu'l-Káf*, on which the *Ta'ríkh-i-Jadíd* is based, in the Bibliothèque Nationale at Paris, rendered the publication of the latter relatively unimportant, and the text of the former ultimately appeared, with a full Introduction and Apparatus Criticus, in 1910 as vol. xv of the "E. J. W. Gibb Memorial" Series. Full accounts of these two books and their relation to one another will be found in the above-mentioned volumes. My transcript, originally intended for the Press, is preserved amongst my MSS., but I have not at present assigned a class-mark to it. In size it is a (12).

F. 56 (7) = BBA. I.

مقالهٔ شخصی سیّاح که در تفصیل قضیّهٔ باب نوشته است،

Besides the full account of this MS. on pp. 663–665 of my *Catalogue and Description of 27 Bábí Manuscripts*, its exact appearance can be judged from the photo-lithographic facsimile forming vol. I of my *Traveller's Narrative, written to illustrate the Episode of the Báb*, published by the Cambridge University Press in 1891, while the Introduction in vol. II, containing the English translation, gives full particulars concerning the work, of which, therefore, no further account need be given here.

F. 57 (9).

رسالهٔ سیّد مهدی دهجی،

Some account of this remarkable tract will be found in my *Materials for the Study of the Bábí Religion* (Cambridge, 1918), pp. 231–233 and 237. The author, Sayyid Mahdí of Dahaj (near Shahr-i-Bábak), was eight years old at the time of the Báb's "Manifestation" in 1844, and became a believer in him at the age of thirteen. Though he never saw the Báb, he was acquainted with many of his chief followers, such as Sayyid Yaḥyà of Dáráb, and in 1858 he went to Baghdád to visit Ṣubḥ-i-Azal, but was much more impressed by Bahá'u'lláh, whom he followed when the schism came, and to whom he remained faithful for thirty-five years. When Bahá'u'lláh died in 1892, the author, Sayyid Mahdí, espoused the cause of his son Muḥammad 'Alí, and repudiated the claims of 'Abbás Efendi 'Abdu'l-Bahá. His long connection with the Bábí community from the earliest days renders his account singularly full and detailed, and enables him to supply many interesting details not to be found elsewhere. He was moved to write it by the perusal of the Persian Introduction to my text of Ḥájjí Mírzá Jání's *Nuqṭatu'l-Káf* ("E. J. W. Gibb Memorial" Series, vol. XV), which he desired to criticize in many details. Unfortunately only the first half of his work reached me, and I do not know whether the other half was actually written and not sent, or lost in the post, or whether old age or illness prevented the fulfilment of his project.

The MS., an autograph, comprises 291 pp. of 20·8 × 13 c. and 18 ll., and is written in a clear *nasta'líq*, with long passages in red ink occurring at intervals. From a passage on p. 254 it appears that it was composed in A.D. 1914. A letter of seven closely written pages from the author is pasted in at the end. The text of the book breaks off abruptly at the bottom of p. 291 after the account of the murder of the Azalís, and in the middle of the account of the *Íqán* (see immediately below, **F. 58** and **F. 59**). My Introduction to the *Nuqṭatu'l-Káf* supplies the text to this elaborate and valuable commentary, the loss of the second half of which is greatly to be deplored.

F. 58 (10) = BBP. 1.

ايقان،

For this MS. of the *Íqán* see pp. 435–438 of my *Catalogue and Description of 27 Bábí Manuscripts*. A French translation of this important work by M. Hippolyte Dreyfus was published in Paris in 1904 under the title of *Le Livre de la Certitude*. See my *Materials for the Study of the Bábí Religion*, pp. 12 and n. 1 *ad calc.*, 179, and 325.

F. 59 (9) = BBA. 2.

Another and much better MS. of the *Íqán*, given to me at Acre on April 20, 1890. See the *Catalogue and Description*, pp. 665–666.

F. 60 (8).

تنبيه النّائمين،

The *Tanbíhu'n-Ná'imín*, or "Awakening of the Sleepers," is described in my *Materials*, pp. 226–227. As there explained, it consists of three separate parts, viz. (1) a letter from 'Abbás Efendi 'Abdu'l-Bahá to the Báb's aunt, called by the Bábís *Khánim-i-Buzurg* ("the Great Lady"), who was still living in Ṭihrán in 1913, inciting her to accept Bahá'u'lláh and abjure Ṣubḥ-i-Azal; (2) her long and caustic reply, which contains much valuable historical material; (3) a homily and refutation by Shaykh Aḥmad of Kirmán, the well-known and unfortunate Azalí. This MS. was received from Dr Sa'íd Khán of Ḥasanábád near Ṭihrán on April 6, 1912. It was transcribed by Mírzá Muṣṭafà and completed on the 3rd of Rabí' II, 1330/ March 22, 1912. It comprises 266 pp. of 17·5 × 10·5 c. and 16 ll., and is written in a clear *naskh*.

F. 61 (9).

Another MS. of the above-mentioned *Tanbíhu'n-Ná'imín*, received from Baḥru'l-'Ulúm of Kirmán on May 20, 1912. It comprises 199 pp. of 21·5 × 14·7 c. and 19 ll., and is written in a clear *naskh* similar to, if not identical with, the last. It is dated 27 Ṣafar, 1330/Feb. 16, 1912.

F. 62 (10).

A number of unbound quires of 22·5 × 15·3 c. received from Mírzá Muṣṭafà in July, 1912, comprising three separate parts, viz.:

(1) A short Preface (*Díbácha*) to the above-mentioned *Tanbíhu'n-Ná'imín* comprising 6 pp. The author does not mention his name, but begins after the doxology (p. 2, l. 7):

و بعد، چنین گوید این افقر و احقر زمرهٔ بشر و این اقصر و اصغر عباد در تمییز خیر و شرّ که پس از طلوع شمس حقیقت از افق غیب الخ

It seems not improbable that it was written by Shaykh Aḥmad of Kirmán, to whose name the following verse quoted from the *Mathnawí* (p. 2, l. 3) may contain an allusion:

نامِ احمد نامِ جمله انبیاست، چونکه صد آمد نود هم پیش ماست،

This Preface ends at the top of p. 6, and p. 7 should contain the letter of 'Abbás Efendi 'Abdu'l-Bahá to the "*Khánim-i-Buzurg*," which constitutes the first part of the two preceding MSS., but actually contains only the title:

صورت مکتوب که جناب میرزا عبّاس افندی بیکی از ورقات مبارکات نگاشته بودند آن مکتوب‌را بعینها در این کتاب با جواب مکتوب که داده شده بی زواید و نواقص می نگارد تا بر ارباب بصیرت پوشیده نماند و آن این است،

In the margin the copyist, Mírzá Muṣṭafà, has written that as the text of this was contained in the MS. previously sent (**F. 60**), he had not considered it necessary to transcribe it again.

(2) Two quires (26 written pages), uniform with the last, headed *Tafáwut-i-nuskhatayn* ("Variation of the two texts"), containing page by page (from p. 1 to p. 273) the variants of the "printed copy" (نسخهٔ چاپی) and the MS. (**F. 60**), and ending with the following note by Mírzá Muṣṭafà:

تفاوتِ نسختین‌را نوشته ارسال داشتم هر کدام که لازم یا واجب است در کتاب درج نمائید و هرگاه لازم نیست بجای خود بوده باشد البتّه آنجناب در این خصوص بصیرتشان بیشتر از حقیر است،

(3) A much corrected and emended copy of the *Risála-i-'Amma*, or "Aunt's Letter," which constitutes the third part of the *Tanbíhu'n-Ná'imín*. Whole paragraphs have been cut out or replaced by others, written in the margin in a small *ním-shikasta*. Apart from such an addition, the text ends on f. 81[a] with the poem ascribed to Bahá'u'lláh which occupies pp. 106–107 in **F. 61**, the last 47 pp. of which (pp. 107–154) appear to be lacking in this MS.

F. 63 (9).

تذكرة الغافلين،

Concerning this work, the *Tadhkiratu'l-Gháfilín*, or "Admonition of the Heedless," see my *Materials*, pp. 227–228. Its anonymous author, a native of Niráq, champions the claims of Ṣubḥ-i-Azal against those of his half-brother Bahá'u'lláh. This MS., the only copy of the work known to me, comprises 228 pp. of 21 × 14·8 c. and 19 ll. It is in the clear *naskh* hand of Mírzá Muṣṭafà, who completed it on Ṣafar 8, 1331/Jan. 17, 1913.

F. 64 (7).

رساله ملّا زين العابدين نجف‌آبادى و جواب آن،

A letter from Mullá Zaynu'l-'Ábidín of Najaf-ábád to one of the "People of the *Bayán*" (*i.e.* the old Bábís), inviting him to accept Bahá'u'lláh as "Him whom God shall manifest" (23 pp.), followed by the much longer reply (198 pp.) of the person so addressed. This MS. also was transcribed by Mírzá Muṣṭafà, from whom I received it through Dr Sa'íd Khán in September, 1920, and was completed on Dhu'l-Qa'da 14, 1337/August 11, 1919. It comprises 221 written pages of 17 × 10·8 c. and 16 ll. This appears to be the last manuscript I received from this excellent old scribe, who has since died, so that his name can be mentioned without imprudence.

F. 65 (7).

Described as follows by Professor Browne in a note written on the back of the cover and dated September 15th, 1922:

"Letter of 'Abbás Efendi 'Abdu'l-Bahá to 'Alí Akbar-i-Mílání, followed by a refutation of the same (pp. 7 *et seqq.*) by Mírzá Muṣṭafà the Bábí scribe (see his letter pasted in opposite), whose real name, as he now tells me for the first time, is Ismá'íl-i-Ṣabbágh of Si-dih, near Iṣfahán, whence he was driven out by the persecutions which took place there about 35 years ago. Received on September 15, 1922, from Dr Sa'íd [Khán Kurdistání] through his son Samuel Sa'íd."

Pp. 82 of 16·3 × 10·8 c. and 16 ll. Dated 19 Sha'bán, 1338/9 May, 1920.

F. 66 (8).

The following note by Professor Browne, dated Christmas Eve, 1924, is written on the fly-leaf:

"Received from Dr Sa'íd Khán Kurdistání on December 23, 1924, with accompanying letter (dated Dec. 3, 1924) pasted opposite.

The author of this work, Ḥájjí Mírzá Mahdí of Iṣfahán, is a son-in-law of Ṣubḥ-i-Azal and is now (1924) 70 years of age. He was formerly in Cyprus and Constantinople, and apparently had some correspondence with me and sent me some books by Ṣubḥ-i-Azal's directions. Being in some ways dissatisfied with my Introduction to the text of Ḥájjí Mírzá Jání's history of the Báb entitled *Nuqṭatu'l-Káf* (published in the Gibb Series) he wrote this treatise criticizing the views there expressed. This MS. is in his own handwriting."

Pp. 246 of 20 × 12·7 c. and 23 ll. Dated 13 Shawwál, 1342/19 May, 1924.

F. 66* (15).

A portfolio containing original letters received by Professor Browne from leading Bábís and Bahá'ís (1889–1913), together with other letters and documents connected with the subject and belonging to the same period.

The following note by Professor Browne is written at the end:

"Full particulars concerning the more important of my Bábí (Azalí and Bahá'í) correspondents whose letters are contained in this volume will be found in my *Traveller's Narrative* (Cambridge University Press, 1891), *New History* (Cambridge University Press, 1893) and *Materials for the Study of the Bábí Religion* (Cambridge University Press, 1918).

Pp. 1–10 contain letters from Mírzá Yaḥyà 'Ṣubḥ-i-Azal'—'the Dawn of Eternity'—himself and from his sons 'Abdu'l-'Alí and Riẓwán 'Alí, his nephew Rúḥu'lláh, and his followers 'Abdu'l-Aḥad of Zanján and Maḥmúd ibn Muḥammad Ja'far of Kirmán, the brother of Shaykh Aḥmad Rúḥí of Kirmán. The Bahá'í letters include those from all Bahá'u'lláh's four sons, *viz.* 'Abbás Efendi 'Abdu'l-Bahá; his rival Muḥammad 'Alí; Badí'u'lláh; and Ẓiyá'u'lláh. Also from Mírzá Muḥammad 'Alí of Yazd; Ḥájjí Sayyid 'Alí of Shíráz; 'Azízu'lláh of Bukhárá (a converted Jew); Muḥammad Jawád and his son Ghulámu'lláh of Qazwín, two of the partisans of Muḥammad 'Alí."

Most of the letters have been numbered by Professor Browne, who has usually noted the writer's name, the date at which the letter was written or posted, and also in many cases the date at which it was received, while some indication is often given as to the nature of its contents. The letters are not always arranged in their exact numerical order; different letters are occasionally denoted by the same number; and there are one or two numbers to which no letter appears to have been assigned[1].

I. Letters from Ṣubḥ-i-Azal, his sons and his adherents, etc.

No. 1 (facing f. 4). From Ṣubḥ-i-Azal, written July 29, 1889, enclosing a copy of Ṣubḥ-i-Azal's appointment by the Báb.

No. 2 (facing f. 4). From Ṣubḥ-i-Azal, posted from Famagusta on Oct. 1, 1889, treating chiefly of the writings of the Báb and his early disciples.

No. 2*a* (facing f. 5). Transcript of a letter of Qurratu'l-'Ayn to Mullá Shaykh 'Alí. Both the transcript and the autograph were received from Ṣubḥ-i-Azal on Oct. 11, 1889. The text of the former, with facsimile of the original, was published in Professor Browne's translation of the *Ta'ríkh-i-Jadíd* (see pp. 421 and 434–437).

---

[1] [The following list should be compared with that given by Prof. Browne in *Materials for the Study of the Bábí Religion*, pp. 234–237, the existence of which I had forgotten at the time when I drew up mine. In Prof. Browne's list the letters sent to him by each of his correspondents are arranged under the writer's name, and as a rule nothing is added except the date.]

No. 3 (facing f. 6). From Ṣubḥ-i-Azal, posted from Famagusta on Dec. 3, 1889. Brief account of Bábí history and martyrs, published at the end of the translation of the *Ta'ríkh-i-Jadíd*, pp. ٢٦-١, under the title, "A succinct account of the Bábí Movement written by Mírzá Yaḥyà Ṣubḥ-i-Ezel." An English translation is given in *op. cit.*, Appendix III, pp. 397–419.

No. 4 (facing f. 6). From Ṣubḥ-i-Azal, posted from Famagusta on Jan. 14, "a short letter, thanking me for a present of a writing-desk which I sent through Captain Young, and which reached him on Christmas Day."

No. 5 (facing f. 7). "First letter from Ṣubḥ-i-Azal after my visit to Cyprus, received May, 1890." It is accompanied by a slip of paper containing the names of the 19 Bábí months, "written out for me by Ṣubḥ-i-Ezel while I was in Cyprus in April, 1890."

No. 5* (facing f. 7). From Ṣubḥ-i-Azal's son, Mírzá 'Abdu'l-'Alí, received May, 1890.

No. 5** (facing f. 7). From 'Abdu'l-Aḥad of Zanján, received May, 1890.

No. 6 (facing f. 8). From Ṣubḥ-i-Azal, written Nov. 25, 1890, and sent along with two MSS., namely, Commentaries by the Báb on Súra II (سورة البقرة) and Súra CIII (سورة العصر).

No. 6*. There seems to be no letter corresponding to this number.

No. 6** (facing f. 8). From 'Abdu'l-Aḥad of Zanján, received Dec. 8, 1890.

No. 7 (facing f. 8). From Ṣubḥ-i-Azal, dated Jumádà II, A.H. 1308, *circa* Jan. 20, 1891.

No. 8 (facing f. 8). From 'Abdu'l-'Alí, dated Jumádà II, A.H. 1308, *circa* Jan. 20, 1891.

No. 8* (facing f. 8). From 'Abdu'l-'Alí, written May 26, 1891.

No. 8** (facing f. 8). From 'Abdu'l-Aḥad of Zanján, written May 26, 1891.

No. 8 *sic* (facing f. 9). This letter from Ṣubḥ-i-Azal, enclosing letters from his son 'Abdu'l-'Alí and from 'Abdu'l-Aḥad of Zanján, was posted from Famagusta on May 26, 1891.

No. 9 (facing f. 9). From Ṣubḥ-i-Azal, written about August 18, 1891. It contains explanations of certain difficult expressions and allusions in a letter (No. 2*a*) from Qurratu'l-'Ayn to Janáb-i 'Aẓím (Mullá Shaykh 'Alí), and of the brief account of the Bábí movement written by Ṣubḥ-i-Azal (No. 3).

No. 9* (facing f. 9). From 'Abdu'l-'Alí, dated 12 Muḥarram, A.H. 1309 (Aug. 18, 1891).

No. 9** (facing f. 9). Two poems by 'Abdu'l-Aḥad of Zanján. These are followed by a Bábí talisman (هيكل) received from Ṣubḥ-i-Azal about Aug. 29, 1891.

No. 10 (facing f. 9). From Ṣubḥ-i-Azal, dated Rabí' II, A.H. 1309 (about Nov. 17, 1891).

No. 10* (facing f. 9). From 'Abdu'l-Aḥad of Zanján, dated 7 Rabí' II, A.H. 1309 (Nov. 10, 1891).

No. 11. A letter from Ṣubḥ-i-Azal, of which only the addressed envelope is preserved in this volume. It was received on Feb. 12, 1892.

No. 11* (facing f. 9). From Ṣubḥ-i-Azal, dated 11 Jumádà II, A.H. 1309, posted Jan. 25, 1892.

No. 12 (facing f. 9). From Ṣubḥ-i-Azal, dated 13 Sha'bán, A.H. 1309, posted March 15, 1892. Accompanying it is an unnumbered letter, enclosed in a letter of August 17, 1891, from Captain Arthur Young, concerning the escape or departure of 'Abdu'l-Ghaffár, the Bahá'í, from Cyprus.

No. 13 (facing f. 10). From Ṣubḥ-i-Azal, identifying the five Gobineau Bábí MSS. in the Bibliothèque Nationale at Paris, received May 31, 1892.

No. 14. This number refers to the three following letters.

No. 14* (facing f. 9). From Rúḥu'lláh, Ṣubḥ-i-Azal's nephew, received June 17, 1896.

No. 14** (facing f. 10). From 'Abdu'l-'Alí, dated June 5, 1896. It is accompanied by a letter from C. D. Cobham, stating that 'Abdu'l-'Alí died at Varoshia, a suburb of Famagusta, in Sept. 1902.

No. 14*** (facing f. 10). From 'Abdu'l-Aḥad of Zanján, received June 17, 1896.

No. 15 (facing f. 10). From Ṣubḥ-i-Azal's son, Riẓwán 'Alí, received June 17, 1896.

No. 16 (facing f. 10). From Maḥmúd ibn Muḥammad Ja'far Kirmání, brother of the Shaykh Aḥmad Rúḥí of Kirmán who was put to death at Tabríz in the summer of 1896 (see *Persian Revolution*, pp. 93–96). Written on Muḥarram 25, A.H. 1314 (July 6, 1896). Professor Browne has added an abstract of the contents in English.

II. Letters from 'Abbás Efendi ('Abdu'l-Bahá), the other three sons of Bahá'u'lláh, and several well-known Bahá'ís.

No. 1 (facing f. 11). From Bahá'u'lláh's son, Mírzá Ẓiyá'u'lláh, dated 10 Shawwál, A.H. 1307 (May 30, 1890).

No. 1* (facing f. 11). Covering letter from Áqá Muḥammad 'Alí Yazdí, the Bábí agent at Alexandria, dated 12 Shawwál, A.H. 1307.

No. 2 (facing f. 11). From Bahá'u'lláh's son, Mírzá Badí'u'lláh, dated 22 Shawwál, A.H. 1307 (June 11, 1890).

No. 2* (facing f. 11). Covering letter from Áqá Muḥammad 'Alí, dated June 21, 1890.

No. 3 (facing f. 12). From 'Abbás Efendi, received Aug. 20, 1890.

No. 3* (facing f. 12). Covering letter from Áqá Muḥammad 'Alí, dated 26 Dhu'l-Ḥijja, A.H. 1307 (Aug. 12, 1890).

No. 4[1] (facing f. 13). From Mírzá Badí'u'lláh, answers to questions arising out of the text of the *Traveller's Narrative*, written Aug. 20, 1890.

No. 4[2] (facing f. 13). From Mírzá Badí'u'lláh.

No. 4* (facing f. 13). Covering letter from Áqá Muḥammad 'Alí, dated 10 Muḥarram, A.H. 1308 (Aug. 25, 1890).

No. 5* (facing f. 14). From Ḥájjí Sayyid 'Alí Shírází, written from Beyrout on 4 Muḥarram, A.H. 1308 (Aug. 20, 1890).

No. 6 (facing f. 14). From Mírzá Ẓiyá'u'lláh, dated 19 Muḥarram, A.H. 1308 (Sept. 3, 1890).

No. 6* (facing f. 14). Covering letter from Áqá Muḥammad 'Alí, dated 25 Muḥarram, A.H. 1308 (Sept. 9, 1890).

No. 7 (facing f. 15). From Mírzá Badí'u'lláh, dated 18 Ṣafar, A.H. 1308 (Oct. 2, 1890).

No. 7* (facing f. 15). Covering letter from Áqá Muḥammad 'Alí, dated 30 Ṣafar, A.H. 1308 (Oct. 14, 1890).

No. 7** (facing f. 15). Covering letter from Áqá Muḥammad 'Alí, dated 5 Rabí' I, A.H. 1308 (Oct. 19, 1890).

No. 7*** (facing f. 15). From Ḥájjí Sayyid 'Alí Shírází, dated 29 Ṣafar, A.H. 1308 (Oct. 13, 1890).

No. 8 (facing f. 16). From Mírzá Badí'u'lláh, dated 15 Rabí' I, A.H. 1308 (Oct. 29, 1890).

No. 8* (facing f. 16). Covering letter from Áqá Muḥammad 'Alí, dated 24 Rabí' II, A.H. 1308 (Dec. 6, 1890).

No. 9* (facing f. 16). From the same, dated 20 Rabí' II, A.H. 1308 (Dec. 2, 1890).

No. 10 (facing f. 17). From 'Abbás Efendi, dated April 3, 1891.

No. 10* (facing f. 16). Covering letter from Áqá Muḥammad 'Alí, dated 28 Sha'bán, A.H. 1308 (April 7, 1891).

No. 11 (facing f. 16). From Mírzá Badí'u'lláh, with a pair of gold spectacles. Dated 17 Dhu'l-Ḥijja, A.H. 1308 (July 25, 1891).

No. 11* (facing f. 17). From Áqá Muḥammad 'Alí, dated 21 Dhu'l-Ḥijja, A.H. 1308 (July 29, 1891).

No. 12 (facing f. 20). Letter from 'Abbás Efendi, dated Aug. 19, 1891, containing an account of the persecution of Bábís at Yazd in Ramaḍán, A.H. 1308.

No. 12 *sic* (facing f. 20). An account of the same persecution written on Aug. 21, 1891, by Mírzá Badí'u'lláh.

No. 12* (facing f. 17). From Áqá Muḥammad 'Alí, dated 19 Muḥarram, A.H. 1309 (Aug. 24, 1891).

No. 12** (facing f. 18). Account of persecution of Bábís at Yazd on 23 Ramaḍán, A.H. 1308 and following days, by Áqá Muḥammad 'Alí Yazdí. Enclosed in the preceding letter.

No. 13 (facing f. 18). From Ḥájjí Sayyid 'Alí concerning publication of the facts of the Yazd persecution. Written from 'Ishqábád on 23 Dhu'l-Ḥijja, A.H. 1308 (July 30, 1891).

No. 13* (facing f. 18). From Áqá Muḥammad 'Alí, dated 5 Ṣafar, A.H. 1309 (Sept. 8, 1891).

No. 14 (facing f. 19). From Áqá Muḥammad 'Alí, dated 21 Jumádà I, A.H. 1309 (Dec. 23, 1891).

No. 15 (facing f. 20). From Mírzá Badí'u'lláh, dated 18 Rajab, A.H. 1309 (Feb. 17, 1892).

No. 15* (facing f. 22). From Áqá Muḥammad 'Alí, dated 23 Rajab, A.H. 1309 (Feb. 22, 1892).

No. 16 (facing f. 22). From the same, dated 28 Ramaḍán, A.H. 1309 (April 25, 1892).

No. 17 (facing f. 22). From the same, dated 14 Shawwál, A.H. 1309 (May 11, 1892).

No. 18 (facing f. 22). From Mírzá Badí'u'lláh, dated 29 Dhu'l-Qa'da, A.H. 1309 (June 25, 1892).

No. 18* (facing f. 22). From Áqá Muḥammad 'Alí, dated June 28, 1892.

No. 19 (facing f. 23). From 'Abbás Efendi, dated March 24, 1893.

No. 19* (facing f. 23). From Áqá Muḥammad 'Alí, dated 3 Shawwál, A.H. 1310 (April 20, 1893).

No. 19^A (facing f. 23). From 'Abbás Efendi, dated Feb. 1, 1901.

No. 19^A* (facing f. 23). From Áqá Muḥammad 'Alí, dated Feb. 3, 1901.

No. 19^B (facing f. 24). From 'Abbás Efendi, dated April 8, 1901.

No. 19^B* (facing f. 25). From Ḥájjí Muḥammad ['Alí] Yazdí, dated April 18, 1901. The writer is the Bahá'í agent at Alexandria, described in the preceding letters as Áqá Muḥammad 'Alí Yazdí.

No. 20 (facing f. 28). From 'Abbás Efendi. Not dated, received about Xmas, 1903.

No. 20* (facing f. 29). From the Bahá'í agent Aḥmad Yazdí, dated Port Said, Dec. 16, 1903.

No. 21 (facing f. 29). From the same, dated June 20, 1904.

No. 21* (facing f. 29). From the same, dated Port Said, Jan. 26, 1904.

The remaining Persian letters are not numbered. They comprise:

1 (ff. 19 and 21). Three letters from 'Azízu'lláh, a Jew of Bukhárá, written in 1892.

2 (facing f. 25). Letter from Bahá'u'lláh's son, Mírzá Muḥammad 'Alí, dated April 3, 1901, together with a covering letter from Muḥammad Jawád, written at 'Akká and dated April 4, 1901.

3 (facing f. 25). Letter from Muḥammad Jawád, written at 'Akká on July 28, 1901.

4 (facing f. 25). Letter from Ghulámu'lláh of Qazwín, son of Muḥammad Jawád, dated March 19, 1901.

5 (facing f. 26). Letter from Muḥammad Jawád, dated Sept. 7, 1901.

6 (facing f. 26). Letter from Ghulámu'lláh of Qazwín to Sir E. Denison Ross, dated April 10, 1901.

7 (facing f. 26). Letter from Muḥammad Jawád, dated 'Akká, Oct. 14, 1901.

8 (facing f. 27). From the same, dated April 14, 1902.

9 (facing f. 27). From the same, dated July 5, 1902.

10 (facing f. 27). From Ḥájjí Sayyid 'Alí "Afnán," dated 'Akká, July 2, 1902.

11 (facing f. 28). From Ghulámu'lláh of Qazwín, dated Aug. 17, 1902.

12 (facing f. 28). From Muḥammad Jawád, dated 'Akká, Oct. 22, 1902.

13 (facing f. 28). "? Letter (undated) from 'Abbás Efendi, to ? 'Azízu'lláh, a Jew of Bukhárá, who sent it to me about July, 1892."

14 (facing f. 28). From Ghulámu'lláh of Qazwín, dated Nov. 22, 1902.

15 (facing f. 29). From Mírzá Badí'u'lláh, dated Sept. 25, 1909.

16 (facing f. 30). From Mírzá Asadu'lláh, dated Chicago, April 21, 1902, and accompanied by a *Lawḥ* or "Tablet" of Bahá'u'lláh's which was sent by Mírzá Asadu'lláh on the same date.

17 (facing f. 30). From Ghulámu'lláh of Qazwín, dated Aug. 10, 1902.

18 (facing f. 31). Manifesto, dated Feb. 4, 1903, of Ḥájjí Mírzá Sayyid 'Alí "Afnán" renouncing his allegiance to the "Náqiḍín," or adherents of Mírzá Muḥammad 'Alí, and declaring his adhesion to 'Abbás Efendi ('Abdu'l-Bahá).

19 (facing f. 31). Manifesto, dated Feb. 4, 1903, of Mírzá Badí'u'lláh, renouncing his allegiance to his brother Mírzá Muḥammad 'Alí and declaring his adhesion to 'Abbás Efendi.

20 (facing f. 31). From Ghulámu'lláh of Qazwín, dated Nov. 11, 1902.

21 (facing f. 31). From Mírzá Badí'u'lláh, dated March 11, 1903, announcing his renunciation of his brother Muḥammad 'Alí and his adhesion to 'Abbás Efendi. (Marked "Important.")

22 (facing f. 31). From 'Abbás Efendi, about March 28, 1903, forwarded by Ḥájjí Sayyid Muḥammad Taqí Minshádí.

23 (facing f. 32). Two letters, dated March 28 and April 1, 1903, from Sayyid Muḥammad Taqí Minshádí.

24 (facing f. 33). Two letters from 'Abdu'l-Bahá, dated Sept. 7, 1911, and Feb. 9, 1913, the latter written from Paris.

25 (facing f. 34). From 'Abdu'l-Bahá, Sept. or Oct. 1911.

26 (facing f. 34). From Mírzá Asadu'lláh, dated March 22, 1902.

27 (facing f. 35). From Ḥájjí Mírzá Ḥusayn Shírází, dated Bombay, March 16, 1896.

28 (facing f. 36). Letter of Baḥru'l-'Ulúm of Kirmán to the Azalís, received from Mírzá Muṣṭafá, the Bábí scribe, about June 3, 1913.

29 (facing f. 37). From Bahá'u'lláh's eldest son, Muḥammad 'Alí, written from 'Akká on Sept. 2, 1922.

G. GENERAL HISTORY.

G. 1[1], G. 1[2] (10).

فتوح ابن اعثم كوفى

Two volumes, equal in size but in different handwritings, of the Persian translation made about the end of the sixth century of the Muḥammadan (twelfth of the Christian) era by Muḥammad b. Aḥmad b. Abí Naṣr b. Aḥmad al-Mustawfí, entitled al-Raḍí al-Kúfí, of the *Futúḥ* or *Ta'ríkh* of Ibn A'tham of Kúfa. The Arabic original, if it ever existed, has hitherto eluded discovery, but is supposed to have been written before 314/926–7. See Rieu's *B.M.P.C.*, pp. 151–152; F. Wüstenfeld's *Geschichtschreiber der Araber*, No. 541 (p. 253); Brockelmann, vol. 1, p. 516.

G. 1[1], defective both at beginning and end, comprises 250 ff. of 25 × 18 c. and 17 ll., good, clear *naskh*, not dated. Probably only f. 1 is missing at the beginning, for what is now the first leaf begins with the concluding words of the doxology, which are followed in l. 3 by the translator's name:

محمّد بن احمد بن ابى نصر بن احمد المستوفى الملقّب الرّضى الكاتب ميگويد...

This volume ends with the murder of 'Uthmán the third Caliph and the brutal treatment of his wife Ná'ila by his murderers.

G. 1[2], written in a fair *nasta'líq* and dated the end of Muḥarram, 924/Feb. 11, 1518, begins after the murder of 'Uthmán with the words:

چون عثمانرا بكشتند مردمان پياپى بخدمت امير المؤمنين على عليه السلام آمدند الخ

and ends with the death of al-Ḥusayn b. 'Alí at Karbalá and what befell his family at the hands of Yazíd. Ff. 188 of 24·5 × 18 c. and 20 ll.

Both volumes were bought by me from the late Ḥájjí 'Abdu'l-Majíd Belshah in 1920.

G. 2 (9).

كتاب الجمان فى اخبار الزّمان

A general history in three sections (*faṣl*) entitled *Kitábu'l-Jumán fí Akhbári'z-Zamán*, ascribed in this MS. to Shaykh Shihábu'd-Dín Aḥmad al-Maghribí al-Fásí, but in Rieu's Arabic Supplement (p. 290, **No. 482**) to Abú 'Abdi'lláh Muḥammad ibn 'Alí...ash-Sháṭibí. Another MS. of the work (not mentioned by Wüstenfeld or Brockelmann) described by Rieu (pp. 318–319, **No. 518, 1**) begins with the same short doxology as the present MS., carries the history of the Caliphate and of the Moors in Spain down to about 667/1268–9, and concludes with an account of the End of the World and the Resurrection.

Ff. 334 of 20·5 × 14·4 c. and 18 ll.; good Maghribí hand with rubrications; transcription completed on Dhu'l-Qa'da 27, 1148/April 9, 1736. From the Belshah collection, 1920.

G. 3 (10).

تجارب السّلف (ترجمهٔ کتاب الفخری)

A Persian version, enriched with much additional matter, especially in the later part, of the Arabic history of the Caliphate commonly known as the *Kitábu'l-Fakhrí*, but here entitled (f. 2[b]) *Munyatu'l-Fuḍalá fí tawáríkhi'l-Khulafá wa'l-Wuzará*. The original work was written by Ṣafiyyu'd-Dín Muḥammad b. 'Alí al-'Alawí aṭ-Ṭiqṭaqá for the library of his lord and patron Jalálu'd-Dín Zangí Sháh ibn Badri'd-Dín Ḥasan ibn Aḥmad of Dámghán. This Persian version was made in 724/1324 by Hindúsháh ibn Sanjar ibn 'Abdi'lláh aṣ-Ṣáḥibí al-Kírání for the Atábek Nuṣratu'd-Dín Yúsuf Sháh ibn Shamsi'd-Dín Alp-Arghún ibn Malik Naṣri'd-Dín Hazárasp, who ruled over Luristán from 696/1296 to 733/1333. The only other known MS. of the Persian version appears to be **Suppl. Pers. 1552** (= **Schefer 237**) of the Bibliothèque Nationale in Paris. See E. Blochet's Catalogue (Paris, 1905), vol. I, p. 251, No. 373.

My MS., bought in January, 1920, from the late Ḥájjí 'Abdu'l-Majíd Belshah, comprises 190 ff. of 22·7 × 16 c. and 19 ll., was transcribed in 1286/1870 in a small, clear, modern *naskh* with rubrications, and contains about 108,000 words. For a fuller description, see my article in the Centenary Volume published by the Royal Asiatic Society in 1924, pp. 21–30.

G. 4 (11).

تأریخ گزیدهٔ حمد اللّه مستوفی قزوینی،

The original of the facsimile edition of the *Ta'ríkh-i-Guzída* published, with an abridged English version by myself, in the "E. J. W. Gibb Memorial" Series (vol. XIV, 1 and XIV, 2, 1910 and 1913). This fine MS., of which the first two pages are particularly beautiful and richly illuminated, was transcribed in 857/1453, and is from the library of the late Prince Farhád Mírzá *Mu'tamadu'd-Dawla*, who has added marginal annotations in several places. It was purchased by me from Ḥájjí Mírzá 'Abdu'l-Ḥusayn Khán of Káshán, entitled *Waḥídu'l-Mulk*, for £50 in the summer of 1907. The work, which is well-known, and is described by Rieu in his Persian Catalogue (pp. 80–81), was composed in 730/1330 by Ḥamdu'lláh Mustawfí of Qazwín. Besides my abridged English translation of the whole, mentioned above, the text of ch. IV, dealing with the Muḥammadan dynasties of Persia, was edited with a French translation by M. Jules Gantin in 1903; while a French translation of the sixth and last chapter, treating of the city of Qazwín, was published by the late M. Barbier de Meynard in the *Journal Asiatique* for 1857 (Série v, tome 10); and in the *J.R.A.S.* for Oct. 1900 and Jan. 1901 I published an English translation of that part of the work (ch. v, section 6, second half) which treats of the Persian poets.

For further particulars of this history and this manuscript of it, see the English Preface and Table of Contents of the above-mentioned facsimile, pp. xi–xix.

G. 5 (12).

تأريخ گزيده،

Another MS. of the *Ta'ríkh-i-Guzída* given to me in January, 1917, by Mr G. le Strange, who bought it from the late Mr Sidney Churchill for £10 in 1909. A modern, but very carefully and neatly written MS. dated in the colophon 23 Muḥarram, 1293 (Feb. 19, 1876). It contains the additional chapter on the Muẓaffarí dynasty (ff. 104^b–128^a = "E. J. W. Gibb Memorial" Series, XIV, 1, pp. 613–755, and XIV, 2, pp. 151–207).

Ff. 158 of 28·5 × 17·3 c. and 31 ll.; small, neat *nasta'líq* with rubrications and numerous marginal notes in a minute hand, which, however, cease a little before f. 80.

G. 6 (10).

روضة اولی الالباب لفخر الدّين البناكتی،

The *Rawḍatu'l-Albáb*, a well-known historical manual composed in 717/1317 by Fakhru'd-Dín-i-Banákatí. See Rieu's Persian Catalogue, pp. 79–80.

This MS., which is defective both at beginning and end, formerly belonged to Prince Bahman Mírzá (died at Ṭihrán in Rabí' II, 1277 = Oct.–Nov. 1860) and afterwards, in 1282/1866, to Prince Farhád Mírzá. It afterwards formed part of the library of the late Sir A. Houtum-Schindler, purchased by me in January, 1917. It is written in an ugly but legible *ta'líq*, and comprises 185 ff. of 23 × 15 c. and 21 ll., and appears to have been transcribed in Shíráz in 1272/1855–6.

G. 7 (10) and G. 8 (10).

مُجمل فصيحى خوافى

Two MSS. of that rare and valuable Persian chronicle entitled the *Mujmal*, or "Compendium," concerning which see my *Persian Literature under Tartar Dominion*, pp. 426–428, and my article in the number of the *Muséon* brought out by the Belgian professors of Oriental Languages, temporarily resident in Cambridge in 1915, at the University Press. So far as I know, only three MSS. of this work exist, *viz.* the two now in my library[1], and a third in the *Institute des Langues Orientales du Ministère des Affaires Étrangères de St Pétersbourg* described by Dorn and Baron Victor Rosen.

The author, Faṣíḥí of Khwáf, is said by Baron Rosen to have been born in 777/1375–6, and spent most of his life in the service of Sháhrukh, for whose use he compiled and to whom he presented this book in 845/1442. It consists of an *Introduction*, containing a sketch of the history of the world from the Creation to the birth of the Prophet Muḥammad; two *Discourses*, of which the first continues the history down to the Flight (*Hijra*) of the Prophet from Mecca to al-Madína, and the second the history of the period after the Flight down to 845/1442; and a conclusion (missing in all three copies) containing a monograph on Herát, the author's birthplace and home. The second Discourse constitutes by far the largest and most important part of the book, which is chiefly remarkable for the large amount of literary history which it contains.

Both the MSS. in my possession are defective, the Raverty MS. (**G. 7**) lacking the years A.H. 718–840 (A.D. 1318–1437), and the Schindler MS. (**G. 8**) the years 834–844 (A.D. 1430–1440).

The Raverty MS. (**G. 7**) was bought in A.D. 1907 from the widow of Colonel Raverty by the Trustees of the "E. J. W. Gibb Memorial Fund" (to whom it really belongs) for £18, together with two other MSS., one of the *Haft Iqlím*[2], and one of part of the *Jámi'u't-Tawáríkh*, each for £6. It comprises 506 ff. of 23·8 × 14·5 c. and 17 ll., and is written in a fine, bold *naskh*, apparently of the fifteenth century, with rubrications and marginal captions, which greatly facilitate reference. The Introduction (*Muqaddama*) occupies ff. 6ᵇ–25ᵃ; the first Discourse (*Maqála*) ff. 25ᵇ–40ᵇ, and the second Discourse the remainder of the volume (ff. 41ᵃ–506ᵇ). There is no colophon, and the book is a good deal wormed.

---

[1] [The Raverty MS., bearing the class-mark **G. 7** in this Catalogue, is now preserved, together with the MSS. and photographic facsimiles belonging to the Trustees of the "E. J. W. Gibb Memorial Fund," in the Library of the School of Oriental Studies, University of London.]

[2] [Numbered **K. 4** in the present Catalogue. It was returned in June, 1927, to the India Office Library, from which, either directly or indirectly, it must have come into the hands of Colonel Raverty before its purchase by the Trustees of the "E. J. W. Gibb Memorial Fund."]

The Schindler MS. (**G. 8**) was presented to me on July 7, 1913, by Mr G. le Strange, who had bought it from Sir A. Houtum-Schindler a few days previously. Though defective at the beginning, it is a much more complete, though more modern, copy than **G. 7.** It comprises 511 written leaves of 21·8 × 14·8 c. and 20 ll., and is written in a good, clear modern *naskh* with rubrications and marginal captions.

For description of the St Petersburg Codex see B. Dorn at the beginning of the second volume of the *Bulletin de la Classe historico-philologique de l'Académie Impériale des Sciences de St Pétersbourg*, and Baron Victor Rosen in the third volume of his *Collections Scientifiques* (1866), **No. 271**, pp. 111–113. In this MS. the Introduction (defective at the beginning) occupies ff. 10^a–33^b (the preceding leaves being blank); the first Discourse ff. 34^a–35^b; and the second Discourse the remainder (ff. 36^a–507^a) of the volume. One of the last events recorded is the death of "God's Physician" (*Ṭabíbu'lláh*) Sayyid Ni'matu'lláh on Thursday, Rajab 22, 844 (December 17, 1440). This is followed by five blank pages, presumably corresponding to a lacuna in the original, after which come four pages chiefly containing the necrology of the year A.H. 845 (A.D. 1441–2).

G. 9 (12).

زُبْدة التواريخ تأليف حافظ ابرو،

The second of the four volumes of Ḥáfiẓ Abrú's great history compiled in 828/1425. This fine manuscript was completed on Friday, 15 Sha'bán, 829 (June 22, 1426) during the lifetime of the author, who died, according to the *Mujmal* of Faṣíḥí, on Sunday, 3 Shawwál, 833 (June 25, 1430). It is written throughout in a clear, good *naskh* hand with rubrications, comprises 484 ff. of 31 × 22 c. and 29 ll., and contains the life of the Prophet Muḥammad and the history of the Caliphate. Ff. 1–53^a deal with the period before the Flight (*Hijra*); the account of the Four Orthodox Caliphs begins on f. 114^b; that of the Umayyads on f. 177^b, and that of the 'Abbásids on f. 271^a.

Concerning Ḥáfiẓ Abrú and his work, see Rieu's Persian Catalogue, pp. 421–424, and his Persian Supplement, p. 16, and for a much fuller and more detailed discussion of this rare and important history, of which only the first half (vols. I and II) appears to be extant, Baron Victor Rosen's *Collections Scientifiques*, vol. III, *Manuscrits persans* (St Petersburg, 1866), pp. 52–111.

G. 10 (13).

نسخ جهان‌آرای للقاضی احمد الغفّاری

An incomplete copy, ending with the year 927/1521, of the *Nusakh-i-Jahán-áráy*, a general history from the earliest times to 972/1564–5, by the Qáḍí Aḥmad ibn Muḥammad, author of the better-known *Nigáristán*. See Rieu's Persian Catalogue, pp. 111–115.

Ff. 113 of 31·8×19·6 c. and 25 ll.; written in a fairly legible but ungraceful *nasta'líq* with rubrications; conclusion and colophon missing. From the library of the late Sir A. Houtum-Schindler.

G. 11 (12).

(۱) خاتمهٔ روضة الصّفا، (۲) عجائب الأشیا،

A manuscript of 72 ff. of 27·4×19·2 c. and 25 ll.; written in a clear modern *naskh* with rubrications, and containing:

(1) The *Khátima* or Conclusion (Book VIII) of Mírkhwánd's *Rawḍatu'ṣ-Ṣafá*, treating of geography and biography (ff. 3ᵇ–44ᵃ). See Rieu's Persian Catalogue, p. 93.

(2) The *'Ajá'ibu'l-Ashyá* (or *—u'd-Dunyá*), "Wonderful Things," or "Wonders of the World," by Abu'l-Mu'ayyad Abú Muṭí'al-Balkhí (ff. 44ᵇ–72ᵇ), who wrote it for Abu'l-Qásim Núḥ ibn Manṣúr the Sámání (reigned over Khurásán from 366/976 until 387/996–7). The text before us must, however, be a much later translation of an Arabic or recension of a Persian original, for on f. 46ᵇ, l. 9, occurs the following passage:

حکایت، در سنه ثلاث و عشر و ستّمائة که من بنده در سفر حجاز بودم بکنار دریای مصر رسیدم و از آن جماعت که آنجا مقیم اند پرسیدم که عجایب دریا چیست، گفتند که سنگ این دریا شکل خرچنگ دارد بزرگ و کوچك چنانکه گویا خرچنگ بوده است که بسنگ شده و آنرا سرطان بحری گویند و در داروهای چشم بکار برند و عظیم سودمند است،

"*Anecdote*.—In the year 613/1216–7 when I was travelling to the Ḥijáz I arrived at the shore of the Egyptian Sea, and enquired of the people who abode there what were the marvels of the Sea. They answered, 'The stones of this sea have the shape of crabs, great and small, so that one would say that they were crabs which had become stone.' These they call 'marine crabs,' and they use them in eye-salves, where they are mighty useful."

The work consists entirely of short anecdotes like this, preceded by the following brief introduction:

رسالهٔ عجایب الاشیاء من کلام ابو مطیع البلخی رحمة الله علیه،
بسم الله الرّحمن الرّحیم وبه نستعین،

چنین گوید ابو المؤیّد ابو مطیع بلخی رحمة الله علیه که مرا از طفلی هوس گردیدن عالم در سر افتاده بود و از مردم تجّار و اهل بحث عجایبها شنیدم و آنچه در کتب خواندم جمله بنوشتم و جمع کردم و از بهر پادشاه جهان امیر خراسان ملك مشرف ابو القسم نوح بن منصور مولی امیر المؤمنین تا اورا از آن مطالعه مؤانست بود و حقّ نعمت اورا گذارده باشم که بر من و عالمیان واجب است میسّر باد، آغاز کتاب، چنین گوید ابو مطیع بلخی که در هندوستان درختیست الخ

The anecdotes refer to India, Andalusia, Rúm (Asia Minor), Syria, Ṭabaristán, Bukhárá, Turkistán, Yaman, Nubia, Daylam, Khurásán, Niháwand, Ádharbayján, Samarqand, China, Egypt, Sístán, Kísh (Persian Gulf), the China Sea, etc. It is worth noting that on f. 68ᵃ occurs a quotation from the *Firdawsu'l-Ḥikmat* of 'Alí b. Rabban aṭ-Ṭabarí, of which the Arabic original has been found by Mr M. Z. Ṣiddíqí, formerly Government of India Research Student in the University of Cambridge, on f. 241ᵃ of the British Museum MS. of this work.

G. 12 (12).

طبقات محمودشاهی (تأریخ صدر جهان)

The *Ṭabaqát-i-Maḥmúd-sháhí*, or *Ta'ríkh-i-Ṣadr-i-Jahán*, a general history from the earliest times down to 838/1434–5 by Fayḍu'lláh ibn Zayni'l-'Ábidín ibn Ḥusám, entitled *Maliku'l-Quḍát Ṣadr-i-Jahán*, compiled about 907/1501–2. See Rieu's Persian Catalogue, pp. 86–87, 885ᵃ, and 1079.

Ff. 550 of 27 × 17 c. and 21 ll., written in legible *ta'líq* with rubrications, incomplete at both beginning and end and lacking colophon and date.

The first half of the work is historical, the second biographical. There appear to be some dislocations, but the principal contents are as follows:

The Prophets and Patriarchs, from Adam to Jesus Christ (ff. 1–30).
The Ancient Kings of Persia (ff. 31ᵃ–61ᵃ).
The *Tubba's* of Yaman (ff. 61ᵇ–70ᵃ).
The Prophet Muḥammad and the Imáms and Orthodox Caliphs (ff. 70ᵃ–170ᵃ).
The Umayyad Caliphs (ff. 170ᵇ–198ᵇ).
The 'Abbásid Caliphs (ff. 199ᵃ–231ᵇ).
The Post-Muḥammadan Dynasties of Persia, etc. (ff. 231ᵇ–306ᵃ).
The Mongols (ff. 306ᵃ–347ᵃ).
The Kings of Dihlí (ff. 347ᵇ–396ᵃ).

The Poets, Arabian and Persian (ff. 396ᵇ–421ᵃ). The particulars concerning the Persian poets are largely derived from the *Chahár Maqála* of Niẓámí-i-'Arúḍí-i-Samarqandí.

The Companions (f. 421ᵇ) and Followers (f. 439ᵇ).

Pious and Learned Men (f. 454ᵇ).

Notable Women (f. 527ᵃ).

Notable Ministers (f. 530ᵇ).

G. 13 (12).

احسن القصص و دافع الغصص،

The *Aḥsanu'l-Qiṣaṣ wa-Dáfi'u'l-Ghuṣaṣ*, an abridgement of the *Ta'ríkh-i-Alfí* (*i.e.* "the Millennial History," or history of the thousand years succeeding the Flight of the Prophet from Mecca to al-Madína) made in 1248/1832–3 by Aḥmad ibn Abi'l-Fatḥ ash-Sharíf al-Ḥárí al-Iṣfahání. Concerning the *Ta'ríkh-i-Alfí*, see Rieu's Persian Catalogue, pp. 117–119, where mention is made of the present abridgement with a reference to the *Mélanges Asiatiques*, vol. VI, p. 121.

Pp. 534 of 28·4 × 17 c. and 19 ll.; fair *ta'líq* with rubrications; the last few pages much discoloured by damp; no date or colophon. The year 994/1586 appears to be the last mentioned.

Begins:

بسم الله والحمد لله تعالی،

بیا و بنگر اگر چشم خوردبین داری، که سنگریزهٔ بطحا عقیق و مرجان است، العبد الراجی احمد بن ابو الفتح الشریف الحاری الاصفهانی معروض میدارد که در هنگام کتابت کتاب تاریخ الفی که جامع جمیع تواریخ و وقایع سلاطین ذوی الاقتدار از زمان اتّفاق امّت در سقیفه الی یکهزار سال آنچه در اسلام بعد از رحلت حضرت خیر البشر صلوات الله علیه وآله واقع شده از حادثات و سیر خلفاء ثلاثه و خلافت جناب امیر المؤمنین علیه السّلام و بنی اُمیّه چهارده نفر در هزار ماه و بنی عبّاس سی و هفت نفر در پانصد و بیست و چهار سال و بقولی مطابق لفظ شرك و حُکّام طاهریّه و سلاطین سامانیّه و صفّاریّه و غزنویّه و آل بویه و سلجوقیّه و خلفاء اسمعیلیّهٔ مصر و دُعاة ایشان در عراق و غیره و خوارزمشاهیّه و ملوك غور و سلاطین هند و چنگیزخانی که در اطراف عالم نسلاً بعد نسلٍ سلطنت کردند الخ

The author continues the enumeration of the dynasties down to the rise of the Ṣafawís in Persia in 906/1500–1 and their establishment of the Shí'a doctrine in that country according to the chronogram مذهبنا حق, "Our doctrine is true," and of the Tímúrid (or "Moghul") dynasty in India down to the time of Akbar. Of the sources used for the compilation of the *Ta'ríkh-i-Alfí* or "Millennial History" (so called because it was compiled in 1000/1591–2) he mentions the works of ad-Dínawarí, Ibn Khallikán, Shaykh Khúrí, Ibn A'tham al-Kúfí, al-Yáfi'í, Ḥáfiẓ Abrú, and al-Mas'údí, the *Rawḍatu'ṣ-Ṣafá* of Mírkhwánd, the *Maṭla'u's-sa'dayn*, and other special histories of Egypt, Baghdád, Turkey (*Rúm*), India, Persia and Turkistán. Having made numerous copies of the *Ta'ríkh-i-Alfí*, an enormous compilation comprising 180,000 *bayts*, the author of the present compendium in the year 1248/1832–3[1] resolved to extract from it the most instructive and entertaining portions and narrate them in a simple and agreeable style for the benefit of those who found the original too long and wearisome, and to give to this compendium the title of *Aḥsanu'l-qiṣaṣ wa-Dáfi'u'l-Ghuṣaṣ* ("the Best of Stories and Dispeller of Sorrows").

The period preceding the fall of the 'Abbásid Caliphate occupies a much greater space (to p. 380) than the later period, the account of the Ṣafawí dynasty only beginning on p. 515, and Bábur's conquest of India on p. 524. The latest date mentioned is 994/1586, the year in which died the Turkish Sulṭán Sulaymán "the Magnificent." The work ends somewhat abruptly:

در وصفش همین بس که مزیّن شد بنام نامی و القاب گرامی بخشید،

There is no colophon.

G. 14[1-5] (15).

خُلْد برین،

An enormous general history bound in five volumes, but really consisting of eight, each entitled *Rawḍa* ("Garden"), composed by Muḥammad Yúsuf in 1078/1667–8 in the reign of Sháh Sulaymán the Ṣafawí, and entitled *Khuld-i-Barín* ("High Heaven"). Two incomplete MSS. are described by Rieu in his Persian Supplement, pp. 22–24, **Nos. 34** and **35**, but no other complete copy appears to exist. The first four volumes (*Rawḍas i–vii*) were transcribed in 1271–2/1854–5 for Prince Bahman Mírzá *Bahá'u'd-Dawla* by Áqá Bábá Sháhmírzádí son of Mullá Muḥammad Mahdí; the fifth and last volume (*Rawḍa viii*, containing the years A.H. 1037–1071 = A.D. 1627–1660–1) is in a different and poorer hand, and was copied in Jumádà II, 1236 (March, 1821). Vols. I, II and III contain two *Rawḍas* each, and treat of the history of Islám, and especially of Persia, before the rise of the Ṣafawí dynasty. Vol. IV (= *Rawḍa vii*) contains the history of the Ṣafawís down to the death of Sháh 'Abbás the Great in 1037/1627–8, and vol. V (= *Rawḍa viii*) their subsequent history almost down to the date of composition.

[1] He must, however, have begun the work before this date, for on p. 404 he mentions 1244/1828–9 as the current date.

The author mentions his name in vol. I, f. 2^a, l. 13, and the title of his work on f. 2^b, l. 5. The contents are then described as follows:

Introduction (*Iftitáḥ*). On the first created beings, the Banu'l-Jánn, and how Iblís obtained sovereignty over them.

Rawḍa i. Account of pre-Islámic Prophets and Kings.

Rawḍa ii. History of the Prophet Muḥammad and the Twelve Imáms.

Rawḍa iii. History of the Umayyad and 'Abbásid Caliphs, described as the "Usurpers of the office of the Caliphate and Imámate."

Rawḍa iv. History of the dynasties contemporary with the 'Abbásids.

Rawḍa v. History of Chingíz Khán and his successors.

Rawḍa vi. History of Tímúr and his successors.

Rawḍa vii. History of the Turkmán dynasties of the "Black Sheep" and the "White Sheep," and other successors of the Tímúrids.

Rawḍa viii. History of the Ṣafawí dynasty.

Conclusion (*Khátima*). History of the reigning King Sháh Sulaymán.

The contents and size of the five volumes are briefly as follows:

G. 14^1 (15).

Ff. 564 of 35·3 × 21·5 c. and 31 ll. *Introduction* (ff. 2^b–5^a):

Rawḍa i. (*a*) The Great Prophets (ff. 5^a–115^b); (*b*) pre-Islámic Kings (ff. 115^b–152^a). The history of Alexander the Great (ff. 132^b–135^a) is followed by accounts of the chief Greek philosophers, such as Pythagoras (f. 135^b), Socrates (f. 136^a), Diogenes and Plato (f. 137^a), Aristotle (f. 137^b), Hippocrates (f. 138^a), etc. *Rawḍa i* ends on f. 152^a with a colophon giving the scribe's name and the date 8 Rabí' II, 1271 (Dec. 29, 1854).

Rawḍa ii. The Prophet Muḥammad to his death in A.H. 11 (ff. 153^b–275^a); the "Usurpers" Abú Bakr (ff. 275^a–281^b), 'Umar (ff. 281^b–294^b); 'Uthmán (ff. 294^b–301^a); table of the "Fourteen Immaculate ones" (*i.e.* Muḥammad, Fáṭima, and the Twelve Imáms, ff. 301^b–302^a), giving in each case the name, ***kunya***, title, day, month and year of birth, reigning king, mother's name; inscription on signet-ring, number of wives and children, duration of life, date and cause of death, place of burial, etc.

The account of the Twelve Imáms, which constitutes the second part of *Rawḍa ii*, occupies the remainder of the volume, *viz.* (1) 'Alí (ff. 303^b–412^a); (2) al-Ḥasan (ff. 412^a–420^a); (3) al-Ḥusayn (ff. 420^a–493^b); (4) 'Alí Zaynu'l-'Ábidín (ff. 493^b–498^a); (5) Muḥammad al-Báqir (ff. 498^a–503^a); (6) Ja'far aṣ-Ṣádiq (ff. 503^a–509^b); (7) Músà Káẓim (ff. 509^b–516^b); (8) 'Alí ar-Riḍá (ff. 516^b–529^a); (9) Muḥammad at-Taqí (ff. 529^a–534^a); (10) 'Alí an-Naqí (ff. 534^a–539^a); (11) Ḥasan al-'Askarí (ff. 539^b–544^b); (12) the Imám Mahdí (ff. 544^b–563^b). The colophon at the bottom of this last page states that the transcription of this second *Rawḍa* was completed on the 27th of Muḥarram, 1271 (Oct. 20, 1854), by Áqá Bábá Sháhmírzádí ibn Mullá Muḥammad Mahdí for [Prince Bahman Mírzá] Bahá'u'd-Dawla.

G. 14² (15).

Ff. 287 of 35·2 × 22 c. and 31 ll.; good plain *naskh* with rubrications, copied by the same scribe as the volume last described for Prince Bahman Mírzá *Bahá'u'd-Dawla* in 1270/1854.

This second volume comprises *Rawḍa iii*, containing the history of the Umayyad and 'Abbásid Caliphs (ff. 2ᵃ–96ᵃ), and *Rawḍa iv*, containing the history of the post-Islámic Persian dynasties from the Ṭáhirids to the Muẓaffarids (ff. 99ᵇ–287ᵃ). There are several lacunae (*e.g.* at the beginning of *Rawḍa iii*) due to a defective original. The colophon at the end of *Rawḍa iii* (f. 96ᵃ) is dated 18 Shawwál, 1270 (14 July, 1854), and that at the end of *Rawḍa iv* (f. 287ᵃ) 14 Ramaḍán, 1270 (10 June, 1854).

The chief contents of the whole volume (both *Rawḍas*) are as follows:

Umayyad Caliphs, ff. 2–54.

'Abbásid Caliphs, ff. 54–96.

Ṭáhirids (ff. 99–101); Ṣaffárids (ff. 101–106); Sámánids (ff. 106–120); Ziyárids (ff. 120–122); Ghaznawís (ff. 122–138); Buwayhids (ff. 138–150); Ismá'ílís of the Maghrib and Egypt (ff. 150–157); —of Alamút (ff. 157–167); Saljúqs (ff. 167–198); (ff. 199–200) blank; Qará-Khitá'ís (ff. 218–221); Muẓaffarids (ff. 221–251); Atábeks (ff. 251–259); Ghúrids (ff. 259–270); Bámiyán branch of the same (ff. 270ᵇ–279ᵇ); Sarbadárís (ff. 279ᵇ–287).

G. 14³ (15).

Ff. 310 of 34·8 × 21·2 c. and 31 ll.; copied in 1270/1854 by the same scribe and in the same handwriting as the two preceding volumes.

This volume contains *Rawḍa v* (ff. 1ᵇ–134ᵃ) and *vi* (ff. 135ᵇ–291ᵇ) and the beginning of *vii* (ff. 292ᵇ–310ᵇ).

Rawḍa v contains the history of the Mongols and kindred peoples. The principal contents are: Ethnology of the Mongols and Turks, and ancestry and birth of Chingíz Khán (ff. 3ᵃ–9ᵃ); reign and conquests of Chingíz Khán (ff. 9ᵃ–28ᵇ); Jújí (ff. 28ᵇ–29ᵃ); Chaghatáy (ff. 29ᵃ–30ᵃ); Ogotáy (f. 30ᵃ); Túlí (f. 38ᵃ); Túrákíná Khátún (f. 38ᵇ); Kuyúk (f. 39ᵇ); Mangú (f. 39ᵇ); Qubiláy (f. 44ᵇ); Húlágú (f. 51ᵃ); Conquest of Baghdád (f. 52ᵇ); Abáqá (f. 62ᵇ); Aḥmad Khán Nikúdár (f. 72ᵇ); Arghún (f. 75ᵇ); Gaykhátú (f. 78ᵃ); Gházán (f. 82ᵇ); Uljáytú (f. 92ᵃ); Abú Sa'íd (f. 104ᵇ); Arpa (f. 118ᵃ); Músà (f. 119ᵇ); Ṭughá-tímúr (f. 120ᵃ); Ḥasan-i-Kúchak (f. 120ᵇ); Malik-i-Ashraf (f. 124ᵃ); Jání Beg (f. 126ᵃ); Sulṭán Uways (f. 127ᵃ); Ḥusayn b. Uways (f. 129ᵇ); Aḥmad b. Uways (f. 130ᵇ). Dated (on f. 134ᵃ), Rajab 4, 1270 (April 2, 1854).

Rawḍa vi contains the history of Tímúr and his successors down to Muḥammad Bábur and Sulṭán Ḥusayn b. Bayqará. The principal contents are: Genealogy and birth of Tímúr (f. 136^{a}); beginning of his reign (f. 148^{b}); birth of Sháhrukh (f. 153^{b}); massacre at Iṣfahán (f. 162^{b}); fate of the Muẓaffarid princes (f. 173^{a}); war with the Ottoman Sulṭán Báyazíd (f. 194^{a}); death of Tímúr (f. 213^{b}); Khalíl Sulṭán (f. 216^{a}); Tímúr's children (f. 216^{b}); Sháhrukh (f. 217^{a}); Ulugh Beg (f. 246^{b}); 'Abdu'l-Laṭíf (f. 253^{a}); Báysunghur (f. 254^{a}); 'Alá'u'd-Dawla (f. 255^{b}); Abu'l-Qásim Bábur (f. 261^{a}); Sulṭán Abú Sa'íd (f. 271^{b}); Muḥammad Bábur (f. 285^{b}); Sulṭán Ḥusayn b. Bayqará (f. 287^{b}); Amír 'Alí Shír (f. 290^{b}).

Rawḍa vii (ff. 292^{b}–310^{b}) contains an account of the "Black Sheep" (*Qará-qoyúnlú*) and "White Sheep" (*Áq-qoyúnlú*) Turkmán dynasties, the escape from captivity of the Ṣafawí princes (f. 305^{b}), and the Uzbek rulers (f. 309^{b}).

G. 14⁴ (15).

Ff. 500 of 33·8 × 20·5 c. and 31 ll.; this volume is in the same handwriting and by the same scribe as the preceding ones, and was copied in the same year, 1270/1854.

This volume contains *Rawḍa viii*, dealing with the history of the Ṣafawí Kings down to the death of Sháh 'Abbás the Great in 1037/1627–8, and comprises five sections entitled *Ḥadíqa*, as follows:

Ḥadíqa i (ff. 10^{a}–74^{b}), defective at the beginning, contains the history of Sháh Ismá'íl I, called *Sulṭán-i-Sikandar-shán*, and his ancestors, concluding with an account of the notable scholars and poets of his reign (ff. 71^{b}–74^{b}).

Ḥadíqa ii (ff. 75^{b}–109^{a}) contains the history of Sháh Ṭahmásp, called *Kháqán-i-Jannat-makán*, followed (ff. 92^{b}–109^{a}) by an account of the notables of his reign, including Mír Dámád, Shaykh 'Alí b. 'Abdi'l-'Alí, Shaykh Bahá'u'd-Dín 'Ámilí, and the poets Ḍamírí, Muḥtasham, Waḥshí, Malik-i-Qummí, who went to the Deccan and entered the service of 'Ádil Sháh, etc.

Ḥadíqas iii and *iv* (ff. 110^{a}–186^{a}). Of these two sections the former deals with Ismá'íl Mírzá (sometimes called Sháh Ismá'íl II), entitled *Shahriyár-i-Rustam-shi'ár*, and the latter with Sulṭán Muḥammad Khudá-banda, entitled *Kháqán-i-'Illiyyín-áshiyán*; but owing to a lacuna on f. 124^{b} (indicated not only by half a page left blank but by the words افتاده دارد written in red in the margin), it is not clear where the division between the two occurs.

Ḥadíqa v, which occupies the remainder of the volume (ff. 187^{b}–500^{a}), deals with the reign of Sháh 'Abbás the Great, which is related in great detail from the year of his accession, 996/1588, to the year of his death, 1037/1627–8. The last 10 leaves (ff. 490^{a}–500^{a}) deal with the eminent men of his reign, including Ministers, *Mustawfís*, and other officers of State, but unhappily omitting poets and learned men, whose biographies should have followed, but are wanting in this manuscript.

G. 14⁵ (14).

This volume, which is in an entirely different handwriting to the preceding ones (an indifferent *ta'líq*), is dated in the colophon 3 Jumádà II, 1236 (March 8, 1821), and comprises 175 ff. of 33·6 × 21 c. and 23 ll. It contains the reign of Sháh Ṣafí (A.H. 1038–1052, A.D. 1629–1642) and of 'Abbás II down to 1071/1660–1, omitting the last six or seven years of his life. The title *Khuld-i-Barín* only occurs in a note of acquisition (in 1271/1854–5) on f. 2ᵃ, and in the opening words of the second part (f. 94ᵇ):

از حدایق پر گل و شقایق روضهٔ هشتم از روضات جنان خُلد برین الخ

From these words it also appears that this volume contains the continuation of *Rawḍa viii*. A long account of the eminent men of Sháh Ṣafí's reign, including men of learning, occupies ff. 81ᵃ–93ᵇ, and includes short biographies of Mír Dámád, Abu'l-Qásim Findariskí, and Mullá Ṣadrá.

G. 15 (13).

زُبدة التواريخ

Zubdatu't-Tawáríkh, a general history in Persian from the time of Adam to the date of composition (1154/1741–2) by Muḥammad Muḥsin-i-Mustawfí, *'Ámil-i-Díwán* in Iṣfahán, where he was resident during the siege of that city by the Afgháns in 1134–5/1722. See Rieu's Persian Supplement, pp. 24–25, **No. 36**, where another MS. (probably an autograph) bearing the class-mark **Or. 3498** is fully described.

Ff. 258 of 30 × 20·9 c. and 23 ll., written in good *ta'líq*, with an admixture of *raqam* or *siyáq*, in double columns, without date or colophon.

The history of the pre-Islámic Prophets, Patriarchs and Saints extends to f. 41ᵇ; that of the Prophet Muḥammad and his ancestors to f. 70ᵇ; that of the Four Orthodox Caliphs to f. 109ᵇ; the Imáms who succeeded 'Alí to f. 133ᵇ; the pre-Islámic Kings of Persia to f. 142ᵇ; the post-Islámic dynasties of Persia; Ṭáhirids, f. 145ᵃ; Ṣaffárids, f. 145ᵇ; Sámánids, f. 146ᵃ; Ghaznawís, f. 147ᵃ; Ghúrís, f. 148ᵃ; Buwayhids, f. 149ᵃ; Saljúqids, f. 150ᵃ; Khwárizmsháhs, f. 152ᵃ; Atábeks, f. 153ᵃ; Ismá'ílís, f. 155ᵃ; Qará-Khitá'ís of Kirmán, f. 156ᵇ; the 'Abbásid Caliphs, f. 157ᵃ; Mongols, f. 159ᵃ; Suldúzís or Chúpánís, f. 163ᵃ; Ílkánís, f. 164ᵃ; Muẓaffarids, f. 165ᵃ; the Kurt dynasty of Herát, f. 167ᵃ; the Sarbadárs, f. 168ᵃ; Tímúr and his successors, f. 169ᵃ; the Qará-qoyúnlú and Áq-qoyúnlú Turkmán dynasties, f. 177ᵃ; the Ṣafawís, f. 180ᵃ. The history here becomes much more detailed, the principal contents being as follows: Sháh Ismá'íl I, f. 182ᵃ; Ṭahmásp, f. 184ᵃ; Ismá'íl II, f. 192ᵃ; Muḥammad Khudá-banda, f. 193ᵃ; Sháh 'Abbás I "the Great," f. 194ᵃ;

Sháh Ṣafí, f. 200ᵃ; Sháh ʻAbbás II, f. 202ᵃ; Sháh Sulaymán, f. 202ᵇ; Sháh Sulṭán Ḥusayn, f. 203ᵃ; he is put to death by the Afgháns, f. 209; Sháh Ṭahmásp II, f. 210ᵃ; the infant ʻAbbás III, f. 216ᵇ; account of the Afgháns from Mír Ways onwards, f. 218ᵃ; European and Christian rulers, f. 224ᵃ; legend of Hárút and Márút, Búdásf, etc., f. 233ᵃ; wonders of the world, f. 253ᵃ.

G. 16¹ (13) and G. 16² (14).

زينة التواريخ

The *Zínatu't-Tawáríkh* ("Ornament of Histories") compiled about 1218/1803–4 by Mírzá Muḥammad Riḍá of Shaháwar for and by order of Fatḥ-ʻAlí Sháh Qájár, in two volumes, not quite uniform in size. See Rieu's Persian Catalogue, pp. 135–136, and Aumer's Munich Catalogue, p. 79.

Vol. I comprises 412 ff. of 31·3 × 19·7 c. and 29 ll.; large, clear *naskh* with rubrications. A colophon on f. 100ᵇ gives the date 1288/1871–2, and another on f. 331ᵃ 1289/1872–3; the latter adds that the MS. was copied by ʻAlí Muḥammad ibn Muḥammad Ḥasan for Mírzá Músà *Mu'tamanu's-Sulṭán*. This volume contains the Introduction (*Ágház*) and the first *Píráya*.

Vol. II, written in a different hand (a small, neat *ta'líq*), comprises 453 ff. of 33·7 × 22 c. and 27 ll., and is incomplete at the end. There is a colophon on f. 374ᵇ in which 1227/1812 is given as the date of transcription. This volume contains the second *Píráya*, down to 1222/1807–8, but not, apparently, the Conclusion (*Anjám*), which should contain biographies of the notable poets and learned men of Fatḥ-ʻAlí Sháh's reign.

The contents of this history are as follows:

Introduction (*Ágház*). On the creation of heaven and earth.

Píráya I. On the great Prophets, Saints, Sages and Doctors, in two sections entitled *Wajh*, of which the second deals with the Prophet Muḥammad and the first with his predecessors. Each of these sections comprises two subdivisions entitled *Gúna*, the subjects of these being:

(i) The Prophets who preceded Muḥammad (ff. 8ᵇ–100ᵇ).

(ii) The Philosophers and Sages who preceded him (ff. 100ᵇ–114ᵇ).

(iii) The Prophet Muḥammad and the Imáms who succeeded him (ff. 114ᵇ–269ᵃ).

(iv) The leading Divines and Doctors of Islám (ff. 269ᵃ–331ᵃ).

This last section comprises four subsections, treating of:

(1) The Relations and intimate Friends and Companions of the Prophet Muḥammad and of the Imáms who succeeded him (ff. 269–289).

(2) Notable Divines, Doctors, Philosophers and Schoolmen of the Muslims, especially of the Shíʻa (ff. 289–296).

(3) Notable Physicians, Astronomers and Mathematicians from the beginning of Islám to the time of writing (ff. 296–313).

(4) Poets, Gnostics and Metaphysicians, Persian and Arabian (ff. 313–331ᵃ).

Here follows (ff. 333ᵇ–342ᵇ) an account of the Ṣafawí Kings from the death of Sháh ʻAbbás the Great and accession of Sháh Ṣafí to the death of Sháh Sulṭán Ḥusayn, taken from the *Zínatu't-Tawáríkh* of Mírzá Raḍí of Tabríz. The earlier history of the Ṣafawís is omitted, says the author, because it is exhaustively treated in the *Ta'ríkh-i-ʻÁlam-ára-yi-ʻAbbásí*. The history of Nádir Sháh occupies ff. 342ᵇ–343ᵇ, and is followed (ff. 343–411) by the history of the Qájárs down to the year 1218/1803–4.

The last three subsections (ff. 289–331) of the biographical portion of this work constitute its most interesting part, since they contain good and readable notices of many notable theologians and scholars of the Ṣafawí period, as well as of earlier Shíʻa worthies.

The second volume of this MS. (**G. 16²**) contains the second *Píráya*, of which the first part (*Wajh* I, *Gúna* I, ff. 1ᵇ–36ᵃ) deals with the ancient Kings of Persia down to the Arab conquest, and the second (*Wajh* I, *Gúna* 2, of Rieu's description, but not so entitled in this MS.) with the post-Muḥammadan dynasties from the beginning of the Caliphate to the death of Luṭf-ʻAlí Khán and the fall of the Zand dynasty (ff. 36ᵃ–374ᵇ), including at the end brief accounts of the Ottoman Sulṭáns (f. 348ᵃ), the Tímúrid or Moghul and other Kings of India (f. 357ᵇ), and the Uzbeks of Turkistán (ff. 362ᵃ–374ᵇ).

Wajh II, *Gúna* 2 (so entitled here, but Rieu indicates no such subdivision of the second *Wajh*, nor is it clear in this MS. what constitutes its first *Gúna*), begins on f. 375ᵇ, and contains the history of the Qájár dynasty down to 1222/1807–8 (f. 422ᵃ). The MS. is incomplete at the end, and breaks off abruptly at the end of the third line of the Conclusion (*Khátima*).

G. 17 (9).

شمس التواريخ

A general history of the Muḥammadan dynasties down to the rise of the Qájár dynasty in Persia, with an Introduction (*Muqaddama*) on the Prophet Muḥammad and his predecessors and successors, compiled in the reign of Muḥammad Sháh (A.D. 1834–1841) by ʻAbdu'l-Wahháb of Chahár Maḥáll, poetically named *Qaṭra*, and entitled *Shamsu't-Tawáríkh* ("the Sun of Histories"). A brief notice of the author is given in Riḍá-qulí Khán's *Majmaʻu'l-Fuṣaḥá*, vol. II, pp. 422–424, with numerous citations from his poems.

This history comprises, besides the above-mentioned *Muqaddama* (ff. 3ᵇ–13ᵇ) and two Conclusions (*Khátima*), forty chapters, arranged as follows: (1) Umayyads;

(2) Ancient Kings of Persia; (3) Kings of Yaman; (4) Arabian Kings; (5) Ismá'ílís, including the Fáṭimid Caliphs of Egypt and the West and the Assassins; (6) Ṭáhirids; (7) Ṣaffárids; (8) Sámánids; (9) Ghaznawís; (10) Saljúqs; (11) Khwárizmsháhs; (12) Qará-Khitá'is of Kirmán; (13) Muẓaffarids; (14) the Injú dynasty in Fárs; (15) Buwayhids; (16) Ziyárids; (17) Ghúrids; (18) Khiljís; (19) Kings of Nímrúz or Sístán; (20) Kurts; (21) Sarbadárán; (22) Atábeks; (23) remnants of the dynasties 8–10 and 15 *supra* which survived in various parts of Persia; (24) Ayyúbids of Egypt; (25) Turkish dynasties of Egypt and Syria; (26) Circassian dynasties of Egypt and the West; (27) Chaláwí rulers of Ṭabaristán; (28) rulers of Mázandarán; (29) rulers of Gílán; (30) Shírwánsháhs; (31) Dhu'l-Qadr dynasty; (32) the Almohade (*Muwaḥḥidí*) dynasty of N. Africa; (33) Chingíz Khán the Mongol and his descendants; (34) the Jalá'ir or Ílkání dynasty; (35) Tímúr and his descendants; (36) the "Black Sheep" and "White Sheep" Turkmán dynasties; (37) the Ṣafawís; (38) the Afgháns; (39) Nádir Sháh; (40) the Zand dynasty. The Conclusion (*Khátima*) comprises two parts, of which the first treats of the Qájárs (ff. 192ᵇ–197ᵇ) and the second of the Ottoman Sulṭáns (ff. 198ᵃ–210ᵃ).

The MS. comprises 210 ff. of 21·8 × 17·5 c. and 16 ll.; small, neat *nasta'líq* with rubrications. There are numerous marginal additions and corrections which suggest the idea that this was the author's autograph, an idea supported by an inscription at the end in a different hand by Luṭfu'lláh the son of 'Abdu'l-Wahháb of Niháwand (presumably the author) dated Ramaḍán, 1256 (November, 1840).

G. 18 (9).

زبدة التواریخ سنندجی،

A general history of Persia, entitled *Zubdatu't-Tawáríkh-i-Sinandají*, compiled by the Qáḍí of Ardalán Muḥammad Sharíf, son of Mullá Muṣṭafá Shaykhu'l-Islám, for Khusraw Khán, the governor of that district, in 1215/1800–1. It begins with the pre-Islámic Kings of Persia and the early Prophets, but the narrative is very jejune until the Ṣafawí period is reached (Section x, ff. 118ᵃ–184ᵇ). This section is continued down to 1168/1754–5, and is followed by Section xi (ff. 184ᵇ–239ᵃ) "on the genealogy of the Kurds, and of the rulers and governors of Ardalán":

فصل یازدهم، در بیان نسب اکراد و نسب وُلات و امراء اردلان،

Section xii (ff. 239ᵇ–246ᵃ) contains a brief account of the Qájár dynasty, and is followed by the Conclusion (*Khátima*), which sets forth, along with other matters connected with the final revision and production of this book, the historical sources on which it is based, and which include the *Mir'átu'l-Janán* of al-Yáfi'í, the *Ta'ríkh-i-Ál-i-Ayyúb*, the *Kitáb-i-Khamís*, the seven volumes of Mírkhwánd's *Rawḍatu'ṣ-Ṣafá*, the *Rawḍatu'l-Aḥbáb* of Shaykh Jamálu'd-Dín al-Muḥaddith al-Ḥusayní, the histories of Ṭabarí, Waṣṣáf and Ḥáfiẓ Abrú, the *Kitáb-i-Mustaqṣí*, the *Hasht Bihisht* of Mullá Idrís of Bitlís, the *Ta'ríkh-i-Guzída*, the *Ḥabíbu's-Siyar*, the *Mir'át-i-Ká'inát* (in Turkish), the *Murúju'dh-Dhahab* (of al-Mas'údí), the *Mi'ráju'n-Nubuwwat*, the *Nafá'isu'l-Funún*, the *Jahán-gushá-yi-Nádirí*, the *Kitáb-i-Dharra wa-Sanglákh*, the *Ta'ríkhu'l-Akrád* (History of the Kurds), and the *Kitáb-i-Sharafi'd-Dín* (probably the well-known *Ẓafar-náma* of Sharafu'd-Dín 'Alí of Yazd).

The account of Ardalán and its rulers, fairly circumstantial from 953/1546–7 to 1215/1800–1, constitutes the most valuable part of the MS., which was copied for Bahman Mírzá *Bahá'u'd-Dawla* by his amanuensis Áqá Bábá Sháhmírzádí and completed on the 27th of Ramaḍán, 1275 (April 30, 1859). It comprises 251 ff. of 21·4 × 14 c. and 12 ll., and is written in a clear *ta'líq* with rubrications.

G. 19.

Two note-books comprising 246 ff. of 22·8 × 17·8 c. and 21 ll. containing the first 6885 verses of that portion of the *Ẓafar-náma* of Ḥamdu'lláh Mustawfí of Qazwín which deals with the history of the Mongols, copied from the unique British Museum manuscript **OR. 2833** about 1917 by an Indian scribe named Ismá'íl 'Alí in a legible *ta'líq*. The very valuable original, transcribed in 807/1405, is fully described by Rieu in his Persian Supplement (**No. 263**, pp. 172–174). It contains in the margins the whole of Firdawsí's *Sháh-náma*, to the establishment of a critical text of which Ḥamdu'lláh had devoted six years, and his own continuation of that great epic down to his own times. This continuation, which he entitled the *Ẓafar-náma*, exceeded the *Sháh-náma* in length, for it contains 75,000 verses, of which 25,000 are devoted to the Arab conquerors of Persia, 20,000 to the Persian post-Islámic dynasties, and 30,000 to the Mongols. The portion copied in these note-books begins with the legendary origins of the Turks and Mongols (f. 447^b of the original) and ends with Khwárizmsháh's march against Chingíz Khán entitled:

رفتن خوارزمشاه بجنگ چنگیز خان ،

The text breaks off abruptly after l. 15 of this section.

H. HISTORY OF SPECIAL PERIODS, DYNASTIES, ETC.

H. 1 (11).

كتاب الملل و النّحل للشهرستانى،

A fine old MS. of Shahristání's well-known "Book of Sects and Schools" (*Kitábu'l-Milal wa'n-Niḥal*), compiled in 521/1127, excellently edited by the Rev. William Cureton (London, 1846), and translated into German by Haarbrücker (Halle, 1850–1). See Brockelmann, vol. 1, pp. 428–429.

This MS., bought from the late 'Abdu'l-Majíd Belshah in Jan. 1920, comprises 431 ff. of 25·1 × 16·3 c. and 15 ll., and is written in a fine, large clear old *naskh*, fully vocalized, but the first page has been supplied in a later hand. The colophon is dated the 6th of Dhu'l-Ḥijja, 542 (27 April, 1148). The volume belonged at one time (apparently in 1095/1684) to the endowments of a college at Amásiya in Asia Minor.

H. 2 (11).

مفتاح القلوب (جلد ٢) تأليف شمس الدّين اصيل،

The second volume of a general history entitled *Miftáḥu'l-Qulúb* ("the Key of Hearts") by Shamsu'd-Dín al-Aṣíl. The author mentions his name and the title of his work at the top of f. 3ª immediately after the doxology:

چنین گوید راوی این روایات ماضیه و آتیه جامع این حکایات مختلفه اضعف عباد الله الملك الجلیل شمس الدین الاصیل بلغ الله تعالی که چون خاطر خطیر این فقیر حقیر از ترتیب جلد اوّل تاریخ مفتاح القلوب که مبنی بود بر هفده مقاله باز پرداخت اکنون بترتیب و تکمیل جلد دویم که مشتمل است بر چهل و چهار مقاله مشغول شد

The author's royal patron, in spite of the many high-sounding titles with which he is celebrated in the passage immediately following that cited above, I have not been able to identify. As regards the contents of the preceding (first) volume, it appears from the following passage on f. 3^b that it concluded with an account of the Prophet Muḥammad, and presumably contained the history of the preceding Prophets and Kings:

چون انتهای جلد اوّل تاریخ مفتاح القلوب بذکر بعضی از صفات و خصال پسندیدهٔ آن خیر البریّه باتمام رسیده ختم شد اکنون واجب چنانست که صدر دفتر ثالث (ثانی ؟) نیز بذکر بعضی از کلمات دُرربار آن قدوهٔ اخیار زیب و زینت پذیرد،

That "third volume" is a mistake for "second volume" in the above extract seems to be proved by the concluding words of the manuscript (f. 445[a]):

لله الحمد والمنّة که بتأیید الهی و فیض فضل نا متناهی جلد دویم از مجلّدات تاریخ مفتاح القلوب که مشتمل است بر ذکر حالات ائمّهٔ اثنی عشر صلوات الله علیهم و خلفاء بنی امیّه و عبّاسیّه و سلاطینی که معاصر ایشان بوده اند باتمام رسید، الحال خاطر این ذرّهٔ بیمقدار مشعوف بآنست که بترتیب و تکمیل دفتر سیوم پردازد و این اراده صورت نبندد مگر بیمن توجّه پادشاه صاحب حشمت صاحب اقبال مهر سپهر (f. 445[b]) علم و کمال خورشید فلك فضل بیت...اعنی پادشاه عالیشان رفیع القدر والامکان که شرح کمالات سلاطین دوران نسبت به کمالات آنحضرت رشحهٔ دریای عمان و وصف مقالات خواقین جهان [نسبت] بآن صاحب شوکت قطرهٔ از بحر بیکران، امید که سایهٔ معدلت این کریم جهان و جهان کرم بر مفارق عباد خصوص این کمینه پاینده و مستدام باد، بالنّبی وآله الامجاد،

This volume contains forty-three chapters (*maqála*) treating of the following dynasties: (1) the Imáms; (2) Umayyads; (3) Umayyads of Spain; (4) 'Abbásids; (5) 'Alawís of Andalusia; (6) 'Alawís of Mecca; (7) Aghlabids; (8) Ṭáhirids; (9) Ṭúlúnids; (10) Ikhshídís; (11) Ṣaffárids; (12) Ḥamdánids; (13) Sámánids; (14) Kings of Gílán; (15) Ziyárids; (16) Ghaznawís; (17) Buwayhids; (18) Ismá'ílís of the West, including the Fáṭimids; (19) Assassins (*Maláḥida*) of Rúdbár; (20) Saljúqs; (21) Ílak Khán, Bughrá Khán and other Kings of Turkistán; (22) House of Dánishmand; (23) Ortuqids; (24) House of Salíq at Erzeroum; (25) House of Mankúḥak of Erzinján; (26) Khwárizmsháhs; (27)[1] Kings of Yaman; (28) Circassians; (29) House of 'Abdu'l-Mu'min; (30) Ayyúbids; (31) Fáṭimid Caliphs who ruled with the support of the Circassians; (32) House of Mirdás; (33) Banú 'Aqíl; (34) Banú Kiláb; (35) Qará-Khitá'ís; (36) House of Injú in Fárs; (37) Muẓaffarids; (38) Atábeks of Yazd; (39) Atábeks of Mawṣil; (40) Atábeks of Tabríz; (41) Atábeks of Fárs; (42) Atábeks of Luristán; (43) Kings of Nímrúz or Sístán. It will be noticed that many very small and unimportant dynasties are mentioned, and hence the number appears inordinately large. The enumeration in the table of contents on f. 3 does not exactly correspond to the actual division of the text. Thus on f. 439[a] we find a section numbered 42 dealing with the Kurt Kings of Herát.

Ff. 447 of 25·7 × 15 c. and 21 ll.; good, clear *ta'líq* with rubrications; not dated. From the library of the late Sir Albert Houtum-Schindler, Jan. 5, 1917.

---

[1] Wrongly numbered 26 in the text (f. 355[b]), and the following sections are all one out.

H. 3 (9).

مواهب آلهی، تألیف معین الدّین یزدی،

The *Mawáhib-i-Iláhí*, a history of the Muẓaffarí dynasty by Mu'ínu'd-Dín Yazdí. See Rieu's Persian Catalogue, pp. 168–169, and his Persian Supplement, **No. 50**, p. 33. For a MS. dated 778/1377 (eleven years before the author's death) see my *Supplementary Hand-list*, **No. 1277**, p. 211. This present MS. was transcribed only a year later, in Sha'bán, 779 (December, 1377). It is written in a large, clear, archaic *nasta'líq* with rubrications, and concludes with a prayer for the reigning King Sháh Shujá'. It appears at one time (1015/1606) to have belonged to the well-known Turkish euphuist Waysí (Veysí).

Ff. 216 of 21·1 × 13·5 c. and 21 ll.

H. 4 (10).

Another MS. of the same work, not dated, but considerably more modern than the last. It comprises 264 ff. of 24·4 × 13 c. and 19 ll., and is written in a clear neat *ta'líq* with rubrications. One leaf at least is missing at the beginning. It was acquired by Prince Bahman Mírzá *Bahá'u'd-Dawla* for his library on the 28th of Rabí' I, 1269/Jan. 9, 1853, and by me from the library of the late Sir A. Houtum-Schindler on Jan. 5, 1917.

H. 5 (7).

فتحنامهٔ صاحب قرانی،

This book is something of a puzzle, for though its title *Fatḥ-náma-i-Ṣáḥib-Qiráni* occurs on f. 10^b, and the place and date of composition are given on f. 9^a as Shíráz in 828/1425, and it comprises an Introduction (*Muqaddama*) and three Discourses (*Maqála*), and [Sharafu'd-Dín] 'Alí of Yazd is indicated in several places (*e.g.* ff. 126^b, 131^a and 135^a) as the author, and though it begins like **No. 190** of Ethé's India Office Persian Catalogue (col. 82), it is in no sense "a plain and simplified edition of...the *Ẓafar-náma*," but rather a collection of letters and prefaces (*díbácha*), headed at the beginning in red:

دیباچهٔ تاریخ امیر تیمور گورکانی،

The chief contents, after the somewhat bombastic doxology, are as follows:

گفتار در سبب تألیف (f. 3^b): ذکر مقدّمات مذکوره و بیان ترتیب نتیجه بر آن (f. 5^b): گفتار در کیفیّت این تألیف شریف و اشارتی بمؤلّف عالیشان متعالی مکانش (f. 8^a): گفتار در فهرست کتاب (f. 10^a): مقدّمه در ذکر بعضی انبیا و سلاطین که تبیین نسب حضرت صاحب قرانی

موقوفست بآن والله المستعان (ff. 10b–11a): دیباچهٔ دیوان مولانا قوام الدّین محمّد قدّس سرّه (f. 11b):
دیباچهٔ مرقّع خواجه عبد القادر گوینده (f. 16b): دیباچهٔ چنگ که خواجه رکن الدّین مسعود صاعدی
جهت امیرزاده اسمعیل بن ابراهیم سلطان می نوشت (f. 39b): دیباچهٔ جامع السلطانی (f. 44b):
دیباچهٔ جمع اشعار (f. 49a): دیباچهٔ مولود خواجه ناصر الدّین منصور بن ضیاء الدّین محمود
طالبی (f. 53a): دیباچهٔ احکام تقویم (f. 53b): کتابهٔ قبر خواجه شاه علی کهجوئی (f. 54a): کتابهٔ
قبر مولانا ضیاء الدّین محمود قاری شیرازی مشهور بصغیر (f. 54a): کتابهٔ پس و پیش زینی (f. 55a):
مثل همانست (f. 55a): مکاتیب مصر از زبان امیرزاده ابرهیم سلطان (f. 55b): از همو بوالی
مصر (f. 56a): از همو بسلطان مصر (f. 57b): از همو بسلطان احمد والی گلبرگه (f. 58b): از همو در
جواب سلطان گلبرگه (f. 60b): چهار تعزیت نامه بوارثان والی گلبرگه از زبان امیر ضیاء الدّین نور
الله (f. 63b): تعزیت نامهٔ ثانی بوارثی دیگر (f. 65a): تعزیت نامهٔ ثالث بوارثی دیگر (f. 67a): تعزیت
نامهٔ رابع بوارثی دیگر (f. 68b): از بزرگی بوالی گلبرگه (f. 70b): از امیر خلیل بسلطان گلبرگه (f. 74b):
مثله (f. 77a): از همو بامیر جلال الدین فیروز شاه (f. 78b): از همو بامیر سیّد زین العابدین (f. 79b):
از همو بامیر اویس صدر (f. 79b): از همو بسیّد غیاث الدّین علی وزیر (f. 82a): از همو بابی الوفا ملك
خلف (f. 82b): از بزرگ زادهٔ در جواب پدرش (f. 83b): از همو بامیر سیّد زین العابدین (f. 85a): از
همو بامیر عماد الدّین پسر سیّد مذکور (f. 86a): از همو بخواجه پیر احمد وزیر (f. 87a): از همو
بامیر اویس صدر (f. 88a): از همو در جواب درویش حسن گیلانی (f. 90b): از نبیرهٔ سیّد زین
العابدین باو (f. 91a): از بزرگ زادهٔ ببرادرش (f. 91b): از بزرگ زادهٔ بجدّش امیر خلیل الله (f. 92b):
از همو بهمو (f. 93a): از همو بربّه‌اش (f. 94a): از بزرگ زادهٔ بسلطان محمّد بهادر (f. 94b): از همو
بمولانا محمّد صدر (f. 94b): از همو بمولانا زین الدّین صدر (f. 95a): از همو بسلطان محمّد
بهادر (f. 95b): از قاضی سمنان بیکی از خویشانش (f. 95b): از خواجه جمال الدّین محمّد ترکه
بداروغای اصفهان (f. 96*): از همو بخواجه شمس الدّین محمّد طاهر وزیر اصفهان (f. 96b): از مولانا
قطب الدّین گیلانی ببرادرش مولانا حکیم الدّین طبیب (f. 97a): از مولانا نجم الدّین سالوك به
پسران ناصر کیا پادشاه لاهجان (f. 98b): مکاتیب متفرّق که بالتماس عزیزان نوشته شده (f. 100a):
و منها بمذهّبی (f. 110a): و منها بقنّادئی (f. 111a): و منها بمنجّمی (f. 114b): در جواب مکتوبی
که مبارکشاه نامی جمیل آورده بود (f 115b): و منها بمجلّدی (f. 121a): و منها بنقّاشی (f. 121b):
آنچه بنفس مبارك خود مرتکب نوشتن شده اند بحضرت علیّهٔ صاینیّه (f. 126b): تعزیت نامهٔ حضرت
علیّهٔ صاینیّه بفرزندانش (f. 127b): بخواجه فضل الدّین محمّد ترکه (f. 128a): بسیّد تاج الدّین
داماد سیّد شریف سفارش فقیری‌را (f. 129b): جواب مکتوب شیخ محبّ الدّین ابو الخیر خزری (f. 130b):
بامیر جقماق داروغای یزد (f. 131a): در جواب مشورت بزرگی (f. 131b): سفارش حافظ سرایی (f. 132b):
جواب مکتوبی (f. 133b): بتلامذهٔ سمنان (f. 134a): جواب مکتوبی که امیر محبّ الدّین حبیب
الله با تبرّکات از گلبرگه فرستاده بود (f. 134b): آزاد نامهٔ غلامی مبارك نام (f. 135a).

The MS. therefore appears to contain a series of elegant extracts, letters, and other documents including at least three or four from the pen of Sharafu'd-Dín 'Alí Yazdí, the historian of Tímúr.

Ff. 135 of 16·7 × 10 c. and 15 ll.; clear *nasta'líq* of the fifteenth Christian (ninth Muḥammadan) century, with rubrications; no colophon or date. The date 849/1445–6 (indicated by the chronogram هاج بعتقه مبارك) occurs on f. 135ª in the deed of manumission of an Indian slave named Mubárak by [Sharafu'd-Dín] 'Alí Yazdí.

H. 6 (11).

ظفرنامهٔ شرف الدّین علی یزدی،

A good old MS. of the *Ẓafar-náma*, the well-known history of Tímúr by Sharafu'd-Dín 'Alí Yazdí. See Rieu's Persian Catalogue, pp. 173–175, etc.

This MS., which lacks the first and last pages, comprises 366 ff. of 24·2 × 16·5 c. and 21 ll., and is written in a large, clear fifteenth century *nasta'líq*. The initial words correspond to vol. I, p. 2, l. 14, of the *Bibliotheca Indica* edition, and the concluding words to vol. II, p. 743, l. 1. The colophon, if there ever was one, is naturally missing. A note in Sir A. Houtum-Schindler's hand states that he bought the MS. in Ṭihrán in January, 1909.

H. 7 (12).

ظفرنامهٔ نظام شامی،

A copy of the British Museum MS. **Add. 23980** of the older *Ẓafar-náma* composed by Niẓám-i-Shámí, relating the history of Tímúr down to 806/1403–4. The original MS. is fully described by Rieu on pp. 170–172 of his Persian Catalogue. This copy, written in a large, clear *naskh* hand on one side of the paper only, was made for me by Dr Aḥmad Khán.

It comprises ff. 403 of 28·8 × 22 c. and 21 ll.

H. 8 (15).

مطلع السّعدَیْن

The *Maṭla'u's-Sa'dayn*, a well-known and valuable history of the period (A.H. 716–875 = A.D. 1316–1470–1) intervening between the accession of Abú Sa'íd the Mongol (b. 704/1305; d. 736/1335–6) and the death of Abú Sa'íd the Tímúrid (the "Busech" of the Venetian travellers in Persia) and accession of Abu'l-Ghází Sulṭán Ḥusayn. It is in allusion to these two Abú Sa'íds that this history (though it deals chiefly with the reign and career of Tímúr, who was born in the same year as that in which the first Abú Sa'íd died) is entitled *Maṭla'u's-Sa'dayn* ("the Rising-place of the two Fortunate Planets"). Full particulars concerning the work and its author, Kamálu'd-Dín 'Abdu'r-Razzáq of Samarqand, are given by Rieu on pp. 181–182 of his Persian Catalogue. Besides the authorities there cited, see my *Persian Literature under Tartar Dominion*, pp. 428–430. There is a good MS. in the library of Christ's College, Cambridge, marked **Dd. 3. 5.**

Ff. 441 of 36·8 × 28·7 c. and 31 ll. Vol. I ends on f. 180 and is dated in the colophon the 22nd of Jumádà II, 1019 (Sept. 12, 1610). Vol. II lacks a colophon, but a note of ownership is dated 1095/1684. Written throughout in a coarse but legible *ta'líq* with rubrications.

H. 9 (11).

هشت بهشت (جلد هفتم)،

The seventh volume of the *Hasht Bihisht* ("Eight Paradises"), a well-known Persian history of the first eight Sulṭáns of the House of 'Uthmán ('Osmán), compiled by Mullá Idrís of Bitlís in 908–911/1502–5. See Rieu's Persian Catalogue, pp. 216–218, and references there given. This volume contains the history of Sulṭán Muḥammad II.

Ff. 250 of 26·7 × 14·8 c. and 17 ll., written in poor but legible *ta'líq* with rubrications and dated in the colophon 1 Ṣafar, 1099/7 Dec. 1687. This was one of 80 MSS. acquired from the late Ḥájjí 'Abdu'l-Majíd Belshah in 1920.

H. 10 (12).

شرفنامهٔ شرف الدّین بتلیسی،

A history of the Kurds and their chieftains, called by Sir A. Houtum-Schindler *Akrád-náma* and described on the title-page in Persian as

تأریخ مولانا اشرف الدّین فی احوال امرآء و خوانین و خصوصیّات ایشان

but properly entitled *Sharaf-náma*, by Sharafu'd-Dín of Bitlís. See Rieu's Persian Catalogue, pp. 208–210, his Persian Supplement, **Nos. 95** and **96**, pp. 64–65, and Ethé's Bodleian Persian Catalogue, **Nos. 312–314**. The text was published by Veliaminof-Zernof at St Petersburg in 1860, and a French translation by F. B. Charmoy at the same place in 1868–1875. Further bibliographical references are given by Rieu.

The history comes down to 1005/1596–7, and this MS. was transcribed in 1027/1618. The MS. comprises 184 ff. of 28·6 × 17·9 c. and 25 ll., and is written in a fair *ta'líq* with rubrications.

H. 11 (7).

عقد العُلى للموقف الأعلى،

'Iqdu'l-'Ulà li'l-Mawqifi l-A'là, a history of the conquest of Kirmán by the Ghuzz chieftain Malik Dínár in 581–3/1185–7, by Afḍalu'd-Dín Aḥmad ibn Ḥámid of Kirmán. See Rieu's Persian Supplement, **Nos. 90–91**, pp. 62–63. This MS. seems to have been copied in 1269/1853 from the same original (dated Rabí' I, 649 = May-June, 1251) as the two British Museum MSS., the colophon of the original being prefixed to the colophon of the copy as follows:

تمّ كتاب عقد العلى للموقف الاعلى فى ربيع الاوّل سنه ٦٤٩ تسع و اربعين و ستّمائة والحمد لله شكرًا، تمّ فى شهر ذى قعدة الحرام سنه ١٢٦٩ تسع وستّين ومائتين بعد الالف من الهجرة النبويّة

الخطّ يبقى زمانًا بعد كاتبه، وصاحب الخطّ تحت الأرض مدفون،

Ff. 77 of 15·4 × 9·8 c. and 17 ll.; neat and legible modern *naskh* with rubrications. The text was lithographed in Ṭihrán in 1293/1876.

H. 12 (11).

سلسلة النّسب صفويّه

A very rare and interesting monograph on the Ṣafawí Kings and their ancestors, entitled *Silsilatu'n-Nasab-i-Ṣafawiyya*, compiled in the reign of Sháh Sulaymán (A.H. 1077–1105 = A.D. 1667–1694) by Shaykh Ḥusayn ibn Shaykh Abdál-i-Záhidí, one of the *Pír-zádas* or descendants of Shaykh Ṣafiyyu'd-Dín's spiritual director (*Pír*) Shaykh Záhid of Gílán. I have described this work in some detail in an article entitled *Note on an apparently unique Manuscript History of the Ṣafawí Dynasty of Persia* published in the *J.R.A.S.* for July, 1921, pp. 395–418. There appears, however, to be at least one other MS. at St Petersburg[1]. The text is now being printed from photographs of my MS. by Mírzá Ḥusayn Káẓimzáda, editor of the *Íránshahr* at Berlin[2]. The last date mentioned in the text is 1059/1649, when Qandahár was taken by the Persians.

Ff. 88 of 26·3 × 16·5 c. and 15 ll.; fair *ta'líq* with rubrications; no date or colophon. Miniatures representing some of the incidents described occur on ff. 13ª, 19ª, 26ᵇ, 35ᵇ, and 80ª.

---

[1] See an article by Khanikof and Brosset in the *Mélanges Asiatiques* (St Petersburg, 1852), I, pp. 580–583, entitled *Sac d'Ardebil vers l'an* 1203. I am indebted for this reference to my friend M. V. Minorsky.

[2] [The text was published by the Íránshahr Press, Berlin, in 1924.]

H. 13 (12) and H. 14 (13).

تأريخ عالمآراى عباسى،

A complete copy of the *Ta'ríkh-i-'Álam-árá-yi-'Abbásí*, a very detailed history of Sháh 'Abbás the Great, compiled by Iskandar Munshí in 1025/1616, in two volumes, not uniform. For particulars of the work, see Rieu's Persian Catalogue, pp. 185–188, etc.

Vol. I (**H. 13**) contains twelve preliminary Discourses (*Maqálát*), followed by the first *Ṣaḥífa*, describing the course of events down to the accession of Sháh 'Abbás the Great (reigned A.H. 996–1038 = A.D. 1588–1629). The chief contents are:

INTRODUCTION (*MUQADDAMA*) comprising 12 Discourses (*Maqála*) as follows:

Maqála i (f. 6^{a}). Genealogy and ancestors of Sháh 'Abbás (Shaykh Ṣafiyyu'd-Dín, f. 12^{a}; Ṣadru'd-Dín, f. 14^{b}; Sháh Ismá'íl, f. 24^{a}; Sháh Ṭahmásp, f. 45^{b}; Sháh Muḥammad Khudá-banda, f. 104^{b}).

Maqála ii (f. 106^{b}). Piety and devoutness of Sháh 'Abbás.

Maqála iii (f. 106^{b}). His wisdom, knowledge, and state-craft.

Maqála iv (f. 107^{b}). His escapes from many perils and his worthiness to be entitled *Ṣáḥib-qirán*, or "Lord of a fortunate planetary conjunction."

Maqála v (f. 108^{b}). His well-considered measures to increase public security and the happiness of his subjects.

Maqála vi (f. 109^{a}). His inflexible severity.

Maqála vii (f. 110^{a}). His rules of government and maxims of administration.

Maqála viii (f. 110^{b}). His simplicity and informality in private life.

Maqála ix (f. 110^{b}). His consideration for his attendants and dislike of flattery.

Maqála x (f. 111^{a}). His knowledge of men and their characters.

Maqála xi (f. 111^{b}). His charitable bequests and pious foundations.

Maqála xii (f. 113^{a}). His wars and victories.

PART I [FIRST ṢAḤÍFA] contains the history of Sháh 'Abbás from his birth at Herát on Ramaḍán I, 978 (Jan. 27, 1571), or Ramaḍán I, 979 (Jan. 17, 1572), until his accession. Some of the principal topics are: the birth and childhood of Sháh 'Abbás (f. 114^{b}); children and grandchildren of Sháh Ṭahmásp (f. 118^{a}); notable men of his reign, including *Amírs* (f. 119^{a}), *Sayyids* and *'Ulamá* (f. 120^{b}), Ministers (f. 129^{b}), physicians (f. 132^{b}), calligraphists (f. 134^{a}), painters and illuminators (f. 136^{b}), poets (f. 138^{b}), singers and minstrels (f. 144^{b}); detailed and connected history of the Ṣafawís from the murder of Ḥaydar Mírzá (in 984/1576) and accession of Sháh Ismá'íl II (ff. 145^{b} *et seqq.*) to the murder of Ḥamza Mírzá (994/1586) and accession of his brother Sháh 'Abbás in the following year.

This MS., transcribed in 1095/1684, comprises 279 ff. of 27·2 × 16·5 c. and 19 ll., and is written in a small, neat *ta'líq* with rubrications. It once formed part of the library of Muḥammad Ḥasan Khán *Ṣaní'u'd-Dawla*, whose book-plate it bears.

Vol. II (**H. 14**) contains the history of the reign of Sháh 'Abbás. This was originally carried down to the year 1025/1616, but a second volume (*maqṣad*) or continuation, subsequently added, extended the history to 1037/1627–8, almost to the death of the King, which took place in the following year. The volume begins with the first year of Sháh 'Abbás's reign, 996/1588, corresponding to the "Year of the Pig" of the Tartar cycle. The subsequent years run as follows: A.H. 997, f. 5^{b}; 998, f. 16^{b}; 999, f. 26^{b}; 1000, f. 31^{a}; 1001, f. 34^{a}; 1002, f. 39^{b}; 1003, f. 54^{a}; 1004, f. 61^{a}; 1005, f. 66^{a}; 1006, f. 72^{a}; 1007, f. 78^{b}; 1008, f. 98^{b}; 1009, f. 102^{b}; 1010, f. 107^{b}; 1011, f. 112^{a}; 1012, f. 119^{b}; 1013, f. 128^{a}; 1014, f. 140^{a}; 1015, f. 158^{a}; 1016, f. 170^{b}; 1017, f. 192^{a}; 1018, f. 204^{b}; 1019–20, f. 215^{a}; 1021, f. 226^{a}; 1022, f. 229^{b}; 1023–4, f. 234^{a}; 1024–5, f. 240^{a}; 1025, f. 244^{b} (here ends the first volume, or *maqṣad*, of *Ṣaḥífa* II); 1026, f. 255^{b}; 1027, f. 261^{a}; 1028, f. 267^{b}; 1029, f. 269^{b}; 1030, f. 273^{b}; 1031, f. 279^{a}; 1032, f. 290^{b}; 1033, f. 299^{a}; 1034, f. 304^{b}; 1035, f. 314^{a}; 1036, f. 322^{a}; 1037, f. 326^{b}. The volume ends with the account of Sháh 'Abbás's death on Thursday, 24 Jumádà I, A.H. 1038 (Jan. 19, A.D. 1629) on ff. 329^{b}–331^{a}. This is followed (ff. 331^{a}–332^{a}) by a further encomium on the deceased monarch; an account of notable persons who died in the same year (f. 332), including a fairly long notice of the poet Shifá'í; and a list of Sháh 'Abbás's most notable nobles and ministers, arranged in categories (ff. 333^{a}–337^{a}).

This MS., from the library of the late Sir A. Houtum-Schindler, comprises 338 ff. of 31·6 × 19 c. and 23 ll., and is written throughout in a small, neat, legible *ta'líq* with rubrications. There is a colophon dated Rabí' I, 1055 (= May, 1645) on f. 254^{a}, at the end of the first part, volume or *maqṣad* of the second *Ṣaḥífa*. The lower portion of the last leaf of the MS. (f. 338) has been torn off, so that if there were another colophon there, it has perished.

H. 15 (13).

منتخب اللّباب (جلد ٣)٠

Part of vol. III of the *Muntakhabu'l-Lubáb* of Muḥammad Háshim Khán, better known as Kháfí Khán, who died in 1144/1731–2. See Rieu's Persian Catalogue, pp. 232–236, and references there given, especially pp. 235^{b}–236^{a}, where a much more complete MS. (**Add. 26265**) of this same volume is described.

The MS., which is defective and breaks off abruptly at the end, comprises in its present state 105 ff. of 31·2 × 18·6 c. and 17 ll., is undated, and is written in a very ugly Indian *ta'líq*.

H. 16 (15).

تأريخ سلطانى،

The *Ta'ríkh-i-Sulṭání* ("Royal History"), composed by Sayyid Ḥasan ibn Sayyid Murtaḍà al-Ḥusayní for Sháh Sulṭán Ḥusayn the Ṣafawí in 1115/1703–4.

The MS., which is defective at the end, comprises 435 ff. of 36·5 × 23·7 c. and 21 ll.; is written in a large, clear *naskh*, with rubrications; and is undated. It begins with a poem of six verses, of which the first is:

افتتاح سخن آن به که کنند اهل کمال، به ثنای ملك الملك خدای متعال،

It comprises the following three chapters:

(1) On the Angels, Devils and *Jinn*, the creation of the World, and the history of the Prophets and Imáms from Adam to the Islámic period (ff. 5^b–247^a).

(2) History of the pre-Islámic and post-Islámic Kings down to the Ṣafawí period (ff. 247^a–290^b).

(3) History of the Ṣafawí Kings and their ancestors down to 1051/1641–2.

From the library of the late Sir A. Houtum-Schindler.

H. 17 (13).

گلدستهٔ گلشن راز در تعریف سلطان محمّد عادل شاه،

Guldasta-i-Gulshan-i-Ráz, dar ta'ríf-i-Sulṭán Muḥammad 'Ádil Sháh, a history of Muḥammad 'Ádil Sháh by Abu'l-Qásim al-Ḥusayní, beginning:

بسم الله الرّحمن الرّحيم،
بس بود اين سكّه بنام حكيم،
حمد و سپاس بی قياس مر ذات مستجمع جميع صفات كمال الخ

The MS., which is from the late Sir A. Houtum-Schindler's library, and is defective at the end, comprises 223 ff. of 29·2 × 17 c. and 15 ll., and is written in a poor and coarse but legible Indian *ta'líq* with rubrications.

Of the few dates given in this book, the earliest (f. 14^b) appears to be 1038/1628–9, and the latest (f. 202^a), 1057/1647–8.

H. 18 (12).

تأريخ نادرى،

The *Ta'ríkh-i-Nádirí*, or History of Nádir Sháh, composed by Mírzá Muḥammad Mahdí Khán of Astarábád in or about A.D. 1757. See Rieu's Persian Catalogue, pp. 192–195. A lithographed edition of the text appeared in 1282/1865–6, and Sir William Jones published translations into French (Paris, 1770) and English (London, 1773).

This MS. was one of thirteen bought from J. J. Naaman for £25 in May, 1902. It comprises 120 ff. of 29·4 × 19·2 c. and 23 ll., and is written in a fair Persian *ním-shikasta*. The copyist, Muḥammad-qulí ibn Mullá Dargáh-qulí of Tabríz, states that he completed it in Rabí' II, 1244/Oct.—Nov., 1828, being then seventy years of age, for a certain Ma'ṣúm ibn Mírzá Bábá Shuturbání of Tabríz, who was himself sixty-nine years of age, having been born in 1175/1762.

H. 19 (9).

تأريخ آل قاجار،

A history of the Qájár dynasty down to 1220/1805, composed in 1269/1852–3 by Muṣṭafà-qulí ibn Muḥammad Ḥasan al-Músawí as-Saráwí (of Saráw or Saráb) as-Sabalání for Qahramán Mírzá, the governor of Ádharbáyján.

The book, which has no proper title, begins abruptly with eight verses of poetry, of which the first three are as follows:

پس از حمدِ یزدان و نعتِ رسول، ثنا باد زی ما باهل قبول،
که اخبارِ شاهانِ پیشینیان، بباید شنودن بصد گوش و جان،
که اندر رهِ دین چه سان مرده اند، بگیتی چگونه بسر بُرده اند،

and then continues abruptly in prose (f. 2[a]):

نوّاب محمّد حسن خان خدیو دانشمند و خسرو سعادتمند و سلطان عادل و خاقان باذل و ملك وافی العهد و پادشاه صادق الوعد بود الخ

The text forms a continuous narrative devoid of divisions or chapter-headings, except for the Conclusion (*Khátima*), which begins on f. 57[b], and treats of matters connected with the author and his patron more appropriate to a preface.

Ff. 74 of 22·7 × 13·8 c. and 13 ll.; good, clear *ta'líq* within gold-ruled margins; copied in Muḥarram 1274/August—September, 1857. From the library of the late Sir A. Houtum-Schindler.

H. 20 (9).

كتاب كلام الملوك،

Kalámu'l-Mulúk, a brief account of the Qájár dynasty down to the death of Fatḥ-'Alí Sháh on the 19th of Jumádà II, 1250/Oct. 23, 1834, of doubtful authorship, copied for Mr Lyne[1], at that time in charge of the Indo-European telegraph-office

[1] See my *Year amongst the Persians*, p. 184.

at Qum, in Ramaḍán, 1290/October, 1873, by ʻAlí Akbar, formerly custodian of the Holy Shrine of Qum. This was one of three small MSS. from the library of the late Mr Lyne bought for 13*s.* from Messrs Luzac and Co. in February, 1907.

Begins, after the title and the *Bismi'lláh*:

لك الحمد يا ذا الجود والمجد والعلى تبارکت تعطى من تشآء و تمنع، تحسين و درود مر نخستين صدور ورود عرصهٔ شهود احمد محمود... (f. 3^{b}, l. 5) تفصيل اين اجمال آنكه ايل جليل قاجار از اروغ ميمون آق قويونلوى تركمانيّه و آن قبيلهٔ نبيله از اولاد ترك بن يافث بن نوح كه بيافث اغلان مذكور و بكثرت اولاد و احفاد مشهور بود قبايل و عشاير (f. 4^{a}) نتيجهٔ يك نسل و فرع يك اصل از او منشعب گشته پس از تسخير ممالك شرق و شمال در تركستان و چين و ثقلاب (sic for صقلاب) و ختاى و ختن جاى‌گير شدند و طائفهٔ از آن ملقّب به آق قويونلو و قرا قويونلو اكثرى از بلاد روم و شامات و ديار بكر بحيطهٔ تملّك و تصرّف در آورده بعزيمت ايران مصمّم در اندك زمان ايران‌را مسخّر و آنرا بسه قسمت كردند كه متون تواريخ و بطون اخبار از آثار و كردار سلاطين با (f. 4^{b}) اقتدار از دو طائفه حاكى و حاويست جمعى در تبريز و ايروان و گنجه ساكن و رايت سلطنت در ممالك آذربايجان و كرج و عراق و فارس افراختند، آباى كرام و اجداد با عدل و داد ما در استراباد و گرگان بعد از استيلاى بر تركمان و دشت قفچاق تمكّن و بهره در مرو شاهيجان توطّن يافته بر اكثر بلاد خراسان حكمران و فرمان‌روا شدند، شاهقليخان پدر پنجم ما كه سرخيل آن انجم بود پس از انقضاى مدّت حكمرانى از اين (f. 5^{a}) جهان فانى در گذشت زمام اختيار آن حدود بفرزند ارشد فتحعلى خان باز گذاشت

From the expression "*our* noble forefathers and first and righteous ancestors" in the above citation, it may be inferred that the author of this little book himself belonged to the Qájár tribe.

Ff. 38 of 20·8 × 15 c. and 9 ll., written in a very large *naskh*, with occasional headings in blue to indicate the occurrence of verses in the text.

H. 21 (11).

تأريخ ذو القرنين،

Ta'ríkh-i-Dhu'l-Qarnayn, a history of the reign of Fatḥ-ʻAlí Sháh Qájár, by Mírzá Faḍlu'lláh al-Ḥusayní ash-Shírází, poetically surnamed Kháwarí (f. 3^{a}, fourth line from the bottom). He was secretary (*munshí*) to the Prime Minister (*Ṣadr-i-Aʻẓam*) Muḥammad Shafíʻ, and this copy is his autograph, as stated in a note at the beginning in the hand of ʻAbdu'l-ʻAlí Mírzá the son of Farhád Mírzá, to whom the MS. belonged, and as appears from the colophon at the end of the first volume on f. 185^{a}, where the compilation is stated to have been completed on Thursday the 6th of Rabíʻ II, 1249 (August 23, 1833), and the transcription of this copy on Monday the 10th of Shaʻbán, 1257 (September 27, 1841).

The work comprises two volumes and a Conclusion (*Khátima*).

Vol. I (ff. 2ᵇ–185ᵃ) contains the first thirty years of Fatḥ-'Alí Sháh's reign (A.H. 1212–1241 = A.D. 1798–1826).

Vol. II (ff. 185ᵇ–272ᵇ) contains the remainder of his reign (A.H. 1242–1250 = A.D. 1826–1835).

The Conclusion (ff. 273ᵇ–321ᵃ) contains a list of his descendants. A copy of this last was presented by Farhád Mírzá to the Hon. C. A. Murray in 1855, and is now **Or. 1361** in the British Museum (see Rieu's Persian Catalogue, p. 201). The same library possesses another complete MS. **Or. 3527** (see Rieu's Persian Supplement, **No. 71**, pp. 47–48).

This MS., obtained from the library of the late Sir A. Houtum-Schindler, comprises 321 ff. of 24·5 × 17·8 c. and 25 ll., and is written in a small and cursive but fairly legible *ta'líq* with rubrications.

H. 22 (9).

تأریخ میرزا مسعود وغیره،

A volume of 176 ff. of 21 × 16·4 c. and 11 ll. written in a rather cursive modern Persian *ta'líq* containing the five following treatises:

(1) An account of the disasters of the year 582/1186–7, as foretold by the stars, beginning:

چون این ترجمه بآخر رسید طرفی از احوال روزگار و انواع فتنه و تشویش که در ایّام فتور و عجایب اتّفاقات و سرهای بزرگان که در سر کار شد و خرابی خطّهٔ عراق و خال جرفاذقان بر وجه ایجاز و اختصار آورده شد بعون الله تعالی،

بسم الله الرّحمن الرّحیم،

شکل حوادث ایّام در شهور سنه اثنی و ثمانین و خمسمائة کواکب هفتگانه‌را در برج میزان اتّفاق اجتماع افتاد و مدّتها بود که در افواه افتاده بود و منجّمان در کتب احکام آورده که درین زمان طوفان باد باشد الّخ

In consequence of this conjunction of the Seven Planets in the Sign of Libra, terrible storms and floods were anticipated by the astrologers, and some even held that the end of the world was at hand, supporting their opinion by an alleged saying of the Prophet, who, when asked "When will be the Resurrection (*Qiyámat*)?" replied several times "*Al-Qiyámat*"; which word, though at first it seemed no answer to the question, was found by the *abjad* notation to yield the number 582. Compare the story told by Dawlatsháh (pp. 85–86 of my edition) in connection with the poet Anwarí; the year is not there specified, but if, as asserted by Dawlatsháh, he died in 547/1152–3, he had been dead for thirty-five years before the fulfilment of the prediction fell due. The same story is told of the astronomer Abu'l-Faḍl al-Kházimí in al-Qifṭí's *Ta'ríkhu'l-Ḥukamá* (ed. Lippert, pp. 426–428), and the year A.H. 582 is given as the date of the conjunction in question both by al-Qifṭí and by the historian Ibnu'l-Athír. See my *Literary History of Persia*, vol. II, p. 367 and footnotes.

This extract occupies ff. 9^a–18^a, was copied in 1272/1855–6, and deals with the history of the period in question, and the struggle between the last Saljúqs and the Khwárizmsháhs. There is nothing to indicate from what book it is taken.

(2) A short history of the Ottoman Sulṭáns down to the accession of Salím II in A.D. 1566 by a certain Asadu'lláh (ff. 19^b–57^a), beginning:

حمد و سپاس و ستایش پادشاهی‌را سزاست که سلاطین جهان بر آستان جلالش کمینه بندگان الخ

(3) A short account of another unlucky year (1212/1826–7), occupying only two pages (ff. 65^b and 66^a), and beginning:

قران نحسَیْن سرطانی که بالذات مخرّب دین و دولت و باعث آشوب بلاد و عباد است الخ

(4) An account of 'Abbás Mírzá, Fatḥ-'Alí Sháh's eldest and favourite son, by Mírzá Mas'úd (ff. 67^b–142^a), beginning:

تاریخ احوال مرحوم نایب السّلطنه عبّاس میرزا که جناب میرزا مسرور وزیر دول خارجه نوشته است' در ذکر خصومتی که فیما بین دولت ابد مدّت قاهره [ایران] و دولت بهیّهٔ روس اتّفاق افتاد

This is also evidently an extract from some larger work, as proved by the expression "as has been previously mentioned" occurring at the beginning. The end is equally abrupt, and there is no colophon or date.

(5) A list of the plate, manuscripts, and other valuables contained in the Ṣafawí shrine at Ardabíl, drawn up, apparently, on the occasion of their inspection by Muḥammad Qásim Beg the *Mutawallí* (Custodian) in Rajab, 1172 (March, 1759), or possibly Rajab, 1272 (March, 1856), entitled:

موجودی اجناس و اسباب و متروکات آستانهٔ مقدّسهٔ منوّرهٔ متبرّکه از قرار باز دید عالیشان رفیعمکان سلالة الساداة العظام محمّد قاسم بیگ متولّی بتاریخ شهر رجب المرجّب سنه ۱۱۷۲ بارس ییل

This list, which occupies ff. 145^b–173^b, is unfortunately very difficult to read, being written in the cipher called *raqam*.

H. 23 (11).

This MS. contains:

(1) An anonymous Arabic introduction to Logic (ff. 1ª–9ᵇ), slightly defective at the beginning, with many interlinear and marginal glosses. It begins:

با (*sic*) الله انّه مفيض الخير والجود الظ (*sic*) ايساغوجى اللفظ الدالّ بالوضع على تمام ما وضع له بالمطابقة

(2) A number of legal questions and answers, written in Turkish (ff. 11ª–11ᵇ).

(3) *Risála-i Nának Sháh* (ff. 12ª–35ᵇ), a Persian history of the Sikhs down to 1178/1764–5, by Budh Singh, generally known as Arúrá (اروڑا), an inhabitant of Lahore in the service of Major James Mordaunt. It was composed *circa* 1200/1785–6; see Rieu's Persian Catalogue, p. 860, where its contents are briefly described. The present copy, which is defective at the end, begins:

كارپردازان ايجاد و تكوين كه عبارت از قضا و قدر باشد

(4) An account, written in Persia without title or author's name, of Niẓámu'l-Mulk Áṣafjáh of the Áṣafí dynasty of Ḥaydarábád and his sons, followed by historical notices relating to the Deccan (ff. 36ᵇ–44ᵇ). It resembles, but is not identical with, **Or. 1391** described in Rieu's Persian Catalogue, p. 323.

Begins:

آصفجاه غفران‌پناه جدّ مادرى او سعد الله خان وزير اعظم صاحبقران ثانى شاه‌جهان است

(5) Part of the *'Iyár-i Dánish* (ff. 47ᵇ–156ᵇ), the well-known version (in sixteen chapters) of the *Anwár-i Suhaylí*, that was made for Akbar by Abu'l-Faḍl ibn Mubárak in 996/1587–8. This copy is incomplete.

Ff. 157 of 26·2 and 18·5 c. and 17 ll., written for the most part in Indian *nasta'líq*.

Ff. 1–45 are of smaller size and in different handwritings. The MS., which is worm-eaten in places, formerly belonged to J. P. Edmond.

I. LOCAL HISTORIES.

I. 1 (9).

رساله فى محاسن اصفهان للمافرّوخى،

This MS., which was given to me on June 18, 1913, by the late Sir Albert Houtum-Schindler, was originally transcribed in 1277/1860 for Prince Bahman Mírzá *Bahá'u'd-Dawla*, who, according to a note in Schindler's writing attached to the volume, died in the Caucasus in A.D. 1883. Schindler subsequently bought the MS. from one of his sons in Ṭihrán. It is carefully written in a good, clear *naskh*, fully vocalized, within margins of gold, blue and red, was copied by Ḥabíbu'd-Dín Abú Ya'qúb Muḥammad ibn 'Alí al-Aṣghar of Jarbádhaqán (Gulpáyagán), and completed on Friday the 5th of Rabí'u'l-awwal, 1277 (Sept. 21, 1860).

This is the original Arabic treatise on the Charms of Iṣfahán (*Maḥásinu Iṣfahán*) by al-Mufaḍḍal ibn Sa'íd al-Máfarrúkhí of which the MS. to be next described (**I. 2**) contains the much later and better-known Persian version. The Arabic original is very rare: indeed I know of no other copy but this. The title and initial words are as follows:

هذه رسالةٌ فی محاسن اصفهان تأليف الاستاذ

المفضّل بن سعيد المافروخی،

بسم الله الرّحمن الرّحيم،

اِنَّ لِلّٰهِ تَقَدَّسَتْ اَسْمَاؤُهُ وَعَظُمَتْ آلاؤُهُ وَجَلَّ ثَنَاؤُهُ وَعَزَّ كِبْرِيَاؤُهُ نِعَماً صَافِيَةَ ٱلْمَشَارِعِ ضَافِيَةَ ٱلْمَدَارِعِ عَلَّ كَافَّةَ ٱلْعِبَادِ زُلَالَ مَنَاهِلِهَا وَعَمَّ عَامَّةَ ٱلْبِلَادِ ظِلَالَ ذَلَاذِلِهَا الخ

No precise information is to be derived from the very ornate and rhetorical Preface. The description or praise of Iṣfahán begins on f. 7[b], penultimate line, with the words:

اصفهان بلدةٌ قد اسنى الله من اياديه البيض قِسْمَهَا و وفّر من مواهبه الغُرّ سَهْمَهَا و صدر فی جريدة البلاد (f. 8[a]) اسمها و اَلْحَقَ برسوم الجنان رَسْمَهَا الخ

The work is to a large extent an anthology of poems in praise of Iṣfahán, but also contains a good deal of historical and archaeological matter of interest besides many legends of a less authentic character. Concerning himself the author gives hardly any information, but from the Persian version to be described immediately we learn that he composed his treatise in 421/1030. Unlike the Persian translation there is in the original Arabic no division into chapters, and the arrangement of matter is very unsystematic.

Ff. 88 of 21·7 × 14 c. and 18 ll.; excellent modern *naskh*, fully vocalized; transcribed, as stated above, in 1277/1860.

I. 2 (9).

رسالهٔ محاسن اصفهان (ترجمهٔ فارسی)،

A MS. of the Persian version of the *Maḥasin-i-Iṣfahán* made by Ḥusayn ibn Muḥammad ibn Abi'r-Riḍá al-Ḥusayní al-'Alawí in or about the year 729/1329. Another MS. of this work belonging to the Royal Asiatic Society was fully described by me in the *Journal* of that Society for 1901 (vol. XXXIII, pp. 411–446 and 661–704), to which I added in a postscript some account of another MS. formerly belonging to M. Charles Schefer, and now preserved in the Bibliothèque Nationale under the class-mark **Suppl. Persan 1573.** The translator has dealt very freely with his original, both as regards rearrangement of matter and additions and suppressions, but in most cases the parallel passages can be found. The translator divides his work into eight chapters entitled *dhikr* as follows (f. 11):

ذکر اوّل (ff. 12ᵇ–17ᵃ) بر وصف اصفهان بر سبیل اجمال،

ذکر دوم (ff. 17ᵃ–30ᵃ) در تفصیل آن بر سایر بلدان بطریق تفصیل،

ذکر سیم (ff. 30ᵃ–38ᵃ) در حدیث گاوخوانی و خواصّ و نوادر نواحیآن،

ذکر چهارم (ff. 38ᵃ–52ᵃ) در محاسن داخلی و خارجی از تعداد مقامات و اماکن و عمارات و تعیین حقوق و متوجّهات قدیم الایّام و عصر مترجم،

ذکر پنجم (ff. 52ᵃ–60ᵇ) در فرمان‌برداری اصفهانیان حاکمرا و قوّت نفس و تأثیر همّت ایشان و آنکه هرکس قصد ایشان ببدی کرده زیانی مالی یا مضرّتی نفسی بدو عاید گشته،

ذکر ششم (ff. 60ᵇ–74ᵇ) در اسامی ملوك و فراعنه و اکاسره که منشأ و منجم ایشان آنجا بوده مضاف با بعضی نوادر و غرایب کلمات ضعفاء ناس مانند زنان و مجانین و مخنّثین،

ذکر هفتم (ff. 74ᵇ–84ᵇ) در فصول اربعه و آثار و نتایج آن و کیفیّت تنعّم و تعیّش اهل بقعه،

ذکر هشتم (ff. 84ᵇ–98ᵃ) در وصف کوهچه و مصلّی و اسماء الرّجال و فضلا و علما و فلاسفه و فقها و مشایخ و اکابر متقدّمان و متأخّران عصر صاحب محاسن و مترجم و بعضی قصاید و اشعار عربی و پارسی در وصف آن،

ذیل کتاب (ff. 98ᵃ–106ᵃ)

This MS. formerly belonged to the Iḥtishámu'd-Dawla, whose seal it bears on the last page (f. 106ᵃ), and came to me from Sir A. Houtum-Schindler's library in January, 1917. It comprises 108 ff. of 21·9 × 14·7 c. and 15 ll., and is written in a good, clear *ta'líq* between gold and coloured borders with rubrications, but has no colophon or date. For a detailed description of the work, see my article above-mentioned in the *J.R.A.S.* for 1901.

I. 3 (9).

نصف جهان فی تعریف اصفهان،

Another Persian work on the history and topography of Iṣfahán composed in 1303/1885–6 by Muḥammad Mahdí ibn Muḥammad Riḍá al-Iṣfahání, who entitled it *Nisf-i-Jahán* ("Half the World," a title formerly given to the old Ṣafawí capital).

This MS., from the library of the late Sir A. Houtum-Schindler, comprises ff. 242 of 21·7 × 14·6 c. and 18 ll.; written in an excellent and very clear modern

Persian *naskh* with rubrications and completed in Rajab, 1308 (Feb.—March, 1891). Begins after the *Bismi'lláh* and brief doxology:

امّا بعد، اقلّ بندگان حضرت سبحانی محمّد مهدی ابن محمّد رضا الاصفهانی بر رای بیضا ضیای صاحبان خبرت و بصیرت عرضه میدارد آلخ

The author tells us (f. 2[a]) that this is a revised and enlarged recension of a work on the same subject which he composed in 1300/1882–3. Of his life we gather little, except that he spent some time in Bombay and associated with the Parsees there (ff. 8[b] and 88[b]) and was in Ṭihrán in 1275/1858–9 (f. 89[a]). He also appears to have some knowledge of European ideas and methods (which he contrasts favourably with those of his own country) and of the Old Testament and the works of Sir John Malcolm, Kaempfer and other European writers on Persia. Of the two works mentioned above (that of Máfarrúkhí and its Persian version) he has made extensive use, which he fully acknowledges, but he justly criticizes them for their lack of geographical material, and has endeavoured to supplement them especially in this particular. His account of the various buildings and gardens, and his sketch of the history of Iṣfahán, especially in Ṣafawí times, are amongst the most valuable parts of the book, which is divided into six sections (*faṣl*) preceded by a Preface (*Muqaddama*), as follows:

مقدّمه (f. 2[a])،

فصل اوّل، در بیان کلّیّات حالات اصفهان و ناحیهٔ آن و تغییرات اسمی و نسبی که درآن روی نموده است (f. 4[a])،

فصل دویم، در قسمت این ناحیت بشهر و بلوك و غیر آن و وضع شهر و حدود آنست (f. 13[b])،

فصل سیّم، در اجزای صناعی اصفهان و امور متعلّقه بآنست (f. 18[a])،

فصل چهارم، در امور طبیعی اصفهان (f. 52[a])،

فصل پنجم، در تاریخ اصفهان و ابتدای بنای آن و وجه تسمیهٔ آن بدین اسم (f. 90[a])،

فصل ششم، ذکر بلوکات اصفهان (f. 212[b])،

I. 4 (14).

قُم‌نامه (تأریخ قُم)،

Part of the Persian history of the city of Qum (entitled *Qum-náma*, or *Ta'ríkh-i-Qum*) described by Rieu in his Persian Supplement, pp. 59–60, **No. 88**. The Arabic original on which it is based was written in 378/988–9 for the celebrated Ṣáḥib Ismá'íl ibn 'Abbád by Ḥasan ibn Muḥammad ibn Ḥasan al-Qummí (see Brockelmann's *Gesch. d. Arab. Litt.*, vol. 1, p. 516). The Persian version (of which this MS. contains only a fragment, namely, part of the first of the twenty chapters into which the book is divided) was made in 806/1403–4[1] by Ḥasan ibn 'Alí ibn Ḥasan ibn 'Abdi'l-Malik of Qum. The British Museum MS. contains the first five chapters, or about one quarter, of the work, and the present MS. only seven of the eight sections which constitute the first chapter. It comprises 65 ff. of 34 × 21·2 c. and 17 ll., and is written in a large and clear but untidy *ním-shikasta*. The original from which it was copied appears to have been dated Monday the 17th of Dhu'l-Ḥijja, 837/July 25, 1434, but the date of this copy (evidently modern) is not given. A table of contents of the whole work occupies ff. 11ᵇ–14ᵇ. Of the six sections (*faṣl*) contained in this volume the first begins on f. 15ᵃ; the second on f. 20ᵇ; the third on f. 23ᵃ; the fourth on f. 27ᵃ; the fifth on f. 30ᵃ; the sixth on f. 39ᵃ; and the seventh on f. 62ᵃ.

Prefixed to the *Qum-náma* and bound up in the same volume is a smaller tract entitled:

كتابچهٔ تفصيل احوالات دار الايمان قُم از بدو آبادى او الى يومنا هذا،

It was composed at the request of a physician named Mírzá 'Alí Akbar Khán who was entitled *Ḥakím-báshí*, and this copy was completed on the 6th of Ṣafar, 1305/Oct. 24, 1887. It comprises 36 ff. of 22·4 × 17 c. and 16 ll., and is written in a cursive *ním-shikasta*.

I. 5.

تأريخ دار الامان قُم،

Another more complete copy of the History of Qum described above, copied for Prince Jalálu'd-Dín *Iḥtishámu'l-Mulk* in 1286/1869–70 when he was governor of Káshán, and containing a few marginal notes in his hand.

This MS. contains the first five chapters of the twenty which constitute the whole work, comprises 110 ff. of 28·4 × 17 c. and 25 ll., and is written in a small, neat modern *naskh* with rubrications. It ends abruptly without any colophon, the date of transcription being given in a note on f. 3ᵃ. The chapters and sections occur as follows:

Table of Contents, ff. 7ᵇ–8ᵇ.

Chapter I, § **1**, f. 8ᵇ; § **2**, f. 11ᵇ; § **3**, f. 13ᵃ; § **4**, f. 15ᵃ; § **5**, f. 16ᵇ; § **6**, f. 21ᵇ; § **7**, f. 33ᵃ (*on the Fire-Temples*); § **8**, f. 34ᵃ.

Chapter II, § **1**, f. 37ᵇ; § **2**, f. 39ᵇ; § **3**, f. 44ᵇ; § **4** (*title omitted*); § **5**, f. 61ᵃ.

Chapter III, § **1**, f. 65ᵇ (*on the Imáms*); § **2**, f. 70ᵇ.

Chapter IV, § **1**, ff. 83ᵃ–84ᵃ; § **2**, f. 85ᵃ.

Chapter V, f. 93ᵃ.

---

[1] So on f. 3ᵃ, l. 2, but Rieu gives 825/1422 as the date of composition.

It is to be regretted that the latter portion of this monograph, which would seem to be far more interesting to students of Persian than the earlier part, which deals almost exclusively with the Arab invaders and governors, appears to be lost, or at any rate undiscovered. Chapter XVIII, containing notices of 130 poets of Qum who wrote in Arabic and Persian, and chapter XIX, dealing with the Jews, Magians and Christians of Qum, would probably be of especial interest.

I. 6 (10).

تأريخ طبرستان،

A good modern copy of the *History of Ṭabaristán* compiled about 613/1216 by Muḥammad ibn al-Ḥasan ibn Isfandiyár, of which I published an *Abridged Translation* in 1905 as vol. II of the "E. J. W. Gibb Memorial" Series. This translation was based on the India Office MS. (**No. 1134** = **No. 568** in Ethé's Catalogue) and the two British Museum MSS. **Add. 7633** and **Or. 2778**, and from it full information concerning this important and interesting book can be derived.

The present MS., which formed part of the Schindler collection, comprises 173 ff. of 24·8 × 15·5 c. and 21 ll., is written in a fair *ta'líq* with rubrications, and was completed in Jumádà I, 1268/Feb.—March, 1852. It formerly belonged to Prince Farhád Mírzá *Mu'tamadu'd-Dawla*, and bears on ff. 1^b and 2^a a number of quatrains in the Mázandarání dialect apparently composed and certainly transcribed by Riḍá-qulí Khán "Hidáyat," commonly known as "*Lala-báshí*." The preliminary note runs as follows:

درین تاریخ طبرستان بعضی رباعیّات بلغت طبری آورده که وزنی مخصوص دارد من بنده رضاقلی متخلّص بهدایت‌را بخاطر رسید که بچند رباعی بدآن سیاقت طبع‌آزمائی کنم و از آنجمله است و هرکه آن لغت داند داند که نه من از آنان بدتر گفته‌ام بلکه بهتر و واضح‌تر سروده ام،

I. 7 (12).

تأريخ مازندران ظهير الدّين،

The History of Mázandarán by Ẓahíru'd-Dín ibn Sayyid Naṣíri'd-Dín-i-Mar'ashí. The work was composed in 881/1476–7, and the text was published by Dorn in St Petersburg in A.D. 1850. See Rieu's Persian Supplement, pp. 63–64, **No. 93**. The text of the author's companion volume on the history of Gílán (see Ethé's Bodleian Persian Catalogue, **No. 309**) was printed at the 'Urwatu'l-Wuthqà Press at Rasht for Mr H. L. Rabino in 1330/1912.

Ff. 132 of 28·4 × 18·5 c. and 25 ll.; written in clear *naskh* with rubrications and dated Ṣafar 14, 1271 (Nov. 6, 1854). Copyist, Muḥammad Ḥasan ibn 'Abdi'lláh al-Kátib. This MS. formerly belonged to Prince Bahman Mírzá *Bahá'u'd-Dawla* and subsequently to Sir A. Houtum-Schindler.

I. 8 (9).

تذكرهٔ شوشتريه

A History of Shúshtar from the earliest times until 1169/1755–6, by Sayyid 'Abdu'lláh ibn Núri'd-Dín ibn Ni'mati'lláh (d. 1173/1759–60). See Rieu's Persian Catalogue, pp. 214–216, and his Persian Supplement, p. 67, where the contents of the work are described.

This MS., bought from Major Salmon on May 21, 1906, comprises 162 ff. of 20·4 × 16 c. and 9 ll. It is written in a clear but coarse *naskh*, is dated 25 Shawwál, 1313/April 9, 1896, and was copied for Major (then Captain) Salmon by Muḥammad Ḥasan ibn Muḥammad Riḍá ibn Ḥabíbi'lláh *Wazír-i-Shúshtarí*.

I. 9 (9).

در احوال سيوند الخ

This little MS. contains an account of Síwand in Fárs and the peculiar dialect there spoken, followed by a selection of other poems in various dialects of Persian, with some remarks on their characteristics. M. Clément Huart, in an article contributed to the *Journal Asiatique* for March—April, 1893, and entitled *Le dialecte persan de Sîwend*, published a translation of the account of Síwand with which the MS. begins (ff. 1–2) and of the greater part of the succeeding vocabulary of the dialect (to f. 15[a], l. 2). This, according to his statement, was drawn up in 1888 by Mírzá Ḥusayn of Ṭihrán, poetically named *Thurayyá*, for *Iḥtishámu'd-Dawla*, the son of Prince Farhád Mírzá *Mu'tamadu'd-Dawla*, when he was Governor of Fárs. M. Huart's copy was made from a MS. belonging to Mírzá Ḥabíb of Iṣfahán by Mírzá Faḍlu'lláh ibn Muḥammad Yúsuf, and completed on Dec. 14, 1888.

My MS. was sent to me from Constantinople on Sept. 2, 1891, by the late Shaykh Aḥmad Rúḥí of Kirmán, and is fully discussed and described in the *Journal of the Royal Asiatic Society* for 1895 (New Series, vol. XXVII, pp. 773–825) in an article entitled *Notes on the Poetry of the Persian Dialects*. It comprises 44 ff. of 20 × 13 c. and 18 ll., and is written in a small and legible Persian *ta'líq* with rubrications, but lacks date and colophon. Concerning the unfortunate Shaykh Aḥmad of Kirmán, to whom I am indebted for many interesting MSS., see my *Persian Revolution*, pp. 10–12, 63, 64, 93–96, and 414–415.

I. 10 (9).

نزهة النّاظرين

A History of Egypt from the Muḥammadan conquest till the restoration of Sulṭán Muṣṭafà I on Rajab 8, 1031/May 19, 1622, entitled *Nuzhatu'n-Náẓirín fí ta'ríkhi man waliya Miṣr mina'l-Khulafá wa-'s-Saláṭín*, by Mar'í ibn Yúsuf al-Maqdisí al-Ḥanbalí. See Ḥájjí Khalífa (ed. Flügel), **No. 13742**, vol. VI, p. 336; Brockelmann's *Gesch. d. Arab. Litt.*, vol. II, p. 369, No. 18, and references there given; and my *Hand-list*, p. 235, **No. 1175**, and *Supplementary Hand-list*, p. 42, **No. 241**, where the title is given as *Ta'ríkhu'l-'Árifín, etc.*

This MS., obtained from the late Ḥájjí 'Abdu'l-Majíd Belshah in November, 1920, comprises 73 ff. of 20·2 × 15 c. and 21 ll., and is written in a fair *naskh* with rubrications, without date or colophon.

I. 11 (13).

شرح نسب اردلان که جدّ والیهای کردستان است،

An account of Ardalán, the supposed ancestor of the Governors, or *Wálís*, of Kurdistán. This MS., given to me by Mr H. L. Rabino and temporarily mislaid, comprises the Persian text, written in a coarse but legible *ta'líq* on 98 ff. of 32 × 20 c. and 15 ll., and completed by a copyist named Muḥammad Riḍá on the 2nd of Rabí' II, 1324 (May 26, 1906), and also an English translation or abridgement, with some genealogical tables, by Mr Rabino written on 37 ff. of flimsy paper and dated January, 1906.

J. BIOGRAPHICAL WORKS.

J. 1 (10).

يتيمة الدّهر للثعالبى،

The second volume of ath-Tha'álibí's well-known biographies of the post-classical Arabic poets entitled *Yatímatu'd-Dahr*, of which the text has been printed in four volumes at Damascus in 1304/1886–7. See Brockelmann's *Gesch. d. Arab. Litt.*, vol. I, p. 284, and references there given.

This MS., bought of Messrs Luzac for 30*s.* on May 25, 1911, contains the poets of the Buwayhid period. It comprises 188 ff. of 23·6 × 16 c. and 21 ll., and is written in a clear *naskh* with rubrications. It was copied by 'Alí Amín al-Yázají of Constantinople for a lady called Mína or Munīra Hánum (هانم for خانم), and was completed on the 20th of Rabí' II, 1272/Dec. 30, 1855.

J. 2 (8).

وفيات الاعيان لابن خلّكان (الجزء الاوّل)،

A MS. of the first volume of Ibn Khallikán's celebrated biographical dictionary entitled *Wafayátu'l-A'yán*, composed in the years 654/1256–672/1274. See Brockelmann's *Gesch. d. Arab. Litt.*, vol. I, pp. 326–328, and the references there given.

This MS., one of five bought of J. J. Naaman on December 9, 1911, comprises 200 ff. of 18·8 × 13·8 c. and 26 ll., is written in a good *naskh* with rubrications, and was completed in Rajab, 997/May—June, 1589.

J. 2* (10).

ايضا (الجزء الخامس)،

The fifth and concluding part of the same work, containing **Lives 817–865** of Wüstenfeld's edition.

This MS. comprises 331 pp. of 24·8 × 17·5 c. and 21 ll., is written in a good, clear *naskh* with rubrications, and was copied in forty days by Aḥmad ibn Muṣṭafà ibn Khalíl, who completed it on the 17th of Ramaḍán, 742 (Feb. 24, 1342).

J. 3 (7).

منتخبات از تذكرة الاولياء شيخ فريد الدّين عطّار،

Selections from the *Tadhkiratu'l-Awliyá*, or "Memoirs of the Saints," of Shaykh Farídu'd-Dín 'Aṭṭár, the well-known Persian poet and mystic, who died (slain by the Mongols according to the popular belief) early in the thirteenth century of the Christian era. References to his life and works (which are to be found in all the larger Persian Catalogues) will be indicated under his poems in section **V** *infra*. A critical edition of this work in two volumes was published by Dr R. A. Nicholson (Brill, Leyden, 1905 and 1907).

This MS. was sent to me as a gift by the poet *Sarkhush* by the hand of my old friend the Nawwáb Mírzá Ḥusayn-qulí Khán when he came from Persia to England in 1892. In the accompanying letter, dated 14 Rajab, 1309/13 Feb., 1892, *Sarkhush* says that he transcribed these extracts when he was only fourteen years old, so that, as the colophon is dated Sha'bán, 1297/July, 1880, he must have been born in or about 1283/1866–7.

Ff. 174 of 16·8 × 10·6 c. and 12 ll.; excellent *ta'líq* with rubrications.

J. 4 (9).

تذكرة الاوليا،

Another somewhat abridged MS. of ʻAṭṭár's *Tadhkiratu'l-Awliyá*, made in 1269/1852–3. It contains forty out of the ninety-seven biographies in Dr Nicholson's edition.

Ff. 228 of 20·8 × 13·5 c. and 15 ll., neat and fairly legible Persian *ta'líq* with rubrications.

J. 5 (10).

ترجمهٔ سير النّبى،

A Persian translation by Uways ibn Fakhri'd-Dín ibn Ḥasan ibn Ismá'íl of Mu'minábád of the Arabic biography of the Prophet Muḥammad composed by Sa'íd ibn Mas'úd ibn Muḥammad ibn Mas'úd of Kázarún, who died in 758/1357, probably the work entitled *al-Muntaqà fí Síratí'n-Nabíyyi'l-Muṣṭafà*. See Brockelmann's *Gesch. d. Arab. Litt.*, vol. II, p. 195. The translator completed his task, as he informs us in the colophon on f. 274[a], on Monday the 27th of Rabí' I, 896/Feb. 7, 1491. A note under the colophon states that this MS. (which is very probably an autograph) became the property of Mawláná Quṭbu'd-Dín ibn Ḥusayn ibn ʻUmar of Táyábád on the 12th of Rabí' II, 899/Jan. 20, 1494. A note in the hand of the late Sir A. Houtum-Schindler, to whom the MS. formerly belonged, states that Mu'minábád is a district in the Qá'in province of Khurásán with ruins of the old Castle of Mu'minábád, formerly a stronghold of the Assassins, and that Táyábád is a village near Búshanj in the Herát province.

Begins:

حمد و سپاس بى قياس خدايرا كه نور محمّدرا عليه الصلوة والسلام پيش از همه چيزها آفريد، و بعد از آن عرش و كرسى و لوح و ارواح ديگر پيغمبران و مقرّبان‌را از آن موجود گردانيد الخ

The author of the original Arabic work is mentioned on f. 4[a], ll. 13 *et seqq.*, as follows:

مؤلّف كتاب خادم احاديث نبويّه شاگرد اخبار مصطفويّه سعيد بن مسعود بن محمّد بن مسعود كازرونى اسكنه الله بحبوحة الجنان وأفاض عليه سجال الرّحمة والغفران گفته كه هر شغلى‌را مردمانند كه اعلام آن بر دست ايشان افراشته و اكمام آن بر زبانشان شكافته و هر عالمى‌را درين علم طريقيست الخ

The book is divided into four parts called *Qism*, each of which is subdivided into numerous chapters (*Báb*) and sections (*Faṣl*). The contents are fully stated on ff. 6^{a}–7^{b}, as follows:

قسم اوّل، در بیان آنچه از اوّل خلق نور نبوّت تا زمان حضرت رسالت صلوات الله وسلامه علیه بوده و درین قسم هشت باب است

باب اوّل، در بیان کیفیّت تابیدن نور حضرت رسالت صلوات الله وسلامه علیه پیش از وجود و صورت او و ذکر خلق طیّبهٔ او پیش از طینت آدم و حدیث صورتهاء پیغمبران علیهم السّلام، (f. 7^{b})

باب دوم، در بیان بشارات کتب قدیمه و انبیا و دیگران به بعثت رسول صلّی الله علیه وسلّم، (f. 14^{a})

باب سیوم، در بیان اخبار جنّیان به بعثت رسول خدای صلّی الله علیه وسلّم، (f. 17^{a})

باب چهارم، در بیان و ذکر کیفیّت منتقل شدن نور او صلّی الله علیه وسلّم از اصلاب بارحام طاهره، (f. 19^{b})

باب پنجم، در بیان و ذکر عجایب و غرایب که در مدّت حمل او صلّی الله علیه وسلّم بظهور آمده، (f. 30^{b})

باب ششم، در بیان و ذکر ولادت و ظهور یمن و برکت او در حال حمل و کیفیّت وضع حضرت رسالت صلّی الله علیه وسلّم (f. 31^{a})

باب هفتم، در بیان حوادث که در شب ولادت او صلّی الله علیه وسلّم ظاهر شده (f. 35^{b})

باب هشتم، در بیان ذکر نسب آبا و امّهات و کیفیّت وفات عبد الله و ذکر اسماء او صلّی الله علیه وسلّم و درین باب بعدد مذکورات پنج فصل است (f. 37^{a})

فصل اوّل، در بیان ذکر نسب او صلّی الله علیه وسلّم (f. 37^{a})

فصل دوم، در بیان ذکر پدران او صلّعم (f. 37^{a})

فصل سیوم، در بیان ذکر مادران حضرت رسالت صلّعم (f. 39^{a})

فصل چهارم، در بیان و ذکر وفات عبد الله (f. 39^{b})

فصل پنجم، در بیان ذکر اسامی رسول خدای صلّعم (f. 40^{a})

قسم دوم، در بیان آنچه از اوّل ولادت تا زمان نبوّت او صلّعم جاری شده و درین قسم نه باب است (f. 41^{a})

باب اوّل، در بیان آنچه در سال اوّل از ولادت او صلّعم حادث شده (f. 41^{a})

باب دوم، در بیان حلیمه و اوضاع او و کیفیّت شقّ صدر و حدیث کاهن وغیره در شان او صلّعم (f. 41^{b})

باب سیوم، در بیان آنچه در سال سیوم از مولد او صلّعم بوده (f. 48^{a})

باب چهارم، در بیان آنچه در سال چهارم و پنجم و ششم از مولد او صلّعم بوده و درین باب بعدد هر سالی فصلیست (f. 50^{b})

فصل اوّل، در بیان آنچه در سال چهارم بوده (f. 50^{b})

فصل دوم، در بیان آنچه در سال پنجم بوده (f. 51^{a})

فصل سیوم، در بیان آنچه در سال ششم واقع شده (f. 51ᵃ)

باب پنجم، در بیان آنچه در سال هفتم از مولد او صَلَّعَم بوده و حدیث سیف بن ذی یزن (f. 51ᵇ)

باب ششم، در بیان آنچه در سال هشتم تا آخر یازدهم از مولد او صَلَّعَم بوده (f. 54ᵃ)

باب هفتم، در بیان آنچه در سال دوازدهم تا آخر سال بیست و سیم از مولد او صَلَّعَم بوده (f. 56ᵃ)

باب هشتم، در بیان آنچه در سال بیست و پنجم از مولد او بوده و قصّهٔ راهب و تزویج خدیجه رضی الله عنها و ذکر اولاد او صَلَّعَم (f. 58ᵇ)

باب نهم، در بیان آنچه در سال بیست و پنجم از مولد او بوده تا آخر چهل‌سالگی او صَلَّعَم در مکّه بوده (f. 61ᵇ)

قسم سیوم، در بیان آنچه در زمان نبوّت و مدّت اقامت حضرت رسالت علیه الصّلوة والسّلام در مکّه بوده و درین قسم نُه باب است (f. 62ᵇ)

باب اوّل، در بیان ذکر امارت و نبوّت او صَلَّعَم (f. 62ᵇ)

باب دوم، در بیان آنچه در سال اوّل از نبوّت او صَلَّعَم بوده و صفت نزول وحی و ذکر آنکه اوّل که مسلمان شد، (f. 66ᵃ)

باب سیم، در بیان آنچه در سال چهارم و پنجم از نبوّت او صَلَّعَم بوده و مکاره که از مشرکان کشیده و کیفیّت هجرت حبشه و درین باب چهار فصل است (f. 72ᵃ)

فصل اوّل، در بیان آنچه در سال چهارم از نبوّت واقع شده (f. 72ᵃ)

فصل دوم، در بیان آنچه در سال پنجم از نبوّت واقع شده (f. 73ᵃ)

فصل سیوم، در بیان آنچه از مشرکان بحضرت رسالت صَلَّعَم رسیده (f. 73ᵇ)

فصل چهارم، در ذکر هجرت بحبشه امّ سلمه رضی الله عنها (f. 74ᵇ)

باب چهارم، در بیان آنچه در سال ششم و هفتم از نبوّت او صَلَّعَم بوده و ذکر اسلام حمزه و عمر رضی الله عنهما (f. 77ᵃ)

باب پنجم، در بیان آنچه در سال هشتم از نبوّت او صَلَّعَم بوده و ذکر عهد و سوگند خوردن قریش بر دشمنی بنی هاشم و بنی مطّلب (f. 80ᵇ)

باب ششم، در بیان آنچه در سال دهم از نبوّت او صَلَّعَم بوده و وفات خدیجه و ذکر ثقیف و جماعتی جنّیان و تزویج عایشه و سوده رضی الله عنهما (f. 83ᵇ)

باب هفتم، در بیان آنچه در سال یازدهم از نبوّت او صَلَّعَم بوده (f. 87ᵇ)

باب هشتم، در بیان آنچه در سال دوازدهم از نبوّت او صَلَّعَم بوده و ذکر معراج و کیفیّت فرض شدن نماز درآن شب، (f. 88ᵃ)

باب نهم، در بیان آنچه در سال سیزدهم از نبوّت او صَلَّعَم بوده (f. 95ᵇ)

قسم چهارم، در بیان آنچه در مدّت سالهای هجرت حضرت رسالت صَلَّعَم جاری شده و درین قسم یازده باب است و خاتمة الکتاب (f. 97ᵇ)

باب اوّل، در بیان آنچه در سال اوّل از هجرت بوده و درین باب پنج فصل است (f. 97ᵇ)

فصل اوّل، در ذکر سبب هجرت رسول صَلَّعَم (f. 97ᵇ)

فصل دوم، در ذکر خروج حضرت رسالت صلعم و ابو بکر رضی الله عنه از مکّه بغار (f. 98[b])

فصل سیوم، در بیان آنچه در راه مدینه واقع شده و قصّهٔ اُمّ مَعْبَد (f. 101[b])

فصل چهارم، در انواع اوصاف رسول خدای صلعم (f. 104[a])

فصل پنجم، در ذکر استقبال کردن اهل مدینه مر حضرت رسالت [را] صلعم و حالات و حوادث که در آن زمان جاری شده و قصّهٔ وفات (f. 115[a])

باب دوم، در بیان آنچه در سال دوم از هجرت بوده و ذکر نکاح و دامادی علی با فاطمه رضی الله عنهما الخ (f. 124[b])

باب سیم، در بیان آنچه در سال سیم از هجرت بوده (f. 140[b])

باب چهارم، آنچه در سال چهارم از هجرت بوده (f. 151[a])

باب پنجم، در بیان آنچه در سال پنجم از هجرت بوده (f. 158[a])

باب ششم، در بیان آنچه در سال ششم از هجرت بوده و بعث رسول بملوك اطراف (f. 172[a])

باب هفتم، در بیان آنچه در سال هفتم از هجرت بوده (f. 184[b])

باب هشتم، در بیان آنچه در سال هشتم از هجرت بوده (f. 189[b])

باب نهم، در بیان آنچه در سال نهم از هجرت بوده (f. 201[b])

باب دهم، در بیان آنچه در سال دهم از هجرت بوده و قصّهٔ حجّة الوداع (f. 214[b])

باب یازدهم، در بیان آنچه در سال یازدهم بوده و ذکر مسیلمهٔ کذّاب (f. 220[b])

خاتمة الکتاب، در انواع اشیا که جمله عاید بتعظیم و توقیر حضرت رسالت صلعم می‌شود و درآن هفت فصل است (f. 239[b])

فصل اوّل، در بیان ثناء خدای تعالی و اظهار عظم قدر آن حضرت نزد حقّ عزّ شانه (f. 239[b])

فصل دوم، در بیان بعضی از معجزات رسول صلعم (f. 240[b])

فصل سیوم، در رعایت حقوق حضرت رسالت صلعم که بر خلایق واجب و لازم است (f. 246[a])

فصل چهارم، در ذکر لزوم محبّت حضرت رسالت صلعم و فوائد بسیار (f. 251[a])

فصل پنجم، در بیان صلوات بر رسول صلعم و ذکر فرض و استحباب و کیفیّت آن و مذهب تارك آن (f. 256[b])

فصل ششم، در بیان آنچه در حقّ حضرت رسالت صلعم سبّ و نقص و تکفیر عایب و سبّ کننده و مکذّب آن حضرت علیه الصّلوة والسّلام و تأدیب آنکس که اضافت و نسبت غیر لایق بآن حضرت کند و ذکر سبّ پیغمبران و ملایکه علیهم السّلام و اهل بیت و صحابه رضوان الله علیهم اجمعین (f. 261[a])

فصل هفتم، در بیان عرس حضرت رسالت صلعم فی الاوّلین و الآخرین (f. 271[b])

The MS. comprises 275 ff. of 24·8 × 17·2 c. and 20 ll., and is written in an antique and very legible *naskh* with rubrications. It belonged formerly to the Iḥtishámu'l-Mulk and afterwards to Sir A. Houtum-Schindler.

J. 6 (10).

نفحات الانس

A fine MS. of Jámí's well-known hagiography entitled *Nafaḥátu'l-Uns* of which the text was printed at Calcutta under the supervision of W. Nassau Lees in 1859. See also Rieu's Persian Catalogue, pp. 349–351.

This MS., which belonged to Prince Farhád Mírzá *Mu'tamadu'd-Dawla* in 1285/1868, and afterwards to Sir A. Houtum-Schindler, comprises 312 ff. of 24·2 × 16·3 c. and 21 ll., and is written in a good, clear *naskh* with rubrications. Its transcription was completed in Rajab, 902/March, 1497, only nineteen years after its composition.

J. 7 (9).

مجالس النّفايس

The *Majálisu'n-Nafá'is*, a well-known biography of contemporary poets compiled in Chaghatáy Turkish by Mír 'Alí Shír Nawá'í in 896/1490–1. See Rieu's Turkish Catalogue, pp. 273–274, and references there given.

The MS., of the acquisition of which I have no note, comprises 94 ff. of 21·5 × 16 c. and 18 ll., is written in a good *ta'líq* with rubrications, and was copied in 937/1530–1 by Muḥammad 'Alí ibn Yár 'Alí of Samarqand.

J. 8 (10).

تذكرة الشعراء دولتشاه،

A MS. of the well-known *Tadhkiratu'sh-Shu'ará*, or "Memoirs of the Poets," of Dawlatsháh of Samarqand, for full particulars of which see the Preface to my edition of the text published by Messrs E. J. Brill of Leyden in 1901.

Ff. 185 of 22·2 × 16·2 c. and 21 ll., good, clear *ta'líq* with rubrications, transcribed in 908/1502–3 or 980/1572–3. From the library of the late Sir A. Houtum-Schindler.

J. 9 (9).

ريحانة الاولياء وزهرة الحياة الدّنيا،

The title ordinarily given to this biographical work of Aḥmad ibn Muḥammad ibn 'Umar al-Khafájí al-Miṣrí (d. 1069/1659) differs slightly from the above, and is *Rayḥánatu'l-Alibbá* (not *Awliyá*) *wa-Nuzhatu* (not *Zuhratu*) *'l-Ḥayáti'd-Dunyá*. See Brockelmann's *Gesch. d. Arab. Litt.*, vol. II, pp. 285–286, and Rieu's Arabic Supplement, pp. 705–706.

This MS., bought of the late Ḥájjí 'Abdu'l-Majíd Belshah in November, 1920, comprises 227 ff. of 21·5 × 15 c. and 15 ll., and is written in a good, clear modern *naskh* with rubrications. The transcription was completed in Dhu'l-Qa'da, 1300/September, 1883.

J. 10 (8).

رسالة فى مناقب الصّحابة وغيره،

An acephalous and untitled Arabic MS. on the virtues of the Prophet's companions (*aṣ-Ṣaḥába*), given to me in Constantinople in April, 1908, by Dr Riḍá Tawfíq. The first complete article with title begins on f. 3[b]:

ومن مناقب الامام أبى بكر رضى الله عنه، قال العلماء افضل المهاجرين السيّد أبى (*sic*) بكر الصّدّيق وأقدمهم اسلامًا وأكرمهم وأعزّهم بعد رسول الله صلّعم آلخ

Then follow similar articles on 'Umar (f. 16[a]) and 'Alí (f. 29[a]), but the latter breaks off abruptly on f. 37[a] and is followed by a blank page. F. 38[a] begins:

قال رسول الله صلّعم من سرّه أن ينظر الى آدم عليه السّلام فى علمه آلخ

Another similar break occurs after f. 77, and the remainder of the volume (ff. 78[b]–101[a]) is filled with prayers.

Ff. 101 of 17·8 × 13·3 c. and 19 ll., large, coarse *naskh* with rubrications, dated Rajab 27, 885/Oct. 3, 1480.

J. 11 (12).

دستور الوزراء

The *Dastúru'l-Wuzará*, containing biographies of eminent *Wazírs*, or Ministers of State, from the beginning of Islám to 910/1504–5, by Khwándamír. See Rieu's Persian Catalogue, p. 335.

This MS., bought from the late Ḥájjí 'Abdu'l-Majíd Belshah in January, 1920, formerly belonged to Mírzá Muḥammad Taqí *Lisánu'l-Mulk* of Káshán, author of the *Násikhu't-Tawáríkh*, whose poetical pen-name was *Sipihr*, and afterwards to his son 'Abbás-qulí, whose note to this effect is dated 1318/1900. It comprises 209 ff. of 28·7 × 18·6 c. and 15 ll., is written in a good, clear modern *naskh* with rubrications, and was completed on Shawwál 15, 1268/August 2, 1852. A note at the end states that it has been collated with the original from which it was copied, but that this original was itself very incorrect.

J. 12 (8).

حديقة الوزراء

The *Ḥadíqatu'l-Wuzará*, containing biographies of the Grand Wazírs of the Ottoman Empire from the origin of the dynasty down to the reign of Sulṭán Aḥmad III, composed in or about 1120/1708–9 by 'Uthmán ('Osmán)-záda Aḥmad Efendi, poetically surnamed Tá'ib (d. 1136/1723–4). See Rieu's Turkish Catalogue, p. 73, and references there given. A printed edition appeared at Constantinople in 1271/1854–5.

This MS., bought at Constantinople on April 23, 1908, comprises 160 ff. of 20·4 × 12 c. and 15 ll., and is written in a good Turkish *naskh*, not dated.

J. 13 (10).

ذيل يوسف نابى

The Continuation or Supplement (*Dhayl*) of Yúsuf Nábí (d. 1124/1712) to the unfinished Life of the Prophet Muḥammad, entitled *Durratu't-Táj*, of Waysí (Veysí), d. 1037/1627–8. See Rieu's Turkish Catalogue, p. 37.

Ff. 175 of 23·5 × 14·6 c. and 27 ll.; written in a small, neat, fairly legible modern Turkish hand; dated Dhu'l-Qa'da, 1310/May—June, 1893. Bought of the late Ḥájjí 'Abdu'l-Majíd Belshah in November, 1920.

J. 14 (11).

آثار احمدى

Áthár-i-Aḥmadí, an acephalous and anonymous Persian work containing anecdotes of the Prophet Muḥammad. The beginning of the Preface is missing, and the author only speaks of himself as "this erring and sinful servant" (اين بندهٔ عاصى جانى), but he gives the title of the book as above in the last line of f. 2b, and says that he compiled it at the request of certain friends whose commands it was his duty to obey. Amongst his sources he mentions the *Rawḍatu'l-Aḥbáb*, a work composed about 930/1523–4, and described on p. 147 of Rieu's Persian Catalogue. The following note by a former owner on the blank page at the beginning of the MS. ascribes it to "one of our men of learning in the time of the Ṣafawí kings":

هذا كتاب الآثار الأحمدى لبعض علمائنا فى زمن السلاطين الصّفويّة وقد انتقل الى العبد الفقير محمّد باقر بن محمّد تقى بن محمّد باقر الاصفهانى فى شهر محرّم من شهور سنة ١٣٢٤

One leaf at least seems to be missing between the remains of the Preface and the body of the work, the first complete section of which is entitled:

گفتار در ذکر حلیمه خاتون بمکّه آمدن و آنحضرترا بوی سپردن بجهة شیر دادن و عجائب و غرائب از آن سرور بظهور آمدن و باز آوردن آنحضرترا بمکّه و بعبد المطّلب سپردن و باقی از حالات آن سرور

The end of the MS. is also missing. The last section (f. 248[a]) is headed:

گفتار در ذکر کرامات امام محمّد مهدی هادی علیه السلم،

Ff. 250 of 25·7 × 15·6 c. and 20 ll.; good *ta'líq* with rubrications. Bought of Ḥájjí 'Abdu'l-Majíd Belshah in 1920.

J. 15 (8).

مناقب اولیای شریفی،

Anecdotes of Turkish Shaykhs and Ṣúfí saints, especially the ancestors of the author, Sharíf ibn Sharífí (f. 4[b], l. 8), more particularly his grandfather Shaykh Burhánu'd-Dín Muḥammad ibn Muḥammad az-Zayní al-Ḥusayní, and his great-great-grandfather Sulṭán Shaykh. The work was composed in 1005/1596–7, and is dedicated to Sulṭán Muḥammad III. It begins:

حمد و سپاس، و شکر بی قیاس، اول خالق خلق و رازق ناس، واهب عقل و حواس، فایض فکر و قیاس حضرتنه اولسونکه آلخ ...امّا بعد، اشبو فقیر حقیر خاکپای اولیای اتقیا، غلام کمترین آل عبا و زمرهٔ علمانك کمتری، و فرقهٔ مدرّسینك احقری شریف ابن شریفی ایدر که آلخ

On f. 79 the author traces his genealogy up to the Imám Músà al-Káẓim and through him to 'Alí ibn Abí Ṭálib and Fáṭima, the Prophet's daughter. There is no date or colophon.

Ff. 70 of 19·9 × 11·8 c. and 15 ll.; good ***naskh*** within gilt margins.

J. 16 (9).

تذکرة الاولیاء (ترکی)

Lives of Prophets and Saints in Turkí, without title or author's name, beginning:

اعوذ بالله من الشیطان الرجیم، بسم الله الرّحمن الرّحیم، ۱۸۴۹ ده،

خبرده بویله گلمشدور کم الله تعالی جهنّمده ایکی خلق یراتدی بری ارکك آرصلان صورتنده و بری دشی آرصلان صورتنده آلخ

The anecdotes range over the whole period between Adam and the Imám Ḥusayn ibn 'Alí, and deal with nearly all the Patriarchs and Prophets. The colophon (f. 124^a) is dated April 11, 1849. Then follows (ff. 124^b–127^b) a Turkí poem on the death of the Prophet's son Ibráhím, beginning:

اوّل الله یادنی یاد ایتالوم، بر سوزوم وار هم صونکره بیان ایتالوم،

This in turn is followed (ff. 128^a–137^a) by a short account of the Torment of the Tomb (فی بیان عذاب القبر), in the colophon of which the scribe gives the date as April 18, 1849, and his name as Muḥammad Khalaf ibn Mullá Sulaymán al-Marjání (?) al-Bulghárí. This is followed by two other short religious poems of 27 and 6 verses respectively, and four lines of Arabic, written in red.

The MS., which, according to a signed note by Dr E. H. Minns, was "bought of Muḥammad al-Ab al-Ab 'Abd-ul-Karím" on October 10/22, 1898, at Kazan, comprises 138 ff. of 20·5 × 16·5 c. and 17 ll., and is written in a clear but outlandish *ta'líq* with rubrications and marginal indications of contents.

J. 17 (8).

رياض الشّعراء رياضى،

The *Riyáḍu'sh-Shu'ará*, a biography of Turkish poets completed after two years' labour in Rajab, 1018/Oct. 1609, by Riyáḍí (b. 980/1572–3, d. 1054/1644–5), and dedicated to Sulṭán Aḥmad I. See E. J. W. Gibb's *History of Ottoman Poetry*, vol. III, pp. 200–201 and 284–286.

Begins:

صد هزار سپاس و ثنا اول دیباجه پرداز انّ هذه تذکرة جنابنه سزادر الخ

Ff. 90 of 19·7 × 13·5 c. and 21 ll.; fair *ta'líq* with rubrications, dated Sha'bán, 1102/May, 1691. Bought of J. J. Naaman in May, 1905, for £4.

J. 18 (14).

تذكرهٔ دلگشا تأليف على اكبر شيرازى،

The *Tadhkira-i-Dilgushá*, containing biographies of modern Persian poets with specimens of their verse, by 'Alí Akbar of Shíráz. To this is prefixed an account of Shíráz and its most notable buildings, mosques and gardens, including somewhat lengthy selections from the poems of Sa'dí (ff. 12^b–24^b) and Ḥáfiẓ (ff. 24^b–28^b). The author, who himself wrote poetry under the pen-name of *Bismil*, began this book in 1237/1821–2 at the command of Ḥusayn 'Alí Mírzá, son of Fatḥ-'Alí Sháh. According to a note of Sir A. Houtum-Schindler (from whose library I acquired the MS. in January, 1917) it was largely used by Sayyid Ḥasan in the compilation of his *Fárs-náma*.

After a fairly short and simple Preface (ff. 2^b–4^a) beginning:

این روضهٔ دلگشاست باغی ز جنان، از فضل خدای اکبر ایمن ز خزان،
هر صفحهٔ اوست غیرت عارض حور، هر سطری ازوست رشك زلف غلمان،

the work is divided into:

Gulzár (ff. 4^a–40^b) on Shíráz, its history, monuments, gardens, etc. This comprises three sections entitled *Gulbun*, occupying ff. 4^a–7^a, 7^a–12^a, and 12^a–40^a respectively.

Bústán i (ff. 41^a–48^a). Poems by Fatḥ-'Alí Sháh and other members of the Royal Family.

Bústán ii (ff. 48^a–116^b). Other poets, arranged alphabetically under the final letter of the *Takhalluṣ*, or *nom de guerre*, *e.g.* under *alif*:

بینوا، شیدا، صبا، صفا، فدا، مینا، نوا، وفا، هما، یغما،

Khátima (ff. 116^b–125^b) containing an autobiography of the author and selections from his poems, and concluding with an account of the earthquake of the 4th of Shawwál, 1239/June 2, 1824.

Ff. 126 of 33·5 × 21·3 c. and 20 ll., excellent and clear *naskh* with rubrications. No date or colophon, but numerous erasures and corrections, especially in the early part of the book, make it appear that this MS. was written by or for the author.

J. 19 (10).

تذکرهٔ متأخّرین شعراء فارس،

This MS., unhappily defective both at beginning and end, was given to me by my friend Mr W. A. Smart, and to him at Shíráz in the spring of 1913 by Faṣíḥu'l-Mulk, poetically surnamed *Shúrída*, by whom I think it must have been transcribed, in return for eight volumes of Persian texts which I had sent to Mr Smart for presentation to men of letters in Persia. The Faṣíḥu'l-Mulk's letter to this effect, dated the 10th of Rabí' II, 1331/March 19, 1913, and also a poem by him in praise of Mr Smart and myself, are bound in the volume at the end.

The volume as I received it comprised 292 pp. of 22 × 15 c. and 12 ll., but pp. 1–2, 5–20, and an unknown number at the end were wanting. It contains short notices of modern Persian poets, chiefly of Fárs, with copious extracts from their poems, and is written in a good, clear *ta'líq* with rubrications and some marginal glosses. The poets mentioned seem to be arranged alphabetically from **A** (ا) to **R** (ر), so that half the book must be missing. Those mentioned include *Ázád* (d. 1328/1910), *Akhtar* (d. 1302/1884–5), *Afsurda* (d. 1320/1902–3), *Ulfat* (d. 1300/1883), *Adíbu'l-Mamálik* (born 1277/1860–1, d. 1335/1917), *Amín-i-Khurásání* (d. 1312/1894–5), *Anjám-i-Shírazí* (d. 1322/1904–5), *Anjám-i-Arrajání*,

Awrang-i-Shírází, *Ízadí of Kázarún* (d. 1322/1904–5), and some twenty-seven more, the four whose names begin with **R** (*Rághib*, *Raḥmat*, *Rukhṣat* and *Rashíd*) being followed by a long notice (pp. 276–292) of *Sayyid Muḥammad Faṣíḥu'z-Zamán*.

J. 20[1] (10) and **J. 20**[2] (10).

روضة الأُحباب فى سير النبى والآل والأُصحاب

لعطاء الله بن فضل الله الملقّب بجمال الحسينى،

A history of the Prophet Muḥammad, his Family, Companions and Followers, entitled *Rawḍatu'l-Aḥbáb fí siyari'n-Nabí wa'l-Ál wa'l-Aṣḥáb*, by Shaykh 'Aṭá'u'-lláh ibn Faḍlu'lláh, called Jamálu'l-Ḥusayní. See Rieu's Persian Catalogue, pp. 147–149, and Pertsch's Berlin Persian Catalogue, **No. 553**, pp. 531–532. The work was completed, as stated at the end, on Sunday, the 11th of Dhu'l-Ḥijja, 888 (Jan. 10, 1483): cf. Rieu's description of **Or. 146**.

The two volumes, of which the first comprises 360 and the second 346 ff. of 22·8 × 16·2 c. and 17 ll., form a continuous text, the division falling in the course of the year A.H. 7. They appear to contain only *Maqṣad I*, the seventh section of which begins at the bottom of f. 330[a] of the second volume. The handwriting is a clear, cursive *ta'líq* with rubrications, undated. Bought of J. J. Naaman on December 9, 1911.

J. 21 (12).

قصص الانبياء

Qiṣaṣu'l-Anbiyá ("Tales of the Prophets") translated into Persian by Muḥammad ibn As'ad ibn 'Abdi'lláh al-Ḥanafí at-Tustarí, beginning:

سپاس بی حدّ و ستایش بی عدد خالقی‌را کی جندین هزار نقطهٔ نبوت‌را از مرکز عدم در دایرهٔ وجود جهت ارشاد خلایق بظهور رسانید الخ ...جنین گوید بندهٔ ضعیف محمّد بن اسعد بن عبد الله الحنفی التستری عفا الله عنه که جون طباع سلیمه‌را بخواندن و شنودن احوال گذشتگان و اسماء و قصص ایشان شعغی تمام می‌باشد الخ

The name of the author of the Arabic original is given in the Preface as Shaykh Abu'l-Ḥasan ibnu'l-Hayṣam (? Haytham) al-Búshanjí, of whom I have hitherto found no other mention[1]. A note by Mr E. Edwards of the British Museum expresses the opinion that this work is probably identical with that mentioned by Ḥájjí Khalífa (vol. IV, p. 518) and by him ascribed to Sahl ibn 'Abdi'lláh at-Tustarí, but states that it is not identical with the British Museum MS. **Add. 25,783**. The chief

[1] [He may be identified with Abú Nu'aym Ḥamza ibnu'l-Hayṣam al-Búshanjí at-Tamímí, who is mentioned by Sam'ání, *Ansáb*, p. 433[b], l. 20.]

contents are indicated by rubrications and are as follows: the Creation, f. 4[a]; Paradise, f. 7[b]; the Sun, Moon and Stars, f. 10[a]; Iblís, f. 14[b]; Adam, f. 15[b]; Cain and Abel, f. 22[a]; Idrís (Enoch), f. 24[b]; Hárút and Márút, f. 27[b]; Noah, f. 29[a]; 'Ád, f. 32[b]; Thamúd, f. 36[b]; Abraham, f. 40[a]; Lot, f. 49[a]; Ishmael, f. 52[a]; Jacob, f. 56[b]; Joseph, f. 58[a]; Job, f. 79[a]; Moses, f. 83[a]; Dhu'l-Kifl, f. 102[a]; Samuel, f. 104[a]; David, f. 105[b]; Solomon, f. 116[a]; Bilqís (the Queen of Sheba), f. 119[b]; Luqmán, f. 130[b]; Jonah, f. 135[a]; Ezra, f. 145[a]; Zakariyyá and John the Baptist, f. 146[a]; Jesus, f. 149[a]; his Disciples, f. 158[a]; the *Aṣḥábu'l-Kahf*, or "Seven Sleepers," f. 160[a]; Dhu'l-Qarnayn, f. 176[a]; Barṣíṣá, f. 178[b]; the *Aṣḥabu'l-Ukhdúd*, f. 182[b]; Jirjís, f. 184[a]; Paul, f. 189[a]; Samson, f. 189[b]; the *Tubba's*, or Kings of Yaman, f. 190[a]; the Prophet Muḥammad, f. 195[a].

The account given of St Paul is particularly curious, since he is made responsible for the schisms amongst the followers of Christ, and, indeed, plays exactly the same part as the Jewish *wazír* in the second story of the First Book of the *Mathnawí*. This passage is as follows[1]:

ذکر بولس؛ قال الله تعالی فَٱخْتَلَفَ ٱلأَحْزَابُ مِنْ بَيْنِهِمْ اهل اخبار گویند که بعد از آنك حق تعالی عیسی‌را بآسمان برد ترسایان طریقهٔ نیکو داشتند تا آنگاه که بولس ایشان‌را از راه برد و او مردی بود از جهودان و با عیسی و اهل ملّت او بد بودی و پیوسته مساوی ایشان گفتی و دشمنی کردی چون پیر شد گفت که نخواهم که شرّ من از ایشان منقطع شود پس یك چشم خودرا کور کرد و ترسایانرا گفت مرا می‌شناسید گفتند بلی بدترین خلق خدا توئی گفت من دوش عیسی‌را بخواب دیدم لطمهٔ بر چشم من زد و مرا کور کرد و گفت تا کی اهل ملّت مرا برنجانی من بلرزیدم و از خواب بر جستم یك چشم من از کار افتاده است پیش شما آمدم تا دین و ملّت شما گیرم تا عیسی از من خشنود شود که من طاقت عتاب او ندارم ترسایان اورا قبول کردند و بخانهٔ بردند و او طریقهٔ رهبانان پیش گرفت و همه روز روزه داشتی و همه شب نماز کردی چندانك مردم برو فتنه شدند آنگاه گروهی‌را بخواند و گفت شما نه بینید که لشکر از پیش ملك آید گفتند بلی گفت ما می‌بینیم که آفتاب و ماه و ستارگان از مشرق بر آیند و مغرب فرو روند بی شك خدا در مشرق باشد گفتند بلی گفت پس اولی آن باشد که در نماز روی سوی مشرق کنیم آن گروه از بیت المقدس روی بر گردانیدند و نماز سوی مشرق کردند بعد از مدّتی گروهی دیگررا بخواند و گفت حق تعالی همه چیزرا نه از بهر منفعت آدمی آفریده است گفتند بلی گفت چرا باید که گوشت گاو حلال باشد و گوشت خوك حرام من چنان بینم که گوشت خوك حلال است آن گروه گوشت خوك بر خود حلال کردند بعد از مدّتی جمعی دیگررا بطلبید و گفت زنده کردن و آفریدن جز خدای تعالی دیگری‌را میسّر نشود گفتند نه گفت پس عیسی باید که خدا باشد که او مرغ آفرید و مرده

[1] [The text and translation of this passage were published in the last article written by Browne before his death, entitled "A parallel to the Story in the *Mathnawí* of Jalálu'd-Dín Rúmí of the Jewish King who persecuted the Christians" (*Islamica*, vol. II, fasc. i, pp. 129–134), which forms part of the "Festschrift" in honour of Professor A. Fischer of Leipzig.]

زنده کرد بعد از مدّتی خلق‌را جمع کرد و گفت دوش عیسی‌را بخواب دیدم گفت اکنون از تو راضی شدم و دست بر روی من نهاد حق از برکت دست او چشم مرا روشن کرد و مرا سخنی چند گفت که با شما بگویم از علما و بزرگان خود جمعی‌را اختیار کرده حاضر کنید تا پیغام بگزارم ایشان سه مرد از اکابر علماء خود پیش (f. 189b) او حاضر کردند گفت یك یك پیش من در آیند اوّل یکی‌را طلب داشت و اورا گفت عیسی مرا گفت چرا مرا بنده خوایند و شما دایند که من مرده زنده کرده‌ام و مرغ آفریدم و کور مادرزادرا بینا کردم و اینها جز خدا نتواند کردن من خدا ام باید که مرا خدا خوانید آن مرد قبول کرد که چنین گوید و از پیش او بیرون آمد' پس آن دیگررا طلب داشت و اورا گفت عیسی مرا گفت که امّت مرا بگو که من چیزها کردم که جز خدا نکند چرا مرا بندهٔ خدا خوایند من شریك خدا ام باید که در حق من این اعتقاد کنید آن مرد ازو قبول کرد و از پیش او بیرون آمد پس سدیگررا طلب داشت و گفت مرا عیسی گفت من پسر خداام و شما دیدید و شنیدید که من چه آفریدم و چگونه مرده زنده کردم باید که در انجیل همچنین خوانید آن مرد ازو قبول کرد و از پیش او بیرون آمد پس بولس هم آن شب خودرا بکشت و بعضی گویند بولس گفت چون پیغام او رسانیدم پیش او خواهم رفت و پیش خلق خودرا بکشت روز دیگر مردم چون آن حال بدیدند پیش ایشان هر سه رفتند و گفتند بولس پیغام عیسی بشما چه رسانید هر کس گفتند دیگر دیگررا خلاف کردند و اختلاف میان ایشان بر خاست و بعضی کویند بولس هر سه‌را گفت که عیسی مرا گفت که من پسر خدا ام پس هر سه خلاف کردند که این چگونه باشد و اختلاف بدین سبب میان ایشان واقع شد و نام ایشان یکی نسطور بود و یکی ملکا و دیگری مار یعقوب و چون مقالات ایشان طولی دارد و در این...چندان فایده نیست در آن شروعی نرفت'

This fine old MS., bought of the late Ḥájjí 'Abdu'l-Majíd Belshah in January, 1920, comprises 216 ff. of 28 × 20·5 c. and 23 ll., is written in a large, clear, archaic *naskh* with rubrications, and is dated the 5th of Dhu'l-Qa'da, 731/August 10, 1330.

J. 22 (8).

شمایل اتقیا

A Persian treatise on the Attributes of the Pious (*Shamá'il-i-Atqiyá*), beginning abruptly, without indication of authorship:

الحمد لله الّذی انار بانوار معرفته قلوب الابرار الخ ...بیان انواع ایمان عوامّ و خواصّ و خاصّ الخاصّ و زیادة و نقصان و مخلوق و غیر مخلوق ایمان و اسلام و فرق میان مؤمن و مسلم

The MS., acquired with some thirty others in January, 1924, comprises 188 ff. of 20 × 14 c. and 15 ll., and is written in a good, clear, modern *naskh* with rubrications, without colophon or date. A complete table of contents is prefixed. Amongst the books cited are the *Jáwíd-náma* of 'Aynu'l-Quḍát, the *Kashfu'l-Asrár*, the *Risála-i-'Unwán*, the *Fawá'idu'l-Fu'ád*, the *Iḥyá'u'l-'Ulúm* (of al-Ghazálí), the *Qútu'l-Qulúb*, the *Kashf-i-Maḥjúb*, and many others, and the author often introduces verses of his own in which, however, I have not been able to discover any clue to his identity.

K. GEOGRAPHY AND TRAVELS.

K. 1 (13).

صور الاقاليم

A Persian treatise on Geography, imperfect at both beginning and end, containing sixteen crude coloured maps, beginning:

و از آنجا تا دریا دو میل باشد و هم چند فید بود و فید در ولایت بنی‌طیّ باشد

In its present state the MS. comprises 97 ff. of 31·5 × 23 c. and 15 ll. and is written in a large, clear *ta'líq*, apparently of the sixteenth or seventeenth century. The maps occur on ff. 5ᵃ (Persian Gulf), 9ᵃ (Western Mediterranean, Spain and North Africa), 16ᵇ (Syria), 19ᵃ (region of the Tigris and Euphrates), 22ᵃ ('Iráq), 28ᵃ (Mediterranean), 38ᵃ (S.W. Persia), 41ᵇ (Fárs), 43ᵃ (S.E. Persia), 48ᵇ–49ᵃ (Khurásán and Transoxiana), 60ᵇ–61ᵃ (Khwárizm, Sughd, etc.), 87ᵇ–88ᵃ (map of the Old World from Spain to China), and 94ᵇ (the Arabian Peninsula). There are certainly some dislocations, and some of the leaves at the end of the MS. should come at the beginning. The regions are treated in the following order. Arabia (ff. 1 and 95–97); the Maghrib (N.W. Africa) and Spain (f. 11); Egypt (f. 15); Syria (f. 17); Mesopotamia (f. 19); 'Iráq (f. 21ᵇ); Khúzistán (f. 26ᵃ); the Mediterranean Sea (f. 27); Fárs (f. 30), including an account of its fire-temples; Khúzistán (f. 40); the Kurds (f. 42); Sístán (f. 44); Khurásán (f. 47); Transoxiana (f. 60); Khwárizm (f. 83).

The work appears to have been translated from an Arabic original of which the authorship is uncertain, but of which the date is indicated by two passages on ff. 11ᵇ and 13ᵇ, where Spain is spoken of as "still in the hands of the Umayyads," and as ruled by 'Abdu'r-Raḥmán III ibn Muḥammad ibn 'Abdi'lláh ibn Muḥammad I ibn 'Abdi'r-Raḥmán II ibn al-Ḥakam I ibn Hishám I ibn 'Abdi'r-Raḥmán I ibn Mu'áwiya ibn Hishám, who reigned A.H. 300–350 (A.D. 912–961) and adopted the title of Caliph in 317/929. The mention of numerous fire-temples in Fárs also points to an early date, *e.g.* on f. 33ᵃ:

ذکر آتشکدهای فارس، هیچ ناحیتی و روستائی نیست که نه درو آتش‌گاهی هست آنچه بزرگترست و معروفتر ازآن یاد کنیم،

Unfortunately, though the writing is generally clear, many diacritical points are omitted, so that the reading of the place-names is often very uncertain.

Bought of Ḥájjí 'Abdu'l-Majíd Belshah in January, 1920.

K. 2 (10).

نزهة القلوب،

Ḥamdu'lláh Mustawfí's well-known geographical work, the *Nuzhatu'l-Qulúb*, of which the portion relating to Persia has been published by G. le Strange with an English translation as vol. XXIII of the "E. J. W. Gibb Memorial" Series. Concerning this work see Rieu's Persian Catalogue, pp. 418–419, and for some account of the author pp. 80–82 of the same.

This MS., from Sir Albert Houtum-Schindler's library, comprises 235 ff. of 23 × 17·5 c. and 20 ll.; small neat *nasta'líq* with rubrications; no date or colophon; numerous marginal annotations and variants in Sir A. Houtum-Schindler's hand in the latter (Persian) portion; bought in Dámghán in 1876.

K. 3 (12).

نزهة القلوب،

Another much more modern copy of the *Nuzhatu'l-Qulúb*, also from Sir A. Houtum-Schindler's library. In the colophon the scribe gives his name as Suhráb ibn Ḥájjí Alláh-Karam of Sinandaj, and the date of completion as Ṣafar of...but omits the year.

Ff. 273 of 28 × 20·4 c. and 19 ll.; clear *ta'líq* with rubrications.

K. 4 (13).

هفت اقليم

The *Haft Iqlím* ("Seven Climes") of Amín Aḥmad-i-Rází, a valuable and well-known geographico-biographical dictionary compiled in 1002/1593–4. See Rieu's Persian Catalogue, pp. 335–337 and references there given, and Ethé's India Office Persian Catalogue, coll. 380–499. A printed edition by Khán Ṣáḥib Mawlawí 'Abdu'l-Muqtadir was begun at Calcutta in 1918, but apparently only one fasciculus (x + 112 pp.) was published, and the work was then discontinued.

This MS. belonged formerly to Colonel Raverty, and was bought from his widow by the Trustees of the "E. J. W. Gibb Memorial" in 1907 with two other MSS., the *Mujmal* of Faṣíḥí of Khwáf (see **G. 7** *supra*) and vol. II of the *Jámi'u't-Tawáríkh* of Rashídu'd-Dín Faḍlu'lláh, for £30. Some other MSS. of his were bought by the India Office[1].

[1] [This MS. of the *Haft Iqlím* is now in the India Office Library, to which it was returned by the Trustees of the "E. J. W. Gibb Memorial Fund" in June, 1927. See note 2 on p. 91 *supra*.]

Ff. 525 of 32·2 × 16·8 c. and 23 ll.; legible but ungraceful *ta'líq* with rubrications; undated. The account of the first Clime begins on f. 3ᵃ; the second on f. 12ᵇ; the third on f. 36ᵇ; the fourth on f. 187ᵃ; the fifth on f. 442ᵃ; the sixth on f. 505ᵇ; and the seventh on f. 523ᵃ.

K. 5 (13).

هفت اقليم،

Another MS. of the *Haft Iqlím* from the library of the late Sir Albert Houtum-Schindler, to which is prefixed a table of contents occupying 6 pages.

This MS., undated, was made in Aḥmad-ábád, comprises 548 ff. of 28·8 × 17 c. and 21 ll., and is written in an excellent *ta'líq* with rubrications. The first Clime begins on f. 3ᵃ, the second on f. 13ᵇ; the third on f. 37ᵇ; the fourth on f. 190ᵇ; the fifth on f. 443ᵇ; the sixth on f. 525ᵇ; and the seventh on f. 545ᵇ.

K. 6 (14).

شهرستان و غيره،

A MS. from the late Sir A. Houtum-Schindler's library containing four Persian treatises on geography, cosmography and the like, namely:

(1) A geographical poem in the *mutaqárib* metre, composed in Sha'bán, 977/January, 1570, by Ḥukmí or Ḥikmatí of Turkistán (ff. 1ᵇ–57ᵇ), incomplete at end, beginning:

آغاز كتاب شهرستان رشك بوستان و گلستان من كلام حكمى شاعر تركستان برغم دوشمنان (*sic*) بكام دوستان،

بنام خداوند جان و جهان، كه باشد خدا بر خداوندگان،
بحقّ رسول طريق يقين، شهِ دين و دنيا محمّد امين،
على ولى شاه مردان دين، مطيع رسول جهان آفرين،

The date of composition is mentioned in the 14th *bayt*, and the title in the sixteenth. The chief cities and districts celebrated are Mashhad, Jám, Bákharz, Sarakhs, Herát, Qandahár, Sístán and other towns in Khurásán, Jurján, 'Iráq, Mázandarán, Ádharbáyján, Fárs, China, Central Asia, Georgia and Kurdistán. Probably only one page is missing at the end, since the last section (p. 57) is described as the "Conclusion of the Book" (ختم كتاب). The poem is of little interest, and the verse is very bad, being full of false quantities.

(2) A Persian work entitled *'Ajá'ibu'l-Makhlúqát* ("the Wonders of Creation"), ascribed to Muḥammad ibn Maḥmúd ibn Aḥmad aṭ-Ṭírí (? aṭ-Ṭabarí) as-Salmání, beginning:

حمد و سپاس خدايرا كه صورت مارا از قطرهٔ آب بنگاشت و بخودى خود برآن ثنا گفت قال الله تبارك وتعالى وصوّركم فاحسن صوركم الخ

It occupies ff. 58ᵃ–207ᵃ and is divided into ten chapters called *Rukn*, of which the *first* (f. 62ᵇ) treats of the Angels, spirits and celestial bodies; the *second* (f. 74ᵃ) of fire, meteors, lightning, rainbows and winds; the *third* (f. 76ᵇ) of the earth, waters and mountains; the *fourth* (f. 94ᵇ) of notable cities, countries and buildings; the *fifth* (f. 116ᵃ) of trees; the *sixth* (f. 121ᵇ) of talismans, buried treasures, and the tombs of famous kings and prophets; the *seventh* (f. 126ᵇ) of the psychology, vanity and races of man, of prophetic miracles, the natural sciences, especially Alchemy and Medicine, and of Predestination and the Resurrection; the *eighth* (f. 156ᵃ) of the Jinn, and various diabolic creatures; the *ninth* (f. 162ᵃ) of wonderful birds; the *tenth* (f. 167ᵃ) of wonderful beasts and reptiles, concluding with an account of seventy-two *dívs* or demons and the talismans appropriate to each.

(3) An anonymous treatise on geography and cosmography entitled *Risála dar Masáḥat u Jaghráfiyá u Hay'at* (ff. 207ᵇ–240ᵇ), beginning:

الحمد لله الّذى زيّن السّمآء الدنيا بزينة الكواكب ونوّر وجه الغبرا باشعتها الثواقب...امّا بعد، بر ضمير منير ارباب فطنت و خاطر مستنير اصحاب خبرت واضح و لايح است كه معرفت هيئت اجسام سفلى و اوضاع اجرام علوى از اشرف مطالب و اعلى مراتب است

It comprises an Introduction (f. 208ᵃ) on elementary geometrical conceptions, two Discourses, the first (f. 209ᵃ) dealing with the measurements of the earth's surface and the definition of the Seven Climes, and the second (f. 233ᵇ) with the measurements of the heavens, planets and stars, and a Conclusion (f. 237ᵇ) dealing with certain religious obligations demanding some knowledge of these sciences. The colophon (on f. 240ᵇ) is dated Saturday, the 2nd of Ramaḍán, 1085/Nov. 30, 1674.

(4) The Conclusion (*Khátima*) of Mírkhwánd's *Rawḍatu'ṣ-Ṣafá* (ff. 241ᵇ–305ᵇ), entitled:

خاتمه در بيان بدايع صنايع ملك صانع و آنچه نگاشتهٔ كلك قدرت اوست بى مانع و منازع،

Copied by Khán Muḥammad ibn 'Abdi'lláh ibn 'Abdi'l-Kháliq ibn 'Abdi'l-Jalíl in 1085/1674–5.

Ff. 305 of 34 × 22·3 c. and 21 ll., legible *ta'líq* with rubrications.

K. 7 (9).

مخزن الاسفار،

Makhzanu'l-Asfár ("the Treasury of Travels"), an account of the mission of Farrukh Khán *Amínu'l-Mulk* to Europe in A.D. 1857–8, in connection with the negotiations which followed and concluded the Anglo-Persian War, compiled by Mírzá Ḥusayn ibn 'Abdi'lláh of Tabríz. The book comprises two parts, (1) an account of the journey from Ṭihrán (which they left on Monday the 11th of Dhu'l-

Qa'da, 1273 = July 3, 1857) to Paris, London and Constantinople (ff. 5[a]–212[a]), and (2) an account of the government and organization of France (ff. 212[b]–275[b]), especially Paris.

This MS., from the library of Sir A. Houtum-Schindler, was copied for Bahman Mírzá *Bahá'u'd-Dawla* by Áqá Bábá Sháhmírzádí, the son of Mullá Muḥammad Mahdí, and completed on Sunday, the 18th of Rajab, 1276/Feb. 10, 1860. It is written in a large, clear *naskh* with rubrications, and comprises 276 ff. of 21·4 × 14 c. and 19 ll.

K. 8 (14).

A modern Persian gazetteer or geographical dictionary, without title, author's name, preface or colophon, containing the names and brief particulars concerning a number of towns and countries in all parts of the world, especially the Western Hemisphere, arranged alphabetically and written in red with full vocalization. Amongst the British towns and places mentioned are Aberdeen, Edinburgh, Oxford, Exeter, Anglesea, Ailsa Crag, etc. The spelling of the Oriental (except the Persian) names often indicates that they have been taken from European geographies. In most cases the population, distance from the capital, and other particulars are given, and some of the articles are of considerable length. The following account of Cambridge (f. 105[a]) may serve as a specimen:

كَمْبَريج شهريست در مملكت انكليس دوازده فرسخ از شهر لندن دورست بسمت مشرق هفده مدرسه خيلى بزرگ دارد و ابتداى اين مدرسه‌ها هفتصد سال پيش ازين بوده كتابخانه‌ها كه در اينجا دارند بزرگترين كتابخانه‌هاى دنياست چهار نفر وكيل از آنجا بپاى تخت ميفرستند جمعيّتش بيست هزار نفرست،

This MS., which is curious rather than valuable, is from the Schindler library, and comprises 166 ff. of 33 × 21 c. and 21 ll., written in a small, clear modern *ta'líq* with rubrications.

K. 9 (9).

A list or census of all the houses and other buildings in Ṭihrán, compiled in 1269/1852–3 by command of Náṣiru'd-Dín Sháh:

عدد خانها و ساير بناهاى دار الخلافهٔ باهرهٔ طهران حفّت بالامن والامان كه حسب الامر قدر قدر وارث گاه جمشيد و ثالث ماه و خورشيد شاهنشاه جمجاه ادام الله ايّام دولته وزمان شوكته در آخر سال سيچقان ئيل مطابق با سنهٔ ١٢٦٩ هجرى تشخيص يافته غير از بيرون دروازها كه در آخر كتابچه جداگانه نوشته شده و علاحده ميزان بسته گشته دخلى بشهر ندارد،

This MS., from the Schindler library, constitutes a directory of the Persian capital for the year indicated (A.D. 1853), the character, size and ownership of each house, small and great, being specified. It is evidently the original MS., and would be of great value to anyone concerned with the topography, size and social life of Ṭihrán at that period. Unfortunately for the non-Persian reader many of the particulars given are written in the hand called *raqam* or *siyáq* commonly used in Persia for keeping accounts.

Ff. 188 of 21·5 × 15 c. and from 10 to 15 entries in four or five columns on each page. The writing, a small, neat *ním-shikasta*, is good of its kind. There is no colophon.

L. OFFICIAL PAPERS, LETTERS, ETC.

L. 1 (7), L. 2 (9), L. 3 (9).

مُنْشَآت رشیدی،

A very interesting collection of some fifty-two letters written to various contemporaries by the great minister, physician and historian Rashídu'd-Dín Faḍlu'lláh, who was finally put to death in A.D. 1318 at the age of seventy by Abú Sa'íd the Mongol. The best and fullest account of this remarkable man is that given by Quatremère in his *Histoire des Mongols de la Perse* (Paris, 1836), but the main facts about his life and literary activity will be found in my *History of Persian Literature under Tartar Dominion* (Cambridge, 1920), pp. 46–47, 49, 51–52 and 68–87. Some account of the present collection of letters (of which, so far as I know, I possess the only two existing MSS.) is given on pp. 80–86 of the above-mentioned work.

L. 1, the original MS., was given by Sir A. Houtum-Schindler in July, 1913, to Mr G. le Strange who gave it to me on September 8, 1917. It is defective both at the beginning and the end, comprises 182 ff. of 17·6 × 11·8 c. and 15 ll., and was bought by Sir A. Houtum-Schindler in Ṭihrán in December, 1908. It is written in a good, clear old *naskh* with rubrications and other titles in blue and dark red, and begins abruptly in the middle of the preface of the editor Muḥammad Abarqúhí:

...و سایه‌بان سرو و شمشادرا بر افراشت، و عروس گلشن خضرارا از آب سحاب سیراب ساخت که وَأَنْزَلْنَا مِنَ ٱلسَّمَآءِ مَآءً الخ

The first letter begins on f. 4[b] and is entitled:

مکتوبی که مصنّف مذکور علیه الرّحمة بمولاناء اعظم مجد الدّین اسمعیل فالی قدّس سرّه نوشته است، عطارد که وزیر شاهنشاه فلك است از لآلی متلالی ارقام اقلام مخدوم حقیقی ملتقط فراید فواید باد، دیروز از فضلای این ملك در باب معنی وزیر و وزارت و اشتقاقات آن بحثی می کردند و چنانکه می خواستند نهال سخن می پیراستند الخ

Unfortunately very few of these letters are dated, *viz.* No. 7 (f. 9[b]), Sha'bán 690/August, 1291, from Sulṭániyya; No. 15 (f. 28[a]), Thursday, mid-Sha'bán, 670/March 17, 1272, from Ṭús; and No. 42 (f. 142[b]), 690/1291, from Caesarea. They vary much alike in length and interest. In several cases long lists of herbs, drugs, and essential oils are demanded from the governors of different towns and provinces for the hospitals founded and maintained by Rashídu'd-Dín; in one (f. 33[b]) forty young men and maidens of Rúm are required to populate one of the villages in the Rab'-i-Rashídí at Tabríz; others refer to the marriages arranged for his sons (No. 23, f. 70[a]); another (No. 36, f. 120[b]) contains the will made by Rashídu'd-Dín during a dangerous illness, including bequests of books to the library founded by him in the Rab'-i-Rashídí, and to his children, fourteen sons and four daughters, enumerated by name. One letter (No. 45, f. 145[b]) is addressed to Shaykh Ṣafiyyu'd-Dín of Ardabíl, the ancestor of the Ṣafawí dynasty, while another (No. 49, f. 161[a]) especially commends him to Amír Aḥmad the Governor of Ardabíl. Several others specify gifts in money or kind to be made to men of learning (in one case residents in N. Africa) who have dedicated books to Rashídu'd-Dín. It will thus be seen that an immense amount of interesting matter rarely to be found in Persian histories is contained in these letters, which should certainly be published[1].

L. 2, the second MS., is merely a modern copy of **L. 1**, beginning with l. 1 of f. 1[b] and ending identically, made in 1266/1849–1850 at Ṭihrán for Prince Bahman Mírzá *Bahá'u'd-Dawla*. It comprises 139 ff. of 21·5 × 16 c. and 17 ll., and is written in a legible *ta'líq* with rubrications.

L. 3 is an English "*Summary of the Contents of the Persian MS. Despatches of Rashīd-ad-Dīn*, copied from notes supplied by Sir A. Houtum-Schindler and afterwards corrected by him, Dec. 1913," made by Mr G. le Strange. Nearly half the book has been left blank. The written portion comprises 93 ff. of 19·6 × 15·2 c. and about 19 ll. + 30 ff. (numbered *1 to *30) slightly larger in size, concluding with a list of the Despatches in Mr le Strange's hand. Only the *recto* of each leaf is written on, the *verso* being left blank.

L. 4 (9), L. 5 (9).

Two volumes of fictitious letters about the ancient glories and present misery of Persia, supposed to have been written by an imaginary Prince of India named Kamálu'd-Dawla to an equally imaginary Prince of Persia named Jalálu'd-Dawla, but really composed by Mírzá Áqá Khán of Kirmán, who was secretly put to death at Tabríz with Shaykh Aḥmad Rúḥí of Kirmán and the Khabíru'l-Mulk on July 15, 1896. See Colonel D. C. Phillott's English Introduction to the Persian translation of Morier's *Haji Baba* (Calcutta, 1905, pp. vii–viii), and my *Persian Revolution*, pp. 93–96.

---

[1] [Some years ago Muḥammad Shafí', now Vice-Principal and Professor of Arabic at the Orienta College, Lahore, who at that time was a Government of India Research Scholar at Cambridge, made an abridged and annotated English translation of the Letters of Rashídu'd-Dín. It is hoped that the publication of this work, in which Professor Browne took the keenest interest, will not be long delayed.]

Both these volumes were transcribed for me in A.D. 1911 by the Bábí scribe Mírzá Muṣṭafà, who supplied me with so many Bábí MSS. They are uniform in size (21·8 × 14·5 c. and 18 ll.) and script (a clear but not very graceful *naskh*), and were received by me together in October, 1912.

L. 4 comprises 160 ff., and is incomplete, for of the hundred letters or addresses (*khiṭába*) to Jalálu'd-Dín which it should contain it actually contains only forty-two. It is headed:

بنام ایزد یکتا،

صورت یکصد خطابه است که شاهزادهٔ آزاده کمال الدّوله دهلوی که پدرش در زمان شاه تیمور از ایران بمرز و بوم هندوستان هجرت کرده بدوست محترم خود نوّاب جلال الدّوله شاهزادهٔ ایران نوشته است و شرح خرابی آنرا نگاشته،

The imaginary writer, Kamálu'd-Dawla, begins by expressing his regret that, contrary to the advice of his friend Jalálu'd-Dawla, he returned from his travels in Europe to India by way of Persia, the condition of which caused him the deepest mortification:

خطابهٔ اوّل، دوست عزیز من جلال الدّوله عاقبت سخن ترا نشنیده در مراجعت از فرنگستان از راه تبریز وارد بخاك اندوهناك ایران شدم، ایكاش نیآمده و هموطنان قدیم و خویشان كهن و وطن اصلی پر بلا و محن خودرا ندیده بودم و از احوال و عادات و اخلاق و روش و کیش و مذهب و آئین ایشان مطّلع نمیگشتم، دلم خون و آب و جگرم پارچه پارچه و کباب شد،

The leading motive of the book is the glorification of ancient and the disparagement of modern Persia. The Arabs are denounced as barbarians, and Islám, especially the Shí'a doctrine, is sharply criticized, while not only Zoroaster but even the communist Mazdak (f. 65^b) is applauded. The author makes a great display of his knowledge of European, especially French, words, and constantly puts forward the most absurd popular etymologies. Thus he detects the Persian word *núr* or *khur* (sun) in such place-names as Europe, Urús (Russia), Urúm (Rúm, Asia Minor), Arman (Armenia), and Arnawd (Albania), and deduces from this a Persian origin or suzerainty for all these people. He derives *Khidíw* (Khedive) from *Mahádíw*; Astronomy from *Sitára-náma*; *Múbadán* from *Mah-ábádiyán* (a mythical ancient dynasty of Persian kings mentioned in the spurious *Dasátír*); *'Ibrání* (Hebrew) from *'abara,* "to cross over," because they crossed over the Euphrates to go into Egypt. He praises the open antagonism to Islám of the Carmathians, Isma'ílís and Assassins (ff. 86^b–88^a), but condemns the later *'ulamá*, philosophers, and heresiarchs of Persia, including Mullá Ṣadrá, Shaykh Murtaḍà, Shaykh Aḥmad al-Aḥsá'í and the Báb, whose ignorance, he says (f. 53^b), is such that "not one of them has hitherto uttered two words calculated to benefit Persia," while the Ṣúfís and mystics are also held up to contempt (f. 95^b), as well as poets like Qá'ání. Polygamy is condemned, the miserable position of Persian women deplored, and the Persian character disparaged to such a point that the author says (f. 139[b]) that though, except the Arabs and savages of Africa, there are no people more filthy and unclean than the Persians, the Jews resident in Persia, and the Hindús, these are the very people who regard everyone else as unclean. The evil effects of the *rawḍa-khwáns* and Muḥarram mournings, especially on women and their unborn offspring, are also emphasised. These *rawḍa-khwáns*, says the author (f. 155[b]), ought to be publicly flayed alive as a warning to others:

حق روضه‌خوان این است که اورا زنده در ملاء عام پوست کنند و عبرت دیگران سازند تا دیگر کسی بندگان خدارا باین جرئت دعوت بر هدم ارکان شریعت و خرق پردهٔ دیانت ننماید، گمان ندارم آنقدر ظلمیکه بر اولاد و احفاد و جنینهای رحم زنان ایران و نطفهای کمر مردان از روضه خوانان می شود از فرعون که هزاران طفل سر بریده شده باشد زیراکه ما از پیش نوشتیم که حالات عارضی مادران در اطفال رحم البتّه خو و طبیعت اصلی می‌شود،

L. 5, the companion volume, comprises 170 ff., and is described as containing three letters from the same Indian Prince Kamálu'd-Dawla to his Persian friend Jalálu'd-Dawla, but only the title of the first letter, supposed to have been written from Tabríz in Ramaḍán, 1282/Jan.—Feb., 1866, appears (on f. 8[a]) in the text. The book begins:

هو الله تعالی،

زاهد از کوچهٔ رندان بسلامت بگذر، تا خرابت نکند صحبت رندانی چند،

صورت سه طغرا مکتوبی است که شاهزادهٔ آزاده کمال الدّوله هندوستانی در جواب جلال الدّوله ایرانی مرقوم داشته،

The writer begins by explaining some score of European words and expressions which, he says, cannot be properly rendered in Persian, and which he therefore proposes to use in the course of his book. These include the words Despot, Civilization, Fanatic, Philosopher, Revolution, Progress, Poetry (*Poésie*), Patriot, Change (*Changement*), Politics, Protestant, Free (*Libre*), Electric, Charlatan, Parliament, Petrarch, Voltaire, Chemistry (*Chimie*), etc. The contents of this volume closely resemble the preceding one; the same abuse of the Arabs; the same absurd popular etymologies (*Shayṭán* derived from Scythian; the magical word *badúḥ*, written on letters to ensure their arrival, from *bi-daw*, "run," etc.); the same condemnation of the *'ulamá*, especially the Shí'a *'ulamá*, of Islám; the same glorification of Zoroastrianism and pre-Islamic Persia; and the same denunciations of her later theologians, philosophers, *darwíshes* and *rawḍa-kḥwáns*. Some account of the great persecution of the Bábís in the summer of A.D. 1852 is given on ff. 109[b]–115[b]. An imaginary dialogue between a tyrannical governor entitled *Súsmáru'd-Dawla* ("the Lizard of the State") and the *Kalántar* occupies ff. 120[a]–155[b], while almost at the end of the book an attempt is made to prove on etymological grounds (jeune = *juwán*; mort = *murd*; père = *pidar*; porté = *burda*; apporté

= *áwurda* ; entrez = *andar á* ; dent = *dindán* ; lèvre = *lab* ; genou = *zánú* ; ville = *bí* in *Ardabíl*, etc.) the close affinity between the French and the Persians.

Perhaps the most interesting passage in either of these depressing volumes is an account of an observance of the Zoroastrians of Yazd and Kirmán entitled *Sufra-sabzí* and "the entertainment of the Daughter of the King of the Fairies" (**L. 4**, ff. 20ª–22ᵇ).

The transcription of **L. 5** was completed on the 8th of Dhu'l-Ḥijja, 1329 (Nov. 30, 1911).

L. 6 (7).

Described by Professor Browne on f. 1*r.* as follows:

"From the Library of the late Sir Albert Houtum-Schindler. Bought from his heirs, Jan. 5th, 1917.

The **first part** of this MS. appears to consist of a series of telegrams sent to Sir A. Houtum-Schindler by various Persian statesmen and grandees during the year 1293/1876, the earliest dated Ṣafar 11 (= March 8) in that year.

The **second part** contains Sir A. Houtum-Schindler's answers to the above, despatched from various places on the road."

Ff. 67 of 16·5 and 10·3 c. Ff. 20*v.*–32*v.* are blank.

M. ENCYCLOPAEDIAS.

M. 1 (8).

دانش‌نامهٔ جهان،

Dánish-náma-i-Jahán, a Persian manual of Natural Science by Ghiyáthu'd-Dín 'Alí ibn 'Alí Amírán al-Ḥusayní al-Iṣfahání, a writer who seems to have flourished in the 7th or 8th century of the *hijra* (13th or 14th of the Christian era). See Rieu's Persian Catalogue, pp. 439–440, and Ethé's Bodleian Catalogue, **Nos. 1456, 2173** and **2174** (cols. 891–892 and 1186–1187). I bought the MS. for 7/6 on March 30, 1899, at a shop in Farringdon Street.

The book comprises ten sections (*faṣl*), twenty subsections (*aṣl*), four "results" (*natíja*), and a conclusion (*khátima*), *viz.*:

Faṣl I (f. 6ª). The Universal Intelligence and the Universal Soul.
Faṣl II (f. 6ᵇ). The Heavens.
Faṣl III (f. 7ᵇ). The revolutions and cycles of the Heavens.
Faṣl IV (f. 9ª). The Elements.
Faṣl V (f. 9ᵇ). The division of the Elements.
Faṣl VI (f. 10ᵇ). Conditions inseparable from the Elements.
Faṣl VII (f. 12ª). Classes of the Elements.

Faṣl VIII (f. 12^b^). Shape of the Heavens and the Elements and how the earth subsists.
Faṣl IX (f. 14^b^). The meaning and true nature of a body.
Faṣl X (f. 16^a^). Division of simple and compound bodies.
Aṣl I (f. 19^a^). Metamorphosis of bodies.
Aṣl II (f. 24^b^). How vapour and smoke are produced.
Aṣl III (f. 27^a^). How wind is produced.
Aṣl IV (f. 30^a^). How clouds are produced.
Aṣl V (f. 31^b^). How rain is produced.
Aṣl VI (f. 33^a^). How snow is produced.
Aṣl VII (f. 34^a^). How hail is produced.
Aṣl VIII (f. 35^a^). How mist and fog are produced.
Aṣl IX (f. 36^a^). How thunder is produced.
Aṣl X (f. 37^b^). How lightning is produced.
Aṣl XI (f. 39^a^). How thunderbolts are produced.
Aṣl XII (f. 40^b^). How shooting stars are produced.
Aṣl XIII (f. 41^b^). Indications of redness in the sky.
Aṣl XIV (f. 42^b^). Mock suns.
Aṣl XV (f. 44^b^). Meteors.
Aṣl XVI (f. 45^a^). Rainbows.
Aṣl XVII (f. 51^b^). Cause of the halo.
Aṣl XVIII (f. 56^b^). Earthquakes and their causation.
Aṣl XIX (f. 57^b^). On the issue from the earth of voices, winds and fire.
Aṣl XX (f. 59^a^). On springs, wells and underground water-courses.
Natíja I (f. 61^a^). Minerals, metals and mines.
Natíja II (f. 85^a^). Plants and their virtues.
Natíja III (f. 95^a^). Animals.
Natíja IV (f. 100^a^). Man.
Khátima (f. 182^a^). Human Anatomy, comprising a *tabṣira* and 32 *waṣlas*.

The MS. comprises 235 ff. of 17·9 × 9·6 c. and 12 ll.; clear *ta'líq* with rubrications; not dated, but probably sixteenth or seventeenth century of the Christian era.

M. 2 (11).

معرفتنامهٔ حقّی

A Turkish Encyclopaedia of Sciences entitled *Ma'rifat-náma-i-Ḥaqqí*, compiled in 1170/1756–7 by Ibráhím Ḥaqqí. See Pertsch's Berlin Turkish Catalogue, pp. 96–97, and Rieu's Turkish Catalogue, pp. 115–116. At least three editions of the text have been printed.

The MS. was transcribed in Erzeroum by ‘Ubaydu’lláh ibn Fayḍi’lláh, a disciple of Sayyid Ḥájjí Tímúr al-Kamálí, and completed in Rabí‘ II, 1234/Feb., 1819. It comprises, besides a very full table of contents of 10 ff., 330 ff. of 27·2 × 15·5 c. and 37 ll., and is written in a small, neat *naskh* with rubrications and punctuation in gold, within gold and red ruled borders. The two opening pages (ff. 1ᵇ–2ᵃ) are elaborately if rather crudely illuminated.

N. PHILOSOPHY.

N. 1 (6).

مجمل الحكمة

Mujmalu’l-Ḥikmat (“Compendium of Philosophy”), a Persian abridgement of the well-known *Rasá’il*, or Treatises, of the *Ikhwánu’ṣ-Ṣafá*, or “Brethren of Purity,” as is stated in the (undated) colophon on f. 139ᵇ as follows:

سری شد کتاب مجمل الحکمة که اختیار و خلاصهٔ رسایل اخوان الصّفا و همگی سپاس و ستایش خدای‌راست جلّ جلاله و درود بی نهایت محمّد مصطفی‌را صلّی الله علیه وآله وسلّم که سرور انبیاست و پیشوای اولیا و زبده و خلاصهٔ حکما و اصفیا علیهم السّلام،

After the doxology, which is chiefly remarkable for its invocation of blessings on the philosophers after the Prophet Muḥammad and ‘Alí ibn Abí Ṭálib, the text begins:

امّا بعد، بدانکه کتابهای حکمت بسیار است و بیشتر بلغة تازی و اندکی بلغة پارسی و در آن کتابها هیچ حظّی نیست مانند سرود اختران و کتاب تام بار خدای و مرزبان‌نامه و آنچه بدین ماند و ما هیچ کتابی نیافتیم که آنچه در حکمت بکار آید از ریاضی و منطق و طبیعی و الهی جمله در وی باشد مگر دانش‌نامه و آن لفظی است بس مشکل و بیشتر اشارتست و بعضی رمزست و کتاب مجمل الحکمة مجموعست و لیکن همچنین مرموز است و در آن حشو بسیار است و بسیار مکرّر است و ما یکدو جای دیدیم که این کتاب‌را بپارسی نقل کرده بودند و همچنان برموز فرو گذاشته اند و حشورا بجای مانده پس رای مجلس سامی احلق (?) سیدی بهآء الدین سیف الملوك شجاع الملك شمس الخواص تیمور کورکان ادام الله علوّه چنان اتّفاق افتاد که این ضعیف آن کتابرا بپارسی دری نقل کند و هرچه حشو است ازو دور کند و هرآنچه مرموز است (f. 3ᵃ) آشکارا کند و از حدّ رمز تصریح کند خواهش ایشانرا اجابت کردم، و این اوّل رسالهٔ ایست که همچون مدخلی است در کتاب ارثماطیقی

Only 39 of the 51 treatises of the original are represented here, the last “On Cause and Effect” (در علّت و معلول) being followed by a blank page (f. 137ᵇ) on the margin of which is written in Persian “several tracts are omitted from the original,” nor is it apparent to which tract the remaining four pages (ff. 138^{a}–139^{b}) which follow the lacuna belong. The contents of the volume are as follows:

I. Arithmetic (f. 3^{a}).
II. Geometry (f. 9^{b}).
III. Astronomy (f. 13^{b}).
IV. Music (f. 23^{b}).
V. Geography (f. 31^{a}).
VI. Geometrical Progression (f. 36^{b}).
VII. Classification of Sciences (f. 40^{a}).
VIII. Classification of Arts (f. 42^{b}).
IX. Nature of Man (f. 43^{b}).
X. Introduction to Logic (f. 46^{b}).
XI. The Categories (f. 49^{b}).
XII. باريرمينياس (بحث قضايا) (f. 52^{a}).
XIII. Logic (f. 54^{b}).
XIV. افرديطيقا *sic* (قياسات).
XV. Matter and Form (f. 59^{b}).
XVI. Heaven and Earth (f. 63^{a}).
XVII. Growth and Decay (f. 67^{a}).
XVIII. Celestial Influences (f. 69^{a}).
XIX. Production of Metals and Minerals (f. 71^{a}).
XX. Nature (f. 75^{a}).
XXI. Production of Plants (f. 78^{a}).
XXII. Structure of the Body (f. 79^{a}).
XXIII. The Senses (f. 83^{b}).
XXIV. Pre-natal Influences (f. 87^{b}).
XXV. Man as the Microcosm (f. 94^{a}).
XXVI. State of the Soul after Death (f. 95^{b}).
XXVII. Man's Capacity for Knowledge (f. 99^{a}).
XXVIII. The Philosophy of Death (f. 102^{a}).
XXIX. On Pains and Pleasures (f. 104^{b}).
XXX. On Diversity of Languages (f. 107^{b}).
XXXI. The Beginnings of Understanding according to Pythagoras (f. 109^{a}).
XXXII. The same according to other Philosophers (f. 111^{a}).
XXXIII. The Macrocosm is a great Animal (f. 112^{a}).
XXXIV. The Intelligence and the Intelligible (f. 114^{b}).
XXXV. On the Aeons and Cycles (f. 118^{b}).
XXXVI. On the Nature of Love (f. 126^{a}).
XXXVII. On the Resurrection (f. 129^{b}).
XXXVIII. On Movements (f. 133^{a}).
XXXIX. On Cause and Effect (f. 134^{b}).

This is incomplete and is followed by the lacuna mentioned above, and that in turn by four pages (ff. 138^{a}–139^{b}) containing Sections IX and X of an unidentified tract.

A lithographed edition of this work, entitled *Rasá'il-i-Ikhwánu'ṣ-Ṣafá*, and comprising fifty treatises, was published in Bombay in 1301/1884.

This MS. formerly belonged to Prince Farhád Mírzá, and was presented by him to the *Iḥtishámu'l-Mulk* at Ja'farábád in Ramaḍán, 1302/June—July, 1885. It is written in a small, neat *naskh* with rubrications, and contains 140 ff. of 13·3 × 9 c. and 17 ll.

N. 2 (14).

کیمیای سعادت،

The second half (third and fourth *Rukns*) of al-Ghazálí's well-known *Kímiyá-yi-Sa'ádat*, or "Alchemy of Happiness," a Persian recension of his *Iḥyá'u 'Ulúmi'd-Dín*. Concerning the latter, see Brockelmann's *Gesch. d. Arab. Litt.*, vol. I, pp. 422–423; and concerning the former (lithographed at Lucknow in 1311/1894), see Rieu's Persian Catalogue, pp. 37–38, etc.

This fine MS., written in a large, archaic *naskh* with rubrications, was transcribed by Ḥusayn ibn Muḥammad ibn 'Alí al-Kátib ("the Scribe"), known as Ibn Ḥamámí, of Shíráz, and was completed on Thursday the 22nd of Shawwál, 727/Sept. 10, 1327. It comprises 330 ff. of 31·3 × 21·2 c. and 18 ll., and was bought by me from J. J. Naaman in August, 1901, for £6. *Rukn iii* (= pp. 254–400 of the Lucknow lithograph mentioned above) occupies ff. 3^a–158^a, and *Rukn iv* (= pp. 401–567 of the lithograph), ff. 159^b–330^a.

N. 3 (10).

شوارق الالهام فی شرح تجرید الکلام،

Shawáriqu'l-Ilhám, a commentary by 'Abdu'r-Razzáq al-Láhijí, a well-known Persian theologian and philosopher who flourished in the middle of the seventeenth century of the Christian era, on the *Tajrídu'l-Kalám* (or -'*Aqá'id*) of Naṣíru'd-Dín Ṭúsí (d. 672/1273–4). This commentary, according to Rieu (Persian Catalogue, p. 32), was printed at Ṭihrán in 1280/1863–4. The contents of the highly esteemed *Tajríd* are given by Ahlwardt (Berlin Arabic Catalogue, vol. II, p. 331, **No. 1745**). See also Brockelmann's *Gesch. d. Arab. Litt.*, vol. I, p. 509, and the *Kashfu'l-Ḥujub wa'l-Astár* (Calcutta, A.H. 1330), **No. 452** (pp. 97–98). Begins:

ربّنا افتح بيننا وبين قومنا بالحقّ وانت خير الفاتحين، امّا بعد، ...فيقول العبد الرّاجى وبباب ربّه الملتجى عبدُ الرزّاق اللّاهيجى بن على بن حسين اللّاهيجى الخ

This MS., one of those bought of Ḥájjí 'Abdu'l-Majíd Belshah in 1920, comprises 195 ff. of 24·6 × 15 c. and 21 ll., and is written in a small, neat and fairly legible *naskh*, without date or colophon.

N. 4 (9).

گوهر مراد،

Gawhar-i-Murád ("the Pearl of Desire"), a well-known treatise on scholastic philosophy (*'Ilm-i-Kalám*) according to the Shí'a doctrine, by the above-mentioned 'Abdu'r-Razzáq al-Láhijí. See Rieu's Persian Catalogue, p. 32. I possess two lithographed editions of this work, one published at Ṭihrán in Jumádà II, 1277/Dec. 1860, and the other in Bombay in 1301/1883–4.

Ff. 204 of 22·1 × 12 c. and 19 ll.; small, neat *nasta'líq* with rubrications; no date or colophon. A table of contents occupying two pages (ff. 1[b]–2[a]) is prefixed.

N. 5 (7).

كتاب المشاعر وغيره لمولانا صدر الدّين الشيرازى،

Two short metaphysical tracts in Arabic, the first (pp. 2–70) described on the title-page as the *Kitábu'l-Mashá'ir* of Mullá Ṣadrá, beginning:

نحمد الله ونستعينه بقوّته الّتى أقام بها ملكوت الأرض والسّمآء وبكلمته الّتى أنشأ بها نشأتى الآخرة والاولى آلخ

The second tract treats of the future life and the Resurrection (pp. 72–111) and begins:

بسم الله ربّ الآخرة والاولى آلخ...فقد سألت يا أخى أطال الله بقاءك فى سبيل المعرفة والهدى وسدّدك فى سلوك المحجّة البيضا عن حشر جميع الأشياء اليه تعالى حتّى طبايع الجماد والنّبات والعجما فضلًا عن غيرها من ذوات العلم والحيوة آلخ

Pp. 112 of 17·5 × 11·2 c. and 16 ll.; neat, modern *naskh*; no date or colophon. From the Belshah collection of MSS.

N. 6 (10).

ذخيرة الملوك،

A well-known Persian treatise on ethics and politics by Sayyid Alí b. Shiháb al-Hamadání (d. 786/1385). See Rieu, B.M.P.C., 447; Ethé, I.O.P.C., No. 2176; Ivanow, A.S.B.P.C., No. 1380, where further references are given.

Ff. 235 of 23·5 and 14·8 c. and 16 ll. Good *ta'líq* with rubrications. No date. Ff. 169*r.*–174*v.* have been supplied by another hand. The MS. was transcribed by Muḥammad b. Sháh Muḥammad and afterwards carefully collated and corrected by a certain Ḥasan b. Ḥusayn b. Ghaybí (?) b. Shaykh Aḥmad. According to a note by Professor Browne on f. 1*r.* it was bought at the auction at Sotheby's on June 18, 1922, for 10*s.*

O. MATHEMATICS AND ASTRONOMY.

O. 1 (10).

زیج المفرد،

A very fine and rare old Persian manuscript of Astronomical Tables, Chronology and Eras, entitled *Zíju'l-Mufrad*, by Abú Ja'far Muḥammad ibn Ayyúb al-Ḥásib aṭ-Ṭabarí, who flourished in the early part of the thirteenth century of the Christian era. No other copy is known to exist, but a fragment of 26 pages preserved at Munich may possibly be from this MS., which is incomplete at the end. It appears to have been copied during the author's life-time by or for a certain Yúsuf ibn Abí..., but is not dated.

Begins, after the *Bismi'lláh* and short doxology:

بعد ثنای ایزد سبحانه و تعالی که آفریذگار دو جهان و روزی‌ده بندگانست و پروردگار جانورانست و کردگار آسمانها و زمینهاست و دارندهٔ هرج در میانشانست و درودش بر خاتم پیغمبران علیهم السلم و بر جملهٔ یارانش و گزیذگانش چنین گویذ محمّد بن ایّوب الحاسب الطّبری کی چون بپرداخته بودم از عمل نخستین عملی زیج مفرد آغاز کردم بابتدا کردن مقاله دوم که اورا مقاله علمی خواندم و اندرو پدیذ کردم هر علمی‌را که اندر مقالهٔ نخستین بجدول یاذ کرده بوذم و بنموذه اندرین مقاله جمله‌را بحساب نموذیم و آنچ ازین دانش است نیز تمامی (?) بنموذیم از حساب و عمل و علم و هیئه و برهان چنانك در مقالهٔ نخستین وعده داده و پذیرفته بوذم و این مقالت‌را دو فصل نهاذم فصل نخستین در حساب و عمل و فصل دوم در هئات و برهان و از ایزد سبحانه و تعالی توفیق خواستم بر تمام شدن هریك کی او تواناست بر آنك توفیق دهذ،

The work comprises four sections (*Faṣl*), each containing many subsections, and a *Kitábu'l-Istikhráját* (ff. 100^a–180^b), consisting almost entirely of astronomical tables. There are no catch-words at the foot of the pages, and some lacunae and dislocations certainly exist, *e.g.* between ff. 1 and 2.

Section I (ff. 1^b–38^a) contains 77 subsections.
Section II (ff. 39^a–60^a) contains 23 subsections.
Section III (ff. 60^b–76^b) contains 30 subsections.
Section IV (ff. 77^a–99^b) contains 45 subsections.

The first nineteen chapters of Section I deal with the years and festivals of the Arabs, Persians, Jews and Christians (Greeks), as follows:

الاوّل در مدخل سنون العرب، الثانی در مدخل سنون الفرس، الثالث، در مدخل سنون الیهود، الرابع، در مدخل سنون الروم، الخامس، در معرفة کبیسة العرب، السادس، در معرفة کبیسة سنون الفرس، السابع، در معرفة سنون کبیسة الیهود، الثامن، در شناختن سالهای کبیسهٔ روم، التاسع، در بیرون آوردن روزها از سالهای رومی، العاشر، در بیرون آوردن سالها و ماههای رومی از روزها، الحادی عشر، در بیرون آوردن روزها از سالها و ماههای یهود، الثانی عشر، در بیرون آوردن سالها و ماههای

یهود از روزها، الثالث عشر، در بیرون آوردن روزها از سالها و ماههای عرب، الرابع عشر، در بیرون آوردن سالها و ماههای پارسی از روزها، الخامس عشر، در بیرون آوردن روزها از سال و ماه پارسی، السادس عشر، در بیرون آوردن سال و ماه پارسی از روزها، السّابع عشر، در استخراج تاریخی مجهول از تاریخی معلوم، الثامن عشر، در استخراج صوم نصاری، التاسع عشر، در معرفة توقیعات و اعیاد اهل الملل،

Most of these chapters are very short, the 19 enumerated above being all included in 8 ff.

The following titles, some entirely in red, some partly in red and partly in black, stand at the heads of the different sections:

الفصل الاوّل من مقالة العلمية من كتاب زيج المفرد تصنيف الشيخ الجليل الاوحد ابى جعفر محمّد بن ايّوب الحاسب الطبرى ادام الله تمكنّه صاحبه ومالكه يوسف بن ابى...طوّل الله عمره، (f. 1[a])

الفصل الثانى من مقالة العمليّة من كتاب زيج المفرد تصنيف الشيخ الجليل الاوحد ابى جعفر محمّد بن ايّوب الحاسب الطبرى ادام الله تمكينه، صاحبه ومالكه يوسف بن...طوّل الله عمره، (f. 39[a])

فصل سيم از مقالهٔ عملى، (f. 60[b])

فصل چهارم از مقالهٔ عملى، صاحبه و مالكه يوسف بن...متّعه الله عمره، (f. 77[a])

The owner's name recurs in the corner of this page with the date 700/1300–1 (as in Section II).

كتاب الاستخراجات، (f. 100[a]) تصنيف الشيخ الجليل الخ

I cannot decipher the name of the father of the owner Yúsuf satisfactorily in any one of the four places where it occurs, though it is mutilated only in the first, where it appears to be ...ابى. In the others it looks like لحابه, with only the one diacritical point and a puzzling ligature of the first three or four letters.

On f. 108[a] occurs a circular figure indicating the appearances of the new moons, ascribed to Abú Rayḥán [*i.e.* al-Bírúní], to whom the title *ash-Shaykhu'r-Ra'ís*, commonly applied to Avicenna, is given, as follows:

دايرة روية الاهلّة من عمل الشيخ الرئيس الحكيم برهان الحقّ أبى ريحان رحمه الله تعالى،

This MS., bought of the late Ḥájjí 'Abdu'l-Majíd Belshah in January, 1920, comprises 180 ff. of 24·2 × 16·2 c. and 21 ll., and is written for the most part in a beautiful archaic *naskh*, with rubrications, though some pages (*e.g.* ff. 39[b]–59[b]) are in a poorer and cruder, though quite legible, hand.

O. 2 (7).

زيج ايلخانى،

Zíj-i-Ílkhání (or *Khání*, as it is here entitled), containing the Astronomical Tables constructed by Naṣíru'd-Dín Ṭúsí by command of Hulákú Khán the Mongol. See Rieu's Persian Catalogue, pp. 454–455, and Brockelmann's *Gesch. d. Arab. Litt.*, vol. I, pp. 511–512.

This beautiful little MS., obtained from the late Ḥájjí 'Abdu'l-Majíd Belshah in January, 1920, is not dated, but was probably transcribed in the fifteenth century of our era. It comprises 148 ff. of 17·2 × 12·5 c. and 19 ll., and is written in a small, neat *naskh* with rubrications and many Tables (ff. 27^b–93^a, 99^a–118^a, etc.). Of the four Discourses (*Maqála*) into which it is divided, of which the subjects are given by Rieu, the *first* begins on f. 3^a, the *second* on f. 20^b, the *third* on f. 93^b, and the *fourth* on f. 137^b.

O. 3 (7).

الاحكام العلائية،

This MS., from the Schindler collection, comprises 126 ff. of 16·6 × 12 c. and from 17 to 19 ll. It presents many lacunae and dislocations, and appears to contain portions of at least two separate Persian treatises on Astronomy or Astrology, one entitled as above *Al-Aḥkámu'l-'Alá'iyya*, ascribed on f. 1^a to Fakhru'd-Dín ar-Rází, and the other entitled in the colophon on f. 79^a *ar-Risálatu'l-Mu'íniyya*.

Concerning the former, composed for 'Alá'u'd-Dín Khwárazmsháh (d. 596/1199) by Fakhru'd-Dín ar-Rází (b. 543/1149, d. 606/1209), see Brockelmann's *Gesch. d. Arab. Litt.*, vol. I, pp. 507–508. It begins, after the doxology:

...امّا بعد، هيچ طاعت بعد از طاعت خداى تعالى و متابعت رسول عَلَيم بهتر از خدمت پادشاه نيست كه أطيعوا الله وأطيعوا الرسول وأولى الأمر آلخ

and is in fact dedicated to 'Alá'u'd-Dín Abu'l-Muẓaffar Takín Khwárazmsháh Íl-Arslán ibn Atsiz Burhánu Amíri'l-Mu'minín. Amongst the authorities on whose work it is based mention is made of Ptolemy, Abu'l-Ma'shar al-Balkhí, 'Umar ibn Farrukhán (?) aṭ-Ṭabarí, Aḥmad ibn 'Abdi'l-Jalíl as-Sijzí, Ya'qúb ibn 'Alí an-Naṣrání, Muḥammad ibn Ayyúb aṭ-Ṭabarí, Gúshyár, etc. The title occurs on f. 6^a, l. 2, and the work is divided into two Discourses (*Maqála*), the first (f. 6^a), in nine sections (*faṣl*) on General Principles (*Kulliyyát*), the second (f. 22^a) on Details (*Juz'iyyát*) or special applications, apparently in seventy sections. It is not clear where the acephalous *Risálatu'l-Mu'íniyya* begins: the colophon with which it ends occurs on f. 79[a] and runs as follows:

تمّ استنساخ هـذه الرسالة الموسومة بـالمعينيّة فى النصف من شهر ربيع الاوّل سـنـة اربع وسبعين وستّمائة، الكاتب مودود بن... الدستجردى،

This date, the middle of Rabí' I, 672, if correct, is equivalent to Oct. 1, 1273.

Owing to the absence of catch-words and the numerous lacunae and dislocations in the manuscript, it is very doubtful whether it would be possible to arrange the pages in their proper order, or to make any serious use of the MS.

O. 4 (9).

كتاب اقليدس ترجمة نصير الدين الطوسى،

A good and very clearly written, but quite modern copy, made in 1298/1881, of Naṣíru'd-Dín Ṭúsí's Arabic version of Euclid's Geometry, a brief account of the various recensions of which in Greek and Arabic is given on ff. 8[b]–9[a]. See Brockelmann's *Gesch. d. Arab. Litt.*, vol. I, pp. 510–511, where copious references to the extensive literature connected with it are given. Begins, after the prefatory note above-mentioned:

الحمد لله الّذى منه الابتدآء واليه الانتهآء وعـنـده حقايق الانباء وبيده ملكوت الاشيآء وصلوته على محمّد وآلـه الاصفيا، وبعد، فلمّا فرغنت من تحرير المجسطى رأيت أن أحـرّر كـتـاب اصول الهندسة والحساب المنسوب الى اقليدس الصّورى بـايجاز غـيـر مخلّ واستقصى فى تثبيت مقاصده استقصاء غير مملّ واضيف اليه مـا يليق به ممّا استفدته من كتب هذا العلم و استنبطته بقريحتى وافرز مـا يوجد من اصل الكتاب فى نسختى الحجّاج وثابت عـن المزيد عليه امّا بالاشارة الى ذلك او باختلاف الوان الاشكال وارقامها ففعلت ذلك متوكّلًا على الله سبحانه انّه حسبى وعليه ثقتى، اقول الكتاب يشتمل على خمس عشرة مقالة مع الملحقتين بآخره وهى أربع مائة وثمانية وستّون شـكـلًا فى نسخة الحجّاج وبزيادة عشرة اشـكـال فى نسخة ثابت وفى بعض المواضع فى الترتيب ايضًا بينهما وانـا رقمت عدد اشكال المقالات بالحمرة للثابت و بالسّواد للحجّاج اذا كان مخالفًا لـه، المقالة الاولى سبعة واربعون شكلًا، الخ

Ff. 138 of 21·5 × 14·6 c. and 20 ll.; good, clear, modern *naskh* with rubrications, but without geometrical figures. From the Belshah collection, fourth division, obtained on Nov. 12, 1920.

O. 5 (6).

شرح ملخّص الجغمينى لقاضى‌زاده،

The Commentary of Músà ibn Maḥmúd Qáḍí-záda (d. *circa* 823/1420) on the treatise on Astronomy entitled *al-Mulakhkhaṣ* of Maḥmúd ibn Muḥammad al-

Jaghmíní, who wrote it in 618/1221. See Brockelmann, *Gesch. d. Arab. Litt.*, vol. I, p. 473, and Rieu's Arabic Supplement, **No. 760**, p. 520.

This MS., which was given to me in March, 1911, by Dr Riḍá Tawfíq (known in Turkey as *Feylesúf Riẓá*, "Rizá the Philosopher"), comprises 110 ff. of 15·4 × 10·6 c. and 16 ll., and is written in a modern, slovenly but fairly legible hand, without date or colophon.

O. 6 (7).

رسالة فى العمل بالرّبع المجيّب، وغيره،

(1) A small treatise on the use of the sinuated Quadrant (ff. 1^b–7^a), by Badru'd-Dín Muḥammad ibn Aḥmad Sibṭu'l-Máridíní, beginning after the brief doxology and the mention of the author's name:

وبعد، فهذه رسالة فى العمل بالربع المجيّب مشتملة على مقدّمة وعشرين بابًا وسمّيتُها الرسالة الضحمه فى الاعمال الجيبيّة آلخ

(2) A treatise on the *Dhátu'l-Kursí* (ff. 10^b–22^b) by Muḥammad ibn Shaykh 'Alí al-Ḥamídí, comprising an Introduction and eighteen chapters.

(3) A treatise on the Astrolabe (ff. 23^b–35^b), comprising an Introduction and fifteen chapters, ascribed in the colophon to Naṣíru'd-Dín Muḥammad aṭ-Ṭúsí.

(4) A treatise on the "Bridged Quadrant" (رُبْع المقنطرة), comprising an Introduction, ten chapters, and a Conclusion (ff. 36^b–49^a), with special reference to its use in determining the times of prayer, etc.

Ff. 49 of 16·8 × 10·6 c. and 21 ll.; poor, modern *nasta'líq* with rubrications; given to me by Dr Riḍá Tawfíq, with the MS. last mentioned, in March, 1911.

O. 7 (7).

بلوغ المرام فى معرفة اقسام العام،

A treatise on the Four Seasons, comprising an Introduction, four Sections, and a Conclusion, and entitled *Bulúghu'l-marám fí Ma'rifati Aqsámi'l-'Ám*, by Muḥammad ibn Ráḍí an-Najafí (pp. 2–68), followed by another treatise (pp. 68–98) on the Mansions of the Stars (*fí Ma'rifati Manázili'n-Nujúm*).

Pp. 98 of 17·1 × 11·3 c. and 19 ll.; modern, cursive *nasta'líq* with rubrications; transcribed in Jumádà II, 1205/Feb. 1791, or 1305/1888. From the Belshah collection, November, 1920.

O. 8 (9).

ثمرة الشّجرة فى احكام النّجوم٬

Thamaratu'sh-Shajara fí Aḥkámi'n-Nujúm, a Persian treatise on Judicial Astrology by 'Alí-Sháh ibn Muḥammad Qásim al-Khwárazmí, known as al-Bukhárí, comprising five chapters called *Shajara* ("Tree"), each of which is subdivided into numerous sections called *Shu'ba*, and subsections called *Thamara* ("Fruit"). The work was compiled for a Minister or Governor entitled Shamsu'd-Dín Muḥammad Mubárakshah. Begins:

حمد و ثنا آفریده‌گاری‌را که افلاك دوائر نجوم و سواتر بیافرید و شکر و سپاس واجب الوجودیرا که عناصر ارکان در وجود آورد...وبعد٬ چنین میگوید مؤلّف این مسوّده علیشاه بن محمّد قاسم الخوارزمی المعروف بالبخاری حرسه الله تعالی نوائب الزمان که چون ایادی واکراه خداوند خواجهٔ معظّم دستور ممالك العالم شمس الدولة والدین سیف الاسلام والمسلمین محمّد الصدّ (?) السعید مبارکشاه اطال الله فی الدولة در حقّ این فقیر بسیار شد و مخدوم زادگانرا که گوهران کان واختران آسمان اند اشارت شده بود تا بعد از وظائف تحصیلات دیگر چیزی ازین علم شریف حاصل معلوم کند٬ چون از حساب هندی و زیج جدید ایلخانی و زیخ عمده که منتجب جمع کرده است این فقیر فارغ شد مجمل الاصول احکام که بحکیم گوشیار رحمة الله علیه منسوبست در تحت آوردند و چند کرّت فرو خواندند الّخ

The contents of the book, which is here entitled *Ashjár wa-Athmár* ("Trees and Fruits"), are briefly stated as follows on f. 3[b]:

...چون شرایط معلوم گشت بدانند که این فقیر بناء این کتاب بر پنج اشجار نهاد و هر شجرهٔرا شعبات و اثمار٬ شجرهٔ اوّل٬ در صفات و منسوبات بروج و کواکب٬ شجرهٔ دوم٬ در احکام قرانات واتّصالات دیگر٬ شجرهٔ سیوم٬ در احکام عالم٬ شجرهٔ چهارم٬ در احکام موالید٬ شجرهٔ پنجم٬ در اعمال تسییرات٬ و اورا اشجار و اثمار الّخ

Shajara i begins on f. 3[b]; *Shajara ii* on f. 37[a]; *Shajara iii* on f. 60[b]; *Shajara iv* on f. 76[a]; *Shajara v* on f. 133[a]. The date of composition, 1176/1762–3, is given in the following verse (f. 153[b]) which concludes the book:

این کتاب‌را که نوشت مفتی زار٬ شش و هفتاد و صد و بعد هزار٬

From the Belshah collection, November, 1920. Ff. 154 of 20·8 × 14·8 c. and 23 ll.; clear *naskh* with rubrications; no date except that given in the above verse.

P. MEDICINE, NATURAL SCIENCE, MINERALOGY, ETC.

P. 1 (7).

كتاب التّشريح لجالينوس ترجمة حنين بن اسحق،

An Arabic translation (apparently much abridged) of Galen's Anatomy, by Abú Zayd Ḥunayn ibn Isḥáq at-Tarjumán ("the Translator"). It comprises five Discourses (*Maqála*), the *first* (ff. 1ᵇ–30ᵇ) on the Bones; the *second* (ff. 31ᵃ–90ᵃ) on the Muscles; the *third* (ff. 90ᵇ–105ᵃ) on the Nerves; the *fourth* (ff. 105ᵇ–127ᵇ) on the Veins; and the *fifth* (ff. 128ᵃ–136ᵃ) on the Arteries.

This MS., which was presented to me by the late Sir Albert (then Dr) Houtum-Schindler on Dec. 10, 1901, comprises 136 ff. of 16·9 × 9·9 c. and 11 ll., and is written in a good *ta'líq*. Copied by Abu'l-Ḥusayn ibn Muḥammad Ibráhím, and completed on the 10th of Jumádà I, 1070/Jan. 23, 1660.

Concerning the full and complete Arabic translation of Galen's Anatomy, see Dr Max Simon's *Sieben Bücher Anatomie des Galen...zum ersten Male veröffentlicht nach den Handschriften einer Arabischen Übersetzung des* 9 *Jahrh. N. Chr. ins Deutsche übertragen und kommentiert* (2 vols., Leipzig, 1906).

P. 2 (7).

كتاب الكُنّاش المعروف بالفاخر لمحمّد بن زكريّا الرّازى،

The *Kunnásh*, or *Kitábu'l-Fákhir*, of the celebrated physician Abú Bakr Muḥammad ibn Zakariyyá ar-Rází (d. 311/923 or 320/932). See Brockelmann's *Gesch. d. Arab. Litt.*, I, pp. 233–235, especially p. 235, No. 41. A MS. of the second half of this work (= ff. 229ᵇ–465ᵃ of this MS.), numbered **6259**, exists in the Berlin Library, and is described by Ahlwardt (Berlin Arab. Cat., vol. v, pp. 516–517), though the conclusions of the two MSS. do not agree. The MS. here described contains a chapter on Smallpox and Measles after the account of the Fevers, and ends:

...فان كان سبب الغشى كثرة الاستفراغ بالعرق فيجب أن يقطع ذلك بما هو موصوف فى باب ادرار العرق و قطعه، فهذا آخر الكلام فيها و هو آخر كتاب الفاخر لمحمّد الزكريا (*sic*) الرازى رحمه الله، تمّ الكتاب بعون الملك الوهّاب على يدى العبد محمّد بن عبد الرزّاق الكاشانى فى سنة ١٠٠٥ هجريّة،

This MS., bought of the late Ḥájjí 'Abdu'l-Majíd Belshah in January, 1920, and transcribed, as we learn from the above colophon, by Muḥammad ibn 'Abdi'r-

Razzáq al-Káshání in 1005/1596–7, is written in a small, neat *naskh* with rubrications, and comprises 465 ff. of 15·8 × 11 c. and 18 ll. Begins:

بسم الله الرّحمن الرّحيم و له الحمد بلا نهاية ‘

اللّهمّ اعصمنا من الذلل وأعذنا من الخطل و وفّقنا لصلاح القول والعمل انّه لا حول ولا قوّة الّا بك ‘ قال محمّد بن زكريا الرازى وهو جامع هذا الكتاب ومؤلّفه انّ من اعظم نعم الله على عباده وجليل تطوّله على خلقه الصّحّة الخ

The chief contents are as follows:

(1) *Diseases of the Head* (ff. 1^{b}–92^{a}), beginning with *Alopecia* and other diseases of the scalp and hair, and including *Headache* (ff. 18^{a}–40^{b}), *Lethargy*, *Phrenitis*, *Insanity*, *Apoplexy*, *Paralysis*, etc.

(2) *Diseases of the Eye* (ff. 92^{a}–117^{a}).

(3) *Diseases of the Ear* (ff. 117^{a}–126^{a}).

(4) *Diseases of the Nose* (ff. 126^{a}–131^{b}).

(5) *Diseases of the Teeth and Mouth* (ff. 131^{b}–142^{b}).

(6) *Diseases of the Throat* (ff. 142^{b}–156^{b}).

(7) *Diseases of the Lungs* (ff. 156^{b}–188^{b}), including *Pleurisy* (f. 175^{b}) and *Pneumonia* (f. 180^{b}).

(8) *Diseases of the Heart* (ff. 188^{b}–194^{a}).

(9) *Diseases of the Stomach* (ff. 194^{a}–228^{b}), including *Hiccough* (f. 214^{b}). Part I of this volume ends on f. 228^{b} with a short colophon repeating the title of the book and dated Rabí‘ II, 1005/Nov.—Dec., 1596.

The contents of vol. II are fully given in the Berlin Arabic Catalogue, *loc. cit.*, and are briefly as follows:

(10) *Diseases of the Liver* (ff. 229^{b}–247^{a}), including *Jaundice* (f. 240^{b}).

(11) *Diseases of the Spleen* (ff. 247^{a}–252^{a}).

(12) *Dropsy* (ff. 252^{a}–263^{a}).

(13) *Diarrhoea* (ff. 263^{a}–289^{b}), *Worms* (f. 289^{b}), *Rupture* (f. 292^{a}), and *Colic* (f. 294^{b}).

(14) *Diseases of the Kidneys and Bladder* (ff. 312^{a}–336^{a}).

(15) *Gout and other Diseases of the Joints* (ff. 336^{a} *et seqq.*), *Elephantiasis* (f. 355^{b}), *Boils and Abscesses* (f. 360^{a}), *Cancer* (f. 362^{a}), etc.

(16) *On Sexual Intercourse* (ff. 371^{a}–377^{a}).

(17) *Diseases of Women* (ff. 377^{a}–393^{a}).

(18) *Care of Children* (ff. 393^{a}–395^{a}).

(19) *Treatment of Poisons, Bites and Stings* (ff. 395^{a}–409^{b}).

(20) *Drugs and their Properties and Doses* (ff. 409^{b}–411^{b}).

(21) *Fevers* (ff. 411^{b}–439^{a}).

(22) *Smallpox and Measles* (ff. 439^{a}–457^{b}). In the Berlin Codex this section forms part of that numbered (15) above, being placed between *Diseases of the*

Joints and *Abscesses*. This is probably its correct place, for in this MS. the article on *Quartan Fever*, which should evidently come in section (21) above, appears on f. 457ᵇ, and is followed on f. 462ᵇ by that on *Putrid Fever*.

P. 3 (9).

تذكرة الكحّالين لعلّى بن عيسى‘

A fine old MS. of the *Tadhkiratu'l-Kaḥḥálín*, or "Oculists' Reminder," of 'Alí ibn 'Ísá, a celebrated oculist who flourished at Baghdád about A.D. 961. A notice of him is given by Ibn Abí Uṣaybi'a (vol. I, p. 247), who speaks in high terms of this book, which is also discussed by Professor Julius Hirschberg in *Die Arabischen Lehrbücher der Augenheilkunde* (Berlin, 1905), pp. 6, and 24 *et seqq*., and described as "the oldest manual of our branch of the Healing Art which we possess in full in the original language." In 1904 Hirschberg in cooperation with Lippert published at Leipzig a complete German translation of the work, entitled *Erinnerungsbuch für Augenärzte, aus Arabischen Handschriften übersetzt und erläutert*. A second volume containing translations of three other Arabic works on Ophthalmology was published by the same scholars in the following year. The text from which they made their translation, but which unfortunately remained unpublished, was based on the first five of the ten MSS. enumerated on p. 29 of the *Arabischen Lehrbücher*, more fully described and classified on pp. xxvi–xxix of the Introduction to the *Erinnerungsbuch*, which gives the fullest information as to the character, scope and value of this remarkable work.

The present MS. (not known to Hirschberg) was one of those bought of the late Ḥájjí 'Abdu'l-Majíd Belshah in January, 1920, and, with the exception of f. 1, which has been supplied in a modern hand, is entirely written in a fine old *naskh*, with rubrications, of the eleventh century of the Christian era. The colophon on f. 108ᵃ with which the MS. ends is unfortunately damaged, so that all that can be read of the date of completion is "Tuesday the twenty-first...and four hundred." It comprises 108 ff. of 20 × 15 c. and 15 ll.

The first Book (*Maqála*) or Discourse (ff. 2ᵃ–11ᵃ = *Erinnerungsbuch*, pp. 7–30) comprises 21 chapters.

The second Book (ff. 11ᵃ–83ᵇ = *Erinn.*, pp. 31–236) comprises 73 chapters.

The third Book (ff. 83ᵇ–108ᵃ = *Erinn.*, pp. 237–321) comprises 27 chapters. Begins:

هذه رسالة على بن عيسى الكحّال جوابًا عمّا سأله بعض اخوانه فى معرفة امراض العين وعلاجاتها‘
وصل كتابك ايّها الأخ الأجلّ الفاضل حفظك الله برأفته وارشدك الى الصواب بحكمته تسأل
عن جواب مع كتب جالينوس فى امراض العين وعلاج كلّ مرض منها لأنّ الاسكندرانيّون (*sic*) ذكروا
عدد الأمراض فى العين ولم يذكروا علاجاتها آلخ

For a description of another MS., transcribed in Rabí' II, 555/April—May, 1160, see the *Catalogue of the Arabic and Persian MSS. in the Oriental Public Library at Bankipore*, vol. IV (Arabic Medical Works), pp. 36–37.

P. 4 (8).

مقالة فى خلق الانسان لأبى الحسن سعيد بن هبة الله٬

A fine old eleventh century MS. of a very rare, if not unique, work on Midwifery, Embryology, Diseases of Children and Psychology, entitled *Maqála fí Khalqi'l-Insán* ("Discourse on the Creation, or Nature, of Man") by Abu'l-Ḥasan Sa'íd ibn Hibati'lláh ibni'l-Ḥasan aṭ-Ṭabíb (b. 436/1045, d. 495/1101), who was Court Physician to the Caliph al-Muqtadí. See Ibn Abí Uṣaybi'a, vol. I, pp. 254–255.

This MS., bought from the late Ḥájjí 'Abdu'l-Majíd Belshah in January, 1920, was transcribed before Ṣafar, 489/Feb., 1096, when a copy was made from it by a certain Muḥammad ibnu'l-Ḥusayn...ash-Shaybání for his own use. It comprises 126 ff. of 18·7 × 14·c. and 18 or 19 ll., written in an ancient but rather cursive *naskh* with rubrications. It has been collated throughout (غ مقابلة) and contains numerous marginal notes and emendations.

The Preface and Table of Contents of the fifty chapters which compose the work are as follows:

بسم الله الرحمن الرحيم وبه أستعين٬

قال الشيخ الجليل ابو الحسن سعيد بن هبة الله بن الحسن الطبيب الحمد لله الّذى له فى كلّ ما تأمّلتْه العيون و تفكّرتْ منه العقول دليلٌ يدلّ على حكمته وشاهدٌ يشهد بتدبيره وعنايته٬ فضّل الانسان على ساير مخلوقاته بعقله وجعل له فى العلوم مراتب مختلفةً بحسب استنارته فى علومه فبقدر شرف العلوم ومنافعها يجب العناية بها وعلى قدر الاجتهاد فيها يكون الاجتنآء من ثمرها ولما كانت العوايق العالمية والحاجات البدنيّة قاطعة لكثير ممّن يتطلّب الفضايل ويهواها صار ميلهم فى مطالبهم الى المعانى المختصرة لا الى المكرّرة منها والمطوّلة فلهذا توخيّتُ فى هذه المقالة الايجاز حاكياً فيما اوردت فيها اقاويل القدمآء واختلاف الفضلآء ومن الله استمدّ التوفيق فيما قصدْتُهُ والعون على ما نويْتُهُ من الغلط والذلل [و هو يسلم] و يحرس من الخطر والخلل بمنّه ورحمته٬

و عدد ابواب هذه المقالة خمسون باباً والله المعين فى جميع الا[حوال]٬

الباب الاوّل (f. 5b) فى العلّة الّتى من اجلها جعلت الطبيعة نوع الانسان مقسومًا بالذكر والانثى٬

الباب الثانى (f. 6a) فى صفة آلات التناسل واولاها فى هيئة القضيب٬

الباب الثالث (f. 7a) فى صفة الانثيين واوعية المنى٬

الباب الرابع (f. 8b) فى هيئة الرحم وعدد النقار الموجودة فيه وعدد الأرحام٬

الباب الخامس (f. 10a) فى اختلاف آراء القدماء فى علّة كون الذكور والاناث٬

الباب السادس (f. 11[b]) فى منافع الجماع للبدن،

الباب السابع (f. 13[a]) فى ذكر الوقت الموافق للجماع،

الباب الثامن (f. 13[b]) فى مضارّ الجماع للبدن،

الباب التاسع (f. 15[a]) فى ذكر الاسباب المانعة للباه،

الباب العاشر (f. 16[a]) فى العلامات الدّالّة على صنفٍ صنفٍ من هذه الاصناف،

الباب الحادى عشر (f. 16[b]) فى مداواة صنفٍ صنفٍ من هذه الاصناف،

الباب الثانى عشر (f. 17[a]) فى ذكر الأغذية المفردة والمؤلّفة الزايدة فى الباه،

لباب الثالث عشر (f. 19[b]) فى ذكر الأدوية المفردة والمركّبة وذكر المسوح والحقن الزايدة فى الباه،

الباب الرابع عشر (f. 24[a]) فى علاج من ضعف من كثرة الباه وفى ذكر الاشياء الّتى تمنع من كثرة خروج المنى وسيلانه وفى مداواة سرعة الانزال وفى الرعدة الّتى تصيب الانسان عند الجماع وبعد الجماع وفى مداواة الانعاظ،

الباب الخامس عشر (f. 26[a]) فى ذكر الاسباب الّتى تقطع الباه،

الباب السادس عشر (f. 26[b]) فى تدبير البكر عند الاقتضاض وفى ذكر الاشياء الّتى تُعين على الحبل وتعديد الأسباب الّتى تمنع منه،

الباب السابع عشر (f. 29[b]) فى ذكر العلامات الدالّة على الحبل وفى ذكر الفروق الّتى يميّز بها بين الحبل بالذكر والحبل بالانثى،

الباب الثامن عشر (f. 31[b]) فى ذكر الأدوية الّتى تسقط الطفل قبل أن يعظم وفى الأدوية الّتى تمنع من الحبل،

الباب التاسع عشر (f. 34[a]) فى ذكر آرآء القدمآء فيما منه يتكوّن الجنين،

الباب العشرون (f. 35[b]) فى ذكر احوال النطفتين عند حصولهما فى الرحم،

الباب الحادى والعشرون (f. 36[a]) فى ذكر خلقة الجنين،

الباب الثانى والعشرون (f. 39[b]) فى علّة استدارة الرّأس وما فيه من الدلايل وانفصال اطراف الجنين،

الباب الثالث والعشرون (f. 40[b]) فى ذكر منافع الشعر والأظفار والأسنان،

الباب الرابع والعشرون (f. 42[a]) فى ذكر الخلاف الّذى بين القدمآء فى اوّل ما يتكوّن من [عضو] الجنين،

الباب الخامس والعشرون (f. 43[a]) فى ذكر الاوقات الّتى يستكمل فيها الجنين،

الباب السادس والعشرون (f. 45[a]) فى تدبير الحامل وحفظ الجنين،

الباب السابع والعشرون (f. 55[b]) فى تسهيل الولادة وتدبير النُفسآء،

الباب الثامن والعشرون (f. 63[a]) فى تعديد الاشيآء الّتى تعسر لأجلها الولادة،

الباب التاسع والعشرون (f. 64[a]) فى ذكر العلّة الّتى من اجلها صار المولود لثمانية أشهر لا يعيش،

الباب الثلثون (f. 68[b]) فى تدبير الطفل حين يولد وفى ذكر الآفات العارضة له بعد خروجه،

الباب الحادى والثلثون (f. 70[a]) فى علّة شبه المولودين بالّذين أولدوهم ولا شبههم وفى ذكر

التشويهات وفى علّة زيادة الاعضاء ونقصانها وفى علّة كبر المولود وصغره واختلاف الوان البدن وجعودة الشعر وسباطته ،

الباب الثانى والثلثون (f. 72ª) فى علاج الأمراض العارضة للأطفال ،

الباب الثالث والثلثون (f. 83ª) فى اختيار الظير واعتبار اللبن وفى ذكر الاشياء الّتى تدرّ اللبن وتزيده وما ينقصه ويقطعه ،

الباب الرّابع والثلثون (f. 87ᵇ) فى تربية الاطفال ،

الباب الخامس والثلثون (f. 92ª) فى علّة شباب الانسان وشيبه ،

الباب السادس والثلثون (f. 95ª) فى العلّة الموجبة لانتصاب قامة الانسان من دون ساير الحيوانات وفى ذكر العلّة الّتى من اجلها صار العمر الطبيعى للانسان مائة وعشرين سنة ،

الباب السابع والثلثون (f. 97ª) فى عدد القوى المدبّرة للانسان وفى ذكر الفوايد المقترنة بكلّ واحدة منها ،

الباب الثامن والثلثون (f. 100ª) فى ذكر الجهة الّتى صدرت عنها كلّ واحدة من هذه النفوس ،

الباب التاسع والثلثون (f. 103ª) فى ذكر الخلاف بين القدماء فى اخلاق النفس ولاىّ القوى يتبع ،

الباب الأربعون (f. 107ª) فى تحقيق الكلام فى العقل الهيولانى الموجود فى الانسان ،

الباب الحادى والاربعون (f. 109ª) فى ذكر الخلافات الموجودة بين القدماء فى مسكن القوّة الفكريّة ،

الباب الثانى والاربعون (f. 110ᵇ) فى جوهر العقل الهيولانى وهل هو مُحْدَثٌ او قديم ،

الباب الثالث والاربعون (f. 111ᵇ) فى ذكر مراتب العقل الانسانى ،

الباب الرابع والاربعون (f. 113ª) فى ذكر مذاهب الفلاسفة فى علم العقل للمعقولات ،

الباب الخامس والاربعون (f. 114ᵇ) فى السؤال عن وجود الشخص وفساده وأيّهما اشرف ،

الباب السادس والاربعون (f. 118ᵇ) فى الفرق بين الرّوح والنفس ،

الباب السابع والاربعون (f. 120ª) فى البيّانات الدالّة على بقاء العقل بعد المفارقة لهذه الهيولى الكثيفة وذكر الشكوك الطارية على بقائه بعد المفارقة ،

الباب الثامن والاربعون (f. 121ª) فى ذكر احوال الصّور الحاصلة فى العقل الانسانى وهل يبطل منه عند المفارقة لهذا الجسم أم يبقا ،

الباب التاسع والاربعون (f. 124ª) فى اللذّة الّتى يصل اليها العقل الهيولانى بعد المفارقة ،

الباب الخمسون (f. 125ᵇ) فى ذكر آراء القدمآء فى التناسخ اعنى عود النفس الّتى كانت فى بعض الأشخاص الى شخص آخر وفى ايراد الشكّ الطارى المفسد لهذا الاعتقاد ،

The order of the chapters in the text does not entirely agree with that in the Table of Contents. Such disagreement is indicated in the margin by such words as يقدّم لانّه التاسع والعشرون opposite the title of Ch. XXX, which really belongs to Ch. XXIX.

P. 5 (10).

قانون الشيخ أبى علی بن سینا.

A very fine old MS. of part of the third Book of the *Qánún* of Avicenna, not dated, but certainly of the twelfth century of the Christian era, since it was transcribed by the somewhat notable physician Hibatu'lláh ibn Ṣá'id, who died in 560/1164 (see Brockelmann, vol. I, pp. 487–488), from the dictation of Sa'íd ibnu'l-Ḥasan.

This MS., bought of the late Ḥájjí 'Abdu'l-Majíd Belshah in January, 1920, was formerly (1298/1881) in the library of Muḥammad Ḥasan Khán *Ṣaní'u'd-Dawla*, whose book-plate it bears. It lacks the first leaf, and in its present state comprises 216 written leaves of 23·3 × 15·1 c. and 19 ll. It is carefully written in a large, clear ***naskh*** with rubrications, and contains the first nine sections (*Fann*) of Book III, treating of the diseases of the head, eyes, ear, nose, mouth and tongue, teeth, gums and lips, throat and uvula, and tonsils. The opening words correspond with p. 281, l. 14, of the edition of the text printed at Rome in A.D. 1593, and the conclusion with p. 385 of the same.

For the most important references to the copious literature on Avicenna (Shaykh Abú 'Alí Ḥusayn ibn 'Abdi'lláh ibn Síná, b. 370/980, d. 428/1037) see Brockelmann, vol. I, pp. 452–458, and especially for the celebrated *Qánún*, p. 457, No. 82.

P. 6 (12).

شرح الموجز فى علم الطبّ.

A Commentary on *Al-Mújaz fí 'Ilmi't-Ṭibb*, the well-known Compendium of Avicenna's *Qánún* by 'Alá'u'd-Dín Abu'l-Ḥasan 'Alí ibn Abi'l-Ḥaram (not-Ḥazm, as in this MS.) al-Qarshí, commonly called Ibnu'n-Nafís (d. 687/1288 or 696/1296). See Brockelmann, vol. I, p. 493.

This MS., bought with 46 others from the late Ḥájjí 'Abdu'l-Majíd Belshah in January, 1920, is written in a good, clear *nasta'líq* with rubrications, and comprises 402 ff. of 27·2 × 16·7 c. and 23 ll. There is no date or colophon, but the date of transcription can hardly be earlier than the sixteenth or seventeenth century.

The book is divided into four sections called *Fann* as follows:

Fann I (f. 2[b]). General principles and considerations.
Fann II (f. 116[b]). Drugs and diet.
Fann III (f. 168[a]). Special Pathology *a capite ad calcem* (f. 168[a]).
Fann IV (f. 337[b]). General Pathology.

The Commentary appears to be that of Burhánu'd-Dín Nafís ibn 'Awaḍ (?) al-Kirmání (composed at Samarqand in 841/1437), since its opening words correspond with the MS. of that work described in vol. IV, p. 64, of the Bankipore Library by 'Aẓímu'd-Dín Aḥmad (Calcutta, 1910).

P. 7 (10).

حلّ الموجز

Another Commentary on the above-mentioned *Mújaz* entitled *Ḥallu'l-Mújaz* by Jamálu'd-Dín Muḥammad ibn Muḥammad al-Áq-sará'í (d. *circa* 800/1397), beginning, after the short doxology:

و بعد، فانّ الطبّ علم شريف لشرف موضوعه ووثاقة دلايله وشدّة الحاجة اليه الخ

The author says that he read with his father most of the well-known abridgments of the *Mújaz*, besides many longer works generally ignored by contemporary physicians, of which he especially mentions the *Ḥáwí*, or "Continens," of ar-Rází, the *Kámilu'ṣ-Ṣaná'at* of al-Majúsí, the *Qánún* of Avicenna, and the writings of Najíbu'd-Dín of Samarqand.

The MS., bought of Ḥájjí 'Abdu'l-Majíd Belshah in January, 1920, comprises 263 ff. of 23·6 × 14 c. and 20 ll., and is written in a clear, fairly modern *naskh* with rubrications and some marginal notes in various hands. The Arabic text ends on f. 260ª, and the remaining leaves contain notes in Persian. On f. 262ᵇ is an inscription in the *Khaṭṭ-i-sarwí*, or "Cypress-writing," described in my *Year amongst the Persians*, pp. 391–392 [426–428 in the reprint published by the Cambridge University Press], which appears to read:

اين كتّاب مال حسين عمّ

P. 8 (13).

(١) تقويم الأدوية، (٢) تقويم الأبدان،

Two Arabic medical works, *viz.* (1) the *Taqwímu'l-Adwiya*, a tabulated list of remedies by Kamálu'd-Dín Ḥubaysh ibn Ibráhím of Tiflís (*circa* 600/1203–4); and (2) the *Taqwímu'l-Abdán*, a tabulated list of diseases, showing the aetiology, symptoms and treatment of each, by Yaḥyà ibn 'Ísà ibn Jazla (d. 493/1099–1100).

This MS., one of the Belshah MSS. bought in January, 1920, comprises 121 ff. of 31 × 20·5 c. and a variable number of lines, and was formerly in the library of Muḥammad Ḥasan Khán *Ṣaní'u'd-Dawla* (1298/1881), whose book-plate is affixed to f. 1ª.

(1) The *Taqwímu'l-Adwiya* (ff. 1b–71a) begins:

الحمد لله مستحقّ الحمد والثناء ومستوجب العباد بما اولاهم من الآلاء وأفاض عليهم من الكرم والنعما آلخ...قال ابو الفضل حبيش بن ابرهيم المتطبّب التفليسى لمّا قرأتُ كتب جالينوس السّتّة عشر الّتى هى اصول الطبّ وتصحّفْتُ ما دوّنه الأطبّاء المتقدّمون والمحدثون فى صناعة الطبّ وطالعْتُ ما صنّفوه فى الأدوية المفردة والاغذية الّتى هى مادّة الطبّ وبها يتمّ حفظ الصّحّة وشفاء الأمراض وقدَّمْتُ النظر فى كتاب ديسقوريدس الّذى له السبق فى المعرفة (*sic*) الأدوية واجتنائها من البستانى والبّرى والسهلى والجبلى والمبالغة فى تحقيق معرفتها فى سبعة مقالات آلخ

Amongst the writers on Materia Medica mentioned in this Preface are, besides Dioscorides, Galen, Oribasius, Ḥunayn ibn Isḥáq, ar-Rází (the *Ḥáwí* or "Continens"), Ibn 'Abdán al-Ahwází, al-Majúsí (the *Kámilu'ṣ-Ṣaná'at*), Abú Sahl al-Masíḥí, Ibn Buṭlán, and Avicenna (the *Qánún*). The title of the work is given as *Taqwímu'l-Adwiya*, and it is dedicated to

...مولانا الوزير الصاحب العادل الرحيم المؤيّد المنصور شرف الدّين معزّ الاسلام والمسلمين عضد الانام شمس الملّة بحر الائمّة خاصة خليفه ظهير الملوك والسلاطين سيّد الوزراء صدر الشرق والغرب صفىّ أمير المؤمنين على بن طراد الرسى (?) ادام الله على الاسلام ظلاله وضاعف على الأوقات اقباله وبلّغه فى الدّارين آماله كما اسبغ على الخليفة [الخليقة] افضاله بمحمّد وآله'

The *verso* of each leaf (ff. 2–58) contains a table ruled in red into thirteen horizontal spaces, each allotted to one drug and divided by vertical lines into twelve compartments. The drugs are arranged alphabetically, according to their Arabic names, of which the Persian, Syriac, Romaic and Ancient Greek equivalents (all written in the Arabic character) are given in the next four columns. The seven remaining columns give (1) the nature (*Máhiyyat*) of the drug in question; (2) the indications for its use; (3) its properties; (4) its uses and (5) misuses; (6) its appropriate excipient; (7) its dose. Needless to say, the foreign equivalents of the Arabic and Persian names of the drugs are terribly corrupt and in many cases hardly to be identified. About 734 drugs are thus enumerated. The opposite page (*i.e.* the *recto* of each leaf) contains selected medical opinions as to the value and use of each drug, arranged in thirteen corresponding vertical spaces, not divided in this case by horizontal lines.

The remainder of the *Taqwímu'l-Adwiya* (ff. 59–70), each divided into 36 (18 × 2) compartments, contains lists of drugs classified under their properties (sweet, bitter, astringent, laxative, etc.), with short notes on each. About 836 medicinal substances are included in these tables. The text ends on f. 71a, and is undated, but is written in a fairly modern *ta'líq*, apparently of the eighteenth century.

(2) The *Taqwímu'l-Abdán* of Yaḥyà ibn 'Ísà ibn Jazla (see Brockelmann, vol. I, p. 485) occupies the remainder of the MS. (ff. 73–121), and is also arranged in tabular form. The Preface (ff. 73ᵇ–74ᵃ) begins:

الحمد لله الّذى خلق وسوّى وقدّر وهدى وأمرض وشفا الّخ

The Table of Contents occupies ff. 74ᵇ–75ᵃ, and is headed:

ذكر ما ضمّنت كلّ ورقة من علم الأمراض،

The diseases are classified under forty-four categories, under each of which eight of the principal species are enumerated, *viz.* (1) quotidian fevers; (2) "putrid" fevers, including tertian and quartan; (3) tumours; (4) and (5) skin-diseases; (6) external diseases of the head and face; (7) same of hands and feet; (8) wounds and ulcers; (9) ulcers and burns; (10) poisonous bites and stings; (11), (12) and (13), animal and vegetable poisons; (14) headache; (15) and (16) diseases of the brain; (17) nervous diseases; (18) and (19), diseases of the eyelids; (20) diseases of the conjunctiva; (21) same of the cornea; (22) same of the humours; (23) same of the optic nerve and ear; (24) same of the ear and nose; (25) same of the olfactory sense and tongue; (26) same of the lips and teeth; (27) same of the teeth, gums and uvula; (28) same of the throat, lungs and trachea; (29) haemoptysis, pleurisy, etc.; (30) cardiac diseases; (31), (32), (33) and (34), diseases of the stomach and oesophagus; (35) same of the intestines; (36) same of the liver; (37) same of the gall-bladder and spleen; (38) same of the spleen and kidneys; (39) and (40) same of the bladder and testicles; (41) and (42) same of the uterus; (43) same of the uterus and breasts; (44) same of the lower extremities.

A page (ff. 75ᵇ–118ᵇ) is devoted to each of these forty-four categories. An initial table, ruled in eleven columns, contains (1) the name of each disease mentioned in each class; (2) five columns indicating the temperament, age, season, and country favourable to the genesis of the disease, and its prognosis; (3) four columns headed السبب, العلامة, الاستفراغ, التدبير الملكى, التدبير السهل الوجود، dealing with aetiology, symptoms, blood-letting, and the simpler and more complicated treatment. A fuller note on the treatment of each disease occupies a corresponding portion of the opposite page. The last 5 pages (ff. 119ᵇ–121ᵇ) contain the Conclusion. The MS. ends with the following colophon, dated Friday, 11 Shawwál, 954 (Nov. 24, 1547):

رتّبه الشيخ الجليل الحكيم يحيى بن عيسى بن على بن جزلة صاحب كتاب منهاج البيان...
قد فرغ من كتابته يوم الجمعة الحادى عشر شهر شوّال سنة اربع وخمسين وتسعمائه،

P. 9 (11).

منهاج البيان لابن جزله،

The *Minháju'l-Bayán*, a well-known Arabic work on simple and compound medicaments by Abú 'Alí Yaḥyà ibn 'Ísà ibn Jazla (d. 493/1100), defective at end. See Brockelmann, vol. I, p. 485; the old *Brit. Mus. Arab. Cat.*, p. 222.

This MS., bought of the late Ḥájjí 'Abdu'l-Majíd Belshah in January, 1920, comprises 309 ff. of 24·0 × 16·2 c. and 21 ll. It is written in a large, coarse *naskh*, with a paucity of diacritical points, and titles in red. On f. 222ᵃ, at the beginning of the second part, is a note of ownership by a Nestorian Christian named Ibráhím Básim, dated 775/1373, so that the MS. was transcribed at some earlier date. Part I occupies ff. 1ᵇ–221ᵃ, Part II, incomplete, ff. 222ᵇ–309ᵇ. The text breaks off in the middle of the article on Oil of Water-lilies (دهن اللينوفر).

P. 10 (13).

رسالة فى طبّ النّبى وغيرها،

A modern Arabic MS. bought of the late Ḥájjí 'Abdu'l-Majíd Belshah in January, 1920, transcribed in a small, neat *naskh*, with rubrications, in 1231/1816. It comprises 28 ff. (written) of 30 × 21 c. and 28 ll. It contains two medical treatises, *viz.*:

I (ff. 2ᵇ–26ᵃ). An anonymous and untitled treatise beginning:

الحمد لله الّذى خلق الانسان من طين ثمّ جعله نطفة فى قرار مكين آلخ...وبعد، فانّ علم الطبّ للأمراض من اهمّ الأغراض لأنّ علم الأبدان متقدّم على علم الأديان وهو مجمع عليه بالكتاب والسنّة واجماع الأُمّة...وبعد فأنّ هذا الكتاب مجتمع وملخّص من كتب الاطبّاء فى الطبّ من المجرّبات الّذى يحصل نفعها انشاء الله تعالى وهو مشتمل على ابواب وفصول فيما يأتى بيانه من ساير انواع الأسقام والأمراض والخواصّات والمنافع ويأتى كلّ فصل فى محلّه بحيث يحصل الانتفاع به وبالله التوفيق،

The work comprises eleven sections (the title of the ninth is missing, but that of the eleventh occurs twice), the last of which is divided into two chapters (*Báb*) as follows:

(١) الفصل الاوّل فى بيان اعشاب المربّيات ومنافعها وخواصّها (f. 3ᵃ)،

(٢) الفصل الثانى فى بيان ما يتعلّق بالاسباب الموجبة لعقر النّسآء ولمنع الحبل (f. 3ᵇ)،

(٣) الفصل الثالث فيما يتعلّق بالاطلية للجرب والكلف والنمش وغيرها ممّا فى معناها (f. 6ᵇ)،

(٤) الفصل الرابع فيما يتعلّق بانبات الشعر وعدم انباته وتطويله وصباغاته وممّا فى هذا المعنى
(f. 8ᵇ) '

(٥) الفصل الخامس فيما يتعلّق بالبواسير والنواسير ووجع العقد والزحير ولد فى(؟) الدم ووجع البطن والقولنج وممّا فى هذا المعنى (f. 10ᵃ) '

(٦) الفصل السادس ما فيها [read فيما] يتعلّق بالأرياح ودهاناتها والنزلات ودهاناتها وتهبيلاتها والطلوعات والبزورات ودهاناتها وذروراتها وريح الفالج ودهاناته وممّا فى هذا المعنى ممّا يحصل النفع به انشاء الله تعالى (f. 11ᵇ) '

(٧) الفصل السابع فيما يتعلّق بأدوية الصفرا والسودا والجذام والبلغم اعاذنا الله من ذلك وممّا فى هذا المعنى ممّا يحصل النفع به انشاء الله تعالى (f. 15ᵃ) '

(٨) الفصل الثامن فيما يتعلّق بالأشربة والشربات ولرمى الدود وجع الآذان وصممها والسعال والبول الفراش وبعسر(؟) البول ووجع المعدة والسرة والاسهال ووجع الأسنان والأضراس واليرقان والصفار وقطع اللعاب ومعافى هذه المعانى وغيرها ممّا يحصل المنفع لها انشاء الله تعالى (f. 16ᵃ) '

(٩) الفصل العاشر [sic, for التاسع] فيما يتعلّق بالمعاجين البالغة النفع للباه ولغيره من المنافع المحقّقة العجيبة نفع الله بها آمين (f. 17ᵃ) '

(١٠) الفصل الحادى عشر [sic, for العاشر] فيما يتعلّق بخواصّ ومنافع اعشاب مستخرجة من القاموس المحيط باللّغة ممّا جرّب وحاصل النفع به انشاء الله تعالى (f. 22ᵃ) '

(١١) الفصل الحادى عشر فيما يتعلّق بمنافع الحيوان الوحشى والأهلى ممّا يحصل النفع به انشاء الله تعالى' باب منافع الغنم...باب منافع الانسان...(f. 23ᵇ)...باب فى منافع البقر (f. 24ᵇ) الّخ

Several other animals, of which various parts are said to possess healing virtues, are enumerated, such as the sheep, the ram, the buffalo, the cow, the horse, the mule, the ass, the camel, the pig, the hare, etc. The short colophon at the end (f. 26ᵃ) contains only the date 1231/1816, and the Arabic verse:

يلوح الخطّ فى القرطاس دهرًا و كاتبه رميمٌ فى التراب '

II (ff. 26ᵇ–28ᵃ). This tract, divided into many short unnumbered paragraphs (*Báb*), appears to contain such Traditions of the Prophet referring to medical matters as are recorded by Abu'l-Qásim an-Naysábúrí. The title and beginning are as follows:

وهذه رسالة فى الطبّ النّبى (sic)...للامام الاستاذ ابو القاسم المحدّث النيشابورى بالاحاديث المروية عن رسول الله الّخ...الحمد لله الّخ...وبعد' فأنّ هذا الكتاب جمعه الاستاذ ابو القاسم الّخ...باب' فى الأدوية قال ابن عمر رضه قال رسول الله...طعام البخيل دآء وطعام السخى دواء' باب' فى منفعة الخبز الّخ

In the colophon at the end (f. 28ᵇ) the copyist's name is given as Qásim ibn Muḥammad an-Naṣrábádí, and the date of completion as Rabí' I, 1231/February, 1816.

P. 11 (8).

تحفة العروس ونزهة النفوس،

A well-known Arabic work on women and marriage entitled *Tuḥfatu'l-'Arús wa-Nuzhatu'n-Nufús*, by Abú 'Abdi'lláh Muḥammad at-Tíjání (fl. 710/1310). See Brockelmann, vol. II, p. 257, and Ahlwardt's Berlin Arabic Catalogue, vol. v, pp. 609–610, No. 6386. The work contains twenty-five chapters (unnumbered), some of which are subdivided into several sections, all of which are enumerated on ff. 6–7. Begins:

الحمد لله الّذى سوّغنا الفضل جزيلًا، وفضّلنا على كثير من خلقه تفضيلًا الخ... امّا بعد، فأنّ الله تعالى بلطيف حكمته وما اورى فى ابداع العالم من عجائب قدرته خلق الانسان مجبولًا على الافتقار الخ

The MS., from the Belshah collection acquired in 1920, comprises 200 ff. of 18·3 × 12 c. and 19 ll., is written in a poor modern *riq'a*, and was completed in Jumádà II, 1306/February, 1889.

P. 12 (10).

مجموعهٔ رسائل در علم طبّ،

Three Persian treatises on Medicine and Materia Medica, mostly translated from Turkish versions of the originals by Muḥammad Báqir al-Músawí, court physician to Sulṭán Ḥusayn the Ṣafawí (reigned A.D. 1694–1722).

This MS., from the Schindler collection, acquired on Jan. 5, 1917, comprises 182 ff. of 23·6 × 13·3 c. and 14 ll., is written in a large, clear, good *naskh* with rubrications, within gilt and coloured margins. A note of purchase in Iṣfahán on f. 182^{b} is dated Jumádà I, 1168/Feb.—March, 1755. The contents are as follows:

I (ff. 3^{b}–47^{b}). A treatise on sexual hygiene, purporting (ff. 5^{b}–6^{a}) to be translated from a Turkish version of the original work of Naṣíru'd-Dín-i-Ṭúsí. The latter is said to have been composed for Gházán Khán, but this appears to be impossible, since he was born about the time (A.D. 1274) when the philosopher of Ṭús died. The Turkish version of this original is said to have been made by a certain 'Abdu'l-Laṭíf for Sulṭán Ya'qúb ibn Dawlat Khán. The first two or three pages have been rendered partly illegible by damp. The words following the doxology are:

و بعد، بر دیدهٔ حقّ بین، و ضمیر حقیقت گزین عارفان دقایق آفرینش، و سالکان مناهج دانش الخ

The work comprises eighteen chapters, of which the contents are stated on ff. 8^b–10^a as follows[1]:

باب اوّل، در مزاجهای مختلفهٔ آدمی و تدبیر هر مزاجی (f. 14^b)،

باب دویم، در غذاهای مفرده که در حفظ صحّت بدن آدمی در کار و مناسب است،

باب سیم، در بیان دواهای مفرده است که (f. 9^a) تقویت افعال متعلّقه بجماع نمایند و مادّهٔ منی‌را زیاد می نمایند،

باب چهارم، در اغذیهٔ مرکّبه و حلواهای چند است که مزاج آدمی‌را باصلاح آورد و سُسْتی اندامها و فالج اعضارا دفع نمایند و افعال جماع‌را قوی نمایند،

باب پنجم، در شرابهاست که خون‌را صاف کنند و مزاج فاسدرا باصلاح آورند و افعال[جماع]را بسیار قوی نمایند،

باب ششم، در معاجین مفرّحه و جوارشهاست که رافع ملال و دلگیری است (f. 24^a)،

باب هفتم، در بیان شیافهاست که سردی کمررا دفع و رطوبت زایده و صفرا و سودا و بلغمرا از معده جذب و رفع کنند و کمررا محکم و افعال جماع‌را قوی نمایند و فواید بسیار دارند (f. 28^b)،

باب هشتم، در حُقْنها که وجع مفاصل و عرق النّسا و درد کمر و ریاح فاسده (f. 9^b) و قولنج‌را دفع کنند و کمررا محکم نمایند و افعال [جماع‌را] قوّت دهند (f. 29^a)،

باب نهم، در پوششها و لباسهاست که در هر یك از فصول چهارگانه موافق مزاج آدمی است و حفظ صحّت مینماید (f. 30^b)،

باب دهم، در بیان شروط و اقسام اوضاع جماع است که بکدام نحو جماع واقع شود که زیانی ببدن نداشته باشد و آدمی‌را زود لاغر و پیر کند (f. 31^a)،

باب یازدهم، در بیان دواهاست که چون بر ذکر بمالند چنانکه باید سطْبر و سخت شود (f. 33^a)،

باب دوازدهم، در بیان دواهای چند است که چون بر ذکر بمالند دراز شود (f. 35^b)،

باب سیزدهم، در بیان دواهاست که چون بر میان انگشتان دست و پا بمالند در قوّت جماع افزاید و ذکررا چنانکه باید محکم کند بمرتبه که چندانکه خواهد جماع تواند کرد و ضعف و سُسْتی عارض نگردد (f. 37^a)،

باب چهاردهم، در بیان دواهائیکه چون در وقت مجامعت در دهان نگاهدارند باعث زیادت لذّت مرد گردد (f. 38^a)،

باب پانزدهم، در بیان دواهائی که از استعمال آن لذّت مرد و زن هر دو زیاد گردد (f. 39^a)،

باب شانزدهم، در بیان ادویه چند که چون زن استعمال نماید مانند باکره گردد و موضع مخصوص او در نهایت گرمی گردد (f. 39^b)،

باب هفدهم، در ادویه که مانع حمل گردد و زن همیشه مانند باکره باشد (f. 40^b)،

باب هیجدهم، در بیان ادویه که زنی که حامل نشود استعمال کند حامله گردد باذن الله تعالی (f. 41^b)،

[1] [The headings of Chh. 2–5 do not occur in the text.]

II (ff. 48[b]–104[b]). Another Persian treatise on the medical virtues of various animals and plants, translated from the Turkish, and supposed to be based on a work of Galen's (f. 49[b]):

بدانکه این کتاب مختصریست در بیان بعضی از منافع انسان و سایر حیوانات و منافع نباتات و احجار و جالینوس آنرا وضع کرده و تجربه نموده و خاصّه و عامّه آنرا استعمال کرده‌اند و این رساله‌را بجهّال و عوالم (read عوامّ) الناس ندهند که مبادا کسی‌را هلاك کنند، منافع انسان، اگر موی سر آدمی‌را بسوزانند و با گلاب ممزوج نمایند زنی که دشوار زاید آنرا بر سر بمالد در همان لحظه بار بنهد آلخ

The virtues of animals other than man begin on f. 50[b]; those of birds on f. 54[a]; those of plants on f. 56[b]. The latter portion of the treatise deals largely with aphrodisiacs and kindred matters.

III (ff. 105[a]–181[b]). Another Persian treatise by the same Muḥammad Báqir on various wounds, injuries and diseases, and their treatment, beginning, after the short Arabic doxology:

امّا بعد، چون عندلیب کلك نوا سنج این غلامزاده از زمزمهٔ ترجمهٔ گلستان دویم کتاب طبّ ترکی باز پرداخت فصل آن آمد که در بوستان دیگر یعنی رسالهٔ سیم کتاب مذکور بپرواز آید آلخ

The ultimate original is said to have been a work entitled *Khuláṣa-i-Díwán* compiled in the time of the Caliph al-Ma'mún at the suggestion or by the direction of a certain Shaykh Abú Ṭáhir ibn Muḥammad ʻArabí (? عرلی), of which a copy (f. 6[a]) fell into the hands of "this weak one, that is Masʻúd," who, finding it written in "a mixture of Persian and Pahlawí," desired to translate it into Turkish "so that matters might be made easy for every beginner." The treatise is divided into three chapters as follows (f. 106[b]):

باب اوّل در دانستن مسایل علمیّه چند، باب دویم در دانستن جراحتها، باب سیم در دانستن معالجها و دواها،

The writing is uniform throughout the MS., and there is no colophon.

P. 13 (8).

قرابادين شفائى،

Qarábádín-i-Shifá'í, a well-known Persian pharmacology by Muẓaffar ibn Muḥammad al-Ḥusayní ash-Shifá'í (d. 974/1556), the drugs being arranged alphabetically. See Rieu's B.M.P.C., pp. 473–474, Fonahn's *Zur Quellenkunde der Persischen Medizin*, pp. 81–84, where the contents are fully stated, etc.

Begins after the short Arabic doxology:

و بعد، پوشیده نماند که فقیر حقیر مظفر بن محمّد الحسینی الشّفائی در مدّتی مدید ترکیب چند

در معالجات امراض که از آن گریزی [گزیری] نبود جمع کرده بود خواست که در سلك ترتیب در

آورد الّخ

This MS. was bought from the late Mr Sidney Churchill by Sir Albert Houtum-Schindler in 1885, and with his other MSS. passed into my possession in January, 1917. It comprises ff. 209 of 18·5 × 11·7 c. and 14 ll., is written in a large, clear *naskh* with rubrications, and was completed on Shawwál 6, 1090/Nov. 10, 1679, by the scribe Ja'far ibn Muḥammad Mu'min al-Fatḥání al-Imámí al-Adíb al-Qárí al-Káshání.

P. 14 (12).

قرابادین نوح بن عبد المنّان،

A Turkish *Qarábádín*, or Materia Medica, compiled by Núḫ ibn 'Abdi'l-Mannán in the reign of Sulṭán Aḥmad III (1115–1143/1703–1730), beginning:

حمد نا محدود، اول حکیم حتّی ودود، درگاهنه عریضه داشته قلنور الّخ...بعد ازین، بو فقیر قلیل

البضاعه، و ضعیف الاستطاعه، الرّاجی من الملك الرّحمان، نوح بن عبد المنّان، عنفوان شبابدن

هنگام کهولته گلنجیه‌دك

The author says that he began the study of Medicine in early youth, and, after practising it privately for twelve years, attracted the favourable notice of Sulṭán Muḥammad IV (1058–1099/1648–1687), during whose reign he held for 27 years the post of Chief Surgeon (ریاست جرّاحین). During the reign of Sulṭán Muṣṭafà II (1106–1115/1695–1703) he was Chief Physician and Chief Minister of Rumelia:

...مدّت سلطنتلری اولان طقوز سنه‌دن متجاوز زمانده سر اطبّا و پایهٔ صدارت روم ایلی (f. 12ª) ایله

کامروا اولوب...

and he continued to enjoy the favour of the succeeding Sulṭán Aḥmad III (1115–1143/1703–1730), to whom, apparently, the present work is dedicated.

The prescriptions are arranged according to the form in which they are made up, such as confections (*ma'jún*), draughts (*sharáʾib*), powders (*sufúf*), etc. A full table of contents occupies ff. 1ᵇ–9ª.

The MS., bought of 'Abdu'l-Majíd Belshah in January, 1920, is dated 1140/1727–8, comprises 210 ff. of 29 × 18·4 c. and 17 ll., and is written throughout in a large, clear *naskh* with rubrications. Many of the prescriptions are ascribed to Galen, Másawayhi, ar-Rází (رازس), Níqúlá, and to the author himself.

P. 15 (10).

قرابادين،

An acephalous and anonymous Arabic work on foods, medicines, etc., arranged alphabetically. The first extant section (*faṣl*) begins on f. 3[a]:

فصل، وامّا الاغذية التى يكره الجمع منها فى المعدة الخ

The next section begins on f. 10[a]:

فصل، وامّا مقادير اوزان الأدوية المفردة المتّحد منها الأدوية المركّبة الخ

The alphabetical list of medicaments (باب الالف) begins with ابرسيم on f. 11[b]; the next letter (باب البا) on f. 29[b] with باقلى; then (باب التا) with تامول or تنبول on f. 44[a]; and finally the (باب الواو) on f. 196[a]. The last entry (on f. 198[b]) is ورد العوسج, in the middle of which article the MS. breaks off.

The MS., bought of Ḥájjí 'Abdu'l-Majíd Belshah in January, 1920, comprises in its present imperfect state 198 ff. of 22·8 × 8·8 c. and about 31 ll. The latter portion (ff. 90–198) is in a much better and more archaic hand (probably thirteenth or fourteenth century) than the earlier supply, which is in a poor *nasta'líq*. There are rubrications in both, and many marginal notes, especially in the older portion. A few of these are in Persian, *e.g.* on f. 150[b] opposite the entry قثا الحمار the Persian *Dhakhíra-i-Khwárazmsháhí* is quoted as follows:

در ذخيره آمده است كى قثا الحمار را علقم خوانند،

P. 16 (13).

ذخيرهٔ خوارزمشاهى،

A large volume containing the whole of the well-known Persian system of Medicine entitled *Dhakhíra-i-Khwárazmsháhí*, composed in 504/1110–1111 by Zaynu'd-Dín Ismá'íl of Jurján for the King of Khwárazm or Khiva. Portions of this celebrated and voluminous work are to be found in most large collections of Oriental MSS., but seldom the entire work in one volume. The best and fullest description of its contents is that given by Adolf Fonahn in his excellent book *Zur Quellenkunde der Persischen Medizin* (Leipzig, 1910), **No. 15**, pp. 7–11, at the end of which article (pp. 10–11) the principal known MSS. are enumerated. See also my *Arabian Medicine* (Cambridge, 1921), pp. 98–100 and pp. 110–111.

This MS., bought of the late Ḥájjí 'Abdu'l-Majíd Belshah for £15 on Dec. 17, 1919, separately from the other MSS. acquired from him, comprises 1403 written pages of 31 × 21·5 c. and 28 ll., and is written in a fairly good modern *ta'líq* with rubrications. There is no date or colophon, but a note of possession at the beginning is dated 1146/1733–4. There are numerous erasures, additions and corrections in the text, besides many marginal notes and glosses.

P. 17 (10).

A fine and ancient but acephalous and incomplete manuscript of most of Books I–III of the above-mentioned *Dhakhíra-i-Khwárazmsháhí*, beginning with the words in the Preface:

...اتّفاقهاء نا موافق اندرین ولایت بسیارست یکی از آن جمله آنست کی هوای بذین درستی و باکیزکی بسبب این بحار بلیذها که اندر شهر هست هوای شهر ناخوش و زیان‌کار می‌شوذ الخ

The full contents of the nine books (*Kitáb*) and of the subdivisions of Book I occupy ff. 1^b–3^a, and the text breaks off in the middle of Book III, *Bakhsh* ii, *Guftár i*, *Juz'* 3, chapter 18, on "Cheese-water" (*Panír-áb*, or *Má'u'l-Jubn*). The chief contents occupy the following portions of the volume:

Book I in six Discourses (*Guftár*) as follows: (i) f. 19^a; (ii) f. 23^a; (iii) f. 30^a; (iv) in five parts beginning respectively on ff. 34^a; 45^a; 59^b; 63^b; and 67^b; (v) f. 70^a; (vi) f. 86^a.

Book II in nine Discourses as follows: (i) f. 93^b; (ii) f. 101^b; (iii) f. 107^a; (iv) f. 121^b; (v) f. 123^b; (vi) f. 142^a; (vii) f. 146^a; (viii) f. 147^b; (ix) in three parts, beginning respectively on ff. 148^b; 156^a; and 161^b.

Book III in two divisions called *Bakhsh*, of which the first (f. 163^a) comprises seven Discourses as follows: (i) f. 163^b; (ii) f. 175^b; (iii) in two parts beginning respectively on ff. 180^b and 186^b; (iv) f. 213^b; (v) f. 223^a; (vi) f. 225^b; (vii) f. 230^a. The second *Bakhsh* (f. 235^a) should also comprise seven Discourses, of which part of the first only is contained in this volume, *viz.* Part I, f. 235^a; Part II, f. 243^a; and Part III on f. 249^a. Of this last Part seventeen complete chapters occur, the last of which (ff. 262^a–280^a) contains a list of the more important drugs and simples arranged alphabetically. Ch. 18, as already mentioned, breaks off abruptly at the bottom of f. 281^b. There is, of course, no date or colophon.

The MS., acquired with 46 others of the Belshah collection in January, 1920, appears to be of the thirteenth or early fourteenth century of the Christian era, and is written in a fine, large, archaic *naskh*. In its present condition it comprises 281 ff. of 23·6 × 15·8 and 25 ll. There are numerous marginal notes and glosses.

P. 18 (12).

A very beautiful old thirteenth century manuscript of another portion of the same *Dhakhíra-i-Khwárazmsháhí*, beginning with Book III, *Bakhsh* i, *Maqála iv*, and extending to the end of Book V. It begins with a table of contents of the 18 chapters into which this *Maqála*, dealing with wine, its uses, abuses, and effects, is divided. The chief contents of the volume are as follows:

Book III, *Bakhsh* i, *Maqála* (or *Guftár*) *iv*, on Wine (18 chapters, ff. 1^a–10^a); *Maqála v*, on Sleeping and Waking (5 chapters, ff. 10^a–12^a); *Maqála vi*, on

Exercise and Rest (6 chapters, of which ch. 4 is omitted, ff. 12^a–16^b); *Maqála vii*, on Clothing and the use of Oils and Scents (4 chapters, ff. 16^b–20^b).

BOOK III, *Bakhsh* ii, *Maqála i*, in 5 parts (*Juz'*), dealing with Phlebotomy, Emesis, Purgation, Diuretics, Diaphoretics, Enemata, etc., ff. 20^b–90^b; *Maqála ii*, on Health and Disease (4 chapters, ff. 90^b–94^a); *Maqála iii*, on the Effects of Mental States on Health (6 chapters, ff. 94^a–96^b); *Maqála iv*, on Abnormal Conditions in Different Regions of the Body indicative of Impending Illness (4 chapters, ff. 96^b–98^a); *Maqála v*, on the Care of Children (8 chapters, ff. 98^a–102^b); *Maqála vi*, on the Care of the Aged (5 chapters, ff. 102^b–104^a); *Maqála vii*, on Precautions to be observed by Travellers (7 chapters, ff. 104^a–106^b). On f. 106^b is the following colophon enclosed in a coloured and ornamented circle:

تمام شذ كتاب سومين از ذخيرهٔ خوارزمشاهى بيد العبد الضعيف الفقير المذنب المحتاج الى
رحمة الله تبارك وتعالى على بن محمّد بن عبد الله النسّاخ الشبابى الشيرازى غفر الله له ولوالديه
ولجميع المومنين والمومنات،

BOOK IV, *Guftár i*, on Diagnosis (3 chapters, ff. 107^b–109^b); *Guftár ii*, on Coction (5 chapters, ff. 109^b–111^b); *Guftár iii*, on Crises (10 chapters, ff. 111^b–126^b); *Guftár iv*, on Prognosis (7 chapters, ff. 126^b–143^b).

BOOK V begins on f. 144^a with a fresh title-page, treats of Fevers, and comprises six *Guftárs*, with many subdivisions of which a full table of contents occupies ff. 144^b–146^b. *Guftár i*, on Fever, its genera, species, signs and treatment (4 chapters, ff. 146^b–149^b); *Guftár ii*, on Quotidian Fever (27 chapters, ff. 149^b–162^a); *Guftár iii*, on Putrid Fevers, in 3 Parts (*Juz'*) containing respectively 5, 10 and 12 chapters, ff. 162^a–206^b; *Guftár iv*, on Phthisis and Wasting Fevers (4 chapters, ff. 206^b–214^b); *Guftár v*, on Smallpox and Measles (13 chapters, ff. 215^a–223^b); *Guftár vi*, on Relapse (5 chapters, ff. 223^b–225^b).

There is a new title-page on f. 226^a indicating the conclusion of Book v and the beginning of Book VI, on Special Diseases *a capite ad calcem*:

تمام شذ كتاب بنجم از ذخيرهٔ خوارزمشاهى بحمد الله ومنّه،
و بعد ازين كتاب ششم آغاز كنيم اندر علاج بيماريها از سر تا پاى

F. 226^b contains part of the table of contents of Book VI.

This precious and beautiful old MS. comprises 226 ff. of 29·3 × 18·4 c. and 27 ll., and is most carefully written throughout in a large, clear, excellent, archaic *naskh*, with numerous headings, titles and sub-titles in red, blue and gold. A better specimen of a Persian MS. of this period is seldom seen.

P. 19 (11).

The latter part of Book VI (from *Guftár xi*, *Juz'* i, *Báb* 1 to *Guftár xxi*, *Báb* 5) of the same *Dhakhíra-i-Khwárazmsháhí*, dealing with local diseases *a capite ad calcem*, beginning in this MS. with the liver, and ending with gout and sciatica.

This MS. was also one of the forty-seven bought from the Belshah collection in January, 1920. It is not only acephalous and incomplete at the end, but the leaves have been bound in the wrong order and there are half a dozen dislocations. They are now numbered correctly, as far as possible, and stand in the following order:

(*A*) Ff. 1–19. *Guftár xi*, i, 1—*Guftár xi*, ii, 1.
(*F*) Ff. 246–256. *Guftár xx*, iii, 6—*Guftár xxi*, 3.
(*E*) Ff. 224–245. *Guftár xx*, ii, 2—*Guftár xx*, iii, 5.
(*B*) Ff. 20–28. *Guftár xi*, ii, 2—*Guftár xi*, iii, 2.
(*D*) Ff. 48–223. *Guftár xiii*, ii, 1—*Guftár xx*, ii, 2.
(*C*) Ff. 29–47. *Guftár xi*, iii, 2—*Guftár xiii*, ii, 1.
(*G*) Ff. 257–262. *Guftár xxi*, 3—*Guftár xxi*, 5.

There are also 26 ff. at the end on medicaments in which chapter-headings 2–8, 10, 12 and 15 occur. The chief preparations described fall under the following headings:

(۱) مفرح، (۲) معجون، (۳) جوارش، (۴) اطريفل، (۵) مربّا، (٦) اشربه و ربوب، (۷) لعوق، (۸) سفوف، (۹) حبّ، (۱۰) قرص، (۱۱) شياف، (۱۲) دهن،

In this portion also there are several dislocations and *lacunae*.

The MS. comprises 288 ff. of 23·8×16 c. and 19 ll., and is written throughout (except in the case of the last 26 ff., which are in a much more modern *naskh* hand) in a clear and archaic *naskh*, apparently of the fourteenth century of the Christian era. There are rubrications throughout.

P. 20 (17).

A complete, but much more modern, MS. of Book VI of the *Dhakhíra-i-Khwárazmsháhí*, comprising twenty-one Discourses (*Guftár*) as follows:

Guftár	*i*	(f. 2ᵇ)	in 5 pts. and	47 chs.	Diseases of the	Head and Brain.
„	*ii*	(f. 38ᵃ)	„ 7 „	78 „	„	Eye.
„	*iii*	(f. 63ᵇ)	„ 1 pt. and	9 „	„	Ear.
„	*iv*	(f. 68ᵇ)	„ 1 „	10 „	„	Nose.
„	*v*	(f. 73ᵃ)	„ 3 pts. and	30 „	„	Mouth and Teeth.
„	*vi*	(f. 83ᵃ)	„ 2 „	9 „	„	Larynx and Pharynx.
„	*vii*	(f. 87ᵇ)	„ 1 pt. and	15 „	„	Respiratory Organs.
„	*viii*	(f. 104ᵇ)	„ 1 „	6 „	„	Heart.
„	*ix*	(f. 108ᵃ)	„ 1 „	10 „	„	Breast.

Guftár	*x*	(f. 109[b])	in 6 pts. and 33 chs.	Diseases of the Stomach and Oesophagus.
,,	*xi*	(f. 123[b])	,, 3 ,, 23 ,,	,, Liver.
,,	*xii*	(f. 133[b])	,, 1 pt. and 4 ,,	,, Spleen.
,,	*xiii*	(f. 136[a])	,, 2 pts. and 15 ,,	Jaundice and Dropsy.
,,	*xiv*	(f. 144[a])	,, 3 ,, 14 ,,	Diarrhoea and Dysentery.
,,	*xv*	(f. 152[b])	,, 1 pt. and 7 ,,	Diseases of the Rectum and Anus.
,,	*xvi*	(f. 157[a])	,, 1 ,, 3 ,,	Intestinal Worms.
,,	*xvii*	(f. 159[b])	,, 1 ,, 10 ,,	Colic and its varieties.
,,	*xviii*	(f. 166[a])	,, 4 pts. and 35 ,,	Diseases of the Kidneys and Bladder.
,,	*xix*	(f. 183[a])	,, 3 ,, 38 ,,	Hernia and diseases of the male organs of generation.
,,	*xx*	(f. 194[a])	,, 3 ,, 28 ,,	Diseases of the female organs of generation.
,,	*xxi*	(f. 208[b])	,, 1 pt. and 10 ,,	Pain in the Back and Loins, Rheumatism, Gout, Sciatica, etc.

This sixth Book thus comprises 434 chapters in 51 parts.

The MS., one of the 47 Belshah MSS. obtained in January, 1920, comprises 212 ff. of 40·4 × 24·5 c. and 31 ll. It is written in a fairly legible but rather negligent *ta'líq* with rubrications, and is dated in the colophon Ramaḍán 10, 1062/August 15, 1652. Scribe, Muḥammad Shafí' ibn Ḥájjí Muḥammad al-Kátib of Dasht-i-Bayáḍ, who wrote it for Amír Muḥammad al-Kabír al-Ḥusayní.

P. 21 (10).

(۱) مختصر در تشریح، (۲) تشریح منصوری،

This MS., also acquired in January, 1920, from the Belshah collection, contains two Persian treatises on Anatomy, *viz.*:

I. The *Mukhtaṣar*, or Epitome (of Anatomy), of Abu'l-Majd aṭ-Ṭabíb al-Bayḍáwí (ff. 2[b]–59[a]). See Rieu's Persian Catalogue, p. 468, and A. Fonahn's *Zur Quellenkunde der Persischen Medizin*, **No. 2**, pp. 4–5. Fonahn gives the author's date as about 687/1288. Begins:

حمد و ثنائی که حاوی قانون تحمید و شاملهٔ کلّیات تمجید بوذ الخ

The author gives his name on f. 3[a], l. 13, and immediately afterwards a full table of contents, which agrees with that briefly given by Fonahn. The work comprises an Introduction (*Muqaddama*, ff. 4^{a}–5^{a}) and two Books (*Kitáb*), of which the contents are as follows:

مقدّمه در بحث اعضا بسبیل اجمال٬

کتاب اوّل در تشریح اعضاء مفرده (f. 5^{b}) و آن مشتمل است بر شش باب٬

باب اوّل در تشریح عظام و آن مشتمل است بر پانزده فصل٬ (١) در تشریح عظام مجملاً٬ (٢) در تشریح عظام سر٬ (٣) ...عظام فكّ اعلی٬ (۴) انف و فكّ اسفل و اسنان٬ (٥) ...فقرات بر سبیل اجمال٬ (٦) فقرات گردن٬ (٧) فقرات صلب٬ (٨) ...عظام قصّ یعنی استخوان سینه٬ (٩) ... ترقوه و کتف٬ (١٠) ...عضد و ساعد٬ (١١) ...رسغ و مشط٬ (١٢) ...اصابع و اظفار٬ (١٣) ...عظم عانه٬ (١۴) ...فخذ و رکبه و ساق٬ (١٥) ...عظام قدم٬

باب دوم در تشریح اعصاب (f. 17^{b}) و آن مشتمل است بر پنج فصل٬ (١) در تشریح اعصاب دماغی٬ (٢) در تشریح [اعصاب] فقرات گردن٬ (٣) ...اعصاب فقرات صلب٬ (۴) ...اعصاب فقرات قطن٬ (٥) ...اعصاب فقرات عجز و عصعص٬

باب سیوم در تشریح اَوْرِدَه (f. 21^{b}) و آن مشتمل است بر پنج فصل٬ (١) در تعریف اَوْرِدَه و منفعت آن٬ (٢) در تعریف ورید که معروفست بباب٬ (٣) در تشریح جزء صاعد از اجوف٬ (۴) ...اَوْرِدَه بر ظاهر بدن٬ (٥) ...جزءِ نازل از اجوف٬

باب چهارم (f. 26^{a}) در تشریح شریانات و آن مشتمل است بر چهار فصل٬ (١) در تعریف شریان و منفعت آن٬ (٢) ...شریان وریدی٬ (٣) ...شریان سباتی٬ (۴) ...شریان اورطی٬

باب پنجم (f. 28^{a}) در تشریح عضلات و آن مشتمل است بر سی فصل٬ (١) در تعریف عضلات و منفعت آن٬ (٢) ...عضل جبهه٬ (٣) ...عضلات چشم٬ (۴) ...عضل جفن٬ (٥) عضل خدّ٬ (٦) ...عضل لب٬ (٧) ...عضل بینی٬ (٨) ...عضل فكّ اسفل٬ (٩) ...عضلات سر٬ (١٠) ...عضل حنجره٬ (١١) ...حلقوم و قصبهٔ ریه٬ (١٢) ...عضل لامی٬ (١٣) ...عضل زبان٬ (١۴) ...عضل گردن٬ (١٥) ...عضلات سینه٬ (١٦) ...عضلات شانه٬ (١٧) ...عضلات بازو٬ (١٨) ...عضلات ساعد٬ (١٩) ...عضلات رسغ٬ (٢٠) ...عضلات اصابع٬ (٢١) ...عضلات صلب٬ (٢٢) ...عضل بطن٬ (٢٣) ...عضل انثیین٬ (٢۴) ...عضل مثانه٬ (٢٥) ...عضل قضیب٬ (٢٦) ...عضل مقعد٬ (٢٧) ...عضلات فخذ٬ (٢٨) ...عضلات ساق و زانو٬ (٢٩) ...عضلات قدم٬ (٣٠) ...عضلات اصابع٬

باب ششم در تشریح جلد و منفعت آن است٬

کتاب دوم (f. 46^{a}) در تشریح اعضاء مرکّبه و آن مشتمل است بر چند باب٬ (١) در تشریح دماغ٬ (٢) ...در تشریح چشم٬ (٣) ...گوش٬ (۴) ...بینی٬ (٥) ...زبان٬ (٦) ...حنجره و حلق٬ (٧) ...حجاب و قصبهٔ ریه٬ (٨) ...قلب٬ (٩) ...مری و معده٬ (١٠) ...جگر٬ (١١) ...مران٬ (١٢) ...طحال٬ (١٣) ...امعا٬ (١۴) ...کلیه٬ (١٥) ...مثانه٬ (١٦) ...قضیب و خصیتین٬ (١٧) ...رحم٬ والله اعلم بالصّواب٬

This portion of the volume ends on f. 59ª with a colophon in which the scribe's name is given as Ḥabíbu'lláh, and the date of completion as the end of Dhu'l-Qa'da, 1055 (Jan. 17, 1646).

II. The *Tashríḥ-i-Manṣúrí* (ff. 60–91) is better known on account of the half dozen curious anatomical diagrams which occur in most copies of the work, and which in this MS. are to be found on ff. 69[b], 74[a], 76[a], 80[b], 82[b] and 91[a]. These have attracted a considerable amount of attention, and are supposed by some scholars to have been handed down traditionally from early times. The author, Manṣúr ibn Muḥammad ibn Aḥmad ibn Yúsuf ibn Faqíh Ilyás, flourished about A.D. 1400. See Fonahn's *Zur Quellenkunde, etc.*, **No. 1**, pp. 3–4, where full references are given, especially to K. Sudhoff's important studies of this work.

This second portion of the volume is on different paper and in a somewhat older handwriting than the first, though the size of the pages (24·5 × 15·8 c.) is the same. The first portion contains 21 and the second 23 lines. Both parts are written in legible *ta'líq*; the second, much better than the first, has no colophon, but the seal of a former owner on f. 60[a] is dated 1033/1623–4. One of the 47 Belshah MSS. acquired in January, 1920.

P. 22 (13).

تشریح منصوری،

Another MS. of the *Tashríḥ-i-Manṣúrí*, obtained at the same time as that last mentioned and from the same collection. The work has been lithographed at Dihlí in 1264/1847–8. This MS. differs from most others, including that described above, in having on the last leaf (f. 64[a]) an additional (seventh) illustration, representing the standing figure of a pregnant woman with the child shown *in situ* in the uterus through the abdominal wall. The other six illustrations occur on ff. 17 (Bones), 26 (Nerves), 29 (Muscles, unfinished), 40 (Veins), 44 (Arteries), and 57 (Viscera).

Ff. 64 of 30·5 × 21·4 c. and 11 ll., large, clear, but rather ill-formed *naskh*. On the blank page facing each of the first six illustrations I have affixed a photograph of the corresponding figure from the India Office MS. **No. 1379**.

P. 23 (13).

طبّ المراد،

A system of Medicine, in Persian, by Murád 'Alí Tálpar, entitled *Ṭibb-i-Murád*, not mentioned by Fonahn or in the usual catalogues. Begins:

حمد بیعدّ و ثنای بیحدّ بارگاه جلال قدس کریمی‌را سزاست الخ ...امّا بعد، بر رای بیضا ضیای نبض شناسان صورت دانش و بینش و ضمیر آفتاب تأثیر تشخیص نمایان ابدان فطرت و دانائی روشن و مبرهن باد که این عاصی پر معاصی محبّ اهل بیت کرام علیهم السّلام مراد علی تالپر بن میر شهید میر صوبدار خان شهید بن میر بهرام خان شهید بن میر شهداد خان تالپررا در دل افتاد که

چون در حدیث علم الابدان خیر من علم الادیان واقع است چیزی از علم طبّ تصنیف کرده شود، پس از کتبهای معتبره این نسخهٔ غریب عجیب موجز و میمونه مسمّی بطبّ مراد که مشتمل است بدفع اصناف امراض و رفع انواع اعراض که مرض و عرض از مستلزمات وجود است بعون حضرت الهی و توفیق نا متناهی تصنیف کردم،

Here follow some verses, among which is a chronogram, giving the date of composition, which was apparently 1216/1801–2:

هاتفم گفت سال تاریخش،   فرحت‌آمیز روح طبّ مراد،

The author was evidently an enthusiastic adherent of the Shí'a sect, and, after enumerating the material methods of treating each disease, constantly adds pious formulae recommended by the Prophet or one of the Imáms as appropriate. Indeed the work as a whole contains more superstition than science, many of the remedies prescribed being grotesque and even disgusting. The elaborate subdivisions characteristic of most Arabic and Persian works on Medicine are here conspicuous for their absence, the only division being into unnumbered sections indifferently entitled *Faṣl* or *Báb*. The principal contents are as follows:

Diseases of the Head, f. 3ᵃ; Eye, f. 64ᵃ; Ear, f. 96ᵃ; Nose, f. 103ᵇ; Lips, Mouth and Tongue, f. 108ᵃ; Teeth and Gums, f. 117ᵇ; Throat, f. 128ᵇ; Lungs, f. 134ᵇ; Heart, f. 157ᵃ; Breast, f. 169ᵇ; Stomach, f. 171ᵃ; Liver, f. 211ᵃ; Spleen, f. 225ᵇ; Rectum and Anus, f. 226ᵇ; Kidneys, Bladder and Urinary organs, f. 236ᵇ; Male organs of Generation, f. 294ᵇ; Gynaecology and Parturition, f. 303ᵇ; Spinal column and Joints, f. 317ᵃ; Wounds and salves, f. 326ᵇ; Haemorrhage, f. 333ᵃ; Excessive perspiration, f. 334ᵇ; Sciatica, f. 336ᵃ; Elephantiasis, f. 337ᵇ; Fevers, f. 338ᵃ; Skin diseases, f. 359ᵃ; Boils and Abscesses, f. 363ᵇ; Cancer, f. 364ᵇ; Leprosy, f. 366ᵃ; Smallpox, f. 368ᵇ.

Amongst the works most often quoted are those of Yúsufí (fl. *circa* A.D. 1500), especially his rhymed treatise on "Foods and Drinks" (see Fonahn, p. 75, **No. 209**), from which a long quotation is given on ff. 188ᵇ–190ᵃ, and a work entitled *Rawḍatu'l-Adhkár* (*e.g.* on f. 225ᵃ), dealing, apparently, with prayers and ejaculations supposed to possess healing virtues.

The MS., obtained from the Belshah collection in January, 1920, comprises 396 ff. of 31 × 19·5 c. and 20 ll., and is written throughout in a neat and legible *ta'líq* with rubrications. The last four leaves are damaged in the lower part, and this damage affects the chronogram at the end which would, apparently, have given the date of composition.

P. 24 (10).

خلاصة التجارب تأليف شاه قاسم نوربخشي،

Another Persian work on Medicine entitled *Khuláṣatu't-Tajárib* ("the Sum of Experience"), composed at Rayy in 907/1501–2 by Bahá'u'd-Dawla ibn Siráji'd-Dín Sháh Qásim ibn Shamsi'd-Dín Muḥammad an-Núr-bakhshí, who died at Rayy in A.D. 1507. See Fonahn's *Zur Quellengeschichte, etc.*, **No. 28**, pp. 28–29, where the author's name (here taken from the colophon on f. 328[a]) is somewhat differently given.

This MS., also acquired in January, 1920, from the Belshah collection, comprises 328 ff. of 24·5 × 16·3 c. and 24 ll., and is written in a small, neat *ta'líq* with rubrications, and, according to the colophon, was copied at three removes from the author's autograph:

...منقول بود از خطّی که منقول بود از خطّی که منقول بود از خطّ مصنّف،

It is dated Monday, 25 Ṣafar, but the year is unfortunately illegible, except the word *alf*, "one thousand...." The scribe's name is Jalálu'd-Dín ibn Muḥammad.... The contents agree with Fonahn's description, the titles of the first eight chapters, which he groups together as "*Bâb* 1–8, *Krankheiten des Kopfes und des Gehirns, Kopfschmerzen, usw.*," being as follows:

باب اوّل در بیان آنچه دانستن آن موقوف علیه حفظ صحّت و مرض است بر وجه کلّی چون طبیعت و مزاج و علامات ثابتهٔ امزجهٔ طبیعیّهٔ حاصله و تغییر و تبدیل المزاج و اخلاط اربعه و اعضاء مفرده و بعضی از مرکّبات اوّلیّهٔ این مفردات و ارواح قوی و افعال بدنیّه و اسباب حدوث کیفیّات در بدن مطلقا و دلالات حالات نبض و نفس و قاروره و براز و عرق بر حالات بدنیّه مطلقا (f. 3[b])،

باب دوم در بیان حفظ الصحّة که اعظم مقاصد طبّی است (f. 22[a])،

باب سوم در بیان تدبیر اطفال و پیران و ناقهان و مرتاضان بتعب و اعراض مفرطهٔ نفسانی و آبهای بد و هواهای مضرّ و استفراغات (f. 32[a])،

باب چهارم در بیان تدابیر آنچه بزینت بدن متعلّق است (f. 61[a])،

باب پنجم در بیان اقسام مرض و امتلاآت منذره بامراض و علامات خیر و شر که اکثر آنها عمومی در امراض دارند و احوال بحرانها و ایّام بحران و انذار و واقع فی الوسط و نضج و منفعت آن و علامات نکس و سبب موت در مرض و اوقات آن و فجاءة بی مرض و وصایا در طریق مراعاة مرضی از روی کلّیه و اصلی چند قیاس با مقتضیات طبایع (f. 69[a])،

باب ششم در بیان حمّیات و اسباب و علامات و معالجات آنها (f. 80[b])،

باب هفتم در بیان حصبه و جدری و سایر بثرها و ورمها و جذام و سرما زدگی و سموم زدگی و کوفتگی و قوبا و قرحها و سوختگیها و عرق مدنی و ریش بلخی و جراحتها و بیرون رفتن سر استخوانها از محلّ خویش و شکستگی استخوانها و اسباب و علامات و معالجات این امراض (f. 107[a])،

باب هشتم در احوال دماغ و بیان آن از ترکیب و وضع مزاج و غیره و علامات امزجهٔ مختلفهٔ
طبیعیّهٔ وی و امراض دماغ و اسباب و علامات و معالجات آنها (f. 136a)،

The remainder of the twenty-eight chapters into which the book is divided are as described by Fonahn, and stand as follows: ch. ix, f. 159b; ch. x, f. 170b; ch. xi, f. 174b; ch. xii, f. 179b; ch. xiii, f. 185a; ch. xiv, f. 198a; ch. xv, f. 202a; ch. xvi, f. 216a; ch. xvii, f. 219b; ch. xviii, f. 232b; ch. xix, f. 235b; ch. xx, f. 252b; ch. xxi, f. 257b; ch. xxii, f. 262a; ch. xxiii, f. 270a; ch. xxiv, f. 277b; ch. xxv, f. 289b; ch. xxvi, f. 294b; ch. xxvii (title omitted); ch. xxviii, f. 325a.

A table of contents in the same hand as the rest of the MS. and prefixed to it occupies ff. 1b–2b.

P. 25 (9).

رسالهٔ علّت مراقیه،

A Turkish treatise on Hypochondriasis, or Melancholy, Syphilis (*Maraḍ-i-Afranj*, "the New Disease"), and a few other diseases not adequately treated in the older Arabic books on Medicine, by Muṣṭafà Feyẓí (Fayḍí), physician to Sulṭán Muḥammad IV (A.D. 1648–1687), beginning after the short doxology:

امّا بعد، بو رسالهٔ صحّت نصاب و نسخهٔ حکمت انتسابك تألیف و ترسیمنه باعث و بادی بو در که
علّت مراقیّهایله سودای مراقیّهنك بین الناس کثرت و فرقی و صغیر و کبیرك بو ایکی مرضه
ابتلالری ظاهر اولوب الخ

The proper title of the work—الرسائل المشفیة للامراض المشکله—("Healing treatises for difficult diseases") is given on f. 2b, ll. 6–7, and it contains nine sections, as follows:

فصل اوّل علّت مراقیّهنك وجه تسمیهسنی و مادّهٔ مراقیّهنك کیفیّت حدوثنی بیاننده در (f. 2b)،
فصل ثانی علّت مراقیّهنك مؤف اولان اعضانك بیاننده در (f. 3b)،
فصل ثالث علّت مراقیّهنك اسبابی بیاننده در (f. 6a)،
فصل رابع علّت مراقیّهنك علامتلری بیاننده در (f. 6b)،
فصل خامس، تقدمة المعرفة بیاننده در (f. 8a)،
فصل سادس علّت مراقیّهنك اجمالاً معالجهسی بیاننده در (f. 14b)،
فصل سابع علّت مراقیّهنك تفصیلاً معالجهسی بیاننده در (f. 15a)،
فصل ثامن علّت مراقیّهده واقع اولان اعراضك تسکینی بیاننده در (f. 25a)،
فصل تاسع بو علّتده اسباب ستّهٔ ضرورینك تدبیری بیاننده در (f. 28a)،

This MS., which was given to me by Dr Riẓá Tevfíq (Riḍá Tawfíq) on August 7, 1909, comprises 30 ff. of 21·8 × 15·4 c. and 17 ll., is written in a clear Turkish *naskh* with the headings of the sections in red, and has no colophon or date. No considerable mention seems to be made of any disease except Hypochondriasis (*Maráqiyya*).

P. 26 (8).

الدُرر النفيسة فى الحكمة الطبيعيّة،

An acephalous super-commentary on a commentary on a treatise on Natural Philosophy entitled *ad-Duraru'n-Nafísa*, copied in Shíráz, in the *Dáru'l-Aytám*, or Orphanage, from the author's autograph in 885/1480–1.

This unattractive little MS., from the last division of the Belshah collection, comprises in its present state 164 pp. of 18·4 × 13 c. and 21 ll. The writing is a minute *ta'líq*, entirely devoid of diacritical points. Some pages are missing at the beginning and between the present pp. 58 and 59. There are no rubrications or divisions into chapters, and the book appears to be of no value.

P. 27 (11).

غاية البيان فى تدبير بدن الانسان،

Another Turkish medical work entitled *Gháyatu'l-Bayán fí tadbíri Badani'l-Insán*, also dedicated to Sulṭán Muḥammad IV, and apparently compiled by a certain Ṣáliḥ ibn Naṣri'lláh. It begins:

جواهر زواهر حمد و ثنا، اول واجب الوجود، و مفيض الخير و الجود، صانع عالم، و دافع امراض بنى آدم آلخ

A full table of contents is prefixed (ff. 1^b–2^b). The work appears to be divided primarily into three Discourses (*Maqála*), of which the third, dealing with diseases of the different organs *a capite ad calcem*, is much the longest. The first deals with hygiene and the second with simple and compound medicaments.

This MS., acquired from the Belshah collection in January, 1920, comprises 105 numbered ff. of text with 3 additional ff. containing the table of contents at the beginning, and 2 ff. at the end; in all 110 ff. of 24·4 × 14·8 c. and 35 ll. It is written in a fair, Turkish *naskh* with rubrications, was copied in Constantinople in Rabí' II, 1089/June, 1678, by 'Alí ibn Sha'bán ibn Muḥammad, known as 'Ajam-záda as-Silistrawí (of Silistria), and has been collated with the original.

P. 28 (8).

الدرّة المنتخبة فى الادويه،

An Arabic treatise on Materia Medica, entitled, *Nubdhat*[un] *Muntakhaba min ad-Durrati'l-Muntakhaba fi'l-Adwiya*. The following table of contents was drawn up by Mírzá Bihrúz of Sáwa, formerly Persian Lecturer at Cambridge:

باب ١ فى ادوية امراض الرأس والوجه وما يتّصل بها (p. 3)،

باب ٢ ... الرئة والقلب والحلق والصدر (p. 18)،

باب ٣ ... المعدة والكبد والطحال والمثانة والكلاء (p. 22)،

باب ٤ ... المعدة والمقعد (p. 27)،

باب ٥ ... اعضاء التناسل والرحم (p. 33)،

باب ٦ ... المفاصل (p. 41)،

باب ٧ ... الجروح والقروح والاورام (p. 46)،

باب ٨ ... الارنبة (p. 57)،

باب ٩ ... فى خواصّ بعض الاشياء (p. 65)،

باب ١٠ فى ادوية امراض السموم المختلطة من سمّها ممّا تقدّم (p. 69)،

باب ١١ فى معرفة شىء من الصناعات المستحسنة وغيرها (p. 81)،

The eleventh and last chapter (pp. 81–283) is much the longest, and contains the following sections:

طبايع الحبوب (p. 127)، طبايع الفواكه (p. 129)، طبايع البقول (p. 135)، طبايع التوابل (p. 139)، طبايع اللحوم والالبان (p. 142)، فى خواصّ اجزاء سباع الطيور (p. 145)، فى ذكر الاحجار وخواصّها (p. 152)، النبات والفواكه وخواصّها (p. 171)، فى البقول الصّغار (p. 219)، فى خواصّ الحيوانات (p. 224)، فى معرفة السموم وعلامة تأثير كلّ واحد منها (p. 242)، فى لدغ الحشرات (p. 260)، فى عضّة الحيوانات (p. 271)،

This MS., from the final division of the Belshah collection in 1920, comprises 286 pp. of 18·8 × 10·5 c. and 13 ll., and is written in a clear, coarse *naskh* with rubrications. It is undated, concluding with the words:

وهذا آخر ما جمعناه فى المجموعة من الفوايد والمجرّبات،

P. 29 (9).

جواهرنامه، تنسوق نامه وغيره،

Three Persian treatises on precious stones, from the Schindler collection, *viz.*:

(I) The *Jawáhir-náma* ("Book of Gems") of Amín Ṣadru'd-Dín Muḥammad ibn Mír Ghiyáthu'd-Dín Manṣúr of Shíráz, who wrote it for Abu'l-Fatḥ Khalíl Báyandarí (A.D. 1478–9), son and successor of Úzún Ḥasan of the "White Sheep" Dynasty. See Rieu's Pers. Cat., pp. 464–465, and also his Pers. Suppl., **No. 158**, pp. 112–113. This MS. was copied from a *Jung*, or volume of miscellaneous contents, in the library of Mashhad, and contains numerous marginal notes and variants, the latter, apparently, taken from the British Museum MS. dated 1206/1791–2. It comprises an Introduction (*Muqaddama*) and two Discourses (*Maqála*), the first containing twenty chapters and a Conclusion (*Khátima*), and the second seven chapters and a *Khátima*, the contents of which are stated on f. 2[b]. This portion of the volume consists of 38 ff. of 21 × 16·3 c. and 14 ll., and is written in a cursive Persian *ta'líq*. It ends abruptly without date or colophon.

(II) The first part of another Lapidary, with the descriptive title of *Risála dar ma'rifat-i-Jawáhir* in Schindler's hand on the blank leaf at the beginning (f. 40[a]), composed by Muḥammad ibnu'l-Mubárak of Qazwín for the Ottoman Sulṭán Salím I "the Grim" (reigned A.D. 1514–1520). It begins:

حمد پاك پاكی‌را سزد كه گوهر پنهان جان انسانرا از خلاصهٔ گوهر معدن آب و خاك پیدا نمود الخ

It is divided into an Introduction (*Muqaddama*), two "Mines" (*Ma'dan*), of which the first contains twenty-one "Caskets" (*Durj*) and the second eight "Treasuries" (*Makhzan*), and two Conclusions (*Khátima*), but the present copy breaks off in the middle of the sixteenth "Casket" on Lapis Lazuli (*Lájiward*). It occupies ff. 40[b]–94[a] of the volume, and is written in a good modern Persian *ta'líq*, quite different from that of the previous portion, and has, of course, no colophon. The contents are stated as follows (f. 42):

مقدّمه در تقسیم موجودات،

معدن اوّل در جواهر، (درج ۱) دُرّ، (۲) یاقوت، (۳) زمرّد، (۴) زبرجد، (۵) الماس، (۶) عین الهّر، (۷) لعل، (۸) فیروزه، (۹) پازهر و احجار حیوانی، (۱۰) عقیق، (۱۱) در بعضی اشباه یاقوت، (۱۲) جزع، (۱۳) مقناطیس، (۱۴) سنباده، (۱۵) دهنه، (۱۶) لاجورد، (۱۷) مرجان، (۱۸) یشب، (۱۹) بلّور، (۲۰) جمست، (۲۱) احجار متفرّقه و نسبت جواهر با یكدیگر،

معدن دویم در فلزّات، (مخزن ۱) طلا، (۲) نقره، (۳) مسّ، (۴) قلع، (۵) اسرب، (۶) آهن، (۷) خارچینی، (۸) در فلزّات و نسبت ایشان بیكدیگر،

(III) An acephalous, incomplete, and probably abridged text of the *Tansúq-náma-i-Ílkhán*, a well-known Persian version of an Arabic work on precious stones and other substances, composed in the thirteenth century of the Christian era by the celebrated philosopher Naṣíru'd-Dín Ṭúsí for Húlákú Khán the Mongol. See Rieu's Persian Supplement, **No. 157**, p. 112. The beginning, of which the initial words down to *az* have been added in pencil, apparently in Schindler's hand, are:

[چنین گوید مصنّف این كتاب ناصر (*sic*) الدّین ابن محمّد ابن محمّد الحسین الطّوسی تغمّد الله برحمته پادشاه عالم هلاكو خان این فقیر حقیررا فرمود و گفت مجموعی از] انواع جواهر معدنی و غیر آن و كیفیّت تولّد و سبب حدوث آن و بهترین و بدترین و شبیه هر یك و خاصیّت و قیمهٔ آن و محافظت‌شان بشرحی تمام بنویس و بما عرضه‌دار الخ

A few lines further on he explains the title as follows:

و این كتاب‌را تنسوق‌نامهٔ ایلخان نام نهادم چه هرچه بخدمت پادشاهان تنسوق آورند در آنجا یاد كرده شود

This portion of the MS. is in the same handwriting as the last, occupies ff. 97[b]–118[a], is incomplete at the end as well as at the beginning, and has no date or colophon. The work should contain four Discourses (*Maqála*), of which the contents are thus stated on ff. 97^b–98^a:

مقالت اوّل در بیان کیفیّت مفردات که جملهٔ معدنیّات و غیرها از مرکّبات عالم سفلی از آن مرکّب شوند و علل معادن بطریق کلّی و آن چهار فصل است'

مقالت دویم در جواهر که از جملهٔ حجر باشد و غیر آن و علل حدوث هر یك و کیفیّت وجود آن و شرح معادن و خواصّ و منفعت و مضرّت و شبیه بطریق صناعت و قیمت هر یك و جلا دادن و آنچه مناسب این نوع باشد'

مقالت سیّم در انواع فلزّات سبعه و علّت حدوث هر یك و خاصیّت و منفعت و مضرّت آن و شرح معادن و هرچه مناسب این کتاب باشد'

مقالت چهارم در انواع عطر و آنچه مناسب این باب باشد'

The text is very incomplete. It appears to comprise the first three sections of the first Discourse. A lacuna, noted in the margin by Schindler, between ff. 101^b and 102^a, extends from the middle of I, 3 to near the end of II, 2, where there is a marginal note in pencil, "here some pages are missing, *Faṣl* 4 of *Maqála* I, and the chapter is faulty...." The whole of the third and fourth Discourses appears to be missing.

Ff. 118 of 21 × 16·5 c. and 18–19 ll. From the library of the late Sir A. Houtum-Schindler.

P. 30 (8).

تنکسوق نامهٔ ایلخانی'

Another older and more complete copy of the *Tansúq-* (or *Tangsúq* as it is entitled in the colophon) *náma-i-Ílkhání*, dated Jumádà II, 973 (January, 1566), comprising 142 pp. of 18·8 × 12·4 c. and 13 ll., written in a large, clear *ta'líq* with rubrications. This MS., like the last, formerly belonged to the late Sir Albert Houtum-Schindler, who, in a pencil-note on the fly-leaf, has described it as "very much abridged, and sequence of chapters different from that of British Museum MS. '**C.**' The first *Maqála* with four *faṣls* and the second *Maqála* up to the middle of the Pearl chapter are missing in this."

The text begins abruptly in the middle of the part dealing with the Pearl:

...و آنچه سوراخ او فراخ بودی بنیم بها بیش نخریدندی و مغولان در آن تفاوت نمی نهند الخ

Lower down on the same page (p. 1) comes:

فصل دوم در آنچه تعلّق به بزرگی و خوردی مروارید باشد الخ

The divisions adopted in the text contained in this volume appear to differ somewhat from those described in the last article. The title *Báb* (Chapter) appears to be substituted for *Maqála* (Discourse). The first chapter deals with 41 precious stones (pp. 1–68); the second with ten valued animal and vegetable products, such as Oil of Balsam, Ivory, Ebony, Terra Sigillata, etc. (pp. 68–91); the third (wrongly called "second") with eight fragrant substances, such as Musk, Ambergris, Aloes, Camphor, Sandal-wood, Saffron and Civet (pp. 92–120); and the fourth and last with eleven metals and fusible substances, such as Gold, Silver, Copper, Tin, Lead, Iron, etc. (pp. 121–136). This is followed (pp. 136–137) by a section entitled:

سخن در نسبت گوهرهای گداختنی با یکدیگر بوزن و مقدار،

and a final section (pp. 137–141):

در انواع ادیم و آنچه تعلّق دارد بآن،

The late Sir A. Houtum-Schindler interested himself greatly in mineralogy and precious stones, and especially in the *Tansúq-náma*. The present MS. he denoted by the letter **A**, the preceding one (**P. 29**, III) by the letter **B**, and the British Museum MS. (apparently the best and most complete) by the letter **C**. He wrote an article on the subject in the *Athenaeum*[1], and the only work he left in a state approaching completion was a type-written translation of one of these Persian Lapidaries which I have not yet succeeded in identifying.

P. 31 (9).

جواهرنامه،

Another good modern copy of the "Book of Gems" (*Jawáhir-náma*) of Muḥammad ibn Manṣúr, already mentioned under **P. 29**. This MS., also from the Schindler collection, is written in a large, clear, modern *naskh* with rubrications, and comprises 84 ff. of 20·1 × 12·5 c. and 15 ll. It appears to have been copied from a *Jung* or Miscellany belonging to a certain Shafí'u'd-Dín Ḥasan ibn Ni'mati'lláh-i-Músawí-i-Shúshtarí as a present to Minúchihr Khán *Mu'tamadu'd-Dawla*, Governor of Iṣfahán in the reign of Muḥammad Sháh Qájár. The actual copyist, however, gives his name (f. 80[a]) as Ḥájjí ibn Ghulám ibn Ḥájjí Shúshtarí. The long note (ff. 80[b]–82[a]), dated 20 Jumádà II, 1260/July 7, 1844, is in a different hand, presumably that of Shafí'u'd-Dín.

The book consists of a Dedication in two sections (ff. 10[a]–12[a]); an Introduction (*Muqaddama*, ff. 12[b]–14[b]); two Discourses (*Maqála*), the first (ff. 14[b]–67[b]), comprising twenty chapters (*Báb*) and a Conclusion (*Khátima*) in twenty sections; and the second (ff. 67[b]–80[a]), comprising seven chapters and a Conclusion. The first Discourse deals with precious stones and the second with metals, and each chapter in the former is subdivided into from three to five sections. The principal divisions are as follows:

مقدّمة در موادّ اجسام معدنی و کیفیّت [تکوّن] ایشان و امور متعلّقه بآن (f. 12[b])،

[1] [I have searched for this article in the files of the *Athenaeum* from 1880 onward, but without success.]

مقالهٔ اولی در جواهر، باب ۱، دُرّ و لؤلؤ و مروارید (ff. 14^b–21^a)، باب ۲، یاقوت (ff. 22^b–27^a)، باب ۳، زمرّد (ff. 28^a–29^b)، باب ۴، زبرجد (ff. 30^b–31^b)، باب ۵، الماس (ff. 31^b–33^b)، باب ۶، عین الهِرّ (ff. 33^b–34^b)، باب ۷، لعل (ff. 35^a–38^b)، باب ۸، فیروزه (ff. 38^b–42^a)، باب ۹، پازهر (ff. 42^a–45^b)، باب ۱۰، عقیق (ff. 45^b–46^a)، باب ۱۱، اشباه یاقوت یعنی بنفش و بیجاده و ماده پنج (ff. 46^a–48^a)، باب ۱۲، جزع (f. 48^b)، باب ۱۳، مقناطیس و آهن ربا (ff. 49^a–50^b)، باب ۱۴، سنباده (ff. 51^b–52^a)، باب ۱۵، دهنة (ff. 52^a–53^a)، باب ۱۶، لاجورد (ff. 53^a–54^a)، باب ۱۷، بُسَّد و مرجان (ff. 55^a–57^a)، باب ۱۸، یشم (ff. 57^a–58^a)، باب ۱۹، بلّور (ff. 58^a–59^b)، باب ۲۰، جمست (f. 60^a)، خاتمه، در احجار متفرّقه و نسبت جواهر با یکدیگر مشتمل بر بیست فصل (ff. 60^b–67^b)، ۱، شیح یا شیق، ۲، خماهن، ۳، طلق، ۴، حجر المطر، ۵، سنگ عقاب، ۶، حجر یرقان، ۷، حجر باغض الخلّ و حجر جاذب الخلّ، ۸، حجر زیت، ۹، حجر الیهود، ۱۰، حجر لبنی، ۱۱، حجر النّساء، ۱۲، حجر الدم، ۱۳، حجر القمر یا بزاق القمر، ۱۴، حجر ذو الوان، ۱۵، حجر النوم و حجر الیقظه، ۱۶، حجر المثقال، ۱۷، مارقشیشا، ۱۸، مغنیسیا، ۱۹، سُرْمه و توتیا، ۲۰، در نسبت بعضی جواهر ببعضی،

مقالهٔ ثانیه، در فلزّات و مشتمل است بر هفت باب (ff. 67^b–78^a)، و خاتمهٔ مشتمل بر هفت فصل (ff. 78^a–79^b)، باب ۱، طلا، ۲، نقره، ۳، مسّ، ۴، ارزیز، ۵، سُرْب، ۶، آهن، ۷، خارصینی، خاتمه، در مرکّب از فلزّات و نسبت ایشان با یکدیگر، فصل ۱، برنج که آنرا شبه گویند، ۲، سفیدروی، ۳، کان‌روی که آنرا تال گویند، ۴، درارو، ۵، درطالیقون، ۶، در سایر اموریکه از فلزّاتند، ۷، در نسبت فلزّات با یکدیگر،

P. 32 (9).

جواهرنامه و غیره،

Another copy of the *Jawáhir-náma*, described above, with two other treatises on precious stones, the *Mukhtaṣar* of Zaynu'd-Dín Muḥammad of Jám, and the *Majmú'atu'ṣ-Ṣanáyi'*.

The MS. (marked **D** by its former owner), acquired from the Schindler collection in January, 1917, comprises 118 ff. of 24·4 × 14·5 c. and 18 ll. It is written throughout on paper of various colours, in a small, neat *ta'líq* with rubrications, and is dated, on f. 56^a, Rabí' II, 1259 (May, 1843).

I. The *Jawáhir-náma* of Muḥammad ibn Manṣúr of Shíráz (ff. 1^b–56^a). The table of contents (ff. 4^b–5^a) agrees with the copy described above, but the text is much less accurate and less legible.

II. *Mukhtaṣar dar bayán-i-shinákhtan-i-Jawáhir* ("Epitome on the recognition of Gems," ff. 57^a–73^b), composed for Sháhrukh Bahádur Khán by Zaynu'd-Dín Muḥammad-i-Jámí, beginning:

شکر و سپاس و حمد بیقیاس مر دهندهٔ عقل و بخشندهٔ حواس‌را الخ

The work comprises twelve chapters, dealing with (1) the Diamond, الماس; (2) the Corundum (ياقوت); (3) the Ruby (لعل); (4) the Emerald (زمرّد); (5) the Pearl (مروارید); (6) the Turquoise (فیروزه); (7) the Bezoar (پازهر); (8) Ambergris (عنبر); (9) Lapis Lazuli (لاجورد); (10) Coral (مرجان); (11) Cornelian (عقیق); (12) Jasper (یشب). From Chapter III onwards the rubrications have been omitted, and the number has been inserted in pencil in Roman figures, no doubt by Sir Albert Houtum-Schindler.

III. The third treatise, anonymous (ff. 74ᵇ–118ᵃ), has a somewhat wider scope, dealing with artificial and artificially coloured gems, pigments of all sorts, sympathetic inks, gilding and decoration of all kinds, fireworks, and the like. It begins:

...امّا بعد، این رساله ایست که حکما تألیف کرده اند که صفت (صنعت؟) بسیار و حکمت بیشمار در این مجموعه جمع است که هر یك از آن بحریست و هر چشمه ازان نهری است که شهرهٔ شهری است و چون طالب بکنهٔ معرفت او اطّلاع یابد و بکمال رساند مقصود کلّی حاصل شود بتوفیق اللّه تعالی، و در این مجموعهٔ صد و شصت هنر است هر یك در ذات خود بی نظیر و پسندیده و بر گزیده و در چهل و دو باب تقسیم شد و در یکصد و چهل فصلست،

The table of contents (ff. 74ᵇ–76ᵇ) gives a list of the 42 chapters, but not of the 160 "artifices" (هنر) or the 140 sections (فصل) which they comprise. In a somewhat abridged form it is as follows:

باب ۱، در ساختن مروارید، باب ۲، در ساختن لعل و یاقوت که با کانی اصل برابر باشد، باب ۳، در ساختن و در جلا دادن مروارید که برنگ قدیم باز رود و نورانی گردد، باب ۴، اندر حلّ کردن زر که بعضی در ملمّع (?) بکار آید و بعضی در نوشتن و نقّاشی و پوست کمان برو ساختن و غیره، باب ۵، در ساختن زمرّد و زبرجد لطیف بلا نظیر، باب ۶، در ساختن فیروزه و الماس قوسی و سیلی و مرجانی که از کانی فرق نتوان کرد، باب ۷، در رنگ کردن عاج از هر رنگ، باب ۸، در تلاویح بلّور و رنگهای غیر مکرّر و آن هفت رنگ است که بسیار کارها از آن آید، باب ۹، در رنگهای فرنگی و بطانهٔ چینی و در صدف کاری بسته بطانه است، باب ۱۰، در ساختن تیغهای فرنگی که چون کاغذ میتوان پیچید و بُرّان (f. 75ᵃ) باشد و هیچ چیز بر او رخنه نکند و آهن و آبگینه ببُرّد و این از عجایب است، باب ۱۱، در ساختن تیغ پیکان و سر نیزه که چون دشمن از آن نصیب یابد زخمش بهیچ گونه به نشود، باب ۱۲، در آب دادن تیغ و کارد که بیمثل باشد و از آن آب همچون آئینهٔ چینی روشن باشد و آهن باشد (تراشد؟) و ببُرّد، باب ۱۳، در رنگ کردن بلّور اگرچه در باب دویم گفته شد فامّا اینجا در قلم آمد و شرح هفت نوع رنگ کردن گفته شود، باب ۱۴، در عمل میناکاری و نگینهای هفت رنگ بغایت اعلا، باب ۱۵، در صفت خضابی که عورتان دست و انگشتان‌را بآن رنگ کنند و این از جملهٔ حسن و جمالست و موجب شهوت و محبّت است، باب ۱۶، در ریختن شنگرف رومی و رُمّانی (?) و زاولی و مصفّا و فرسی (قدسی؟) و فارسی و فرنگی و غیره، باب ۱۷، در رنگ کردن کاغذ قدیم و جدید و الوان غیر مکرّر، باب ۱۸، در ساختن زنگار و آن هفت نوع است نقره و سبز ذهبی و ترسائی و فرعونی و مصفّا و فرنسیّه و فیروزه، باب ۱۹، در

جلا و ساختن لاجورد و از بابت آن از آب دادن و شش زنگار محض و آمیختن و این جمله هنرهای غریبه است، باب ۲۰، در شنگرف بردن و صاف کردن جهت نقّاشی و غیره، باب ۲۱، در ساختن کوره جهت شنگرف پختن و ساختن جهت مروارید و غیره و این ضرور است در این کارها و کل حکمت و قلقند و قلقطار و قلندیس و قلقت ساختن جهت رنگ کردن بلّور و غیره (f. 75b)، باب ۲۲، در رنگ ضروف (*sic* for ظروف) مثل کاسه و پیاله و کوزه که مانند آن زمرّد نمایند و در غایت خوبی بود، باب ۲۳، در حلّ کردن نقره و مسّ و فولاد و سرب و قلعیز (قلعی؟) و زرنیخ و غیر آن و این در بسیار جایها بکار آید، باب ۲۴، در کشش (کشتن؟)[1] زر و فولاد و ابرك که آن‌را طلق گویند و کشش (کشتن؟) سیماب جهت خوردن و قوّة باه، باب ۲۵، در عمل سفیداب که سفیداب‌را در لسان عرب سفیداج گویند نیکوترین او پاك و سفید و خوشبوی کاشفری (کاشغری؟) و سفیداب ریش و سفیداب گل‌مهره، باب ۲۶، در صفت نخل‌بندی از زر و سیم که از گل یاسمن و موکره و دیگر گلها فرق نتوان کرد و بو دهد و لرزان و متحرّك باشد و این فنّی غریب است، باب ۲۷، در صنعت در حلیة الکتاب و روغن از کاغذ بر داشتن و قلم نقّاشی ساختن یعنی مداد و دوده گرفتن و کاغذرا مسطّر کردن که مثل بغدادی شود و آمیختن رنگها جهة نوشتن چیزهای غریبه و آن ده فصلست، باب ۲۸، در ساختن مکینه تاکینه و کشیدن من خراطین جهت مکینه تاکینه که آن پازهر همه زهرهاست و لایق خزانهٔ پادشاهان باشد، باب ۲۹، در حکمت گل حکمت و ساختن اسکندری روغن و تعبیه دادن روغن نی جهة آتش در قلاع و شهر دشمنان افگندن و این از اسرار غریبه است و حکمت عجیبه است و کاری بزرگ باشد، باب ۳۰، در ساختن کوتکهای مجرّب جهة امساك که آنرا در دهان گیرند امساك شود تا از دهان بیرون نیاورند انزال نشود و این هفت نوع است و چهار عقد این فصل، باب ۳۱، در صنعت الکُتّاب که چون بنویسند پیدا نباشد و چون بر آتش (f. 76a) بزند (برند؟) هر رنگ پیدا شود و از هر داروئی رنگی پدید آید غیر مکرّر، باب ۳۲، در شناختن صنعتهای دستهٔ کارد و ساختن لاجوردی و سبز و سرخ و زرد و صدف‌کاری که از سنگ پارهٔ قدری فرق نتوان کرد و نتوان شناخت، باب ۳۳، در عجایبها که خداوندان زرق نمایند مثل آنکه اگر او چیزی در دست گیرد غایب شود و آتش در دهان گیرند و در جامه کنند نسوزد و شعله‌ها و چراغها لعبتهای غیر مکّرر و صفتهای غریب و عجیب و آن انواع است، باب ۳۴، در عمل سریشم پنیر(؟) و این‌را جواهر سریشم گویند چندین عمل که در این کتاب گفته شد بعضی موقوف باین سریشم است در قلم آمد که چرا استادان این‌را مخفی داشتند که رکن هنر اینست، باب ۳۵، در داروئی که چون پر تیر بآن بچسپانند اگر در آب باران ده روز بماند پر بر نیآید و زیان نکند، باب ۳۶، در ساختن سیب سخن‌گوی که اگر هزار بار بجنبانند چون بلبل آواز دهد و بوی مشك از او آید و ساختن طوسی کمان از هر رنگ و غیر مکرّر غریبه، باب ۳۷، در ساختن برنج دمشقی و ساختن سیماب و بند کردن سیماب و حلّ کردن طلق و ساختن صلایه منوّر از جوهر جسد مصری و کحل الجواهر شامی و ساختن تیزآب فاروق، باب ۳۸، در رنگ کردن یاقوت سفید که لعل شود و قیمت یاقوت سرخ شود، باب ۳۹، در صنعت خطّ نوشتن بر عقیق و نگینها و سنگها و ساختن مسّ از آهن و ساختن اقلیمیای سیم و ساختن رو سوخته بجهة رنگ بلّور و صنعت

[1] [کُشِش, which occurs in the *Mathnawī*, VI, 1112, may be the correct reading here.]

تعویذها و دکمها و دانستن هر اناری که چند دانه دارد، باب ۴۰، در صنعت بر رنگ که در جامه چکد از نیل و روغن و سیاهی (f. 76b) از ابرشیم و کمخا و اطلس و قطنی و صوف بآسانی از آن دور کند، باب ۴۱، در رنگ کردن موی و داروئی که موی‌را برویاند و داروئی که موی‌را منع کند و سیاه کردن موی سفید و سفید کردن موی سیاه و رنگ کردن اسپ و این نیز انواع است و چهار فصل، باب ۴۲، در آتش‌بازیهای از هر رنگ طاوسی و سبز و هفت‌رنگ در خل (خلاء؟) هوائی و طوطك اندر قفس و گل چنار و گل سرو و گلهای غیر مکرّر و این انواع بود در دو فصل و اکنون یکان یکان در قلم آوردن واجبست تا طالبان ازین فایده گیرند و مقصود ازآن حاصل شود،

The contents of this treatise should be of considerable interest to chemists and artisans, for they deal with a variety of ingenious devices not often discussed in Persian books.

P. 33 (8).

جواهرنامه

Another MS. of the *Jawáhir-náma*, or "Book of Gems," of Muḥammad ibn Manṣúr of Shíráz, one of 13 MSS. bought of J. J. Naaman for £25 in May, 1902. It is incomplete, ending with ch. xvii of the first Discourse, treating of Lapis Lazuli (*Lájiward*), but, as far as it goes, appears to correspond with **P. 29** and **P. 31** described above. The rubrications, indicating the beginnings of chapters and sections, have been inserted only in the first few pages, and are represented by blank spaces throughout the remainder of the MS.

Ff. 56 of 19·2 × 11·7 c. and 13 ll.; small, neat *ta'líq*; no colophon or date. Ff. 54b–56b contain notes on the Interpretation of Dreams, the Microcosm (from Sulṭán Walad's *Áfáq wa-Anfus*, etc.). The date 995/1587 occurs on f. 56b.

P. 34.

خلاصة الحساب للشيخ بهآء الدّين العاملی،

Khuláṣatu'l-Ḥisáb, a treatise in Arabic on Arithmetic, by the celebrated theologian Shaykh Bahá'u'd-Dín al-'Ámilí (b. 953/1546, d. 1031/1622), followed, on p. 117, by a Persian treatise on Precious Stones which appears to be part of the *Tansúq-náma* of Naṣíru'd-Dín Ṭúsí, already described.

I. The contents of the *Khuláṣatu'l-Ḥisáb* are fully stated by Mírzá Bihrúz on one of the fly-leaves at the beginning, as follows:

المقدّمة [فی تعریف علم الحساب] صٓ ۴،

الباب الاوّل، فصل ١، فی الجمع صٓ ٧، فصل ٢، فی التنصیف صٓ ١٠، فصل ٣، فی التفریق صٓ ١١، فصل ۴، الضرب وقواعده صٓ ١٣، فصل ٥، فی التقسیم صٓ ٢٧، فصل ٦، فی استخراج الجذر المضروب فی نفسه... صٓ ٣١،

الباب الثانى فى الكسور وفيه ثلاث مقدّمات، مقدّمه ١، ص ٣٦، مقدّمه ٢، فى مخرج الكسر، ص ٣٨، مقدّمه ٣، التجنيس والرفع، ص ۴٢، فصل ١، جمع الكسور وتضعيفها، ص ۴٣، فصل ٢، تنصيف الكسور وتفريقها، ص ۴۴، فصل ٣، ضرب الكسور، ص ۴۴، فصل ۴، قسمة الكسور، ص ۴٦، فصل ٥، استخراج جذر الكسور، ص ۴٧، فصل ٦، تحويل الكسر من مخرج الى مخرج، ص ۴٨،

الباب الثالث، فى استخراج المجهولات الاربعة المتناسبة، ص ۴٩،

الباب الرابع، فى استخراج المجهولات بحساب الخطائين، ص ٥٢،

الباب الخامس، فى استخراج المجهولات بالعمل بالعكس وقد يسمّى بالتحليل والتعاكس، ص ٥۴،

الباب السادس، فى المساحة، المقدّمة، ص ٥٦، فصل ١، فى مساحة السطوح المستقيمة الاضلاع، ص ٦١، فصل ٢، فى مساحة بقيّة السطوح، ص ٦۴، فصل ٣، فى مساحة الاجسام، ص ٦٧،

الباب السابع، فيما يتبع المساحات من وزن الارض لاجراء القنوات ومعرفة ارتفاع المرتفعات وعروض الانهار واعماق الآبار، فصل ١، فى وزن الارض لاجراء القنوات، ص ٦٩، فصل ٢، فى معرفة ارتفاع المرتفعات، ص ٧٢، فصل ٣، فى معرفة عروض الانهار واعماق الآبار، ص ٧٥،

الباب الثامن، فى استخراج المجهولات بطريق الجبر والمقابلة، فصل ١، فى المقدّمات، ص ٧٧، فصل ٢، فى استخراج المجهولات بالجبر والمقابلة، ص ١٠٢،

This part of the MS. ends on p. 116 without a colophon, and appears to be incomplete.

II. The remainder of the volume is occupied by part of the Persian *Tansúq-náma*, viz. the Introduction (*Muqaddama*) and the chapters on the Precious Stones beginning with the Turquoise and Pearl, and ending with Amber (*Kahrubá*) and Jet (*Jaza'*). It fills 23 pp. bearing a fresh numeration. There is no colophon except the words تمّت بعون الله تعالى.

The MS., acquired in the final partition of the Belshah collection, comprises 144 pp. of 15·4 × 10·5 c. and 8 ll. Both parts are written in *ta'líq*, but not in the same hand or on the same paper.

P. 35 (10).

كتاب فى الطّب لخليل الله بن حسن بيگ الجنابدى،

An acephalous and untitled work on Medicine, apparently composed in Rajab 1113/December 1701 by Khalílu'lláh ibn Ḥasan Beg al-Janábadí, and, as appears from the following colophon on p. 225, an autograph:

هذا آخر ما اوردنا وليكن هذا القول من كلامنا المختصر فى الاصول الكلّيّة لصناعة الطّب كافيًا ولنأخذه فى الأدوية المفردة والحمد لله على التوفيق لاتمامه، فرغت من تحرير هذه النسخة الشريفة

والمقالة المنيفة فى يوم الاثنين من اواخر شهر رجب المبارك من شهور سنة ثلث عشر ومائة بعد الالف من الهجرة... فى قرية بيلند من توابع جنابد حين مراجعتى من دار السلطنة هرات وآبتلائى بسكنى الرستاق لاسباب شتّى احدها انسداد الطرق باعتبار كثرة قُطّاعها، وأنا الواثق بلطف ربّه الجليل النبيل القديم السرمدى ابن حسن بيگ المرحوم المغفور خليل الله الجنابدى،

The work is divided into four main divisions called *Fann* and about fourteen subdivisions called *Ta'lím*, of the contents of which Mírzá Bihrúz has constructed the following table, which replaces the original pp. 1–2, now missing:

الفنّ الاوّل، التعليم الاوّل... التعليم الثانى فى الاركان، صـ ٥، التعليم الثالث فى الأمزجة، صـ ٥، التعليم الرابع، فى الأخلاط، صـ ١٣، التعليم الخامس فى الأعضا، صـ ٢٠، الجملة الاولى فى العظام، صـ ٢۴، الجملة الثانية، فى العضل، صـ ۴٠، الجملة الثالثة، فى العصب، صـ ٥۴، الجملة الرابعة، فى الشرايين، صـ ٦٠، الجملة الخامسة، فى الاوردة، صـ ٦٣، التعليم السادس، فى القوى، صـ ٦٨،

الفنّ الثانى، التعليم الاوّل، فى الأمراض، صـ ٧٥، التعليم الثانى وفيه جملتان، الجملة الاولى فى الأشياء الّتى تحدث عن سبب من الأسباب السّتة العاميّة وهى تسعة عشر فصلًا صـ ٨١، الجملة الثانية فى تعديد سببٍ سببٍ لكلّ واحد من العوارض البدنيّة وهى تسعة وعشرون فصلًا صـ ١٠٦، التعليم الثالث احد عشر فصلًا وجملتان، صـ ١١٣، الجملة الاولى فى النّبض صـ ١٢۴، الجملة الثانية فى البول والبراز صـ ١٣٥،

الفنّ الثالث، فى حفظ الصحّة وهو فصل وخمسة تعاليم، الفصل فى سبب الصحّة والمرض وضرورة الموت صـ ١۴٩، التعليم الاوّل فى التربية، صـ ١٥١، التعليم الثانى، فى التدبير المشترك للبالغين صـ ١٥٩، التعليم الثالث فى تدبير المشايخ صـ ١٧٩، التعليم الرابع فى تدبير بدن من مزاجه غير فاضل صـ ١٨٢، التعليم الخامس فى الانتقالات وهو فصل وجملة، الفصل فى تدبير الفصول صـ ١٨٣، الجملة فى تدبير المسافرين صـ ١٨۴،

الفنّ الرابع فى نصف (بعض؟) وجوه المعالجات احد وثلثون فصلًا صـ ١٨٩،

This MS., from the Belshah collection, comprises 226 pp. of 24·7 × 12·5 c. and 25 ll., and is written throughout in a small, neat, legible *ta'líq* with rubrications.

Q. OCCULT SCIENCES.

Q. 1 (12).

الفلك الدّائر.

An acephalous Arabic work, without author's name, of a cabbalistic character, dealing to some extent with astrological matters, but chiefly with the virtues of certain verses of the *Qur'án* (خواصّ القرآن), the Names of God (اسماء الله الحُسْنى, ff. 47ª–83ª), etc. The title *al-Falak* (or *al-Fulk*) *u'd-Dá'ir* is inscribed in a modern hand on the remnant of f. 1 (more than half of which has been torn away), but I cannot find it in the body of the book. It can hardly be the work of the name mentioned by Brockelmann in vol. I, p. 283, of his *Gesch. d. Arab. Litt.*, but may be the *Kitábu'l-Falaki'd-Dawwár li'sh-Shamsi'l-Munír wa'l-Qamari's-Sayyár* of al-Manáshírí (d. 1039/1630) mentioned on p. 326 of vol. II of that work.

The work is divided into many unnumbered sections (*faṣl*), beginning with an account of the planet ruling each hour of each day in the week, *e.g.*:

يوم الثلاثا، اوّل ساعة منه للمرّيخ يكون العمل فيها للبغضا والفساد والفرقة ونزف الدم والأسقام والأمراض، الساعة الثانية للشمس لا تعمل فيها شيئًا ابدًا آلخ

There are several circles and other diagrams, *e.g.* on f. 4ª, thus described on f. 3ᵇ:

فصل، فى احكام منازل القمر الثمانية وعشرين الفلكيّات ونذكر هنا جدولًا غطيم الفايدة يعلم منه هلال كلّ شهر بأيّ منزلة هو آلخ

This MS., obtained in the last partition of the Belshah collection, comprises 147 ff. of 22·3 × 18·5 c. and 25 ll., and is written in a large, clear, coarse *naskh* with rubrications. It ends on f. 147ª without any mention of title, author, scribe's name, or date of transcription.

Q. 2 (9).

رسالة فى علم الرّمل.

An anonymous and untitled Arabic treatise on Geomancy, beginning abruptly, without even the *Bismi'lláh*:

باب فى حلال الرمل، اعلم ان اوّل بيت النفس والثانى بيت المال آلخ

The book contains a good many obscure poems, *e.g.* (f. 3ª) one beginning:

وطالع فى جوده كالبحر، ضاحكًا بنور وفخر،
يبين لاهل الدين يا خليلى، وانه من احسن الدليلى،

This MS. was acquired from the same source and on the same occasion as the last. It comprises 96 ff. of 22·2 × 15·8 c. and 17 ll., and is written throughout in a bold but indifferent *naskh*, not dated, but modern.

Q. 3 (9).

اسرار قاسمی،

A Persian treatise on the Five Occult Sciences (علوم خمسه، محتجبه) called *Kímiyá* (Alchemy), *Límiyá*, *Hímiyá*, *Símiyá* and *Rímiyá*, the initials of which give the words *Kulluhu Sirr* ("All of it is Mystery"). A lithographed edition of this book appeared at Bombay in 1302/1885.

This MS. has lost the first leaf, but comparison with the lithographed edition shows that only 8½ lines are missing at the beginning, the opening words being:

......چون جان بود، رایحه، روضه، رضوان بود،

In a short preface the author enumerates the five occult sciences and the chief works on each, and defines their scope. *Kímiyá* (Alchemy) is that which treats of the production of the Elixir and the Transmutation of Metals, and on which Jaldakí, Majríṭí, Khálid [ibn Yazíd], Ṭughrá'í, "*Ḥaḍrat-i-Mawlawí*" (*i.e.* Jalálu'd-Dín Rúmí), Sulṭán Walad and others have written. Next comes the science of Talismans (presumably *Límiyá*, though this word is not mentioned), defined as "that science whereby is known the method of mating the Active Superior with the Passive Inferior Powers, so that some strange action may be produced; and this they call 'the Alchemy of Talismans.'" The third, called *Hímiyá*, is the science of Subjugation or Control (*'Ilm-i-Taskhír*), and deals with Planetary Influences, Spells, Incantations, Control of the *Jinn*, and the like. The fourth, called *Símiyá*, deals with the Control of the Imagination for the evocation of forms which have no outward or independent existence, and appears to be equivalent to Mesmerism and Hypnotism. The fifth and last is *Rímiyá*, which appears to be mere Conjuring or Leger de Main (*'Ilm-i-Shu'bada*). Amongst the authors and books dealing with the last, or the last two sciences, are Khusraw Sháh, Ibn 'Iráqí, Abú 'Abdi'lláh al-Maghribí (*Siḥru'l-'Uyún*, also known as the *Lubáb* of Ibnu'l-Ḥalláj), and Ḥakím Abu'l-Qásim Aḥmad as-Samáwí (*'Uyúnu'l-Ḥaqá'iq* and *Anfáḥu't-Ṭaríq*). The last two "great masters" (*Buzurgán*) are said to have translated from the Greek into Arabic, and, apparently, are credited with the invention of that cabbalistic secret writing of which the author of this book also makes use to disguise from profane eyes certain words which should not be known save to Adepts, and those whom they trust, according to the verse:

بیجرعهٔ غم کسی بجامی نرسد، تا خون نشود دلی بکامی نرسد،
از گلشنِ حکمتِ گلستان هنر بوئی که دهد بهر مشامی نرسد،

The *soi-disant* author, Ḥusayn ibn 'Alí al-Wá'iẓ al-Káshifí (d. 910/1504–5), dedicates the book to Sayyid Qásimu'l-Anwár (d. 837/1433–4). Some account of these two men will be found in my *Persian Literature under Tartar Dominion*, pp. 503–504 and 473–486. From the chronological point of view it seems almost impossible that this authorship and this dedication can be genuine, and E. Edwards (*Cat. of Persian Books in the British Museum*, cols. 278–279) is no doubt right in regarding this attribution as false, for Qásimu'l-Anwár, on whom are bestowed laudatory titles innumerable, is spoken of as still living.

This MS., acquired in Nov. 1920 in the fourth partition of the Belshah collection, was transcribed by Áqá Bábá Sháhmírzáda, son of Mullá Muḥammad Mahdí, who copied many books for Prince Bahman Mírzá *Bahá'u'd-Dawla*, and was completed on Shawwál 14, 1268/Dec. 9, 1851. It comprises 172 ff. of 21·9 × 13·7 c. and 20 ll., and is written in a clear, good *naskh*. At the end is a table of the cabbalistic letters in red, with their Arabic equivalents in black. Though entitled "Greek writing" (قلم یونانی) and "Syriac writing" (قلم سریانی), these letters bear no resemblance to any known script.

Q. 4 (9).

کتاب اصول ملاحم وغیره

(I) A Persian work on Omens, beginning:

بدانکه نخست اصل این کتاب ملحمهٔ دانیال پیغمبر علیه السّلام نام نهاده است و بعد از او حکماء قدیم چون حرمس و بوذرجمهر و نحسکان (*sic*) و والیس حکیم هر کس بروزگار خود تجربه کرده‌اند و در کتابهای خویش تجربتی باز نموده‌اند الخ

The author, who does not mention his name, says that the word *Malḥama* means in Persian *Razm-gáh* ("Battle-field," "Place of Carnage") and is applied to these visions because they abound in portents of slaughter and bloodshed. The book is said to comprise two Discourses (*Maqála*), of which the first is divided into 25 and the second into 28 sections, each treating of the significance of some particular portent, *viz.* (1) eclipses of the Sun; (2) eclipses of the Moon; (3) other signs in the disc of the Sun; (4) — of the Moon; (5) the rising of New Moons; (6) comets; (7) shooting stars; (8) rainbows; (9) meteors; (10) redness in the sky; (11) other wondrous signs in the heavens; (12) appearance in the air of the semblance of a person; (13) thunder; (14) the glittering of snow; (15) fire falling from heaven; (16) heavy rain; (17) hail; (18) falling of red dust from the air; (19) falling of frogs or worms; (20) dust-storms; (21) darkness of the air; (22) noises in the air; (23) earthquakes; (24) unseasonable heat; (25) unseasonable cold; (26) unseasonable snow. As a matter of fact the arrangement indicated at the beginning of the book does not seem to be observed, and the whole work appears to be divided into numerous sections (*faṣl*) with recurring numeration. This part of the volume ends on f. 70[a] with a colophon stating that it was copied for Shír Khán Beg and completed on Muḥarram 4, 1278/July 12, 1861.

(II) The second part of the volume (ff. 70[b]–159[a]) containing a Persian treatise on fortunate and unfortunate days by Muḥammad Báqir ibn Muḥammad Taqí, beginning:

...امّا بعد، چنین گوید احقر عباد الله الغنی محمّد باقر بن محمّد تقی عفی الله عن جرائمهما که این رساله ایست در بیان آنچه [از] احادیث معتبرهٔ اهل بیت علیهم السلام معلوم میشود از سعادت و نحوست ایّام هفته و ماه و روز و ساعات و سایر ضروریّات که از کتب علماء سلف استخراج شده،

The first section deals with the days of the month from the 1st to the 30th, the next with the days of the week from Friday to Thursday, the next with the Muḥammadan months from Muḥarram to Dhu'l-Ḥijja, others with eclipses, seasons, the seven climes, the seas, rivers, sources and springs, wells, the order of creation and the six Zoroastrian *Gáhanbárs* (گاهنبار), etc.

This MS. was acquired in Nov. 1920 in the final partition of the Belshah collection. It comprises 160 ff. of 22 × 16 c. and 15 ll., and is written in a fair modern *ta'líq* with rubrications, dated 1278/1861.

Q. 5 (7).

(۱) تعبیر خواب منظوم، (۲) رسالهٔ شیخ عبد الله انصاری،

A little MS. of 30 ff. of 15·9 × 9 c. and 12 ll., written in a small, neat *ta'líq* within gilt borders, undated, but probably of the sixteenth century, bought by me in Constantinople in April, 1910. It contains two separate works, *viz.*:

I (ff. 1[b]–23[a]). An anonymous Persian poem on Oneiromancy, beginning:

وقت خواب درست نشستن (*sic*)، لازم آمد نخست دانستن،
آب از بیخ سوی شاخ رود، خواب مردم درست و راست بود،
ور سوی بیخ آمد از شاخ آب، در چنان فصل راست نآید خواب،

Ends on f. 23[a]:

هیزم آمد دلیل نمّامی، ناکسی و افترا و بدنامی،
تخمه‌را گیر بر ریا برهان، توبه از آن ریا قی و غشیان،

II (ff. 24[b]–28[b]). A Persian prose mystical treatise ascribed in the title to Shaykh 'Abdu'lláh Anṣárí, beginning:

دل از جان پرسید که اوّل این کار چیست و ثمره چیست، جان جواب داد الخ

Ends without colophon:

سپری شد سخن شیخ الاسلام عبد الله انصاری قدّس الله روحه،

Q. 6 (9).

مفتاح اسرار الحسینی،

A Persian mystical treatise entitled *Miftáḥ-i-Asrár al-Ḥusayní*, which title is a chronogram giving the date 1160/1747, by 'Abdu'r-Raḥím ibn Muḥammad Yúnus of Damáwand, beginning:

الحمد لله الّذی نجانا من العلوم الرسمیّة بنبیّه وسقانا كأس المحبّة من ید خلیفته وأذاب قلوبنا بتجلّیاته حتّی بلّغنا الی الكشف والمعاینة آلخ...امّا بعد، میگوید این فقیر الی الله و خاك روبهٔ آستانهٔ مرشدم جناب سیّد الشّهدا علیه السّلام عبد الرّحیم بن محمّد یونس دماوندی كه این كتابیست مشتمل بر بعضی اسرار كه در كتب و رسائل اكابر عرفا وحكما نیست آلخ

The work is divided into 37 chapters called *Miftáḥ* ("Key"), which are fully enumerated on ff. 2^b–3^a, and of which the first nine are as follows:

(۱) در اثبات صانع، (۲) در بیان دلیل مبدأ و معاد من كلام عالم ربّانی ملّا محمّد صادق اردستانی قدّس سرّه، (۳) در عینیّت وجود واجب و دلیل آن، (۴) در بیان توحید واجب الوجود بمعنی نفی شركت از واجب در مفهوم وجوب وجود، (۵) در بیان توحید وحدت بطریق عرفا، (٦) در بیان فرق میان علم و معرفت وعالم وعارف، (۷) در شرح لفظی كلام معجز نظام مولانا امیر المؤمنین صلوات الله علیه، (۸) در بیان تنزیه و تقدیس و تشبیه، (۹) در بیان بطلان اعتقاد جماعتی از اهل سلوك آلخ

This MS., acquired from the Belshah collection in 1920, comprises 118 ff. of 21·6 × 16·5 c. and 19 ll., and is written in a large, plain, modern *naskh* on greenish-blue paper, not dated. It should have been placed in **Class D** rather than in **Q.**

R. ART, CALLIGRAPHY, MUSIC, ETC.

R. 1 (10).

(۱) بهجة الرواج، (۲) رسالهٔ كرامیّه، (۳) ملفوظات امیر تیمور،

Two Persian treatises on Music, the first, entitled *Bahjatu'r-Rawáj*, professedly translated from Greek and Arabic originals, the second entitled *Risála-i-Kirámiyya*. These are followed by an abridged or imperfect text of the so-called "Institutes of Tímúr."

This MS., acquired in January, 1917, from the Schindler library, comprises 70 ff. of 21·8 × 15·5 c. and 11–12 ll. It is written throughout in a small, neat Persian *ta'líq* of the latter part of the nineteenth century.

I. The *Bahjatu'r-Rawáj* (ff. 1^b–22^b) is said to have been translated into easy Persian for Sulṭán Maḥmúd of Ghazna (reigned A.D. 998–1030) by 'Abdu'l-Mu'min ibn Ṣafiyyi'd-Dín ibn 'Izzi'd-Dín ibn Muḥyi'd-Dín ibn Ni'mat ibn Qábús ibn Washmgír of Gurgán, a chronological absurdity, since Qábús reigned from A.D. 976–1012, so that his fifth descendant in the direct line could not possibly have written in the eleventh century. Moreover on f. 7ᵇ, last line, mention is made of Malik Sháh the Saljúq (A.D. 1072–1092). The work begins, after the short doxology:

...امّا بعد، فهذه رسالة شريفة وجيز الباهرة (*sic*) فى علوم الادوار من قول الحكما الفلسفة (*sic*) بدلايل المرضيّة المطبوعة يعنى اين رساله ايست بزرگ قليل اللفظ و كثير المعنى متبحّر در علم موسيقى از كلام حكماء يونان زمين بدليل ظاهر روشن قابل صحيح از كتب متقدّمين افلاطون الهى نامش حكيم ادريس نبى عليه السّلام كه از روى كواكب سبعهٔ سيّاره استنباط كرده و از طبّ روشن ساخته تا عارفان سراپردهٔ شوق و طالبان صاحب ذوق از تأثير آن پردهٔ پندار از پيش جان بر اندازند و بر عالم الوهيت لواى عشق بر افرازند الخ

The work comprises an Introduction, ten chapters, and a Conclusion, of which the contents are stated as follows (ff. 2ᵇ–3ᵃ):

مقدّمه در آنكه هر مقامى از چه استخراج كرده اند، الباب الاوّل فى مبدأ هذا العلم من قول الحكماء الفلاسفة اجمالًا وتفصيلًا، باب دوم در اقاويل بعضى از حكما درين علم و چگونگى آن، باب سيم در نسبت اين علم بوجود انسان، باب چهارم در نسبت اين علوم بكواكب سبعه، باب پنجم در بيان بحور اصول و حركات هر يك، باب ششم در بيان اين علم فى النظم، باب هفتم در تركيب پرده بحسب سير عطارد و زهره، باب هشتم در بيان آنكه مناسب هر كه چه نغمه گويد، باب نهم در بيان آنكه هر پرده چند بانگ بود، باب دهم در سلوك صاحب اين علم با خواصّ و عوامّ، خاتمه در نسبت پردها بكواكب و عناصر و فصول اربعه،

This treatise contains numerous tables and circles, concluding on f. 22ᵇ with the most elaborate, which shows the relations of the 12 *Maqáms*, the 24 *Shu'bas*, the 48 *Gúshas*, the 6 *Áwázas*, and the 24 *Baḥr-i-Uṣúls*.

II. The *Risála-i-Kirámiyya* (ff. 23ᵇ–29ᵃ), beginning:

نغمه اولى است ز فيض كريم، رباعى اى بلبل جان نغمه سراى از غم تو، چون دايره دل بيسر و پا از غم تو، عشّاق هميشه بينوا از غم تو، درد از تو و دردرا دوا از غم تو، حمد و سپاس و ستايش بيقياس پادشاهى‌را كه بساط اهل نشاطرا در مأمن حفظ و حضور و مهد عيش و سرور ارباب عشرات‌را در مقام و مسكن سرور انداخت الخ

...امّا بعد، چون سرگشتهٔ هر وادى ساكن كوى نامرادى دورهٔ سفرچى ميخواست كه آنچه بقدر وسع خود در فنّ موسيقى از اقوال حكما فرا گرفته بعمل در آورده بود تحرير كند شايد كه منظور نظر كيميا اثر حضرت عاليمقام...سلطان تاجبخش شاه‌نشان عليقلى خان گردد...بنابرين اين رسالهٔ موسوم‌را بكراميّه دوره بر سه اصل بنا نهاد، اصل اوّل در بيان دوازده مقام، ...اصل دوم در بيان شعبه و آوازه، اصل سيم در بيان اصول و بعضى از فوايد موسيقى،

This tract ends on f. 29ᵃ, and was completed in 1280/1863.

III. The *Malfúzát* or *Túzuk-i-Tímúrí*, or "Institutes of Tímúr" (ff. 31ᵇ–68ᵇ), a well-known work of doubtful authenticity. Both beginning and end correspond with the text published at Oxford in A.D. 1783 by Major Davy and Joseph White (pp. 2 and 408), but this tract is so much shorter than the printed text that much of the intervening part has evidently been omitted or greatly condensed.

R. 2 (7).

رساله میر علی تبریزی،

A small treatise on Calligraphy by Mír 'Alí-i-Tabrízí, beginning:

باید دانست که تعلیم نسخ و تعلیق واضح الاصل میر علی تبریزیست نوّر الله مرقده بدین طریق
است، الف باید (f. 2ᵃ) که سه نقطه درازیش باشد الّخ

The letters of the alphabet are discussed in their proper succession.

Ff. 12 of 17 × 10·3 c. and 6 ll.; fine, large *ta'líq* with rubrications between gilt and coloured margins and an illuminated *'unwán*; transcribed by Riḍá-qulí Adíb. No indication of date or place of acquisition.

R. 3 (8).

کتاب المفاخرة والحروب الباترة للسّیوطی،

Kitábu'l-Mufákhara wa'l-Ḥurúbi'l-Bátira, ascribed on the title-page to the celebrated polygraph Shaykh Jalálu'd-Dín as-Suyúṭí, and comprising three *Maqámát*, the first two dealing with fruits and the third with gems. Begins abruptly:

قال الشیخ العالم العلّامة، والبحر الهمّام الفهّامه، فرید عصره وأوانه، ووحید دهره وزمانه، سألنی
بعض الاصدقاء أن اعمل مختصرًا لطیفا، لیکون فرجة للناظرین وسمّیته بکتاب المفاخرة والحروب
الباترة (p. 3) امّا بعد، ایّها الناس فإنّ الله تعالی آتی انواع الطیب شرفا عمیما وجعل لها فی الدنیا
والآخرة والبرزخ فضلا عظیما الّخ

The following Table of Contents was drawn up by Mírzá Bihrúz:

المقدّمة فی فضل الطیب والأحادیث الواردة فیها صّ ۳،

المقامة التفاحیّة صّ ۱۴، الرّمان صّ ۱۶، الاترج صّ ۱۸، السفرجل صّ ۲۳، التفّاح صّ ۲۵،

الکمثری صّ ۲۷، النبق صّ ۲۹، الخوخ صّ ۳۱،

المقامة الزمرّدیّة فی الخضروات صّ ۳۴، الفُستق صّ ۳۵، اللـوز صّ ۳۶، الجوز صّ ۳۸، البندق
صّ ۳۹، الشاهبلوط صّ ۳۹، حبّ الصنوبر صّ ۴۰،

المقامة الیاقوتیّة صّ ۴۱، قال الیاقوت صّ ۴۱، قال اللؤلؤ صّ ۴۴، قال الزمرّد صّ ۴۷، قال المرجان،
صّ ۴۹، قال الزبرجد صّ ۵۱،

This MS. comprises 55 pp. of 17·9 × 12·3 c. and 15 ll., but presents several lacunae, which have been filled by blank pages. It contains no indication of origin, but I think was acquired at the final partition of the Belshah MSS. It is written in a clear but shaky and senile *naskh* with rubrications, and is undated.

R. 4 (11).

"PERSIAN PICTURES."

A collection of 51 Persian miniatures illustrating episodes from the *Sháhnáma* of Firdawsí, apparently all by the same artist, and, so far as I can judge, of no special excellence. On the back of each the subject represented is indicated in a poor, modern Persian *ta'líq*. The volume formerly belonged to the late E. J. W. Gibb, and bears his *ex Libris*. The leaves measure 25·7 × 14·5 c. Most of the episodes illustrated are taken from the earlier part of the Epic, but no chronological order is observed. Thus the subjects of the first twelve are: (1) Suhráb killed by Rustam; (2) Bahrám's war with the Faghfúr, or Emperor of China; (3) Túr killed by Qáran; (4) not indicated; (5) Kay-Ká'ús informed of the coming of Afrásiyáb; (6) death of Surkha (?) at the hands of Farámurz; (7) Rustam comes to the help of Gúdarz and Ṭús; (8) Kay-Khusraw takes counsel with the Persians; (9) execution of (? name illegible) in the presence of Afrásiyáb; (10) Kundraw (?) comes before Afrásiyáb; (11) an Ambassador coming to Bahman; (12) Ká'ús informed of the coming of Siyáwush, etc.

R. 5 (11).

An Album, with one of the Persian lacquered covers missing, containing seven mediocre miniatures, six specimens of calligraphy (one modern imitation of Kúfic writing), and two ingenious specimens of "nail-work" (شغل ناخن), all, apparently, quite modern. The cardboard leaves on which these are mounted measure 24·5 × 15·5 c. and are joined at their outer edges, so that they can be displayed in one row simultaneously, like a map. They are: (1) head and shoulders of a Persian lady, European style, labelled in English "this is painted on canvas"; (2) three-quarter length picture of a European lady, bearing a Persian inscription saying that it was drawn by an artist named Rafá'íl, and has been injured by fire; (3) a book, by Áqá Ṣádiq; (4) imitation Kúfic writing described as "Abú Sa'ídí," bearing the seal of one Muḥammad Taqí ibn Muḥammad Báqir; (5) *ta'líq* writing by Mushtáq 'Alí Sháh; (6) Persian woman playing the *tár*; (7) Persian woman with castanets, dancing; (8) and (9) two specimens of *ta'líq* writing by Mírzá Ghulám 'Alí; (10) and (11) two designs drawn with the nail by Prince 'Alí Akbar Mírzá, the first a youthful full-length figure holding a bouquet of flowers, the second a gazelle under a very ornate tree; (12) and (13) two more specimens of Mírzá Ghulám 'Alí's writing.

Bought for £1 at a sale amongst other Persian articles.

S. DICTIONARIES.

S. 1 (10).

مقدّمة الأُدب للزّمخشری،

A fine old copy, dated Muḥarram 721/Feb. 1324, of the *Muqaddamatu'l-Adab min Tarjumáni'l-'Ajam wa'l-'Arab* of the celebrated philologist and commentator of the *Qur'án* Maḥmúd ibn 'Umar az-Zamakhsharí (d. 538/1143). See Brockelmann, vol. I, pp. 289–293, and J. G. Wetzstein's edition, 2 vols., Leipzig, 1844. Begins, after the *Bismi'lláh*:

اَلْحَمْدُ لِلّٰهِ الَّذِی فَضَّلَ علی جَمِیعِ الاَلْسِنَةِ لِسَانَ الْعَرَبِ الخ

سپاس و ستایش مرخدای‌را آنك تفضیل کرد بر همهٔ زبانها زبان تازی عرب‌را

The Persian interlinear translation is written in a smaller *naskh* hand than the Arabic text, but very clearly. The work is dedicated to the Sipahsálár Bahá'u'd-Dín 'Alá'u'd-Dawla Abu'l-Muẓaffar Atsiz ibn Khwárazmsháh (reigned A.D. 1127–1156), and is divided into five parts (*Qism*), the first treating of nouns, the second of verbs, the third of particles, the fourth of the declension of nouns, the fifth of the conjugation of verbs.

The MS., acquired at the fourth partition of the Belshah collection on Nov. 12, 1920, comprises 66 ff. of 23·5 × 15 c., with 8 lines of Arabic text and an equal number of Persian interlinear translation, the former in a larger and bolder *naskh* hand and vocalized. It is dated Muḥarram 721/Feb. 1321.

S. 2 (8).

معیار جمالی،

An acephalous but otherwise complete copy of the *Mi'yár-i-Jamálí*, by Shams-i-Fakhrí, of which the fourth and last part, edited by Salemann, was printed at Kazan in 1887. This good MS., apparently of the fifteenth century of the Christian era, was given to me by Dr Riẓá Tevfik [Riḍá Tawfíq] in August, 1909. It lacks at least one leaf at the beginning, the opening words (in the part dealing with the origins of Poetry and the nature of the Poet) being:

...و در مجمعی که اکابر اقارب او و اعیان آن قبیله حاضر بودند بخواند، ایشان گفتند ما هذا الترتیل الّذی ما کنّا شعرنا بك قبل یومنا هذا آلخ

It comprises 176 ff. of 18·2 × 13 c. and 15 ll., and is written in a clear and excellent archaic *nasta'líq*, apparently of the fifteenth century. In the colophon the date "Monday, the 18th of Ramaḍán" occurs, but the year is unfortunately omitted. The contents are as follows:

Part I (ff. 1–43[a]), on Poetry and Prosody, in nine chapters.

Part II (ff. 43[b]–67[b]), on Rhyme, various forms of Verse, etc., concluding with a prayer for Shaykh Abú Isḥáq Injú (killed in 758/1356) to whom the work is dedicated.

Part III (ff. 68[a]–97[b]), on Rhetorical Devices, Tropes, etc.

Part IV (ff. 98[a]–176[a]), on Persian Lexicography, an alphabetical list of rare Persian words with verse citations illustrating their use. This is the portion published by Salemann at Kazan in 1887 under the title *Shams i Fachrîi Ispahanensis Lexicon Persicum, id est libri Mi'jâr i Ǵamâlî pars quarta, etc.* See also Ḥájjí Khalífa, ed. Flügel, vol. v, p. 640, No. 12,440.

S. 3 (12).

مجمع الفرس،

A good, clear modern copy of the well-known Persian-Persian Lexicon entitled *Majma'u'l-Furs*, compiled in 1008/1599–1600 by Muḥammad Qásim ibn Ḥájjí Muḥammad of Káshán, better known as Surúrí, and dedicated to Sháh 'Abbás the Great. See Rieu's Persian Catalogue, pp. 498–499, etc.

This MS., acquired from the Schindler collection in Jan. 1917, comprises 258 ff. of 29 × 17·3 c. and 24 ll. It is written in a clear and very legible *naskh* with rubrications, and the transcription was completed on the 8th of Jumádà I, 1254/ July 30, 1838. A second preface, composed in pure Persian after the completion of the work and occupying both sides of f. 1, is written in small but clear Persian *ta'líq*, and is dated two days later than the date in the principal colophon given above. It is headed:

این دیباچه خلاصة المجمع است که بعد از اتمام مجمع الفرس نوشته شد الخ

Ff. 2[b]–4[a] are blank, but on f. 2[a] is a short note in English in Sir A. Houtum-Schindler's hand giving the title and authorship of the book, with a reference to "Flügel I, 101" (*i.e.* the Vienna Catalogue), and adding that "the author is mentioned by Pietro della Valle as living in Iṣfahán in A.D. 1622."

S. 4 (13).

برهان قاطع،

A good, complete copy of the well-known Persian-Persian Lexicon entitled *Burhán-i-Qáṭi'* ("the Trenchant Argument"), compiled in 1062/1652 by Muḥammad Ḥusayn ibn Khalaf of Tabríz, poetically surnamed Burhán. See Rieu's

Persian Catalogue, p. 500; E. Edwards's *Catalogue of printed Persian Books in the British Museum*, cols. 484–486, etc.

This MS. was sent by Prince Muḥammad 'Alí Mírzá on the 17th of Rabí' II, 1330/April 5, 1912, from Ṭihrán to Dr Aḥmad Khán, at one time Persian lecturer in Cambridge, from whom I received it. It comprises 489 ff. of 30 × 19 c. and 25 ll., and is written in a small, neat *ta'líq* with rubrications. The copyist gives his name as Ibnu'l-Ma'ṣúm 'Abdu'l-'Alí, and the date on which he completed his work as the 28th of Shawwál, 1149/March 1, 1737.

S. 5 (11).

فرهنگ رشیدی،

A good seventeenth-century MS. of the well-known Persian-Persian Lexicon compiled in 1064/1653–4 by 'Abdu'r-Rashíd ibn 'Abdi'l-Ghafúr al-Ḥusayní al-Madaní at-Tatawí, and entitled *Farhang-i-Rashídí*. See Rieu's Persian Catalogue, pp. 500–501; Ethé's India Office Persian Cat., cols. 1350–1351, etc.

This MS., like so many others in the library of the late Sir A. Houtum-Schindler, formerly belonged to Prince Farhád Mírzá *Mu'tamadu'd-Dawla*, whose note of ownership is dated the 28th of Jumádà I, 1293/June 21, 1876. It comprises 297 ff. of 27 × 16 c. and 24 ll., is written in an excellent *ta'líq* with rubrications, and was completed on the 6th of Dhu'l-Qa'da, 1084/Feb. 12, 1674.

S. 6 (9).

An incomplete Persian-Turkish Vocabulary, followed by an acephalous and incomplete Arabic Vocabulary. The former begins on f. 1[b] abruptly after the *Bismi'lláh*:

باب الالف المفتوحة من الاسماء آبْ آب ماه آبه

صو آغستوس، صوڭیای آیی صافی صو

Next follow words beginning with *i* (المكسورة), and *u* (المضمومة), then infinitives and imperfects of verbs beginning with a vowel, then (f. 6[b]) words beginning with *b*, and so on, up to verbs beginning with *sá* and *sa* (f. 41[b]). Here the Arabic glossary begins abruptly with words ending in *s*:

...فی النّفْی، النَمْسُ راز پنهان داشتن، الهَجْسُ فرا دل آمدن اندیشه الخ

Ends abruptly on f. 148[b]:

المعتلّ الیای، سَ، اَلْیَأْسُ نَوْمِید شُدَن، الیبْسُ وَالْیَبْسُ خشك شدن ویَیْبَسُ لُغَةٌ، تم الکتاب،

The colophon (on f. 149[a]) gives the name of the copyist as Aḥmad ibn 'Abdi'l-Mannán, and the date of completion as the middle of Jumádà I, 877/October, 1472.

This unattractive MS., obtained at the fourth and last partition of the Belshah collection in November, 1920, comprises 149 ff. of 20·9 × 14·8 c. and 13 ll. Written in a large, clear **naskh** with rubrications.

S. 7 (8).

مصرّحة الأسْماء مع قصد التأريخ فى الإسْماء٬

A vocabulary of Arabic words arranged alphabetically, with Persian interlinear glosses, entitled as above *Muṣarriḥatu'l-Asmá*, composed for and dedicated to Sulṭán Báyazíd II (reigned A.D. 1481–1512).

Begins:

انّ من لطف الله بالثبات٬ حمد المنطق باللّغات٬ وشكر المنعم بالجهات آلخ...

...وبعد فهذه مجلّة الادب وحديقة الارب رتّبتُها وزيّنتها قاصدًا بجمهرة الاسمآء الصحاح بالبيان السّامى وتوضيح ما وُضع له الالفاظ الكثيرة التداول من الاسامى باسلوب عامّ النفع للواقفين بقواعد الاشتقاق وغير الواقفين بأُصول الصبغ (الصيغ) لمزيد الاشفاق لأُتمّم الخدمة لمن نُصِبْتُ لخدمته وغرِقْتُ فى بحار نعمته وهو المخدوم الاعظم والاقنوم الافخم سلالة السلاطين ونتيجة الخواقين...أعنى السّلطان بن السلطان سلطان بايزيد بن محمّد خان خلّد الله تعالى سلطانهما واوضح على العالمين برهانهما واعتبرْتُ بترتيب حروف التهجّى من اوّل الكلمة الى آخرها الّا تاء التأنيث والوحدة وقدّمتُها على الالف فرقاً عن التّاء والهاء الاصليّتين فى البنية واعرضْتُ من (عن) متعسّف ارباب اللغة من انّ نحو تمرٍ جمع تمرةٍ وانبعث الجموع لمفرّداتها ولا ضرورة فى اتيانها واثباتها والزمْتُ بجمع الاسماء المذكورة فى المقدّمة والسّامى بأسرها مع زيادات من الصّحاح والجمهرة والمُجْمَل وغيرها فسمّيتُها مُصرّحة الاسمآء مع قصد التأريخ فى الإسماء وما غرضى الّا دعاءٍ يُستجاب وثناءٍ يُستطاب وبلطف الله وفضله يُفْتَح الأبواب وينال الآمال والارباب (والآراب)٬ حرف الالف

اءأَنْتَ اَمْ رُوحِى اَتَعْلَمُ حالى اَسلْطانى

توى يا جان من مى دانى حال من اى پادشاه من

This MS. was one of 13 bought from J. J. Naaman for £25 in May, 1902. It comprises 158 ff. of 20·3 × 14·5 c. and 10 ll., with the Persian interlinear glosses between them, is written in a good, clear *naskh*, vocalized, with rubrications, and was completed on the 28th of Ramaḍán, 906/April 17, 1501.

S. 8 (14).

Specimens of the Gílakí dialect.

A large, thin volume of 28 ff. of 34·7 × 21 c. and about 29 ll. in double columns, written in a very cursive modern Persian *ním-shikasta*, containing specimens of Gílakí, the dialect spoken in Gílán, in most cases with Persian translation opposite. A few of the extracts are in verse; the prose pieces are mostly short stories, and there is no preface, doxology, title or author's name. The compilation was probably made for Mr H. L. Rabino, formerly H.B.M. Consul in Rasht, who kindly gave it to me with other papers.

S. 9 (10).

لطائف اللُّغات،

A glossary of rare words occurring in the *Mathnawí* of Jalálu'd-Dín Rúmí, compiled by 'Abdu'l-Laṭíf al-'Abbásí of Gujrát (d. circa 1048/1688–9), who also wrote two commentaries on the poem. See Rieu, B.M.P.C., p. 590; Ethé, I.O.P.C., **No. 1091**. The language to which the words included in the glossary originally belonged is indicated by means of letters placed opposite them in the margins.

Ff. 200 of 24·5 × 14·5 c. and 17 ll. Good clear *nasta'líq*, with blue and gold borders. Dated Tuesday, ——th of Rajab, 1257/1841–2.

S. 10 (9).

نصاب الصبيان،

A popular versified vocabulary entitled *Niṣábu's-Ṣibyán*, giving the Persian synonyms of common Arabic words, by Abú Naṣr Faráhí, who wrote it in 617/1220/1. See Rieu, B.M.P.C., p. 504, Ethé, I.O.P.C., **No. 2375**, etc.

Ff. 18 of 21·5 × 16 c. and 15 ll. Fair *nasta'líq* with rubrications, gold borders, and coloured vignettes. Dated 1198/1783–4. The colophon is in Turkish.

T. ACROSTICS, RHYME, RHETORIC, ETC.

T. 1 (9).

معاهد التّنصيص على شواهد التّلخيص،

An excellent copy of the *Ma'áhidu't-Tanṣíṣ 'alà Shawáhidi't-Talkhíṣ* of 'Abdu'r-Raḥím ibn 'Abdi'r-Raḥmán al-Qáhirí al-'Abbásí, composed in 901/1495–6. See Ahlwardt's Berlin Arabic Catalogue, **Nos. 7224–5** (vol. VI, pp. 383–384); Brockelmann, vol. I, p. 296, etc.

The MS., obtained from the Belshah collection in January, 1920, comprises 306 ff., of which the first seven contain a Table of Contents. The leaves measure 21 × 14 c. and 33 ll. The writing, a neat, small *naskh* with rubrications, is that of 'Abdu'l-Qádir ibn 'Umar, who completed it in 1146/1733–4, and who prefaces to his own colophon a copy of the original colophon, which states that the author completed the composition of this work in Cairo in 901/1495–6, and completed his autograph of the fair copy in Ramaḍán, 934/May—June, 1528.

T. 2 (8).

رسالهٔ معمّا،

Jámí's Treatise on Acrostics and Riddles, entitled *Risála-i-Mu'ammá*, beginning:

ای اسم تو گنج هر طلسمی، قانع ز تو هر کسی باسمی،
هم اسم توئی و هم مسمّا، عاجز شده عقل ازین معمّا،

معمّا کلامیست موزون که دلالت کند بر اسمی از اسما، بطریق رمز و ایما، دلالتی که پسندیدهٔ طبعهای سلیم، و ذهنهای مستقیم، باشد و ناظم معمّارا ناچارست از دو امر الخ

A copy of the same work is contained in the collection of Jámí's *Rasá'il* described by Flügel, Vienna Catalogue, vol. III, p. 542 foll. (**No. 2010**, ff. 67–74).

This MS., of the acquisition of which I have no note, comprises 44 ff. of 19 × 12 c. and 13 ll., and is written in a graceful and legible *ta'líq* with rubrications, dated in the colophon 959/1552.

T. 3 (9).

رسالهٔ معمّا،

Surúrí's Turkish translation and explanation of a Persian Treatise on the Acrostic, composed in 856/1452 by Jámí, different from that mentioned above, undertaken, as the translator states in a short Turkish Preface, at the request of some friends. Begins:

حمد اول احده که ذاتی معمّاسی غیر اسمادن چقمق مشکل، و کنهی لغزی اوصاف و سمات ایله بلنمگه دگل قابل الخ ...امّا بعد، بو حقیر و دمبسته، سروری خاطر شکسته، اهل دللردن بعضی یاران، و طالبلردن خیلی خُلّان، ایله صحبت دلگشا و مصاحبت معمّی ایدوب الخ

The Persian text commentated begins:

بسم الله الرحمن الرحيم، بعد از گشایش مقال سوز اچدقدن صکره بستایش خجسته مآل مآلی مبارك اُوکُش ایله دانائیرا که بر عالمه که الخ

This MS. was bought on May 7, 1903, for £2. 10*s*. 0*d*. from J. J. Naaman. It comprises 108 ff. of 21·5 × 12·4 c. and 17 ll., is written in a small, clear *ta'líq* with rubrications, and was completed at the beginning of Rabí' II, 941/Oct. 10, 1534.

T. 4 (8).

رساله در قوافی،

The Treatise on Rhyme composed in Persian for Mír 'Alí Shír *Nawá'í* in 892/1487, by Núru'd-Dín ibn Aḥmad ibn 'Abdi'l-Jalíl.

Begins:

نورانی اختری که مطلع انوار بیانرا شاید و روحانی جوهری که مخزن اسرار جنانرا بیاراید الخ

I have no note of the acquisition of this MS., which comprises 58 ff. of 18·7 × 11·7 c. and 15 ll., and is written in an excellent sixteenth-century *ta'líq* with rubrications and some marginal notes. The colophon records neither the scribe's name nor the date of transcription, but only the date of composition, as given above.

T. 5 (9).

A fragmentary and worthless treatise on Arabic Grammar in Arabic, containing loose leaves numbered 30–68, measuring 20·4 × 15·2 c., and comprising 12 lines of text, with many interlinear and marginal notes and glosses, the former written in a poor, modern *naskh*, the latter in *ta'líq*. There is no note of acquisition.

U. ARABIC POETRY.

U. 1 (9).

المعلّقات السّبع،

The Seven *Mu'allaqát* (of Imru'u'l-Qays, Zuhayr, Ṭarafa, Labíd, 'Antara, 'Amr ibn Kulthúm, and al-Ḥárith ibn Ḥilliza) and the *qaṣída* of Khálid ibn Ṣafwán al-Qannáṣ.

This MS., acquired in the final division of the Belshah collection, comprises 76 ff. of 21 × 15·5 c. and 17 ll., and is written in an indifferent though legible *naskh* of no great antiquity with rubrications. It is undated, nor does the copyist give his name, but only says at the end of the last *qaṣída* that it was one of the things he read with his "righteous and martyred Master and Brother Sayfu'd-Dín Yúsuf ibn Muḥammad al-'Alawí al-Ḥusayní."

A Table of Contents has been prefixed by Mírzá Bihrúz.

U. 2 (9).

ديوان المتنبّى،

A fine MS. of the *Díwán* of the celebrated Arabic poet al-Mutanabbi (b. 303/905; d. 354/965). See Brockelmann, I, pp. 86–89, R. A. Nicholson's *Literary History of the Arabs*, pp. 304–313, etc.

This MS., bought on Oct. 31, 1902, for £10 from J. J. Naaman, comprises 173 ff. of 22·5 × 12·1 c. and 20 ll. It was transcribed in Nakhjuwán by Sulṭánsháh ibn Sanjar ibn 'Abdi'lláh, and was completed in Jumádà I, 692/April, 1293. It is written throughout in a beautiful, clear *naskh*, fully vocalized, with a good many marginal notes in a very minute hand, especially in the earlier part.

U. 3 (10).

ديوان ابى فراس الحمدانى،

The *Díwán* of Abú Firás al-Ḥamdání (b. 320/932; d. 357/968). See Brockelmann, I, p. 89; Nicholson, *op. laud.*, pp. 270 and 304.

This MS., also acquired from the Belshah collection on Nov. 12, 1920, comprises 76 ff. of 22·8 × 15 c. and 17 ll. It is written in a good fairly modern *naskh*, unvocalized, with rubrications, and has no date or colophon. The short prose preface begins:

قال ابو عبد الله الحسين بن محمّد بن احمد بن خالويه من حلّ من الشرف السامى والفضل النامى والكرم الداعى والأدب البارع والشجاعة المشهورة والسماحة المأثورة محلّ أبى فراس الحرث بن سعيد بن حمدون بن الحرث العدوىّ آلخ

U. 4 (8).

سقط الزند لأبى العلاء المعرّى،

A fine old MS., acquired from the Belshah collection in January, 1920, of the poems of Abu'l-'Alá al-Ma'arrí (b. 363/973; d. 449/1057), most or all of them from the *Siqṭu'z-Zand*. See Brockelmann, I, pp. 254–255; Nicholson, *op. laud.*, pp. 313–324, etc.

This MS., written in a large, bold *naskh*, the verses fully vocalized, the intervening commentary in a rather smaller hand less fully vocalized, is, unfortunately, defective both at the beginning and end, but appears to have been transcribed in the 13th or 14th Christian century. In its present state it comprises 174 ff. of 18·7 × 14·3 c. and 14 ll., and begins:

وَانْ تَوَافَقَ فِى مَعْنًى بَنُو زَمَنٍ، فَإنَّ جُلَّ المعَانِى غَيْرُ مُتَّفِقِ،
قَد يَبْعُدُ الشَّئُ مِنْ شَئٍ يُشَابِهُهُ، اِنَّ السَّمَآءَ نَظِيرُ الماء فى الزرق،

U. 5 (9).

ديوان الشريف الرضى،

A very modern MS., copied in Baghdád in 1283/1867, of the *Díwán* of ash-Sharíf ar-Raḍí (b. 359/970; d. 406/1015), concerning whom see Brockelmann, I, p. 82. It was transcribed for his own use, as stated in a note on f. 1ᵃ, by Anṣárí-záda Ḥasan al-Qádirí, a Treasury official during the governorship of Muḥammad Námiq Pasha.

Begins:

هذا ما الّفه وصنّفه الرضى رضى الله عنه من الشعر ويبداء فى كلّ قافية بالمدايح والتهالى ثم بالافتخار وشكوى الزمان ثمّ بالمراثى والزهد الّخ

A brief account of the Sharíf's genealogy, with the dates of his birth and death, follows, and then (f. 2ᵃ) the first poem, beginning:

جزاء امير المؤمنين ثنائى، على نعم ما تنقضى وعطائى،

The MS., obtained at the final division of the Belshah collection in November, 1920, comprises 297 ff. of 20·4 × 14·8 c. and 27 ll., and is neatly written in a small and fairly legible *naskh*. In the colophon the copyist gives his name as Ḥusayn ibn Amín al-Qá'imí al-Baghdádí, and states that he completed his work on Ramaḍán 6, 1283/Jan. 12, 1867.

U. 6 (11).

ديوان عمر بن الفارض
مع شرح الشيخ عبد الغنى النابلسى،

The *Díwán* of the celebrated Egyptian mystical poet 'Umar ibnu'l-Fáriḍ (b. 586/1181; d. 632/1235) with the extensive prose commentary of Shaykh 'Abdu'l-Ghaní an-Nábulusí (b. 1050/1641; d. 1143/1731). Concerning the latter, see Brockelmann, II, pp. 345–348, where 85 of his works are enumerated; and for Ibnu'l-Fáriḍ see the same, I, pp. 262–263, and R. A. Nicholson's *Literary History of the Arabs*, pp. 394–398.

This MS. was given to me in Constantinople in April, 1910, by Dr Riẓá Tevfíq (Riḍá Tawfíq). It comprises 520 ff. of 27 × 17 c. and 37 ll., is written throughout in a small, neat, and legible, though ungraceful *naskh*, the text in red, and was copied by 'Abdu'l-Qádir ibn Muḥammad al-'Aṭífí, who completed his work on Monday the 13th of Ramaḍán, 1141/April 12, 1729, *i.e.* during the Commentator's life-time. The work is divided into two parts, of which the first ends on f. 292ᵃ, and the second begins on f. 293ᵇ.

U. 7 (9).

ديوان القاضى ابى بكر ناصح الدّين الأُرّجانى وغيره·

The Arabic *Díwán* of the Qáḍí Náṣiḥu'd-Dín Abú Bakr Aḥmad ibn Muḥammad ibn al-Ḥusayn al-Arraján. See Brockelmann, I, pp. 253–254, according to whom he was born in 460/1068 and died in 544/1149. A note in red on f. 1[a], under the principal title, says that this is followed by the *Díwán* of Ḥusámu'd-Dín (? الحاهرى), but I find no sign of this.

Begins after the *Bismi'lláh*:

قال القاضى ناصح الدّين ابو بكر احمد بن محمّد بن الحسين الأرّجانى رحمة الله عليه يمدح بعض الرؤسا هو ضياء الدّين رئيس بلدة اوران (?)

يرمى فوادى وهو فى سودآيه· اتراه لا يخشى على حوبآيه·

This MS. was acquired in the last division of the Belshah collection on Nov. 12, 1920. It comprises 137 ff. of 20·2 × 13·8 c. and 23 ll., is written in a fair ***naskh***, and was transcribed by Ibráhím ibn Muḥammad Abu'l-Ma'álí ad-Dayrí in Damascus and completed in Jumádà II, 995/May, 1587.

U. 8 (6).

ديوان الصّبابة·

The *Díwánu'ṣ-Ṣabába*, a well-known anthology of erotic verse in Arabic compiled by Ibn Abí Ḥajala of Tilimsán (Tlemçen), who was born in 725/1325 and died in 776/1375. See Brockelmann, II, pp. 12–13; Rieu's Arabic Catalogue, p. 348[a], and Arabic Supplement, **No. 1113**, pp. 702–703. The text has been printed in Cairo in 1291/1874. It comprises an Introduction (*Muqaddama*), thirty chapters, and a Conclusion (*Khátima*).

This MS. was one of those acquired at the final division of the Belshah collection on Nov. 12, 1920. It comprises 210 ff. of 14·5 × 9·10 c. and 15 ll., and is written in a good, legible ***naskh***, not vocalized, with an extensive use of red and green ink. There is no date or colophon.

U. 9 (9).

وتريّات·

An anonymous Arabic poem in praise of the Prophet Muḥammad, somewhat in the style of the celebrated *Burda* of al-Búṣírí, beginning:

صلوٰتى وتسليمى وأزكى تحيّتى· على من له وجهٌ من الشمس اضوأُ·

The poem is in the form of a *takhmís*, or "fivesome," four half-verses rhyming together being followed by a fifth which maintains the same rhyme throughout the canto, the cantos being arranged under these principal rhymes in alphabetical order. Thus under the isolated verse already cited the first stanza (حرف الالف) begins:

بدأتُ بذكر الله مدحًا مقدّما، وأثنى بحمد الله شكرًا معظّما،
وأختم قولى بالصلوة وإنّما، أُصلّى صلوةً تملأُ الارض والسما،
على من له اعلى العُلا متبوّأُ

نبىّ له فى حضرة القدس منزلُ، وحُجّابه الاملاك وهو مبجّلُ،
أتى آخرًا فى بعثه وهو اوّلُ، أُقيمَ مقامًا لَمْ يَقُمْ فيه مرسلُ،
وأمست له حُجْب الجلال توطّأُ

Each canto comprises about twenty stanzas of five hemistichs, like the two given above. The title *Witriyyát* occurs only in a later hand on f. 1[a].

The MS., acquired from the Belshah collection with that last mentioned, comprises 62 ff. of 20·8 × 14·8 c. and 15 ll. It is written in a large and rather coarse but legible *naskh* with rubrications, and is dated 1200/1785–6.

U. 10 (12).

شرح البديعيّة لابن حجّة

وهو الموسوم بخزانة الأُدب وغاية الأرب،

Part of a didactic poem in praise of the Prophet, designed to exemplify the use of rhetorical figures and illustrate علم البديع, together with a commentary by the author, Abu'l-Maḥásin Taqiyyu'd-Dín Abú Bakr b. 'Alí b. 'Abdi'lláh b. Ḥijja al-Ḥamawí (Brockelmann, II, 15), who died in 837/1434. The *Badí'iyya* is avowedly an imitation of the *Burda* of al-Búṣírí; and the author's commentary, completed according to his own statement (f. 186[a]) in Dhu'l-Ḥijja, 826/November, 1423, bears the titles *Taqdím Abí Bakr* and *Khizánatu'l-Adab wa-Ghâyatu'l-Arab*. The *Khátima* (ff. 185[b]–186[a]) runs as follows:

قال المؤلّف تغمّده الله برحمته هذا المصنّف المبارك اعنى البديعية وشرحها اذا ملكه متأدّب شرفت نفسه عن النظر الى غيره من تذاكر الأدب فانّى ما تركت ما وقع من جيّده ورديّه ونصبت البحث بين المقصرين والمجيدين...وقد انتهت الغاية بحمد الله الى حسن الختام وأوردت فيه ما لا خفيت محاسنه على المتأمّل ولا ضمنه صدر كتاب وأنا اسأل الله حسن الخاتمة ببركة الممدوح عليه افضل الصلوة والسلام،

قال المصنّف رحمه الله فرغت من تأليفى هذا الكتاب فى شهر ذى الحجّة الحرام سنة ستّ وعشرين وثمانمائة وحسبنا الله ونعم الوكيل....

Colophon:

وقع الفراغ من تكميله يوم الجمعة عاشر شهر شعبان الكريم سنة ثلاث وثمانين ومائة وألف وذلك بعناية سيّدنا الفقيه الافضل الآدب الاكمل شمس الدّين احمد بن اسمعيل الفضل ادام الله تعالى بقاه

See Ḥájjí Khalífa, vol. II, No. 1737; Pertsch, Gotha Cat., p. 488, **No. 2795**; and for other MSS. and commentaries, Brockelmann, II, 16. The complete work has been printed at Búláq and Cairo. An abridgment, entitled لمع حجّة من شرح بديعيّة ابن حجّة, by Muḥammad b. Aḥmad as-Samannúdí, is preserved at Paris in the Bibliothèque Nationale (De Slane, *Cat. des manuscrits arabes*, **No. 3218**).

Of this copy, which originally contained ff. 433, more than half has been lost. It begins on f. 1a = f. 246a:

اخذه الشيخ جمال الدّين نباتة وتقوّى عليه بالسيف فقال

ادعو السيوف صقيلة من لحظه　　واذا دعوتُ لماهُ جاوبنى الصدا

Ff. 187 of 29·1 and 19·5 c. and 19 ll. Ff. 159a–186a are written in a smaller hand and have 27 ll. on each page. Excellent large *naskhí* with headings of different colours. Vowel-points and other orthographical signs are frequently inserted. The date of transcription is that given above, *viz*., Sha'bán, 1183/November—December, 1769.

U. II (13).

الشعاع الشائع باللمعان، فى ذكر اسمآء أئمّة عمان، وما لهم فى العدل من الشّان،

A *qaṣída*, in praise of the Imáms of 'Umán, together with a copious historical commentary containing many citations in verse, by an author whose name is not mentioned.

Begins:

الحمد لله الذى جعل ائمّة العدل هم الضيآء المنجاب به الظلام، بعد الانبيآء عليهم السلام، ...امّا بعد لقد سألنى بعض الاخوان فى الدين، ان انظم قصيدة فى ائمّة عمان الصالحين، ...وأن اشرحها شرحا مختصرا مفيدا، او شرحا بسيطا لا يطلب العارف له مزيدا،

The opening verse of the *qaṣída* (f. 2a) lacks the double rhyme:

عمان (*sic*) عن لسان الحال رُدّى　　جوابا منك لى ارجو الجوابا

On f. 9a the author enters on his proper subject with the verse

كفى فخرًا عمان بالجَلَنْدا　　اذا اصطخبت بمفخره اصطخابا

referring to Julandá ibn Mas'úd, "the first of the rightful Imáms of 'Umán" (elected *circa* 134/751), and the list of his successors is carried down to the Imám Sulṭán ibn Murshid al-Ya'rubí, elected 1151/1738 (f. 131a). See G. P. Badger, *History of the Imâms and Seyyids of 'Omân* (Hakluyt Society, 1871).

Ff. 138 of 38 × 22 c. and 18 ll. Large coarse *nasta'líq* with rubrications. No colophon or date.

V. PERSIAN POETRY.

V. 1 (8).

قصائد منوچهری،

A very neat, modern MS. of the poems of Minúchihrí, copied in Bombay in 1290/1873 for a certain Ismá'íl Khán. The text appears to agree with that published by A. de Biberstein Kazimirski with a French translation and critical and historical Introduction in Paris in 1886–7. The text was also lithographed in Persia in 1297/1880. The poems are preceded by a short account of the poet in prose (ff. 1^b–3^a).

This MS., which I obtained from the Nawwáb Mírzá Ḥusayn-qulí Khán, the well-known Persian diplomatist, about 1884, when he was a student in London, comprises 132 ff. of 19·9 × 12 c. and 12 ll., and is written in a very elegant Persian *ním-shikasta* with rubrications.

V. 2 (9).

قصائد منوچهری،

Another copy of the above given to me by Dr Riẓá Tevfíq (Riḍá Tawfíq) in August, 1909, on one of his visits to England. It appears to agree with the last, and begins with the same biography of the poet. It comprises 140 ff. of 19·9 × 12·5 c. and 15 ll., and is written on tinted paper, between borders ruled in gold and red, in a good clear *ta'líq* with rubrications. At the end of the prose Introduction the copyist, Muḥammad Rashíd, states that he began to transcribe it on Muḥarram 22, 1295/Jan. 26, 1878, intending to present it, together with the *Díwán* of Yaghmá, to the *Fakhru'l-'Ulamá*. In the colophon on f. 138^a he states that he completed it on the 2nd of Rabí' 1 (March 6) of the same year, and asks consideration from the reader for any errors he may detect on the ground of the badness of his original and his own inadequate knowledge of literature:

چون مواد چندانی ندارم و نسخه هم خیلی غلط بود مستدعیم از ملاحظه کنندگان از غلط او چشم بپوشند و به تصحیح او بکوشند والسّلام،

V. 3 (9).

دیوان قطران،

A neatly written modern MS. of the poems of Qaṭrán of Tabríz, where Náṣir-i-Khusraw met him in 438/1046. Much light has been thrown on this poet and the attribution of many of his poems to his more celebrated predecessor Rúdakí by Sir

E. Denison Ross (who made use of this MS. amongst others in his researches) in an article entitled "Rúdakí and Pseudo-Rúdakí" published in the *J.R.A.S.* for October, 1924, pp. 609–644.

This MS., which formerly belonged to Riḍá-qulí Khán *Hidáyat*, and was apparently used by him in the compilation of his *Majma'u'l-Fuṣaḥá*, was obtained from the Belshah collection in January, 1920. It comprises 178 ff. of 21 × 12·5 c. and 17 ll. and is dated (on f. 95[b]) the 7th of Jumádà I, 1261/May 14, 1845, the copyist's name being given as 'Alí Akbar of Tafrísh. Written in a small, neat modern Persian *ta'líq*. On f. 3[a] Riḍá-qulí Khán has written in his own hand some account of the poet (whose death he places in 465/1072–3), together with a chronological list of contemporary and earlier princes and poets.

V. 4 (7).

ديوان ازرقى،

The *Díwán* of Azraqí (died about A.D. 1130), concerning whom see the second volume of my *Literary History of Persia*, p. 323.

This little MS. was given to me on June 6, 1913, by Mírzá 'Alí Akbar Káshif. It comprises 90 ff. of 16 × 9·8 c. and 12 ll., is written in a good, clear Persian *ta'líq* with some marginal notes in red, a short prose notice of the poet (ff. 1[b]–2[a]), and two rather faded miniatures, apparently depicting the poet reading and then presenting his book to his young patron, presumably Ṭughán-sháh. The text ends abruptly without date or colophon on f. 90[b].

V. 5 (8).

ديوان امير معزّى،

A neat modern MS. of the poems of Amír Mu'izzí, the poet-laureate of Sulṭán Sanjar the Saljúq, who died about 542/1147–8. See vol. II of my *Literary History of Persia*, pp. 327–330, etc.

This MS., obtained from the Belshah collection in January, 1921, comprises 248 ff. of 19·5 × 12·5 c. and 16 ll. It is written in a small, neat Persian *ta'líq*, and was completed on the 19th of Jumádà II, 1252/Oct. 1, 1836. A blank line has been left at the head of each *qaṣída* in which the copyist, son of Mashhadí 'Alí Akbar of Ashtiyán and Qum, probably intended to insert in red ink the name of the patron to whom it is dedicated.

V. 6 (9).

حديقة الحقيقة،

A good copy of the well-known *Ḥadíqatu'l-Ḥaqíqa*, or "Garden of Truth," composed in A.D. 1131 by Saná'í of Ghazna or Balkh, who is accounted the first of the three great mystical poets of Persia, the others being Shaykh Farídu'd-Dín 'Aṭṭár and Jalálu'd-Dín Rúmí. See vol. II of my *Literary History of Persia*, pp. 317–322, etc.

This MS., which I bought of Messrs R. D. Dickinson of 89 Farringdon Street, E.C., on March 30, 1899, for a guinea, comprises 316 ff. (some, such as ff. 312–315, missing) of 21 × 12·5 c. and 15 ll., written in a good and clear *ta'líq* with rubrications, undated, the first two pages ornamented with floral designs in gold.

V. 7 (14).

كلّيات شيخ فريد الدّين عطّار،

A fine large MS. with pictorial lacquer sides illustrating incidents in the lives of Ṣúfí saints, containing the *Kulliyyát*, or complete works, of the eminent mystical poet Shaykh Farídu'd-Dín 'Aṭṭár. See vol. II of my *Literary History of Persia*, pp. 506–515, and especially pp. 509–511, where attention is called to the extraordinary discrepancies of various biographers as to the year of his death, the dates given for which vary between 589/1193 and 632/1234–5. According to the most circumstantial account (given by Dawlatsháh, whose inaccuracy is, however, notorious) he perished in the sack of Níshápúr, his native town, by the Mongols in 627/1229–1230. Other MSS. of the *Kulliyyát* of 'Aṭṭár, or portions of them, are described by Rieu (Persian Catalogue, pp. 576–580); Ethé (Bodleian Pers. Cat., cols. 498–506; India Office Pers. Cat., cols. 612–627), etc.

This MS. was brought to Cambridge with others by Prince Ẓahíru's-Sulṭán in November, 1908, when he was driven into exile during the period of reaction which followed the destruction of the Persian *Majlis* and Constitution by Muḥammad 'Alí Sháh and his Russian aiders and abettors in the preceding summer; and was bought from him by me for £15, a small price for so excellent a book. It comprises the following 21 works of 'Aṭṭár, the list of which is given on f. 2^a, and the beginning of each of which is indicated by a small tag of red cloth attached to the margin of the initial page.

(1) *Tadhkiratu'l-Awliyá*, or "Memoirs of the Saints," the only prose work in the collection, of which the text, edited by Dr R. A. Nicholson, was published in my "Persian Historical Texts" Series in two volumes in 1905 and 1907. This occupies ff. 2^b–142^b of the MS.

(2) The *Jawharu'dh-Dhát* (ff. 143^b–253^b). At the end are written, in a cursive modern hand dated 1307/1889–90, two quatrains on the mutability of life and the transitoriness of all possessions. Beneath them is the signature "Ṣafá 'Alí."

(3) The *Iláhí-náma* (ff. 254^b–312^a). The same two quatrains with the same signature appear at the end of this poem also.

(4) The *Muṣíbat-náma* (ff. 313^b–391^b).

(5) The *Kanzu'l-Ḥaqá'iq* (ff. 392^{b}–405^{b}).

(6) The *Tarjamatu'l-Aḥádíth* (ff. 406^{b}–426^{a}). The last verse of this poem gives 699/1299–1300 as the date of completion, which throws great doubt on its authenticity, though 'Aṭṭár's name is mentioned in the third verse from the end:

گناهی نیز عطّار از برونست، که من از هرچه میگویم فزونست،
بیآمرزد بنقد آن بندهٔ حق، دهد این نسخه‌را با خلق رونق،
رساند نفع این بر خاص و عام این، که در ششصد نود نُه شد تمام این،

(7) The *Maẓharu'l-'Ajá'ib* (ff. 427^{b}–500^{a}). It is divided into two parts called *Daftar*, of which the second begins on f. 477^{b}, and contains answers to twenty-four questions.

(8) The *Asrár-náma* (ff. 501^{b}–534^{b}).
(9) The *Khusraw wa Gul* (ff. 535^{a}–619^{b}).
(10) The *Wuṣlat-náma* (ff. 620^{b}–635^{a}).
(11) The *Haft Wádí* (ff. 636^{b}–642^{b}).
(12) The *Khayyáṭ-náma* (ff. 643^{b}–653^{a}).
(13) The *Manṣúr-náma* (ff. 654^{b}–657^{b}).
(14) The *Miṣbáḥ-náma* (ff. 658^{b}–664^{b}).
(15) The *Pand-náma* (ff. 665^{b}–667^{b}).
(16) The *Manṭiqu'ṭ-Ṭayr* (ff. 668^{b}–699^{b}).
(17) The *Bulbul-náma* (ff. 700^{b}–704^{b}).
(18) The *Ushtur-náma* (ff. 705^{b}–732^{b}).
(19) The *Lisánu'l-Ghayb* (ff. 733^{b}–787^{a}).
(20) *Qaṣídas* and *Ghazals* (ff. 788^{b}–854^{a}).
(21) The *Mukhtár-náma* (ff. 855^{b}–914^{b}).

The MS. comprises 915 ff. of 33·5 × 20 c. and 25 ll. in four columns (*i.e.* two *bayts* or verses to the line). Written throughout in a small, neat, clear Persian *ta'líq* of no great antiquity with rubrications and illuminated *'unwáns* at the beginning of each component part. No date or colophon.

The former owner of this MS., Ẓahíru's-Sulṭán, though of the blood royal, was an enthusiastic supporter of the Constitution. After the *coup d'état* of June 23, 1908, he was one of those imprisoned by Muḥammad 'Alí Sháh in the *Bágh-i-Sháh* ("King's Garden"), and it was said that his cousin the Sháh only refrained from killing him because his mother (the Sháh's aunt) threatened to kill herself if he persisted in this intention. It was during his subsequent exile that he visited Cambridge on November 20, 1908. See my *Persian Revolution*, pp. 204, 208 and note, and 209. His father Ẓahíru'd-Dawla, whose proper name was 'Alí Khán Qájár, was Master of the Ceremonies (*Wazír-i-Tashrífát*) under Náṣiru'd-Dín Sháh, with whom he was a great favourite, and who gave him his daughter Furúghu'd-Dawla (the lady above mentioned) in marriage. He was a notable *Murshid*, or spiritual guide, and the Head of an Order of Dervishes.

V. 8 (9).

مظهر العجايب شيخ عطّار،

A MS. written in a very cursive Persian *ta'líq* and completed in Ṣafar 1286/May—June, 1869, of the *Maẓharu'l-'Ajá'ib* of Shaykh Farídu'd-Dín 'Aṭṭár. It was obtained from the Belshah collection in January, 1920, and comprises 264 ff. of 21·3 × 15·9 c. and 16 ll. (*bayts*) in the body of the text with 12 in the margin. It appears to contain at least two different poems. The first, beginning:

آفرين جان آفرين بر جان جان، زآنكه او هست آشكارا و نهان،

is the *Maẓharu'l-'Ajá'ib*. It ends on f. 142[b], and is followed, after a short colophon and a new *Bismi'lláh*, by a "second book" (دفتر ثانى), another *mathnawí* poem in a different metre (*hazaj* instead of *ramal*) beginning:

شوى واصل بدرياى يقين تو، انا الحق گوئى و منصور بين تو،

From a prose statement on ff. 262[a]–263[b], beginning "here ends the Book of the *Maẓharu'l-'Ajá'ib*," it would appear that the copyist's object was to prove that it was really written by 'Aṭṭár, a fact denied by the *'ulamá* of Samarqand, who caused it to be publicly burned as spurious and heretical in the beginning of Rajab 882/Oct. 9, 1477, and that similar Shí'a tendencies are to be found in other poems by 'Aṭṭár. Presumably some of the citations given are from these, for the contents of the volume seem too extensive to represent only this one poem. On f. 263[b] a number of citations from various poets are given to show how highly 'Aṭṭár was esteemed by such men as Shaykh Maḥmúd Shabistarí, Jámí, Kátibí of Níshápúr, and Jalálu'd-Dín Rúmí.

V. 9 (10).

ديوان كمال الدّين اسمعيل،

A fine old MS. (incomplete at end and undated, but apparently of the 14th century of the Christian era) of the *Díwán* of Kamálu'd-Dín Ismá'íl of Iṣfahán, for whose death dates ranging between 628/1230–1 and 639/1241–2 are given by different authorities, though Dawlatsháh and most other historians and biographers say that he perished in the massacre made by the Mongols in 635/1237–8. See Rieu's Persian Cat., pp. 580–581, and my *Literary History of Persia*, vol. II, pp. 540–542, etc. A list of his chief patrons is given in both places. Others to whom poems are addressed in this volume include:

الصاحب السيّد نظام الملك (f. 31[b])، الصاحب تاج الدّين على بن كريم الشرف (f. 32[b])، صدر الدّين عمر الخجندى (f. 120[a])، الصاحب نظام الدّين محمّد (f. 126[b])، الصاحب فخر الدّين بن نظام الدّين (f. 129[a])، الامير ضياء الدّين البيابانكى (f. 133[a])، الصاحب عميد الدّين الفارسى (f. 136[a])، الصاحب شهاب الدّين عزيزان الساوى (f. 138[a])، الصدر بهاء الدّين عبدوس (f. 141[b])، ضياء الدّين زنگى (f. 163[b])،

The *qaṣídas* (ff. 1^b–174^b) also include an elegy on the death of his father Jalálu'd-Dín 'Abdu'r-Razzáq (f. 55^a) and an "answer" to a *qaṣída* by Ruknu'd-Dín *Da'wá-dár* (? *Dawídár*: f. 153^b). There is also a *mathnawí* (ff. 174^b–177^a) satirizing the *Ra'ís-i-Lunbán*, beginning:

تا زبانم بکام جُنبانست، در ثناء رئیس لنبانست،
چه رئیس آن خسیس پر تلبیس، مایهٔ ظلم و سایهٔ ابلیس،

The "Fragments" (*Muqaṭṭa'át*) occupy ff. 177^a–242^b, and include panegyrics on Zaynu'd-Dín as-Suhrawardí (f. 216^b) and the Amír Náṣiru'd-Dín al-Mankalí (f. 218^a). The Odes (*Ghazaliyyát*), not arranged in alphabetical order and containing no *takhalluṣ*, occupy ff. 242^b–275^b, and the Quatrains (*Rubá'iyyát*) the remainder of the volume.

The MS., acquired from the Belshah collection in January, 1920, comprises 290 ff. of 24·2 × 16·9 c. and 24 ll., and is written in a clear but ungraceful old *naskh* with rubrications. The spelling as well as the writing is archaic. To the initial *qaṣídas*, which are in praise of God, is prefixed, instead of the *Bismi'lláh*, the illuminated heading:

و لذکر الله اعلى و اجلّ،

V. 10 (14).

ديوان شمس تبريز،

A very large collection of the Odes of Jalálu'd-Dín Rúmí, commonly known as the *Díwán-i-Shams-i-Tabríz*. See R. A. Nicholson's *Selected Odes* from that *Díwán* (Cambridge, 1898), which contains a full and excellent critical study of the whole subject; and my *Lit. Hist. of Persia*, vol. II, pp. 515–525, etc.

This MS., acquired from the Belshah collection in January, 1920, comprises 426 ff. of 33·8 × 21·8 c. and 31 ll., is written in a small and legible, but ungraceful *ta'líq*, and was completed by "the least of physicians" Mírzá Muḥammad 'Alí of Ṭihrán on the 21st of Shawwál, 1282/March 9, 1866. The volume cannot contain much fewer than 49,000 verses (*bayts*).

V. 11 (7).

مثنوی معنوی،

A neat and compactly written MS. of the celebrated *Mathnawí* of Jalálu'd-Dín Rúmí, given to me on April 26, 1903, by the late Sir Mark Sykes, who bought it in Syria.

Ff. 268 of 16 × 11 c. and 27 ll. in four columns (two *bayts* to the line). Copied in 1040/1630–1 in Saráy by a Mevleví dervish named Muṣṭafá in the then new monastery or retreat (*Záwiya-i-Jadída*) recently established for that Order.

V. 12 (10).

مثنوی معنوی،

Another complete MS. of the *Mathnawí*, copied at Yazd in 1012/1603, and formerly in the possession of the late Professor Cowell, who thought highly of its accuracy. The MS. has been badly wormed, but has been carefully repaired, in the earlier part by Professor E. B. Cowell and Professor E. H. Palmer, and in the later part by the binder, Mr F. E. Stoakley of Green Street, Cambridge, to whom I entrusted its restoration. Professor Cowell appears, from a note at the beginning, to have bought it in 1850 from Messrs Allen and Co., from one of whose catalogues the printed slip describing it which is affixed to the opposite leaf is presumably taken. Under his signature is the following note in Professor Cowell's handwriting:

"A well-written MS., but sadly worm-eaten. It has a good text, though occasionally abridged, and the scholia are very useful. E. B. C.

"Written at Yazd A.H. 1012 (A.D. 1603).

"The handwriting of the text and the notes appears to be the same, and in some places where the notes are numerous the lines of the text are much fewer than usual, as, *e.g.*, fol. 56[a] in Book I."

Ff. 396 of 23·6 × 13·6 c. and 19 ll. (*bayts*) in the centre of the page and 32 ll. (16 *bayts*) in the margin. In the outer margin are many notes and glosses. Written in a small and legible *ta'líq* with rubrications, the marginal notes in a very minute hand, and dated in the colophon (on f. 394[a]) Ramaḍán 27, 1012/Feb. 28, 1604. The scribe's name, except the first part, "Ḥusayn ibn...," is illegible.

V. 13 (10).

مثنوی معنوی (دفتر اوّل)،

A fine old (probably fourteenth century) copy of Book I of the *Mathnawí*, defective at both ends, and presenting many dislocations and lacunae. Thus f. 12[a] contains part of the first story, with the rubric:

فرستادن باذشاه رسولان بسمرقند بآوردن زرگر،

while the first rubric on f. 5[a]:

دزدیدن مارگیر ماری‌را از مارگیری دیگر،

comes from a later part of the text.

The last rubric (on f. 108[b]) is:

گفتن بیغامبر علیه السلم مر زیدرا که این سررا فاش‌تر ازین مگو و متابعت نگه دار،

In its present state the MS. comprises 108 ff. of 24·7 × 16 c. and 19 ll. (*bayts*) to the page; in all something under 4000 *bayts*. It is written in a large, clear, archaic ***naskh***, probably of the fourteenth Christian (eighth Muḥammadan) century. It was acquired from the Belshah collection in January, 1920.

V. 14 (7).

منتخبات مثنوی،

A small MS. volume containing (ff. 3^b–30^b) selections from the *Mathnawí*, compiled in 943/1536–7. At the end the compiler has added the five following verses of his own:

چونك كرد الطاف مولی فتح باب، مفردات مثنوی شد انتخاب،
بر امید آنك آن سلطان عشق، سازد این درمانده‌را درمان عشق،
این دل گمراه‌را ره‌بین کند، غرق بحر عشق شمس الدین کند،
اختیارم می کند آن پاك ذات، مثنوی شد انتخاب مفردات[1]،
بدین (?) تاریخ گزینش بشنوی، هست لولوهای درج مثنوی،
تاریخ سنه ثلث و اربعین و تسعمائه،

As the chronogram appears to give 901/1495–6, the date 943/1536–7 may indicate the date of transcription.

These extracts are followed (ff. 31^b–40^a) by an anonymous Persian tract entitled *Mir'átu'l-Qulúb*, beginning, after the doxology:

...امّا بعد، بدان ای طالب علم یقین و ای کاشف اسرار دین که این فقیر چند کلمه از کنوز واردات غیبی در معنی حدیث نبوی صلّعم ادا کرده تا سالکانرا مرات رؤیت گردد...و این رساله مشتمل است بسه دایره و این رساله‌را نام نهاده شد مرآت القلوب تا در میان اهل اشارت محبوب گردد والله الموفّق والمعین، قال رسول الله صلّعم من أراد ان یجلس مع الله فلیجلس مع اهل التصوّف الخ

There are diagrams of the "three circles" to which allusion is made above, and at the end a *qaṣída* of some eighty verses beginning:

اشجار باغ‌راست ز دیبای چین قبا، ازهار تاج‌وار ز مبدع شدش عطا،

The MS. was one of thirteen bought of J. J. Naaman for £25 in May, 1902. It comprises 40 ff. of 16·6 × 12·3 and 13–15 ll., and is written throughout in an ungraceful but legible *ta'líq*.

V. 15 (9).

كلّيات سعدی،

A neatly written MS. of the *Kulliyyát*, or Complete Works, of Sa'dí, bought of Gejou for £4 on Nov. 1, 1904. It comprises 443 ff. of 22 × 14·6 c. and 17 ll. in the body of the page and 12 in the margin, and is written in a good and legible *ta'líq* with rubrications. It is undated, but the copyist gives his name as Shaykh

[1] So corrected in pencil. Originally مفردات stood at the beginning instead of the end of the line.

Murshidu'd-Dín Muḥammad, while a note on f. 1ª states that in the year 1210/1795–6 it was in the possession of one of the inmates of the *Mevleví* [*Mawlawí*]-*Khána* of Galata, Constantinople, whose name has been cut off by the binder, but who describes himself as خادم میدان غالب دده.

There is inserted at the beginning the following table of contents:

رسالهٔ مجالس ۲، رسالهٔ سؤال صاحب دیوان ۱۷، رسالهٔ عقل و عشق ۱۸، نصیحة الملوك ۲۰، رسالهٔ سلطان اباقا ۲۸، حکایهٔ ملك انکیاتو ۲۹، حکایت ملك شمس الدّین تازیگوی ۳۰، گلستان ۳۱، بُسْتان ۹۹، قصاید عربی ۱۹۵، قصاید فارسی ۱۹۹، کتاب المراثی ۲۲۷، کتاب الملمّعات ۲۳۱، کتاب الترجیعات ۲۳۶، کتاب طیّبات ۲۴۱، کتاب البدایع ۳۳۲، کتاب خواتیم ۳۷۴، غزلیّات قدیم ۳۸۷، کتاب صاحبیّه ۳۹۶، کتاب رباعیّات ۴۱۷، کتاب المفردات ۴۲۴، کتاب المطایبات ۴۲۷، کتاب الخبیثات ۴۳۵، مجلس ثانی فی الهزل ۴۳۸، مضحکات ۴۴۲،

V. 16 (8).

بُسْتان سعدی،

A neatly written and undated but fairly modern copy of the *Bustán* of Sa'dí, given to me in Cairo, in March, 1903, by Ḥájjí Niyáz of Kirmán. Ff. 142 of 20 × 12·5 c. and 14 ll.; small, neat and legible *ta'líq* with headings in blue.

V. 17 (8).

بُستان با شرح سودی،

The *Bustán*, with the Turkish translation and commentary of Súdí the Bosnian, who died in or after Shawwál, 1006/May, 1598, when he completed this work. See Rieu's Turkish Catalogue, pp. 158–159, and Flügel's Vienna Catalogue, vol. 1, p. 541.

This MS. was one of my earliest acquisitions, and was, I think, bought from Quaritch about 1883. It comprises 176 ff. of 20 × 14 c. and 27 ll., and is written in a legible but ungraceful Turkish *ta'líq* with rubrications, the Persian text also being overlined with red. It was copied by one Aḥmad ibn Bálí and completed in Jumádà II, 1065/April—May, 1655.

V. 18 (9).

گلستان سعدی،

A very pretty MS. of the *Gulistán* of Sa'dí, given to me by the late Mr E. J. W. Gibb about 1883. It comprises 134 ff. of 22·5 × 15·5 c. and 11 ll., and is written in a good *ta'líq* hand between gold and blue marginal lines with gold headings and pages powdered with gold, and is undated.

V. 19 (9).

گلستان (ترجمه‌سی)،

An anonymous Turkish translation of the *Gulistán*, transcribed by one 'Abdí ibn Nabí (?) in the middle of Jumádà I, 1011/Nov. 1, 1602. The verses are given in the original Persian, followed by a Turkish prose translation.

This MS., which was given to me by Dr Riḍá Tawfíq (Riẓá Tevfíq) in August, 1909, comprises 101 ff. of 20·4 × 13 c. and 15 ll., is written in a large, clear *naskh*, fully pointed.

V. 20 (6).

مقطّعات ابن يمين،

A neat little manuscript of the "Fragments" (*Muqaṭṭa'át*) of Amír Maḥmúd ibn Yamíni'd-Dín (d. 769/1367–8), commonly called Ibn-i-Yamín, a notable poet of the Sarbadárí court. His father, Amír Yamínu'd-Dín, settled at Faryúmad in the reign of the Mongol Khudá-banda, and died in 724/1324. See my *Persian Literature under Tartar Dominion*, pp. 211–222. An edition of the "Fragments" (but much less extensive than this MS.) was printed at Calcutta in 1865, and a German verse-rendering of many of them by Schlechta-Wssehrd was published at Vienna in 1852.

This MS., concerning the acquisition of which I have no note, comprises 142 ff. of 13·3 × 7·8 c. and 11 ll., and is written in a small and beautiful *ta'líq* with headings in blue. The transcription was completed on Rajab 5, 881/October 24, 1476.

V. 21 (6).

گلشن راز،

A poor and modern copy of the *Gulshan-i-Ráz*, or "Rose-garden of Mystery," of Shaykh Maḥmúd-i-Shabistarí, a celebrated compendium of Ṣúfí doctrine in Persian *mathnawí* verse first made known in Europe by Dr Tholuck a century ago, and edited with English translation by E. H. Whinfield in 1880. See my *Persian Literature under Tartar Dominion*, pp. 146–150, Rieu's Persian Catalogue, pp. 608–609, etc. The work was composed in 710/1311 in answer to questions submitted to the author from Khurásán. The text of this work occupies ff. 1ᵇ–48ᵇ, and is followed by two short prose treatises, the first on Oneiromancy (ff. 49ᵃ–58ᵇ), the second on the Science of the Breath (ff. 59ᵃ–66ᵇ).

Ff. 66 of 15 × 10·5 c. and 12 ll.; poor but legible *ta'líq*; dated 1223/1808.

V. 22 (7).

ديوان سلمان ساوجی،

A good MS. of the *Díwán* of Salmán of Sáwa, who was born about 700/1300 and died about 778/1376. See my *Persian Literature under Tartar Dominion*, pp. 260–271, where reference is made to the best studies of his life and works, and pp. 296–298, where parallels between his poems and those of Ḥáfiẓ are given.

This MS. is undated, but the scribe gives his name (f. 125ᵇ) as "Ḥáfiẓ of Shíráz" (كتبه الفقير الحقير حافظ شيرازى)—not, of course, the great Ḥáfiẓ. I bought it for 13*s.* at the sale by auction, on June 5, 1890, of the Fiott-Hughes collection, when many fine MSS. were disposed of at very low prices. I had an opportunity of examining and cataloguing all these MSS. before the sale, for which my catalogue was printed, and which I attended, noting the prices at which the MSS. were sold, and acquiring a few which were knocked down at prices within my then available means. Another of the MSS. I then acquired, which will be described immediately under the class-mark **V. 25**, is in the same writing and bears the name of the same scribe, with the addition of the date 869/1464–5. I only noticed this identity of handwriting and of the scribe's name immediately before the sale. The two MSS. are identical in form as well as script, but the effect of **V. 25** being dated was to raise its price to £3. 7*s.* 6*d.*

Ff. 128 of 17·1 × 11·8 c. and 15 or 16 ll.; written in a curious, rather stilted *nasta'líq* with rubrications.

V. 23 (10).

ديوان سلمان ساوجی،

Another MS. of the *Díwán* of Salmán of Sáwa, bought with 12 other MSS. from J. J. Naaman for £25 in May, 1902.

Ff. 110 of 24·5 × 17 c. and 17 ll., written in a good, clear *ta'líq*, undated. There is an erasure at the end (f. 109ᵇ) where there may have been a colophon, though it looks more like the beginning of a poem, in which case the MS. probably lacks one leaf or more at the end.

V. 24 (10).

جام جم اوحدی،

A good, neatly written MS. of the *Jám-i-Jam* ("Cup of Jamshíd") of Awḥadí of Marágha, who died about 738/1337–8. See my *Persian Literature under Tartar Dominion*, pp. 141–146, where reference is made (p. 141, n. 2) to this MS.

This MS., bought for £4. 10*s.* 0*d.* from J. J. Naaman on May 7, 1903, comprises 154 pp. of 24 × 14 c. and 15 ll., is written in a large, clear *ta'líq* between margins ruled in blue and gold, and is dated Dhu'l-Ḥijja, 916/March, 1511. This may, however, be the date of the original from which it was copied, as the present MS. looks a good deal more modern.

V. 25 (7).

دیوان خواجوی کرمانی،

The *Díwán* of Khwájú of Kirmán, who died about 742/1341–2. See my *Persian Literature under Tartar Dominion*, pp. 222–229, and references there given.

This MS., bought at the auction of the Fiott-Hughes MSS. (**No. 75** of the Catalogue) on June 5, 1890, for £3. 7*s*. 6*d*., as already mentioned above in the article on **V. 22**, comprises 155 ff. of 17·6 × 13·2 c. and 15 ll., and is written in the same curious, angular *nasta'líq* as its companion volume, **V. 22**, but has the fuller colophon on f. 152^b:

كتبه الفقير الحقير المحتاج الى رحمة الله تعالى درويش حافظ شيرازى غفر الله له ولجميع المسلمين سنة ٨٦٩

The total number of verses is given as 4000.

V. 26 (9).

دیوان خواجوی کرمانی،

Another quite modern MS. of the *Díwán* of Khwájú of Kirmán, sent to me as a gift by Mírzá 'Alí Akbar Káshif, by whom I think the copy was made, on June 6, 1913.

The MS. comprises 159 pp. of 20·6 × 13·3 c. and 17 ll., is written in a cursive *ním-shikasta* hand, and was completed in Ṭihrán on Ramaḍán 25, 1330/Sept. 7, 1912.

V. 27 (10).

مهر و مشتری تألیف عصّار تبریزی،

The romance of *Mihr u Mushtarí* by 'Aṣṣár of Tabríz, who completed it on Shawwál 10, 778/Feb. 20, 1377, only a year or two before his death. See Rieu's Persian Catalogue, pp. 626–627, and, for a full analysis of the poem, Sir Gore Ouseley's *Biographical Notices of Persian Poets*, pp. 201–226.

This MS. I bought in Constantinople with two others for 200 piastres on April 23, 1908. It comprises 173 ff. (of which f. 1, containing the opening lines of the poem, is missing) of 24·3 × 16·5 c. and 12 ll., is written in a fairly good *ta'líq*, and is without date or colophon.

V. 28 (8).

غازان‌نامه،

A very interesting and rare (if not unique) account in Persian verse of the reign of Gházán Khán the Mongol (reigned A.D. 1295–1304: see my *Persian Literature under Tartar Dominion*, pp. 40–46), composed in 758/1357 for Sulṭán Shaykh Uways of the Jalá'irí or Ílkhání dynasty (reigned A.H. 757–777 = A.D. 1356–1375) by Khwája Núru'd-Dín, whose father Shamsu'd-Dín appears to have been a Minister (*Wazír*) of Gházán Khán, and who earned the favour of Shaykh Uways by curing him within a prescribed period of fourteen days of an illness with which he was afflicted, and which baffled the other physicians.

This fine MS., which was given to me in August, 1909, by Dr Riḍá Tawfíq (Riẓá Tevfíq), was made in Tabríz by Khuṭúṭí of Shírwán, and was completed on the 9th of Dhu'l-Ḥijja, 873/June 20, 1469. It appears from an Arabic dedication written in gold in a fine large *naskh* on ff. 1ᵇ–2ᵃ that it was made for the library of the Sulṭán Abú Naṣr Ḥasan Bahádur Khán, on whom a whole page of high-sounding titles are bestowed. This dedication is followed on ff. 2ᵇ–3ᵃ by the following prose account of the circumstances which led to the composition of the poem:

هذا لنسخه (*sic*) من كلام قدوة العرفا خواجه نور الدّين،

گفتار اندر بيان تصنيف كتاب غازان‌نامه من كلام قدوة العرفا والمحقّقين زبدة الحكماء المهندسين و نقاوة الاطبّاء المتأخّرين نتيجة الصحابة سيّد المرسلين ابّد الله تعالى روحه بخلد البرين، نقل است كه در ايّام زمان دولت سلطان المغفور المبرور غازان خان انار الله برهانه محمودًا پدر خواجه نور الدّين خواجه شمس الدّين محمّد الاژدرى موسوم باسم وزارت بوده است و بانواع فنون و كمالات آراسته، چون نوبت زمان دولت غازان‌خانى بپادشاه رعيّت‌پرور عدل‌گستر سلطان اويس رسيد خواجه نور الدّين در سنّ چهارده سالگى بعلم طبّ و نجوم و اصناف علوم رياضى مشغول بوده و اتّفاقًا درآن روزگار سلطان اويس‌را در موضع بردعه عارضهٔ مهلكه حادث شده چنانچه جماعت اطّبا از معالجهٔ آن مرض عاجز مانده و سلطان فرموده كه كرهًا و جبرًا خطّى بدهيد كه بچند وقت اين علّت مرتفع شود هر يك در حالت اضطرارى بى اختيار وعدهٔ دور و نزديك ميداده از جهت قابليّتى كه خواجه نور الدّين‌را بوده (f. 3ᵃ) با وجود صغر سنّ در اوان تحصيل از شهر تبريز احضار كرده اند و او متعهّد شده و خط داده تا مدّت چهارده روز و اطبّارا اجازه گفته و بموعود مذكور حضرت واهب العطايا عزّ اسمه از دار الشفاء غيب سلطانرا صحّت كرامت كرده سلطان بعد از صحّت و خلاص از علّت تربيت و شفقت در حقّ خواجه نور الدّين باعلى مرتبه فرموده و گفته كه هرچه ملتمس او باشد مبذول گردد، مولانا مشار اليه التماس امضا احكام ادرار موروثى غازانى نموده و آن ادرار مذكور مبلغ صد هزار دينار غازانى بوده بدو مسلّم داشته اند، بعد از آن مولانا مشار اليه در صدد آن آمده كه از عهدهٔ شكر اين نعمت بيرون آيد از الهامات غيبى ملهم شده كه چون از آن خاندان بزرگوار بدين بندهٔ حقير اين عارفهٔ عامّه عايد گشت واجب ديد و لازم شمرد

که خدمتی بجای آورد که بر بیاض صفحات اوراق ایّام سواد نقوش معانی آن صورت مرقوم گشته باقی ماند، چون اعتماد بر قوّت و قدرت طبع موزون خود داشت در وزن شصت هزار بیت شاهنامه ده هزار بیت غازان‌نامه باتمام رسانید والله اعلم،

This poem, therefore, is one of the many imitations of Firdawsí's *Sháh-náma*, recording in some 10,000 verses the history of Gházán Khán and his predecessors; and, though it contains many fanciful legends, it probably contains also historical matter of importance, since it was composed little more than fifty years after his death. It seems, therefore, worth while to give the headings of the sections. It begins on f. 3[b] under a beautiful *'unwán*:

سر آغاز دفتر نخستین سخن، بنام خداوند چرخ کهن،
بر آرندهٔ گوهر تابناک، نگارندهٔ کشور آب و خاک،

The subsequent headings are as follows:

در مراتب خرد و سخن گوید (f. 4[b], end)،
در مراتب نفس گوید (f. 5[b])،
در آفرینش عالم گوید (f. 6[a])،
در ستایش پیغمبر علیه السلام گوید (f. 6[b])،
در ستایش پادشاه اسلام شیخ اویس (f. 8[a])،
در نصیحت فرزند گوید (f. 10[a])،
در سبب نظم کتاب گوید (f. 12[a])،

In this section the author says that he was fifty years of age at the time of writing:

مرا سالیان چون به پنجه کشید، جوانی شد و روز پیری رسید،

and gives the date of composition (f. 13[a], l. 5) as 758/1357:

پس از هفتصد سال و پنجاه و هشت، که از دور سالار دین بر گذشت،
نهادم یکی گنج پر مایه رنج، کزو پر گهر شد سرای سپنج،

Sulṭán Shaykh Uways, to whom the poem is dedicated, is then mentioned (f. 14[b], l. 2):

بماناد این شاهِ فرّخ نژاد، که تا نام او زنده دارد بداد،
سر سرکشان جهان شیخ اویس، کزو هست با آب و با رنگ بیس،
جهانگیر و با ارج و گیتی ستان، خردمند و با رای و روشن روان،

The narrative now begins with the reign of Chingíz Khán and his successors:

پادشاهی جنگیز خان بیست [و] پنج سال بود (f. 14[a])،
پادشاهی اوکتای شش سال [و] دو ماه بود (f. 16[a])،
پادشاهی هولاکوه خان نه سال [و] سه ماه بود (f. 16[b])،
پادشاهی اباقا خان هفده سال [و] سه ماه بود (f. 17[b])،
ولادت غازان خان از مادر (f. 18[a])،

The date of Gházán Khán's birth in Mázandarán is given as Friday, 20th Ádhár, 670 A.H.:

چو از گاه هجرت ز دور هلال، بهفتاد و ششصد گرائید سال،
به نیکوترین ساعتی صبحگاه، شب جمعه عشرین آذار ماه،
هلالی ز برج بزرگی بتافت، کزو تاج و تخت و نگین زیب یافت،

طلب کردن اباقا غازانرا (f. 20b)،

پادشاهی احمد خان دو سال و دو ماه بود (f. 23b)،

پادشاهی ارغون خان هفت سال بود (f. 25b)،

رفتن نوروز بخراسان بجنگ بوقای شهریار (f. 27a)،

رزم کردن غازان با نوروز (f. 31b)،

نامه نوشتن غازان بنزد ارغون و مدد خواستن لشکر (f. 34a)،

لشکر فرستادن ارغون بمدد غازان بخراسان (f. 35b)،

گریختن نوروز بترکستان و آوردن دو شهزاده ابوکان و ایکوتمر (f. 38b)،

خراب کردن ابوکان شهر اسفرائین‌را و رفتن بترکستان زمین (f. 43b)،

گرفتن غازان حصار دامغان‌را (f. 45b)،

پادشاهی کی‌خاتو خان سه سال [و] نه ماه بود (f. 48a)،

دیدن غازان دختر مهراب‌را بخواب و عاشق شدن بر وی (f. 49b)،

دیدن دخت مهراب درد غازانرا و عاشق شدن بر وی (f. 53a)،

پشیمان شدن نوروز و آشتی جستن با غازان خان (f. 59a)،

صفت زمستان (f. 63b)،

پادشاهی بای‌دو خان نه ماه بود (f. 68b)،

آمدن غازان خان بآذربیجان و رزم کردن بایدو با او (f. 69b)،

رزم کردن غازان با بای‌دو خان (f. 74a)،

گرفتن بایدو و نوروزرا و حیلت کردن نوروز با او (f. 79b)،

اسلام پذیرفتن غازان محمود بر دست شیخ صدر الدّین حموی علیه الرحمة (f. 83b)،

فرستادن بایدو شیخ محمودرا برسولی بغازان و فریب دادن نوروز رسولانرا (f. 86b)،

مهمانی کردن رسولان و جاده کردن نوروز (f. 89a)،

رسیدن نوروز بشهر تبریز و گرفتار شدن بایدو خان (f. 91b)،

آمدن غازان بشهر تبریز و سزا دادن امرای گناه‌کار (f. 98a)،

بد گفتن امرا در حق نوروز پیش شاه غازان و متغیّر شدن غازان برو (f. 99b)،

عروسی کردن غازان با بلغان خواتون (f. 102a)،

پادشاهی غازان نه سال بود (f. 104a)،

رفتن نوروز بجنگ ترکان بخراسان زمین (f. 106b)،

جنگ کردن نوروز با سوکا و گریختن او بجانب کرهرود (f. 109b)،

گرفتن هورقداق سوکارا بشهر خرقان [و] کشته شدن سوکا (f. 116a)،

رفتن هورقداق بجانب مرغان و قهر کردن غازان خان دشمنانرا (f. 118a)،
جنگ کردن ارسلان با امرای غازان خان (f. 119b)،
شکار کردن غازان بکوههای گیلان و پند دادن شیخ زاهد غازانرا (f. 123a)،
پاسخ دادن غازان محمود شیخ زاهدرا (f. 129a)،
جواب دادن زاهد غازان‌را (f. 129b)،
رفتن غازان بجانب بغداد بعزم قلامیشی (f. 134b)،
وزارت صدر جاوی[1] و فتنه انگیختن میان نوروز [و] غازان (f. 138a)،
نامه نوشتن صدر جادی[1] بنوروز از زبان غازان و بازی دادن اورا (f. 139a)،
گرفتار شدن قیصر جاسوس (f. 144a)،
نامه نوشتن نوروز بشاه مصر [و] شام (f. 144b)،
پاسخ نامهٔ نوروز (f. 145b)،
مکر انگیختن صدر جادی و کشته شدن قیصر و پسر و برادر نوروز (f. 147b)،
رفتن قتلوغشاه بگرفتن نوروز بخراسان (f. 153b)،
رزم نوروز با قتلوغشاه (f. 156a)،
گریختن نوروز بشهر هری و پناه بردن بملك فخر الدّین (f. 161a)،
اندیشه کردن ملك فخر الدّین با بزرگان شهر در گرفتن نوروز (f. 166b)،
صفت بهار (f. 172a)،
نامه نوشتن غازان باطراف جهان بدلخوشی رعایا و کشته شدن صدر جادی و وزارت خواجه رشید الدّین (f. 175b)،
داستان درویش با نوشیروان و مثل نیکوکاران (f. 179b)،
وزارت خواجه رشیدین (f. 182b: *sic*)،
لشکر کشیدن سولامیش از مرز روم و جنگ کردن جوبان و سوتای و قتلوغشاه با او (f. 185a)،
آغاز داستان (f. 186a)،
رفتن سولامیش بمصر و آوردن لشکر و جنگ کردن با امراء ایران (f. 189a)،
خبر بردن سولامیش بغازان خان طاب ثراه (f. 191a)،
شکار کردن غازان بکوهها کردستان و رفتن بدیر رهبان و سؤال و جواب با او (f. 192a)،
آمدن غازان بایران زمین و کشتن سولامیش‌را (f. 201a)،
خواستن غازان خان کرمون‌را و عروسی کردن (f. 202b)،
سخن گفتن امرای مصر [و] شام با غازان خان محمود (f. 205a)،
گرد کردن غازان لشکررا و رفتن بجنگ مصر و شام (f. 212b)،
لشکر کشیدن غازان بدیار مصر [و] شام (f. 213a)،
نامه نوشتن غازان بملك ناصر (f. 215b)،
پاسخ نامهٔ غازان محمود (f. 217a)،
جنگ بزرگ (f. 224a)،

---

[1] It is impossible to say for certain whether this name is جادی or جاوی.

رزم کردن زواره با زاور (f. 225^{a})‘
رزم کر[دن] مظفّر با زاور و کشته شدن زاور (f. 225^{b})‘
رزم کردن مظفّر با جهان پهلوان (f. 226^{a})‘
رزم کردن مظفّر با ارکوان (f. 226^{b})‘
رزم کردن مظفّر با نرّ دیو (f. 227^{a})‘
رزم کردن مظفّر با قرای جندی (f. 228^{a})‘
رزم کردن مظفّر با ازکبوس (f. 228^{b})‘
رزم کردن مظفّر با پولاد رومی (f. 229^{a})‘
رزم کردن مظفّر با اسکندر دیوبند (f. 230^{a})‘
باز آمدن غازان محمود بآذربیجان (f. 239^{b})‘
مهمانی کردن خواجه نصیر الدّین طوسی غازانرا و سؤال پادشاه از وی و تاریخ احکام سلطان الزّمان ابو ٱلنّصر حسن بیگ بهادر خان (f. 242^{a})‘

This section presents a somewhat curious chronological puzzle, for while, as we have seen, the poem was composed in 758/1357 for Sulṭán Uways, this manuscript was written for Abú Naṣr Ḥasan Beg Bahádur Khán in 873/1469. How, then, can mention of the latter occur in a poem written more than a century earlier? His name occurs only in the title of this section, not in the poem itself, so that the most likely conjecture is that it was inserted there by the scribe to give an unwarranted precision to the vague prophecies ascribed to Naṣíru'd-Dín Ṭúsí.

لشکر کشیدن غازان محمود بار دوم بجانب مصر [و] شام (f. 245^{a})‘
نامه کردن غازان محمود بملك ناصر (f. 247^{a})‘
پاسخ غازان محمود (f. 248^{a})‘
شکار کردن غازان بکوههای لگزستان (f. 249^{a})‘
آغاز داستان (f. 249^{b})‘
رفتن غازان در غار و کشتن اژدها و ره نمودن پیر دانا بسر گنج اسکندر (f. 250^{a})‘
سؤال و جواب غازان با پیر غار (f. 251^{b})‘
آگهی دادن پیر غار غازان‌را از گنج اسکندر (f. 253^{b})‘
بندهایی که بر کنار تاج اسکندر نبشته بود (f. 256^{a})‘
زاری کردن بلغان خواتون از دوری غازان (f. 259^{a})‘
باز آمدن غازان بلشکرگاه خود (f. 261^{b})‘
صفت خرگاه که از بهر غازان ساخته بودند و خطبه کردن در وی (f. 263^{b})‘
خطبه خواندن غازان (f. 264^{b})‘
بر انداختن آیینهاء بد و نهادن رسمهای نیکو (f. 267^{b})‘
آثاری که از غازان محمود بظهور آمده است (f. 268^{b})‘
نکته (f. 269^{a})‘ (f. 271^{a})‘ (f. 273^{a})‘ (f. 274^{a})‘ (f. 275^{b})‘ (f. 276^{a})‘ (f. 280^{b})‘ etc.

تنبیه (f. 270^{a})‘ (f. 271^{a})‘ (f. 284^{a})‘

فایده (f. 272^{b})‘ (f. 273^{b})‘ (f. 274^{b})‘ (f. 277^{b})‘ (f. 278^{a})‘ (f. 282^{b})‘ (f. 283^{b})‘ etc.

لطیفه (f. 277^{a})‘ (f. 281^{b})‘ (f. 283^{a})‘

مکاشفه (f. 279^{a})‘

حکایت (f. 280^{b})‘

اندرز کردن غازان خان رعایارا و ولی عهد کردن خدابنده محمّد سلطان (f. 289^{a})‘

بنا نهادن قبّه و مسجد و مدارس و ابواب البرّ و وقفهای آن (f. 291^{b})‘

شرطهایی که غازان محمود فرموده است (f. 293^{a})‘

وفات غازان محمود طاب ثراه (f. 295^{a})‘

The poem, which, as we have seen, was begun in 758/1357, seems not to have been completed until 763/1361–2, as appears from the following verses on f. 300^{a}:

ز هجرت شده هفتصد و شصت و سه‘ مر این نامهٔ نامداران مه‘

بروز دوشنبه بماه حرام‘ شد این نامه بر دست ناظم تمام‘

The last written page (f. 301^{a}) contains the following very ungrammatical Arabic colophon and Persian historical note:

تمّت الکتاب الغازان‌نامه بعون الملك الّوح والخامه فی تاسع ذا الحجه سنه ثلثه وسبعین وثمانمایة الهجریه النبّویه‘ کتبه العبد الحقیر خطوطی شروانی فی مدینة التبریز‘ مّ‘

در سال سته عشر و سبعمایه پادشاه اسلام سلطان سعید پدر ابو سعید غیاث الدّنیا والدّین اولجایتو خدابنده محمّد ابن ارغون در بلدهٔ سلطانیّه روح مطهّر پاکش از قالب خاکی برون آمد و بر اعلای علّیین آشیان ساخت و آنچنان بود که در سلطانیّه قسلامیسی فرمود و بشکار بر نشست و مرضی عارض شد مراجعت نمود روز پنجشنبه سلخ رمضان وفات کرد علیه الرحمة والرضوان

چو قدراز[1] برتر از قدر جنان بود‘ خباب[2] قدس اعلی شد مکانش‘

روان بادا بهر دم صد هزاران‘ درود از حضرت حق بر روانش‘

The MS. contains 303 ff. of 18 × 13 c. and 15 ll., and is written in a good, clear *ta'líq* with headings and borders in gold.

V. 29 (9).

دیوان نزاری قهستانی‘

A copy of the British Museum MS. **Or. 7909**, containing the *Díwán* of Nizárí of Quhistán, made for me in 1913 by an Indian named Ismá'íl 'Alí. See my *Persian Literature under Tartar Dominion*, pp. 154–155.

This copy is chiefly written (ff. 59–168) in a note-book of 20·3 × 17 c. and 23 ll., but the first 58 ff. are on paper of a slightly different size. The writing is a clear and careful Indian *ta'líq*.

---

[1] Probably the correct reading is قدرش. [2] Or جناب. Possibly it should be قباب.

V. 30 (9).

قصائد انوری،

A MS. of the poems of Anwarí, bought of R. D. Dickinson, 89 Farringdon Street, E.C., for 10*s*. 6*d*. on March 30, 1899. It should, of course, have been placed higher in this class, since Anwarí flourished under the House of Saljúq in the twelfth century, but was overlooked.

Ff. 103 of 20·2 × 11·5 c. and 14 ll.; fairly good *ta'líq* between marginal lines of red and blue; no date or colophon.

V. 31 (9).

دیوان حافظ،

A very poor Indian MS. of the *Díwán* of Ḥáfiẓ, given to me on May 13, 1903, by my former pupil Harináth Dè of Dacca College. It was copied in 1177/1764 by a certain Fatḥu'lláh Ákhúnd, and in March, 1839, belonged to "Baboo Chunder Narain Moostofee." I have not thought it worth while to number the leaves, which measure 20·5 × 13·3 c. and contain 13 ll. each of poor *ta'líq* writing.

V. 32 (6).

دیوان جهان،

The *Díwán* of a poetess[1] using the pen-name (*takhallus*) of Jahán, who was contemporary with Sháh Shujá' the Muẓaffarí, and is probably identical with the Jahán-Khátún satirized by 'Ubayd-i-Zákání. See my *Persian Literature under Tartar Dominion*, p. 233, n. 1.

The MS., apparently bought by me in Constantinople, since I have marked it in pencil "20 piastres," comprises 38 ff. of 14·9 × 10·4 c. and 15 ll., and is written in a small, neat *ta'líq* with rubrications. In the colophon the month of completion is given as Dhu'l-Ḥijja, but the year is almost obliterated, though it looks most like 1028 (this would be equivalent to Nov.—Dec., 1619).

The poems are for the most part *ghazals*, with a few *muqaṭṭa'át* (fragments) and *rubá'iyyát* (quatrains) at the end. Prefixed to them is a prose preface celebrating the virtues and titles of Jalálu'd-Dín Abu'l-Fawáris Sháh Shujá'. The poems are as usual arranged in alphabetical order of the final letter, except the first three, of which the first, in praise of God, begins:

ای ز امر کُنْفَکَانَت گشته پیدا کاینات، ذات بیچون ترا ترک صفت عین صفات،

---

[1] The sex is shown by the occurrence in the prose preface of the expression این ضعیفه.

the second, in praise of the Prophet, begins:

ای افتخار نام نبوّت ز نام تو، افزوده حشمت رسل از احتشام تو،

and the third, in praise of Sháh Shujá‘, begins:

کسی که شمع جمال تو در نظر دارد، ز آتش دل پروانه کی خبر دارد،

. . . .

جلال دنیا و دین کهف ملك شاه شجاع، که صیت معدلتش ملك بحر و بر دارد،

V. 33 (10).

دیوان کمال خجندی،

A good MS. of the *Díwán* of Kamál of Khujand, a poet contemporary with Ḥáfiẓ. See my *Persian Literature under Tartar Dominion*, pp. 320–330, where a number of extracts from this MS. are given. It was bought for £4 from J. J. Naaman on May 1, 1901, comprises 186 ff. of 22·5 × 14·4 c. and 17 ll., is written in a neat, clear *ta‘líq*, and has no date or colophon.

V. 34 (9).

دیوان مغربی،

A good but undated MS. of the *Díwán* of Maghribí. See my *Persian Literature under Tartar Dominion*, pp. 330–344.

This MS. was one of seven which I bought for £20 from J. J. Naaman in September, 1901. They were originally numbered **W. 113**, and **W. 124–129**, this being **W. 125**. It comprises 50 ff. of 22·2 × 14·3 c. and 15 ll. and is written in a small, neat, and very pretty *ta‘líq*. It has no colophon or date.

V. 35 (7).

دیوان قاسم الانوار وغیره من آثاره،

An excellent MS. of the *Díwán* of Qásimu'l-Anwár, transcribed in 861/1456–7, only 24 years after the poet's death in 837/1433–4. See my *Persian Literature under Tartar Dominion*, pp. 473–486.

This MS., bought of J. J. Naaman in August, 1901, comprises 268 ff. of 16·3 × 12 c. and 15 ll., is written in a clear and beautiful *nasta‘líq* between margins ruled in gold, and was copied by Muḥammad ibn Muḥammad ibn Khurram-Pír of Gílán, who completed it at the end of Ramaḍán, 861/Aug. 21, 1457. The *ghazals* extend to f. 204^b, and are followed by a *tarjí‘band* (ff. 204^b–209^a), after which come some poems in Turkish and in a Persian dialect (probably that of Gílán), fragments, quatrains, etc., ending on f. 227^b. Next follows (ff. 228^b–251^a), after a blank page, a treatise entitled *Anísu'l-‘Árifín* in *mathnawí* verse, to which is prefixed a prose

Preface in which the author gives his full name as "'Alí ibn Naṣír ibn Hárún ibn Abi'l-Qásim al-Ḥusayní at-Tabrízí, commonly known as Qásimí," which latter pen-name he uses alternatively with Qásim. The title of the poem is given in the following verse (f. 235[a], l. 7):

خوش نماید گر دهم ترتیب ازین، نسخهٔ نامش انیس العارفین،

The volume concludes with another treatise in prose interspersed with verse entitled *Anísu'l-'Áshiqín* (ff. 252[b]–266[a]), and ends with the following colophon:

قد فرغ من تحرير هذا الكتاب الشريف المبارك الميمون المنظوم العبد الفقير الحقير المحتاج الى رحمة حضرة السبحانى محمّد بن محمّد بن خرّم‌پير الجيلانى للبحر الزخّار وسالك الاطوار ومخزن الاسرار وسيّد الاحرار وقطب الفلك الدوّار قاسم الانوار سلام الله عليه وعلى من اتّبعه الهدى فى اواخر شهر رمضان المبارك سنة احدى ستّين وثمانمائة،

This colophon would seem to imply that the MS. was copied for Qásimu'l-Anwár himself, but the chronological difficulties involved are obvious.

V. 36 (7).

ديوان قاسم الانوار،

The same *Díwán* without the *Anísu'l-'Árifín* and the *Anísu'l-'Áshiqín*.

Ff. 200 of 17·2 × 12·8 c. and 17 ll.; written in a good, clear *naskh* within lines ruled in red, the last page or two in a smaller *ta'líq*; no date or colophon. Bought of J. J. Naaman for £3. 10*s*. 0*d*. on May 1, 1901.

V. 37 (8).

ديوان كاتبى،

A good copy of the *Díwán* of Kátibí of Níshápúr (d. 838/1434–5). See my *Persian Literature under Tartar Dominion*, pp. 487–495.

This MS., which was one of thirteen bought for £25 from J. J. Naaman in May, 1902, comprises 115 ff. of 18·3 × 11·4 c. and 15 ll., is written in a neat, small *ta'líq* with rubrications, and was copied by Murád ibn Khudá-verdi Beg in 923/1517.

V. 38 (13).

كلّيات جمالى،

A MS. of the very rare poetical works of Pír Jamálu'd-Dín Muḥammad of Ardistán, poetically named Jamálí. A notice of him is given in Riḍá-qulí Khán's *Riyáḍu'l-'Árifín*, pp. 53–57, according to which he died in 879/1474–5. The only other MS. I have seen was in the possession of the late Ḥájjí 'Abdu'l-Majíd Belshah, but I do not know what became of it[1]. This MS. was given to me by my friend Mírzá 'Abdu'l-Ḥusayn Khán of Káshán, entitled *Waḥídu'l-Mulk*, on October 12, 1912.

This large and compactly written volume comprises 330 ff. of 32 × 21 c. and 33 ll., is written in six columns to the page in a small, neat *ta'líq* with rubrications, and was transcribed by Sayyid 'Alí Akbar al-Hirawí (? الهمروی or الهمردی) who completed it on Ṣafar 10, 1235/Nov. 28, 1819. The contents, which are fully set forth on two additional (unnumbered) pages at the beginning, are as follows:

(1) *Miṣbáḥu'l-Arwáḥ* (ff. 1ᵇ–27ᵇ), a *mathnawí* poem beginning after a short prose Preface:

شحنهٔ دل میل صحرا میکند، ترك مستش فکر غوغا میکند،

(2) *Aḥkámu'l-Muḥibbín* (ff. 28ᵃ–39ᵃ), beginning after a short prose Preface:

مژده مژده مژده ای دلدادگان، کآمد آن یاریِ دهِ افتادگان،

(3) *Niháyatu'l-Ḥikmat* (ff. 39ᵇ–59ᵇ), beginning after the Preface:

الصلوة ای عاشقان کآمد امام، بر رخش آرید ایمان و سلام،

(4) *Bidáyatu'l-Maḥabbat* (ff. 60ᵃ–71ᵃ), beginning after the Preface:

اسپِ همّت زین کن ای همّت بلند، تا ز پای روح بگشائیم بند،

(5) *Hidáyatu'l-Ma'rifat* (ff. 71ᵇ–97ᵃ), beginning after the Preface:

با محبّت رو بیار آور دلا، کاندرین بحرست سیر آشنا،

(6) *Fatḥu'l-Abwáb* (ff. 97ᵇ–130ᵃ), beginning after the Preface:

ربّنا افتح ربّنا افتح بیننا، بین قوم الحقّ وانصر واحدنا،

(7) *Mihr-afrúz* (ff. 130ᵇ–133ᵃ), beginning after the Preface:

به محبّت در آی و شو تسلیم، تا که همّت ترا کند تعلیم،

It will be noticed that in this poem there is a change of metre from the hexameter *Ramal* hitherto employed.

(8) *Kanzu'd-Daqá'iq* (ff. 133ᵇ–143ᵇ), beginning after the Preface:

مشعلهٔ صبح سعادت دمید، وسوسهٔ ظلمت عادت رمید،

(9) *Sharḥu'l-Kunúz* (ff. 144ᵃ–161ᵃ), beginning without Preface:

باسم عظیم و بذات قدیم، که عشقست و بس هرچه هست ایحکیم،

(10) *Rúḥu'l-Quds* (ff. 161ᵇ–171ᵃ), also described as the third part of the above *Sharḥu'l-Kunúz*.

---

[1] [It is now in the Library of the India Office. I have described its contents in an article contributed to the '*Ajab-náma* (a volume of Oriental Studies published by the Cambridge University Press in 1922 and presented to Professor Browne on his 60th birthday), pp. 364–370.]

(11) *Tanbíhu'l-'Árifín* (ff. 171^{b}–187^{a}), beginning after a rather long Preface:

ساقی قدحی که نو بهار است، چشم دل و جان در انتظار است،

(12) *Maḥbúbu'ṣ-Ṣiddíqín* (ff. 187^{b}–214^{a}), beginning without Preface, but with interspersed passages of prose later on:

روز از نور عشق شد خرّم، ظلمت شب درید جامهٔ غم،

(13) *Kashfu'l-Arwáḥ* (ff. 214^{b}–240^{a}), beginning:

بنامت نامه‌را سر بر گشایم، که اندر کوی عشقت میسرایم،

(14) *Miftáḥu'l-Qaṣr* (ff. 240^{a}–242^{b}), beginning after a longish Preface:

بود چه ایّوب زآل خلیل، خواست خدا تا که شود او جلیل،

(15) *Mishkátu'l-Muḥibbín* (ff. 242^{b}–243^{b}), beginning:

ای گزیده جهان و هرچه دروست، جان عالم توئی و عالم پوست،

(16) *Kitáb-i-Ma'lúmát* (ff. 243^{b}–244^{b}), beginning:

ای رفیق ره و حریف مدام، ای طلبکار رند درد آشام،

(17) *Kitáb-i-Mathnawiyyát* (ff. 245^{a}–248^{a}), beginning:

عشق تو مرا به باد بر داد، خوشنودم از آنکه سخت‌تر باد،

(18) *Sharḥu'l-Wáṣilín* (ff. 250^{a}–275^{a}), beginning:

این شجر با آن ثمر پیوسته است، بیثمر باشد کز این بگسسته است،

(19) *Istiqámat-náma* (ff. 275^{b}–281^{b}), beginning:

استقم دل که باز حسن حبیب، میکند عشوها بعشق غریب،

(20) *Kitáb-i-Núr^{un} 'alà Núr^{in}* (ff. 282^{a}–285^{a}), beginning, after a longish prose Preface:

روز اوّل که دوست آئینه (آینه) خواست، عقل بنمود روی و قامت راست،

(21) *Kitáb-i-Náẓir wa-Manẓúr* (ff. 285^{b}–290^{a}), beginning:

مصطفی هور و نور مشهور است، علی بو العلا علی نور است،

(22) *Kitáb-i-Mir'átu'l-Afrád* (ff. 290^{b}–313^{a}), in prose interspersed with verse, beginning:

ای آنکه مشتاق جمال دوستی و میخواهی که معرفت آلهی ضمّ کنی الخ

(23) *Kitáb-i-Qaṣá'id* (ff. 313^{b}–316^{b}), beginning:

صبح روشن گشت یا مهتاب بر بالاستی، یا ز نور دلبرم عالم چنین زیباستی،
یا شب قدر است یا خود نغمهٔ روح القدس، کاینچنین دیر مغان چون مسجد الاقصاستی،

The *qaṣídas* are followed (ff. 316^{b}–319^{b}) by two *tarjí'-bands*, a *tarkíb-band* and other shorter poems.

(24) *Ghazals*, with the *takhalluṣ* of Jamálí (ff. 320^{a}–327^{b}).

(25) *Rubá'iyyát* and *Mufradát* (ff. 327^{b}–330^{a}).

V. 39 (7).

دیوان ریاضی،

The *Díwán* of the Persian poet Riyáḍí of Samarqand, who died about 884/1479–80. See Rieu's Persian Catalogue, p. 1074. The *ghazal* which comes first in the British Museum MS. occurs on f. 8^b in this MS., which begins:

صنع او آندم که نقش گنبذ افلاك بست، نامهٔ حیرت ببال طایر ادراك بست،

This MS., which I appear to have bought in Constantinople for 15 piastres, comprises only 29 ff. of 16 × 11·6 c. and 11 ll., is written in good, clear *ta'líq*, and lacks date and colophon.

V. 40 (8).

دیوان هلالی، دیوان ریاضی،

The *Díwáns* of Hilálí (ff. 2^b–36^a) and of the above-mentioned Riyáḍí (ff. 40^b–68^a), a pretty but undated MS., which, with three others, I bought of J. J. Naaman for £15 on May 22, 1901. Concerning Hilálí of Astarábád, who was put to death by the Uzbeks in 935/1528–9, see my *Persian Literature in Modern Times*, pp. 234–235. His first ode in this MS. begins:

ز آب چشم من گِل شد براه عشق منزلها، ندانم تا چه گُلها بشگفد آخر ازین گِلها،

and the *Díwán* ends with the following quatrain:

با هر که نشینی و قدح نوش کنی، از رشك مرا خراب و مدهوش کنی،
گفتی که چو می خورم ترا یاد کنم، ترسم که شوی مست و فراموش کنی،

In the *Díwán* of Riyáḍí contained in this MS. the *ghazal* which comes first in the British Museum MS. comes second, the first beginning:

گر طبیب آید که گیرد نبضِ جانانِ مرا، من همی میرم که می گیرد رگِ جانِ مرا،

The MS. comprises 68 ff. of 12 × 11 c. and 13 ll.; ff. 1, 2^a, 36^b–40^a and 68^b are blank; the writing is a small, neat *ta'líq*, and there is no date or colophon.

V. 41 (8).

تحفة الاحرار جامی، دیوان ریاضی،

This MS., bought of J. J. Naaman for £2. 10*s.* 0*d.* in May, 1905, bears on f. 1^a a seal which a marginal note declares to be that of the Ottoman Sulṭán Salím, called "the Grim" (*Yáwúz*). It comprises 88 ff. of 19·8 × 11·9 c. and 15 ll., is written in a small, neat *ta'líq* with rubrications, and is divided into two parts, separated by several blank leaves (ff. 64ª–68ª), of which the first only has a colophon, giving 886/1481 as the date of completion[1]. These two parts contain:

I. The *Tuḥfatu'l-Aḥrár* of Jámí (b. 817/1414, d. 898/1492), of whom a full account is given in my *Persian Literature under Tartar Dominion* (pp. 507–548), with a short notice of this book (pp. 526–528). The text has been edited by Forbes Falconer. This occupies ff. 1ᵇ–63ᵇ of the MS.

II. Another copy of the *Díwán* of Riyáḍí of Samarqand (ff. 68ᵇ–88ᵇ), beginning like **V. 39** *supra*.

V. 42 (7).

سبحة الابرار و ديوان جامی،

A neatly written but undated MS., bought by me in Constantinople in April, 1910, from 'Abdu'r-Raḥmán Efendi for two or three *mejídiyyés*, containing:

I (ff. 6ᵇ–59ᵇ). The *Subḥatu'l-Abrár* of Jámí, incomplete at end, concerning which see my *Persian Literature under Tartar Dominion*, pp. 528–531.

II (ff. 60ª–251ª). The First *Díwán* of Jámí, entitled *Fátiḥatu'sh-Shabáb*, incomplete at the beginning. The alphabetical arrangement only begins at the eighth *ghazal* (f. 62ª), of which the text and translation are given on pp. 543–544 of my *Persian Literature under Tartar Dominion.* See also Ethé's India Office Persian Catalogue, col. 743.

The MS. comprises 251 ff. of 15 × 10 c. and 14 ll. written in a small and neat but rather angular *ta'líq*.

V. 43 (7).

سلسلة الذهب جامی،

Jámí's *Silsilatu'dh-Dhahab*, or "Chain of Gold," concerning which see my *Persian Literature under Tartar Dominion*, pp. 516–523.

This MS. was bought with twelve others for £25 from J. J. Naaman in May, 1902. It comprises 301 ff. of 15·5 × 9·2 c. and 12 ll., was transcribed in 997/1589, and is written in a small, neat *ta'líq* with headings in red and blue between margins ruled in gold and colours. The first of the three *Daftars*, or Books, into which the poem is divided occupies ff. 2ᵇ–177ª; the second ff. 177ᵇ–251ª; and the third ff. 251ᵇ–301ª.

---

[1] The completion of the poem is evidently meant, Jámí's original colophon having been copied from the archetype.

V. 44 (9).

ليلى و مجنون مكتبى،

A MS. of the *Laylà ú Majnún* of Maktabí, which I bought in Constantinople on August 31, 1882. It is written in a fairly good *ta'líq*, without date or colophon, but contains eighteen rather crude miniatures, of which the first (on f. 6[a]) represents the Prophet's Ascension (*Mi'ráj*), and the others various episodes in the romance of Laylà and Majnún.

Ff. 105 of 21·8 × 13·3 c. and 11 ll. The Persian lacquer binding has been greatly damaged. Concerning Maktabí, who composed this poem in 895/1490, and is believed to have died about 900/1494–5, see Rieu's Persian Supplement, pp. 191–192, **Nos. 298–299**.

V. 45 (7).

ليلى و مجنون هاتفى،

A pretty and well written little MS. of the *Laylà ú Majnún* of Hátifí (d. 927/1520–1), concerning whom see my *Persian Literature in Modern Times*, pp. 227–229. This poem, one of the "Quintet" (*Khamsa*) which he composed in imitation of Niẓámí, was published at Calcutta by Sir W. Jones in 1788.

Ff. 96 of 17 × 10·5 c. and 11 ll.; good *ta'líq* with rubrications between gold lines; no date or colophon.

V. 46 (7).

ديوان محيى،

A small, neatly written MS. containing the *Díwán* of a poet using the pen-name of Muḥyí (so scanned, though generally written Muḥí, مُحى), but described in the colophon as that of Abú Muḥammad Muḥyi'd-Dín Shaykh 'Abdu'l-Qádir-i-Gílání. This celebrated saint died in 561/1165–6, and is certainly not the author of these much more modern poems. The real author is probably Muḥyí of Lár (d. *circa* 933/1526–7), whose *Futúḥu'l-Ḥaramayn* has been similarly ascribed to Shaykh 'Abdu'l-Qádir. See Rieu's Persian Catalogue, p. 655. The first *ghazal* begins:

گر بیآئی بسر تربت ویرانهٔ ما، بینی از خون جگر آب زده خانهٔ ما،

The *Díwán* concludes with sixteen quatrains.

Ff. 32 of 17 × 11 c. and 13 ll.; small, neat *ta'líq*. The MS. appears from the colophon to have been copied for a certain Ḥusní Efendi of the Naqshbandí Order of Dervishes in 1162/1749.

V. 47 (8).

صفات العاشقين هلالى،

The *Ṣifátu'l-'Áshiqín* ("Attributes of Lovers") of Hilálí, who was killed by the Uzbeks in 935/1528–9. See my *Persian Literature in Modern Times*, pp. 234–235; Rieu's Persian Supplement, **No. 302**, p. 192; Ethé's Bodleian Persian Catalogue, **No. 1026**, cols. 650–651.

This MS., bought of J. J. Naaman in September, 1901, with six others for £20, comprises 40 ff. of 19·8 × 12·2 c. and 12 ll., and is written in a good *ta'líq* between gold borders. There is no colophon or date.

V. 48 (8).

ديوان عرفى،

An undated modern MS. of the *Díwán* of 'Urfí of Shíráz (d. 999/1590–1). See my *Persian Literature in Modern Times*, pp. 241–249, and Ethé's Bodleian Persian Catalogue, **No. 1051**, col. 662. The first poem begins:

اى متاع درد در بازار جان انداخته، گوهر هر سود در جيب زيان انداخته،

This MS., bought of J. J. Naaman on May 1, 1901, for £1, comprises 94 ff. of 20·2 × 12·4 c. and 17 ll., and is written in a small, clear, neat Persian *ta'líq*, without date or colophon.

V. 49 (7).

ديوان عرفى،

Another MS. of the *Díwán* of 'Urfí, defective at beginning and end, given to me by Dr Rizá Tevfíq (Riḍá Tawfíq) in August, 1909. Though imperfect, this MS. contains a much larger selection of 'Urfí's poems than the preceding one. It begins in the middle of a *qaṣída* with the verse:

تا رايت عفو و غضبش سايه نيفگند، هُيات متصوّر نشد آرامش و رمرا،

In its present state the MS. (which appears to suffer from numerous dislocations and lacunae) comprises 154 ff. of 16·8 × 9·5 c. and 15 ll., and is written in a small, neat Persian *ta'líq* between gold lines. A colophon at the end of the *ghazals* on f. 143 is ١٠٧, which may be meant for 1007/1598–9, or 1070/1659–60.

V. 50 (8).

نل و دمن فيضى،

A small, plainly written, modern MS. of the *Nal ú Daman* of the Indian poet Fayḍí (Fayẓí), concerning whom see my *Persian Literature in Modern Times*, pp. 241–245. He died in 1004/1595, and composed this poem in the preceding year. See Rieu's Persian Catalogue, pp. 670–671.

This MS. was one of thirteen bought of J. J. Naaman for £25 in May, 1902. It comprises 111 ff. of 20·3 × 11·2 c. and 19 ll., and is written in a small, fairly good Persian *ta'líq*. The copyist was Muṣṭafà ibn Muḥammad called Sirrí (Sarí)-záda, but there is no date.

V. 51 (11).

ديوان صائب،

A good MS. of the *Díwán* of Ṣá'ib (d. 1088/1677–8), concerning whom see my *Persian Literature in Modern Times*, pp. 265–276.

This MS., for the gift of which I am indebted to Sir John Tweedy, who kindly gave it to me on March 7, 1922, comprises 598 ff. of 25·6 × 13·5 c. and 17 ll., written in excellent *ta'líq* between borders ruled in blue and gold. The last written page (f. 597[a]) is in a coarser and apparently later hand, and seems to have been supplied to replace a lost leaf. It ends with a colophon dated 10 Shawwál, 1044/March 29, 1635. If this be correct the MS. was written not only during the poet's lifetime, but soon after he came at an early age from Persia to India.

V. 52 (10).

ديوان صائب،

Another MS. of the *Díwán* of Ṣá'ib, bought of Quaritch on May 14, 1901, for 15*s*. It comprises 349 ff. of 22·3 × 13·7 c. and 15 ll., is written in a clear and fairly good Indian *ta'líq*, and has no date or colophon. The poet's pen-name (*takhalluṣ*) is invariably written in red.

V. 53 (10).

ديوان شيخ على حزين،

A beautifully written and illuminated MS. of the *Díwán* of Shaykh 'Alí Ḥazín (b. 1103/1692, d. 1180/1766–7), concerning whom see my *Persian Literature in Modern Times*, pp. 277–281, and Rieu's Persian Catalogue, pp. 715–716.

This MS. formerly belonged to my friend the late Mr E. J. W. Gibb, and was given to me on Dec. 5, 1901, by his widow and his mother. It is finely bound in Persian lacquer covers, comprises 450 ff. of 23·7 × 14·7 c. and 15 ll., and is written in a small and very elegant Persian *ta'líq* between blue and gold borders. The whole ground of each page, as well as the margins, is ornamented with gilt floral designs. There are two colophons, one on f. 39^b^, at the end of the prose Preface (*Díbácha*), dated Rajab, 1233/May, 1818, and another fuller one on f. 449^a^, dated Muḥarram, 1234/November, 1818. The scribe omits his own name, but gives the name of the person for whom he made this copy, preceded by three lines of honorific epithets which even the greatest sovereigns might deem exaggerated, but unhappily the name was written in gold letters which are now illegible. The contents of the MS. are as follows:

I (ff. 3^b–39^b). Prose Preface (*Díbácha*), beginning:

نحمده ونسأله التقی ونعتصم بعروته الوثقی... رباعی، یارای زبان کو که ثنای تو کنیم، الخ

II (ff. 41^a–104^b). *Qaṣídas*, beginning:

غیر نفی حکمت یکتای بیهمتاستی،

III (ff. 105^b–379^b). *Ghazals*, beginning:

ای نام تو زینت زبانها، حمد تو طراز داستانها،

IV (ff. 380^b–407^a). *Rubá'iyyát*, beginning:

شد صید خم زلف رسائی (رشائی) دل ما، افتاده بدام اژدهائی دل ما،
از بوی کباب میتوان دانستن، کز عشق در آتشست جائی دل ما،

V (ff. 407^b–448^b). *Muqaṭṭa'át*, beginning:

یا (*sic*) ابا حسن القیت حبّك منفذی، ولو بذنوب الخلق کنت محاسبا،

V. 54 (13).

کلّیّات نشاط،

The complete works (*Kulliyyát*) of Mírzá 'Abdu'l-Wahháb, entitled Mu'tamadu'd-Dawla and poetically surnamed Nasháṭ, who died in 1244/1828–9. See the *Majma'u'l-Fuṣaḥá*, vol. II, pp. 509–514, and my *Persian Literature in Modern Times*, pp. 225, 307 and 311. A lithographed edition appeared at Ṭihrán in 1282/1865–6.

This MS. was one of those obtained from the Belshah collection in the spring of 1920. It comprises 194 written ff. of 30 × 19 c. and 17 ll., is written in a fairly good cursive Persian *ta'líq* between margins ruled in red, gold and blue, and was completed on the 19th of Rabí' II, 1282/11 September, 1865, at Ṭihrán. The scribe's name appears to be Muḥammad Ibráhím, and in a marginal note he gives the day as well as the year of Nasháṭ's death as the 5th of Dhu'l-Ḥijja, 1244/June 8, 1829.

The volume contains both prose and verse. The first section of the prose selections (ff. 1^{b}–62^{a}) is headed by the following rubric:

مشتمل است بر دیباچه و خطبه و وقف‌نامه و نکاح نامجات و توصیف بعضی از ولات '

It contains many letters, despatches, etc., besides the longer pieces and is interspersed with a certain amount of poetry. It is preceded by a rather crude illuminated *'unwán*, and has a colophon dated 5 Rabí' I, 1282, only a fortnight earlier than the final colophon mentioned above.

The second prose section (ff. 62^{b}–82^{b}) also contains prose pieces interspersed with verse, some devotional, some anecdotal in character. There is a colophon at the end of this part, dated the 17th of Rabí' I, 1282/Aug. 10, 1865.

The poems fill the remainder of the volume, first a *mathnawí* (ff. 83^{b}–107^{b}) beginning:

ای خوشا آغاز غم پرواز عشق ' ای خوشا انجام به از آغاز عشق '

This is dated in the colophon nine days later than the preceding one. Next come the *qaṣídas* (ff. 108^{b}–117^{b}), beginning:

هوا باد و هوس باران طمع خاك و خطر خضرا '
در این گلشن بسی نادان که بندد دل گشاید پا '

The colophon at the end of this portion gives the 28th of Rabí' I, 1282/Aug. 21, 1865, as the date of completion. The *ghazals* (ff. 118^{b}–184^{a}) are immediately followed by *tarkíb-bands*, *muqaṭṭa'át* and *rubá'iyyát* (ff. 184^{a}–194^{a}).

V. 55 (8).

دیوان ناظم '

The Persian *Díwán* of a poet called Náẓim, who may or may not be identical with one of the two poets who made use of this pen-name mentioned in Rieu's Persian Catalogue, pp. 370 and 692. The first *ghazal* begins:

عشق ناظم شد چو دیوان دل آگاه‌را '
آهی انشا کرد و مصرع داد بسم الله‌را '

This little MS., given to me by Dr Riẓá Tevfíq (Riḍá Tawfíq) in August, 1909, comprises 50 ff. of 20·5 × 11·4 c. and 15 ll., is written in a small, neat Persian *ta'líq*, and is dated in the colophon 21 Dhu'l-Ḥijja, 1242/July 16, 1827.

V. 56 (7).

دیوان شیخ صافی،

The Persian *Díwán* of a poet called (Shaykh) Ṣáfí, consisting entirely of *ghazals* except for two quintets (*mukhammas*) and two quatrains at the end. The first *ghazal* begins:

ای اسم تو سر دفتر هر نامهٔ غرّا، وی بی همه و با همه در اسم و مسمّا،

This MS., one of thirteen bought for £25 from J. J. Naaman in May, 1902, comprises 104 ff. of 17·7 × 13·6 c. and 13 ll., is written in a plain *nasta'líq* hand, and is dated 919/1513–14.

V. 57 (11).

دیوان سحاب،

The *Díwán* of Saḥáb, son of the more celebrated Hátif of Iṣfahán, and one of the leading poets of the court of Fatḥ-'Alí Sháh. See Rieu's Persian Supplement, pp. 88–89, 118–120, and 379.

This MS., bought of Quaritch for 28*s.* on May 14, 1901, is bound in Persian lacquer covers with floral designs inside, and comprises 175 ff. of 27 × 17·5 c. and 12 ll.

The first part of the volume (ff. 1[b]–54[a]) contains *qaṣídas*, *muqaṭṭa'át*, etc., and ends with several chronograms, of which three of the last five give the dates 1214/1799–1800 and 1215/1800–1, two 1216/1801–2, and one the much earlier date 1193/1780–81. All of them celebrate the completion of gardens or buildings (*Dil-gushá*, *Dil-furúz*); Fatḥ-'Alí Sháh is explicitly mentioned in three of the four bearing the later dates, and Áqá Muḥammad Khán in the remaining one.

The second part of the volume (ff. 55[b]–174[b]) contains the *ghazals* and *rubá'iyyát*.

V. 58 (9).

کتاب شیخ صنعان [و] ترسا،

The story of Shaykh Ṣan'án and the Christian girl, for love of whom he contravenes the precepts of Islám by drinking wine, acting as a swine-herd, and worshipping an idol, until finally the girl, moved by his love, embraces Islám, while he recovers his odour of sanctity amongst his astonished and scandalized disciples, is well known, and occurs in Shaykh Farídu'd-Dín 'Aṭṭár's *Manṭiqu'ṭ-Ṭayr*. For other versions see Rieu's Pers. Suppl., **No. 376**, p. 234[b], and also his Turk. Cat., pp. 185^b and 302^b. The poem contained in this MS. I cannot identify, nor can I find any mention of the author's name, but it is dedicated (f. 13^b) to Sulṭán 'Abdu'l-Majíd:

در مدح پادشاه اسلام پناه سلطان البرّ والبحر صاحب الكرّ والفرّ مالك الحرّ والقرّ السلطان عبد المجيد خان الغازى مدّ الله ظلّه الى آخر الزّمان،

If the king in question be the Ottoman Sulṭán 'Abdu'l-Majíd, the poem is quite modern, of the nineteenth century, and the following reference to artillery appears to support this view:

ز رشك بانگ طوپش بر عراده، بجان برق صد آتش فتاده،

The poem, which comprises about 1700 verses, begins:

خداوندا دلم بی نور گشته، ز قسوت سرمه سنگ طور گشته،

The actual story begins on f. 19^b:

کهن پیران سخن آغاز کردند، درِ دیرِ فصاحت باز کردند،
که اندر شهرِ صنعان بُود پیری، گروه مردمان‌را دستگیری،

The MS., one of thirteen bought in May, 1902, for £25 from J. J. Naaman, comprises 58 ff. of 19·6 × 13·7 c. and 15 ll., and is written in a large and clear but ungraceful *ta'líq* with rubrications, and dated 1272/1855–6.

V. 59 (7).

كتاب حسين و حسن،

A short *mathnawí* poem on the Imáms Ḥasan and Ḥusayn, beginning:

شود یاورم گر مُعین اله، بنظم آورم قصّهٔ آن دو شاه،

It comprises about 300 verses, is entirely unhistorical in character, being filled with marvels, and is, I am informed, commonly learned by heart by Persian children, with the "Cat and Mouse" (*Músh ú Gurba*) of 'Ubayd-i-Zákání and the *Niṣáb* of Abú Naṣr-i-Faráhí.

This copy, in a poor, cursive *ním-shikasta*, was made at the end of 1285/March —April, 1869, by a woman named Zahrá Bíbí, and was acquired with the other Schindler MSS. in January, 1917. It comprises 24 ff. of 16·3 × 10·2 c. and 7 ll.

V. 60 (9).

نامهٔ باستان،

The *Náma-i-Bástán*, or "Book of the Ancients," an imitation of the *Sháhnáma*, supposed to embody the researches of European savants and archaeologists into Persian antiquities, composed by Mírzá 'Abdu'l-Ḥusayn Khán of Kirmán, better known as Mírzá Áqá Khán, during his detention in Trebizond in Ramaḍán, 1313 (Feb.—March, 1896). He was put to death on July 17, 1896, at Tabríz, together with Shaykh Aḥmad "Rúḥí" of Kirmán and the Khabíru'l-Mulk, on suspicion of complicity in the assassination of Náṣiru'd-Dín Sháh on May 1, 1896. See my *Persian Revolution*, pp. xi, 10–12, 63–64, 93–96, 409–414, where an extract from this poem, suppressed in the lithographed edition published two years after the author's death, is given. Of his numerous writings he enumerates twenty on the last page (f. 82[a]) of this MS. Several of these, such as the *Hasht Bihisht* (**F. 53** and **F. 54**) and the *Kitáb-i-Riḍwán* (**X. 11**), are noticed elsewhere in this Catalogue. The full title of this poem, an autograph copy, is:

نامهٔ باستان مشتمل بر تاریخ راستین قدیم ایران از روی آثار عتیقه و خطوط قدیمه که سیّاحان اروپ درین عصر کشف نموده اند اثر عبد الحسین کرمانی الشهیر بمیرزا آقا خان کرمانی هنگام توقّف طرابزون فی شهر رمضان ۱۳۱۳،

Ff. 82 of 20·5 × 14·5 c. and 18 ll.; small, neat Persian *ta'líq* with rubrications.

The book begins with a prose table of contents, enumerating eleven ancient Persian dynasties "according to the beliefs of European historians." These are entitled (1) *Ábádiyán*; (2) *Ájámiyán* (or *Píshdádiyán*, *Jamshídiyán*, *Gilsháhiyán*, or *Jamsháspiyán*); (3) *Márdúshiyán* (i.e. Ḍaḥḥák and his descendants, or the "Nimrods" of Babylon, or the "Shepherd Kings" who also subdued Egypt); (4) Ábtín and Firídún and their descendants; (5) the *Pahlawání*, or Heroic Epoch of Záb, Karshásp, Sám, Naríman and Rustam; (6) the Achaemenians; (7) the Medes; (8) the *Sháhinsháhs* of Párs, of whom the first was Cyrus the Great (**سیروس اعظم**), whom the author identifies with Kay-Khusraw; (9) the Seleucidae; (10) the *Ashkániyán*, or Parthians; and (11) the Sásánians. This table is followed (on f. 3[a]) by a note (**افادهٔ مخصوصه**) setting forth how much greater European researches have shown the Persians to be than ever Firdawsí imagined.

The actual poem, written, like the *Sháhnáma*, in the *Mutaqárib* metre, begins:

سرِ نامه بر نام (زروان) پاك،   که رخشید ازو (هرمز) تابناك،

There are copious foot-notes explaining the archaic and obsolete words used in the poem, such words being placed in parentheses in the text and written in red in the notes. The latter part of the poem, lamenting the departed glories of Persia and her present miserable condition, satirizing Náṣiru'd-Dín Sháh, and giving some account of the author's life (ff. 71–81), is the most interesting. The section last mentioned (ff. 76[b], l. 13–78[a], end in the MS.), entitled:

در مقام اندرز و شرح حال خود گوید—

تو تا باشی ای خسرو نامور،   مرنجان کسی‌را که دارد هنر،

will be found printed *in extenso* (60 verses), with English translation, at the end of my *Persian Revolution* (pp. 409–411). As a further specimen, I here give the Conclusion (*Khátima*) of the poem:

چو آمد به بُن این کهن داستان، بنامیدمش نامهٔ باستان،
ز تاریخ هجرت ز بعد هزار، یکی سیصد و سیزده بر شمار،
که پایان شد این نامبردار گنج، بیك ماه بردم درین کار رنج،
سپاسم ز یزدان پیروزگر، که این نامهٔ نامی آمد بسر،
غرض بود تاریخ نی شاعری، که طبع من از شعر بودی عری،
بویژه که بودم به بند اندرون، چه لطف آید از طبع بندی برون،
درین نامه از هر دری گفته شد، گهرهای معنی بسی سفته شد،
ز گفتار فردوسی پاکزاد، بسی کرده ام اندرین نامه یاد،
نبوذ اندرین ره مرا توشهٔ،
هم از خرمن او شدم خوشهٔ،

V. 61 (8).

اشعار یحیی ریحان (مدیر گل زرد)،

The Persian poems, mostly political and composed during the Great War, of a young poet named Yaḥyà Rayḥán, who sent this little volume to me in November, 1918. According to the accompanying letter (dated Shawwál 10, 1336/July 19, 1918) he was born at Ṭihrán in 1313/1895–6 and received his education there until 1328/1910, when he accompanied his family to Khurásán. In the following year some of his poems were published in the *Naw Bahár* (No. 42), of April 20, 1911. In 1334/1915–6 he returned to Ṭihrán and entered a department of the Ministry of Finance. In the spring of 1336/1918 he began publishing his fortnightly paper, entitled *Gul-i-Zard* ("the Yellow Rose"), of which he sent me the first four numbers, published on June 7, June 21, July 6 and July 21, 1918. A photograph of the poet, taken in 1335/1917, is pasted into the beginning of the book, which comprises 98 written pages (numbered by the copyist, probably the author himself) of 17·5 × 13 c. and 14 to 18 ll., written in a fair cursive *ta'líq*. For his lighter verse the author uses the pen-name of Jújí.

The collection consists of about 34 poems, mostly in the new style, and with such titles as:

"At the beginning of the International War." در اوائل جنگ بین المللی،

"The plaint of the victim, the philosophy of the oppressor." فریاد مظلوم فلسفهٔ ظالم،

"A moral ode." یك غزل اخلاقی،

"Awaiting spring in a garden." در یك گلزار بانتظار بهار،

Rayḥán is very fond of the *mustazád*, so popular amongst the poets of the Revolution, many specimens of which are given in my *Press and Poetry of Modern Persia* (*e.g.* Nos. 4, 5, 40 etc.). This type of verse, however, is not so modern as I had originally supposed, for it goes back at least to Yaghmá of Jandaq, who flourished in the middle of the nineteenth century. See my *Persian Literature in Modern Times*, pp. 339–343.

V. 62 (6).

كتاب ملّا پريشان،

A little volume given to me by the Rev. W. St Clair Tisdall on July 24, 1912, containing a Kurdish *mathnawí* poem of about 500 verses, beginning:

من ژ بسم الله من ژ بسم الله، ابتدا مكم من ژ بسم الله،
پريشان نامه ذكر مكم لله، نه آراى هر كس پى قافى الله،
لا رطب و لا يابس الّا فى كتاب، كتاب درج و حمد و فصل الخطاب،
حمد و بسم الله مندرج بين، او نيژ ژ پاى باغ هزار گل چين،

The title, *Kitáb-i-Mullá Paríshán*, is given in the colophon on f. 21b, also the copyist's name, Mírzá Muḥammad Káẓim Fílí of the Sa'dawand tribe, who wrote it for an ecclesiastic named Áqá Bahá'u'd-Dín, apparently in 1302/1884–5.

Ff. 21 of 14·2 × 9·5 c. and 13 ll.; clear though rather inelegant *naskh*.

V. 63 (10).

محيط اعظم عبد القادر بيدل و نكات،

A MS. given to me in August, 1909, by Dr Riḍá Tawfíq (Riẓá Tevfíq), containing two works of 'Abdu'l-Qádir Bí-dil, who died in 1133/1720–1. For his life see Rieu's Persian Catalogue, p. 706; Ethé's Bodleian Persian Catalogue, cols. 712–713, etc.

The first of the two works contained in this volume (ff. 4b–94a) is a *mathnawí*, apparently entitled *May-Khána* ("the Wine-Tavern") in eight sections (called *Dawr*, "Round" or "Circuit" of the wine-cup), preceded by a prose preface beginning:

حمد نشأ آفرينى‌را كه ميخانهٔ حقيقت انسانى‌را از نشأ وَلَقَدْ كَرَّمْنَا بَنِى آدَم علوّ مفاخرت بخشيد الخ

After a doxology concluding with seven verses of *mathnawí*, it continues:

امّا بعد، بدانكه اين خمخانهٔ طهور حقايق است نه ساقى‌نامهٔ اشعار طهور الخ

The actual poem begins on f. 6b:

ازين ميخانه نتوان بود غافل، كه درها مى گشايد بر رخ دل،

The eight *dawrs* which it comprises are as follows:

دور اوّل، جوش اظهار خم بزم وجود (f. 6b)،

دور ثانی، جام تقسیم گلستان شهود (f. 9b)،

دور ثالث، موج انوار در بحر وجود (f. 17b)،

دور رابع، شور سرخوش می فیض حضور (f. 24a)،

دور خامس، رنگ اسرار گلستان کمال (f. 32a)،

دور سادس، بزم نیرنگ خط لوح بیان (f. 49b)،

دور سابع، حلّ اشکال در عقد بیان (f. 81b)،

دور ثامن، ختم طومار رنگ بوی زبان (f. 88b)،

The title *Muḥíṭ-i-A'ẓam* ("Most Mighty Ocean") occurs in a quatrain at the end of f. 94a:

این نسخه که از خامهٔ الهام رقم، گردید مسمّی بمحیط اعظم،

در یافت دبیر خرد از روی حساب، سال اتمام [آن] بنامش مُدْغم،

This appears to imply that the title of the poem, *Muḥíṭ-i-A'ẓam* (= 1078/1667–8), gives the date of its composition, in which case it must have been composed in the author's youth.

The second part of the MS. (ff. 96b–205b) contains the same author's prose *Nikát* (نکات), concerning which see Rieu's Persian Catalogue, p. 745b. Numerous verses are scribbled on what should have been the blank leaves at the beginning and end of the volume, including some in Turkish by Fuḍúlí (Fuẓúlí) of Baghdád.

Ff. 210 of 24·2 × 12·2 c. and 13 ll.; poor Indian *ta'líq* with rubrications; dated 1223/1808–9 on f. 205b.

V. 64 (8).

گوهر شاهوار (اشعار ذرّه)،

Gawhar-i-Sháhwár ("the Royal Pearl"), a collection of poems (*mathnawís, qaṣídas, ghazals* and *rubá'iyyát*), mostly in praise of Maḥmúd Mírzá, one of the numerous sons of Fatḥ-'Alí Sháh, by Mírzá 'Abdu'l-Ghaní of Tafrísh, poetically surnamed *Dharra*. The work begins (ff. 1b–11a) with a prose Preface in which the author mentions a few particulars about himself, and in the concluding sentence gives the title of the work. The initial *mathnawí* (ff. 11a–34a), headed *Ḥikáyát* (Stories), begins:

بنام خداوند فرهنگ و هوش، پدید آورِ انس و جنّ و وحوش،

کریمی که گیتی است ازو فیضیاب، یکی ذرّه از نور او آفتاب،

It is followed by *qaṣídas* (ff. 34ᵃ–50ᵃ) and *ghazals* (ff. 50ᵇ–59ᵇ), mostly in praise of Maḥmúd Mírzá, who is generally referred to as "Maḥmúd Sháh," and a few quatrains.

This little MS., obtained in the final division of the Belshah MSS., comprises 61 ff. of 20 × 13 c. and 9 ll., is written in a fair *ta'líq*, and is undated.

V. 65 (7).

مجموعهٔ دیوانهای قدیم،

A fine old Anthology of Persian poetry, transcribed by one Maḥmúd Sháh Naqíb, and completed on Ramaḍán 27, 827/August 23, 1424[1]. I bought it in Constantinople in April, 1910, for £13 T. from a bookseller named 'Abdu'r-Raḥmán Efendi.

The selected poems are arranged according to form in the following twelve categories: (1) *Tawḥíd*; (2) *Na't*; (3) *Manqabát*; (4) *Qaṣá'id*; (5) *Tarjí'át*; (6) *Ghazaliyyát*; (7) *Mathnawiyyát*; (8) *Muqaṭṭa'át*; (9) *Mukhammasát*; (10) *Rubá'iyyát*; (11) *Mu'ammayát*; (12) *Abyát* (isolated verses). About eighty poets (of whose names a list is given in an illuminated Table of Contents on ff. 2ᵇ–3ᵃ) are represented in the collection. They are as follows:

(1) 'Aṭṭár; (2) Kamálu'd-Dín Ismá'íl; (3) 'Iráqí; (4) Anwarí; (5) Khwájú of Kirmán; (6) Sirájí; (7) Sa'dí; (8) Athíru'd-Dín Akhsíkatí; (9) Salmán-i-Sáwají; (10) Ḥasan-i-Káshí; (11) Saná'í; (12) Kháqání; (13) Ẓahíru'd-Dín Fáryábí; (14) 'Abdu'l-Wási'-i-Jabalí; (15) Mu'izzí; (16) Mujíru'd-Dín-i-Baylaqání; (17) Mas'úd-i-Sa'd-i-Salmán; (18) Azraqí; (19) Súzaní; (20) 'Abdu'r-Razzáq-i-Iṣfahání; (21) Sayfu'd-Dín-i-Isfarangí; (22) Mukhtárí; (23) Rashídu'd-Dín Waṭwáṭ; (24) Jalálu'd-Dín Rúmí; (25) Awḥadu'd-Dín Awḥadí; (26) Abu'l-Mafákhir-i-Rází; (27) Niẓámí; (28) Amír Khusraw; (29) Amír Ḥasan of Dihlí; (30) Ḥamídu'd-Dín-i-Samarqandí; (31) Náṣir-i-Khusraw; (32) Ḥusámu'd-Dín Ḥasan; (33) Falakí-i-Shírwání; (34) Qiwámí-i-Rází; (35) Qaṭrán; (36) Minúchihrí; (37) 'Izzu'd-Dín-i-Shírwání; (38) Waḥíd-i-Samarqandí; (39) Sharafu'd-Dín-i-Rází; (40) Shamsu'd-Dín Shufurwah; (41) Maḥmúd Ibn Yamín; (42) Faríd-i-Aḥwal; (43) Imámí-i-Hirawí; (44) Athíru'd-Dín Awmání; (45) Siráju'd-Dín Qumrí; (46) Amír-i-Kirmání; (47) 'Imád-i-Faqíh; (48) Jalál-i-'Aḍud; (49) Jalálu'd-Dín-i-Khwáfí; (50) Jalálu'd-Dín-i-Ṭabíb; (51) Sa'd (or Sa'íd)-i-Hirawí; (52) Púr-i-Bahá-yi-Jámí; (53) Náṣir-i-Bukhárí; (54) Mahmúd-i-Abharí; (55) 'Ubayd-i-Zákání; (56) 'Iṣmat-i-Bukhárí; (57) Humámu'd-Dín-i-Tabrízí; (58) Nizárí-i-Quhistání; (59) Ḥusámu'd-Dín-i-Hirawí; (60) Amír 'Abdu'l-Majíd; (61) Jalálu'd-Dín 'Atíqí; (62) Ḥáfiẓ-i-Shírází;

[1] So in the colophon on f. 479ᵃ, but the year 857/1453 or 859/1455 is given on f. 3ᵃ at the end of the Table of Contents.

(63) Kamál-i-Khujandí; (64) Jamálu'd-Dín Laṭífí; (65) Fatḥu'lláh-i-Qazwíní; (66) Karímu'd-Dín-i-Tabrízí; (67) Naṣíru'd-Dín-i-Manṣúr; (68) Maḥmúd ibn Qamar; (69) Sharafu'd-Dín...; (70) Ashrafu'd-Dín Sharaf; (71) Khwája 'Abdu'l-Malik; (72) Kamálu'd-Dín Sábiqí; (73) Aḥmad-i-Khákí; (74) Áqá-yi-Tiflís; (75) Qáḍí Raḍí; (76) Sháh Shujá'; (77) Sulṭán Aḥmad-i-Baghdádí; (78) Amír Sayyid Ḥusayní; (79) Shaykh Aḥmad-i-Jám; (80) Sayyid Ni'matu'lláh; (81) Firdawsí-i-Ṭúsí. Many of these poets, of course, recur in several of the twelve sections into which the work is divided. The total number of verses contained in the volume does not fall far short of 20,000.

Ff. 479 of 15·8 × 11·6 c. and 17 ll. (*bayts*) in the body of the page and 12 ll. (6 *bayts*) in the margin. Written throughout in a small neat *nasta'líq*, with headings in gold and red and ornamental designs in the outer corners of each page, and more elaborate illuminations on ff. 4ª, 4ᵇ and 5ª.

V. 66 (10).

جواهر خمسه،

Selections from the *Díwáns* of five Persian poets who flourished about the end of the fifteenth and beginning of the sixteenth centuries of the Christian era, namely, Áṣafí, Hilálí, Áhí, Sháhí and Ahlí, to which is prefixed a much later prose Preface written in 1120/1709, for Prince Muḥammad Farrukh-Siyar (reigned 1124/1713–1131/1719) before he succeeded to the throne.

This finely-written and finely-bound MS. was one of seven bought of J. J. Naaman in September, 1901, for £20. It comprises 234 ff. of 22·3 × 14·5 c. and 14 ll. and comprises:

(1) The prose Preface (*Díbácha*) mentioned above (ff. 1ᵇ–8ᵇ), beginning:

انواع حمد و ثنای [بی] مر ذات پاك بی نیاز بی انبازیرا آلخ ...(f. 4ª) مکشوف ضمایر ارباب بصایر گردانیده می آید که چون نسخهٔ دیوان شاهی و آصفی و هلالی و اهلی و آهی از جملهٔ دیوانها بجهة ترشیح و تنقیح مبانی و تقریر و تحریر معانی و علوّ مضامین مطالب و سموّ مقاصد و مآرب ممتاز بوده آلخ

The date of this Preface (1120/1709) is given in the following chronogram (f. 7ᵇ):

شیری شکار کرد که آسود خلق ازو، شیر از ستم بمانده بود سال این شکار،

The Preface is in a good, legible *ta'líq*, larger and more modern than the remainder of the MS.

(2) The *Díwán of Áṣafí* (ff. 9ᵇ–79ª), beginning:

ساز آباد خدایا دل ویرانیرا، یا مده مهر بتان هیچ مسلمانیرا،

Áṣafí died on Sha'bán 16, 923/Sept. 3, 1517. See Rieu's Persian Catalogue, pp. 651–652.

(3) The *Díwán of Hilálí* (ff. 80^{b}–124^{a}), dated in the colophon 990/1582 and beginning:

ای نور خدا در نظر از روی تو مارا، بگذار که در روی تو بینیم خدارا،

Hilálí was killed by the Uzbeks in 939/1532–3. See Rieu, *loc. cit.*, p. 656.

(4) The *Díwán of Áhí* (ff. 125^{b}–154^{a}), dated in the colophon 990/1582 and beginning:

ای صد خجالت از گل روی تو لاله‌را، مانند غزال چشم تو چشم غزاله‌را،

Áhí died in 927/1521. See Ethé's Bodl. Pers. Cat., col. 644.

(5) The *Díwán of Sháhí* (ff. 155^{b}–192^{b}), also dated 990/1582 and beginning:

بیا ای از خط سبزت هزاران داغ بر دلها، مرو کز اشك مشتاقان بخون آغشته منزلها،

Sháhí died in 857/1453. See Rieu, *op. cit.*, p. 640.

(6) The *Díwán of Ahlí* (ff. 194^{a}–234^{a}), lacking the opening lines of the first or the first and second *ghazals*, f. 193^{b}, though ruled, being left blank. The first complete *ghazal* (f. 194^{a}, l. 5) begins:

تا چو شمع افتاد در سر آتش سودا مرا، نیست بیم از کشتن و از سوختن پروا مرا،

There were two well-known poets who wrote under the pen-name of Ahlí, one of Shíráz, who died in 942/1535–6, and the other of Turshíz, who died in 934/1527–8. See Rieu, *op. cit.*, pp. 657–658. This portion of the MS. is undated, but was copied by Mírzá Ṣáliḥ Gháziyání, whereas the name occurring in two previous colophons (ff. 124^{a} and 192^{b}) is Mír Ḥilmiyya.

The writing is throughout an excellent *ta'líq*, though older, smaller and better in the body of the manuscript than in the Preface, which was added to it a century and a quarter later.

V. 67 (7).

دیوان مظهر، رباعیّات جامی، رباعیّات سرمدی،

A composite volume, containing (1) the Persian *Díwán* of a poet called Maẓhar; (2) a selection of the quatrains of Jámí; (3) the same of Sarmad in manuscript; (4) a lithographed edition of the last-named, published at Dihlí in 1314/1897; (5) a short prayer in Arabic.

(1) The *Díwán of Maẓhar* was given to me in Constantinople in April, 1908, by Dr Riḍá Tawfíq (Riẓá Tevfíq). It comprises only 17 written leaves of 15·8 × 9·5 c. and 13 ll. and is written in a fairly good, small, modern *ta'líq*. From a brief prose autobiography prefixed to the poems we learn that the author was an 'Alawí by descent, Indian by habitation, of the Ḥanafí sect and the Naqshbandí Order. As he states that he was sixty years of age at the time of writing (1170/1756–7), he was presumably born about 1110/1698–9. The *Díwán* is incomplete, containing only poems rhyming in *alif*, *tá* and *dál*. The first begins:

آبی نزد بروی گرانخواب بخت ما، با آنکه گریه داد بسیلاب رخت ما،

The next three portions of the volume were given to me in 1920 by Umraosingh Sher Gil, who selected and copied the quatrains of Jámí, and attempted to reconstruct by conjecture (no MSS. being available) the faulty quatrains of Sarmad published in the above-mentioned lithographed edition.

(2) Of Jámí's quatrains (ff. 2^a–7^a) he gives only twenty, headed:

بنام یزدان، انتخاب مرتّبه از رباعیّات جامی،

and beginning:

در مسجد و خانقه بسی گردیدم، بس شیخ و مریدرا که پا بوسیدم،
نی یکساعت ز هستئ خود رستم، نی آنکه ز خویش رسته باشد دیدم،

(3) The Quatrains of Ṣarmad are preceded by a short prose Preface (ff. 10^b–11^b) from which we learn that the poet was a Jewish merchant of Káshán who migrated to India, fell in love, assumed the guise and attributes of a *qalandar*, *malámatí*, or antinomian *darwísh*, and was ultimately put to death for refusing to wear any clothes in 1072/1662 in the reign of ʿÁlamgír. About 150 of his quatrains are given, which are arranged in an order differing from that of the lithographed edition, the corresponding number of which is, however, added in the margin. Thus No. 1 in the MS. = No. 224 of the lithograph, and runs:

با فکر و خیالِ کس نباشد کارم، در طورِ غزل طریقِ حافظ دارم،
امّا برباعیم مریدِ خیّام، نی جرعه‌کشِ بادهٔ او بسیارم،

This portion of the volume occupies ff. 10–50, beginning with a rudely-illuminated title, followed by the preface above-mentioned, and ending with a symbolical drawing, signed "U. S. [Umraosingh], 7. iii. 1920," described as "Life of Sermed symbolized," and representing, apparently, a fiery star, a burnt moth, a broken sword, on the hilt of which a bee or fly is walking, and a smoking saucer (of opium ?) on the cross-bar of a sort of retort-stand. Underneath is written the following hemistich of Saʿdí:

همین بود انجام عشق ای پسر،

This is followed by the subjoined account of the labours of the editor and transcriber:

"These Quatrains of *Sermed* were restored, selected and arranged after reading very many times, by *Umraosingh* Sher Gil, 1st January, 1920.

"Red numerals to the right, in English, represent the serial numbers of the quatrains in the little edition.

"Note: the historical account is from the same lithographed edition, which does not mention the source.

"These quatrains of Sermed were selected after innumerable readings from the collection of three hundred and twenty-nine quatrains in alphabetical order published in 1897 at the Fárúqí Press, Dehli, by Sayyid Mohammad Isháq.

"I have tried to restore the text, which has many corrupt and erroneous readings, partly, at any rate, due to the calligraphist of the little Press. I had no manuscript to refer to, and had to depend in this work on my own intuition. Some faulty readings were easy of restoration by a slight addition or transposition of the words to bring the verse into the right metre and meaning, which should not contradict the context; but others were very difficult to guess, and a few—not quoted here—entirely escaped my ingenuity. The selected quatrains here are arranged more or less in the topical order, as well as what I conceive to be the chronological order of the poet's spiritual development.

"Umraosingh Sher Gil, 18th March, 1920."

(4) The volume concludes with the little lithographed edition published at Dihlí in 1314/1897, which comprises 80 pp., and is copiously annotated by Umraosingh, who kindly presented me with these portions of the volume.

(5) At the end of the volume is a short Arabic prayer, copied out for his private use by a certain Sayyid Muṣṭafà, "the servant of the shoes of the learned," whose master Shaykh Muḥammad Amín Naqshbandí had given him permission to recite it once a day.

V. 68 (13).

تذكرهٔ درويش بينوا،

An immense anthology of Persian verse compiled by Darwísh Ḥusayn of Káshán, called Darwísh Bí-Nawá, who died about 1288/1871–2. See Rieu's Persian Supplement, **No. 115**, pp. 81–82. Besides the British Museum MS. (**Or. 3386**) some information is also given there concerning another MS. known to Mr Sidney Churchill in the library of the late historian *Lisánu'l-Mulk*, poetically surnamed *Sipihr*. The present MS. resembles this last in including not only the earlier poets enumerated by Rieu (ff. 1–417 = ff. 5[b]–408[a] of this MS.) but an enormous number of minor poets (*Ṭabaqa* 1, *Silsila* 2) enumerated on ff. 408[a]–412[a], extending to f. 484[a], some as ancient as Abu'l-Faraj-i-Sijzí, Abu'l-Fatḥ al-Bustí, Shahíd of Balkh, Abú Ṭáhir al-Khátúní, and the great Avicenna (Abú 'Alí ibn Síná) himself, others at least as modern as the Ṣafawí period. A third section, bearing no special title, beginning on f. 484[a] with the *Bismi'lláh* and a further list of poets mostly quite modern, and including such nineteenth-century poets as Mijmar, Wiṣál and Yaghmá, occupies the remainder of the volume, but appears to be incomplete, ending in the middle of the letter ص on f. 500[a]. The following page is blank, and the remainder of the volume (ff. 501[a]–524[a]) contains poems, without any very obvious arrangement, and at the end some medical prescriptions, in a much more cursive hand. The volume thus has an appearance of incompleteness, and has no date or colophon. It was one of the MSS. bought of the late Ḥájjí 'Abdu'l-Majíd Belshah in January, 1920, and comprises 524 ff. of 30·5 × 21 c. and 25 ll., written as far as f. 500[a] in a neat Persian *naskh* with rubrications, the remainder in a rather cursive and slovenly *ta'líq*.

V. 69 (5).

قصّهٔ حیدر و دختر قاضیٔ کشمیر،

The following note by Professor Browne is written on the fly-leaf:

"From the Library of the late Sir Albert Houtum-Schindler. Bought from his heirs, Jan. 5th, 1917.

A Persian poem on the adventures of one Ḥaydar, supposed to have lived in the time of Sháh 'Abbás the Great (16th—17th century), and the daughter of the Qáḍí of Kashmír. The author's name does not appear, nor the title of the poem, which shows little skill in verse and is probably quite modern. It is also incomplete at the end."

Begins:

الا ای طوطیٔ نطق شکرخای   بزندان قفس تا کی کنی جای

Ff. 95 (the last 30 blank) of 18 × 10·7 c. Fair Persian *shikasta-ámíz*. The oblong pages, each of which contains five verses, are arranged in note-book form and follow each other in the same order as those of a European book.

V. 69* (14).

شاهنامهٔ فردوسی،

An imperfect copy of the *Sháhnáma*, comprising about five-eighths of the poem, *viz.*, from the beginning to the death of Rustam. The verse with which it concludes

بدو دست بگرفت و (*sic*) پیچان سرش   بدان تا که از مار سازد خورش

corresponds to p. 1241, *v.* I in vol. III of Turner Macan's edition.

This copy has the older Preface (see Ethé, I.O.P.C., **No. 860**), the first part of which, beginning

سپاس و آفرین خدایرا که این جهان وآن جهان آفرید

is supplied on the inner fly-leaf. The Preface ends on f. 3ᵇ and is followed by the satire on Sulṭán Maḥmúd. The poem itself begins on f. 4ᵇ:

بنام خداوند جان و خرد

Ff. 393 of 34·4 × 21·5 c. and 25 ll., written in four columns. Good but rather ungraceful *nasta'líq*. Blank spaces for pictures on ff. 8ᵇ, 19ᵃ, 20ᵃ, 30ᵃ, 31ᵇ, 41ᵇ, 43ᵃ, 44ᵃ, 54ᵇ, 57ᵃ, 69ᵇ, 83ᵃ, 87ᵇ, 88ᵇ, 102ᵇ, 109ᵃ, 112ᵃ, 120ᵇ, 133ᵃ, 141ᵃ, 143ᵇ, 154ᵇ, 160ᵃ, 162ᵇ, 183ᵃ, 190ᵃ, 204ᵃ, 209ᵃ, 219ᵇ, 227ᵃ, 243ᵃ, 255ᵇ, 271ᵃ, 294ᵃ, 295ᵃ, 305ᵇ, 307ᵇ, 320ᵃ, 338ᵃ, 350ᵇ, 371ᵃ, 388ᵇ, 392ᵃ.

V. 70 (11).

مثنوی معنوی،

The first three Books of the *Mathnawí* of Jalálu'd-Dín Rúmí: Book I on ff. 1b–114b, Book II on ff. 115b–205b, and Book III on ff. 209b–308b. The prefaces to Books I and II are wanting.

Ff. 309 of 27·6 × 15·3 c. and 21 ll. Fair Indian *nasta'líq* with rubrications. Dated Ṣafar 1053/April, 1643. The copyist describes himself as

بهیکه (?) بن سیّد حسین حسینی ساکن بلده گره

V. 70* (9).

Four Persian works by the famous poet 'Urfí of Shíráz (d. 999/1590–1):

1. (ff. 1b–39a.) *Majma'u'l-Abkár*, an imitation of Niẓámí's *Makhzanu'l-Asrár*. See Rieu, B.M.P.C., p. 667; Ethé, I.O.P C., **Nos. 1451–3.**

Begins:

بسم الله الرّحمن الرّحیم موج نخستست ز بحر قدیم

2. (ff. 39a–55a.) *Farhád ú Shírín*, another *mathnawí* by 'Urfí, beginning:

خداوندا دلم بی نور سنگ است دل من سنگ و کوه طور سنگ است

3. (ff. 56a–158b.) The *Díwán* of 'Urfí, comprising *qaṣídas*, *ghazals* and *rubá'ís*.

Begins (defectively):

گر ز لطفم ناامید امیدوارم از عتاب

گر ندارم سبحه بر کف در میان زنّار

4. (ff. 159b–171b.) A prose discourse, Ṣúfistic and homiletic in character, which derives its title, *Nafsiyya*, from the circumstance that it consists of successive paragraphs, each beginning with the words ای نفس, *i.e.* "O soul!" This work is rare. Another copy, described by Ivanow in A.S.B.P.C., **No. 675**[2], has "a long flowery preface" by an anonymous editor, which is wanting in this MS.

Begins:

حمدی که از نهایت شایستگی منزّه

Ff. 173 of 22 × 11·6 c. and 19 ll. Bought at the auction at Sotheby's on June 18, 1923, for 30*s*. Poor *nasta'líq*. No date. On ff. 171b–173a an account is given (under rubrications in Turkish) of two saints, Ḥakím Mír Abu'l-Fatḥ and another, belonging to Kashmír, whose name is illegible.

V. 71 (9).

يوسف و زليخا،

A modern copy of the *Yúsuf ú Zalíkha* of Firdawsí, presented to Professor Browne on February 22, 1924, by Sayyid Ḥasan Taqí-záda, whose letter is enclosed. This MS. omits *vv.* 1–130 in Ethé's edition, and begins:

نشسته یکی روز اندوهناك   بکنج غم از درد دل چاك چاك

The next passage (ff. 1ᵃ–4ᵃ) includes the section headed in Ethé's edition گفتار اندر یاد کردن سبب این قصّه (*vv.* 169–250), though the version given in the present MS. is almost entirely different in form. As Taqí-záda remarks in his letter, this section on the origin of the poem is wanting in most copies and occurs in one only of the five MSS. used by Ethé, *viz.*, the Bland codex = **No. 200** in Rieu, B.M.P.C. (Suppl.). Then comes an account of the revelation of the سورة یوسف (Ethé, *vv.* 131–168), illustrated with a miniature (f. 5ᵃ) in which four figures (three of them veiled) —apparently the Prophet, ʻAlí, Ḥasan and Ḥusayn—are depicted sitting together, while angels descend from above. The passage headed آغاز داستان (f. 6ᵇ–7ᵃ) corresponds to *vv.* 319–336 in Ethé's edition, and is followed by the story of the birth of Jacob.

Ff. 229 of 20·8 × 13·3 c. and 15 ll. Good *ta'líq* with illuminated headings and borders. Written for Amír Muḥammad Ḥusayn by Ibn Muḥammad Riẓá Muḥammad Ḥasan آغ اولی, and dated 10 Rajab, 1242/7 February, 1827. A loose half-page, richly gilded, which accompanies the MS., contains the opening verses of the *Sháhnáma*.

V. 71* (7).

بوستان سعدی،

This copy of the *Bústán* of Sa'dí has lost a leaf at the end, containing *vv.* 97–112 of the tenth chapter, the last verse being *v.* 96 in Graf's edition, p. 442:

بر آورده مردم ز بیرون خروش   تو پاینده در پردهٔ پرده پوش

Ff. 174 of 16·9 × 10·5 c. and 12 ll. Distinctly written in *nasta'líq* with rubrications. The first page has been supplied by a later hand.

V. 72 (9).

گلستان، نصاب الصّبیان،

Contains:

1. (ff. 2ᵇ–142ᵃ.) The *Gulistán* of Sa'dí.

2. (ff. 143ᵇ–186ᵇ.) The *Niṣábu's-Ṣibyán* of Abú Naṣr Faráhí, the same work as **S. 10** (9), described on p. 211 above.

Ff. 189 of 21·4 × 15 c. Ff. 1, 2ᵃ, 187–189 blank. Fair *ta'líq*. The *Gulistán* is dated 10 Shawwál, 1296/September, 1879. Name of copyist (f. 186ᵇ): Yaḥyà ibn Muḥammad Taqí Sumayramí Iṣfahání.

V. 73 (9).

مهر و مشتری،

The celebrated love-romance of Mihr and Mushtarí, completed in 778/1377 by Muḥammad 'Aṣṣár of Tabríz. See Rieu, B.M.P.C., p. 626; Ethé, I.O.P.C., **No. 1244**. Begins (f. 2^b):

بنام پادشاه عالم عشق [که نامش هست نقش خاتم عشق]

Ff. 169 of 20·7 × 13 c. and 15 ll. Fair *nasta'líq* with rubrications. F. 2, on which the poem begins, is supplied by a later hand, and the upper part of the page has been torn off. The MS. is defective at the end. It appears to have been written in the 17th or early 18th century.

V. 74.

[No manuscript bearing this number has been found.]

V. 75 (8).

دیوان حافظ،

A fairly good copy of the *Díwán* of Ḥáfiẓ. It contains:

1. (ff. 10^b–13^b.) The preface by Muḥammad Gulandám, a friend of the poet and the first editor of his works.
2. (ff. 15^b–175^b.) *Ghazals* in alphabetical order.
3. (ff. 176^a–183^b.) *Qiṭ'as.*
4. (ff. 183^b–184^b.) The *mathnawí*, beginning:

الا ای آهوی وحشی کجائی مرا با تست هر دم آشنائی

5. (ff. 184^b–188^b.) The *mathnawí*, beginning:

بیا ساقی از باده پر کن بطی مغنّی کجائی بزن بربطی

6. (ff. 188^b–190^b.) *Rubá'iyyát.*
7. (ff. 191^a–201^a.) *Qaṣídas*, etc.

Ff. 210 of 18·2 × 11 c. and 17 ll. Good clear *ta'líq*. No date, probably 18th century. Some complete *ghazals*, many separate verses, and several Turkish glosses have been inserted in the margins by former owners. One of these, a Turk, has numbered the *ghazals* and added a *fihrist* (index) in which they are arranged under their rhyme-letters.

V. 76 (8).

سبحة الابرار،

Another copy (see **V. 42**) of the *Subḥatu'l-Abrár* of Jámí. It begins with the *rubá'í* of which the first two lines are printed as prose by Ethé, I.O.P.C., col. 746, No. 5.

Ff. 99 of 20·5 × 12 c. and 15 ll. Clear but ungraceful *ta'líq* with rubrications. No colophon or date, probably 17th century. The last page is wanting.

V. 77 (8).

سلسلة الذهب،

Another copy (see **V. 43**) of Jámí's *Silsilatu'dh-Dhahab.* See Ethé, I.O.P.C., col. 747, No. 9. In this copy the beginning of Daftar I is not indicated; Daftar II begins on f. 142^{b}, and Daftar III on f. 206^{b}.

Ff. 250 of 20·4 × 11·8 c. and 13 ll. Fair *ta'líq* with rubrications. Dated A.H. 1018/A.D. 1609–10. The copyist, who gives his name as Núḥ al-Wadnawí (**الوودنوى** in the MS.), says that he was encouraged to transcribe Jámí's poem by the Qáḍí of Wadna (**ودنه**), Muḥammad ibn Maḥmúd.

V. 78 (8).

يوسف و زليخا،

The well-known *mathnawí* of Jámí entitled *Yúsuf ú Zalíkhá.* See Ethé, I.O.P.C., col. 746, No. 6.

Ff. 111 of 19·6 × 13·3 c. and 17 ll. Distinct but inelegant *ta'líq* with rubrications. No colophon or date. A seal-inscription on the back of f. 1 shows that the MS. was bequeathed to a mosque, of which the name is illegible. Many glosses in Turkish are written on the margins.

V. 79 (9).

تيمورنامهٔ (ظفرنامهٔ) هاتفى،

An old but slightly defective copy of the *Tímúr-náma* or, as it is also styled, *Ẓafar-náma* of Hátifí (d. 927/1521), the nephew of the famous Jámí, a poem written to celebrate the conquests of Tímúr. See Rieu, B.M.P.C., p. 653; Ethé, I.O.P.C., **No. 1410.**

Begins:

ز مهمانیش مه خجل شد نخست   که بر سفره کم دید نان درست

The first complete section (f. 3[a]) begins with an address to the reigning sovereign:

شها شهریارا سرا سرورا   خداوندگارا جهان‌پرورا

Ff. 113 of 21·5 × 11·5 c. and 14 ll. Fair *nasta'líq* with rubrications and illuminated borders. The date of transcription appears to be Jumáda'th-thání, 960/May, 1553.

V. 80 (8).

خسرو و شیرین عُرفی، قصائد عُرفی،

1. (ff. 1[b]–18[a].) The *Khusraw ú Shírín* (entitled in some copies *Farhád ú Shírín*) of 'Urfí of Shíráz. See Ethé, I.O.P.C., cols. 799 and 800; Rieu, B.M.P.C., p. 667 *b*, IV.

Begins:

خداوندا دلم بی نور تنگست   دل من سنگ و کوه طور سنگ است

Colophon:

تمّت الکتاب بعون الملك الوهّاب تمام شد خسرو و شیرین بحمد الله [و] حسن توفیقه

2. (ff. 18[b]–75[b].) The *qaṣídas* of 'Urfí, beginning:

اقبال کرم میگزد ارباب همم را   همّت نخورد نشتر آری و نعم را

After f. 75[b] one or more pages are missing. F. 76[a], which is pasted on the back of the cover, begins with the verse:

از خجلت این گنه که عفوش   بر تست نه بر عطای یزدان

Ff. 76 of 18 × 10·1 c. and 14 ll. Written in a small, poor *ta'líq* with illuminated 'unwáns and coloured borders. No date.

V. 81 (10).

دیوان ظهوری،

A large collection of the lyrical poems of Ẓuhúrí of Turshíz (d. 1024/1615). See *Persian Literature in Modern Times*, p. 253, and Ethé, I.O.P.C., cols. 820–827.

1. (ff. 1[a]–209[a].) *Ghazals* in alphabetical order. One or more pages have been lost at the beginning, and the first verse is:

قصد خمخانهٔ افلاك پی دوران کنند   آسمانها قطرهای ساغر سرسار ما

2. (ff. 209[a]–216[a].) *Rubá'ís*, beginning:

یا رب چکنم که چشم جان باز کنم   یا رب جگری که رزم خود ساز کنم

Ff. 216 of 25·1 × 13 c. and 19 ll. Indifferent *ta'líq*. No colophon or date.

V. 82 (9).

دیوان کلیم،

The shorter poetical works of Mírzá Abú Ṭálib Kalím of Hamadán, the poet-laureate of Sháhjahán. He died 1061 or 1062/1651–2. See Rieu, B.M.P.C., p. 686; Ethé, I.O.P.C., **No. 1563**.

Contents:

1. (ff. 3ᵇ–30ᵃ.) *Qaṣídas*, beginning:

شوق هر کس‌را که در راه طلب سر میدهد　　گر در آرد اوّل از پا آخرش بر میدهد

2. (ff. 30ᵃ–41ᵃ.) *Muqaṭṭa'át.*

3. (ff. 41ᵃ–68ᵇ.) *Mathnawís.* The first of these is entitled کتابهٔ دولتخانهٔ پادشاهی, and the second کتابهٔ دولتخانهٔ اکبرآباد. There are about twenty poems in this section of the *Díwán*.

4. (ff. 71ᵃ–128ᵃ.) *Ghazals* in alphabetical order, beginning:

بدل کردم بمستی عاقبت زهد ریائی‌را　　رسانیدم بآب از یمن می بنیاد تقوی‌را

5. (ff. 128ᵃ–133ᵃ.) *Rubá'ís.*

Ff. 135 of 22·7 × 12·2 c. and 15 ll. in centre, 26 ll. in margins. Cursive *ta'líq* approximating to *ním-shikasta*, with rubrications, gilt borders, and two vignettes. No date. The names of several former owners (including at least one European, T. or J. Zovianoff) are inscribed at the beginning and end.

V. 83 (12).

کلّیات نشاط،

This volume, bought from the Trustees of the British Museum, comprises several works by Mírzá 'Abdu'l-Wahháb Nasháṭ of Iṣfahán, who died in 1244/1828 (see *Persian Literature in Modern Times*, pp. 225, 307 and 311), but is not such a complete collection as **V. 54** (pp. 247–248 *supra*).

1. (ff. 1ᵇ–59ᵇ.) Various pieces in ornate prose intermingled with verse. The contents agree closely with those of **Add. 19,533**, ff. 17–55 and 75–142, as described by Rieu (B.M.P.C., p. 722), and include (*a*) a preface to the *Díwán* of Fatḥ 'Alí Sháh, beginning on f. 1ᵇ ناظم العوالم بدیع المناظم; (*b*) a preface (f. 20ᵇ) to the *Sháhin-sháh-náma* of Fatḥ 'Alí Khán of Káshán who took the pen-name Ṣabá and was the poet-laureate of Fatḥ 'Alí Sháh (see *Persian Literature in Modern Times*, p. 309); (*c*) *khuṭbas* in Arabic, Persian, and Turkish; (*d*) letters addressed to various Oriental and European sovereigns, among the latter being Napoleon and George III of England.

2. (ff. 62ᵇ–130ᵃ.) *Ghazals* in alphabetical order, with a *tarkíb-band* and some *rubá'ís*. The *ghazals* begin as follows:

پیداست سرّ وحدت از اعیان اما تری   العکس فی المرایا والنفس فی القوی

Ff. 130 of 29·1 × 19·8 c. and 17 ll. There is a lacuna after f. 59ᵇ, and ff. 60 and 61 are left blank. Written in clear *ta'líq* with illuminated 'unwáns and borders. No colophon or date.

V. 84 (7).

دیوان نوا،

This MS. is described (f. 1ᵇ and f. 68ᵇ) as a collection of *ghazals* by Mír Naṣr Nawá, who received the title of *Táju'sh-Shu'ará* ("Crown of the Poets"). Begins:

زآن کنم حمد خالق یکتا   که زبان شد بحمد او گویا
حقّ حمدش کجا توان گفتن   قطره کی وصف گوید از دریا

The author was a native of Shíráz, as appears from the following verses (f. 21ᵃ):

بدار اکنون زشعر و شاعری دست   که جز غم حاصلی در شاعری نیست
اگرچه چون نوا در ملك شیراز   تورا همتا بگفتار دری نیست

and f. 21ᵇ:

ای نوا گشتم جهانرا سر بسر   هیچ ملکی خوشتر از شیراز نیست

The title *Táju'sh-Shu'ará* occurs in a verse on f. 20ᵃ:

تاج الشعرا چو نوا می نتوان گفت   در عالم معنی چو تو صاحب هنری هست

Ff. 70 of 16·3 × 10·5 c. and 10 ll. Small cursive *ta'líq*. Dated 1313/1895–6.

V. 85 (16).

شاهنشاه‌نامهٔ صبا،

A fine copy of the *Sháhinsháh-náma*, an epic poem composed in honour of Fatḥ 'Alí Sháh Qájár (1797–1834) by his poet-laureate Fatḥ 'Alí Khán of Káshán (d. 1238/1822–3), whose pen-name (*takhalluṣ*) was Ṣabá (see *Persian Literature in Modern Times*, p. 309; Ethé, I.O.P.C., col. 563, **No. 901**). The text was lithographed in Bombay in 1890.

Begins:

بنام خداوند آموزگار   نگارندهٔ نامهٔ روزگار

Ff. 438 of 39·5 × 26·5 c. and 20 ll. Good *nasta'líq*, with rubrications, written on thick paper in four columns within blue and gold borders. It was evidently intended that the history of the hero should be illustrated with pictures, and for this purpose blank spaces, some of which occupy the whole or nearly the whole page, have been left on ff. 19^{a}, 45^{b}, 49^{a}, 53^{b}, 57^{b}, 77^{b}, 88^{a}, 97^{a}, 100^{a}, 101^{a}, 102^{a}, 103^{a}, 104^{a}, 105^{a}, 106^{a}, 120^{b}, 135^{b}, 137^{b}, 141^{b}, 144^{b}, 150^{b}, 155^{a}, 161^{a}, 167^{b}, 178^{a}, 212^{a}, 232^{b}, 238^{a}, 244^{a}, 257^{a}, 306^{b}, 327^{a}, 330^{b}, 343^{a}, 369^{a}, 374^{a}, 383^{a}, 416^{a}. As these blank spaces are ruled with vertical lines, the latter would seem to have been added subsequently. The MS. was bought from the Trustees of the British Museum in January 17, 1924.

V. 86 (8).

دیوان طرزی،

A collection of erotic odes by a poet whose pen-name (*takhalluṣ*) is Ṭarzí and whom I am unable to identify. It begins:

ای دل بشاد و از غم هجران باضطراب   چون قطب ساکنیده فلکسان باضطراب

The work, though contemptible in every other respect, derives some lexicographical interest from the author's habit of coining verbs unknown to the dictionaries by adding the termination ـیدن to Arabic and Persian nouns, adjectives, and participles. Besides ساکنیدن (in the verse cited above), we find such monstrosities as تحصیلیدن, تغافلیدن, طلوعیدن, مجنونیدن, آبادیدن, آزادیدن, etc., etc.

From the words in the colophon دیوان مختصر مرحوم طرزی افشاررا در دار الخلافه طهران تحریر...(?) it would appear that the author was an Afshár Turk, and probably he belongs to the 19th century.

Ff. 157 (nearly 100 of which are blank) of 17·9 × 11 c. and 12 ll. Transcribed at Ṭihrán in Ṣafar, 1284/June, 1867, in a cursive *ta'líq* approximating to *ním-shikasta*.

V. 87 (9).

A collection of Persian poems by various authors.

Contents:

1. (ff. 1^{b}–10^{a}.) *Ghazals* and *rubá'ís* from the *Díwán-i Shams-i Tabríz* by Jalálu'd-Dín Rúmí.

2. (ff. 10^{b}–13^{b}.) The well-known *tarjí'-band* by Sayyid Aḥmad Hátif of Iṣfahán, beginning:

ای فدای تو هم دل و هم جان   وی نثار رهت هم این و هم آن

of which Professor Browne has given the text, with an English prose translation, in *Persian Literature in Modern Times*, pp. 284–297.

3. (ff. 14^{a}–21^{b}.) A *mathnawí* by Mírzá Naṣír, whom I have not been able to identify, beginning:

شبی با نو جوانی گفت پیری   کهن دردی کشی صافی ضمیری

4. (ff. 22ᵃ–25ᵇ.) The *Sarápá*, a *mathnawí* describing the human body, by Mír Sayyid 'Alí Mihrí of Iṣfahán, who flourished in the reign of Sháh Ḥusayn, the last Ṣafawí monarch (1105–1135/1694–1722). See Rieu, B.M.P.C., p. 796; Ethé, I.O.P.C., **No. 1640**. Begins:

ای بت چابك شیرین حرکات جلوهٔ ناز تو چون آب حیات

5. (ff. 26ᵃ–28ᵃ.) *Rubá'ís* and couplets by Ẓiyá, *i.e.*, probably, Ẓiyá'u'd-Dín Káshí (Ethé, I.O.P.C., **No. 1743**, 29).

6. (ff. 28ᵇ–30ᵃ.) Selections from Waḥshí of Báfq (see Ethé, I.O.P.C., **No. 1444**) and the above-mentioned Ẓiyá. These are followed by a *ghazal* of Jámí.

7. (ff. 30ᵇ–35ᵇ.) *Qaṣídas* and *ghazals* by Sa'dí.

8. (ff. 36ᵇ–85ᵇ.) The *qaṣídas* of Qá'ání, arranged in the order of their rhyme-letters from ا to ه.

9. (ff. 85ᵇ–99ᵃ.) A large number of short extracts from the poems of Qá'ání.

10. (ff. 99ᵃ–108ᵇ.) *Qaṣídas* of Qá'ání rhyming in the letter ی.

Ff. 109 of 21·2 × 13 c. and 14 ll. Cursive *ta'líq* with vignettes. No date.

V. 88 (7).

دیوان عنصری، قصائد لامعی، مجموعهٔ اشعار،

A valuable Persian Anthology, comprising specimens of the work of many poets who lived in the Sámánid, Ghaznavid, and Saljúq periods. The contents are as follows:

1 (pp. 2–139). The *Díwán* of 'Unṣurí, the poet-laureate of Sulṭán Maḥmúd of Ghazna, beginning:

دل مرا عجب آید همی زکار هوا که مشکبوی سلب گشت و مشکبوی صبا

See Rieu's Pers. Suppl., **Nos. 204** (ii), **205**. Pp. 2–132 contain *qaṣídas* in alphabetical order, which are followed by three *qiṭ'as* and about thirty *rubá'ís*. The transcription was completed on 25 Sha'bán, 1266/6 July, 1849.

2 (pp. 144–179). The *qaṣídas* of Abu'l-Ḥasan Lámi'í of Jurján, a poet who wrote panegyrics on Malikshâh and Niẓámu'l-Mulk and died in the reign of Sulṭán Sanjar. See Rieu, Pers. Suppl., **No. 212** (ii). Begins:

مانوی نقش است رویت ای نگار آذری کز تو در دلها چنین نقش است چندین داوری

3 (pp. 180–186). Two *qaṣídas* by Ḥakím Azraqí (see *Literary History of Persia*, vol. II, p. 323). 4 (pp. 186–190). Two *qaṣídas* by Súzaní of Samarqand (see *ibid.*, p. 342). 5 (p. 190). A *qaṣída* by Manshúrí of Samarqand. See the *Lubábu'l-Albáb* of 'Awfí, Pt. II, p. 44, where twelve verses of the same *qaṣída*, beginning یکی دریا پدید آمد الخ, are cited. 6 (p. 192). A *qaṣída* by Manṣúr ibn 'Alí Manṭiqí of Rayy (see *Literary History of Persia*, vol. II, pp. 93–94, and *Lubáb*, Pt. II, pp. 16–18), beginning:

نگار سمن‌بوی و ماه سمن‌بر لبش جای جان و رخش آز آزر

7 (p. 193). A *qaṣída* by Bahrámí of Sarakhs (see *Lit. Hist. of Persia*, vol. II, p. 156, and *Lubáb*, Pt. II, pp. 55–57), beginning

همیشه خرّم و آباد باد ترکستان   که قبلهٔ شمنانست و جایگاه بتان

8 (p. 195). A *qaṣída* by Abu'l-Ma'álí of Rayy (see *Lubáb*, Pt. II, pp. 228–236, where two complete odes by him are cited). 9 (p. 196). A *qaṣída* in praise of the vine (در وصف رز) by Bashshár-i Marghazí[1], beginning:

رزرا خدای از قبل شادی بیآفرید   شادی و خرّمی همه از رز شود پدید

10 (p. 198). A *qaṣída* by 'Am'aq of Bukhárá (see *Lit. Hist. of Persia*, vol. II, p. 335, and *Lubáb*, Pt. II, pp. 181–191), beginning:

نماز شام چو پنهان شد آتش اندر آب   سپهر چهره بپوشید زیر پرّ غراب

11 (p. 199). Part of the celebrated "Candle" *qaṣída* by Minúchihrí, of which the full text is given in Kazimirski's edition, pp. 86–93. 12 (p. 200). A *qaṣída* by Qaṭrán (see *Lit. Hist. of Persia*, vol. II, p. 271). 13 (p. 202). A *qaṣída* by Ẓahír of Fáryáb. 14 (p. 204). A *qaṣída* by Saná'í of Ghazna. 15 (p. 205). A *qaṣída* by Mu'izzí. 16 (p. 206). A *qaṣída* by Mukhtárí of Ghazna (see Rieu, B.M.P.C., p. 543). 17 (p. 207). A *qaṣída* by Sayfu'd-Dín A'raj of Isfarang (see Dawlatsháh, pp. 126–128). 18 (p. 208). A *qaṣída* by Rúdakí, beginning:

آمد بهار خرّم با رنگ و بوی و طیب   با صد هزار زینت و آرائش عجیب

19 (p. 209). A *qaṣída*, defective at the beginning, by Daqíqí. The first verse is:

پری چهره بتی عیّار و دلبند   نگاری سرْوقد و ماهمنظر

20 (p. 212). Two *qaṣídas* by Saná'í. 21 (p. 219). A short extract from a *qaṣída* by Farrukhí. 22 (p. 220). A similar extract from a *qaṣída* by Badru'd-Dín of Shásh (see Rieu, B.M.P.C., pp. 1031–1032). 23 (p. 222). The opening verses of a *qaṣída* by Daqíqí. 24 (p. 222). A *qaṣída* by Lámi'í of Jurján (see No. 2 *supra*). 25 (p. 225). The famous *qaṣída* by Rúdakí, beginning

مادر می بکرد باید قربان   بچّهٔ اورا گرفت و کرد بزندان

which has been edited by Mirzá Muḥammad Khán, with an introduction and English translation by Sir E. Denison Ross, in *J.R.A.S.* for 1926, p. 213 foll. The text given in this MS. contains 95 verses, one more than the printed text. 26 (p. 228). A *qaṣída* by Mukhtárí of Ghazna. 27 (p. 229). Two *qaṣídas* by Wiṣál, possibly Wiṣál of Shíráz (d. 1263/1847), who composed a sequel to the *Farhád ú Shírín* of Waḥshí (see Rieu, Pers. Suppl., **No. 308**). 28 (p. 233). A *qaṣída* by Abu'l-Faraj Rúní of Lahore (d. *circa* 1100 A.D.; see *Lubáb*, Pt. II, p. 238).

---

[1] [*Marghazí* is a dialectical form of *Marwazí*, *i.e.* of Merv. I cannot find any notice of this poet.]

It is scarcely necessary to state that many of the poems mentioned in the above list are not complete *qaṣídas*, but only extracts comprising the customary *tashbíb* or prelude. Pp. 238 of 17 × 10 c. and 16 ll. Small cursive *ta'líq*. Dated on p. 139 A.H. 1266/A.D. 1849. On p. 1 Professor Browne has written the following note: "Given to me by Mírzá 'Alí Akbar Káshif, June 6, 1913." Facing p. 1 is a Persian table of contents prepared by Mírzá Bihrúz.

V. 89 (8).

دیوان کمال خجندی،

A good, fairly old, but very incomplete copy of the odes of Kamál of Khujand (cf. **V. 33** *supra*). It is defective both at the beginning and the end, but while it contains *ghazals* rhyming in ی—ف, none of those rhyming in ا—غ is included. There is also a lacuna after f. 31[b], where some *ghazals* rhyming in ه and all those rhyming in و have fallen out.

Ff. 44 of 17·9×12·5 c. and 13 ll. Clear but somewhat inelegant *ta'líq*. No colophon or date.

V. 90 (8).

گلستان سعدی،

A defective copy of the *Gulistán*. The portions missing are (1) the latter part of the Introduction, (2) the whole of Book I, (3) the earlier part of Book II, occupying pp. 46–51, l. 4, in Platts's edition.

Ff. 102 of 16·8 × 10·5 c. and 13 ll. Fair *ta'líq* with rubrications. Dated 948/1541–2. Professor Browne has noted that this was one of 34 MSS. bought by him from the Trustees of the British Museum in December, 1923, for £14.

V. 91 (10).

گلستان سعدی،

The following description by Professor Browne is written on the fly-leaf: "The *Gulistán* of Sa'dí, received as a present from Muftí-záda 'Izzí Bey of Nicosia, Cyprus, with letter [which is pasted on the last page] dated March 5, 1925, on March 15 of the same year. From the *Table of Contents* on ff. 1[b]–2[a] it would appear that this formed only a small part of a large volume of selected Persian writings.

Ff. 41 of 24·8 × 14 c. and 23 ll. Excellent *ta'líq* with rubrications; dated in colophon Rabí' 1, 1061/Feb.—March, 1651."

W. TURKISH POETRY.

W. 1 (8).

ديوان نجاتى،

The *Díwán* of Najátí (d. 914/1509; see E. J. W. Gibb, *Hist. of Ottoman Poetry*, vol. II, p. 93 foll.), which he dedicated to Prince Maḥmúd, son of Báyazíd II. See Rieu, B.M.T.C., p. 171, and Flügel, Vienna Cat., vol. I, p. 624.

Contents:

Preface (f. 2^b), beginning:

كلّگوز اوللمر گه و بيگاه   ذاكر لا اله الّا الله

Qaṣídas (f. 4^b), beginning:

شو سوز كمر اوله مثال كلامر اهل كمال   سلاستنده خجل اوله سلسبيل و زلال

Ghazals (f. 51^b), beginning:

واركن جانانه كوكلمر جانه اولمز آشنا   شمعى قويب غيرله پروانه اولمز آشنا

The *ghazals* are followed by a number of short poems, including some *rubá'ís*.

Ff. 174 of 19·7 × 14·2 c. and 15 ll. Good Turkish *naskh*. No date. Bought for £1 in Cairo, Feb. 10, 1903.

W. 2 (7).

ديوان فضولى،

The Turkish *Díwán* of Fuẓúlí of Baghdád (d. 963/1555–6 or 970/1562–3). See *Hist. of Ottoman Poetry*, vol. III, p. 70 foll.), Rieu, B.M.T.C., p. 207, and Flügel, Vienna Cat., vol. I, p. 638. The preface is wanting.

Begins:

قد انار العشق للعشّاق منهاج الهدى   سالك راه حقيقت عشقه ايلر اقتدا

Ff. 81 of 16·8 × 11 c. and 17 ll. Dated 20 Ṣafar, 1218/12 June, 1803.

W. 3 (8).

ديوان نفعى،

The poetical works of Nef'í of Erzerúm, who flourished in the reign of Sulṭán Murád IV and was put to death, according to most authorities, in 1044/1634–5 (*Hist. of Ottoman Poetry*, vol. III, p. 252 foll.). See Rieu, B.M.T.C., p. 192

Ff. 1ᵇ–60ᵇ comprise Persian *qaṣídas*, *ghazals*, and *qiṭ'as*, beginning:

دلم سرمست جام عشق و عقل کل زباندانش   نگوید نشنود هر دو جز از توحید یزدانش

The Turkish poems (ff. 62ᵇ–214ᵃ) begin:

عقدهٔ سررشتهٔ راز نهانیدر سوزم   سلك تسبیح دُر سبع المثانیدر سوزم

Ff. 214 of 18×12·5 c. and 15 ll. Good *ta'líq* with rubrications. No colophon or date. Bought from J. J. Naaman in May, 1902.

W. 4 (8).

عين الحيوة.

A Turkish mystical *mathnawí*, entitled *'Aynu'l-Ḥayát* or "The Fountain of Life," by Áq-Kirmání Naqshí (according to the rubric on f. 1ᵇ of **W. 5**), written partly in the *hazaj* metre and partly in *ramal*, and beginning:

ایا گل گور بو گون عین الحیاتی   نه یوزده شرح ایدر بو کائناتی

The work, which is defective at the end, consists of a versified exposition of Qur'ánic texts and traditions of the Prophet.

Ff. 206 of 20×15 c. and 11 ll. Coarse Turkish hand, a mixture of *riq'a* and *díwání*. Bought from J. J. Naaman in Sept., 1901.

W. 5 (9).

عين الحيات،

A complete copy of the same poem, presented to Professor Browne by Dr Riẓá Tevfíq in August, 1909.

Ff. 90 of 22·2×15 c. and 22 ll. Clear Turkish *naskh* with rubrications. Transcribed by Darwísh 'Abdu'l-Fattáḥ Yáziji and dated 9 Rajab 1217/5 November, 1802.

W. 6 (9).

ذمّ الفناء،

A collection of *qaṣídas*, bearing the title *Dhammu'l-Fanā*, which (as الفناء must here signify دار الفناء) is equivalent to *De contemptu mundi*. According to the late Mr E. J. W. Gibb, whose letter accompanies the MS., this work was composed by a certain Muṣliḥu'd-Dín-oghlu of Ṣirṣirat (صِرْصِرَت, probably for سرستاد, Siristád) in Bozqir (بُوْزقِر), a district in the south-west of the viláyet of Qoniya.

Begins:

ثنا و حمد لا يُحْصَى سكا اى خالق فيّاض
كه يُوقْدُر سكا هيچ امثال كه سنسن قادرُ (*sic*) فيّاض (قبّاض)

Ff. 122 of 21 × 15·4 c. and 16 ll. Defective at the end. Poor but legible Turkish *naskh*. Bought at Kazan by Professor E. H. Minns in September, 1898.

W. 7 (9).

The first of the two works contained in this volume is a long Turkish *mathnawí* on religious topics, without title or author's name. It comprises many edifying anecdotes, stories of the Prophets, expositions of Qur'ánic texts, etc.

Begins:

ابتدا قيلديم حق آدين اى كوكل

The colophon (f. 124[a]) is as follows:

كتب هذه نسخة شريفة حبيب الله بن محين (?) در زمين قزان و راه آلاط در تريته (?) بوسكا (?)
و فى مدرسة عبد الرحيم بن مولا بيكچتاش (?)

The second work (ff. 125[a]–196[b]) is an Arabic treatise on *fiqh*, defective both at the beginning and the end. The contents include كتاب النكاح (f. 141[a]), كتاب العتاق (f. 159[a]), and كتاب البيع (f. 169[a]).

Ff. 197 of 20 × 15·8 c. and 17 and 10 ll. Coarse Transoxanian *nasta'líq*. As the MS. was written in Kazan and bears the name of a former owner who belonged to that town, it probably came from there.

W. 8 (7).

طريقت‌نامهٔ هُدائى، نجاة الغريق هُدائى، پندِ ظريفى بابا،
تصوّف‌نامهٔ ظريفى،

This MS., which was given to Professor Browne by Dr Riẓá Tevfíq, contains the following works:

1. (ff. 1[b]–13[a].) The *Ṭaríqat-náma*, or "Book of the Mystic Path," by Shaykh Ḥelváji-záde Maḥmúd of Scutari, with the *takhalluṣ* (pen-name) of Hudá'í (d. 1038/1628; see Gibb, *Hist. of Ottoman Poetry*, vol. III, p. 218 foll.). Another copy is described in Flügel's Vienna Catalogue, vol. III, p. 541. The treatise is written in prose, beginning الحمد لله الذى تجلّى بذاته لذاته, and concludes with two short pieces in verse.

2. (ff. 13[a]–31[a].) *Najátu'l-Gharíq*, or "The Rescue of the Drowning," a *mathnawí* by Hudá'í which, as described by Mr E. J. W. Gibb (*loc. cit.*, p. 219),

"consists of a series of riming paraphrases of certain well-known Apostolic traditions and sayings of prominent Ṣúfí saints."

Begins:

خدایه حمد [و] منّت اوّل آخر   که اولدر ظاهر [و] باطنده ظاهر

3. (ff. 33^b–79^a.) The *Pand* or "Counsel" of Ẓarífí Bábá, a *mathnawí* on ethical topics, beginning:

حمد بی‌حد اول خدایه ابتدا   حکمتینه یوقدر آنڭ انتها

4. (ff. 79^b–91^b.) Another treatise by the same Ẓarífí on various *iṣṭiláḥát* or technical terms used by the Ṣúfís. It is written partly in prose and partly in verse.

Begins:

حمد بی‌حد اول خدای عزّته   لایق اولدر مدح شکر منّته

and ends:

گل ظریفی ناقص اولمه کامل اول   اون سڭز بیڭ عالمی کندنده بول

5. (ff. 92^a–96^b.) The *Taṣawwuf-náma* or "Book of Ṣúfism" by Ẓarífí, beginning:

خدایه اوّلا حمد هزاران   یارتدی کائناتی جنّ انسان

Ff. 97^a–98^a contain tables of *iṣṭiláḥát* (1) of the great Shaykhs and (2) of Ḥáfiẓ, with the explanations written below.

Ff. 102 of 16·6 × 11·2 c. and 13 ll. No colophon or date. Written by different hands. No. 3 is a small, neat, and carefully pointed *ta'líq*.

W. 9 (8).

ترجمهٔ پندنامهٔ عطّار

A metrical Turkish translation of the *Pand-náma* of Farídu'd-Dín 'Aṭṭár by Amrí of Adrianople (d. 988/1580). See Flügel, Vienna Catalogue, vol. III, p. 415, where another copy of the work is described, and Rieu, B.M.T.C., pp. 154 and 261.

Begins (f. 2^b):

ابتدا کردم بنام آن کریم   مبدع کونین سلطان قدیم

The translation, written in the same metre as the original poem and dedicated to Prince Báyazíd, a son of Sulṭán Sulaymán I (see Gibb, *Hist. of Ottoman Poetry*, vol. III, pp. 10–11), begins on f. 4^a:

حمد بی‌حدّ اول خدای عالمه   نور ایمان ویردی خاك آدمه

and is followed by miscellaneous Turkish and Arabic verses (ff. 37^a–40^b).

Ff. 43 of 19·8 × 13·6 c. and 15 ll. Clear *naskh*, pointed, with rubrications. Transcribed by Darwísh Safar and completed in 1035/1625–6. This MS. was presented to Professor Browne in April, 1908, by Dr Riẓá Tevfíq.

W. 10 (9).

دیوان میر علی شیر نوائی،

The Chaghatáy or Eastern Turkí poems of Nawá'í, which is the pen-name of Mír 'Alí Shír (d. 906/1501), the accomplished minister of Sulṭán Ḥusayn ibn Manṣúr ibn Bayqará. See *Persian Literature under Tartar Dominion*, p. 505, and Rieu, B.M.T.C., pp. 294–298.

Ff. 1^b–21^b. Preface in prose, beginning:

فصاحت دیوانی‌نینك غزل سرالاری

Ff. 24^b–305^b. *Ghazals* in alphabetical order, beginning:

اشرقت من عکس شمس الكأس انوار الهدا

Ff. 306 of 22 × 12·7 c. and 9 ll. Fair *ta'líq* between gold and coloured borders. Copied at Káshghar in 1241/1825–6. Professor Browne has written on the fly-leaf, "A Christmas Present to me from Professor A. von Le Coq of Berlin, 25. xii. 1923," and the latter's book-plate with inscription signed "A. v. Le Coq" is pasted inside the cover.

X. STORIES AND EPISTOLARY MODELS.

X. 1 (9).

كمال البلاغة،

Kamálu'l-Balágha or "The Perfection of Eloquence," an Arabic anthology in prose and verse compiled by 'Abdu'r-Raḥmán ibn 'Alí al-Yazdádí and comprising in the first place the letters (*rasá'il*) of Shamsu'l-Ma'álí Qábús ibn Washmgír, Prince of Ṭabaristán (d. 403/1012; see *Lit. Hist. of Persia*, vol. II, p. 101), which are followed, for the purpose of comparison, by specimens in the same style selected from the correspondence of the royal author's eminent contemporaries. Ḥájjí Khalífa (ed. Flügel, vol. v, p. 240, **No. 10858**) attributes this work to Qábús ibn Washmgír himself.

Begins:

قال عبد الرحمن بن على اليزدادى كنت انظر فيما ألفه قدامة بن جعفر فى ذكر الكتّاب وأورده فى فصول مستخرجة من اثناء رسايل الكتّاب وكلام البلغاء وأبان عنه من محاسن معان وألفاظ فصيحة

The book to which al-Yazdádí refers in this passage is no doubt the *Ṣiná'atu-'l-Kitába* by Qudáma ibn Ja'far (d. 310/922 according to Brockelmann, *Gesch. d. Arab. Litt.*, I, 228), which seems to have formed part of the same writer's *Kitábu-'l-Kharáj* (see De Slane in *Journal Asiatique*, Série v, vol. 20, p. 156).

Al-Yazdádí goes on to say that, finding nothing in Qudáma's work comparable to the epistles of Qábús ibn Washmgír, he resolved to edit the latter in order that they might serve as a perfect model to secretaries,

ولهذا سمّيتُ الكتاب كمال البلاغة لبلوغه مبلغ النهاية فى الكلام

He adds that he has not included the answers written to these epistles, making an exception, however, in favour of the *Ṣáḥib* Ismá'íl ibn 'Abbád (and in one instance, of Abú Isḥáq Ibráhím ibn Hilál aṣ-Ṣábí)[1]. In the heading prefixed to each epistle he states the number of pairs of rhymed clauses (قرائن الاسجاع) which it contains.

In addition to the correspondence of Qábús ibn Washmgír, this volume comprises epistles or poems by the following: Abú Isḥáq ibn Ibráhím aṣ-Ṣábí (f. 18^b), the *Ṣáḥib* Ismá'íl ibn 'Abbád (ff. 21^a, 22^a), Abú Bakr al-Khwárizmí (ff. 22^b–23^a), Muḥammad ibn 'Abdi'l-Jabbár al-'Utbí (ff. 24^a–25^b), Muḥammad ibn 'Abdi'l-'Azíz as-Sulamí an-Nishábúrí (f. 25^b), ar-Ra'ís Aḥmad ibn Ibráhím aḍ-Ḍabbí (f. 26^b), as-Sayyíd Abu'l-Ḥasan 'Alí ibnu'l-Ḥasan al-'Alawí (ff. 26^b–27^b), Abú Sa'íd ar-Rustamí (f. 28^a), Abu'l-Faraj ibn Hindú (f. 28^b), Abú Sa'íd ibnu'l-Khalaf al-Hamadání (ff. 29^a–31^b), al-Imám Abú Ja'far Muḥammad ibn 'Abdi'lláh ibn Ṣáliḥ az-Zawzaní (f. 32^a), Abu'l-Ḥasan al-Bákharzí (ff. 32^b–33^b), Badí'u'z-Zamán al-Hamadání (ff. 34^b–38^a, 45^b, 46^b, 58^b–59^b), Abú Naṣr Aḥmad ibn Muḥammad al-Míkálí and his son Abu'l-Faḍl (ff. 40^a–42^a), Rashídu'd-Dín Waṭwáṭ (ff. 46^b–56^a), Abú Sa'íd ibn Abi'l-Khayr and Ibn Síná (ff. 57^a–58^b), and many others.

Ff. 60 of 21·5 × 14·2 c. and 17 ll. Neat, clear modern *naskh* with rubrications. No colophon or date. This is one of eighty-four MSS. of the Belshah collection which were divided at the British Museum on Nov. 12, 1920.

X. 2 (10).

صرف الهمّ (?)،

A collection of edifying tales by an anonymous writer. The words صرف الهمّ, which occur in the description of the work immediately after the *Bismi'lláh*, are given in the colophon as its title; they also form the title of a book ascribed in the *Fihrist* (p. 130, l. 24) to Qudáma ibn Ja'far (d. 310/922). The title written in red above the *Bismi'lláh* is كتاب الفرج بعد الشدّة, and Professor Browne has noted on the fly-leaf that "This seems to be an abridgement of the *Kitábu'l-Faraj ba'da'sh-Shidda* of at-Tanúkhí, entitled *Ṣarfu'l-Hamm*." The contents, however, show that

[1] [In this letter (f. 17^b) aṣ-Ṣábí replies to a letter (f. 16^b) in which Qábús had asked for two astrolabes and other astronomical instruments in aṣ-Ṣábí's *khizána*, and excuses himself for his inability to comply with the request.]

the present compilation, though much of its matter is taken from at-Tanúkhí, must be regarded as an independent work.

Begins :

كتاب الاخبار المعينة على ادب النفس و صرف الهمّ وهو اثنا عشر باباً

The headings of the twelve chapters into which it is divided are as follows :

الباب الاوّل، فى الاخبار المعينة على الدّيانة وحسن النيّة والاقلاع عن المعصية والخطية، (f. 2^{b})

الباب الثانى، فى الاخبار المعينة على الشكر وعلى تجنّب الكفر، (f. 20^{a})

الباب الثالث، فى العفّة وتجنّب الفجور، (f. 30^{a})

الباب الرابع، فى الاخبار المعينة على التواضع وعلى تجنّب الكفر (الكبر)، (f. 39^{b})

الباب الخامس، فى الاخبار المعينة على الرحمة وعلى تجنّب القساوة، (f. 47^{b})

الباب السادس، فى الاخبار المعينة على التوبة وعلى تجنّب الاصرار، (f. 52^{b})

الباب السابع، فى الاخبار المعينة على استعمال الحزم والمداراة وطلب العلم والحكمة وعلى تجنّب التهوّر والجهل وتطبيع (?وتضييع) الحزم، (f. 60^{a})

الباب الثامن، فى الاحوال المعينة على استعمال المشاورة وعلى تجنّب الاستبداد بالرأى، (f. 65^{b})

الباب التاسع، فى الاخبار المعينة على مكارم الاخلاق وتجنّب سوء الخلق، (f. 72^{b})

الباب العاشر، فى الاخبار المعينة على الكرم وعلى تجنّب البخل، (f. 82^{a})

الباب الحادى عشر، فى الاخبار المعينة على استعمال العدل وعلى تجنّب الظلم والجور، (f. 96^{a})

الباب الثانى عشر، فى الاخبار المعينة على استعمال الحلم وعلى تجنّب الغضب والسفه، (f. 104^{a})

As regards the books which the compiler has mentioned by name in the rubrics introducing each anecdote, there are twenty-six excerpts from the *Kitábu'l-Faraj ba'da'sh-Shidda* of at-Tanúkhí; ten (ff. 4^{b}, 36^{a}, 39^{a}, 40^{a}, 48^{a}, 55^{b}, 56^{a}, 109^{b}, 113^{b}, 114^{a}) from the *Kitábu'l-Firdaws*; six (ff. 108^{b}, 112^{b}, 114^{b}, 118^{a}, 119^{a}, 119^{b}) from the *Safaṭu'l-Jawhar* (سفط الجوهر); three (ff. 72^{b}, 98^{b}, 99^{a}) from the *Ta'ríkh* of Abu'l-Ḥasan Thábit ibn Sinán (aṣ-Ṣábí; d. *circa* 365/975); three (ff. 120^{b}, 121^{a}, 121^{b}) from the *Kitábu Naqli'ẓ-Ẓiráf* (نقل الظّراف); two (ff. 45^{a}, 46^{a}) from the *Kitábu'n-Naṣíḥa* of Abu'l-Qásim Hibatu'lláh ibn Masarra; and two (ff. 82^{a}, 104^{a}) from the *Kitábu'l-Wuzará* of [Muḥammad ibn 'Abdús] al-Jahshiyárí (d. 331/942). Although the last-named work is one of at-Tanúkhí's sources, the extracts from it which are given in this MS. are not likely to have been copied from the *Faraj*; the other five books were not, apparently, excerpted by at-Tanúkhí in his great collection, and at any rate they are not cited by him (see Alfred Wiener, *Die Farağ ba'd aš-Šidda-Literatur* in *Der Islam*, vol. IV, 1913, p. 403 foll.). While our author has derived the greater part of his materials from the *Faraj*, his work is planned on different lines and to that extent possesses a character of its own.

Ff. 122 of 23·7 × 13·3 c. and 17 ll. Excellent *naskh* with rubrications. Dated 1033/1623–4. No. 3 of eighty-four MSS. of the Belshah collection divided at the British Museum on Nov. 12, 1920.

X. 3 (12).

جوامع الحکایات ولوامع الروایات، قسم اوّل،

The First of the Four Parts of the celebrated collection of anecdotes compiled in 625/1228 by Muḥammad 'Awfí. For a full account of the author and his work see *Introduction to the Jawámi'u'l-Ḥikáyát* by Dr Muḥammad Niẓámu'd-Dín (E. J. W. Gibb Memorial, New Series, vol. VIII). The present MS., which is designated as X and numbered 28 in Dr Niẓámu'd-Dín's descriptive list of the MSS. of the *Jawámi'*, is characterized by him (*op. cit.*, p. 122) as modern and unreliable. It contains 967 anecdotes.

Begins:

شکر و سپاس بی‌قیاس که مقاطع اوهام انسان از مطالع آن نشان ندهد

Ff. 396 of 28·6 × 19·5 c. and 19 ll. *Nasta'líq*, no date; probably written in Turkey in the 18th century. Bought of J. J. Naaman, April 12, 1901.

X. 4 (16).

جوامع الحکایات ولوامع الروایات،

This apparently complete MS. of the *Jawámi'u'l-Ḥikáyát* of 'Awfí is designated as P and numbered 20 in Dr Niẓámu'd-Dín's descriptive list (*op. cit.*, p. 121), but though it contains all the Four Parts into which the work is divided, many anecdotes are omitted and Chs. V, VI, VII in Part IV are almost entirely wanting. Dr Niẓámu'd-Dín, who worked upon this MS. for four years, has numbered the anecdotes correctly, marked with an asterisk on the margin those which are missing, and added a *Table of Contents* in comparison with the preceding MS. (**X. 3**), the India Office MS. **595** (L), and the British Museum MS. **Add. 16,862** (J). He describes its textual value as very uncertain.

Begins:

شکر و سپاس ...ی‌را که اثر ابتدای صباح وجود تا ابتدای رواح عدم هرچه هست در قبضهٔ تقدیر اوست

Ff. 404 of 38 × 24·5 c. and 25 ll. Small legible *nasta'líq* with rubrications. The first few pages are damaged. Dated 27 Muḥarram 1059/11 February, 1649. Transcribed by 'Abdu'r-Raḥím ibn Muḥammad Niyásarí (Niyástarí). Bought from the heirs of the late Sir Albert Houtum-Schindler on Jan. 5, 1917.

X. 5 (14).

لطایف الظرایف،

A collection of anecdotes in Persian. There appears to be no indication of authorship.

Begins:

اوّل ثنای دوست فصیحان ادا کنند آری طعامرا به نمك آشنا کنند

حمد بیحد و شکر بی عدد حضرت فرد و صمد و خداوند احد

The work ends on f. 188[a] and is followed by various poems, some by Yaghmá, *rubá'ís*, etc.

Ff. 215 of 32·3 × 18·7 c. and 15 ll. in the middle of the page and 26 in margins. Dated (on f. 188[a]) 1253/1837–8. Large and rather illegible *ta'líq*.

X. 6 (10).

بستان للعارفین و گلستان للعابدین،

A Persian work on Ṣúfism, anecdotal in character, treating of ethical and religious topics and written partly in prose and partly in verse. I have not found any notice of it elsewhere.

Begins:

حمد و ثنا خالق زمین و زمانرا صانع بی آلتی همین و همانرا

The author's name, Zaynu'l-'Ábidín, is mentioned in the following passage (f. 4[a]):

چنین گوید متوقّد این شمع و مترتّب این جمع تراب اقدام صلحا و فقرا

خاك راه زمرهٔ اهل یقین بندهٔ بیچاره زین العابدین

که چون توفیق باری عزّ اسمه رفیق شد الخ

He states that on retiring from his employment as an official secretary and accountant he devoted himself to the religious life and composed the present work, which is dedicated to the Tímúrid Prince Nuṣratu's-Salṭana Sulṭán Khalílu'lláh (807–812: d. 814/1411–12).

The title is given on f. 12[a]:

بستانًا للعارفین و گلستانًا للعابدین موسوم شد

The work consists of three chapters, which are subdivided into ten, five, and two *faṣls* respectively.

Table of contents:

Chapter I, *Faṣl i*, فی التوبة; *Faṣl ii*, فی کثرة الطاعة; *Faṣl iii*, فی التوکل; *Faṣl iv*, فی طلب الحلال; *Faṣl v*, فی ریاضة النفس; *Faṣl vi*, فی کثرة البکا عن خشیة الله; *Faṣl vii*, فی اخلاص عند الدع; *Faṣl viii*, فی الحلم والعفو; *Faṣl ix*, فی السخا ومذمّة البخلا; *Faṣl x*, فی صفاء الباطن.

Chapter II, *Faṣl i*, فى حالات العجيبة عن اولياء الله; *Faṣl ii*, فى الصبر عند البلاء ونجاتها; *Faṣl iii*, فى رؤية منام الصلحا بعد موت الفقرا; *Faṣl iv*, فى كرامات الاوليا; *Faṣl v*, فى زهد الامرا وعفّت النساء.

Chapter III, *Faṣl i*, فى حكايات المتفرّقه; *Faṣl ii* (*Khátima*), فى كرامات الدولة السلطانيّه.

Owing to a lacuna after f. 51[b], *faṣls ix* and *x* of Ch. I and *faṣl i* with part of *faṣl ii* of Ch. II are wanting in this copy.

Ff. 114 of 24·6×16·4 c. and 19 ll. Dated in the colophon 23 Shawwál, 891/22 October, 1486, and written in a rather archaic *ta'líq*, which is quite legible though the scribe has recorded that on account of his infirmities—he was then seventy-five years old—and his weak sight he copied the last pages hastily بعين زجاجيّة فرنجيّة. The MS. was bought from the heirs of Sir Albert Houtum-Schindler on January 5, 1917.

X. 7 (9).

چهل ناموس، منتخب سعيدى،

The first of the two treatises contained in this MS. is the *Chihil Námús*, also known as *Námús-i Akbar* and *Juz'iyyát ú Kulliyyát*, of Ẓiyá'u'd-Dín Nakhshabí (d. 751/1350–1), author of the *Silku's-Sulúk* (see **D. 21**, No. 8, p. 41 *supra*) and several other works. As the title indicates, it is a description, in belletristic and poetical style, of forty parts of the human body, arranged under forty *námús*. See Rieu, B.M.P.C., vol. II, p. 740, and Ivanow, A.S.B.P.C., **No. 335**. The author says (f. 13[b]):

و هر جزورا که درین مجموعه ذکر کرده آمد از بسکه آن جزو در محلّ خویش بمنزلهٔ کلّ بود این مجموعهرا جزئيّات و کلّيّات نام نهاده آمد... و این مجموعهرا که لقب ناموس اکبر زیبد بر چهل ناموس ترتیب کرده آمد

Begins:

تحمید حمد (*sic*) احدی که قل هو الله احد الله الصمد

Table of Contents (ff. 13[b]–14[b]). The poem which concludes the work (ff. 276[b]–279[b]) is incomplete.

Ff. 280[b]–458[b] are occupied by an extensive collection of moral and religious sayings in prose and verse, anecdotes, homilies, etc., on which the copyist has bestowed the title (f. 280[a]): الجز اول (*sic*) نسخه منتخب سعیدی. The compiler, who describes himself (f. 281[a]) as Ḥáfiẓ Muḥammad Sa'íd ibn Ḥáfiẓ Karami'lláh ibn Ḥáfiẓ Sulṭán Muḥammad ibn Ḥáfiẓ 'Ayni'd-Dín کهوتکهر کهکی (?) ثم الکولوی, composed the present work in Dhu'l-Qa'da of the thirty-fourth year of Aurangzeb = A.H. 1102/July, A.D. 1691, at Islámábád[1] (Mathurá).

Begins:

حمدی که حضرت آفریدگاررا سزد جلّ جلاله

[1] [The author gives منتخبى as a chronogram for the date of his work (f. 283[a]).]

It comprises a preface and five chapters, of which the contents are as follows:

مقدّمه، در بیان شمّهٔ از حقیقت و کیفیت آدمی‌زاد و وضع اهل زمانه، (f. 219a)

باب اوّل، در اجناس فضایل انسان که مکارم اخلاق عبارت از آنست، (f. 335b)

باب دویم، در تهدید اهل جرم و خطا و لطایف و نکتهٔ دل بر کرم خداوند فضل و عطا (f. 345b)

باب سیوم، در بیان دوست و دشمن و مناسب آن، (f. 361b)

باب چهارم، در تدبیرات امور و مواعظ حکما و فواید سکوت و کم گفتن، (f. 372b)

باب پنجم، در کلمات و نکات و لطایف متفرقه و کلام سعادت انجام ختم خلافت امیر المومنین حضرت مرتضی علی رضی الله تعالی عنه وکرّم الله وجهه (f. 412a)

This work, like the preceding one, is incomplete at the end, and there is no colophon.

Ff. 458 of 21 × 11·5 c. and 15 ll. Poor Indian *ta'líq* with rubrications. The fly-leaf bears the signature of Standish O'Grady by whom the MS. was presented to Professor Browne.

X. 8 (6).

اخبار الغزالی، ایّها الولد،

A collection of moral and religious anecdotes, especially legends of the prophets and saints, compiled from the *Iḥyá'u 'ulúmi d-Dín* of Abú Ḥámid al-Ghazálí and possibly from other works by the same author. These excerpts, which occupy ff. 30a–194b, are preceded by the well-known ethical work of al-Ghazálí entitled *Ayyuha'l-Walad* (Brockelmann, *Gesch. d. Arab. Litt.*, vol. 1, p. 423, No. 32), beginning on f. 2b:

الحمد لله ربّ العالمين والعاقبة للمتّقين

Ff. 195 of 14·5 × 9·7 c. and 10 ll. Dated 1295/1878–9. The text is very carelessly written and abounds in grammatical errors. This is one of the MSS. of the Belshah collection divided at the British Museum on Nov. 12, 1920.

X. 9 (8).

قرق وزير تأريخى،

An imperfect copy of the well-known Ottoman Turkish version of the *History of the Forty Wazírs* made in the 15th century by Aḥmad-i Miṣrí or Sheykh-zádeh, which has been translated into English by E. J. W. Gibb. See Rieu, B.M.T.C., pp. 216–219, Flügel, Vienna Cat., vol. 1, p. 417, and cp. Gibb, *Hist. of Ottoman Poetry*, vol. 1, p. 430, n. 1, and vol. v, p. 13, n. 1.

Begins:

حمد و ثنا بی منتها اول بار تعالی حضرتنه

Ff. 78 of 19 × 13·8 c. and 19 ll. Written in clear *nasta'líq* and dated Muḥarram, 1155/Feb.—March, 1742. There is a lacuna of twenty or thirty folios between f. 1[b] and f. 3[a], and the catch-words indicate other omissions. Professor E. H. Minns has noted on the fly-leaf that he bought the MS. at Kazan in Sept. 1898.

X. 10 (10).

همایون نامه٬

A fine old copy of the *Humáyún-náma*, the well-known Turkish version of the *Anwár-i Suhaylí* (Fables of Bídpáy), composed by 'Alí Chelebi of Philippopolis (d. A.H. 950/1543) and dedicated to Sulṭán Sulaymán I. See Rieu, B.M.T.C., pp. 227–228; Flügel, Vienna Cat., vol. III, pp. 299–301.

Begins:

حضرت حلیم خلّاق و حکیم علی الاطلاق جلّت حکمته

Ff. 345 of 24 × 16·2 c. and 21 ll. Excellent *ta'líq* with rubrications. Transcribed by Khalíl ibn Yúsuf in Jumádà I, 982/August, 1574. According to Professor Browne's note on the fly-leaf, this MS. was given to him in April, 1908, in Constantinople by Dr Riẓá Tevfíq.

X. 11 (9).

کتاب رضوان٬

The following description has been written by Professor Browne on the fly-leaf: "This book, entitled *Kitáb-i Riẓwán*, is written in imitation of the famous *Gulistán* of Sa'dí. It is quite modern, being adorned with a panegyric on Sulṭán 'Abdu'l-Ḥamíd, and was composed (see p. 22) in A.H. 1304 (=A.D. 1886–7). It comprises:

Pp. 23– 53: (1) A Preface. On the Happiness of Men and the Vicissitudes of Fortune.

Pp. 54–101: (2) Chapter I. On Love, Beauty, and Youth.

Pp. 102–150: (3) Chapter II. Ethical.

Pp. 151–209: (4) Chapter III. Characteristics of the Great.

Pp. 210–282: (5) Chapter IV. Witticisms and quaint Anecdotes.

Pp. 283–310: (6) Conclusion. Philosophical Maxims.

I think the author of this work is Mírzá Áqá Ján of Kirmán, or possibly Shaykh Aḥmad Rúḥí of Kirmán, concerning whom see my *Persian Revolution* [pp. 93–6]."

A full account of these men, both of whom were Azalís, and their numerous writings will be found in *Materials for the Study of the Bábí Religion*, p. 221 foll., where Professor Browne definitely assigns the *Kitáb-i Riẓwán* to Mírzá Áqá Ján of Kirmán.

Begins :

بنام ایزد متعال، تعالی ذات لم یزل که وحدتش منشاء کثرت است و بوصف اندرش مزید حیرت

Pp. 310 of 20·5 × 14 c. and 18 ll. Clear *naskh* with rubrications. The transcription of Mírzá Muṣṭafà, the Bábí scribe, was completed on 6 Sha'bán, 1331/11 July, 1913.

X. 12 (12).

تحفة الالباب [ونخبة الاعجاب]،

The work entitled *Tuḥfatu'l-Albáb*, of which this MS. contains the second volume comprising the last twenty-four chapters, is noticed by Ḥájjí Khalífa (ed. Flügel, vol. II, p. 222, **No. 2548**) and is mentioned by Maqqarí (Leyden ed., vol. I, pt. 2, p. 617, No. 147), but, so far as I am aware, no complete copy of it is extant. According to Ḥájjí Khalífa, it comprises a Preface and four chapters (اربعة ابواب); it actually contains forty, but the first sixteen are wanting in the present MS., which begins as follows :

الباب السابع عشر فی خبر الحسان من الجواری والقیان، حکی ان جاریة من جوار المأمون الخ

Concerning the author, Abú 'Abdi'lláh (or Abú Ḥámid) Muḥammad ibn 'Abdi-'r-Raḥím al-Mázini al-Qaysí of Granada, we learn from Maqqarí (*loc. cit.*) that he was born in 473/1080–1, studied in Alexandria, Cairo, Damascus and Baghdád, stayed for some time in Khurásán, finally returned to Syria, and died at Damascus in Ṣafar, 565/Oct.—Nov., 1169.

The historian adds that the subject of the *Tuḥfatu'l-Albáb* is the wonders which its compiler had seen in the course of his travels, and that his account of them brought him into disrepute (ونسبه بعض الناس بسبب ذلك الى ما لا یلیق). On the whole, however, the contents of this MS. do not correspond with the above description. In the colophon the work is correctly described as a general *Adab*-book (جامعة لفنون الادب). The headings of the twenty-four chapters have been written by a modern hand on a page of foolscap facing p. 1, as follows :

Ch. xvii (p. 1):	فی خبر الحسان من الجواری والقیان
Ch. xviii (p. 13):	فیما یستغرب من خبر النساء ویستملح
Ch. xix (p. 38):	فی المنادمة والغناء وأخبار المغنّین
Ch. xx (p. 47):	فی الهزل والمجون الجاری فی الاحادیث التی هی شجون
Ch. xxi (p. 50):	فی خبر بعض المجانین ومن فی معناهم من البله والمغفلین
Ch. xxii (p. 55):	فی الفصاحة والبلاغة فی الکلام
Ch. xxiii (p. 69):	فی اخبار الشعراء وذکر ملح من اشعارهم
Ch. xxiv (p. 95):	فی المدیح والهجاء

Ch. xxv (p. 102): فى الهفوات والزلّات اللسانيّة فى الشعر وغيره
Ch. xxvi (p. 106): فى اخبار المتكبّرين والجبابرة وسوء عاقبتهم الخاسرة
Ch. xxvii (p. 112): فى تقلّبات الدهر بأهله آلخ
Ch. xxviii (p. 134): فى غرائب الاتّفاق التى وقعت فى الآفاق
Ch. xxix (p. 139): فى اشياء عجيبة ونوادر غريبة
Ch. xxx (p. 160): فى ذكر صنائع نافعة ومطالع رائقة
Ch. xxxi (p. 166): فى الاذكار والادعية المجرّب نفعها وعواقب فعل الخيرات والمعروف
Ch. xxxii (p. 181): فى الرقى والخواصّ
Ch. xxxiii (p. 190): فى السحر والكهانة وشئ من علم ا...(?)
Ch. xxxiv (p. 193): فى الزجر والعيافة والتنجيم والفال
Ch. xxxv (p. 203): فى الوعظ والوصيّة والحكم واخبار الحكماء من سائر الامم
Ch. xxxvi (p. 266): فى الزهد فى الدنيا والثقة بما عند الله
Ch. xxxvii (p. 271): فى حسن الظنّ بالله تعالى آلخ
Ch. xxxviii (p. 276): فى خبر من رُزق الثبات عند تحقّق الموت والفوات
Ch. xxxix (p. 282): فى الرثاء والتعزية آلخ
Ch. xl (p. 285): جامع لمسائل من العلم والسير والتأريخ واخبار بعض العلماء وفضل العلم

Pp. 299 of 29 × 20·3 c. and 31 ll. Written in a fair Maghribí hand, with rubrications, and dated 20 Ṣafar, 1176/10 September, 1762. The author's name does not seem to occur anywhere in the volume, but the title of the work is given in the colophon.

X. 13 (9).

نگارستان كمال پاشازاده،

The *Nigáristán* or "Picture-gallery," composed in Persian in imitation of Sa'dí's *Gulistán* by the famous Ottoman legist and historian, Kamál-Páshá-záde (d. 941/1535; cf. Brockelmann, *Gesch. d. Arab. Litt.*, vol. II, p. 449; Flügel, Vienna Cat., vol. III, p. 285).

Begins:

منّتهاى بى منتها خداى بى همتاى‌را

The work consists of a Preface and eight chapters, which bear the same titles as those of the *Gulistán*.

Ff. 174 of 20·6 × 12·6 and 21 ll. Good *nasta'líq* with rubrications. Dated 973/1565–6. Bought for 10*s*. at Sotheby's sale on June 18, 1923.

X. 14 (9).

نگارستان کمال پاشازاده،

Another copy of the *Nigáristán* of Kamál-Páshá-záde, bought at the same auction as the MS. described above.

Ff. 124 of 21·3 × 15·5 c. and 22 ll. Curious *nasta'líq* with rubrications. Dated Jumádà I, 963/March—April, 1556. The colophon is on f. 115[a], and ff. 115[b]–121[a] are filled with a large number of Persian and Turkish apophthegms, proverbs, etc.

Y. COLLECTANEA, MISCELLANEA, AND UNCLASSIFIED.

Y. 1 (8).

Contents:

1. Several MS. Persian *taṣnífs* or ballads collected and sent to Professor Browne by George Grahame, then H.B.M. Consul at Shíráz, in October, 1905.

2. Lithographed Muḥarram poems (*ta'ziyas* and *rawẓa-khwáns*), including the following six *ta'ziyas*:

(۱) كتاب درّة الصدف،

(۲) شهادت حُرّ بن يزيد رياحى،

(۳) كتاب شهادت حضرت سيّد سجّاد و امام زين العابدين،

(۴) مجلس امير تيمور با وفات زينب خاتون،

(۵) مجلس تعزيهٔ خروج نمودن عبد الله يزدجرد با لشكر بيارئ سيّد الشهداء و آمدن بدشت كربلا و مجلس تعزيهٔ غارت،

(۶) مجلس شهادت امام،

3. A MS. Bábí poem by Mírzá Na'ím of Ábádé (see *A Year amongst the Persians*, p. 567 of the reprint), received from G. Grahame in August, 1902, with a letter in which the writer says that Mírzá Muḥammad or Mírzá Na'ím really came from Sidih.

4. A MS. Kurdish poem received from the Rev. W. St Clair Tisdall in 1912.

5. MS. poems by Mírzá Dáwarí of Shíráz, a son of the poet known as Wiṣál (see *A Year amongst the Persians*, reprint, pp. 130 and 292). They were given to Professor Browne in the winter of 1887–8 at Ṭihrán by the Nawwáb Mírzá Ḥasan-'Alí Khán.

6. A *qaṣída* composed in 1887 for Queen Victoria's Jubilee by Mírzá-yi Farhang of Shíráz, a younger brother of the above-mentioned Mírzá Dáwarí (see *A Year amongst the Persians, loc. cit.*), and copied by Professor Browne from the original belonging to the Nawwáb Mírzá Ḥasan-'Alí Khán. It is followed by a *ghazal* composed in honour of Professor Browne by Ḥájjí Pír-záda.

7. Bábí MS. tracts given to Professor Browne by Basil Williams, Feb. 7, 1897, comprising (α) مناجات, (β) لوح زردشتیان, (γ) لوح بشارات, (δ) رسالهٔ سیاسیّه.

8. Professor Browne's pencil copy, made in Cambridge, Nov. 4, 1900, of the text of a "Tablet" (لوح) revealed by "the Most Great Branch" ('Abbás Efendi) to Mr A. P. Dodge.

9. MS. commentary by 'Abbás Efendi on the *Ḥadíth* كنتُ كنزًا مخفيًّا, "I was a Hidden Treasure," written for 'Alí Shevket Páshá and obtained from Áqá Jawád the *dallál* in Iṣfahán on March 1, 1888.

10. A short life of the famous philosopher Ḥájjí Mullá Hádí of Sabzawár composed by his pupil Mírzá Asadu'lláh of Sabzawár in Ṭihrán, February, 1888. This is the memoir from which Professor Browne derived the account of Ḥájjí Mullá Hádí given in *A Year amongst the Persians.* See the reprint, p. 146, note 1.

11. A cutting from the *Pall Mall Gazette*, Nov. 26, 1891, containing a letter by Professor Browne on the persecution of the Bábís in Yazd in May, 1891, together with the original rough draft of a MS. Persian translation of the same made for Náṣiru'd-Dín Sháh by Mírzá Ḥusayn-qulí Khán.

12. An Arabic tract, mystical in character, composed by Maḥmúd ibn Muḥammad at-Tabrízí in 1255/1839–40 and dedicated to Muḥammad Sháh Qájár. The lithograph bears the date 1264/1847–8.

Begins:

الحمد لله الذی هدانا شرایع الاحکام

Y. 2 (15).

[This volume is not included in the present collection. According to the description given by Professor Browne in his Slip-catalogue, it is "The original Catalogue of Schindler MSS., containing also the prices paid for them originally, with my additional notes and list of lithographed works."]

Y. 3 (10).

(۱) کنز الاسرار (۲) رساله در اعزّ اوقات (۳) فرّخ نامهٔ جمالی،

This MS. comprises three separate works:

1. (ff. 1ᵃ–77ᵇ.) A Persian translation, entitled *Kanzu* (or *Ganju*) *'l-Asrár*, of a well-known Arabic treatise on marriage and sexual intercourse, *al-Íḍáḥ fí Asrári'n-Nikáḥ.* The original was written by Shaykh 'Abdu'r-Raḥmán ibn Naṣr ibn 'Abdi'lláh ash-Shírází, a physician of Aleppo who died in 565/1169 (see Brockelmann, *Gesch. d. Arab. Litt.*, vol. 1, p. 488, No. 20). The anonymous translator dedicates his work to the Wazír Abu'l-Ma'álí Muḥammad ibn 'Izzi'd-Dín, at whose instance he composed it. It is divided into two Parts (*Juz'*) of which the first (ff. 1ᵃ–38ᵃ) contains a *Muqaddama* and ten chapters, and the second (ff. 38ᵃ–73ᵇ) nine chapters, together with a *Khátima* (ff. 73ᵇ–77ᵇ). Table of Contents on f. 6ᵇ.

The transcription of this copy, which is imperfect at the beginning, was completed on 25 Dhu'l-Qa'da, 886/Jan. 15, 1482, by 'Alí ibn 'Abdi'lláh ibn 'Alí Bákír (?) al-Kátib aṣ-Ṣifáhání. A Turkish version of the *Íḍáḥ* is described in Flügel's Vienna Catalogue, vol. II, p. 538.

2. (ff. 78ᵇ–87ᵇ.) *Risála dar a'azz-i awqát*, a treatise on the most suitable times for sexual intercourse, in seventeen chapters, without author's name or date. Table of Contents on f. 79ᵇ.

Begins: بسم الله تيمّنًا بذكره الاعلى سپاس و ستايش آفريدگار جهانرا

3. (ff. 88ᵇ–168ᵇ.) *Farrukh-náma-i Jamálí* by Abú Bakr al-Muṭahhar ibn Muḥammad ibn Abi'l-Qásim ibn Abí Sa'íd (Sa'd in this copy) al-Jamál, generally known as al-Yazdí. See Rieu, Persian Catalogue, vol. II, p. 465, where this work is described as "treating of the properties and uses of natural substances, also of divination and astrology." The title, فرّخ‌نامهٔ جمالی, occurs on f. 89ᵇ, l. 11; Ḥájjí Khalífa, ed. Flügel, vol. IV, p. 412, **No. 9011**, reads فرخ‌نامه, which Rieu has adopted. The date of composition is said by Ḥájjí Khalífa to be Ramaḍán 560/Nov.—Dec., 1164. The British Museum MS. gives Ramaḍán 580/Dec. 1184—Jan. 1185, and in the present copy the date given is Rabí', 597/Dec. 1200—Jan. 1201. As the author states in his preface, the work is an imitation of the *Nuzhat-náma-i 'Alá'í* (see Ivanow, A.S.B.P.C., **No. 1358**), which he ascribes on f. 89ᵇ, l. 3, to شهر (*sic*) مردان المستوفی. The contents of the sixteen *Maqálát* or Discourses are enumerated on ff. 91ᵃ⁻ᵇ (cf. Rieu, *loc. cit.*, p. 466).

Begins:

شکر و سپاس بی‌قیاس آن پروردگاری که معلّم اشیا [اسما] و مظهر اسماست [اشیاست]

No colophon or date.

Ff. 168 of 22 × 16·8 c. and 17 ll., written throughout in a legible *ta'líq* and dated on f. 77ᵇ the 25th of Dhu'l-Qa'da, 886/Jan. 15, 1482. From the library of the late Sir Albert Houtum-Schindler.

Y. 4 (7).

كتاب الفرايد والقلايد، شرح الحروف الجامع بين العارف والمعروف وغيره،

The contents of this volume, which is written by different hands, are as follows:

1. (ff. 1ᵇ–36ᵃ.) *Kitábu'l-Faráʼid wa'l-Qaláʼid*, an Arabic work on ethics and belles-lettres by Abu'l-Ḥusayn Muḥammad ibn al-Ḥusayn al-Ahwází (4th cent. A.H.). See Brockelmann, *Gesch. d. Arab. Litt.*, vol. I, p. 96; Dozy, Leiden Cat., vol. I, p. 194, and vol. IV, p. 197; Flügel, Vienna Cat., vol. III, p. 269. In some copies it is falsely ascribed to Tha'álibí or to Qábús ibn Washmgír. The titles of the eight chapters into which it is divided are given on f. 4ᵇ as in the Vienna Catalogue.

Begins: الحمد لله العلىّ الكبير القوىّ القدير

Clear pointed *naskh*, 15 ll. to the page. According to the colophon (f. 36[b]) the date of transcription was A.H. 461, but the words واربع مايه have been supplied by a later hand.

2. (ff. 37[a]–38[a].) A number of sayings attributed to the Prophet, 'Alí, and others

3. (ff. 38[b]–57[a].) *Sharḥu'l-Ḥurúf al-jámi' bayna'l-'Árif wa'l-Ma'rúf*, a treatise in Arabic on the mystical significance of the Letters of the Alphabet, by Ibráhím ibn Muḥammad aṭ-Ṭá'úsí of Qazwín. The present MS., which appears to be unique, is an autograph and is dated 658/1260. Small, neat, and closely written *ta'líq*, 28 ll. to the page.

Begins:

الحمد لله الذى تحيّر من وجدان ريح نَفَسه المتحيّرون

4. (ff. 58[b]–71[a].) A devotional tract written in Persian but consisting almost entirely of Arabic prayers.

Begins:

الحمد لله ربّ العالمين والعاقبة للمتّقين...معيّن و مبيّن است بنزد ارباب بصيرت و اصحاب حقيقت كه حقّ جلّ ذكره انسان‌را كه خلاصه و زبدهٔ موجوداتست الخ

Ff. 71 of 17 × 12·5 c.

One of forty-seven MSS. bought of Ḥájjí 'Abdu'l-Majíd Belshah in January, 1920.

Y. 5 (11).

A Miscellany of Arabic and Persian extracts on biographical, historical, religious, and literary subjects.

Contents:

1. (ff. 2[a]–9[b].) *Munáẓaratu Rukni'd-Dawla ma'a'ṣ-Ṣadúq*, a polemical Shí'ite tract in the form of a debate which is reported to have been held at the court of Ruknu'd-Dawla the Buwayhid (320–366/932–976).

Begins:

قال الملك ايّها الشيخ العالم اختلف الحاضرون فى القوم الذين تطعن عليهم الشيعة

2. (f. 10[a].) Definitions of Love (الحبّ) by 'Abdu'lláh ibn Ṭáhir, Ḥammád ar-Ráwiya, and Mu'ádh ibn Jabal.

3. (ff. 11[a]–13[a].) Extracts from the *Kitábu'l-Anís wa'l-Jalís*. These include part of the celebrated *qaṣída* by 'Abíd ibnu'l-Abraṣ, beginning اقفر من اهله ملحوب (No. I in Lyall's edition) with an Arabic commentary.

4. (ff. 14[a]–32[b].) Various Arabic extracts and anecdotes, most of which display a strong Shí'ite bias, including:

(α) Story of a Shaykh of Kúfa who reviled the Umayyads and their ancestors in the presence of the Caliph Hishám ibn 'Abdi'l-Malik (f. 14[a]).

(β) Story of the poet Abu'l-Ḥasan Naṣru'lláh ibn 'Unayn (see Brockelmann, *Gesch. d. Arab. Litt.*, vol. 1, p. 318) and the ode which he addressed to al-Maliku 'l-'Azíz, the brother of Saladin (f. 17[a]).

(γ) Letter written by Muḥyi'd-Dín Ibnu'l-'Arabí to Fakhru'd-Dín ar-Rází, beginning (f. 20ᵃ):

امّا بعد فانّا نحمد الله الذى لا اله الّا هو ونصلّى على نبيّه وحبيبه

5. (ff. 33ᵃ–45ᵇ.) Selected passages from a work in praise of the *Ahlu'l-Bayt*, by Shaykh Muḥammad ibn Makí, entitled *Duraru's-Simṭ fí akhbári's-Sibṭ*, beginning:

فصل، رحمة الله وبركاته عليكم اهل البيت فروع النّبوّة والرّسالة

6. (ff. 47ᵃ–51ᵃ.) Chronological and genealogical tables, written in Persian, beginning with the pre-Islamic kings and ending with the Ṣafawís and Ottoman Sulṭáns. The latest date mentioned is the accession of Sháh Ṭahmásp II in 1135/1722–3 on f. 50ᵇ.

7. (ff. 51ᵇ–104ᵇ.) A complete table, preceded by a chronological summary, also written in Persian, of the chief historical events from the Fall (هبوط) of Adam to the Hijra (6216 years after Adam), and of the *ta'ríkh-i-Hijrí* from A.H. 1–1066/A.D. 622–1655, where it breaks off with the catch-words وزارت گوزل محمّد.

Ff. 104 of 27·1 × 17·5 c. The first forty-six folios are written in good *naskh*. No. 72 of eighty-four MSS. of the Belshah collection divided at the British Museum on Nov. 12, 1920.

Y. 6 (6).

The contents are as follows:

1. (ff. 1ᵇ–36ᵃ.) A Turkish treatise on prayers and *awrád*, comprising a Preface and seven chapters.

Begins:

حمد و سپاس و ستايش بى قياس اول سامع الاصوات و مجيب الدعوات صفاتنه اولسون

2. (ff. 40ᵇ–44ᵃ.) A Turkish poem, entitled *Risála-i-Irshádiyya*, on the qualities of the soul, beginning:

اى يار طالب اولان مطلوبه هر بار   اگر اولمق ديلرسڭ اهل ديدار

3. (ff. 44ᵇ–46ᵇ.) A Turkish tract on the mystical life, enumerating seven journeys, *viz.*: *sayr ila'lláh*, *sayr lilláh*, *sayr 'ala'lláh*, *sayr ma'a'lláh*, *sayr fi'lláh*, *sayr 'ani'lláh*, *sayr bi'lláh*.

4. (ff. 46ᵇ–51ᵃ.) Another Turkish tract on the same subject, describing forty-one stages of the Way to God.

Begins:

حمد و سپاس و ثناء بى قياس بصانع شهود عالم و مبدع وجود آدم

5. (ff. 51ᵃ–58ᵇ.) A similar Turkish work on the Path (*ṭaríqa*) of the Ṣúfís, beginning:

الحمد لله الّذى تجلّى بذاته لذاته فأظهر ما اظهر

6. (ff. 63ᵇ–95ᵃ.) Short tracts or excerpts in Arabic and Turkish on religious and legal subjects, especially questions connected with the reading of the *Qur'án* (قراءة القرآن).

7. (ff. 95[b]–100[a].) A collection of anecdotes of Abú Ḥanífa, entitled *Laṭá'ifu'l-Imámi'l-A'ẓam* and written in Arabic.

8. (ff. 100[b]–108[b].) The *'aqída* or creed of the Ḥanafite theologian Aḥmad b. Muḥammad aṭ-Ṭaḥáwí (see Brockelmann, *Gesch. d. Arab. Litt.*, vol. I, pp. 173–174, where other MSS. are mentioned).

Begins:

الحمد لله ربّ العالمين...وبعد هذا بيان اعتقاد اهل السنّة والجماعة على مذهب فقهاء الملّة ابى حنيفة النعمان بن ثابت الكوفى الّخ

9. (ff. 109[b]–111[b].) A list (in Arabic) of the seventy-two Muslim sects, giving the name of each sect with a very brief statement of its doctrine.

Begins:

قال النبىّ صلعم من احدث حدثا فى الاسلام فقد هلك

On f. 112 there are some predictions of the Prophet concerning Abú Ḥanífa. The remainder of the volume is occupied by verses (including a *qaṣída* by Dhátí), letters, chronograms, etc., in Turkish and Arabic.

Ff. 120 of 15·8 × 9·5 c. Written by various hands.

Y. 7 (9).

رسالهٔ ادبيّه

A Persian treatise on the education of children by Áqá-yi-Mutarjim Ibn Muḥammad Mahdí-yi-Tabrízí, who transcribed it at Qum in 1295/1878.

Begins:

الحمد لله ربّ العالمين...امّا بعد چون خدمت بر دولت و ملّت فريضهٔ ذمّت و لازمهٔ انسانيّت و مدنيّت است

Pp. 101 of 21·5 × 16·5 c. and 11 ll. Fair *ním-shikasta*. From the library of Mr C. Lyne.

Y. 8 (9).

رسالهٔ اخلاقيّه

A Persian manual of ethics for the instruction of children by the same author, Áqá-yi-Mutárjim Ibn Muḥammad Mahdí of Tabríz.

Begins:

الحمد لله الملك المنّان خلق الانسان علّمه البيان...امّا بعد بر روى حقيقت‌نماى صاحبان تميز و تمكين...مخفى و پوشيده نيست

Pp. 136 of 21·8 × 17·3 c. and 13 ll. *Ním-shikasta*. Transcribed at Qum, in the course of a week, during the month of Jumádà I, 1295/May, 1878, by Mahdí ibn Áqá Shaykh Ḥasan, called Shaykh Ustád-i-Qummí. From the library of Mr C. Lyne.

Y. 9 (9).

A volume of miscellanea in Arabic, Persian, and Turkish. The last two items are lithographed.

1. (ff. 1^b–9^b.) A translation of twelve of La Fontaine's Fables into Persian verse by Mírzá Ḥusayn Dánish Khán (Ḥusayn Dánish Bey, formerly Chef du service de la traduction à l'agence de la banque ottomane à Stamboul), who gave the autograph to Professor Browne in Constantinople in April, 1908.

The Preface, dated 4 Rabí' II, 1311/15 October, 1893, begins:

بر ارباب زبان و اصحاب بیان روشن و عیان است

2. (ff. 11^a–16^b.) A *takhmís* by Mírzá Ḥusayn Dánish Khán on the celebrated *qaṣída* of Kháqání (*Elegia de urbe Madâin*, of which the text is given in Spiegel's *Chrestomathia Persica*, pp. 105–111). The author presented this *takhmís* to Professor Browne in April, 1908. It was subsequently published at Constantinople.

3. (ff. 17^a–73^b.) A Persian commentary on some verses of Ḥáfiẓ by a certain Mushfiq. Given to Professor Browne in Persia (? Kirmán) in 1888.

Begins:

سپاس بیقیاس عالمی‌را روا و ستایش بی آلایش ناظمی‌را سزاست

4. (ff. 75^a–115^a.) A work entitled *Miftáḥu'l-'irfán fí tartíb-i suwar-i'l-Qur'án* or "The Key of Knowledge concerning the order of the Súras of the Qur'án," probably by Mírzá Báqir of Bawánát, whom Professor Browne knew in London in 1882–5 (see *A Year amongst the Persians*, reprint, pp. 13–16). It consists of two parts, the first dealing with the Meccan Súras, and the second with those revealed at Medina.

Part I begins (f. 75^a):

از آنجا که این کتاب مستطاب من حیث السور مقدّم و مؤخّر بود

Part II begins on f. 99^b.

5. (ff. 116^b–129^b.) An unfinished collection of Arabic sentences, dialogues, proverbs, etc., designed for the use of students beginning to read that language.

Begins:

الحمد لله ربّ العالمین... فهذه کلمات من اللغة العربیّة هادیة لمن یقصدها

6. (ff. 133^a–138^a.) A Turkish tract, comprising a preface and three chapters, entitled *Niháyatu'l-i'tiṣám li-Umm Ḥarám bint Milḥán* and compiled by Shaykh Ibráhím from a *risála* and other materials which were left by his father, Shaykh Muṣṭafà Efendi, who died in 1210/1795–6. The work is dedicated to Sayyid Ḥasan Ághá, the Director of Customs (*muḥaṣṣil*) in Cyprus. Umm Ḥarám, whose name is said to have been Rumayṣá or Sahla, was the wife of 'Ubáda ibnu ṣ-Ṣámit (d. 34/654), a well-known Companion of the Prophet. She took part in the expedition against Cyprus in 28/649, and her tomb near Larnaca "is still revered as the greatest Muslim sanctuary in the island" (*Encycl. of Islam*, vol. I, p. 883).

This MS., which gives an account of her life and miracles, was presented by the Shaykh of the Tekyé to C. D. Cobham in 1878 or 1879.

Begins:

حمد نامعدود و ثنای نامحدود اول واجب الوجود و مفیض الخیر والجود حضرتلرینه

7. (ff. 140^b–144^b.) A Persian translation of the Sermon on the Mount and Psalms cxvii–cxix, 81 by Ḥusayn ibn ʻÍsà ibn Muḥammad al-Ḥusayní al-Baḥrání.

8. (ff. 146^a–147^b.) Two chapters (*Súratu'n-Núrayn* and *Súratu'l-Wiláyat*) of the Arabic *Bayán* or Bábí Scripture, with Persian interlinear translation. Dated 1285/1868–9.

9. (ff. 150^a–165^b.) Arabic translations of parts of the Old and New Testaments, *viz.*, the Parable of the Prodigal Son (St Luke xv, 11–32), and Genesis, ch. xxxvii and chs. xxxix–xlv.

10. (ff. 168^a–175^b.) An Arabic translation of St Paul's Epistle to the Romans, chs. v–ix, 7.

11. (ff. 176^b–191^a.) A Persian lithograph containing the story of *Salím-i-Jawáhirí ú Ḥajjáj*, with many illustrations.

Begins:

امّا راویان اخبار و ناقلان آثار و طوطیان شکرشکن شیرین‌گفتار چنین روایت کرده‌اند

12. (ff. 192^b–211^a.) A Persian treatise on *tarásulát* and *siyáq*, lithographed at Ṭihrán in 1263/1846–7.

Begins: شکر و سپاس فزون از فهم و قیاس خالقی‌را

Ff. 211 of various sizes and colours. The MSS. are written by different hands.

Y. 10 (7).

الرسالة الحسينيّة٬

A short Arabic treatise on ethics, etc., in five chapters, by Naṣru'lláh Zaytúní, beginning: الحمد لله معزّ من عدل بسلطانه ومكرّم من حلم باحسانه

I have not been able to find any notice of this work or of its author.

Contents (f. 9^b):

الباب الاوّل٬ فى العدل وما يتعلّق به

الباب الثانى٬ فى الحلم ومحمود عواقبه

الباب الثالث٬ فى الجود والسخآء

الباب الرابع٬ فى الشجاعة والحروب

الباب الخامس٬ فى بعض صناعة البديع والنوادر

Ff. 68 of 17·4 × 11·6 c. and 7 ll. Good *ta'líq* with gilt borders and titles. Copied by the author's son, who completed the transcription on 15 Rabíʻ I, 928/12 February, 1522. It was given to Professor Browne by the *Mir'átu'l-Mamálik* and sent by the hand of Mírzá ʻÍsà Khán when he came to London in March, 1924. Letters from them both are enclosed in an envelope pasted inside the cover.

Y. 11 (7).

A volume of miscellaneous contents.

1. (ff. 1^a–35^b.) A short life of the Prophet, entitled

نور العيون فى تلخيص سير الأمين المأمون

which the author, Abu'l-Fatḥ Muḥammad b. Abí Bakr al-Ya'murí ash-Sháfi'í ibn Sayyidi'n-nás (Brockelmann, *Gesch. d. Arab. Litt.*, vol. II, p. 71), epitomized from his larger work, entitled عيون الاثر فى فنون المغازى والشمائل والسّير. Both are mentioned by Ḥájjí Khalífa, ed. Flügel, **No. 8449**, and the present abridgment is described in Rieu's Suppl. to the Cat. of Arabic MSS. in the British Museum, **No. 1277**[10], and in the Bodleian Arabic Catalogue, **No. 345**[3].

Begins:

بعد حمد الله فاتح ابواب النّدا...فلمّا وضعتُ كتابى المسمّى عيون الأثر الخ

Good, clear *naskh*. The copyist, whose name is illegible, completed the transcription on 10 Dhu'l-Qa'da, 885/11 January, 1481.

2. (ff. 36^b–43^a.) An Arabic *qaṣída* in praise of the Prophet and 'Alí, by as-Sayyid Abú Háshim Ismá'íl ibn Muḥammad al-Ḥimyarí, beginning:

هلّا وقفتَ على المكان المُعشِبِ بين الطُّوَيْلع فاللوى من كبكبِ

3. (ff. 43^b–103^b.) A collection of various prayers, charms, homilies, etc., mostly in Arabic, including a list of the ninety-nine Names of God (f. 48^a) and also a list of names and epithets of the Prophet (f. 50^a).

Ff. 103 of 16·9 × 11·8 c. Written by several hands. This is one of the Belshah MSS. and was acquired at their final division in Nov. 1920.

Y. 12 (9).

(١) البارقة الحيدريّة فى نقض ما ابرمته الكشفيّة،

(٢) اشعار تركيّة للقائمى،

1. The author of the first work contained in this volume (ff. 2^b–61^b) is Ḥaydar ibn Ibráhím ibn Muḥammad al-Ḥusayní al-Ḥasaní, an orthodox Shí'ite theologian, who wrote it in order to refute the doctrines of the Shaykhís and other heretical Shí'ite sects, such as the *Ghulát* and the *Mufawwiḍa*. Most of it appears to be directed against Shaykh Aḥmad Aḥsá'í, the founder of the Shaykhí sect, his successor Sayyid Káẓim of Rasht, and their followers. The work is written in Arabic, but Persian verses are sometimes quoted.

Begins: الحمد لله الذى خلق السموات والارض وجعل الظلمات والنور

Ff. 61 of 21·3 × 14·8 c. and 20 ll. Copied in Dhu'l-Ḥijja, 1256/February, 1841. Clear but common *naskh*.

2. Some Turkish poems by Qá'imí, beginning (f. 65[b]):

بحمد الله بو دملرده بزه توفيق ايدوب باری

The date 1079/1668–9 is given in the line (f. 80[a]):

شمدی بيك يتمش طقوز تاريخيدر گلدی دينور

Another poem (f. 82[a]) gives the date 1083/1672–3:

تاريخن بو پهلوانك ديديلر بيك سكس اوچ

Ff. 22 of 21 × 15·4 c. and 18 ll. Large clear *naskh*. Dated 1138/1725–6. Given to Professor Browne by Dr Riẓá Tevfíq.

Z. NON-ISLAMIC BOOKS.

Z. 1 (7).

صد در،

Ṣad Dar or "The Hundred Gates," a Zoroastrian catechism in Persian verse, completed in 900/1495 by Íránsháh-i-Maliksháh at the request of Dastúr Shahriyár-i-Ardashír-i-Bahrámsháh. See Rieu, B.M.P.C., pp. 48–49; Ethé, Bodleian Persian Catalogue, **Nos. 1945–6**, and for the prose version, on which this work is based, Ethé, I.O.P.C., **Nos. 2820** and **2987**; E. W. West in *Grundriss d. Iran. Philologie*, vol. II, p. 123.

The present copy is imperfect at the beginning, the first verse being

كه تا آدمی زو هويدا شود   خلايق از آن دوار (*sic*) پيدا شود

Ff. 78 of 17·6 × 12 c. and 11 ll. Fair *ta'líq*. Written in Qazwín by Khudá-khusraw-i-Bahrámkhusraw-i-Yazdigird for Bahrám-i-Khudádád-i-Rustam, at the request of the latter's father, and finished on 22 Muḥarram, 1108/21 August, 1696.

APPENDIX

The following list of supernumerary MSS. includes those which Professor Browne neither designated by a class-mark nor described in his Catalogue. In some cases, I think, their omission can only have been due to inadvertence.

Sup. 1 (10).

شبستان خیال،

A fair copy of the euphuistic work entitled *Shabistán-i-Khayál* or *Shabistán-i-Nikát*, consisting of eight *Bábs* and a *Khátima*, which was composed in 843/1439–40 by Yaḥyà Síbak, with the pen-name Fattáḥí, of Nishápúr, the author of the famous allegory *Ḥusn ú Dil.*

Begins:

حمد خدائی‌را که چشم میم حمدش دریائی است

Ff. 143 of 23·4 × 13·2 c. and 11 ll. Clear *nasta'líq* with rubrications and many glosses in the margins. Transcribed at Akbarábád and dated Ṣafar, the 35th year of the reign of Akbar, *i.e.* 998/1589. The name of the copyist is illegible.

Sup. 2 (9).

قواعد علیشیری،

A commentary on some difficult verses in the First Part of the *Sikandar-náma* of Niẓámí, by Muḥyi'd-Dín ibn Niẓám, a disciple of Sayyid Ashraf Jahángír (as-Simnání). See Rieu's Persian Catalogue, p. 859, and Sprenger's Oudh Catalogue, p. 522.

Begins:

سپاس بی‌قیاس مر دایران (دارای) کونین‌را که میزان اشعار نامدار در لسان دُربار شعرا تعبیر فرمود

The author, who studied Persian poetry under Shaykh Muḥammad Lál and Shaykh Muḥaddith, composed the present work in 956/1549 and gave it the title of *Qawá'id-i-'Alí-Shírí* in honour of his patron Naṣíru'd-Dín 'Alí-Shír. Rieu (*loc. cit.*) calls it *Fawá'id-i-'Alí-Shírí*, but this seems to be a mistake.

Ff. 182 of 22 × 13 c. and 17 ll. Excellent *nasta'líq* with rubrications. Dated 1086/1675.

Sup. 3 (9).

This anonymous work, which is lettered on the back of the cover "Persian Gazeteer" (*sic*), comprises an historical and geographical account (apparently translated into Persian from the French) of the countries and peoples of Asia, *viz.*, Persia (ff. 1^{b}–45^{b}), Afghánistán (ff. 46^{a}–50^{b}), Baḥrayn (ff. 50^{b}–51^{b}), Bukhárá (ff. 51^{b}–54^{b}), Balúchistán (ff. 54^{b}–56^{b}), China (ff. 56^{b}–66^{a}), Khiva (ff. 66^{b}–67^{b}), Japan (ff. 67^{b}–73^{a}), Siam (ff. 73^{b}–76^{b}), 'Umán (ff. 77^{b}–81^{b}), Zanzibar (ff. 81^{b}–83^{a}), Korea (ff. 83^{a}–84^{b}), Asiatic countries under European rule (ff. 84^{b}–119^{b}).

Begins:

چون چندی قبل تاریخی از دول اروپ بنحو اختصار مسطور نموده نیز لازم دید که تفصیلی از تواریخ ملك آسیا مختصرًا مرقوم نمایم

Ff. 119 of 22×17 c. and 12 ll. Dated end of Ramaḍán, 1313/March, 1896. This volume formerly belonged to the Library of Sir Albert Houtum-Schindler, from whose heirs it was purchased by Professor Browne, Jan. 5, 1917.

Sup. 4 (9).

A replica of the preceding volume, transcribed by the same copyist and bearing the same date. Purchased from the Schindler collection on Jan. 5, 1917.

Sup. 5 (8).

A Persian Almanac comprising a series of astrological tables for each month of the Muḥammadan year.

Ff. 16 of 19·9×12·5 c. Written in a very small and neat *nim-shikasta* with rubrications and dated 1313/1895–6. This elegant little booklet was presented to Professor Browne on Feb. 2, 1912, by Ḥájjí Mírzá Yaḥyà of Dawlatábád, for whom see *Persian Literature in Modern Times*, pp. 225 and 307.

Sup. 6 (8).

Forty-five unbound leaves, containing:

(1) *Ghazals* of Ḥáfiẓ, some with the rhyme-letters ا and ب, but mostly with the rhyme-letter ت (ff. 1^{a}–16^{b}).

(2) The *Pand-náma* of Shaykh Farídu'd-Dín 'Aṭṭár (ff. 17^{a}–45^{b}), beginning:

حمد بیحدّ آن خدای پاکرا   آنك ایمان داد مشتی خاکرا

The last verse is

در جوانی دارْ پیرانرا عزیز   تا عزیز دیگران گردی [تو نیز]

which occurs near the end (Ch. LXXIV, p. 297) of De Sacy's French translation, so that this copy of the poem would seem to be almost complete.

Ff. 45 of 19·5×13·5 c. and 14 ll. and 22·2×15 c. and 16 ll. Many leaves are torn and water-stained. Probably 17th or 18th century.

Sup. 7 (12).

تأريخ جديد،

This manuscript of the *Ta'ríkh-i-Jadíd* or "New History" of Ḥájjí Mírzá Jání of Káshán is a copy of **F. 55** (p. 77 above) made by Professor Browne in 1890 and collated by him with the British Museum MS. **Or. 2942** (Rieu, Supplement to the Persian Catalogue, **No. 15**), of which he has noted the variant readings in the margins. The original MS. came from Shíráz and was given to him in 1888. With the view of preparing a text for publication, he transcribed it "in a fair legible hand, such as could be easily read by an European compositor, marking the passages which seemed corrupt, or writing them in pencil with a query in the margin, and sometimes a conjectural emendation." See the Introduction to *The New History of the Báb*, p. xliv foll., where the reasons which caused him to abandon his intention of publishing the text are fully set forth. On p. 77 above he refers to this transcript and adds, "I have not at present assigned a class-mark to it."

Ff. 283, written on one side only, of 28·5 × 22 c. and 22 or 23 ll. A note on f. 283 states that the collation was finished at 2 p.m. on Saturday, April 11th, 1891.

Sup. 8 (9) and **Sup. 9** (7).

These two MSS. are Nos. 9 and 10 in a volume of miscellanea, which also contains the following printed or lithographed items:

(1) *Le Fars* (Teheran, June, 1913). Pp. 218 + xi + iv (Tables des matières). With several maps.

(2) Speech of the Náṣiru'l-Mulk on assuming the Regency on 12 Ṣafar, 1329/Feb. 12, 1911, and telegrams from the *Mujtahids*, etc., connected therewith. Lith., Ṭihrán. Pp. ١٣٦.

(3) Persian and Turkish poems of La'lí of Tabríz (lithographed; no place or date). Pp. ٢٥٢.

(4) *al-Islám* (lith.), No. 7 of First Year; Ṭihrán, 18 Rabí' I, 1332/Feb. 14, 1914. Pp. ٤٨.

(5) *al-Maqṣadu'l-Asnà* (printed), on Double Entry. Ṭihrán, Jumádà I, 1323/July, 1905. Pp. ٩٠.

(6), (7), and (8). Three Persian Almanacs, for 1326/1908–9, 1323/1905–6, and 1318/1900–1. Lith., Ṭihrán. Each contains ٣٢ pp.

Sup. 8 (the ninth item in the volume) is a manuscript entitled *Kitábcha-i-Rán-i-Kúh ú Langarúd*, and is described in a note by Professor Browne on the fly-leaf as "'a document which is usually very difficult to obtain,' sent to me by Mr H. L. Rabino, H.B.M.'s Vice-Consul at Mogador (Morocco), formerly of

Rasht (Persia), on April 11, 1914." It appears to be a statistical report on the revenues, products, etc. of the districts of Rán-i-Kúh and Langarúd in Mázandarán.

Ff. 16 of 21·5 × 15·3 c. Written in cursive *ním-shikasta.*

Sup. 9 (the tenth item in the volume) was also received from Mr H. L. Rabino, with a letter of the same date (April 11, 1914). Mr Rabino describes it as "a few leaves from the draft of Mírzá Ibráhím's journal of his journey with Captain Mackenzie, British Consul in Rasht (Persia) in 1859. Melgounoff's book *Das südliche Ufer des Kaspischen Meeres* is based on it." Ff. 19 of 17·5 × 10 c. and 14 to 16 ll. Written in *ním-shikasta.*

In the lettering on the back of the volume these two MSS. are described respectively as "MS. Journal of Travel in Caspian Provinces" and "Kitábcha-i-Langarúd."

INDEX I

The following Index contains the titles of all the manuscripts described in the Catalogue. When a single MS. comprises two or more works by different authors, their titles are given separately. The figures refer to the pages of the Catalogue; those printed in **Clarendon** type denote the page on which the MS. is described. Titles of Oriental works that are not described in the Catalogue but only mentioned incidentally will be found in Index II.

INDEX II

In the following Index the names of authors of works described in the Catalogue are printed in **Clarendon** type, which is also used to indicate the more important of several references to the same name; and the names of copyists are distinguished by means of an asterisk. Titles of books are printed in italics. The alphabetical arrangement takes no account of **Abú** ("Father of...") or **Ibn** ("Son of..."), or of the definite article **al**, so that names like Abú Sa'íd, Ibn Khallikán, al-Majúsí, must be sought under the letter which follows the prefix.

A

Ábádiyán, Persian dynasty, 251
'Abbás I the Great, Sháh, 16, 40, 96, 102, **112**, 113, 208, 260
'Abbás II, Sháh, 100
'Abbás Efendi. *See* **'Abdu'l-Bahá**
'Abbás Mírzá, son of Fatḥ-'Alí Sháh, 118
'Abbás-qulí Khán, Mírzá, the Nawwáb, 57
'Abbás-qulí, son of Muḥammad Taqí *Lisánu'l-Mulk*, 133
Ibn 'Abdán al-Ahwází, 170
'Abdí, Áqá, 31
*'Abdí ibn Nabí (?), 228
Abú 'Abdi'lláh al-Magribí, 200
'Abdu'lláh Anṣárí of Herát, Shaykh, 30, 41, 202. *See* **Anṣárí**
'Abdu'lláh ibn Muḥammad, Shaykh, 14
'Abdu'lláh ibn Muḥammad Zamán, 37
'Abdu'lláh ibn Núri'd-Dín ibn Ni'mati'lláh, Sayyid, 125
'Abdu'lláh ibn Ṭáhir, 289
'Abdu'l-Aḥad of Zanján, 65, 82, 83, 84
'Abdu'l-'Alí, Mírzá, son of Farhád Mírzá, 116
'Abdu'l-'Alí, son of Ṣubḥ-i-Azal, 82, 83, 84
*'Abdu'l-'Azíz ibn Sa'íd [ibn] al-Ḥájj Aḥmad an-Najjár, 15
'Abdu'l-Bahá, 'Abbás Efendi, 53, 66, **67**, 69, 78, **79–81**, 82, **84–87**, **287**
*'Abdu'l-Fattáḥ Yáziji, Darwísh, 273
'Abdu'l-Ghaffár, the Bahá'í, 84
'Abdu'l-Ghaní, Mírzá, of Tafrísh, 254
'Abdu'l-Ghaní an-Nábulusí, 215
'Abdu'l-Ḥamíd, Sulṭán, 283
'Abdu'l-Ḥusayn Khán, Ḥájjí Mírzá, *Waḥídu'l-Mulk*, of Káshán, 89, 240
'Abdu'l-Ḥusayn Khán, Mírzá, of Kirmán, 250. *See* **Áqá Khán, Mírzá**, of Kirmán
'Abdu'l-Laṭíf, translator, 174
'Abdu'l-Laṭíf al-'Abbásí of Gujrát, 211
'Abdu'l-Majíd, Sulṭán, 250
'Abdu'l-Majíd ibn Firishta 'Izzu'd-Dín, 47. *See* **Firishta-záda** *and* **Firishta-oghlu**
'Abdu'l-Malik, Khwája, 256
'Abdu'l-Mu'min ibn Ṣafiyyi'd-Dín...ibn Qábús ibn Washmgír, 204
'Abdu'l-Muqtadir, Khán Ṣáḥib Mawlawí, 142
'Abdu'l-Qádir-i-Gílání, Shaykh, 244
*'Abdu'l-Qádir ibn Muḥammad al-'Aṭifí, 215
*'Abdu'l-Qádir ibn 'Umar, 211
'Abdu'r-Raḥím ibn 'Abdi'r-Raḥmán al-Qáhirí al-'Abbásí, 211
*'Abdu'r-Raḥím ibn Muḥammad Niyásarí (Niyástarí), 279
'Abdu'r-Raḥím ibn Muḥammad Yúnus of Damáwand, 203
'Abdu'r-Raḥmán III, 141
'Abdu'r-Raḥmán Efendi, 243, 255
'Abdu'r-Raḥmán ibn Naṣr...ash-Shírází, 287
'Abdu'r-Raḥmán an-Nujúmí, 9
'Abdu'r-Rashíd ibn 'Abdi'l-Ghafúr al-Ḥusayní al-Madaní al-Tatawí, 209
'Abdu'r-Razzáq-i-Iṣfahání, 255
'Abdu's-Salám ibn Ibráhím al-Laqání, 7
'Abdu'l-Wahháb, Mírzá, entitled *Mu'tamadu'd-Dawla*, 247. *See* **Nasháṭ**
'Abdu'l-Wahháb of Chahár Maḥáll, 102
'Abdu'l-Wahháb Munshí, Mírzá, 62
'Abdu'l-Wáḥid ibn Muḥammad ibn 'Abdi'l-Wáḥid al-Ámidí at-Tamímí, 11
'Abdu'l-Wási'-i-Jabalí, 255
'Abíd ibnu'l-Abraṣ, 289
Ábtín, 251
Achaemenians, the, 251
Adíbu'l-Mamálik, 137
Áfáq wa-Anfus, by Sulṭán Walad, 196

H

I

J

CAMBRIDGE: PRINTED AT THE UNIVERSITY PRESS BY WALTER LEWIS, M.A.